pa

HAWAII

spend less see more

2nd Edition

by Jeanette Foster, Pauline Frommer
& David Thompson

Series Editor: Pauline Frommer

WILEY
Wiley Publishing, Inc.

Published by:

Wiley Publishing, Inc.

111 River St.
Hoboken, NJ 07030-5774

ISBN 978-0-470-18411-0

Editor: Ian Skinnari
Production Editor: M. Faunette Johnston
Cartographer: Guy Ruggiero
Photo Editor: Richard Fox
Interior Design: Lissa Auciello-Brogan
Production by Wiley Indianapolis Composition Services
Front and back cover photo © Bob Barbour/Minden Pictures
Cover photo of Pauline Frommer by Janette Beckmann

For information on our other products and services or to obtain technical support, please contact our Customer Care Department within the U.S. at 800/762-2974, outside the U.S. at 317/572-3993 or fax 317/572-4002.

Wiley also publishes its books in a variety of electronic formats. Some content that appears in print may not be available in electronic formats.

Manufactured in the United States of America

5 4 3 2 1

Contents

List of Maps

An Invitation to the Reader

In researching this book, we discovered many wonderful places—hotels, restaurants, shops, and more. We're sure you'll find others. Please tell us about them, so we can share the information with your fellow travelers in upcoming editions. If you were disappointed with a recommendation, we'd love to know that, too. Please write to:

Pauline Frommer's Hawaii, 2nd Edition
Wiley Publishing, Inc. • 111 River St. • Hoboken, NJ 07030-5774

An Additional Note

Please be advised that travel information is subject to change at any time—and this is especially true of prices. We therefore suggest that you write or call ahead for confirmation when making your travel plans. The authors, editors, and publisher cannot be held responsible for the experiences of readers while traveling. Your safety is important to us, however, so we encourage you to stay alert and be aware of your surroundings. Keep a close eye on cameras, purses, and wallets, all favorite targets of thieves and pickpockets.

About the Authors

A resident of the Big Island, **Jeanette Foster** has skied the slopes of Mauna Kea—during a Fourth of July ski meet, no less—and gone scuba diving with manta rays off the Kona Coast. A prolific writer widely published in travel, sports, and adventure magazines, she's also a contributing editor to *Hawaii* magazine, the editor of *Zagat's Survey to Hawaii's Top Restaurants,* and the Hawaii chapter author of *1,000 Places to See in the U.S.A. and Canada Before You Die.* In addition to writing this guide, Jeanette is the author of *Frommer's Maui; Frommer's Kauai; Frommer's Hawaii with Kids; Frommer's Portable Big Island; Frommer's Honolulu, Waikiki & Oahu; Frommer's Maui & Lanai Day by Day;* and *Frommer's Honolulu & Oahu Day by Day.*

Pauline Frommer is the creator of the award winning Pauline Frommer's Guides. *Pauline Frommer's London* and *Pauline Frommer's New York City* were named "Best Guidebook of the Year" (in 2006 and 2007 respectively) by the North American Travel Journalists Association. She is also a recipient of a Lowell Thomas Medal from the Society of American Travel Writers for her magazine work, and a Webby Peoples Voice award for her work as the first editor of Frommers.com. Every Sunday, she co-hosts "The Travel Show" with her father Arthur Frommer, now heard on over 100 radio stations across the United States. On Wednesdays, she appears on CNNOnline to discuss the latest travel trends; you may also have seen her discussing travel on *Today, The Early Show, Live with Regis and Kelly, The O'Reilly Factor, The CBS Evening News,* CNN, FOX, and MSNBC. Pauline pens a bi-weekly column for MSN.com and contributed a chapter to the book *The Experts Guide to Babies* on traveling with children. She is married to physical therapist Mahlon Stewart and the proud mother of two very well traveled daughters, Veronice (age 9) and Beatrix (age 5).

Big Island–based journalist **David Thompson** grew up in Hawaii and writes about what goes on there for publications such as *Honolulu Magazine* and *Hana Hou!,* the in-flight magazine of Hawaiian Airlines.

Acknowledgments

Pauline would like to thank her family for letting her run off to Hawaii to work on this book without (too many) complaints. Her chapters wouldn't have been nearly as good without the input of publisher Mike Spring and her meticulous editor Ian Skinnari. Gratitude is also owed to the wonderful people she met on the Big Island, Maui, Molokai, and Lanai, all of whom shared their insights and company with her in a most generous manner.

Star Ratings, Icons & Abbreviations

Every restaurant, hotel, and attraction is rated with stars ★, indicating our opinion of that facility's desirability; this relates not to price, but to the value you receive for the price you pay. The stars mean:

No stars: Good
★ Very good
★★ Great
★★★ Outstanding! A must!

Accommodations within each neighborhood are listed in ascending order of cost, starting with the cheapest and increasing to the occasional "splurge." Each hotel review is preceded by one, two, three, or four dollar signs, indicating the price range per double room. Restaurants work on a similar system, with dollar signs indicating the price range per three-course meal.

Accommodations

$	Up to $85 per night
$$	$86 to $130
$$$	$131 to $180
$$$$	$181 and up

Dining

$	Meals for $8 or less
$$	$9 to $14
$$$	$15 to $20
$$$$	$20 and up

In addition, we've included a kids icon (kids) to denote attractions, restaurants, and lodgings that are particularly child friendly.

Frommers.com

Now that you have this guidebook to help you plan a great trip, visit our website at **www.frommers.com** for additional travel information on more than 4,000 destinations. We update features regularly to give you instant access to the most current trip-planning information available. At Frommers.com, you'll find scoops on the best airfares, lodging rates, and car rental bargains. You can even book your travel online through our reliable travel booking partners. Other popular features include:

- Online updates of our most popular guidebooks
- Vacation sweepstakes and contest giveaways
- Newsletters highlighting the hottest travel trends
- Podcasts, interactive maps, and up-to-the-minute events listings
- Opinionated blog entries by Arthur Frommer himself
- Online travel message boards with featured travel discussions

a note from pauline frommer

I started traveling with my guidebook-writing parents, Arthur Frommer and Hope Arthur, when I was just four months old. To avoid lugging around a crib, they would simply swaddle me and stick me in an open drawer for the night. For half of my childhood, my home was a succession of hotels and B&Bs throughout Europe, as we dashed around every year to update *Europe on $5 a Day* (and then $10 a day, and then $20 . . .).

We always traveled on a budget, staying at the Mom-and-Pop joints Dad featured in the guide, getting around by public transportation, eating where the locals ate. And that's still the way I travel today, because I learned—from the master—that these types of vacations not only save money, but offer a richer, deeper experience of the culture. You spend time in local neighborhoods, meeting and talking with the people who live there. For me, making friends and having meaningful exchanges is always the highlight of my journeys—and the main reason I decided to become a travel writer and editor as well.

I've conceived these books as budget guides for a new generation. They have all the outspoken commentary and detailed pricing information of the Frommer's guides, but they take bargain hunting into the 21st century, with more information on using the Internet and air/hotel packages to save money. Most important, we stress "alternative accommodations"—apartment rentals, private B&Bs, religious retreat houses, and more—not simply to save you money, but to give you a more authentic experience in the places you visit.

A highlight of each guide is the chapter that deals with "The Other" side of the destinations, the one visitors rarely see. These sections will actively immerse you in the life that residents enjoy. The result, I hope, is a valuable new addition to the world of guidebooks. Please let us know how we've done! E-mail me at editor@frommers.com.

Happy traveling!

Pauline Frommer

Pauline Frommer

1 The Best of Hawaii

From six islands, hundreds of beaches, & hundreds of sights—how do you choose?

IT'S A QUANDARY, YOU MIGHT THINK. ARE THE ISLANDS DISTINCTIVE, OR are they alike? Don't they all have giant surf, pineapple fields, and big fancy hotels? And which one has the active volcano?

Actually, there are answers: yes, no, maybe, and the Big Island.

A map of Hawaii is like a portrait of siblings lined up in order of birth. Of the six main inhabited islands—Kauai, Oahu, Molokai, Lanai, Maui, and the Big Island—Kauai, on the far left, is the oldest, at close to 6 million years. Just under a million years old and posing on the far right is the Big Island, the baby of the bunch—though not forever. About 20 miles off the Big Island, in 3,000 feet of water, a volcanic seamount is rising. It's been dubbed Loihi, and scientists say it will become the next Hawaiian island, but it won't reach the surface for about another 150,000 years.

Ruling out Loihi, which island—or islands—would best suit you? Here are snapshots of each place to help you decide.

A BRIEF SUMMARY OF THE ISLANDS

KAUAI

The picture of Hawaii in the minds of people who've never been there is often one of Kauai—with rainbows appearing over waterfalls, sunny beaches, and dark, misty mountains. Kauai is the wettest and most weathered island, showcasing heavily sculpted mountains, as well as rivers and streams radiating from its center like spokes. Largely rural and overwhelmingly green, Kauai has a mountain peak in its middle where it almost never stops raining, and beaches around its edges where it almost always feels like summer. Most of the laid-back towns have no big shopping malls (Lihue is the only exception), very little nightlife to speak of, and the entire island has no building taller than the coconut trees (it's the law!). Folks come here to chill out and tap into a different rhythm of life.

OAHU

Home of Honolulu and 75% percent of Hawaii's population, Oahu is the island with the action. Stretching for about 30 miles between iconic Diamond Head and historic Pearl Harbor, Honolulu's got glittering lights, an arts scene, nightlife, shopping, the high-rise canyons of Waikiki, and the Pacific's major military presence, not to mention LA-style freeways and gridlock. In addition to "town," as people call the city, Oahu's got "country"—which includes the North Shore, where the monster winter waves break, and the best surfers in the world push the limits of the sport a little further each year.

MOLOKAI

Molokai is the most Hawaiian of the main islands, with native Hawaiians making up the majority of its population of 7,000. It's also the most rural and the least oriented toward tourism. If you want to get the authentic, undiluted flavor of the Hawaiian Islands, go to Molokai. The accommodations are affordable, eateries are geared toward local tastes, and the beaches blissfully uncrowded. The top tourist attraction here, and it's a doozy, is the Kalaupapa Peninsula, once the most notorious leper colony in the Pacific. You get there on the back of a mule, bumping down the tallest sea cliffs on the planet. Many day-trippers come just to experience Kalaupapa, but a longer stay will reward the visitor—and lower their blood pressure. There are few places anywhere as serene.

LANAI

Lanai is the most exclusive of the Hawaiian Islands, owned almost entirely by billionaire David Murdoch. He's brought in the Four Seasons to manage its resorts, so prices are elevated. Still it retains its small town charm. Its single town, Lanai City, has a handful of bed-and-breakfasts and almost all 3,000 of Lanai's residents live there. A lot of day-trippers from Maui come over to snorkel or drive to the Garden of the Gods, an otherworldly landscape of boulders and spires that glow red and purple at sunset. Also visit-worthy is Hulopoe Beach, one of the most postcard-perfect in all of Hawaii.

MAUI

Maui is the pampered, popular kid of the bunch, spoiled rotten with lavish resorts and idyllic beaches. Less hectic than Oahu but with no fewer things for visitors to do, its protected leeward waters are perfect for sailing, snorkeling, whale-watching, and all sorts of other ocean activities carried out by a fleet of tourist vessels. The deeply creased West Maui Mountains dominate one side of the island, while the smooth slopes of 10,023-foot Haleakala dominate the other. Trade winds trying to find their way around Haleakala gain speed and make for perfect windsurfing and kiteboarding conditions on Maui's north shore. The one-time whaling port of Lahaina is like a little Waikiki with a sense of history and a height ordinance.

THE BIG ISLAND

At just under a million years of age, the island of Hawaii, aka the Big Island, is the youngest and largest of the islands—and still growing. It's the land of the fire goddess Pele, who dwells in the crater of Kilauea volcano, which has been erupting almost continuously since 1983. This is where you go to see earth's fiery creation process unfold before your eyes. The Big Island is also home to Mauna Loa, the largest volcano on earth, which erupted last in 1984 and has been subtly swelling and deflating since. Mauna Kea, the tallest (and sometimes snowcapped) peak in the Pacific and the best site for astronomy on the planet, is there as well. Rainforests cover one side of the island and lava deserts cover the other, with upcountry ranchland resembling the Scottish highlands in between. Deep waters off the Kona Coast bring giant ahi and billfish close to shore, giving Kona its reputation as one of the world's best places for deep-sea fishing.

BEST SIGHTS, ATTRACTIONS & ACTIVITIES

Visit a live volcano. Hike out to the lava flow at Hawaii Volcanoes National Park on the **Big Island** and watch molten rock ooze, pool, spill, and cascade through the flow field, occasionally gushing into the ocean over 80-foot cliffs. See p. 393.

See the Grand Canyon of the Pacific. Nearly 3,600 feet deep Waimea Canyon on **Kauai** was carved from the runoff from Waialeale, one of the world's wettest spots. Drive the rim and watch the rock walls change to purples, greens, blues, grays, and reds. See p. 60.

Snorkel the reef. At Molokini, explore a half-sunken volcanic crater off **Maui;** at Kealakekua Bay on the **Big Island,** the water is so clear you can see the bottom at 100 feet; and at Hanauma Bay on **Oahu,** the fish are so tame you can practically join their schools. See p. 303, 403, and 136.

Pay homage to the dead at Pearl Harbor. An intensely moving memorial, at which you'll learn the history of what Franklin Delano Roosevelt aptly called "A day that will live in infamy."

Go whale-watching. Thousands of humpback whales spend the winter in Hawaii, mating, calving, and making a big splash—especially around **Maui.** See p. 286.

Scale Haleakala. Wake up on **Maui** in the wee hours to see the sunrise from atop Haleakala, "The House of the Sun," a dormant 10,023-foot volcano with a crater so alien NASA trained astronauts for moonwalks there. See p. 288.

Take a sunset cruise. Sip a mai tai under sail as night falls along **Kauai**'s spectacularly rugged Na Pali Coast (p. 51) . . . or off the high-rise urban jungle of Waikiki (p. 95) . . . or upon the tranquil waters around Lahaina (p. 226) . . . or in the deep near-shore waters off Kailua-Kona (p. 334).

Visit a historic leper colony. The Kalaupapa Peninsula was home to thousands of exiles with Hansen's Disease. Hearing their stories and scaling the sea cliffs that back the colony will be one of your most moving and exciting experiences in Hawaii.

BEST PEOPLE-WATCHING BEACHES

Waikiki Beach, Oahu Diamond Head (which has been an extinct volcanic crater for 15,000 years), high-rise hotels, and the turquoise sea frame a sandy shore where thousands of visitors lay out in the sun and play in the long, gentle waves. See p. 133.

Kaanapali Beach, Maui Come for the long, broad swath of sand lined with restaurants, bars, catamarans, and taut, tanned beachgoers. There's good swimming and snorkeling here. See p. 272.

Poipu Beach, Kauai Visitors from nearby hotels and locals from around the island mingle in the water, on the sand, and in the grassy park here. See p. 48.

Big and Little Makena, Maui Big Makena is a long golden beach that draws a huge crowd but never feels crowded. Little Makena is a short stretch of sand, hidden in a cove, where beachgoers bare it all. See p. 269.

BEST SECLUDED BEACHES

Makalawena, the Big Island If you're willing to hike across a withering lava desert, you can discover this perfect Big Island beach where hardly anyone goes. See p. 370.

Red Sand Beach, Maui An eroding red cinder nourishes this vibrantly colored beach at the bottom of a treacherous trail on Maui's lush, rural east side. See p. 275.

Shipwreck Beach, Lanai Visit this windy Lanai beach at the end of a bumpy road to see two old ships rusting on the rocks. See p. 217.

Hanakapiai, Kauai A 2-mile hike along the cliffs of Kauai's Na Pali Coast leads to this idyllic little beach fronting a deep, narrow tropical valley. (Keep hiking and the beaches become even more secluded.) See p. 52.

BEST BEACHES IF YOU'RE A KID

Kanaha Beach Park, Maui The reef far offshore gives windsurfers waves to jump and keeps near-shore waters calm enough for babies to enjoy. See p. 273.

Lydgate County Park, Kauai Here, easy swimming in well-protected pools carved into the reef, as well a community-built playground wonderland—with tall bridges to cross, a lava slide to shoot, and mazes to run—delight children. See p. 48.

Poipu Beach, Kauai An open bay at this beach attracts Kauai's surfers and snorkelers, while a lava-rock jetty creates a sheltered area for kids. See p. 48.

Kapalua Beach, Maui Two rocky promontories do an extremely good job of calming the waters at this perennially popular Maui beach fronting the Kapalua Bay Hotel Resort. See p. 273.

BEST BEACHES FOR OCEAN SPORTS

The North Shore, Oahu Home to Sunset Beach, Pipeline, Waimea Bay, and many more celebrated surfing breaks, this area comes to life in the winter with giant waves. See p. 137.

Makapuu, Oahu A consistent, year-round bodysurfing beach, Makapuu welcomes beginners when the surf is small and eats them for lunch when it gets big. See p. 136.

Hookipa, Maui Also known as the Windsurfing Capital of the World, this is the home base for the Maui Air Force—windsurfers who catch huge air off the faces of breaking waves. See p. 273.

Kite Beach, Maui Practitioners of Hawaii's newest extreme sport, kiteboarding, have claimed this as their very own beach, a safe distance from the airport to keep them out of the flight paths of planes. See p. 273.

Magic Sands, the Big Island The sand here at the islands' best bodysurfing beach—along Alii Drive in Kailua-Kona—comes and goes with the storms. See p. 367.

BEST ACTIVE EXPERIENCES

Surf lessons. Learn to ride the waves with a pro surfer on Oahu, with county lifeguards on the Big Island, or at the old whaling port of Lahaina on Maui.

Blasting down a zipline. You don't swing through the trees on Maui; you zip through them along a series of steel cables strung through a eucalyptus forest, back and forth across a gaping gulch. See p. 310.

Landing a marlin. Some of the world's best deep-sea fishing is just offshore from Kailua-Kona on the Big Island. See p. 405.

BEST "OTHER HAWAII" ACTIVITIES

Kick it. Hang with Hawaiian musicians jamming backyard-style while you nibble on a pupu (appetizer) and knock back beers at a down-home country club in Waimanalo on Oahu. See p. 155.

Relax. Get mellow on *awa* (or *kava* as this mildly narcotic, but perfectly legal, brew is also known) in Honolulu amid candlelight, hushed tones, and Hawaiian-studies students from the University of Hawaii; or in Kailua-Kona amid throngs of tourists; or with Big Island bohemians in the wilds of rural Puna. See p. 398.

Become an ecotourist. Join conservationists in the field; stand watch over the nests of endangered turtles, root out an invasive species from native rainforests, or plant ohia and koa seedlings on the slopes of Mauna Loa. See p. 398.

BEST PLACES TO EAT

Ono Hawaiian Foods, Oahu The poi is thick and fresh, the *laulau* luscious, and the line out front perpetual. See p. 127.

Blossoming Lotus, Kauai At this affordable, gourmet vegan place, you can get roasted-red-pepper curry for dinner and a kava brownie for dessert. See p. 43.

Mama's Fish House, Maui Mama's elegant yet casual fine dinning is tucked in a palm grove in a lovely cove, with South Seas castaway decor so hokey it's chic. See p. 267.

Kilauea Lodge, Big Island French and German classics share the menu with ostrich filet in this restaurant set in a cool, misty rainforest near the volcano on the Big Island. See p. 366.

2 Kauai: Hawaii's Garden of Eden

Nearly everyone has a soft spot for picturesque Kauai.

by Jeanette Foster

AS THE OLDEST OF THE MAIN HAWAIIAN ISLANDS, KAUAI HAS BEEN RIPENING and maturing for more than 5 million years, weathering the passage of time exceedingly well. It has a character that the younger islands lack—visible in its craggy peaks, long and numerous beaches (more than any of the other Hawaiian islands), river-cut valleys, and color-streaked canyons. One of the most spectacularly beautiful places on Earth, it possesses a majesty wrought by the slow, deft forces of geologic time.

And the island's appeal goes deeper than its scenery. Perhaps the best way to explain it is to discuss the mystery here; you can still access the area's primordial roots—in the gold-pink light that tints the ocean whitecaps at sunrise, the straight sheets of blowing rain, and the bits of drifting mist that drape kelly-green mountains. Yes, Kauai has plenty of what Hawaiians call *mana* (spiritual energy). In a culture that defines *wai* (water) as wealth, the island's abundant fresh water is a major source of power. Its flattop volcano, Waialeale, is one of the wettest spots on Earth, receiving nearly 600 inches of rain per year. Much of the water finds its way into the mighty Wailua River, the state's only navigable river (making this island a great pick for kayaking enthusiasts).

Located just 90 miles from Oahu, and the capital of the state Honolulu, Kauai is indeed different, a special and unique place where, by law, no building is taller than a palm tree. That being said, it isn't suited to travelers who seek major shopping centers or lots of choices for nightlife. Its depth and magic are largely lost on those who give the island only a day or two of their time, driving the highway and declaring it seen. But for those who want to quiet down and slow their pace, Kauai is perhaps the closest any of us will come to the Garden of Eden.

DON'T LEAVE KAUAI WITHOUT . . .

Shelling out. Buy a lei or some piece of jewelry strung from the exquisite, tiny shells collected predominantly on the beaches of Niihau. This traditional Hawaiian craft is unique to Kauai and has enjoyed a resurgence in recent years. The work is intricate, painstaking, and truly beautiful. See p. 82.

Exploring Waimea Canyon and Na Pali Coast. The rugged fluted peaks and narrow, verdant valleys of this wilderness area are wonders in the already wondrous Pacific.

Floating in a warm sea filled with rainbow-colored fish. If you only see Kauai on land, you're missing half of the experience. Experience the watery wonders of Kauai by snorkeling, scuba diving, kayaking, or sailing. See p. 72.

Indulging in at least one wellness session. Kauai is known as the healing island, and it's home to a large, eclectic population of body workers, all eager to help you feel better. You'll be amazed at the modalities you can choose from: ayurvedic pancha karma, lomilomi and shiatsu massage, crystal healing, Rolfing, a "vibe" machine—and that's barely scratching the surface. See p. 76.

A BRIEF HISTORY

Of all the major Hawaiian islands, Kauai was the first to be inhabited. Kauai's first settlers are believed to be the Menehune, who displayed extraordinary engineering and stonecutting skills, which allowed them to divert water for agriculture and create fish ponds.

Who were the Menehune? Today they're most commonly portrayed as elflike creatures with superhuman capabilities, who often completed their work impossibly fast and at night. The legend is so popular around the islands that the State Department of Transportation used a grinning, shaka-flashing Menehune graphic on its signs during a lengthy construction project at Honolulu Airport. Experts, however, theorize that the first arrivals may have been from the Marquesas Islands. As the subsequent Polynesian migrations brought waves of new settlers to Kauai, the Marquesans, who were either smaller in stature and less warlike than the Tahitian newcomers (or, because the Tahitians had a strong cast system, they may have considered the Marquesans of a lower caste or "small"), may have been driven out or simply overwhelmed. Or perhaps they sailed away, as some stories contend.

Kauai was the only island never physically conquered by King Kamehameha in his bloody unification drive. But after Kamehameha's warriors were twice beat back by natural forces before they even reached Kauai's shores, the island's king, Kaumualii, peacefully negotiated terms that allowed him to retain power as Kauai's governor, forging the link that for the first time joined the entire island chain under one ruler in 1810.

Kauai has distinguished itself as the site of many important firsts in Hawaii's history. Captain James Cook, who in 1778 ushered in the era of Western contact that led to dramatic and disastrous consequences for the Kingdom of Hawaii, first landed in the bustling village of Waimea, on Kauai's West Side. Cook found a thriving population of several thousand people tending a vast network of taro fields within the natural wetlands, the patches connected by an elaborate series of waterways navigable by canoe. Similar scenes were being played out in fertile river valleys all around Kauai. The island's fertility and abundant water supply were not lost on the Westerners who followed Captain Cook in hopes of reaping fortunes from her red clay and loamy black soils. Massive diversion projects, nearly all of them constructed by Chinese laborers, channeled water out of Kauai's many streams and into the irrigation ditches of sugar-cane and pineapple fields. The sugar industry, which ruled Hawaii for 1½ centuries, got its start on Kauai in the pleasant little South Side town of Koloa and is now struggling to survive here. Gay & Robinson, which maintains fields on the West Side, is one of just two sugar plantations remaining in the state—the other is on Maui.

KAUAI TODAY

Although agriculture has dwindled, the island is still predominantly rural. Kauai produces coffee, wetland taro, tropical flowers, exotic fruits, free-range beef, honey, and goat cheese. Organic farming is expanding—and so is the island's controversial participation in the cultivation of genetically modified crops for both experimental and seed-corn purposes.

The island's resident population of about 57,000 is joined by some one million tourists each year, which largely fuels the economic engines. Kauai has also been discovered by the moneyed crowd, with the concurrent boom in luxury residential construction. The Navy's Pacific Missile Ranch Facility, which conducts rocket launches for the "Star Wars" missile defense program, is a major employer on the West Side.

Socially and culturally, Kauai continues to march to the beat of its own drummer. Despite the island's small size, folks tend to stick close to home, not generally venturing out of their geographic region. Family connections remain important. Kauai also has the highest rate of volunteerism and per capita giving in the state, reflecting the kindness and generosity typical of most residents.

Until recently, Kauai was known as a casual, low-key place where few residents had money, drove fancy cars, or lived in large homes. But things have changed dramatically since 2000, when a spurt of growth seriously frayed Kauai's close-knit social fabric. People from the mainland have arrived more rapidly than they can be assimilated into the tight-knit rural communities; worse, too many of the have erected fences that close off longtime coastal and mountain access ways, built large homes overlooking formerly secluded beaches, and speculated in real estate, driving up home prices and property tax rates to a point where most local residents are excluded from the market.

Today Kauai is clearly at a crossroads. Many longtime residents are stunned at how quickly the island's physical and social landscape is being altered. Folks are starting to question just how much more development the island can take before its charm is lost, and its populace is thoroughly displaced and disaffected by the widening chasm between rich and poor.

LAY OF THE LAND

The island is about 500 square miles, and round. Because the wet, mountainous interior is largely inaccessible, most of the human activity is centered in very small towns strung along a highway that spans about two-thirds of the island. Between the two ends of the highway lies the rugged, impassible Na Pali Coast, another of Kauai's legendary landscapes.

The main roadway that nearly encircles the island changes its name at Lihue; it's called Kuhio Highway (Rte. 56) when you're traveling northeast and Kaumualii Highway (Rte. 50) when you're headed southwest. But be advised when asking directions that most locals use the highway names and may not even know the highway numbers. Lihue is also the unofficial dividing line between the windward side of the island, which lies to its northeast, and the leeward side, which encompasses everything to the southwest.

It's easy to get around on Kauai because two major frames of reference—*mauka* (the mountains) and *makai* (the sea)—are nearly always visible from the highway, and there's essentially one main road. But that doesn't mean it's a breeze to cruise around the island. Traffic moves slowly even on the highway, which is two lanes almost everywhere except a short stretch between Lihue and Wailua and a few passing lanes on the West Side. Side roads are invariably narrow, and you need to watch for potholes everywhere.

DRIVING TIPS

During the usual morning and evening commute hours, traffic often comes to a virtual standstill in the corridors between Wailua and Kapaa, and Lihue and Koloa. Fortunately, Kauai's traffic problems have given rise to a strict and thoughtful driving etiquette that requires motorists to wave to enter or cross traffic. Vehicles are allowed to merge into traffic, one at a time, alternating with through traffic, so be sure to get with the program. It's all very civilized, and you'll appreciate the friendliness and eye contact of most motorists, despite the occasional instance of road rage.

If you're sightseeing and traveling slower than the speed limit, pull over and let the cars behind you pass. Kauai motorists are notorious for pulling out in front of you, too, so drive defensively. And be sure to wear your seatbelt: It's a $70 to $100 fine, and the cops are immune to sad stories.

In that same vein, be aware that the speed limit on the main highways usually drops from 50 mph down to 25 or 35 mph as you go through small towns and communities that may appear to be little more than wide spots in the road with a post office and convenience store. Reduce your speed, not just because police may be using radar to catch scofflaws, but out of courtesy to the folks—and especially to the children—who may be walking, biking, or pulling on and off the highway.

One more hint: On the North Shore there are several one-lane bridges. Remember you are in Hawaii where aggressive driving is out and manners are in. Slow down as you approach the one-lane bridges (there will be a stop sign). Under law you are required to yield if another car is on the bridge (if two cars in opposing direction reach the bridge at the same time, be the generous driver, and allow the other car to cross first). If you are in a long line of cars approaching the bridge, don't just join the train crossing the bridge. Local etiquette calls for six to eight cars to cross the bridge, then yield and give the cars waiting on the other side of the bridge a chance to cross. You'll notice that not everyone will adhere to these rules of thumb (check out the cars that don't—they most likely are rentals), but then, not everyone visiting Hawaii enjoys the spirit of aloha.

Just Direct Your Feet to the Sunny Side of the . . . Island

One note on the weather: Kauai is quite small, but that doesn't mean one sort of weather will blanket the island. Often when it's raining in Poipu, locals will simply pack up and head to the beach on the North Shore (or vice versa). There's usually some way to find the sun in Kauai.

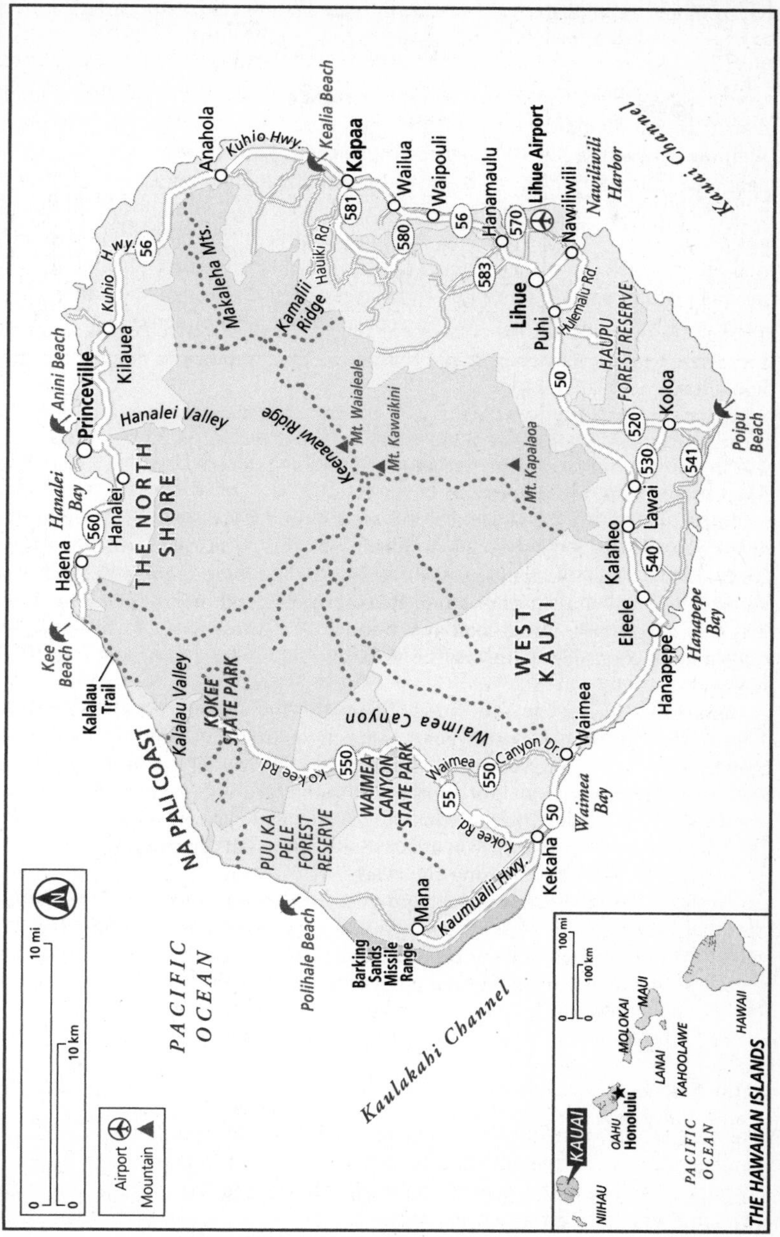
Airport
Mountain
0
10 mi
0
10 km
PACIFIC OCEAN
Kaulakahi Channel
Polihale Beach
Barking Sands Missile Range
Mana
Kaumualii Hwy.
Kekaha
NA PALI COAST
PUU KA PELE FOREST RESERVE
WAIMEA CANYON STATE PARK
Kokee Rd.
55
50
Waimea Bay
Waimea Canyon Dr.
550
Waimea
Kalalau Valley
KOKEE STATE PARK
Waimea Canyon
Kalalau Trail
Kee Beach
Haena
560
Hanalei
Hanalei Bay
THE NORTH SHORE
WEST KAUAI
Hanapepe
Hanapepe Bay
Eleele
Kalaheo
540
Lawai
530
541
Mt. Kapalaoa
Mt. Kawaikini
Mt. Waialeale
Keenaawi Ridge
Hanalei Valley
Princeville
Anini Beach
Kilauea
Kuhio Hwy.
56
Makaleha Mts.
Kamalii Ridge
Hauiki Rd
Anahola
Kuhio Hwy.
Kealia Beach
Kapaa
581
Wailua
580
Waipouli
56
Hanamaulu
570
583
Lihue Airport
Lihue
Nawiliwili
Nawiliwili Harbor
Kauai Channel
Puhi
Hulemalu Rd.
HAUPU FOREST RESERVE
50
520
Koloa
Poipu Beach
NIIHAU
KAUAI
OAHU
Honolulu
MOLOKAI
MAUI
LANAI
KAHOOLAWE
HAWAII
PACIFIC OCEAN
0
100 mi
0
100 km
THE HAWAIIAN ISLANDS

Repatterned Traffic

If you're out early on weekdays, don't be caught off guard by the miles of orange plastic cones that create an entirely different traffic configuration for Kuhio Highway between Kapule Highway and the Coconut Marketplace. The cones, set out before dawn by state highway crews and picked up again after 9am, transform the middle lane, which is normally northbound, into a thoroughfare for southbound commuters. The setup keeps traffic moving smoothly in the busy Lihue-Kapaa corridor during peak travel times, but it can be daunting when first encountered. Just remember that you'll find center turn lanes in all the usual, necessary places, although they're not initially easy to spot amid the mass of cones.

THE AREAS & MAJOR TOWNS

Starting at the north end of the island, the **North Shore** is perhaps one of the most beautiful and lush locations in the state. A series of half-moon cove beaches lines this area with powdery-perfect white sand beaches backed by spectacular sea cliffs. Two towns, **Hanalei** and **Kilauea,** and one resort area, **Princeville,** are located here. Because of the postcard beauty, accommodations tend to be more expensive here than the rest of the island. However, many wintertime tourists find the weather too wet and the ocean too rough for their tastes. The surf definitely comes up between September and May; bays that are turquoise lakes in summer become churning washing machines of white water when the 20- to 30-foot winter swells roll in. Traveling clockwise, the **East Side** (also known as the **Coconut Coast**), which extends from the town of **Kapaa** down to **Lihue** (where the airport is located), is the population and political hub of the island. Hence it's the area with the largest selection of restaurants, shops, and low-cost accommodations. In Lihue, you'll find modern Wilcox Hospital; state and county office buildings, including police headquarters and the courthouse; and most of the usual big box stores and fast-food restaurants.

Kapaa is Kauai's biggest town. It sprang up to serve folks who worked in the vast sugar cane fields and pineapple plantations that once stretched several miles inland from the coast. It's still a real town, with a mix of restored historic buildings and new construction, resort condominiums, and adorable, old-fashioned beach bungalows. Most structures are under three stories tall.

You'll find an eclectic collection of shops and restaurants frequented by residents and visitors alike on the northern end of town, along with Kapaa Beach Park, a fenced, grassy park that lies between Kuhio Highway and the sea. Community fairs and other events are often staged here; check the fence for banners announcing upcoming festivities. The East Side is an excellent, centralized area from which to explore the entire island. In terms of weather and scenery, its windward orientation translates into frequent showers and cooling trade winds year-round, with resulting verdant vegetation.

Most visitors head for the **South Side,** drawn to the large luxury hotels and condominium projects along the coast at sunny **Poipu.** During the rainy months, generally December through March, the Poipu area typically has more sunny days than the rest of the island (important if you're here for a beach vacation). Poipu itself is the largest resort community on Kauai. One very nice feature is a delightful shoreline promenade that connects many of the little coves and beaches that front the resorts. This is the place to take a stroll and watch a picture-perfect sunset. If beaching, golf, ocean sports, horseback riding, hiking, and sightseeing appeal to you, Poipu is a good choice. Shore dives, snorkeling, board- and bodysurfing, boogie boarding, and safe swimming are found here. Poipu is located between commercial harbors at Port Allen, to the west, and Nawiliwili, to the east, making it easy to catch fishing charters and Na Pali Coast tour boats. It's also convenient for day trips to Waimea Canyon, with its numerous hiking trails.

The **West Side** is the least developed region on Kauai, which helps explain why it has managed to retain the look and feel of the old, slow Hawaii. The hot, dry climate of this leeward area and a discernable cowboy culture distinguish it from the rest of the island, as does its geographic isolation. The economy of the predominantly rural West Side is dominated by agriculture, so hotels, shops, lodging, and other commercial services are limited.

GETTING TO & AROUND KAUAI

I'd strongly advise flying direct to Lihue Airport on Kauai (otherwise you are stuck with a 2-hour layover in the not-very scenic Honolulu International Airport). Airlines from the U.S. mainland flying directly into Lihue, Kauai are **United Airlines** (☎ 800/225-5825; www.ual.com), which offers direct service to Kauai, with daily flights from Los Angeles. **American Airlines** (☎ 800/433-7300; www.aa.com) offers a nonstop, daily flight from Los Angeles. **America West** (☎ 800/327-7810; www.americawest.com) has direct flights from Phoenix to Lihue. **SunTrips** (☎ 800-SUN-TRIP; www.suntrips.com) offers a charter from Oakland International Airport (OAK) once a week. **Pleasant Hawaiian Holidays** (☎ 800/742-9244; www.pleasantholidays.com), one of Hawaii's largest travel companies offering low-cost airfare and package deals, has two weekly nonstop flights from Los Angeles and San Francisco using American Trans Air.

All other airlines land in Honolulu, where you'll have to connect to a 30-minute interisland flight to Kauai's Lihue Airport. And with the recent loss of Aloha Airlines, interisland tickets are harder to come by—and subsequently more expensive—while delays are becoming more common (see the box on p. 429 for more information). The two remaining major interisland carriers are **Hawaiian Airlines** (☎ 800/367-5320, 808/245-1813, or 808/838-1555; www.hawaiianair.com) and **go!** (☎ 888/IFLYGO2; www.iflygo.com). ***Budget hint:*** Check fares on the Web, but generally go! has the cheaper airfares.

A View from the Air

Always sit on the left side of the plane for the best view of the island: the craggy slopes of the Haupu Mountain Range and the wind-chopped waters of Kalapaki Bay below. It's only a quick glimpse before the plane circles over the manicured golf courses of the Kauai Marriott Beach Resort and Kauai Lagoons and lands.

Unlike Maui and Oahu, there is a dearth of package deals to Kauai, but if you're planning on using one of the big three websites for booking airfares—Orbitz.com, Expedia.com, or Travelocity.com—it may behoove you to see if booking airfare in tandem with hotels leads to savings. Kauai is not a big "package deal" island, but it can't hurt to try.

GETTING TO & FROM THE AIRPORT

Both the airport and Nawiliwili Harbor, where the cruise ships dock, are about 3 miles east of Lihue, the centrally located county seat. Since the **Kauai Bus** (☎ 808/241-6410) doesn't service the airport, and has limited service to the remainder or the island, I strongly suggest you rent a car. Yes, there are taxis, but they are not only outrageously expensive, but also inconvenient to employ for touring, especially if you want to linger anywhere, as you surely will. This is not New York City, where you can flag down a cab on every corner: The few taxis on the island have to be booked in advance. Even taking a cab to your hotel is pricey: You can expect to pay $15 to $20 to reach a Poipu resort, and a whopping $35 to $40 if your destination is on the North Shore. By comparison, it costs about $30 to $35 a day to rent an economy car.

All the usual rental-car companies do business on Kauai, with service desks located at the Lihue Airport and courtesy vans that shuttle customers to their nearby base yards, where the cars are stored. Another option is to go with the independent local firm **Island Cars** (2983 Aukele St., Lihue; ☎ 800/246-6009 or 808/246-6000; www.islandcars.net), which is located near the Lihue Airport, and has no credit card or minimum age requirement. Consistently, **Rent A Wreck of Kauai** (☎ 808/632-0741) and **Alamo Rent a Car** (☎ 877/603-0615 or 808/245-0645; www.alamo.com) offer the lowest rates, but they may come at a hidden cost. I've received complaints about Rent a Wreck's unreliable vehicles. Alamo tends to overbook its vehicles, meaning that customers have shown up at the airport and had to wait up to an hour or more to get their car. Weigh carefully whether cost or convenience is more important to you.

Important: Reserve a car in advance; rates tend to be lower and you're more likely to get the vehicle you desire. All major car-rental companies operate on Kauai and charge competitive rates. Save money by renting the smallest vehicle you can find. Gas is expensive on Kauai, roads are small, and the maximum speed limit is 50 mph. Jeeps and convertibles often prove a nuisance in the frequent rain showers, and you won't need four-wheel-drive capability.

GETTING TO YOUR ACCOMMODATIONS

Once you're all loaded up and ready to go, follow the one-way road that fronts the airport and stay in the middle lane as it makes a sharp jog to the left; you're now on Ahukini Road, which passes tour-helicopter and charter-plane hangars to your right. Stay in the center lane, and you'll soon reach the well-landscaped intersection with Kapule Highway.

If you're headed to lodgings on the East Side or North Shore—the communities of Wailua, Kapaa, Kilauea, Princeville, and Hanalei—turn right. If you want to reach accommodations on the South Side, including Poipu and Kalaheo, go straight through the intersection and stay on Ahukini Highway until it dead-ends into Kuhio Highway. Here you'll take a left and then, after a short jaunt, a right onto Kaumualii Highway, which leads in about 7 miles to the Maluhia Road turnoff for Koloa and Poipu Beach. It then continues another 23 miles to Waimea, passing Lawai, Kalaheo, and Hanapepe along the way.

ACCOMMODATIONS, BOTH STANDARD & NOT

Lodging can take a big bite out of your Kauai travel budget, requiring value-conscious travelers to be clear about their needs versus desires when looking for accommodations. Simply choosing a room that faces the mountains rather than the shore can save you a bundle. And, obviously, choosing a hotel that's off the beach rather than on is always a huge money-saver (as much as $100 a night, no joke) and not necessarily too much of a hardship. ***Remember:*** All beaches are public in Hawaii, even those that front the sniffy resorts. So you don't have to spring for one of those fancy properties to lounge on their sands. Just go and enjoy.

Both condominiums and hotels are located in the island's resort areas, and these areas do vary greatly in terms of ambience, height of surf, and believe it or not, weather. Take these factors into consideration and don't assume that you're going to be able to zip off quickly to other areas of the island if you're not happy with the one you're in. The Garden Island looks small on the map, but it takes time to get around. I think it's wisest, therefore, to choose a resort area first, looking at its location and perks, and then look for a unit there that fits your budget.

Condos can be a terrific way to save money on lodging. Beyond the often lower price per night, they usually come with cooking facilities (either full kitchens or kitchenettes). That's a worthwhile consideration on Kauai, where restaurant meals are often pricey and much of the food isn't noteworthy. They also tend to be more spacious than standard hotel rooms, and if you're traveling with kids, there'll often be a door that you can shut between you and the little ones at night should the, er, mood strike. For complete info on condo rentals, both the pluses and minuses, see p. 16. You can be assured that the properties we list in this book will be clean and well maintained. They invariably have a pool and barbecue pit. Tennis courts, daily maid service, spas, exercise rooms, golf, Jacuzzis, restaurants, poolside bars, entertainment, concierge desk, and room service are some of the possible amenities. Obviously, the less you need, the less you pay.

The other main source of alternate and budget accommodations is the ever-growing supply of vacation rentals, and we'll point you toward these as well.

Note: When looking at room rates in this chapter, don't forget to add Hawaii's 11.42% accommodations tax to the total.

THE EAST SIDE

If you're looking to pay the lowest rates on Kauai for lodging, head to the East Side, between Lihue and Kapaa, where there aren't as many visitors because the beaches, though long and sandy, aren't considered up to snuff. The windward side

---

Finding Your Place to Stay

The accommodations in the following sections can be found on the maps starting on p. 35.

How Best to Book a Condo

by Pauline Frommer & Jeanette Foster

Ah, yes, that is the question. As anyone who's done this sort of vacation before knows, booking with the right source can mean the difference between spending $70 a night or $170 a night for an identical room in the same condo complex. Booking direct with the owner of the condo is usually the least expensive method, but it comes with more risk, as you won't be sure if the owner is representing his property honestly until you get to the place. Nor do you always have a back-up system should something go wrong (you lose your key, the toilet backs up, you name it). If you decide to go the direct-to-owner route, the most comprehensive websites for this type of booking include: Vacation Rental By Owner (www.vrbo.com), Rentalo (www.rentalo.com), and Home Away (www.homaway.com). For this type of booking, be sure to ask the following questions:

- Do you have a caretaker on-site or nearby that I can contact if something goes wrong? If I use that person, will their services cost extra, or are they included in the cost of the rental?
- Is there a cleaning fee? Daily maid service? It's important to know all your costs up front.
- What equipment, exactly, does the condo have? You may also want to inquire if there's a full stove and fridge, a washer/dryer, a DVD player, Wi-Fi, beach towels, coffeemaker, and so on.
- What are the cancellation and early leave policies?
- Can the unit accommodate people with mobility impairments? If you have any physical limitations, be certain to inquire about the unit's location within the complex. Although Kauai lacks high-rise condominiums, elevators are rare in two- and three-story buildings, so be prepared for stairs unless you request a ground-floor unit. Walkways between units, especially those in Princeville, with its more hilly terrain, may be steep. Bell service is almost never available, so travel light and be ready to handle your own bags.

is fully exposed to trade winds, which take the mugginess out of summer days but kick up the surf and bring rain showers during the winter. One of Hawaii's longest fringing coral reefs hugs the coastline here, making it great for shoreline fishing and miles-long beachcombing walks, but not ideal for swimming.

Along the "Coconut Coast," which runs from Wailua to Kapaa, is your best bet, especially if you're traveling with children. This is Kauai's major population center, with a wide selection of restaurants and shops, as well as hiking, golf, kayaking, bicycling, movie theaters, video arcades, and other activities. The lodging in this area generally lies between the ocean and Kuhio Highway, an area that gets busy and congested during daylight hours. It can be daunting to execute a left turn onto the road.

If you get satisfactory answers to all of these questions, you may want to go for it. Or you could try the two agencies below, which we've personally vetted and can vouch for. We've found their rates to be quite competitive, and as importantly, their service is topnotch.

Those looking for condos in Poipu should call the **Parrish Collection Kauai** (formerly Grantham Resorts), 3176 Poipu Rd., Koloa, HI 96756 (☎ 800/325-5701 or 808/742-2000; fax 808/742-9093; www.parrish.com). It handles more than 100 handpicked rental units for 12 different condo developments in that area, plus dozens of vacation homes, ranging from quaint cottages to elite resort homes. The Parrish Collection has high standards for their rental units and offers extremely fair prices. If the properties are not maintained to their high standards, they have no problem taking the units (and, in one case, an entire condominium project) out of their selected rentals. Condos start at $105 for a spacious one-bedroom, garden-view unit in low season. There's a 5-night minimum for condos and a 7-night minimum for homes.

For elsewhere on the island, call Rosemary Smith of **Rosewood Bed & Breakfast** (☎ 808/822-5216; www.rosewoodkauai.com). For the past 27 years she's been tirelessly peeking under sheets, fingering washcloths, and testing water pressure at the three dozen or so properties she represents around Kauai. Proudly particular, she spot-checks all of these B&Bs, condos, and vacation rentals at least once every 3 months, issuing marching orders to the hosts who don't yet have pillowtop mattresses, or refusing to allow a burned potholder to remain by a stove. "I won't represent anyplace I wouldn't stay myself," she told me. "People are coming here on vacation; the last thing they need to get is a lumpy bed." Best of all, many of the properties she represents are reasonably priced, the country homes and cottages starting at just $95 a night (and going up to $200 per night, though a handful do bounce up to around $400 per night). Rosemary is a terrific source of advice, direct, and highly knowledgeable—which is why we personally recommend her services as a terrific option for those seeking quality lodgings on Kauai.

$ The cheapest place to stay on the east side is the **Kauai International Hostel** (4532 Lehua St.; ☎ 808/823-6142; www.kauaiinternationalhostel.com; AE, MC, V) located in Kapaa. A busy hostel, frequented by 20-year old European backpackers, it's located just a couple of blocks from a beach (not the best swimming beach, but a white sand, generally wind blown beach). After years of neglect and a somewhat shoddy reputation, a new manager has renovated the two-story building, repainted everything, and has told drug users they are not welcome here. The setting is noisy during the day but quiets down considerably at night. If you're really pinching pennies, bunk in the dorm for $25. There are also private doubles for $60 to $75, but at those prices you can do better elsewhere. The bathrooms, kitchen, laundry, and TV room with pool table are shared.

Watch Out for Those Add-On Fees

For years I have been dismayed at major resorts and hotels that tack on "resort fees" for things we used to get for free—parking, local newspaper delivery, and so on. Now, condos, several bed-and-breakfast places, and some vacation rentals are following in these footsteps with a "cleaning fee." Personally, I hate this! Why not just incorporate all costs into the room rate? As a consumer, I want a price for the unit—a total price—but owners of these accommodations tend to think that travelers don't look beyond the base price of the unit. Be sure to read the fine print: If you're getting a unit for $135 a night plus an $80 cleaning fee for a 2-night minimum, you're really buying a $175 a night unit. I hope the owners of these vacation rentals and condos wise up and just give us one bottom-line price.

$ For a few dollars more and infinitely better accommodations than the Kaui International Hostel, try the **Lani-keha** ★ (848 Kamalu Rd. [Hwy. 581], Kapaa; ☎ 800/821-4898 or 808/822-1605; www.lanikeha.com; cash only). Located in a quiet, pastoral setting, this bed-and-breakfast is housed in an old *kamaaina* (long-time Hawaii resident) home built in the sprawling style of the 1940s. It boasts 3 acres of lawn, gardens, and trees. The unbelievably cheap rates (starting at $65 for two) include breakfast and free Wi-Fi. The closest beach is a 10-minute drive.

$ If you plan on doing any watersports, the **Surf & Ski Cottage** ★ (Ohana St. [in Wailua River Lots], off Hwy. 580 [Kuamoo Rd.], Kapaa. Reservations: c/o Kauai Water Ski & Surf Co., 4-356 Kuhio Hwy., Kapaa; ☎ 800/344-7915 or 808/822-3574; surfski@aloha.net; AE, DC, DISC, MC, V) is the place to stay. Owned by the same local family that runs the Kauai Water Ski & Surf Co., they keep prices moderate (doubles start at $90) and offer guests a 20% discount on all outdoor equipment and activities at their company (water-skiing, kayaking, and surfing lessons; boogie board and snorkel rentals; and much more), which translates into significant savings. As for the cottage itself, it's a cozy, wee place (just 220 sq. ft.), basically one airy, high-ceilinged room with a bedroom attached that's within easy walking distance of Kapaa's beaches, stores, and restaurants.

$–$$ Women looking for a safe, inexpensive place to stay, that's a step up from a hostel, should try **Mahina's Women's Guest House** ★ (4433 Panihi Rd., Kapaa; ☎ 808/823-9364; www.mahinas.com; MC, V), where hostess Sharon Gonsalves has turned a four-bedroom old plantation house, just a 2-minute walk from the beach, into a warm and welcoming single-sex environment. Starting at $76 single, with the most expensive room at $110 double, this place offers good bang for the buck. The individual rooms are immaculately clean and very functional (with Sharon's touch of fresh flowers for arriving guests). The four rooms share three bathrooms and there's no phone or TV in the house. Restaurants and shops are just a 5-minute walk away.

$–$$ If your heart is not set on staying on the ocean, and instead you want a quiet, country location, **Inn Paradise** (6381 Makana Rd., Kapaa; ☎ 808/822-2542; www.innparadisekauai.com; AE. DISC, MC, V) should do the trick (and the ocean's still in reach, just a 15-min. drive away). Another gracious plantation style house with a huge wraparound lanai, it sits on 3½ landscaped acres. Depending on your needs, you can choose from a studio ($80) with a tiny kitchenette tucked away in a closet, or one of two family-friendly, two-bedrooms with full kitchens ($115). Not exactly a B&B, guests are greeted with a "welcome basket" with all the makings for your first day's breakfast. My favorite amenity here is the hot tub, which is great for star watching at night.

$$–$$$ **The Kauai Sands** (420 Papaloa Rd.; ☎ 800/560-5553 or 808/822-4951; www.kauaisandshotel.com; MC, V), a plain-looking (think: all concrete), 200-room, single story motel, is one of just a handful in the state that are Hawaiian-owned and operated. This is basic, utilitarian lodging—clean and sparsely furnished, with thin linens and sheets. But at rates running from $98 to $178, it's a good value for a waterfront property that has a few resort amenities—including two pools and a small fitness center—that its neighbors lack. Also, you're doing the right thing by staying here and supporting a Hawaiian business. All rooms have fridges, a few have kitchenettes, and there's a self-service laundry on-site.

$$–$$$$ A recent upgrade lifted the **Hotel Coral Reef** ★ (1516 Kuhio Hwy.; ☎ 800/843-4659 or 808/822-4481; www.hotelcoralreefresort.com; AE, DC, MC, V), the sixth discount property in this neighborhood, out of the dump category—so ignore those old reviews you might read on user generated websites, as they're out of date. It's now quite a cute place with a beach in the backyard, allowing you to stay on the ocean at a fraction of the cost of most oceanfront accommodations. And with the recent renovation, rooms have been transformed and are now quite dignified and modern (with flatscreen TVs, no less!). Other improvements: a pool, useable exercise room, and sauna have been added to the property. Rooms closest to the highway are the cheapest at $125 for a double; one-bedrooms with foldout couches go for $199; oceanfront suites, just 40 feet from the water, with kitchenette and beachfront lanai, go for $249 for a double.

$$–$$$ It's hard to beat Coral Reef's prices at other Coconut Coast resorts, but the condominium **Kapaa Sands** ★ (380 Papaloa Rd.; ☎ 800/222-4901 or 808/822-4901; www.kapaasands.com; MC, V) comes close, and in some ways (though not all), it's a better property—quieter, smaller (just 20 units), with better views from the rooms and nicer grounds. It's walking-distance close to the many shops and restaurants at the Coconut Marketplace. What the rooms here will look like is a crapshoot, as they're individually owned, but all have microwaves, cable TV, VCRs, and either a full or partial ocean view; however, all but the oceanfront rooms are rather dark. Rates range from $120 to $150 for a studio unit (with kitchenette and pull-down Murphy beds that aren't the most comfortable mattresses I've slept on). The two-bedroom units ($170–$185) have full kitchens and private lanais. I suggest booking with the in-house booking desk at Kapaa Sands, listed above: They seem to have the best prices and are located on-site, so if you have any problems they're available to help.

$$–$$$ I'm very fond of this next listing for the simple fact that waking up here in the morning is like waking up in the middle of a botanical garden. That's because **Kakalina's Bed and Breakfast** ★ (6781 Kawaihau Rd., Kapaa; ☎ 800/662-4330 or

808/822-2328; www.kakalina.com; MC, V) is set in a 3-acre working flower farm tucked away in the foothills of Mount Waialeale, just behind Kapaa. The smells here are divine, as are the views. Four units in all are available, and they range from two rooms ($90 double) to an entire house ($155 double). And the decor? It takes its cue from the setting, so expect lots of pastels and floral prints (along with cable TVs and VCRs). Rates cover continental breakfast in some, but not all, units. Be sure to add on the additional one-time $90 cleaning fee.

$$–$$$ Also up in the rolling hill country, **Kauai Country Inn** ★★★ (6440 Olohena Rd., Kapaa; ☎ 808/821-0207; www.kauaicountryinn.com; AE, MC, V) is just what it sounds like: an old-fashioned country inn in bucolic surroundings. Your hosts here are a splendid couple, Mike and Martina Hough, who retired from their successful international advertising agency in Los Angeles and put that creative energy into making sure you have the vacation of your life on their 2-acre slice of paradise. Each of the four units is unique in decor but tastefully done, with Hawaiian Art Deco furnishings, hardwood floors, private baths, kitchen or kitchenette, your own Macintosh computer with Wi-Fi connection, and lots of little amenities (my fav is the hot tub). A separate two-bedroom country cottage on-site is perfect for families with children. One more surprise: Host Mike has his own private Beatles Museum from his decades of collecting Beatles memorabilia (including a Mini Cooper S car owned by Brian Epstein, the Beatles manager; original paintings by John Lennon; and a host of books, records, movies, tapes, T-shirts, and other interesting and unusual rare items). The rooms in the inn are $110 to $165; the two-bedroom cottage is $245 for up to six.

$$$ Back to the beach in a slightly higher price (and amenities) range, the **Wailua Bayview** ★ kids (320 Papaloa Rd., Kapaa; ☎ 800/882-9007 or 808/823-0960, www.wailuabay.com; AE, DISC, MC, V), a condo complex, nonetheless offers great value. I'm talking spacious one-bedroom apartments overlooking the ocean (no sandy beach, though, just rocks), starting from $840 a week ($120 a night). Garden units may be cheaper but get a lot of noise from the highway (if you go that route, ask for one with air-conditioning, good for the temperature and an excellent way to drown out noise). ***A couple of caveats:*** You must book 7 nights to get the best deal and they tack on a "cleaning fee" of $95, which works out to an additional $13.60 a day. The best rates we've seen are with the on-site booking agent (phone number listed above).

Taking into Account the Seasons—or Not—in Kauai

There's minimal variation in the weather or pricing from season to season. Late spring and fall tend to be the cheapest times of the year, and the summer may be negligibly warmer than other times of the year. The changes in the ocean are more drastic; from December through April, "kona storms" at sea can make the waters too rough for ocean activities in all but the most sheltered coves, sometimes for days at a time. As a result, whale-watching cruises are sometimes canceled at this time of year, which is ironic, considering that this is the best time of year to spot these behemoths.

Bidding Blind

It's no secret that websites such as Hotwire.com and Priceline.com often get quite good deals. They place those clients daring enough to pay for a hotel sight unseen into some of the finest hotels on Hawaii for a fraction of what they normally cost. Problem is, you usually don't know what you're getting . . . unless you know where to look. And in the case of Priceline the place to snoop is at www.biddingfortravel.com, a website where ordinary travelers spill the beans about how much they bid and what they got. For Kauai, most folks who are making four-star bids, as we go to press, are getting the **Hilton Kauai Beach Hotel Resort** (4331 Kauai Beach Dr., Lihue; ☎ 800/HILTONS or 808/245-1955; www/hiltonkauairesort.com; AE, DISC, MC, V). The reason? Wind. Though it has a convenient location just 4 miles outside Lihue and close to the shops and restaurants of the Coconut Coast, it's really windy here. Which is a shame because there's a beautiful 3-mile-long, white sand beach out front, but it's so windy, just walking along the beach is like getting sand blasted. And due to offshore currents, the waters off the beach are not very safe for swimming (and certainly not safe for children).

So why are we telling you about this? Because frugal travelers will realize that there are other beaches just a couple minutes drive away and rooms here have been going for between $90 and $130 a night on Priceline (despite the fact that published rates *start* at $179). And this is a cushy place. The renovated rooms feature deep, plush carpeting, marble bath and floors, top-of-the-line bedding, and high-speed wireless Internet service. Plus the property has other resort-type amenities like on-site restaurants, nightly entertainment, four outdoor pools (with water slides), tennis courts, fitness room, two Jacuzzis, watersports equipment rentals, spa, fitness center, and a complimentary shuttle to and from the airport.

There's one big caveat: No matter what price you get at Priceline, you will still have to pay the daily resort fee of $13 per day (it covers parking and a host of things you may or may not use but are charged anyway, like the nightly sunset cocktail party and Polynesian dance show).

$$$–$$$$ The unpretentious **Aloha Beach Hotel Kauai** (3–5920 Kuhio Hwy.; ☎ 888/823-5111 or 808/823-6000; www.abrkauai.com; AE, DC, DISC, MC, V) is a top choice for families, as it allows kids under 18 to stay for free and those under 12 to eat for free. A low-rise resort, it's set on 10 sprawling acres on the banks of the Wailua River and the ocean; on the grounds are two nice pools, volleyball and shuffleboard courts, and a gym. It also adjoins the oceanside Lydgate Park, and is near a number of restaurants and shops, although its otherwise convenient location is slightly marred by the near-constant traffic around its entrance, which makes walking dangerous. In 2006, every room was renovated with new carpet and furniture, oversize Balinese mahogany doors, upgraded bathrooms, and

Hawaiian-style quilts on the beds. But at these prices don't expect the Four Seasons or the Ritz, just clean, comfortable furnishings in a family-type atmosphere. The one-bedroom beach cottages, with kitchenettes, work well if you're traveling with kids. Rooms are $149 to $169, while cottages and suites are $240, but as we went to press, AAA members could get rooms starting at $125 (look on-site for other possible discounts, as well).

LIHUE

$$–$$$ If you have an early flight out in the wee hours of the morning, or arrive late at night and don't want to bother driving long distance after a long plane flight, it makes sense to stay close to the airport in Lihue. The least expensive, decent accommodations nearby can be found at the **Tip Top Motel** (3173 Akahi St., Lihue, HI 96766; ☎ 808/245-2333; MC, V), just a 5-minute drive from the airport. It's no great shakes, a two-story concrete tile building with institutional linoleum tile floors and twin beds sporting well-used mattresses, but rooms are just $70 a night. If you can afford it, head instead to the much more pleasant **Garden Island Inn** (3445 Wilcox Rd.; ☎ 800/648-0154 or 808/245-7227; www.gardenislandinn.com; AE, DISC, MC, V), which lies a couple blocks from the ocean. It offers 21 rooms and 2 suites for $99 to $170—going up in price from the ground floor to the third floor—which is about $240 to $300 less than lodgings at the Marriott, located just around the corner. No, it's not as fancy, but it's clean and fully adequate, with fresh flowers in each room. Plus, the staff is friendly, sharing beach gear with guests and fruit from the grounds. Some units have kitchens, others have kitchenettes, but all have fridges and cable TV. Given its proximity to Nawiliwili Harbor and Lihue Airport, this hotel, like the Marriott, suffers from traffic and aircraft noise, although both drop off at night. Be prepared: If you want to close the windows to block the noise, make sure to request a room with air-conditioning. Otherwise, arm yourself with earplugs.

THE SOUTH SIDE: POIPU BEACH

The sunny side of Kauai, the South Shore, features one of the best resort areas in the state: Poipu beach. It's chock full of eateries, lots of places to stay, and interesting small boutique shops. Activities from golf to snorkeling trips abound. Best of all, the white sand beaches that line the resort are great for swimming, and, in a few areas, terrific for surfing. If you spent your entire vacation in Poipu you'd still have a terrific time. The resort area is located a couple of miles from the old plantation town of Koloa. "Town" is used loosely here, as the entire area is just two streets long, with wooden plantation-style structures lining a main street shaded with large flowering trees. Here you'll find the bank, post office, library, grocery stores, and other services one would expect in a small commercial area.

Poipu has a wide range of accommodations, but mainly in the luxury and moderate price categories—the expression "budget Poipu accommodations" is an oxymoron. The restaurant and shopping choices are correspondingly broad, but remember, this is Kauai, so your options are never numerous.

$$$ If you'd like to go the condo route, two good choices are **Waikomo Stream Villas** ★ or **Poipu Crater Resort** (see the "How Best to Book a Condo box" on p. 16; DC, DISC, MC, V). Bargain hunters will love the one-bedroom **Waikomo Stream Villas** where rates start at just $95 a night. The location is terrific, just a

Big Construction in Poipu

The forecast for the **Poipu Resort** area is plenty of major construction for the next couple of years. By the time all the building is done, the number of condominium and hotel rooms currently under construction (and not counting the ones still in the planning process) will increase the number of visitor accommodations in Poipu by 25%.

The good news is that more accommodations could mean more competitive prices. While all the construction is going on, Kauai County has very strict guidelines for noise and dust abatement, which is vigorously enforced. Just keep in mind that you most likely will have some traffic delays, construction noise, and the general problems with a lot of construction work in a small area.

As we went to press, there were 121 new luxury oceanfront hotel rooms under construction, which should be completed by spring 2008. Plus another 655 condominium units in three different projects have broken ground, with completion dates ranging from 2008 into 2009. And the county is planning a "roundabout" to replace the intersections of Poipu and Lawai Roads to help facilitate the traffic.

In the permit process, with no definite construction timetable yet, are plans for another 280 condominium units, a 64-room luxury hotel, 128 timeshare or vacation rental units, and an 11,000 square foot spa and fitness center.

For more information, contact the **Poipu Beach Resort Association, ☎ 888/744-0888** or www.poipubeach.org.

2-minute walk from your condo to the beach, close to shopping and restaurants. And units are large (1,100 sq. ft. for one-bedroom, 1,500 sq. ft. for two-bedroom), with comfortable lanais to take in the lush gardens surrounding the property, and all the amenities (washer/dryer, complimentary beach towels, high-speed Internet) that you'd have in a very pricey condo. I'd say it's one of the best kept secrets on the island. Just a little farther from the beach, **Poipu Crater Resort** has even lower rates on the two-bedroom garden view units (just $95–$130 through VRBO), though it's a 10-minute walk to the beach. The size of the rooms and amenities you get are similar to what you'll find at Wakomo Steam Villas, though here there's no A/C, just fans, and no maid service (but at these rates you can make the bed yourself). To book these two, compare and contrast what the Parrish Collection is offering with what the rental by owner sites have.

$$$ One of the better Poipu deals for a single person or couple is **Kauai Cove Cottages ★★** (2672 Puuholo Rd.; ☎ 800/624-9945 or 808/651-0279; www.kauaicove.com; DISC, MC, V), which offers cheerful, nonsmoking lodging starting at $135 per night (plus an additional one time $50–$65 cleaning fee). The three self-contained studio units are essentially the same, although only one, the Hibiscus, supplements the shower with a bathtub. Full kitchens are well stocked with cookware, and lush landscaping makes each unit's adjoining patio—complete with a barbecue grill—very private. The four-poster queen-size beds and bamboo furniture aren't especially comfortable, but that's a minor concern when sandy Poipu Beach and Koloa Landing, a popular snorkeling area, are right outside your door. The managers supply towels, chairs, and a cooler so you can linger on the sand. This clean property is ideal if you're seeking some seclusion but still want to be in the thick of things at Poipu.

$$$ If you can't make up your mind between the social atmosphere of a B&B or the privacy of a vacation rental, **Poipu Plantation** (1792 Pee Rd.; ☎ 800/634-0263 or 808/742-6757; www.poipubeach.com; MC, V) offers a hybrid of both. The B&B part features three bedrooms, each with a large, modern, well-functioning private bathroom, and a honeymoon suite with a fireplace in the sitting-room and a private lanai, rented in the charming main house, a nicely restored 1938 plantation-style home ($135–$210). Included in the rate is a full breakfast each morning on a screened lanai. Nine one- and two-bedroom cottages—all of them, like the rooms, cheerful, spacious, and bright—have been built around the house for those who seek more privacy and cooking facilities. The quality of these accommodations and their central Poipu location make them a very good value; the one-bedroom units run $145 to $175, and the two-bedroom units $185 to $210. While these prices are comparable with some condos in the area, they include the cleaning fee and the setting is friendlier and less crowded than most resorts. Discounts are available for stays longer than 3 nights or booked directly with the office or through the website, and there's a 5% discount May 1 to June 15. Rental-car discounts are offered, too.

THE SOUTH SIDE MAUKA: KALAHEO & LAWAI

$–$$$ Once you leave the Poipu resort area and head west to the communities of Lawai and Kalaheo, lodging prices drop considerably. Away from the beach, about a 10-minute drive inland from Poipu, in sleepy one-road Kalaheo town, **Kalaheo Inn** ★ kids (4444 Papalina Rd., Kalaheo; ☎ 888/332-6023 or 808/332-6032; www.kalaheoinn.com; MC, V) rents 14 studio, one-, two-, and three-bedroom suites. It can't compete with the style and luxury of Marjorie's (below), but at rates ranging from $80 to $120 per night, it's a bargain (especially the larger units). Every suite has at least a fridge and microwave; if you want to cook, units 5, 10, 12, and 13 have gas stoves. These are very simple, slightly worn accommodations, but I found them to be extremely clean, and the new pillowtop beds in each room are comfy. Guests have use of barbecue grills, beach towels, mats, chairs, snorkel gear (it's a 15-min. drive to the ocean), coolers, golf clubs (a 9-hole course is just up the street), games, and books. The staff also offers tropical fruit harvested from the grounds.

$ Hidden in an upscale subdivision of multi-million dollar homes, **Hale Ikena Nui** (3957 Ulualii St. Kalaheo; ☎ 800/550-0778 or 808/332-9005; www.kauaivacationhome.com; MC, V) is offering rooms for as little as $75 a night—oh, wouldn't the neighbors be shocked! That's the price for the bed-and-breakfast room (with complete use of the host's kitchen); the downstairs apartment is just $95 a night for two. Personally, I prefer the apartment, as it's a fully equipped vacation rental studio with a full-size kitchen (with dishwasher), private entrance, large dining room and living room areas, and a queen bed and a queen-size sofa bed. The unit easily sleeps four. ***Dog owners note:*** "Bear," a tiny Pomeranian/poodle mix not only greets every guest, but also will be happy to act as "your dog" while you stay here.

$ Glamour of a different sort is offered at **Aloha Estates at Kalaheo Plantation** ★ (4579 Puuwai Rd. Kalaheo; ☎ 808/332-7812; www.kalaheo-plantation.com; cash only). A 1924 plantation house, it's been lovingly restored to its former glory with 1920s and 1930s furniture and fabrics in each room. Stained glass, created by the host, adds to the prettiness of the place. There's a room to fit every visitor's needs and budget, from a small $55 room with king bed, kitchenette, private entrance, stereo, VCR, and lanai; to a $75 room with full kitchen, private entrance, hot tub, VCR, stereo, and private lanai overlooking the koi pond.

$$$ Another excellent B&B in Kalahelo is the tropical **Bamboo Jungle** ★★ (3829 Waha Rd.; ☎ 888/332-5115 or 808/332-5515; www.kauai-bedandbreakfast.com; MC, V). Not quite as rural as Aloha Estates (above), Bamboo Jungle is located in an upscale subdivision on a lushly landscaped property whose best feature is a bubbling fountain and an 82-foot lap pool. You'll stay in a quaint plantation-era home with moderate size bedrooms (each with private entrance through French doors and your own private lanai). The romantic bedrooms are decorated with mosquito netting over the beds (which comes in handy during the rainy season when the mosquitoes vacation in Kauai). Accommodations range from a single room with deck to a studio with minikitchen. Breakfast is served in the "great room" inside the house and is a full breakfast (frittata or waffles, French toast, pancakes, and so on). Golf and tennis courts are nearby, and in-room massage can be arranged. Note that there is no air-conditioning, which 350 days of the year is fine, but on the few days the trade winds stop blowing, it's not so great. ***Another caveat:*** no phone in the rooms. Doubles run $130 to $160, with a one-time $35 to $45 cleaning fee. A minimum stay of 3 to 5 nights (depending on the room) is required.

$$–$$$ Slightly closer to Poipu Beach, but still in the cool hills, **Marjorie's Kauai Inn** ★★★ (3307D Hailima Rd., Lawai; ☎ 800/717-8838 or 808/332-8838; www.marjorieskauaiinn.com; cash only) is a calm and tasteful hideaway that's smoke free inside and out. Perched on a steep hill, the views are spectacular—both from the house itself and from the thrilling cliffside pool. All three rooms have private lanais, those killer views, and kitchenettes stocked with fresh-baked bread, tropical fruits, juice, coffee, and tea. They're carefully furnished and

Neat Freaks, Beware

Island housekeeping and maintenance standards tend to be more relaxed than on the mainland. In other words, prepare yourself: Geckos, bugs, mold, and various little things that don't work, or were never built quite right, might be present to some degree in all but the most luxurious accommodations. And nearly every B&B in Hawaii (and several condos on Kauai) will ask you to remove your shoes before you enter; removing your shoes before you enter a home is a custom in Hawaii (it actually helps to keep the floors clean). If taking off your shoes before you go into a B&B or a condo upsets you, make plans to stay somewhere else.

pretty, with comfortable mattresses, quality linens, and many extras—indoor and outdoor dining tables, minifridge, coffeemaker, toaster and microwave oven, dishes and utensils, a DVD player and small movie library, and books on Hawaiiana topics. Other pluses include a lap swimming pool, a hot tub, and an extremely gracious host who enjoys advising guests. And the beach is just a 10-minute drive away. With rooms renting for $130 to $160 per night, this is one of the best values in this part of the island. Guests under 16 not admitted.

AS FAR WEST AS YOU CAN GO: WAIMEA

$ **Polihale State Beach Park** (end of 5-mile long dirt road from Mana Village, off Kaumuali'i Hwy. [Hwy. 50]; permits are available from the State Forestry and Wildlife Division, 3060 Eiwa St., Room 306, Lihue; ☎ 808/274-3444; www.hawaiistateparks.org/parks/kauai; cash only) holds the distinction of being the westernmost beach in the United States. The beach is spectacular—some 300 feet wide in summer, with rolling sand dunes (some as high as 100 ft.), and the islands of Niihau and Lehua just offshore. Bordered by the Na Pali Coast cliffs to the north, steep valleys to the east, and the blue Pacific to the south and west, this is one of the most dramatic camping areas in the state. The **campgrounds** for tent camping are located at the south end of the beach, affording privacy from daytime beach activities. There's great swimming in summer (even then, be on the lookout for waves and rip currents—there are no lifeguards), some surfing (the rides are usually short), and fishing. The camping is on sand, although there are some kiawe trees for shade. (***Warning:*** Kiawe trees drop long thorns, so make sure you have protective footwear.) Facilities include restrooms, showers, picnic tables, barbecues, and a spigot for drinking water. You can purchase supplies about 15 miles away in Waimea. Camping permits are $5 per night and camping is limited to 3 nights.

$ If you want to camp on the west side but can't get a space at Polihale State Park (see above), the county allows camping at the 4½-acre **Lucy Wright Park** (Alawai Rd., Waimea; for a permit contact Permits Division of Kauai County Parks and Recreation, 4193 Hardy St., Lihue; ☎ 808/241-6660; www.kauai-hawaii.com/activities.php; cash only) located just outside Waimea. Not the best beach park, it's okay for camping in a pinch. The park, located on the western side of the Waimea River, is named after the first native Hawaiian schoolteacher at Waimea, Lucy Kapahu Aukai Wright (1873–1931). More interestingly, this is where Captain Cook first came ashore in Hawaii in January 1778. The beach here is full of flotsam and jetsam from the river, making it unappealing. Facilities at Lucy Wright include the camping area, restrooms, a pavilion, picnic tables, and (cold) showers. To get to Lucy Wright Park, take Kaumualii Highway (Hwy. 50) to Waimea and turn left on Alawai Road, which leads to the park. Permits are $3 per person, per night (children 18 and younger are free). You can stay at the county parks a maximum of 4 nights (or 12 nights if you go from one county park to another).

$$–$$$ Waimea is an arid area surrounded by the blue ocean on one side and lofty mountains on the other. The town itself looks like a setting for an old Western movie, so it seems appropriate that Waimea's friendliest inn is set in the quaint former residence of a church pastor. The **Inn Waimea** (4469 Halepule Rd., Waimea;

☎ 808/338-0031; www.innwaimea.com; cash only) is located just 1 block from the ocean, and a block from "town" (walking distance to restaurants and shops). Its four rooms are individually decorated, each with a hint of flair—a wrought iron screen with banana leaf patterning here, and unusual bedpost there—have all the basic amenities (private phones with free local phone calls, private bathrooms, coffeemakers, fridges, cable TVs, ceiling fans, even free high-speed Internet), plus some unique niceties (one room has a Jacuzzi for two, another room has an ADA-compliant shower). Called Halepule Suites, they range in price from $110 to $125 a night. If you have a family, they also rent one- and two-bedroom cottages in the Waimea area ($150). If you plan to visit the North Shore, this is not a good location, as you will be on the road doing quite a bit of driving.

$$$–$$$$ I have to say I love **Waimea Plantation Cottages** ★★ (kids) (9400 Kaumualii Hwy.; ☎ 800/992-4632 or 808/338-1625; www.waimea-plantation.com; AE, DC, DISC, MC, V) because it's unique, historic, low key, and most importantly, real Kauai—with no glitz. It's also the only resort on the West Side. Among 27 acres, dotted with groves of coco palms, sit clusters of 48 beautifully restored former sugar-plantation cottages (where sugar workers and their families lived from the 1880s to the 1930s), which have been transformed into cozy, comfortable guest units with period furniture and fabrics from the 1930s, when sugar was king on Kauai. It's like stepping back in history (with the addition of an oceanfront pool, tennis courts, and laundry facilities). This is a terrific place for families: Kids can wander and explore, away from traffic. The latest addition is a spa on the property, with a complete menu, while you are pampered in this pastoral setting. The cottages range from studios to five bedrooms, all have sitting porch, modernized large bathrooms (showers are roomy enough for two), cable TV, and telephones. There are some caveats: The gray-and-black-sand beach is not good for swimming (murky water) and the location, like all of Waimea, is remote. If you plan to just relax on property, great; but if you want to see the North Shore, it's a 1½-hour drive away. Other amenities: complimentary wireless Internet access in common areas and in-room dataports. Studios start at $155, one-bedroom cottages start at $225, two-bedroom at $275, and the 3-, 4-, and 5-bedroom units go up from there (ask). Check the website for specials throughout the year.

THE WEST SIDE: KOKEE STATE PARK

The Kokee State Park, nestled above the scenic Waimea Canyon, at a chilly 4,000 feet has limited options for accommodations: a small lodge in the park, a few state camping areas, and a private camping area. Staying here is for nature lovers who happily give up fancy restaurants, shopping, and activities for a chance to stay in a quiet wilderness area, where hiking, bird-watching, and just watching the clouds go by are the choice activities.

$ At 4,000 feet, the nights are cold, particularly in winter, and no open fires are permitted at **Kokee State Park** (to obtain a camping permit, contact Hawaii State Parks Division, Division of State Parks, 3060 Eiwa St., Room 306, Lihue; ☎ 808/587-0300; www.hawaiistateparks.org/camping/fees.cfm; cash only). The state campground at Kokee allows tent camping only. Facilities include showers, drinking water, picnic tables, pavilion with tables, restrooms, barbecues, sinks for dishwashing, and electric lights. The permits are $5 per night; the time limit is 5 nights in a single 30-day period.

$ **Sugi Grove** and **Kawaikoi** in **Kokee State Park** (located about 4 miles from park headquarters on the Camp 10 Rd., an often muddy and steep four-wheel-drive road; permits are available from the State Forestry and Wildlife Division, 3060 Eiwa St., Room 306, Lihue; ☎ 808/274-3444; www.hawaiistateparks.org/parks/kauai) are named for the sugi pines, which were planted in 1937 by the Civilian Conservation Corps. This is a shady backwoods campsite with a single picnic shelter, a pit toilet, a stream, and space for several tents. The Kawaikoi site is a 3-acre open grass field, surrounded by Kokee plum trees and forests of koa and ohia. Facilities include two picnic shelters, a composting toilet, and a stream that flows next to the camping area. There is no potable water—bring in your own or treat the stream water. There's no fee for the permits, but camping is limited to 3 nights.

$$ If you want to stay indoors, the **Kokee Lodge** (3600 Kokee Rd.; 808/335-6061; scotts@hawaiilink.net; AE, DC, DISC, MC, V) is your best choice. Basically 12 rustic cabins with wood-burning stoves (you'll need to buy firewood), I find them a bit austere for long stays; still, they're a great place to crash if you want to get in some serious hiking, which is a delightful way to spend a few days on Kauai. They sleep six in bunk beds; if you're not that cozy with your companions, a few cabins have two bedrooms. Bring groceries to prepare meals in the cabin's kitchenette; the Kokee Lodge dining room, the sole food concession in the park, closes at 5pm. The cabins have no phones or TV sets and rent for $90 a night, plus a one-time cleaning fee of $20.

$–$$ If the Kokee Lodge is full, try the **YWCA of Kauai's Camp Sloggett** (Camp 10 Rd.; ☎ 808/245-5959; www.campingkauai.com/accomodations.html; cash only). Facilities range from a grassy field where you can pitch your tent (be sure it's waterproof) for $10 per night per person to dormitories equipped with bunk and twin beds, kitchenettes, and hot showers to Sloggett Lodge, a mountain house on the National Historic Register that sleeps 11 and has a big commercial kitchen, an 800-square-foot covered lanai, and a fireplace; you provide the firewood, sleeping bags, and linens. For a large group, the house is a steal, renting for $25 per night per person, based on a five-person, 2-night minimum (3 nights during holidays). For a solo traveler or couple, Caretaker's Cottage, which sleeps two, is a great deal. This one-bedroom cottage has a comfy king-size bed, a full kitchen, and a wood-burning stove for just $85 per night on weekdays and $120/night on weekends, for up to four people, with a 2-night minimum and $100 cleaning fee. ***Note:*** If you only stay 2 nights, that raises the amount you pay to $135 a night on weekdays and $170 a night on weekends, which is a bit pricey for what you get. Bring your own towels. Just remember, this is Camp Sloggett, with lodgings tending toward funky rather than luxury.

THE NORTH SHORE

Condominiums and vacation rentals dominate in this region. The bulk of them are found amid the manicured golf courses at Princeville, a master-planned resort community that is set above, but not on, the ocean. Some people find that a drawback, but the upside is that the mountain and ocean views are awesome. Princeville also has the region's widest selection of accommodations. Other lodging is found in the rural communities of Kilauea and Hanalei (one of the cutest towns on Kauai with plenty of hip restaurants, cutting edge shops, and activities).

If you choose to stay on the North Shore, be aware that it's remote, located about an hour's drive from the Lihue Airport. If you want to do a lot of island-wide sightseeing, be prepared to put in some serious road time. It's not pleasant to make the long, dark drive into Kapaa to dine at night. The price of everything, from gas to groceries, is higher here than elsewhere on the island, but it's possible to find a few bargains here and there.

$ Local residents love **Anahola Beach Park** ★★ (Manai Rd., Anahola; for camping permits contact Permits Division of Kauai County Parks and Recreation, 4193 Hardy St., Lihue; ☎ 808/241-6660; www.kauai-hawaii.com/activities.php; cash only) and are here almost every day. They say that this is the one of the safest year-round swimming beaches and great for small children. Tucked behind Kala Point, the narrow park has a shallow offshore reef that protects the sandy shoreline from the high surf visiting the area. Another plus is that board surfing is prohibited in this area. Surfers have to head to the north end of the beach to the sandbar where surfing is allowed. Tall ironwoods provide relief from the sun. Facilities include a camping area, a picnic area, barbecue grills, restrooms, and cold showers. A part-time lifeguard is on duty. When you camp here, don't leave your valuables unprotected. You must have a permit, which costs $3 per person, per night. You can stay at the county parks a maximum of 4 nights, or 12 nights if you are going from one county park to another. To get to Anahola Beach Park, take Kuhio Highway (Hwy. 56 north) to Anahola, turn right onto Anahola Road, and then turn right onto Manai Road.

$ The 12-acre **Anini Beach County Park** ★★ (Anini Beach Rd., Kilauea; to get a camping permit, contact Division of Kauai County Parks and Recreation, 4193 Hardy St., Lihue; ☎ 808/241-6660; www.kauai-hawaii.com/activities.php; cash only) is one of Kauai's safest beaches for swimming and windsurfing. It's also one of the island's most beautiful: It sits on a blue lagoon at the foot of emerald cliffs, looking more like Tahiti than almost any other strand in the islands. One of Kauai's largest beach camping sites, it is very, very popular, especially on summer weekends, when local residents flock to the beach to camp. It's easy to see why: This 3-mile-long gold-sand beach is shielded from the open ocean by the longest, widest fringing reef in Hawaii. With shallow water 4- to 5-feet deep, it's also the very best snorkeling spot on Kauai, even for beginners. On the northwest side, a channel in the reef runs out to the deep blue water with a 60-foot drop that attracts divers. Beachcombers love it, too: Seashells, cowries, and sometimes even rare Niihau shells can be found here. Anini has a park, a campground, picnic and barbecue facilities, outdoor showers, public telephones, and a boat-launch ramp. Princeville, with groceries and supplies, is about 4 miles away. You must have a permit, which costs $3 per person, per night. You can stay at the county parks a maximum of 4 nights, or 12 nights if you are going from one county park to another. To get here follow Kuhio Highway (Hwy. 56) to Kilauea; take the second exit, called Kalihiwai Road (the first dead-ends at Kalihiwai Beach), and drive a half-mile toward the sea; turn left on Anini Beach Road.

$ Camping is allowed at the 2½-acre **Hanalei Beach Park** ★★★ (Weke Rd., Hanalei. To apply for the permit, contact Permits Division of Kauai County Parks and Recreation, 4193 Hardy St., Lihue; ☎ 808/241-6660; www.kauai-hawaii.com/activities.php; cash only) on weekends and holidays only. Reserve in advance, as this is a very popular camping area. Gentle waves roll across the face of half-moon Hanalei Bay, running up to the wide, golden sand; sheer volcanic ridges laced by waterfalls rise to 4,000 feet on the other side, 3 miles inland. Swimming is excellent year-round, especially in summer, when Hanalei Bay becomes a big, placid lake. The aquamarine water is also great for boogie boarding, surfing, fishing, windsurfing, canoe paddling, kayaking, and boating. (There's a boat ramp on the west bank of the Hanalei River.) Facilities include a lifeguard, a pavilion, restrooms, picnic tables, and parking. You must have a permit, which costs $3 per person, per night. You can stay at the county parks a maximum of 4 nights, or 12 nights if you are going from one county park to another. To get here, take Kuhio Highway (Hwy. 56), which becomes Highway 560 after Princeville. In Hanalei town, make a right on Aku Road just after Tahiti Nui, then turn right again on Weke Road, which dead-ends at the parking lot for the Black Pot section of the beach; the easiest beach access is on your left.

$ There are a lot of pluses and minuses to **Haena Beach Park** ★★★ (Hwy. 560, 4 miles past Hanalei; to apply for the permit, contact Permits Division of Kauai County Parks and Recreation, 4193 Hardy St., Lihue; ☎ 808/241-6660; www.kauai-hawaii.com/activities.php; cash only). Its biggest plus is its glorious good appearance: The nearly 6-acre park is bordered by the ocean on one side and a dramatic mountain on the other. In fact, old-timers call this beach Maniniholo, after the local manini fish, which used to be caught in nets during summer. Across the highway from this park are the dry caves, also called Maniniholo. The caves, really a lava tube, run a few hundred feet into the mountain. The area is great for camping, flat and grassy with palm trees for shade. Now the minuses: This is not a good swimming beach because it faces the open ocean, and Kauai's North Shore can be windy and rainy. However, good swimming and snorkeling are available either a quarter mile east of the campground (about a 5-min. walk) at Tunnels Beach, where an offshore reef protects the bay; or at Kee Beach, about a mile west of the campground. Facilities include the camping area, restrooms, outside screened showers, a pavilion with tables, electric lights, a dishwashing sink, picnic tables, and grills; however, there are no lifeguards. The water here is safe to drink. Supplies can be picked up in Hanalei, 4 miles east. You will need a permit, which costs $3 per person, per night. You can stay at the county parks a maximum of 4 nights, or 12 nights if you are going from one county park to another. To get here, take Highway 56 from Lihue, which becomes Highway 560. Look for the park, 4 miles past Hanalei.

$ The ideal spot to stay before or after conquering the Na Pali Trail, **Camp Naue** (Hwy. 560, 4 miles past Hanalei, 2 miles from the end of the road; for permits contact the YMCA ☎ 808/246-9090; cash only) is also a good pick if you just want to spend a few days lounging on fabulous Haena Beach. This YMCA camp sits right on the ocean (two bunkhouses), on 4 grassy acres ringed with ironwood and kumani trees and bordered by a sandy beach that offers excellent swimming and snorkeling in the summer (the ocean here turns really rough in the winter). Each bunkhouse has four rooms with 10 to 12 beds, $12 per bunk. Facilities are coed, with separate bathrooms for men and women. There's no bedding here, so bring your sleeping bag and towels. Large groups frequently book the camp, but if there's room, the Y will squeeze you into the bunkhouse or offer tent space ($12/person). Also on the grounds: a beachfront pavilion, and a campfire area with picnic tables. You can pick up basic supplies in Haena, but it's best to stock up on groceries and other necessities in Lihue or Hanalei. Phone them a few months before your trip (☎ 808/246-9090), and they'll let you know if there's space. Don't e-mail or send a letter; the Y simply is not set up to answer mail.

$ Simply put, **Na Pali Coast Wilderness State Park** ★★★ (for a camping permit contact Kauai State Parks Office, 3060 Eiwa St., Room 306, Lihue; ☎ 808/274-3444; www.hawaiistateparks.org/parks/kauai; cash only) is the loveliest area in the Hawaiian Islands. Hanging valleys open like green-velvet accordions, and waterfalls tumble to the sea from the 4,120-foot-high cliffs; the experience is both exhilarating and humbling. Whether you hike in, fly over, or take a boat cruise past, be sure to see this park. Established in 1984, Na Pali Coast State Park takes in a 22-mile stretch of fluted cliffs that wrap the northwestern shore of Kauai between Kee Beach and Polihale State Park. Volcanic in origin, carved by wind and sea, "the cliffs" (*na pali* in Hawaiian), which heaved out of the ocean floor 200 million years ago, stand as constant reminders of majesty and endurance. Four major valleys—Kalalau, Honopu, Awaawapuhi, and Nualolo—crease the cliffs. The camping season runs roughly from May or June to September (depending on the site). All campsites are booked almost a year in advance, so call or write well ahead of time. Stays are limited to 5 nights. Camping areas along the Kalalau Trail include **Hanakapiai Beach** (facilities are pit toilets, and water is from the stream), **Hanakoa Valley** (no facilities, water from the stream), **Milolii** (no facilities, water from the stream), and **Kalalau Valley** (composting toilets, several pit toilets, and water from the stream). Generally, the fee for a state park camping permit is $5 per campsite per night, but the Na Pali fee is $10 per campsite per night. You cannot stay more than 5 consecutive nights at one campsite. Keep your camping permit with you at all times.

KILAUEA

$–$$ One of the best deals here is **Aloha Plantation** (4481 Malulani St., Kilauea; ☎ 877/658-6977 or 808/828-1693; www.garden-isle.com/aloha; cash only), a plantation manager's house that was built in the 1920s (and is filled with Hawaiian antiques) on a residential street in the rural community of Kilauea. The owners rent out two rooms in the house for $69 to $79 (one room has a half bath but shares a shower with the owner and the other has a private bathroom) and a garage converted into a studio for $99. The rooms are furnished with comfortable wrought-iron beds and ceiling fans, plus they share a screen porch, with a coffeepot and an old 7-Up machine used as a fridge. In the courtyard is an outdoor cooking area with enough appliances to fix dinner, and a fridge. The studio has air-conditioning, TV, phone, and CD, plus a private bath. Located just off the highway (with some highway noise, but not much), the Aloha Plantation is about 15 minutes from Princeville and 20 minutes from Hanalei. Coffee, pastries, and fruit are served each morning.

$$ Serenity incarnate, **North Country Farms** ★ (kids) (Kahili Makai St., off Kuhio Hwy. at mile marker 22, Kilauea; ☎ 808/828-1513; www.northcountryfarms.com;

cash only) offers a slice of real-life Kauai. Lee Roversi rents out a comfortable and reasonably priced cottage ($150 for two; $10 for each extra guest, kids under 18 stay free) on her 4-acre organic farm. The farm supplies about 50 families each week with fruits, flowers, and vegetables, which guests can pick. The setting is rural, a 15-minute drive from the beach, and the handcrafted wooden cottages are very private, with attached covered lanais, kitchenettes, and a country-tropical decor. The bedroom has a queen bed, with additional sleeping arrangements possible in the living room. The full bathroom is complemented with outside shower. Lee is a gracious hostess, supplying cottages with coffee, teas, juice, fruit, granola, and muffins, as well as loads of paperback books and magazines, beach gear, videos, puzzles, and games. ***Note:*** The only thing missing is a TV set. Families and those interested in sustainable living will be especially happy here.

PRINCEVILLE

$$ Aside from some very expensive oceanfront vacation homes at Anini Beach, you won't find many lodgings between Kilauea and Princeville, except for **Mana Yoga** (Ahonui Place, just off the highway, just shy of the resort area, Princeville; ☎ 808/826-9230; www.manayoga.com; cash only). This sweet little vacation rental in a rural subdivision, *mauka* (inland) of Kuhio Highway, offers expansive mountain views. Located downstairs in a family home, the two units include an 800-square-foot two-bedroom apartment and a small studio. Both have private entrances, their own kitchens, bathrooms, and outside lanais. The views are of the verdant hills surrounding the farm. The amenities range from pillowtop mattresses to complimentary Wi-Fi. Guests are welcome to pick the fruit and vegetables in season on the 5-acre farm. Most guests stay here to study with hostess Michaelle Edwards, who has developed the unique YogAlign method, a pain-free way of stretching (but anyone is welcome, even non-stretchers). The studio is $95 and the two-bedroom unit is $145. There is a 3-night minimum and a one-time $70 cleaning fee. The beach is about a 15-minute drive away.

$$–$$$$ If you want to stay in the Princeville area but want a location with a bit more luxury or pampering, try **Princeville Bed and Breakfast** ★ (3875 Kamehameha Dr. [the 3rd street on the right past the entrance to Princeville], P.O. Box 3370, Princeville; ☎ 800/826-6733 or 808/826-6733; www.kauai-bandb.com; MC, V), a very large and luxurious home located on the 6th hole of the Makai Course. This is a true B&B, with the owners living in the house, which serves a full sit-down breakfast daily (pancakes or an egg casserole with plenty of fruit, coffee, tea and pastries). You can choose from two bedrooms, each with a private entrance, for $135 or $145, or rent a 1,000-square-foot suite, replete with whirlpool tub, kitchenette, and king-size beds, for $205 to $300 per night. All the rooms have private bathrooms, fridges, and TV/VCRs, as well as golf-course, mountain, and distant ocean views. The furnishings are very tasteful and comfortable, and the home is extremely clean, with fruit trees growing in the yard. There's a 3-night minimum stay, and it's not appropriate for children.

HANALEI

$$ Once you enter the rural community of Hanalei, lodgings become expensive because of their proximity to a desirable stretch of long, sandy beach. But if you're not super fussy, and don't mind spartan backpackers-type accommodations, you

Cock-a-doodle . . . Aargh!

Kauai folks tend to go to bed early and get up with the roosters, literally. No matter where you stay, you're likely to encounter roosters serving as living alarm clocks. The problem is, they aren't very good at telling time, so they often start crowing at about 3am—or earlier, on nights with big, bright moons—and keep it up through the day.

Flocks of wild chickens are ubiquitous on Kauai. After Hurricane Iniki in 1992, the strong winds picked up and scattered the fowl all over the island, where they have been populating at a prodigious rate ever since. Generally, having a few chickens scratching around in the dirt is quaint and a photo opportunity. However, the "dark side" of the chicken population explosion is the increase in the number of roosters. In fact, a new industry has cropped up: Rooster Eradicators. Resorts hire these eradicators to remove the roosters from the well-manicured grounds because the large number of these male birds has led to crowing contests. Normally, roosters will crow as the sun comes up. But on Kauai, with the rapid population increase, the roosters crow all day long and throughout the night in some places. Just be warned that part of the "charm" of Kauai is the rooster population, and you might want to consider bringing earplugs.

can beat the high prices by staying at **Hanalei Inn** (5468 Kuhio Hwy.; ☎ 808/826-9333; www.hanaleiinn.com; MC, V). Here, you can rent a room with a private bathroom for $109, or a studio with kitchen for just $10 more; you'll also pay a $10 cleaning fee for a 1-night stay. These are very plain and utilitarian accommodations with a ceiling fan, bed, small kitchen, tiny bathroom, small table with a couple of chairs, and a TV—period. Some guests might find the accommodations a bit bare-bones for the price. Most of the clientele are hikers and backpackers who have been out in the jungle and want a clean, soft bed and a shower for the night. ***Warning:*** Located right on the highway; bring earplugs for the traffic noise.

$$–$$$ For a little more comfort and some company, try one of Hanalei's oldest bed-and-breakfasts, **Bed, Breakfast & Beach at Hanalei Bay** (5095 Piikoa St.; reservations ☎ 808/826-6111; www.bestofhawaii.com/hanalei; cash only), which offers quiet accommodations on a residential street, just 150 yards from Hanalei Bay. Hostess Carolyn Barnes has three guest rooms, ranging from a 700-square-foot suite with a 360-degree view to a mini-apartment on the ground floor with a kitchenette and an outdoor shower; prices range from $110 to $170 with breakfast. The location couldn't be better (some guests don't even bother to rent a car). It's a 4-minute walk to Hanalei Bay's 2-mile-long beach, and a 10-minute walk to the shops and restaurants of Hanalei. For families, Carolyn also has a cozy two-bedroom, one-bathroom house a couple of blocks away ($1,250 a week).

$$$ For your "dream vacation," I highly recommend splurging on accommodations and book a studio at the **Hanalei Surf Board House** ★★★ (5459 Weke Rd., Hanalei; ☎ 808/826-9825; www.hanaleisurfboardhouse.com; cash only). Although at first glance it seems pricey ($175 a night), the list of amenities, from location to charming accommodations themselves, actually make this a value property. The first reason to stay here is the incredible location—just a block from the beach (about a 2-min. walk to the ocean), and within walking distance of Hanalei town and its restaurants and shops. The second reason to stay here is the two studio units that host Simon Potts has whimsically designed, which are charming: One studio is outfitted with "cowgirl" decor, and the other in Elvis Presley memorabilia. Both units have kitchenettes, comfy beds, water purification systems, 300-channel TVs, free Wi-Fi, Bose CD players, DVDs, iPod docks, barbecues, and backyard lanais. The third, and best, reason to stay here is your host. Potts is a former record company executive from England who claims he has "retired" to Hawaii. For a guy who is retired, we'd like to have seen him when he was working. Besides renovating the two studio units on the ground floor of his home, he's also the soccer coach on the North Shore. One day Potts got a brilliant idea—he asked the kids he coaches if they had any old surfboards. After he had collected a few dozen he fenced in his yard with the surfboards (standing straight up, one next to another).

DINING FOR ALL TASTES

You'll find the cheapest eateries on the East Side of the island because this area caters to a local clientele. Resort areas like Hanalei, Princeville, and Poipu are significantly pricier, in general, but offer excellent restaurants, a huge selection of cuisines, and the cutting edge in culinary trends.

EAST SIDE: IN & NEAR LIHUE

In Lihue many restaurants cater to the business crowd and close before dark. But if you're sightseeing, it's quite likely you'll find yourself cruising through town during daylight hours, looking for breakfast or lunch. And you'll be in luck, with a choice of some great little "no dinner" eateries that I wish were in my neighborhood.

$ If your kids are hankering for a burger, or if you're in your swimsuit and just want to grab a quick meal, head for **Kalapaki Beach Hut** (kids) (3474 Rice St., Nawiliwili; ☎ 808/246-6330; Tues–Sun 7am–8pm, Mon 7am–9pm; MC, V). This tiny eatery actually has an ocean view, but everything is served on paper plates with plastic cutlery at cheap, cheap prices. Breakfasts are hearty omelets, pancakes, and numerous egg dishes all under $8. Lunches are heavy on the hamburgers (prepared 10 different ways), lots of sandwiches, a few healthy salads, and fish and chips (also all under $8). Kids get their own menu with smaller portions. Located behind the ritzy Marriott Resort in the Nawiliwili Harbor area, the "hut" has window service, a few tables downstairs, and more tables upstairs (with an ocean view out the screen windows).

Where to Stay & Dine on Kauai's East Side

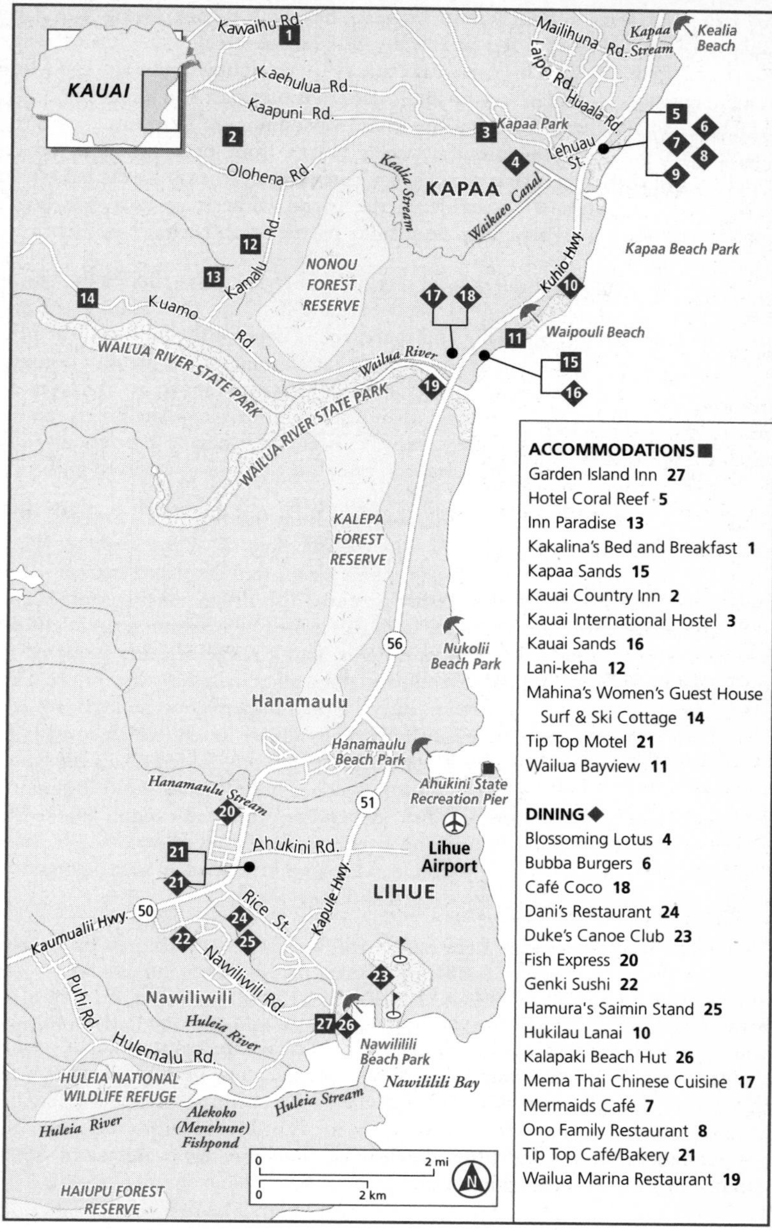

ACCOMMODATIONS ■

- Garden Island Inn **27**
- Hotel Coral Reef **5**
- Inn Paradise **13**
- Kakalina's Bed and Breakfast **1**
- Kapaa Sands **15**
- Kauai Country Inn **2**
- Kauai International Hostel **3**
- Kauai Sands **16**
- Lani-keha **12**
- Mahina's Women's Guest House Surf & Ski Cottage **14**
- Tip Top Motel **21**
- Wailua Bayview **11**

DINING ◆

- Blossoming Lotus **4**
- Bubba Burgers **6**
- Café Coco **18**
- Dani's Restaurant **24**
- Duke's Canoe Club **23**
- Fish Express **20**
- Genki Sushi **22**
- Hamura's Saimin Stand **25**
- Hukilau Lanai **10**
- Kalapaki Beach Hut **26**
- Mema Thai Chinese Cuisine **17**
- Mermaids Café **7**
- Ono Family Restaurant **8**
- Tip Top Café/Bakery **21**
- Wailua Marina Restaurant **19**

$ You can't leave Kauai without at least having breakfast at **Tip Top Café/ Bakery** ★ kids (3474 Rice St., Nawiliwili; ☎ 808/246-6330; Tues–Sun 7am–8pm, Mon 7am–9pm; MC, V). This small cafe/bakery (in the lobby of the Tip Top Motel) is an institution on Kauai, serving local customers breakfast and lunch since 1916. The biggest bang for your buck is breakfast: Most items are $5 or under, and their macadamia pancakes are famous. Lunch ranges from pork chops to teriyaki chicken, but their specialty is oxtail soup. For a real treat, stop by the bakery and take something home (I never leave the island without at least one box of malasadas, which are Portuguese donut-like pastries with no holes in them).

$–$$ If you want to sample a good mix of local-style cuisine, **Dani's Restaurant** (4201 Rice St.; ☎ 808/245-4991; Mon–Sat 5am–1:30pm, cash only) is the place to do it. The dining room is big and spare; you're here for the food and the prices ($4–$10), not the ambience. If you want to eat Hawaiian food without doing the luau thing, order the *laulau* (pork and taro leaves wrapped in ti leaves and steamed) or kalua pig, slow-roasted in an underground oven. Alternately, go with Japanese—tonkatsu (pork cutlet), teriyaki beef, or fish-cake omelets are quite tasty. You'll also find standard American fare, but everything is served with rice.

$–$$ Plan a picnic lunch or dinner with the fresh fish from **Fish Express** ★ kids (3343 Kuhio Hwy., across the street from the Wal-Mart; ☎ 808/245-9918; MC, V). Mon–Sat 10am–6pm; Sun 10am–4pm). This clean, well displayed market is basically a take out fish shop with freshly prepared fish dishes ranging from Cajun-style grilled ahi with guava basil, to fresh fish grilled in a passion-orange-tarragon sauce to fresh fish tacos in garlic and herbs, and a range of other prepared fish dishes, all served with rice, salad, and vegetables, all at incredibly low prices. There are six preparations to choose from, each flavored to perfection and costing $8 to $10. Local residents come here for the Hawaiian plate lunch (which consists of a *"laulau,"* composed of kalua pork, lomi salmon, ahi poi, folded into a big banana leaf and served with white rice and poi), which is not for those counting calories. Other popular dishes are smoked fish (depending what was caught, smoked fish can range from ahi/tuna to swordfish). Every restaurant has its own "secret" smoking technique, but generally the fish is marinated in soy sauce, sugar, ginger, and garlic, then smoked in a smoke oven with kiawe wood.

$–$$ If you have a yen for Japanese cuisine, but don't want to dress up or spend a fortune, stop by **Genki Sushi** kids (Kukui Grove Shopping Center, 3-2600 Kaumualii Hwy., Lihue; ☎ 808/632-2450; Sun–Thurs 11am–9pm, Fri–Sat 11am–10pm; MC, V), an affordable chain that's perfect for families: The sushi is inexpensive (and made fresh), and the kids will love being able to select each dish as it circulates the counter on a conveyor belt. Prices are based on the color of the plate, and range from $2 to $6.

$–$$ Another casual place to sample local style cuisine is **Hamura's Saimin Stand** (2956 Kress St., Lihue; ☎ 808/245-3271; Mon–Thurs 10am–10:30pm, Fri–Sat 10am–midnight, Sun 10am–9pm; cash only). The first thing you'll notice is that there is a crowd at this tiny eatery, all focused on their steaming bowls of saimin, a unique island dish. The menu, mainly saimin (a Japanese noodle soup popular in Hawaii with fish, shrimp, or meats and vegetables served hot) and

Where to Stay & Dine on Kauai's South Side

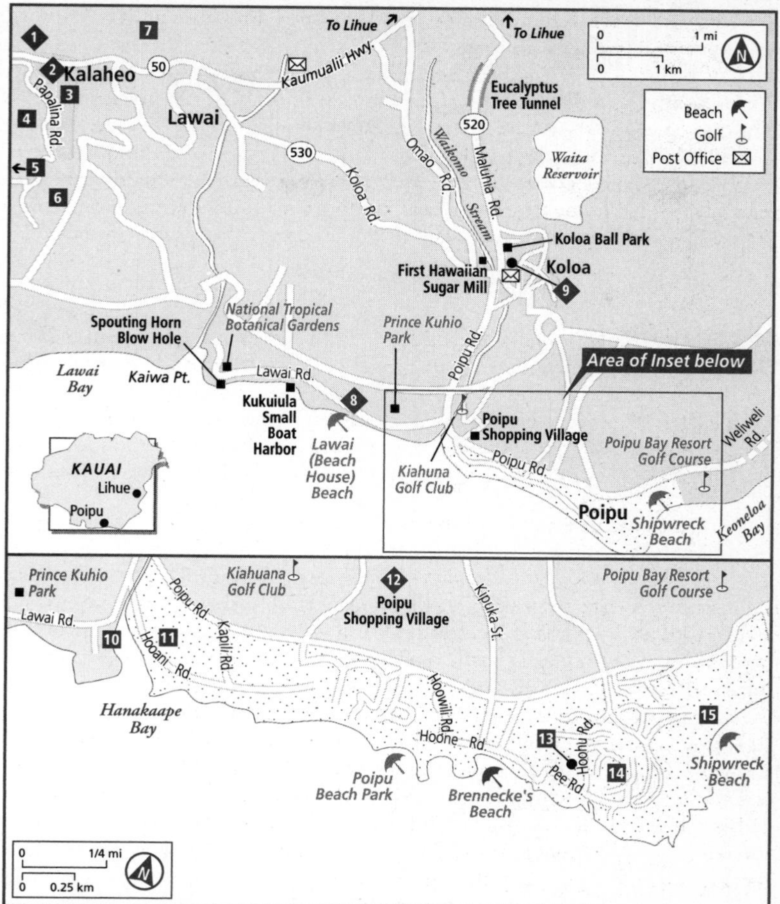

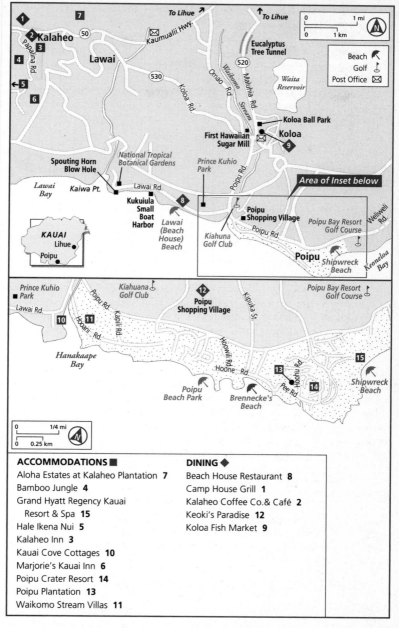

ACCOMMODATIONS ■

Aloha Estates at Kalaheo Plantation **7**
Bamboo Jungle **4**
Grand Hyatt Regency Kauai Resort & Spa **15**
Hale Ikena Nui **5**
Kalaheo Inn **3**
Kauai Cove Cottages **10**
Marjorie's Kauai Inn **6**
Poipu Crater Resort **14**
Poipu Plantation **13**
Waikomo Stream Villas **11**

DINING ◆

Beach House Restaurant **8**
Camp House Grill **1**
Kalaheo Coffee Co.& Café **2**
Keoki's Paradise **12**
Koloa Fish Market **9**

Where to Stay & Dine on Kauai's North Shore

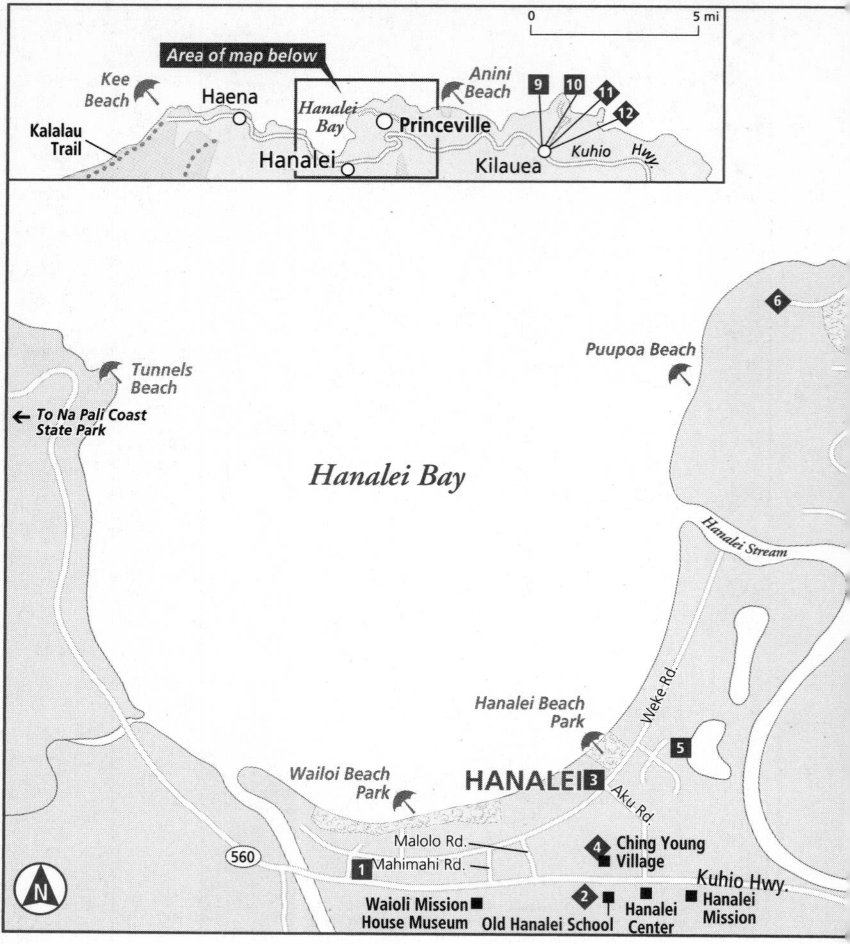

teriyaki barbecue sticks, attract an all-day, late-night, pre- and post-movie crowd. What makes Hamura's so popular are the perfect noodles and generous helpings of vegetables, wontons, hard-boiled eggs, sweetened pork, and condiments. Most dishes are under $10

$$$–$$$$ At least 1 night, plan to splurge and eat right next to the water at **Duke's Canoe Club** (in the Kauai Marriott Resort & Beach Club, 3610 Rice St., Nawiliwili; ☎ 808/246-9599; daily 5–10pm; AE, DISC, MC, V). Overlooking the ocean, this is one of Kauai's "in spots," where 20-something local residents and elegantly dressed visitors come out to play. Duke's not only has a great view, but also a terrific menu (five or six varieties of fresh catch each night), and can be pricey. I suggest that you go during Tropical Friday, when tropical drinks go for

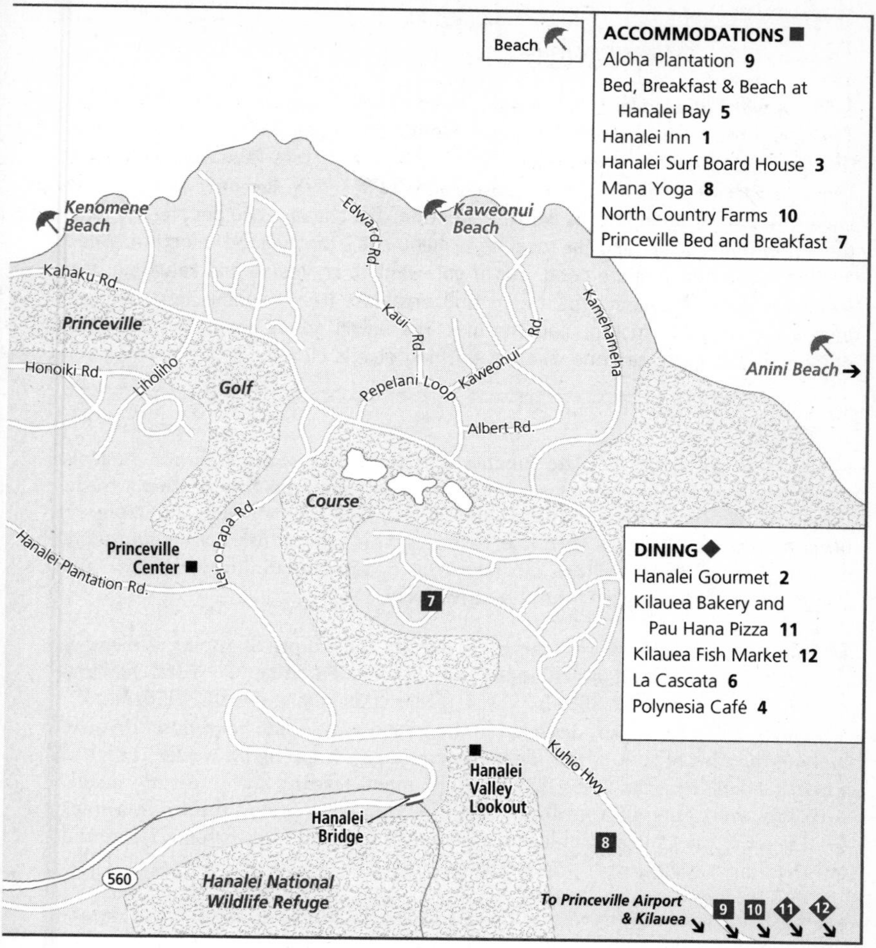

under $6 from 4 to 6pm and live music keeps things happy—plus you can fill up on the pupu (appetizers) and still come out ahead.

THE SOUTH SIDE

The South Side has quite a few restaurants, some of which are truly excellent, but they tend to be expensive. The simple, casual, local-style eateries common to the East Side are in decidedly short supply on this side of the island, in part because many restaurants cater to the well-heeled tourist crowd.

$–$$ One of the better places to grab a low-cost take out lunch or early dinner is **Koloa Fish Market** ★ (kids) (5482 Koloa Rd., Koloa; ☎ 808/742-6199; Mon–Fri 10am–6pm, Sat 10am–5pm; cash only), located on the main drag in Koloa

After-Hours Eats

$–$$ ***A word of advice:*** Don't dawdle, or you might miss dinner. It's difficult in Kauai to find any meal, much less a good one, after 8pm. For that reason alone, **Oki Diner** (3125 Kuhio Hwy., Lihue; ☎ 808/245-5899; Tues–Wed 6pm–midnight, Thurs–Sat and Mon 6pm–3:30am, closed Sun; cash only), the only place on the island that stays open late, is worth a mention. It's cheap—two people can have dinner for under $20—and the local-style menu has a pretty good selection. When available, the dim sum are good, and if you want to try *laulau* and kalua pig, the Hawaiian plate is decent. You'll also find breakfast items, sandwiches, burgers, beef stew, teriyaki chicken, and the like. The baked goods are better than the entrees, but it all tastes fine when everything else is closed.

---

town. They specialize in plate lunches and local-style seafood dishes, such as sashimi and poke (chunks of seasoned raw fish), and the fish is always fresh. Lunch entrees (most under $10) may be teriyaki fish, fried chicken, kalua pig, or other hot dishes, all served with rice. Although this is just a fish market and there are no tables in the store, you can take your delicious plate lunch down to the Poipu Beach Park, only a 10-minute drive away.

$$–$$$ A restaurant worth checking out in the Poipu Shopping Village is the slightly fancier and much more lush **Keoki's Paradise** ★ (2360 Kiahuna Plantation Dr., Koloa; ☎ 808/742-7534; 11am–11pm daily; AE, DC, DISC, MC, V). This plant-filled eatery was designed in the style of a dockside boathouse. If you're looking for a bit of action, this lively restaurant gets hopping on weekend nights, when it offers live music and dancing. The menu features surf-and-turf cuisine, with appetizers ranging from fresh sashimi and poke to grilled shrimp in a spicy Thai sauce. Steaks, burgers, chicken, pasta, pork ribs, and fresh-fish specials round out the dinner menu, with prices ranging from $10 to $24.

$$$–$$$$ If you want to treat yourself to a special dinner in a romantic, ocean-front setting, make a reservation at the **Beach House Restaurant** ★★★ (5022 Lawai Rd., Koloa; ☎ 808/742-1424; www.the-beach-house.com; dinner only 5:30–9pm daily; AE, DC, MC, V) and prepare to enjoy a leisurely meal that showcases Hawaii Regional Cuisine. This is one restaurant where the food is equally paired with the locale, and that's saying something, since the Beach House is tucked between the manicured grass of Prince Kuhio Park, a coastal promenade, and the Pacific Ocean. This is the kind of restaurant where local residents splurge to celebrate a special occasion like a birthday or an anniversary. You must book in advance (like the day you buy your airplane tickets) and be sure to request a table close to the ocean, where you'll have an unobstructed view of the sun slipping into the sea. The dining room, with its oversize windows, also capitalizes on the setting. The menu is sophisticated and original; signature dishes include the hearty paella made with island fish and the spicy fire-roasted ahi. I also recommend the rack of lamb, flavored with a delicate mint-coriander marinade, and the crisp-skinned duck, slow-roasted Chinese-style and served with a little pancake made from risotto and porcini mushroom. The entrees, priced at $18 to $28, are filling and can be shared.

WEST SIDE

Unless you're one of the few who stay on the West Side, it's a little too remote to warrant making a special trip out there for a meal. But if you're heading back to your room after a tour boat ride or day of sightseeing in Kokee State Park or Waimea Canyon when hunger strikes, as it likely will, you can take comfort in knowing there are some good places to eat along the highway.

$–$$ **Camp House Grill** (kids) (1–3959 Kaumualii Hwy.; ☎ 808/332-9755; 6am–9pm daily; AE, DISC, MC, V) is one of those options. It's open for three meals a day, serving up hearty, country-style breakfasts (under $10) and the usual burger, sandwich, and salad fare at lunch (most items under $10). They're good with a grill, whether it's cooking burgers, ribs, steaks, fresh fish, or chicken ($10–$15), and anything barbecued is a good bet on this menu. The homemade pie—chocolate macadamia nut—gets a big thumbs up and can be purchased whole or by the slice. The decor is rustic and funky—think screen doors, paper cups, and wooden tables—but it's clean and suits the menu. Another Camp House Grill (4–831 Kuhio Hwy.; ☎ 808/822-2442), is in the Kauai Shopping Village in Kapaa, but neither the food nor the setting is as noteworthy. In my opinion, if you can't make it to the Kalaheo locale, don't bother.

$–$$ For breakfast, lunch, or an afternoon java jolt, stop by the **Kalaheo Coffee Co. & Café** ★★ (2–2436 Kaumualii Hwy., Suite A-2, Kalaheo; ☎ 808/332-5858; Mon–Fri 6am–3pm, Sat 6:30am–3pm, Sun 6:30am–2pm; MC, V). This little diner is busy but manages to retain its friendly service during the all-day rush. They make wonderful giant cinnamon rolls, as well as the usual breakfast fare: pancakes, eggs and hash browns, and omelets (under $8). At lunch the hefty burgers, deli-style sandwiches, and homemade soups and salads (under $10) are prepared to order. You can take your food out or eat in the small, clean, casual dining room.

$–$$ Heading east, the next town is Eleele, where **Grinds Café & Espresso** (Eleele Shopping Center, Kaumualii Hwy., Eleele; ☎ 808/335-6027; 6am–9pm daily; MC, V) takes fast food up a step or two, while managing to keep the prices low and the service quick. The menu, varied enough to suit a family, is the same all day. Breakfast features omelets ($5.75–$6.25). The pastries and breads are freshly baked, which is a nice touch. And alongside the usual burgers (from $4.25 for a BBQ burger to $8.25 to the Cajun burger with classic Cajun spices, onions, and Jack cheese) and deli-type sandwiches (ranging from an Italian spice-pesto cream cheese sandwich with salami, tomato, and grated parmesan cheese for $4.50 to a Reuben sandwich or a hot roast beef sandwich for $6.50), you'll also find veggie burgers ($5.75), a tasty salad made with hearty chunks of chicken and walnuts ($6.50), fried fish ($7.50), chicken barbecued with a tangy sauce ($6.75), chili and rice ($4.50), and pizza (from $13). There's a covered lanai where you can eat, although the parking-lot view isn't especially pleasing, or you can order takeout.

Bring the Kids

Ohana (family) is the basis of the Hawaiian culture, so it's no surprise that *keiki* (kids) are welcome in restaurants everywhere on Kauai. This takes a lot of the pressure off folks traveling with young children, as even crying kids won't generate stink eye from other diners. Instead, local patrons and restaurant staff tend to do whatever they can to put the smile back on baby's face. High chairs and booster seats are widely available; children's menus are less common, especially at local restaurants, where kids eat what adults do and just bring home their leftovers.

$$–$$$ Way out west in Waimea, **Wrangler's Steakhouse** (9852 Kaumualii Hwy.; ☎ 808/338-1218; Mon–Thurs 11am–8:30pm, Fri 11am–9pm, Sat 5–9pm, closed Sun; AE, DISC, MC, V) is channeling the Old West with its food and cowboy decor (apropos for these parts)—props like *paniolo* saddles and even an old stagecoach fill the historic Ako General Store, which has been lovingly restored. If you're a history buff, you'll enjoy the *kaukau* lunch—a sampling of meat, rice, condiments, and other goodies served up in a two-tiered metal pail that's just like the ones used by plantation hands to transport their meals to the sugar and pineapple fields. Other options: crisp and light vegetable tempura, a 16-ounce steak grilled with garlic, capers, peppers, or a teriyaki sauce, and an assortment of fish, chicken, and pasta entrees ($12–$24). The gift shop is worth a browse, too, since it's stocked with distinctive toys and crafts, many made in Kauai, which you won't see in other island shops. Ask for a table on the back deck, which is really nice on one of those warm, starry nights so common in Waimea.

COCONUT COAST: RESTAURANTS FROM WAILUA TO KAPAA

When you hit the Wailua-Kapaa corridor, you're in Kauai's dining hotspot. You'll find lots of restaurants, many of them local-style, and very few of them budget-busters. Most are simple, casual eateries, but, unlike restaurants in Lihue, they're nearly always open for dinner.

$–$$ If you have a carload of hungry kids, head for **Bubba Burgers** (4-1421 Kuhio Hwy., Kapaa; ☎ 808/823-0069; daily 10:30am–8pm; MC, V), where hamburgers are the attractions, with a few out-of-the-ordinary burgers like the Slopper (open-faced with chili for $4.75), the half-pound Big Bubba (three patties for $4.50), or the Hubba Bubba (with rice, hot dog, and chili for $5.75). There's also a Bubba's plate lunch, featuring a burger patty and Bubba's Budweiser chili. They have a few other items (fish burger, tempeh burgers for vegetarians, even a chicken burger, all priced at $4.25) but this is your basic burger place with a wonderful sense of humor.

$–$$ **Ono Family Restaurant** (1292 Kuhio Hwy., Kapaa; ☎ 808/822-1710; daily 7am–2pm; AE, DC, DISC, MC, V) is my one pick that doesn't serve dinner. Service stops after lunch, but I prefer breakfast here, if I can get a table, and preferably one outside so I can watch for friends passing by on the road. This little cafe has lots of tropical country charm, and it's popular with locals as well as visitors. Prices range from $6 to $12 for omelets—if you are a fan of spicy foods, take a chance and try an omelet with kimchi, Portuguese sausage, and fried rice—and for gourmet concoctions like eggs Canterbury (poached eggs with ham, turkey, Jack cheese, tomato, hollandaise sauce, and mushrooms on an English muffin). Banana macadamia-nut pancakes, breakfast burritos, and such standard lunch fare as burgers, sandwiches, salads, and soups round out the menu. As I said, breakfast is the better choice.

$–$$ Just down the road from the Coconut Marketplace, you'll find **Mema Thai Chinese Cuisine** ★ (Wailua Shopping Plaza, 4–369 Kuhio Hwy., Kapaa; ☎ 808/823-0899; no lunch on weekends; cash only), which is prettier and more elegant than you might expect given the reasonable prices. Two can eat well here for under $35. Excellent Thai and Chinese dishes are served on linen tablecloths, and blooming orchids everywhere create a charming Asian-garden ambience. Nightly specials featuring local produce in season and fresh fish are always good choices. The fragrant, rich curries run from mild to fiery hot.

$–$$ If you're in the mood for a casual but healthy meal, tucked into the store fronts in Kapaa is the tiny **Mermaids Café** ★★ (1384 Kuhio Hwy., Kapaa; ☎ 808/821-2026;. daily 11am–9pm; DC, MC, V), which serves creative healthy cuisine for lunch and dinner from a takeout type window (with a handful of tables available outside) at prices in the $9 to $10 range. Fresh fish in tortilla wrap tops the menu as my favorite; other entrees include tofu or chicken satay, chicken coconut curry plate, and chicken satay wrap, and great salads. I love to take the entrees and go sit by the ocean. At these prices, go ahead and splurge on a glass of fresh-squeezed lemonade.

$–$$$ In a romantic mood? How about a tropical outdoor ambience with lit tiki torches and cuisine that is gourmet cuisine at wallet pleasing prices? **Café Coco** ★★ (4–369 Kuhio Hwy., Wailua; ☎ 808/822-7990; Tues–Sun 5–9pm; MC, V) is your place. Hard to find (get directions when you book your reservations) but it's well worth the hunt for this adorable cafe with its backyard dining amongst fruit trees (pomelo, avocado, mango, tangerine, litchi, and bananas) with a view of the Sleeping Giant Mountain in the background. The menu is limited (salads, fresh fish, tofu-and-roast-veggie wraps) but the specials are always creative. Entrees generally run $7 to $21. Service can be slow, but the atmosphere is so divine, who cares?

$–$$$ Vegetarians will love **Blossoming Lotus** ★★★ (New Pacific House, 4504 Kukui St., Kapaa; ☎ 808/822-7678; www.blossominglotus.com; 5–9:30pm daily; AE, MC, V), which could very well be the best restaurant on the island in terms of quality ingredients and distinctive taste. And in the area of consciousness, it's unsurpassed. Owned by a worker's collective, this is the only restaurant in Hawaii to achieve national "Green Certification" for its eco-friendly practices, including composting and using biodegradable takeout packaging, and its cuisine is organic vegan. But don't worry; you won't find a holier-than-thou vibe in this gourmet veggie restaurant. It's a friendly place, with nightly entertainment in the pleasant, high-ceilinged dining room decorated with Buddha images and rich,

What to Wear When Out to Eat

Unless you're going to a posh restaurant, don't bother to dress up for dinner; dining is extremely casual on Kauai. But that doesn't mean a swimsuit and bare feet are acceptable. Shorts, T-shirts, and sundresses are the norm, except at luxury hotel dining rooms, like La Cascata (p. 45), where men should wear long pants and collared shirts (aloha shirts are fine).

muted colors. Even non-veg-heads will find the food absolutely divine: creative, fresh, healthful, and packed with flavor. For lunch, the nori wraps filled with veggies and the live food pâté du jour are favorites of mine, as is the tangy barbecue sandwich made with seitan. The hearty spanikopita and roasted-red-pepper curry are sound dinner choices. Dinner selections (sorry, no lunch) are reasonable at $12 to $19. Save room for a slice of pie or, better yet, the delectable kava brownies. Organic beers and wines are available. They also have a very wonderful Sunday brunch (10am–2pm) with entrees in the $6 to $7 range (a yummy almond-orange spice French toast, from spelt cinnamon raisin bread; a crepe of the day; south of the border scramble with tofu; a basil fritta with roasted eggplant and Italian tomato relish; and even a gooey cinnamon-pecan bun).

The same folks also operate the **Lotus Root Juice Bar & Bakery** (4-1384 Kuhio Hwy., Kapaa; ☎ 808/823-6658), an ideal snack stop. Try the yummy vegan ice cream, a fresh-fruit smoothie, or a cup of tea with a fresh piece of pie or cake. Best of all, it's good for you. The outdoor tables face Kapaa's main drag, a better choice than a small, stuffy dining room.

$$–$$$ Another place I want to mention before leaving the East Side is **Hukilau Lanai** (4-484 Kuhio Hwy., Kapaa; ☎ 808/822-0600; Tues–Sun, dinner only, 5–9pm; AE, MC, V). It's in the Coconut Marketplace, tucked away off the lobby of the Beachboy resort, but don't hold that against it. On a nice evening you'll want an outside table. The torch-lit dining lanai looks out across manicured lawns to the ocean. Inside or out, it's really a very pleasant spot to linger with a meal, and the food doesn't disappoint. The emphasis is on local ingredients, prepared in satisfying, distinctive ways. Signature entrees, priced at $15 to $25, are shiitake-mushroom meatloaf, sugar-cane shrimp, and Mongolian baby back ribs. I usually order the fresh fish—they often have choices not widely found in island restaurants, like opah and wahoo, both moist and delicious—or pair the creamy-sauced sweet-potato ravioli appetizer with a green salad chock-full of colorful raw veggies. Share if you must, but do try the warm cake made from Big Island chocolate or the Kauai goat cheese crème brûlée for dessert.

$$–$$$ The last good choice in this area is the landmark **Wailua Marina Restaurant** (Wailua River State Park, Wailua Rd., Kapaa; ☎ 808/822-4311; Tues–Sun 10:30am–2pm and 5–8pm; AE, MC, V). To avoid the crowds who catch the tour boats to the Fern Grotto, come here for dinner or a late lunch. The food is popular with locals and visitors and the portions border on humongous.

Besides, the riverfront setting is unique in the state, imparting a soothing, relaxed flow to the service and ambience. Entrees range from $12 to $24, and if you've got an appetite, you'll definitely get your money's worth (or simply split portions to save). The signature dishes are an inches-thick stuffed baked pork chop and fresh ahi (tuna) stuffed with crab, both of which I recommend, as well as the steamed river mullet, a classic island fish dish.

THE NORTH SHORE

Once you leave Kapaa and head north, restaurant pickings get mighty slim. For reasons I've never fully understood, given the brisk tourist trade in Princeville and Hanalei, the North Shore is plagued by a dearth of decent eateries. Restaurants tend to be overpriced and average at best, though they start looking more appealing against the alternative of a 45-minute drive to Kapaa. But there are a handful I can recommend.

$–$$ In Kilauea, the first true North Shore town, you can either order a pizza from **Kilauea Bakery and Pau Hana Pizza** ★★ (Kong Lung Center, Keneke St., Kilauea; ☎ 808/828-2020; 6:30am–9pm daily; MC, V) or stop by **Kilauea Fish Market** (4270 Kilauea Lighthouse Rd., Kilauea; ☎ 808/828-6244; Mon–Sat 11am–8pm; MC, V), where you'll find wraps, plate lunches, salads, and daily specials made primarily with fresh local fish. The **fish market** seems expensive for the simple fare, with most items about $12 to $15, and the bottled drinks are way overpriced. The fish wrap, served in a red flour tortilla, tastes very good, but it's too big and sloppy to hold. You order at a counter and then wait a good piece for your food, which you can eat at an outdoor table or take away.

The gourmet pizzas served at **Kilauea Bakery** aren't cheap (from $12), either, but they're excellent, with chewy sourdough crusts. The Big Blue—topped with smoked fish, capers, and tomato slices—is dynamite, as is the Spartan, with its salty feta cheese and Kalamata olives. Soups and salads round out the very limited menu. In the morning, it's a popular spot for coffee and fresh flaky pastries. The best tables are outside, under the umbrellas, but if it's rainy, the seating inside is pleasantly cozy.

$$$–$$$$ Up the road a few miles, and half a world away, lies the master-planned community of Princeville, home to the overly opulent Princeville Resort, which in turn houses one of the best restaurants on the North Shore: **La Cascata** ★★★ (5520 Ka Haku Rd., Princeville; ☎ 808/826-2760; dinner only 6–9:30pm daily, reservations required; AE, DC, DISC, MC, V). This is one of the splurge spots I mentioned (expect to pay $25–$40 per person, without wine). If you're looking for very romantic ambience, La Cascata is the place.

For romantic fine dining, La Cascata sets the standard with its terra-cotta floors, hand-painted murals, *trompe l'oeil* paintings, and exquisite eats. The chef works local ingredients into a menu dominated by pasta, fresh seafood, beef, and a superb rack of lamb. The food is innovative—brodetto di pesce is a medley of snapper, scallops, clams, and Kauai shrimp served with an Arrabbiata sauce over linguine, and the seared ahi is paired up with artichoke cannelloni, caramelized-onion broth, and toasted pine nuts. The professional, efficient service—not often found on this island—complements the sophisticated food.

HANALEI

Hanalei has a number of eateries, but not many are bargains. This is a splurge location, so plan accordingly.

$–$$$ For a casual, filling meal, **Hanalei Gourmet** ★ kids (5-5161 Kuhio Hwy., Hanalei; ☎ 808/826-2524; Sun–Thurs 9am–10:30pm and Fri–Sat 8am–11:30pm; DC, DISC, MC, V), in the historic Hanalei School Center, features filling food for three meals a day. You can choose to can eat inside the small, dark dining room or at a table set on a rambling, covered porch. The lunches—salads and sandwiches served on fresh-baked breads ($7–$10)—are a better deal than the dinners ($15–$23), which are overpriced for such standard fare as burgers, fresh fish, and pasta with vegetables. There's also a full bar that has live music on weekend nights.

$$–$$$ Although the folks who run **Polynesia Café** (Ching Young Village, 5-5190 Kuhio Hwy., Hanalei; ☎ 808/826-1999; daily 8am–8:30pm; cash only) bill their fare as gourmet, and the meals are pricey, you will be served on paper plates and use plastic utensils. It's a step above a plate lunch, but when you step up to the counter to place your order, you might be surprised to see dinner entrees priced from $15 to $25. Although those prices aren't warranted, given the eatery's casual, bordering-on-scruffy setting in a small shopping center, the food is worth it. The breads, buns, desserts, and pastries are freshly baked; they grind their own beef for the burgers; the huevos rancheros and eggs Benedict are excellently prepared at breakfast; and dinner entrees are creative, with a Pacific Rim and Mexican influence. You'll be contacted via pager when your order is ready, and you can eat at one of the outdoor picnic tables (it's okay to bring your own wine), although it isn't the sort of place you'd want to linger, especially on one of those wet, cool nights so common in Hanalei.

WHY YOU'RE HERE: KAUAI'S BEACHES

Kauai is internationally known for its beautiful beaches, which come in every size, shape, and color: white, green, buff, black, and brown. You'll find crescent-shaped hideaways; long, narrow ribbons edging sheer sea cliffs; and broad expanses that stretch for miles and miles. Some beaches have coral reefs offshore, offering protection from the waves and opportunities for snorkeling. Others face the open ocean, making them more suitable for surfing and boogie boarding. Nearly always, they're wonderfully uncrowded, and sometimes blissfully deserted—just the way I like it.

Finding Your Place in the Sun

The beaches in the following sections can be found on the maps starting on p. 55.

Beach Rules

"Never turn your back on the water," is one water-safety rule drilled into the head of every local child, and it's a maxim wise adults heed, too. Waves can come up unexpectedly and knock you off balance if you're not watching the water. During periods of giant winter surf, people have actually been swept out while walking the beach. Always wear fins when boogie-boarding; never swim or snorkel in rough waters. And keep a close eye on your *keiki* (children). Water wings and other flotation devices cannot be trusted to protect children in the sea. If you have any questions about activities appropriate to a certain beach or current water conditions, ask a lifeguard or local resident, or inquire at a dive shop.

If you ever feel uneasy, get out of the water. Don't take chances—Kauai has more drownings than any other island, averaging one or two each month. Even experienced swimmers shouldn't underestimate Kauai's powerful waves, which grow stronger during periods of big surf and heavy rain, when swollen rivers race to the sea. And there's another reason to stay out of the murky waters that linger a couple of days after a storm—they're favored by sharks. So exercise caution, especially at remote beaches without lifeguards.

Look to your car's safety as well. Like elsewhere in Hawaii, rental car rip offs are a thriving cottage industry. My advice? Leave nothing inside you would mind losing, and keep the doors unlocked (so thieves won't be tempted to break a window to get in).

Finally, Kauai waters are rich in marine life, including many animals on the endangered-species list (green sea turtles, monk seals, humpback whales). Please treat these protected animals with respect and remember it's illegal to do anything that causes a marine mammal to change its behavior (you can be arrested for this, and charged with a federal crime). That means no swimming after dolphins, no riding sea turtles, and no getting chummy with a monk-seal pup, as the mom will give you a nasty nip. Also, avoid stepping on reefs when snorkeling as this damages the slow-growing, living coral.

Each beach has its own personality, which can change dramatically between seasons, and from one day to the next, depending on where the surf is breaking and how the winds are blowing. Beaches on the South Side are typically calmer during the winter, when giant surf often pounds the North Shore. Conditions flip during the summer months, although south swells never reach the legendary heights of North Shore breakers.

BEACHES ON THE EAST SIDE

The scenic eastern shoreline offers one of the best beach walks on Kauai because you can access it at various points along the Coconut Coast, allowing you to explore different sections without walking the entire length. Monk seals often haul out along here to doze in the warm sand, and you can frequently see green turtles feeding on the reef at low tide. (Do *not* approach either one; both are protected by law and you can be arrested for "harassment" just for moving in too close to take a photo.) And if you want to watch the sun and/or moon rise out of the sea, a pastime I highly recommend, this is the place.

The coastline here has full trade-wind exposure, which keeps temperatures cool—sometimes too cool for comfortable wintertime beaching—and it's bordered by one of the largest fringing reef systems in Hawaii, a feature more pleasing to fishermen than swimmers.

Beaches Near Lihue

Sadly, I can't recommend much about the beaches around Lihue, but the blame for that rests squarely on humans, not Mother Nature. She did a fine job with **Kalapaki Beach,** creating a sandy beach that slopes gradually into a horseshoe-shaped bay that fronts the Kauai Marriott Beach Resort on Rice Street (it's open to the public, as are all beaches in Hawaii). It's a pretty place—busy but not overcrowded—with a terrific surf break (there's even a tiny surfing museum here). The Marriott provides clean bathrooms, and the outside showers have hot water, which you won't find at public beach parks. So what's the problem? The water quality is often compromised by urban runoff and a nearby sewage-treatment plant that frequently overflows. I'd avoid it if I were you.

Coconut Coast Beaches

Lydgate County Beach Park ★★ kids (on Leho Dr. behind the Aloha Kauai Beach Resort, adjoining the Wailua River) is a beach ideal for families, popular with both locals and visitors. It has two big draws: Kamalani, a kid-designed, community-built playground with all sorts of neat art and architectural features; and two protected saltwater pools dug out of the reef. One is *keiki*-size; the other is larger and especially suitable for seniors, people with disabilities, and anyone uncomfortable with the ocean or their swimming skills. It's a perfect place to practice snorkeling. The park has clean restrooms with changing rooms, cold outside showers, barbecue grills, and covered pavilions with picnic tables.

The park grounds have significant cultural value, too. The ancient Hawaiians built a string of *heiau* (temples) and other sacred sites along the Wailua River, from the ocean to the summit of Waialeale. The park and hotel occupy the original riverfront site, and you can still see the stone walls of Hikinaakala, a traditional place of refuge that granted asylum to lawbreakers who managed to make it inside its borders. ***Note:*** Show respect by not walking within the walls.

BEACHES ON THE SOUTH SIDE

Visitors love South Side beaches because they're so often hot and sunny, have wonderful sunset views, and many are within walking distance of most Poipu hotels and condos. The sandy beaches tend to be small pockets, or narrow strips, but the waters near shore are often calm and protected enough for kids. The region is good for snorkeling, body- and board surfing, and boogie boarding.

Poipu Beach Park ★★ kids (at Hoowili and Poipu Beach roads) is a particularly good spot for safe watersports. A short breakwater and sand bars offshore create a large, protected swimming area on one side, although rip currents can form during periods of very big summer surf, making it ideal for boogie boarding. On the other side is an open bay for more serious swimmers, snorkelers, and surfers. Families will enjoy the mix of lawn and sand, playground equipment, picnic tables, outside showers, restrooms, and lifeguard station. This is a near-perfect beach, so expect to share it with many other visitors and locals.

Several other nice beaches—none with facilities—lie to the east of Poipu Beach Park, the first of which is **Brennecke,** a choice bodysurfing break with a postage-stamp beach alongside Hoowili Road. At the very end of Poipu Road is **Keoneloa,** nicknamed Shipwreck for a boat that went aground here many years ago. All that remains of the wreck is its motor, lying in "the long sands" that account for the beach's Hawaiian name. The eastern end is a hot windsurfing spot, while the break is favored by bodysurfers and boogie boarders. It fronts the Hyatt Regency, although the resort is built back from the beach.

Mahaulepu is the South Side's unpolished gem, noted for its dramatic sea cliffs, reddish sand dunes, and archaeological sites (try to find the petroglyph of a canoe in the rock). It's not uncommon to come across an endangered Hawaiian monk seal—sometimes with a pup—basking on the sand, as green sea turtles swim offshore. I would not recommend swimming here because there's no lifeguard, but for a taste of the unspoiled beauty of Kauai, this beach has few peers.

Heading west of Poipu Beach Park, you'll encounter a series of small beaches suitable for sunbathing, dipping, and snorkeling. The first is a crescent of sand called **Waiohai Beach,** followed by **Poipu Beach** ★★★, a little pocket of sand that fronts the Sheraton Kauai, facing a small bay. It's also used by windsurfers and surfers. The public access is at the eastern end of Hoonani Road, but parking is hard to come by and virtually impossible to find when the surf is up. At the western end of Hoonani Road lies **Koloa Landing** ★, an excellent spot for shore dives and snorkeling, although the rocky shoreline isn't great for sunbathing. You can also snorkel at Beach House Beach (on the western side of Waikomo Stream, in front of the Beach House Restaurant). Restrooms, showers, and a very small parking lot are directly across the road from the beach. Don't plan on sunbathing unless the tide is out, as the beach pretty much disappears in high tide. The reef here is popular during summer swells with surfers who ride three breaks known as P.K.'s, Centers, and Acid Drop.

BEACHES ON THE NORTH SHORE

The North Shore has no shortage of scenic sandy shoreline. The mountains are close to the sea here and the landscape is lush, giving parts of the coastline a wild, dreamy, primordial feel accentuated by the frequent appearance of misty rainbows and an ethereal late-afternoon golden light.

The waters here are dramatically affected by powerful northwest swells that roll in and out through the winter and spring months, transforming placid, lake-like waters into thundering 20-foot breakers overnight. North Shore beaches are sometimes closed during periods of extremely large surf, because waves totally inundate the sand, even coming onto the road at times. In summertime it's an entirely different story, especially when the trade winds drop and the ocean is flat, barely rippling as it meets the shore. That's when conditions are ideal for kayaking, snorkeling, swimming, diving, boating, and just hanging out.

Anini Beach Park ★★ kids (take the northernmost Kalihiwai Rd. off Kuhio Hwy., then turn west on Anini Rd.) is one of the few North Shore beaches that's equally desirable in summer and winter. The shoreline is flanked by a large offshore reef that serves the double duty of creating a protected swimming lagoon—at many points, the water is only 4 to 5 feet deep—and keeping big surf away from the beach. Teeming sea life along the reef makes this the best spot on the island for snorkelers; on the northwest side, a channel in the reef allows divers to plunge 60 feet down for more intense underwater sightseeing. This also happens to be one of the most spectacular-looking places on Kauai, with towering cliffs fronting an aqua lagoon. Although Anini can get crowded, if you're willing to walk a little ways north or south of the park, you can usually find a private little nook where you can spread your towel or mat beneath the shade of a kamani tree. The park has bathrooms, cold showers, a tent camping area, and a boat launch.

Hanalei Bay ★★★, a big, beautiful, crescent-shaped bay framed by a 2-mile-long sand beach and large homes, is another popular spot—with good cause. In addition to its large size, stunning mountain backdrop, and view of the setting sun, it's an excellent place to swim, canoe, surf, boogie board, fish, walk, and jog in the summer. In the winter, it's another matter as giant swells turn this bowl into an oversize washing machine. Another problem: Though Hanalei Bay is a delightful recreation area, it tends to suffer some of the same water-quality problems as Kalapaki Bay, especially following periods of heavy rain.

Three county beach parks have been built around Hanalei Bay, accessible from Weke Road, which runs roughly parallel to Kuhio Highway along the shoreline. All three parks have lifeguards, restrooms, showers, and picnic tables. The southernmost is **Black Pot** ★ kids, adjoining the Hanalei River. A boat ramp at the end of Weke Road allows small boats to reach the ocean via the river, which is also good for kayaking. Kids enjoy jumping off a pier that juts out into the bay. The waters around the pier are generally calm but can get murky during rainy weather. A surf break is beyond the reef, but it's a long paddle from the beach and suitable for advanced surfers only during periods of high surf.

About a block west is **Hanalei Pavilion** ★★, named for the sheltered picnic areas adjoining the parking lot. The pavilions are separated from the beach by a large lawn with picnic tables and barbecue grills. There's often a shore break here, making it suitable for older kids who want to boogie board, but it's not the best choice for very small children.

At the far western end of the bay, you'll find **Waioli Beach Park,** a small park shaded by ironwood trees that account for its nickname, Pine Trees. Currents tend to be strong here, and it can have a snapping shore break, even in summer, so it's popular with boogie boarders and surfers but not the best place for casual swimming. It tends to be less crowded than the other two parks, but it's still very busy when the surf is up.

Although it's not well-suited to swimming or watersports, **Lumahai Beach** ★★★ (on Kuhio Hwy. about 2 miles west of Hanalei town) is a great spot for sunbathing and picnicking. It's one of the few truly wild beaches left on Kauai, with no houses built along its shores. Swatches of green olivine in the black-brown sand give it a unique color. This is a wonderful place for a long beach walk (though it has no facilities). ***Caution:*** Because there is no protective reef here there is a strong rip current, so do *not* swim here; there have been numerous drownings.

At the very end of Kuhio Highway lies **Kee Beach** ★★, a pretty little spot with reddish-gold sand backed by soaring cliffs that has grown far too popular for its own good. Nearly everyone who comes to Kauai visits this beach because it's at the end of the road, but also because it marks the start of the popular **Kalalau Trail.** If you don't mind crowds, there's much to recommend here, including excellent snorkeling and swimming, especially during the summer; the cove and its swimmers are protected from the North Shore's dangerous currents by a reef. A path on the western end of the beach leads to a *heiau* (temple) dedicated to hula and tended by students from a local hula *halau* (school). It's a sacred spot that should be approached with respect. You'll find the fewest people if you arrive before noon on weekdays.

BEACHES ON THE WEST SIDE

If you're looking for nothing but sun, sand, and surf, head for the West Side beaches. You'll have plenty of room to stretch your legs along a sandy coastline that's the longest in all of Hawaii. At some West Side beaches, the water is murky from river runoff or too rough for swimming. But you can usually find someplace suitable to take a dip, and a bit of privacy, too. The beaches in this area also offer glorious sunsets and views of Niihau, an offshore private island owned by the Robinson family and home to nearly 200 Native Hawaiians who still lead a fairly traditional life.

Salt Pond Beach Park ★★ kids (past Hanapepe off Hwy. 50 on Lokokai Rd.) is one of my personal favorites on the island, thanks to its protected swimming areas (including a rock-ringed toddlers' pool), lifeguard station, clean restrooms, cold outside showers, and covered pavilions with picnic tables. There's also a tent camping area. Never crowded, this is an ideal spot for a sunset picnic or swim. And if you're wondering how the beach got its moniker, it's named for the nearby salt pans where the famed alae salt is harvested to this day. Locals collect seawater in pans and leave them outside until all that hasn't evaporated is this highly prized reddish, local salt.

Visually spectacular **Polihale State Park** ★★ is one of Hawaii's largest beaches, some 17 miles long, though it does have its drawbacks: In the summer it can be unbearably hot, with little shade and flesh-scorching white sand, and in the winter stay out of the water when the surf is up. Kiawe trees grow here, too, and their long, sharp thorns are not compatible with bare feet. The ocean is often too rough for swimming, and you should never leave any valuables in your car here as thefts are routine. So why do I award it two stars? It's a beauty, and the long, sandy beach, with its dramatic mountain backdrop, is one of the drier beaches on the island, meaning this is the place to come if it's raining elsewhere. To reach Polihale, a very remote beach, you'll need to drive to the end of Highway 50, then take an old cane-haul road that can get very rutted and rough, depending on the time of the year and how much rain has fallen since the last time it was graded. You'll find a campground, covered pavilions, and restrooms, but no snack facilities, so come prepared to make a day of it.

BEACHES ON THE NA PALI COAST

Now that you're a little more *akamai* (knowledgeable), it's time to explore the diverse, often wild, and always spectacular coastline that encircles this little green gem in the Pacific. There's only one place to start: the beaches of **Na Pali Coast** ★★★, a 6,500-acre state wilderness park accessible only by boat or on foot. Na Pali Coast, which translates literally as "the cliffs," is comprised of idyllic beaches that front wide and narrow tropical valleys, or lie at the feet of sheer, craggy cliffs plunging into the sea. These are Kauai's most viewed but least visited beaches, as they're typically seen from the boats and helicopters that show tourists this stunning example of nature's handiwork.

Kalalau Trail Beaches

The two Na Pali beaches you're most likely to visit are reached via the 11-mile Kalalau Trail. You can hike in 2 miles to **Hanakapiai** ★★★, where the beach opens onto a bay. Before you take off on the trail make sure you have hiking boots or closed toe shoes (like running shoes, not flip-flops), that you have adequate protection from the sun (sunscreen, hat, T-shirt, not just a swimsuit) and that you are carrying plenty of water, and insect repellant. This short, wide stretch of white sand is framed at either end by unusual rock formations and fronts a lush tropical valley that is wedged in between dramatic mountain ridges, making it one of the most scenic beaches in Hawaii. Unfortunately, it's nearly always unsafe for swimming and has been the site of numerous drownings, so if you're hot, stay out of the sea and instead cool off in the clear freshwater stream that runs through the valley. Also, it's been discovered by many people, and by midday it's usually too crowded for my taste. That's when I either hike out or go *mauka* to find a quiet, shady spot alongside the stream, deeper in the valley.

If you continue on the trail for another 9 miles, you'll arrive at **Kalalau** ★★★, which is both a long sandy beach and a deep, wide, amphitheater-shaped valley. You won't be able to make it in and out of Kalalau in a day unless you're a super athlete, so most folks camp at Kalalau. But don't even think about camping unless you have a permit in your hand. Permits are available from the **Office of State Parks** (3060 Eiwa St., Lihue; ☎ 808/274-3444).

One other caveat: Kalalau has a definite counterculture vibe, so don't be surprised if you see a few bare butts. However, sunbathing in the nude is illegal in Hawaii, and you can be arrested.

You can kayak into Kalalau when the seas are calm (rare in the winter months). Some folks drift down the coast to Kalalau and then turn around and paddle back against the trade winds (you'd best have strong arms if that's your plan).

Coastal Access Beaches

A half-mile west of Kalalau is picturesque **Honopu,** where a lava-rock archway separates two thick patches of sand that often disappear beneath pounding winter surf. No camping is allowed, and while some hardy types do swim in from Kalalau, you'll be a lot safer in a kayak. The next beach is **Nualolo Kai,** which has an extensive reef that in some places extends out 600 feet from shore. The valley has many fascinating archaeological sites, reminding visitors that the ancient Hawaiians once lived and grew taro in all the remote Na Pali valleys. There's no camping at Nualolo, and it's often impossible to land here during rough weather. Some tour-boat companies anchor offshore so their passengers can swim and snorkel in the clear, azure-colored sea.

At the westernmost end of the coastline, and accessible only by boat, lies lovely **Milolii,** once the site of a thriving fishing village. Sheer cliffs tower at each end of a narrow, curving sandy beach that spans nearly a mile of coastline, offering some of the island's best shelling. Camping is allowed, but the rough surf usually deters boaters, except in the summer months.

As their wilderness designation implies, Na Pali beaches have no potable water, lifeguards, or services of any kind, except for primitive toilets and an occasional shelter or picnic table. Permits are required to camp in the park or hike beyond Hanakapiai. To obtain them, or to get more information, visit the **Office of State Parks** (3060 Eiwa St., Lihue; ☎ 808/274-3444).

THE TOP SIGHTS & ATTRACTIONS

Every trip to Kauai begins in Lihue, whether you arrive by sea or air, making it a good starting point for sightseeing.

LIHUE & ENVIRONS

That being said, downtown Lihue has little to lure the tourist. Its only highlight is the **Kauai Museum** ★ (4428 Rice St.; ☎ 808/245-6931; www.kauaimuseum.org; Mon–Fri 9am–4pm, Sat 10am–4pm; $7 adults, $5 seniors, $3 students, $1 children ages 6–12), housed in a historic 1920s stone building. You can get through this small museum in an hour or less, but it offers a good introduction to both Hawaiian culture and the plantation camp lifestyle. On the second floor is a changing exhibit featuring the work of Kauai artists.

Beyond the museum, the view of the mountains is the No. 1 attraction, with the massive and slightly foreboding **Haupu range** dominating the landscape. These are particularly rugged peaks that no roads or trails traverse, forming a nearly impenetrable barrier between Lihue and the southern coast. One of the best places to view the Haupu range is from the area around **Nawiliwili Harbor,** a small, narrow, compact harbor that's a bit of a tight squeeze for the cruise lines and container ships that dock here.

A short drive away, on the northern edge of the Huleia River, lies the **Alekoko,** or **Menehune Fishpond,** which is not just a pretty sight but an archaeological marvel. It's the oldest fishpond on the island, so ancient that its distinctive stonewall construction is attributed to the Menehune, who were perhaps Kauai's first inhabitants. It's also the best example of an inland fishpond in the entire state. A National Historic Landmark, the 102-acre property is privately owned, although a few fishermen have permission to go crabbing or fish for mullet. You'll be able to view it from **a roadside overlook** (take Rice St. to Rte. 58; turn right and then

Fun Facts

- Kauai is the northernmost island in the main Hawaiian chain and the westernmost place in the United States.
- Kauai has more species of endangered forest birds than any other island.
- Kauai's landscapes have been featured in more Hollywood films than any other Hawaiian island, including *Raiders of the Lost Ark, Jurassic Park,* and *Blue Hawaii.*

left onto Niumalu Rd. and right onto Hulemalu Rd.). It's especially nice in early morning or very late afternoon, when you can hear the birds in the valley.

Nearby is the **Grove Farm Homestead Museum** ★★ (Nawiliwili Rd.; ☎ 808/245-3202; tours Mon, Wed, and Thurs; $5; reservations recommended), an estate created in 1864 by former plantation manager George Wilcox, a missionary descendent who found his fortune in sugar. If you've made reservations—which you should—you can join a 2½-hour guided tour of the old house, lovingly restored to give visitors a glimpse into the lifestyle of Kauai's elite in the early days of the lucrative sugar industry. It is by far the most in-depth and interesting plantation tour in the islands. You'll also be taken through the grounds and outbuildings, which offer a fascinating glimpse into the measures required to achieve self-sufficiency on this remote island.

From here, it's easy to catch the two-lane Kaumualii Highway, headed west, a highly scenic drive. You'll find plenty of reasons to pull off the road, and I advise that you do so at every opportunity. Don't do the island, or yourself, the injustice of viewing it only from the inside of an air-conditioned car.

Just west of Kukui Grove, you'll see a sign on your right for **Kilohana** ★ (3-2087 Kaumualii Hwy.; ☎ 808/245-5608; www.kilohanakauai.com; daily 9:30am–dusk; free admission). It, too, is a former plantation manager's house, built in 1935 by George Wilcox's nephew, Gaylord. The 16,000-square-foot Tudor-style mansion has been restored to house a restaurant and gift shops. If you have kids, don't miss the **Kauai Plantation Railway** ★ kids (Kilohana, 3-2087 Kaumualii Hwy., Lihue; ☎ 808/245-RAIL; www.kauaiplantationrailway.com; admission $18 adult, $14 children 2–12; Mon–Sat 10am–2pm) where an old-fashioned diesel train pulls highly polished passenger cars on this scenic/educational/cultural 3-mile tour that takes 40 minutes, as your guide provides a running commentary on Kauai's history and points out the more than 50 different crops which have been planted along the train route (sugar, pineapple, taro, fruit trees, even fragrant plants). The train stops briefly at the "animal farm," where some pigs, goats, sheep, chickens, and cows are available for petting.

POIPU & ENVIRONS

Folks usually come to this area for three reasons: sun, sand, and sea. All are entirely valid vacation pursuits, and the region consistently delivers, which accounts for its popularity.

The resorts of Poipu are a relatively new attraction. This is where Hawaii's sugar industry was born, the site of Kauai's first plantation. Although the South Side plantations have been closed for 2 decades, quite a bit of land remains as pastureland, or produces vegetables and a more controversial crop: plants, especially corn, that contain genetically modified organisms, some of which have been approved for cultivation and sale and others that are still in the experimental stage.

In Poipu, it's worthwhile to drive to the western end, along Lawai Road at mile marker 4, to the **Spouting Horn** ★ kids. This is a natural blowhole formed in the black lava rock that characterizes this very pretty stretch of coastline. The thrill factor of the show depends on the size and direction of the prevailing swell, but even when the geyser is small, it's a lovely sight. Along with the view, you'll hear an odd wailing sound caused by wind going through the other blowholes at this site. A Hawaiian legend, one your kids might enjoy, is that a giant lizard, trapped with a hunter's spear in its gullet, is causing the commotion.

Beaches & Attractions on Kauai's East Side

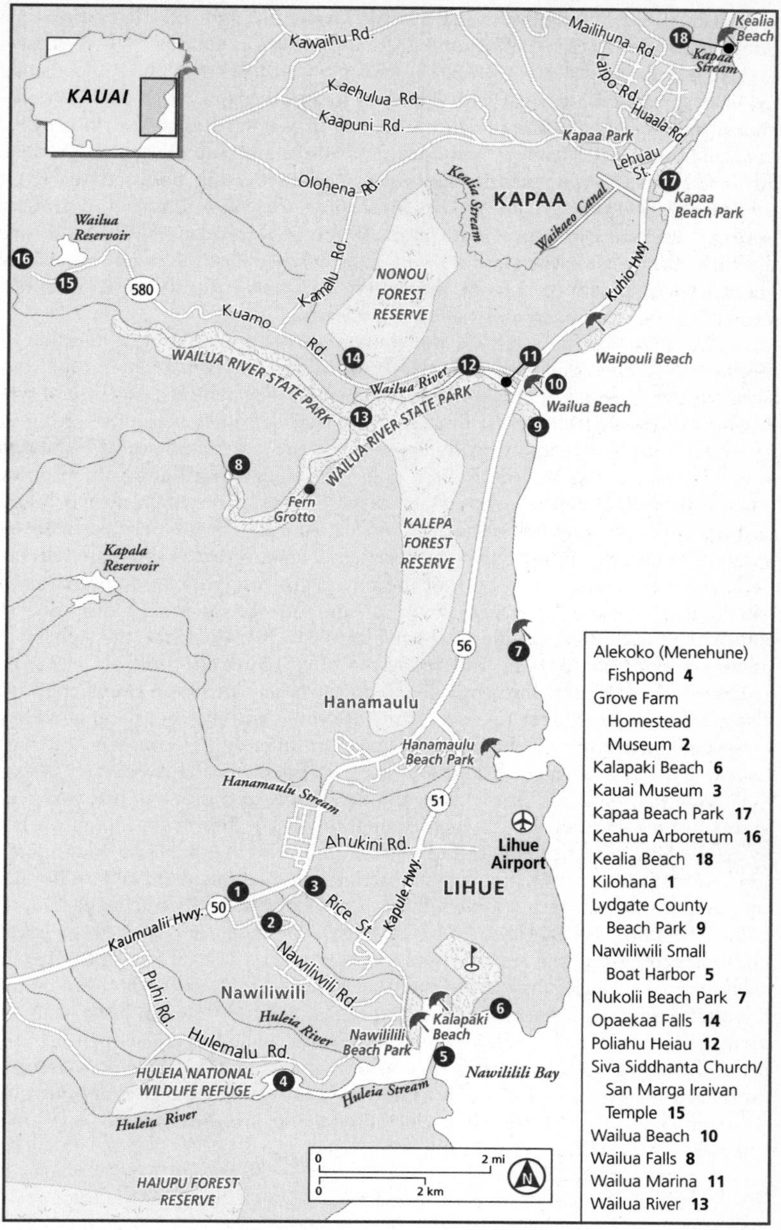
KAUAI
Kawaihu Rd.
Kaehulua Rd.
Kaapuni Rd.
Olohena Rd.
Mailihuna Rd.
Laipo Rd.
Huaala Rd.
Kealia Beach
Kapaa Stream
Kapaa Park
Lehuau St.
Kapaa Beach Park
KAPAA
Kealia Stream
Waikaeo Canal
Kuhio Hwy.
Wailua Reservoir
580
Kamalu Rd.
Kuamo Rd.
NONOU FOREST RESERVE
WAILUA RIVER STATE PARK
Wailua River
Waipouli Beach
Wailua Beach
Fern Grotto
KALEPA FOREST RESERVE
Kapala Reservoir
56
Hanamaulu
Hanamaulu Beach Park
Hanamaulu Stream
51
Ahukini Rd.
Lihue Airport
LIHUE
Kapule Hwy.
Rice St.
Kaumualii Hwy.
50
Nawiliwili Rd.
Nawiliwili
Puhi Rd.
Huleia River
Hulemalu Rd.
Nawiliwili Beach Park
Kalapaki Beach
Nawiliwili Bay
HULEIA NATIONAL WILDLIFE REFUGE
Huleia Stream
Huleia River
HAIJUPU FOREST RESERVE
0 2 mi
0 2 km
N
Alekoko (Menehune) Fishpond 4
Grove Farm Homestead Museum 2
Kalapaki Beach 6
Kauai Museum 3
Kapaa Beach Park 17
Keahua Arboretum 16
Kealia Beach 18
Kilohana 1
Lydgate County Beach Park 9
Nawiliwili Small Boat Harbor 5
Nukolii Beach Park 7
Opaekaa Falls 14
Poliahu Heiau 12
Siva Siddhanta Church/ San Marga Iraivan Temple 15
Wailua Beach 10
Wailua Falls 8
Wailua Marina 11
Wailua River 13

Across the road is one of Kauai's iconic attractions and one of the finest gardens in the United States: **National Tropical Botanical Garden** ★★★ at Lawai (Lawai Rd., Poipu; ☎ 808/742-2623; www.ntbg.org). It's a splendid place, made up of two very different gardens. The first is the Allerton garden, which graced the former summer home of Queen Emma (it was later turned into a private estate), Tours (at 9, 10am, 1, and 2pm; $35 adults and $20 children 6–12 years; advance reservations required) lead visitors past reflecting pools, statuary, and other regal effects tucked among the landscaping. Or you can catch a tram (trams depart every hour between 9:30am and 2:30pm; $15) into Lawai Valley, and wander through the McBryde Garden, with its extensive collection of rare and endangered tropical plants (said to be the largest such collection in the world). It's a veritable Garden of Eden and well worth a visit.

Just west of Eleele, watch for the **Hanapepe Valley Lookout,** a roadside rest stop that overlooks the deep, wide depths of this fertile river valley. Taro, a traditional wetland crop, is still grown in this rugged valley, which has plenty of wild, wide-open spaces. It's a lovely, peaceful sight that definitely warrants getting out of your car to take a look. Equally appealing is the old farm town of **Hanapepe,** which has two parts, the less interesting of which lies along Kaumualii Highway. The historic Main Street forks off on the north side of the highway at a hillside covered with vibrantly colorful bougainvillea. Along its few blocks you'll see old wooden buildings, some of them restored and now in use as shops, restaurants, and galleries displaying the work of the town's growing population of artists. It's fun to poke around here; park your car and browse on foot. Don't miss the **Hanaepepe Swinging Bridge,** just off Hanapepe Rd. (look for the sign in the parking lot). Built in 1911 and renovated after Hurricane Iniki in 1992, this bridge is a thoroughfare for people living on the other side of the Hanapepe River. The bridge definitely lives up to its name; it swings and dances as you cross from one side to the other. If people are crossing in different directions it becomes a Disneyland-like ride as the bridge swoops and slides over the river water below.

The West Side is still firmly rooted in agriculture and is one of just two places in the state where you can see a sugar plantation. **Gay & Robinson,** a longtime family company, farms the land around two communities that are mere wide spots in the road: Makaweli and Kaumakani. Stop in at the small **museum and visitor center** (turn left on Kaumakani Ave., just west of Kaumualii Hwy.'s mile marker 19, and follow the signs; ☎ 808/335-2824; www.hawaiimuseums.org/mc/iskauai_gayandrobinson.htm; tours 9am and 1pm Mon–Fri; $30 adults, $21 for kids under 18) that tells the story of sugar's history on the West Side and the steps involved in cultivation, harvesting, and processing. G&R has branched into tourism to help support its sugar operations, and offers several excursions, including a 2-hour tour of its fields and sugar mill. Another scenic tour goes to Olokele Canyon overlook. A third takes you on four-wheel ATVs through Makaweli Ranch. The tours are quite worthwhile, traversing private land (including a dramatically rugged coastline) you otherwise wouldn't see.

WAIMEA

Waimea is the island's prettiest town, in part because it has such a strong sense of itself. It's one of the few communities that hasn't lost substantial ground to the contrivances of tourism and conveniences of gentrification. Like so many other

Beaches & Attractions on Kauai's South Side

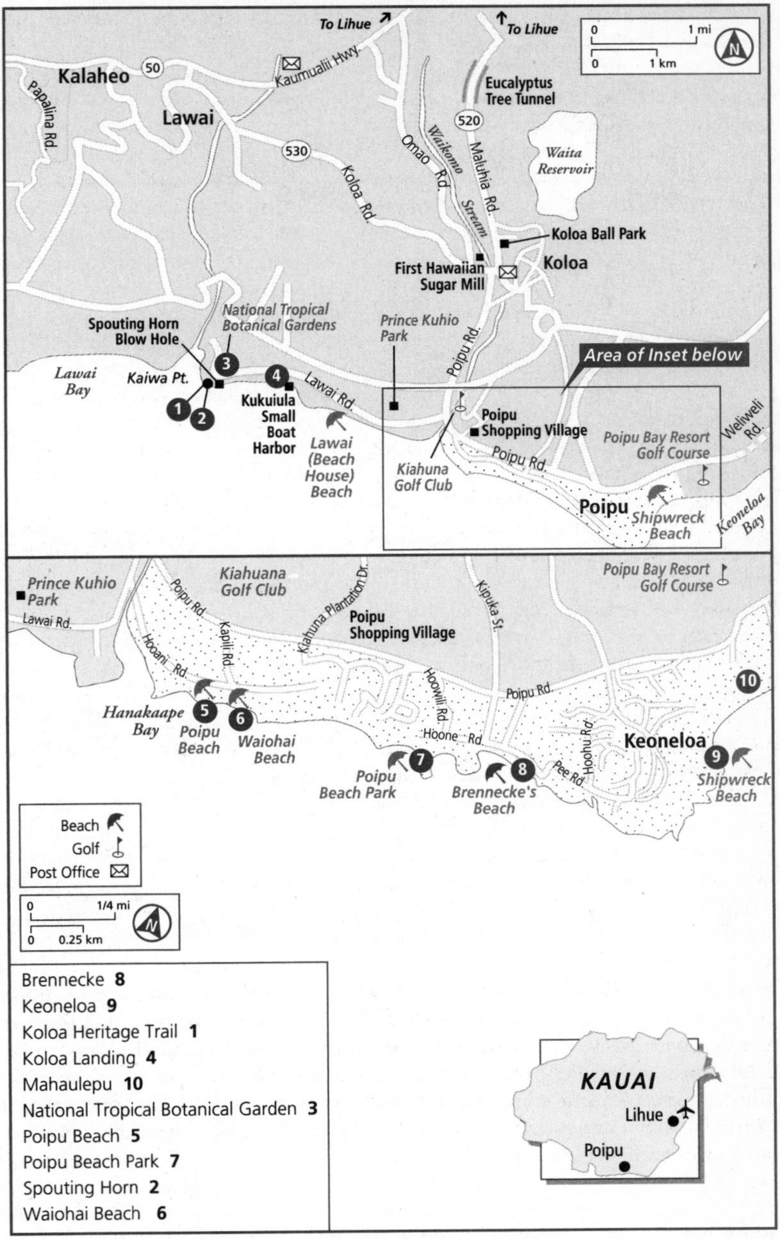

Beaches & Attractions on Kauai's North Shore

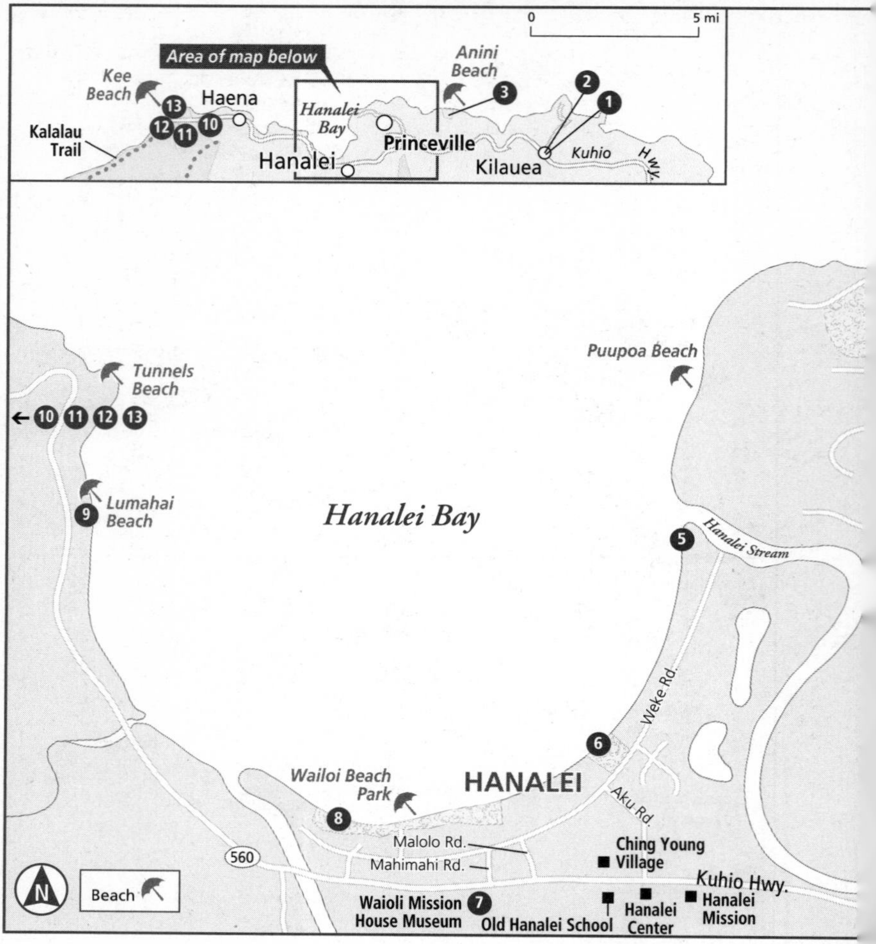

Kauai settlements, it's nestled between the mountains and the sea and bordered by a stream—in this case, the mighty Waimea River. But the similarities end there. This is *paniolo* (cowboy) country—think Old West, island-style—and the landscape is more arid, open, rugged, and colorful than elsewhere on Kauai, with broad swaths of burnt orange, rust red, and mustard yellow running through the dark blue-green of vegetation that covers the mountains behind the town.

Waimea was a large and thriving community—cultivating taro, sweet potato, and paper mulberry in the expansive wetlands that were later drained to grow sugar—when Captain James Cook arrived in 1798, ushering in an era of unprecedented change that dramatically altered both the culture of this island kingdom and its natural environment. A boulder with a large plaque marks the spot where

Anini Beach Park **3**	Kee Beach **12**
Black Pot **5**	Kilauea Point National Wildlife Refuge **2**
Guava Kai **1**	Limahuli Garden **11**
Hanalei Pavilion **6**	Lumahai Beach **9**
Hanalei Valley Lookout **4**	Waikanaloa and Waikapalae caves **10**
Kalalau **13**	Waioli Beach Park **8**
	Waioli Mission House **7**

Kenomene Beach

Edward Rd.

Kaweonui Beach

Kahaku Rd.

Kaui Rd.

Kamehameha

Princeville

Honoiki Rd.

Liholiho

Pepelani Loop

Kaweonui Rd.

Golf

Albert Rd.

Hanalei Plantation Rd.

Lei o Papa Rd.

Course

Princeville Center ■

560

Kuhio Hwy

4 Hanalei Valley Lookout

Hanalei Bridge

Hanalei National Wildlife Refuge

To Princeville Airport & Kilauea

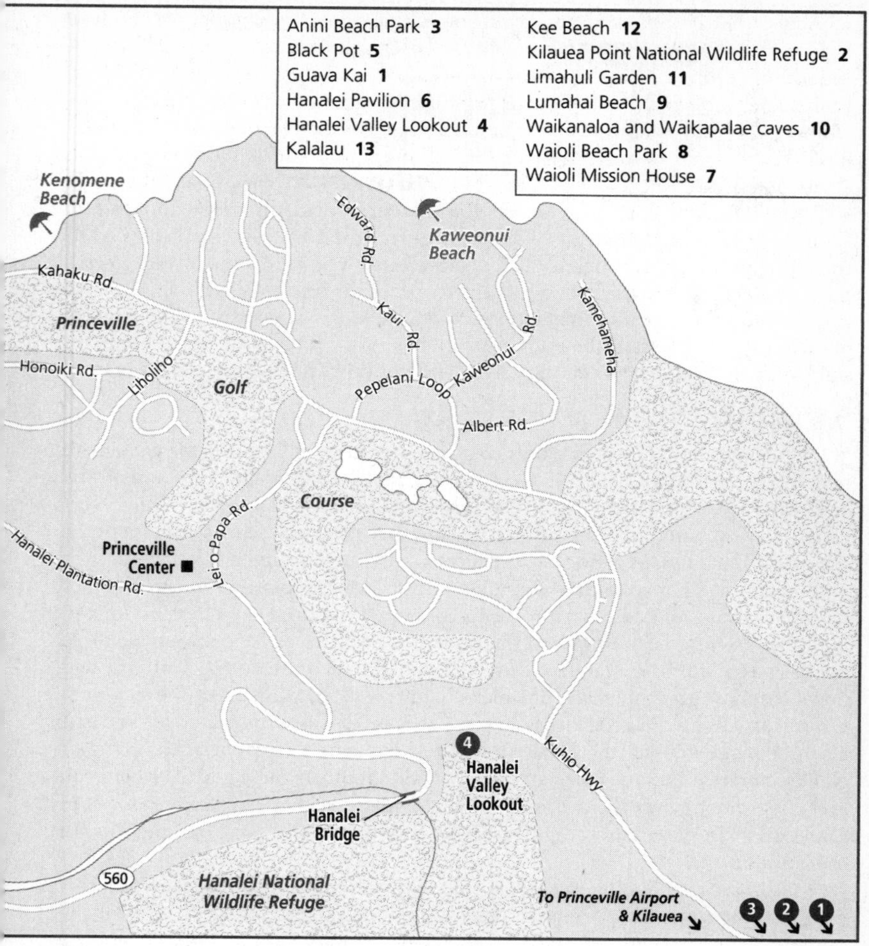

Cook first went ashore in the Hawaiian Islands on what is today Lucy Wright Beach Park, on the western bank of the Waimea River.

If you like historic buildings, the **Waimea United Church of Christ** (4548 Ola Rd.; ☎ 808/338-9962), previously known as the Waimea Foreign Church, was constructed in 1859 from sandstone blocks cut from the reef and transported to the site by bullock cart. You can pick up a map that shows all of Waimea's historic sites at the **West Kauai Technology & Visitor Center** (9565 Kaumualii Hwy.; ☎ 808/338-9957; daily 9am–6pm). The center is small but its exhibits are sophisticated, informative, and well done, delving into Kauai's geology and natural environment, as well as high-tech activities on the island. Other exhibits and artifacts, as well as classes in lei making and a walking tour, celebrate the Hawaiian culture and West Side lifestyle.

Across the river lie the remains of Fort Elizabeth, a fortress that was built in 1815, when Kauai's King Kaumualii was on chummy terms with the Russian-American Company. Russian military forces occupied the fort until 1817, when Kamehameha I expelled all Russians from the Kingdom of Hawaii after that government foolishly tried to claim it as a colony. Hawaiian soldiers used the stone fort—built from lava rocks in a star-shaped formation—until 1864, when it was taken out of service. You can visit the 17-acre **Russian Fort Elizabeth State Historical Park** at any time; watch for the entry road on the *makai* side of Kaumualii Highway, just east of Waimea town, just after mile marker 77. The ruins themselves aren't much to look at now, but if you take a short walk toward the ocean, you'll be rewarded with a lovely view of the western coastline. The park is rather arid, but there's usually a nice wind, making it a good spot for a picnic on a hot day. This could be your first up-close encounter with Kauai's red-clay soil, which has stained all the vegetation and buildings in the park a dark orange.

WAIMEA CANYON & KOKEE STATE PARK

While Waimea has its own charms, it also serves an important role as the gateway to two very special areas on Kauai—Grand Canyon look-a-like **Waimea Canyon** ★★★ and woodsy **Kokee State Park** ★★★. These public lands offer great hiking, bicycling, hunting, camping, and sightseeing, and they give you a chance to experience the island's cool uplands, wet and dry forests, and water-sculpted interior.

You can catch a road that will take you up the mountain either in Waimea town or Kekaha. Because both routes are scenic, I like to take one going up and the other coming back down, so the drive is varied. It's easier on your car to go up the steep, curving Waimea Canyon Road (Hwy. 550) out of Waimea, and down the more gradual incline of Kokee Road (Hwy. 55), which will deliver you to Kaumualii Highway at Kekaha. The scenery is lovely from the get-go and doesn't let up anywhere along the drive, unless you happen to encounter dense fog or clouds. Some of the overlooks are merely wide shoulders on the road, where you literally can hang over the canyon rim, while others, such as the Waimea Canyon Lookout, at an elevation of 3,120 feet, have restrooms and large parking lots for tour buses.

I recommend stopping at every scenic overlook on Kauai, especially the ones you encounter on this upcountry drive. Each one offers a different view of the canyon, and the colors of the rock walls shift through various hues of purples, greens, blues, grays, and reds as the light changes through the day. Rainbows, waterfalls, soaring birds, and drifting mists often make an appearance, so you'll want to keep your camera handy.

After passing through Waimea State Park, you'll climb a bit higher to **Kokee State Park.** Much of its acreage is impossibly lush, standing in sharp contrast to the stark, rocky landscape of Waimea Canyon. While the park has many warm, sunny days, I've found floating mists, light drizzle, and chilly breezes to be more characteristic of Kauai's upcountry climate (bring rain gear or at least a jacket and a pair of long pants). That may be because most of this area is rainforest, in the midst of which is the Alakai Swamp, the largest in Hawaii. Look up: A California redwood may be shading your path. It's a recent transplant here, along with Australian eucalyptus. This is also one of the few places anywhere to see the now rare koa tree.

Kauai's West Side

ACCOMMODATIONS■
Camp Sloggert **18**
Inn Waimea **6**
Kokee Lodge **16**
Waimea Plantation Cottages **7**

DINING◆
Grinds Cafe & Espresso **1**
Wrangler's Steakhouse **8**

ATTRACTIONS●
Gay & Robinson Sugar Museum **4**
Hanapepe Valley Lookout **2**
Kekaha Beach **11**
Kokee Natural History Museum **17**
Kokee State Park **15**
Milolii **13**
Polihale State Park **12**
Russian Fort **5**
Salt Pond Beach Park **3**
Waimea United Church of Christ **9**
West Kauai Technology & Vistors Center **10**
Waimea Canyon **14**

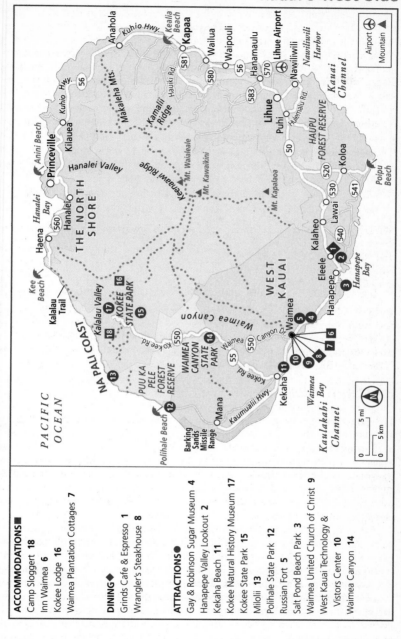

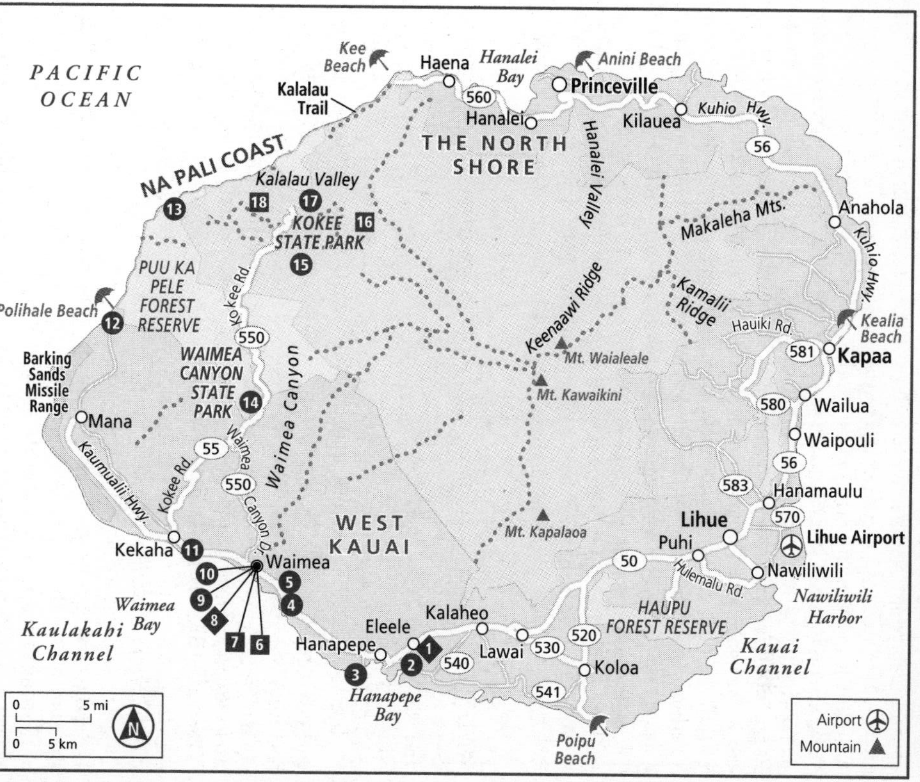

Water, Water Everywhere

Waialeale is one of the wettest spots in the world, receiving an average of 466 inches of rain each year. When that much water is pouring down a mountain for more than 5 million years, it makes an impact.

Waialeale, Kauai's second-highest peak, fed the Waimea River, which in turn made the stunning Waimea Canyon. This landmark is even more spectacular when you consider how it was created through severe, ongoing erosion. The force of water working constantly on rock eventually carved a crevice that is a mile wide, 3,600 feet deep, and 10 miles long.

A number of hikes, ranging from moderate to difficult, can take you along the rim and down into the canyon. The truly rugged can stay in primitive camps in this wilderness area. But before you head out, remember that what goes down must come back up, and the elevation loss is about 2,000 feet in 2½ miles.

At the summit of Waialeale, the heavy rainfall has created vast bogs where the sparse vegetation grows in dwarfed and stunted shapes, like natural bonsai. These bogs and broad stands of native ohia forest comprise Alakai Swamp, a part of which can be traversed on a wooden boardwalk. The strenuous 6-mile hike ends at Kilohana (which, translated, means lookout). Here, if the weather cooperates, you'll be treated to an absolutely magical view into the impossibly lush depths of Wainiha Valley on the northwest shore. Suddenly, it becomes clear that this is, indeed, a little circle of an island where everything is connected by *wai* (water), which is the Hawaiian word for wealth.

Upon entering the park, your first stop should be **Kokee Natural History Museum** ★★ (☎ 808/335-9975; daily 10am–4pm; free). It's run by the nonprofit Hui O Laka, which provides all the interpretive and educational services available in the park, including guided hikes, workshops, cultural programs, and trail-maintenance projects (see p. 74).

At the museum, you can pick up maps, flora and fauna guidebooks, and helpful hints for hiking **Kokee's 45-mile trail system** ★ (kids). There's also a compelling exhibit on Hurricane Iniki, which devastated the island in 1992; and stuffed birds, artifacts, and other collectibles that reflect the forest ecosystem. Next door is the rustic Kokee Lodge, which serves simple meals daily from 9am to 5pm.

If you stay on Kokee Road as you leave the park, you'll head straight to the **Kalalau and Puu O Kila lookouts,** with their scenic bird's-eye views of Na Pali Coast wilderness valleys and remote beaches. I often spot native birds—including the vibrant red iiwi and apapane, and the more rare yellow-green amakihi—in the trees that shade these vistas. And during winter months, I've seen whales breach and spout in placid offshore waters some 1,500 to 2,000 feet beneath me. It doesn't get much better on Kauai, or anywhere else on the planet for that matter, so if you feel the urge to hurry, squash it. You don't see natural beauty like this every day, unless, or course, you live or work in Kokee.

THE EAST SIDE

A quick drive on the East Side will take you to two magnificent waterfalls, afford you a glimpse of ancient royal Hawaii, and allow you to visit an other-worldly, modern Buddhist monastery.

With Lihue again as the starting point, head north out of town on Kuhio Highway. As the road dips down into **Kapaia Valley,** watch for Maalo Road on your left. You'll want to take this 4-mile side trip to **Wailua Falls** ★★, a magnificent cascade featured prominently in the opening segment of the old *Fantasy Island* television show.

Warning: The area surrounding the falls is very wet, overgrown, and treacherous, so stay behind the railing. A number of people have drowned or fallen to their deaths while attempting to hike here.

When you've had your fill of rainbow-hued tumbling water, backtrack to Kuhio Highway and make the odd jog from this highway to Kapule Highway, which you'll take north to Kuamoo Road (Hwy. 58). You'll end up in the heart of Wailua, which is itself the heart of Kauai, due to its direct connection with the replenishing rains of **Mount Waialeale.** In honor of this relationship, the ancient Hawaiians built seven rock-walled *heiau* (temples) that followed the river's course from the summit of Waialeale down to the sea. Bell stones, birthing stones, and other features linked to traditions and protocol practiced by the *alii* (nobles or royals) are found in this rich, fertile river valley favored by Hawaiian royalty. It's one of the most extensive archaeological complexes in the Hawaiian Islands, and much of it is accessible for public viewing.

The easiest sites to find and visit are **Hikinaakala,** a walled city of refuge at the mouth of the Wailua River, adjacent to Lydgate Park, and the **Poliahu *heiau,*** which lies about 2 miles up Kuamoo Road. Its unusual stonework is similar to the style used in the Alekoko Fishpond, prompting speculation that it, too, was built by the Menehune. From here you can easily walk *makai* to pohaku hanau, a two-piece stone that blessed all who were birthed upon it. Parents often tucked a newborn's umbilical cord into the cracks of nearby pohaku piko to gain insights into the child's destiny.

The *heiau* is across the highway from a scenic overlook that offers a view of stunning **Opaekaa Falls** ★, so named for now-scarce freshwater native shrimp that were once so abundant they could clearly be seen in the cascading waters.

As you travel north on Kuhio Highway, see if you can make out the profile of a **"Sleeping Giant"** in the 1,241-foot-high **Nounou Ridge;** it's easy to spot once you reach the **Coconut Marketplace.** Legend holds that the huge creature will one day awaken and rise from his mountaintop slumber.

THE NORTH SHORE & THE ROAD TO HANALEI ★★★

This is Kauai's don't-miss road trip. Every view along the drive is spectacular, as the landscape turns damper and more lush, and your sense of entering a Garden of Eden grows more intense by the mile. The cliff-hugging roadway that stretches from the Hanalei bridge to the pavement's end at Kee Beach is a National Historic Scenic Highway, a designation that could help keep its many charms intact. Chief among them are the old one-lane bridges that cross the region's numerous waterways, and the low lava-rock walls that line the roadway in places with sheer coastal drop-offs. The Na Pali Coast is inarguably one of the Pacific's grandest visions.

The rounded summit of **Crater Hill,** an ancient coastal cinder cone, marks your approach to Kilauea, a former sugar town struggling to retain its rural roots in the face of heightened pressure to expand and urbanize. On the outskirts of town, you can follow Kuawa Road *mauka* for about 2 miles until it ends at the gates of **Guava Kai** (☎ 808/828-6121; daily 9am–5pm; free admission), the biggest guava orchard in the world. The company cultivates some 480 acres of guava trees and also processes the sweet and tart, pink-fleshed fruit into pulp and juice. You can wander among the low-growing trees and browse in a slightly kitschy visitor center that sells jellies, juices, syrup, marinades, and other products made from guava. This isn't an especially compelling attraction, but if you're curious about island agriculture—or hungry—you can cruise through here in a half-hour or so. The mountain scenery is pretty, too.

Architecture and history buffs will want to make a stop at Kilauea's **Episcopal Church** (on Kilauea Lighthouse Rd., just beyond the Menehune Foodmart) to check out the elaborate stained-glass windows, black lava-rock construction, and churchyard cemetery dating back to the 1800s. The doors are generally open during daylight hours, and visitors are welcome. As you travel slowly down Kilauea Lighthouse Road, you'll pass more of the distinctive stone buildings originally built to house the plantation's managers, dispensary, and store. These quaint structures, currently in use as restaurants and upscale shops, comprise the town's minimalist commercial core, which is centered around the intersection of Keneke Street and Kilauea Lighthouse Road.

While the town itself is worth a look, the big attraction here is the **Kilauea Point National Wildlife Refuge** ★★★ kids (at the *makai* end of Kilauea Lighthouse Rd.; ☎ 808/828-0168; daily 10am–4pm; $3 admission), a seabird sanctuary perched on the edge of a sheer sea cliff along a rough and wild coastline. Seabirds spend most of their life on the open ocean, returning to land only to breed and raise their young. These federal lands offer a protected nesting habitat that attracts thousands of Laysan albatrosses, wedgetail shearwaters, boobies, great frigates, and other seabirds, as well as Hawaii's endangered state bird, the nene goose. You can see birds nesting on steep cliff faces and flying low overhead, a spectacle that is even more thrilling in late afternoon, when great numbers of seabirds—some with 8-foot wingspans—return to their roosting areas after a day of fishing. In winter months you'll often see whales spouting and breaching offshore, and the panoramic ocean and mountain views are beyond picture-perfect. As in most natural areas, the view changes constantly, depending on the elements, so it's different every time you visit.

The birds share the grounds with a historic lighthouse built in 1913 to warn ships away from a small offshore islet called Mokuaeae and the generally treacherous coastal waters. That function is now performed by a free-standing signal light, although the original lamp, outfitted with a clamshell lens that is among the world's biggest, is still operational. The lighthouse is currently undergoing a major restoration intended to allow greater public access to the structure, which previously was opened only on special occasions.

The nonprofit **Kilauea Natural History Association** (on the same site as the refuge, at the *makai* end of Kilauea Lighthouse Rd.; ☎ 808/828-0383; daily 10am–4pm) operates an on-site bookstore that's stocked with an excellent collection of nature, environment, and history titles, as well as children's books and toys. Guided hikes and other interpretive services are offered intermittently.

As you continue to drive north on Kuhio Highway, passing the manicured links of the Prince Course and the entryway to Princeville, a master-planned resort community that functions as the hub of North Shore tourism, the mountains and sea both seem to draw nearer, and the scenery sprouts even more shades of green. Before you head down into Hanalei Valley, stop at the **Hanalei Valley overlook** ★★★, located across the highway from the Princeville Shopping Center, for a glimpse of the mountain-framed rural landscape that awaits you.

The region's agricultural value is immediately evident once you cross the **Hanalei Bridge**—which was manufactured in New York City in 1912 and then assembled on Kauai to span the Hanalei River. It's now on the National Registry of Historic Places. This is a relic, too small to allow tourist buses. (At this point, Kuhio Hwy. becomes Hwy. 560.)

Deep, wide **Hanalei Valley** ★★★ has long been a significant food producer on Kauai. Its ancient taro fields—which early missionaries reported as among the most extensive in the islands—were cultivated with rice for nearly a century and then returned to taro in 1961. Kauai now produces about two-thirds of the state's wetland taro, which is milled into poi, the starchy cornerstone of a traditional Hawaiian diet. The taro fields you'll see along the Hanalei River are leased from the U.S. Fish and Wildlife Service, which manages the wetlands as a refuge for endangered Hawaiian water birds.

The traditional crop is also cultivated on private lands around **Hanalei town,** long viewed throughout the state as a near-perfect hamlet with an idyllic, enchanted setting and an old Hawaii lifestyle. In truth, the town no longer lives up to its reputation, as it's experiencing severe culture shock: skyrocketing real estate prices and property tax rates are forcing out longtime residents and dismantling Hanalei's counterculture image, which dates back nearly 40 years to the arrival of the first hippies. Still, one thing has not changed, and that's the town's remarkable locale. Nestled around a large, crescent-shaped bay, with a dense, interior mountain range pressing in close, Hanalei is the quintessential island beach burg, which at least partly explains its perennial popularity. It has a sweet, small-town feel and is easily traversed on foot or bicycle.

Besides the beach and the people-watching scene, Hanalei has few formal attractions other than the **Waioli Mission House** (Waioli Park, Kuhio Hwy., Hanalei; ☎ 808/245-3202; self-guided tours Tues, Thurs, and Sat 9am–3pm; donations accepted), which was built in 1837 by Hanalei's first missionaries, Lucy and Abner Wilcox. I like this little museum, which you can explore at your leisure on a self-guided tour. The rigid New England architecture and heavy, dark koa wood furniture speak volumes about the tightly controlled missionary worldview, offering insights into their influence on both traditional Hawaiian culture and modern island life.

Following the coastline, you'll pass through the lovely Waipa, Lumahai, and Wainiha river valleys before reaching a series of small caves that can be visited if you're interested in the island's volcanic origins. The first is **Maniniholo,** named for the head fisherman of the legendary Menehune. On the *mauka* side of Kuhio Highway, across from Haena Beach Park, it's more widely known as the "dry cave." A bit farther west, also on the *mauka* side of the highway, are two wet caves marked by a roadside directional sign; park in a small dirt lot across the street. **Waikanaloa** is right alongside the road; adjacent **Waikapalae** is a short uphill walk away on a dirt trail. Legend claims these caverns were dug by Pele, the volcano goddess. Some people swim in these caves, which are fed by natural springs, but I've never been tempted to put so much as a toe in the cold, dark, stagnant waters.

It's hard to imagine a man-made attraction could compete with the scenic splendor, but **Limahuli Garden** ★★★ (Rte. 560, Haena; ☎ 808/826-1053; www.ntbg.org; Tues–Fri and Sun 9:30am–4pm; self-guided tours $15, guided tours $25) holds its own, in part because the mountains here have been weathered into dramatically fluted and spiraled peaks. These give the narrow, verdant valley a primordial, almost ethereal quality that's enhanced by the ancient stone-walled terraces carved into the sloping hillside by Hawaiian taro farmers some 700 years ago. The terraces are still cultivated with wetland taro today, while the surrounding grounds have been landscaped with native and introduced coastal plants. You'll be rewarded with panoramic ocean views from a number of vistas on the walking path. Charles "Chipper" Wichman created this garden and nature preserve on land inherited from his grandmother before placing it under the auspices of the National Tropical Botanical Garden, which he now heads on Kauai. This is one of my favorite spots in all of Hawaii; I can guarantee that you'll never find another place quite like it.

Limahuli Stream runs through the garden and collects in a deep pool, known as "cold pond," alongside the highway, just west of the garden entrance. This favorite hot-weather hangout with local folks is the official start of **Haena State Park** ★★. From this point on, the mountains press in close alongside the road, which skirts boggy lands that once grew taro. The pavement ends in less than 2 miles at a parking lot, with restrooms and cold showers nearby. This busy spot is frequented by folks who wish to hike on the Kalalau Trail or swim at Kee Beach. You can join them, or simply turn around and drive back the way you came, spellbound and subdued from a delightful double dose of natural beauty.

THE OTHER KAUAI

People often ask me about the Garden Island's "secret spots" and "hidden places." The fact is, there aren't any places on this island that haven't been revealed to tourists, and there isn't one locale that encapsulates the essence of Kauai to a greater degree than any other. But there are things you can do, and authentic experiences you can share, that will bring you closer to local residents and help you understand how we live in—and look at—our island world.

VOLUNTEER OPPORTUNITIES

If you really want to "mingle" with local residents, you might consider volunteering while on vacation on Kauai. It not only gives you an opportunity to meet Kauaians, but volunteering behind the scenes will also show you a slice of life in Hawaii that most visitors never get to see.

There are several conservation-oriented organizations which welcome volunteers throughout the year. The first is the **National Tropical Botanical Garden at**

Limahuli Garden (½ mile past mile marker 9 on Kuhio Hwy. [Hwy. 560], Haena; contact Lea Taddonio, Volunteer Coordinator, ☎ 808/332-7324, ext 228). The Garden needs volunteers to get their hands dirty helping restore native Hawaiian forests (digging, planting, working in the nursery, pulling weeds, and so on). Depending on how much time you have to volunteer, your skill level, and your interest, NTBG will work to find an area where they need help and that interests you. A similar opportunity is available through the "Weed Busters" program at **Kokee Natural History Museum in the Kokee State Park** (☎ 808/335-9975 or www.kokee.org). Its innovative program employs volunteers to help eradicate alien species from the forest. I was surprised to learn that many of the volunteers were visitors, who cite a desire to get to know the forest more deeply and give back to the land. Whichever you choose, here's a chance to get an insider's view of the important ecological restoration work going on in Kauai.

If you are lucky enough to be in Hawaii during the humpback whale season (Jan–Mar), the **Hawaiian Islands Humpback Whale National Marine Sanctuary** is always looking for volunteers for its annual whale count, which generally takes place the last Saturdays in January, February, and March. The count is done by volunteers on land at 15 designated sites along Kauai's coast. Not only are they counting the whales they see between 8am and 12:15pm, but they're also making a record of the whales' surface behavior.

Even if you can only participate in one Saturday, the count really is a lot of fun. First you must sign up for the mandatory training session (generally given a week or two before the count). The "training" really is a wonderful opportunity to hear from whale experts about the incredible humpback, which weigh up to 40 tons and measure some 50 feet in length. In the past, I've met volunteers who had so much fun that they have arranged their next vacation in Hawaii around the annual whale count. For more information, contact **Jean Souza, Kauai Volunteer Programs Coordinator** (☎ 808/246-2860; www.hawaiihumpbackwhale.noaa.gov).

CULTURE & MUSIC

In laid-back Hawaii, much of the culture is passed down through music and what local residents call "talk story," where old timers sit around and talk about the culture of Hawaii. To experience this firsthand, head to the **Slack Key Guitar Concerts at Hanalei Community Center** (5-5299 Kuhio Hwy., Hanalei; ☎ 808/826-1469; http://www.mcmasterslackkey.com/liveshows.html; Fri 4pm, Sun 3pm; $20 adults, $15 seniors and kids). It's an informal, community oriented event where everyone bring a beach mat or chair and relaxes on the lawn as the soothing Hawaiian music washes over them. In addition to the music, there are always stories about the songs, the legends of Hawaii, and the culture.

Obon Festivals

Like communities throughout the U.S., Kauai's culture has been shaped as much by the immigrants who came to the island as by the native Hawaiians. So it should come as no surprise that one of the most "Kauai-ian" fests of the year is actually a Buddhist ceremony from Japan. Though the Obon Festival has religious roots—it honors those who have died and is a time to express gratitude to ancestors as well as the living—it has become more of a cultural celebration over the

Island of Festivals

In the aftermath of Hurricane Iniki, which hit in 1992, the island's tourism industry was as battered as the landscape. At that time, then-mayor Maryanne Kusaka made a concerted effort to develop local events and market Kauai as the "festival island."

Despite a rather contrived origin, the festivals now held all around the island throughout the year are actually some of the most authentic cultural experiences available to Kauai visitors. Nearly all feature entertainment—most often Hawaiian music and hula—as well as locally made crafts and booths selling plate lunches, shave ice, hot *malasada* (Portuguese donuts), coconuts, and other local food treats. Admission is usually free or low-cost, making them an ideal outing for families. Children are always welcome at these gatherings, with games and activities planned specifically for them. It's worthwhile to stop at any one of them for a few hours; to avoid traffic jams and crowds, go early or late, as they tend to be busiest midday.

Fall and spring are especially popular festival times, although something is scheduled nearly every month of the year. Below is a partial list of the most interesting fests and their usual schedule.

- **February:** Waimea Town Celebration showcases the West Side's cowboy culture.
- **July:** Kaloa Plantation Days Celebration is a weeklong summertime tribute to the island's agricultural heritage.
- **September:** Mokihana Festival is a weeklong celebration of Hawaiian music and hula.
- **October:** Coconut Festival, Queen Emma Festival, Matsuri Festival, Taro Festival, and Pow Wow.
- **December:** Lihue and Waimea's annual "festival of lights" parades, as well as The Christmas Fantasy Fair, which is the island's largest crafts fair (generally scheduled for the first or second weekend of the month).

For an updated schedule, visit www.kauaifestivals.com or check the calendar listings on The Garden Island website at www.kauaiworld.com. When you're on-island, watch for flyers and posters displayed in store windows and posted on public bulletin boards, or check the event listings in the weekly *Kauai Island News.* KKCR, Kauai's community radio station (90.9 or 91.9 on your FM radio dial; www.kkcr.org), also gives a rundown of arts and entertainment activities following the local news at about 5:45pm on weekdays.

years, and many non-Buddhists participate. The festival is celebrated on weekends from June through August at different Buddhist temples around the island. Usually you'll have your choice of two or three temples, but I'd suggest going to the closest one, as the festivities are nearly identical.

The story of Obon originated in India 2,500 years ago, when Moggallana, a leading disciple of Buddha, discovered that the soul of his mother suffered in the realm of hungry spirits. She was hung upside-down because of her greed when she was alive. Hoping to ease her suffering, Moggallana gave her a bowl of food but it turned to fire in her mouth. He then asked Buddha for advice.

Buddha taught him that he must practice great compassion and offer food to his fellow monks. Moggallana followed his instructions, and as a result his mother rose from the world of Hungry Ghosts. He was so happy that he danced with joy, giving inspiration to the Bon Dance celebration. And it's these dances, along with the colorful paper lanterns, that are at the heart of these celebrations.

What makes the Bon Dance unique in Hawaii is the mix of people at the dances. Everyone, regardless of age, gender, and ethnicity, feels welcome. The dances are very easy and repetitive. You'll pick up the simple moves in a few minutes, plus people are happy to help you out if you turn the wrong direction or forget a step. And you'll leave with a host of newfound friends.

Dress like you are going to church: in a nice muumuu or aloha shirt (no shorts, slippers, or T-shirts). You'll see some people in Japanese kimonos. Check the local papers listings of Obon Festivals or call the following Buddhist temples and missions:

West Kauai: Hanapepe Hongwanji Mission, 1–3860 Kaumualii Hwy., ☎ 808/335-3195; **Kauai Soto Zen Temple Zenshuji,** Hanapepe, ☎ 808/335-3521; **Kauai Soto Zen Temple,** Hanapepe, ☎ 808/335-3521; **Waimea Shingon Mission,** 3770 Manehune Rd., Waimea, ☎ 808/338-1854; **West Kauai Hongwanji Mission,** 4675 Manehune Rd., Waimea, ☎ 808/338-1537.

Lihue: Lihue Hongwanji Mission, Kapaia, ☎ 808/245-6262.

Coconut Coast: Kapaa Hongwanji Mission, 1170 Kuhio Hwy., ☎ 808/822-4667; **Kapaa Jodo Mission,** 4524 Hauaala Rd., ☎ 822-4319.

TEMPLE CONSTRUCTION, HINDU-STYLE

For a very different experience on the Garden Isle, plan to spend half a day watching the largest Hindu temple in the U.S. being created. In addition to the good karma, you'll learn a little bit about Hinduism and how it came to Kauai. For half a decade, master craftsmen from India have been building the Saiva Siddhanta Church's **San Marga Iraivan Temple** (☎ 808/822-3012, ext. 198; www.saivasiddhanta.com), scheduled for completion in 2010. The Chola-style temple is the result of a vision by the late Satguru Sivaya Subramuniyaswami, known to his followers as Gurudeva, the founder of the church and its monastery. He specifically selected this 458-acre site in 1970, a spot sacred not only to the Hindu community but to native Hawaiians, who call this location *pihanakalani,* "where heaven touches earth." The temple is huge: The concrete foundation is 68×168 feet and 3 feet thick, designed not to crack under the weight of the 3.2-million-pound structure dedicated to the Hindu god Shiva. It will be built of granite which is being hand-quarried by some 70 stonemasons in India, then shipped to Kauai for final shaping and fitting on the site by the master craftsmen from India. The center of the temple will hold a 700-pound crystal, known as the Sivalingam, now displayed at the monastery's smaller temple on the grounds.

The public is welcome to the monastery temple, open daily from 9am to noon, but I'm recommending the weekly guided tour which includes an opportunity to see the master craftsmen work on the temple (they even let you try your hand at the hand carvings which are being done here), a discussion of the flora and fauna on-site, and background on Hinduism (don't worry; they won't try to convert you). The weekly tour time varies depending on the retreat schedule at the monastery. Bring an umbrella, as it often rains here, and wear closed toed shoes and modest dress (this is a religious site, after all). For information, call ☎ 808/822-3012, ext. 198, or go to www.saivasiddhanta.com.

To get there, turn *mauka* (left, inland) off Kuhio Highway (Hwy. 56) at the lights, just after crossing the bridge, onto Kuamoo Road (between Coco Palms Hotel and the Wailua River). Continue up the hill, for just over 4 miles. A quarter mile past the 4-mile marker, turn left on Kaholalele Road and go 1 block to the end of the road. The Information Center is at 107 Kaholalele Rd. Park on Temple Lane. Enter the open pavilion, where a guide will escort you through the monastery. You can also visit the Sacred Rudraksha Forest, at 7345 Kuamoo Rd., for meditation, open 6am to 6pm; or the Nepalese Ganesha Shrine and Bangalore Gallery, which are located at 107 Kaholalele Rd.

STAR WATCH

One of the most romantic aspects of Hawaii is pondering the stars and the night sky. If you'd like a casual guided tour of the stars above the 50th state, join Kauai residents in the monthly **Star Watch,** sponsored the Kauai Educational Association for Science & Astronomy. Every month, on the Saturday closest to the new or dark moon, folks gather on the softball field in Kaumakani (Hwy. 50 west past Hanapepe just after the 18 mile marker; look for KEASA signs on the right, which will take you behind the school for parking and starwatch).

The event is free, and starts at sunset. Once the sun sets, Rozlyn Reiner, the secretary fore KEASA, generally does an overview of the night sky to the naked eye. You just relax in your lounge chair or on your beach mat, as she uses a laser pointer to orientate everyone to the sky, noting the constellations, various Hawaii stars that people from the mainland may not be familiar with, and pointing to the stars that you probably have heard of but didn't know where to find them in the sky. By this time the astronomers of KEASA have set up their telescopes (ranging from at least 2 to as many as 12) around the field. After the introduction of stars, guests are free to wander around the field to the different telescopes and view whatever each astronomer is focused on that evening (ranging from Saturn's rings to the moons of Jupiter). Everything is very casual, but entertaining, as well as educational, and the Star Gazing events are targeted for beginners. KEASA has chosen this area because of the clear skies (Rozlyn says 90% of the time they have perfect weather), however, for the 10% that may mean rain; check to make sure the event has not be cancelled by calling ☎ 808/332-7827 before you head out. More information is on their website, www.keasa.org.

Although it's very educational, it feels more like a friendly neighborhood gathering with people talking and sharing food before the event gets underway (great way to meet local folks; you'll see people from small kids to grandmas there).

Bring a picnic dinner, a light jacket (it gets chilly), mosquito repellant, a lawn or beach chair to sit on and a mat or blanket to lie down on, and watch the sky. ***One more note:*** The weather can change quickly here—I'd never go without an umbrella.

MEET THE ARTISTS

Kauai may be a small, rural island, but its art scene is surprisingly large and cosmopolitan. Artistic types flock to the Garden Island, where the enchanting light, inspiring scenery, and peaceful lifestyle stimulate and nurture their personal muse as they work in a range of mediums, including glass, silk and dyed fiber paper, clay and ceramics, oils, watercolors, pastels and acrylics, beads, wood, metal, mixed media, and photography.

You can view the fruits of their artistic labors in many different places: galleries, crafts fairs, boutiques, specialty shops, restaurants, museums, and public facilities, including the Lihue Airport, the state office building at 3060 Eiwa St. in Lihue, and the Exhibition Hall at the Kukui Grove Shopping Center. But if you really want to delve into the local art world, you'll need to get acquainted with some artists. This can be done by attending art openings and exhibitions held in various places throughout the year or taking a class, such as the free life-drawing course offered every Wednesday afternoon at the **Aloha Center** (3371 Wilcox Rd., Lihue; ☎ 808/245-6996; www.alohacenter.net).

Art Night, held every Friday from 6 to 9pm on Hanapepe's Main Street, is another fun and festive way to hang out with artists who live or show their work on the West Side. All the local galleries host open houses; sometimes these include demonstrations or live music.

You also can visit some artists in the studios where they work. Just be sure to call and schedule an appointment, because many Kauai artists hold additional daytime jobs. **The Kauai Society of Artists** (P.O. Box 3344, Lihue, HI 96766; www.kauaisocietyofartists.org) maintains a directory of local artists that includes photographs of their work, information on where their art can be seen, and contact information for those who accept studio visits and commissions. Another excellent resource on the local art scene is the **Garden Island Arts Council** (P.O. Box 827, Lihue, HI 96766; www.gardenislandarts.org).

GOING TO MARKET

At "sunshine markets," local farmers gather to sell their fruit, flowers, and vegetables at prices well below those charged by island grocery stores. And since local produce is harvested on market day or the day before, it's much fresher than the limp lettuce and tired tomatoes that spend 1 to 3 weeks in refrigerated cargo containers while in transit to Kauai.

While those two factors alone make it worthwhile to patronize the sunshine markets, they offer other advantages as well. For one thing, you'll get a chance to see the full array of crops cultivated on island farms, most of which are small and family owned. It's an eye-opening experience that's guaranteed to introduce you to fruits and veggies you never knew existed. You'll also gain the satisfaction that comes from putting money directly in the pockets of local farmers, which not only benefits individual growers but supports island agriculture overall. And it's a sector of the economy that needs all the assistance it can get.

Market Days

Every Monday a farmers market starts at noon at the Koloa Ballpark, on Maluhia Road near the entrance to town. On Tuesday there's a 3:30pm market at the Neighborhood Center in Kalaheo and a Hawaiian Farmers Market in Hanalei from 2 to 4pm.

The Kapaa New Town Park, at Kahau and Olohena roads, is the site of a 3pm Wednesday market. On Thursday the start time is 4:30pm in the parking lot of the Kilauea Neighborhood Center, on Keneke Street in Kilauea. In Hanapepe, the Sunshine Market also is on Thursday, behind the fire station from 3:30 to 5:30pm.

Friday's market is in Lihue at Vidinha Stadium parking lot, Hoolako St., beginning at 3:30pm.

Saturday's market moves to the Kekaha Neighborhood Center, at 9am and also in Kilauea at the Christ Memorial Church, 2518 Kolo Rd., from 9am to 11am.

A combination crafts fair and farmers market is held at 9am every Saturday in Hanalei's Waioli Park. If that's too early, you can catch a 10am market in the field adjacent to the Kilauea Post Office.

Within 30 minutes of opening time, the crowd thins considerably. Some farmers who sell out quickly start packing up, while others relax and tidy up their displays. This is the time to "talk story" with farmers and other shoppers, who are usually quite happy to share recipes and tips on determining ripeness and cultivating tropical plants at home.

ACTIVE KAUAI

Like the other Hawaiian islands, Kauai is an ideal place to test your limits and up your adrenaline. Surfing, kayaking, hiking, snorkeling, diving, windsurfing—it's all here for the trying and more. In this section, I cover all your options, including some that allow you to be totally inactive (massage anyone?).

HIKING

Kauai has miles of hiking trails to take you along the coast and into the rugged mountains and lush valleys of this largely undeveloped island. You can pick a day hike or spend a few days wandering through Na Pali Coast State Park or Waimea Canyon if you're in good shape. As far as I'm concerned, any time spent on Garden Island trails is well spent. You're traveling at a speed that allows you to take in the smells, textures, colors, sounds, and sights that together weave the marvelous tapestry of Kauai's natural world.

Tips for a safe and pleasant hike: When hiking on Kauai, be prepared for rain and cool temperatures, especially in the mountains, and bring plenty of water. The best footwear is tennis shoes or light hiking boots, something that gives you traction on soil that tends to be loose and crumbly. Expect that whatever you wear will get wet and likely stained with red Kauai clay, which doesn't wash out.

Kauai trails aren't always especially well marked, so it's useful to have a map. Since most of Kauai's trails are found in the Kokee, Waimea Canyon, and Na Pali

Coast state parks, the **Division of State Parks** (3060 Eiwa St., Lihue; ☎ 808/274-3445) is a good resource. It has maps, trail guides, and information about wilderness camping and hiking permits for lands under its domain. Having a map will help you avoid the narrow, faint paths that often branch off the main trail. These are usually made by pig and goat hunters, who go places you won't want to.

The state's **Na Ala Hele** (www.hawaiitrails.org) project maintains a website with information about *mauka* and *makai* trails and public access ways on each island. **Earthwalk Press** (☎ 800/828-MAPS) publishes an excellent Northwestern Kauai Recreation Map ($8.95; available at www.globecorner.com or the Kokee Natural History Museum), with lots of trails listed.

Kauai's foremost hike is along the world-renowned 11-mile **Kalalau Trail** ★★★, which winds through tropical valleys along the magnificent Na Pali Coast. This challenging wilderness trek starts at the western end of Kuhio Highway, at popular Kee Beach, which accounts for heavy foot traffic along the first 2 miles of the rough and often rocky trail. I like to hike early to avoid the crowds—as well as the heat and humidity, which can be oppressive on a midsummer's day. In 2 miles, or about an hour, you can reach Hanakapiai, a tropical valley with a stream running through the middle of it, framed by towering green mountains on one end and a white-sand beach (where it's usually inadvisable to swim) at the other. The trail is often wet and muddy, and there's no drinking water once you leave the trail head at Kee Beach; be sure to carry a bottle of water with you. It's easy to spend a thoroughly enjoyable day on this hike, although children under 10 will likely need to be coaxed to keep going.

If you're in excellent physical condition and have at least 2 full days and camping gear, you can hike up and out of the valley along a steep switchback trail that climbs 2,000 feet. You won't reach sea level again until Kalalau, 9 miles farther along. In between is Hanakoa, a wet valley and stream at the 5-mile mark. Then it's another 6 miles of hard hiking along the coastline until you drop down to sea level again at Kalalau Valley. No food, drinking water, or other supplies are available along the trail.

Note: A permit is required to hike past Hanakapiai or camp in any of the three valleys; contact the **Division of State Parks office** (on the third floor of the state building at 3060 Eiwa St., Lihue; ☎ 808/274-3444).

Waimea Canyon ★★★ and **Kokee State Park** ★★★ kids are the upcountry hiking hot spots on Kauai, and for very good reason. This is where you'll experience the natural world of Kauai—with native plants and birds that aren't found

---

To Book in Advance or Not, That's the Question

Although you often can save money by booking in advance online, you run the risk of getting to Kauai and finding the weather less than ideal for the activity you've scheduled. Activity booths around the island also offer discounts, but beware that some of the super deals require you to sit through a timeshare sales presentation. Only you can decide if it's a fair exchange.

Don't Drink the Water

If you're planning any backcountry hiking or camping, be sure to treat the water you collect from streams, springs, or other natural sources. All fresh water in Hawaii is potentially contaminated with leptospirosis, a type of bacteria spread through the feces and urine of cats, rats, pigs, goats, and deer, all of which are abundant in Kauai's valleys and forests. You can also contract leptospirosis through your mouth, eyes, and open cuts on your skin, so be very cautious if you want to stand under a waterfall or take a dip in a cool mountain stream. It's also found in wet pastures, taro fields, and other muddy places.

If you experience brutal headaches, wracking body pain, or any mild-to-severe flulike symptoms after drinking fresh water, seek medical help immediately and be sure to inform your doctor about possible leptospirosis exposure. Antibiotics are effective against leptospirosis, but the bacteria can kill you if left untreated—or make you so sick you might wish you were dead.

anywhere else in the world. The scenery is divine, whether you're gazing down into gorges carved through colorful rock, or watching whales frolic along the shoreline from your windy perch 1,500 feet above. The terrain is varied, too; you can walk on a boardwalk through the Alakai Swamp, or descend 1,800 feet into the arid Waimea Canyon, the so-called "Grand Canyon of the Pacific." Some 45 miles of trail in these two parks offer hikes that range in length and difficulty, so families and fitness freaks alike will find something that suits them. For hikes in Waimea Canyon, I'd recommend driving to the east rim (park on Halemanu Valley Rd., between mile markers 14 and 15 on Waimea Canyon Rd.) and taking the Canyon Trail, a round-trip of about 2 hours (it's a bit over 3 miles), which affords marvelous views of the canyon and a stop at Waipoo Falls, a magnificent 800-foot waterfall.

For hikes in Kokee State Park, stop first at **Kokee Natural History Museum** ★ kids (at the meadow, just inside the park entrance; ☎ 808/335-9975) to pick up maps and field guides that will help you identify flora and fauna along the trails; the friendly and knowledgeable staff can also give you an update on weather conditions and help you choose a suitable trek. Volunteers often lead hikes during the summer. If you decide to trek on your own, the **Berry Flat Trail,** which begins on Mohihi Road in Kokee, is suitable for children. This 2-mile hike on level ground through a forested area takes only about 60 to 90 minutes round-trip. If you're in good shape and looking for some views, try the **Awaawapuhi Trail,** a 6.6-mile (round-trip), full-day hike with an elevation loss and gain of 1,600 feet. The trail starts on Kokee Road, about 1½ miles past the park entrance, in a wet forest that generally gets drier as you approach the ridges above Awaawapuhi and Nualolo valleys. You can look down 2,500 feet into these Na Pali Coast valleys from a number of viewpoints along the trail, which ends at a scenic perch, where you turn around and retrace your steps. If you don't mind getting wet, the **Alakai Swamp Trail** ★ is fascinating and not as much of a slog through the bog as it used to be, thanks to the construction of a boardwalk. The trail is especially recommended for bird-watchers, as you'll see many rare species, but be sure to come prepared for rain: This area gets nearly 500 inches per year! You'll walk a little over 3½ miles by the end of the adventure.

Spouting Horn (p. 54) is the starting point for the **Koloa Heritage Trail** ★, a 10-mile ramble that can be walked, biked, or driven. It will take you past 14 coastal and inland historical sites, each with an interpretive plaque. It's very informative, as well as scenic. Pick up a map at your hotel or Koloa shops, or contact the **Poipu Beach Resort Association** (☎ 808/742-7444; www.poipu-beach.org).

If you're looking for a more centralized hike in the heart of the Coconut Coast, I'd suggest the **Nounou Ridge, or Sleeping Giant, Trail.** You can start at one of three trail heads—the easiest to find is right along Kuamoo Road (Rte. 580), about a half-mile *mauka* of Opaekaa Falls. From here, you can hike on level ground for 1.5 miles, or about an hour, making it suitable for kids. At the 1.5-mile mark, all paths converge at a trail that gains about 500 feet in elevation in slightly less than a mile, taking you to the top of a ridge that offers great views of the island's east side. Bring mosquito repellent.

Recommended Hiking Tours

You can hike independently, but if you'd like to have a guide, **Kauai Nature Tours** (P.O. Box 549, Koloa; ☎ 808/742-8305; www.teok.com) leads a number of educational hikes in both ocean and mountain areas around the island. Rated easy to strenuous, they range from a 4-hour stroll along the Mahaulepu Coastline to a difficult 9-mile forest hike. Prices run from $100 to $130 for adults and $75 to $85 for kids ages 12 and under. Fees include transportation, lunch gear (backpacks, rain gear, binoculars, and towels). Custom hiking packages can be arranged.

Another good outfit is **Aloha Kauai Tours** (1702 Haleukana St., Lihue; ☎ 800/452-1113 or 808/245-6400; www.alohakauaitours.com). You can sign up for daylong scenic tours of Kokee State Park and Kilohana Crater conducted in a four-wheel-drive vehicle ($125 adults, $90 for kids under 12) or an easy 3-mile guided hike through a rainforest in the island's interior section ($70 adults, $50 kids).

Princeville Ranch Adventures ★ (P.O. Box 224, Hanalei; ☎ 888/955-7669 or 808/826-7668; www.adventureskauai.com; $129–$145 for hike [children ages 5–10 yeas $89] and $145 for zipline) offers an excellent guided hike on the North Shore's 2,500-acre private Princeville Ranch. You'll walk through pasture and forested lands to a secluded waterfall, where you can swim and have lunch. They also have some routes that include ziplines if you're feeling frisky.

HORSEBACK RIDING

If you'd rather see the countryside on horseback, you can catch a ride at one of several stables around the island. **CJM Country Stables in Poipu** (P.O. Box 1346, Koloa; stables located on a dirt cane-haul road east of the Hyatt; ☎ 808/742-6096; www.cjstables.com) offers a good variety of excursions, ranging from $98 to $125, some of which take you right along the coastline, although it's illegal to ride on the sand beach in Hawaii. On the North Shore, **Princeville Ranch Stables** (corner of Pooku Rd. and Kuhio Hwy., Princeville; ☎ 808/826-6777; www.princevilleranch.com) leads group and individual rides ranging from a 1½-hour

Body & Soul

Kauai acts like a magnet to body workers, attracting practitioners trained in a diverse range of modalities, including Rolfing, lomilomi massage, crystal healing, acupuncture, acupressure, craniosacral work, art therapy, hot stone massage, shiatsu, theta healing, reiki, and much more. Many practitioners work independently, and a good number will travel to you, while others are affiliated with resort spas. If you're looking for straight body work, you'll get the best deals from the independents. Spa services cost more, and the treatment selection is narrower than you'll find on the open market, but you can also enjoy such amenities as steam rooms, dry sauna, and whirlpools.

If you are on Kauai's West End, the **Hart-Felt Massage and Day Spa** (Waimea Plantation Cottages, Kaumualii Hwy., Waimea; ☎ 808/338-0005) is an affordable and highly professional place for body work. It also offers a wide range of massage and structural integration therapies, as well as relaxing spa treatments, at prices ranging from $50 to $145 for treatments from 30 minutes to 90 minutes.

Another favorite establishment, this time on the North Shore, is **Ola's Massage** (4–971D Kuhio Hwy., Kapaa; ☎ 808/821-1100), which offers a variety of massage styles at prices starting at $75 for a 1-hour treatment. Out-call services are also available at $95 an hour. **Hanalei Day Spa** (57132 Kuhio Hwy., Hanalei; ☎ 808/826-6621; www.hanaleidayspa.com) is another respected outfit on this side of the island.

Whatever treatment you choose, plan to do nothing but relax afterward. Allow the healing to settle in and do its job on a deep, cellular level. Take a nap, lounge under a coconut tree, or soak in a tide pool. Let go. Breathe.

ocean bluff ride for $80, an unusual 1½-hour cattle drive for $135, a 3-hour waterfall, swim, and picnic ride for $125 (or the same ride for 4 hr. for $135).

TENNIS

If you're seeking a more competitive pastime, you'll find 20 tennis courts at the **Princeville Resort** (5520 Ka Haku Rd., Princeville; ☎ 808/826-3620; www.princevillehotelhawaii.com/ac_tennis.htm); call to reserve a court ($18 for non-guests for an hour, $12 for guests). You can use the public courts around the island for free (four courts on Lehua St., at the Kapaa New Town Park; and in Hanapepe four courts are on Kaumualii Hwy., at the Hanapepe Ball Park and next to the fire station). Keep in mind, though, that these courts are popular with locals; your best chance of getting an open court is midday in the middle of the week. Rule of thumb is if someone is waiting for a court, limit your play to 45 minutes.

GOLF

Kauai's golf courses are considered some of the prettiest, and toughest, in the state. Most are located along the coast, where golfers are treated to truly gorgeous views that stretch from *mauka* to *makai.* The scenery comes at a price; golf is an expensive outing on Kauai, although hotel and condominium guests often receive special rates at whatever course is affiliated with the property. All the private courses also offer discount "twilight" rates that will save you $20 to $60 on greens fees for play initiated after noon or 1pm.

The best discount deal I've found (also great for last-minute tee times) is **Stand-by Golf** (☎ 888/645-BOOK; www.stand-bygolf.com), which has up to 50% off greens fees on some courses and guaranteed tee times for same-day or next-day golfing.

If you plan to do a lot of golfing at resort courses, you'll save by purchasing the **Golf Challenge package,** which allows you to play the Poipu Bay, Kauai Lagoons, and Prince courses for about $390 (a $50 savings). You can sign up at any of the participating courses.

Among Kauai's private golf courses, the best rates are found at the **Kauai Lagoons Golf Club** (3351 Hoolaulea Way, Lihue; ☎ 808/241-6000). It has two courses, Kiele and Mokihana, both designed by Jack Nicklaus. They lie along a scenic stretch of coastline that's in the direct path of the trade winds and planes approaching Lihue Airport. Fees for 18 holes are $120 at Kiele (tee times 7am–2pm) and $170 at the Mokihana (tee times 7:30am–4pm).

The **Kiahuna Golf Club** (2545 Kiahuna Plantation Dr., Koloa; ☎ 808/742-9595) is one of two resort courses on the South Side, both designed by Robert Trent Jones, Jr. Kiahuna is a par-70 course built on an ancient coastal Hawaiian fishing village. Archaeological sites that could be worked into the course's design were allowed to remain. Greens fees, including cart, are $90; daily tee times are 6:30am to 5pm. Also here are a driving range, snack shop, bar, pro shop, and putting green. The same facilities are available at **Poipu Bay Resort** (2250 Ainako St., Koloa; ☎ 808/742-8711), a posh oceanfront course that's affiliated with the Grand Hyatt Regency Kauai Resort and Spa. It's consistently rated among the nation's top courses, and hosts the annual PGA Grand Slam of Golf. Greens fees, including cart, are a whopping $185, but rates drop to $65 for play begun after 3pm. Kids under 17 can play for half price when accompanied by a paying adult. Tee times are 6:30am to 5:30pm daily.

On the North Shore, you'll find two courses managed by Princeville Resort. The **Makai Course** (4080 Leiopapa Rd., Princeville; ☎ 808/826-3580) combines three 9-hole links to create a par-36, 27-hole course. It winds through the Princeville community, with houses built around its perimeter. The **Prince Course** (5-3900 Kuhio Hwy., Princeville; ☎ 808/826-5000) is far more wild and scenic, with dramatic views of the North Shore mountains and coastline. It's also a lot tougher than the Makai; indeed, it has a USGA course rating of 75.3, making it the most challenging in Hawaii. Greens fees, including cart, are $125 at the Makai and $175 at the Prince. During the winter and spring, Laysan albatross frequently nest on both Princeville courses, allowing you to witness the attentive parenting skills of these big seabirds.

Because locals usually can't afford the high fees charged by private courses, they flock to the county-owned **Wailua Municipal Golf Course** (3-5351 Kuhio Hwy.,

Lihue; ☎ 808/241-6666), which lies between the highway and the ocean, just south of the Wailua River. It's a pretty little course, but the low prices are the real draw. Greens fees—cash only—are just $32 on weekdays and $44 on weekends. Optional carts are $20. Tee times are 6:30am to 5pm daily. Even lower fees are charged at Kauai's other public facility: **Kukuiolono Golf Course** (Papalina Rd., Kalaheo; ☎ 808/332-9151). It costs just $8 to play this par-36, 9-hole course, so it's generally very crowded, but you'll witness lovely views of the hilly Kalaheo countryside. Tee times are 6:30am to 4:50pm daily.

BICYCLING

Island roads tend to be narrow, busy, and devoid of bicycle lanes, so those who bicycle on Kauai highways do so at their own risk. But there is a dandy little bike-pedestrian path that runs along the coast, behind the Coconut Marketplace, that's level and safe enough for young children. You'll also find many good mountain-biking trails in Waimea and Kokee state parks. The state forest reserve at the end of Kuamoo Road in Kapaa, *mauka* of Keahua Arboretum, has a number of dirt roads good for riding, especially the 13-mile Powerline Trail, which takes you over the mountains to the edge of Hanalei Valley.

You can rent bikes at **Kauai Cycle and Tour** (1379 Kuhio Hwy., Kapaa; ☎ 808/821-2115; www.bikehawaii.com/kauaicycle) from $15 a day. To rent beach cruisers and mountain bikes, try **Outfitters Kauai** (2827 Poipu Rd., Koloa; ☎ 888/742-9887; www.outfitterskauai.com; $25–$45 a day). Outfitters Kauai also offers early-morning and late-afternoon 4½-hour excursions that include a 12-mile downhill ride from Waimea Canyon at 3,600 feet to the coast. The cost is $98 for adults and $78 for children ages 12 to 14. Younger children are not allowed.

KAYAKING

Kauai is the only Hawaiian island to excel in river kayaking (as opposed to ocean kayaking). One- and two-man kayaks ply the broad, deep waters of the **Wailua River,** alongside motorized tour boats that hold the permit to land at a lush little cave known as the **Fern Grotto.** You can rent kayaks for around $40 per person per day a day, depending on size, and paddle them on the Wailua, Hanalei (North Shore), and Huleia (Lihue) rivers. Guided tours also are available; they're good for beginning paddlers and some include lunch. **Kayak Kauai** (P.O. Box 508, Hanalei; ☎ 800/437-3507 or 808/826-9844; www.kayakkauai.com) spearheaded the industry on the Garden Island and remains the best. If you're a skilled kayaker, you'll have fun exploring the little coves and crannies of Kauai's coastline when the seas are calm. Na Pali Coast is a popular summertime paddle; you depart from Hanalei and take advantage of the winds and currents to help push you toward Polihale, where a shuttle van picks you up if you booked through a commercial guide.

WHALE-WATCHING & OTHER CRUISES

Given the beauty of the coastline, it's not surprising that Kauai has a sizable commercial-tour-boat industry. You can travel on a range of motorized boats and catamarans, although it's wise to avoid the rubber inflatable-type boats if you're pregnant, frail, have back problems, or under the age of 8, as the ride can be very rough, even punishing, if the winds come up. Although a few commercial boating

Kayak-Rental Outfits

Kayak rentals should always include: life jackets, paddles, dry bags, and, when necessary, roof racks for your car. Among the kayak renters on the island, the following outfitters offer the best value:

- **Kayak Kauai** (☎ 800/437-3507 or 808/826-9844; www.kayakkauai.com): This is the only kayaking company with its own dock on the Hanalei River, along with its shop in Hanalei (on the Kuhio Highway in Hanalei Town). Single kayaks start at $42 a day; doubles go from $62.
- **Outfitters Kauai** (Poipu Plaza, 2827A Poipu Rd.; ☎ 808/742-9667; www.outfitterskauai.com): Cost is $40 per person per day, and along with the gear, they'll give you a brief lesson when you're set into the water. Outfitters also has two locations riverside, where they distribute the kayaks, on the Wailua and Huleia rivers. Like Kayak Kauai, it also offers guided tours.
- **Pedal 'n Paddle** (in the Ching Young Village shopping center, Hanalei; ☎ 808/826-9069; http://pedalnpaddle.com): This is the cheapest of the three at just $20 for a single kayak and $40 for a double, but you can only rent kayaks for paddles along the Hanalei River.

operations depart from Hanalei, nearly all the tour boats leave from Port Allen Harbor on the West Side. In summer, the route is invariably the western approach to Na Pali Coast, and most tours follow a 4- to 6-hour itinerary that includes anchoring off Nualolo for a thrilling deep-water snorkel stop. When big wintertime surf makes Na Pali Coast unsafe, the tour boats offer whale-watching cruises along the South Side coastline instead. Endangered humpback whales frequent waters all around Kauai between November and March, when they give birth and tend their young. You often can see them spouting, skyhopping, and breaching from shore, but a boat trip increases the likelihood of a sighting and definitely brings you closer to the action.

Overall, I've found **Captain Andy's Sailing Adventure** ★★★ (kids) (Port Allen Small Boat Harbor, Eleele; ☎ 808/335-6833; www.sailing-hawaii.com) provides the most consistently excellent service and value—you can save 10% booking online. The 55-foot catamaran is comfortable enough for kids and seniors, and this is one of the few outfits that will take very young children. Plus, you can rest easy knowing it's a longtime company with a good safety record. Their 5-hour Na Pali snorkel cruise costs $139 for adults, $99 for children ages 2 to 12.

Another good choice is **Liko Kauai Cruises** ★★ (kids) (9875 Waimea Rd., Waimea; ☎ 800/732-5456 or 808/338-0333; www.liko-kauai.com), a 49-foot power catamaran owned and operated by Liko Hookano, a local boy from the West Side. A 4-hour Na Pali snorkel cruise is $140 for adults and $95 for kids ages 4–12. **Captain Sundown** ★ (kids) (Hanalei; ☎ 808/826-5585; www.captainsundown.com) is the only sailing catamaran departing from Hanalei and touring the Na Pali coast. You can take a 6-hour Na Pali snorkel sail ($162 for adults, $38 for kids 7–12) during the summer; and a 3-hour whale-watching sail in the winter ($120 adults and $99 kids ages 7–12 years).

FISHING CRUISES

There are two types of fishing on Kauai: deep sea fishing in the ocean and freshwater fishing in Kauai's streams, rivers, and lakes.

The cheaper of the two, freshwater fishing, is big on Kauai, thanks to its dozens of "lakes," which are really man-made reservoirs containing large-mouth, small-mouth, and peacock bass (also known as *tucunare*). The Puu Lua Reservoir, in Kokee State Park, also has rainbow trout and is stocked by the state every year. Fishing for rainbow trout in the reservoir has a limited season: It begins on the first Saturday in August and lasts for 16 days, after which you can only fish on weekends and holidays through the last Sunday in September.

Before you rush out and get a fishing pole, you have to have a **Hawaii Freshwater Fishing License,** available through the **State Department of Land and Natural Resources, Division of Aquatic Resources** (P.O. Box 1671, Lihue, HI 96766; ☎ 808/241-3400; www.hawaii.gov/dlnr/dar/fish_regs/index.htm). The license is also available through any fishing-supply store, like **Lihue Fishing Supply** (2985 Kalena St., Lihue; ☎ 808/245-4930); **Rainbow Paint and Fishing Supplies** (Hanapepe; ☎ 808/335-6412); or **Waipouli Variety** (4–901 Kuhio Hwy., Kapaa; ☎ 808/822-1014). A 1-month license costs $3.75; a 1-year license is $7.50. When you get your license, pick up a copy of the booklet *State of Hawaii Freshwater Fishing Regulations.* If you would like a guide, **Sportfish Hawaii** ★ (☎ 877/388-1376 or 808/396-2607; www.sportfishhawaii.com) has guided bass fishing trips for two starting at $265 per person for a half-day and $375 for a full day.

Deep sea ocean fish is more expensive, and Kauai's fishing fleet is smaller and less well recognized than others in the islands, but the fish are still out there. All you need to bring are your lunch and your luck. The best way to book a sportfishing charter is through the experts; the best booking desk in the state is **Sportfish Hawaii** ★ (☎ 877/388-1376 or 808/396-2607; www.sportfishhawaii.com), which books boats not only on Kauai, but on all islands. These fishing vessels have been inspected and must meet rigorous criteria. Prices start at $1,200 for a full-day exclusive charter (you and five of your closest friends get the entire boat to yourself, $200 each), $925 for a three-quarter day exclusive, and $625 for a half-day exclusive.

DIVING & SNORKELING

If you'd rather view fish than catch them, you can do that, too. Both shore and boat dives are available, primarily on the South Side, and on the North Shore during the summer months. A few travel to the waters around Niihau; an all-day trip runs around $275 per passenger. Prices vary depending on the length of the trip, number of dives, and comforts offered aboard the boat, but certified divers can expect to pay around $85 to $125 for a one-tank dive and $80 to $135 for two-tank dives. Refresher and certification courses are offered, too. Some packages include gear, or you can rent the works for about $25 to $30 a day.

Because the best dives on Kauai are offshore, I recommend booking a two-tank dive off a dive boat. **Bubbles Below Scuba Charters** (6251 Hauaala Rd., Kapaa; ☎ 808/822-3483; www.aloha.net/~kaimanu) specializes in highly personalized, small-group dives, with an emphasis on marine biology. The 35-foot dive boat, *Kaimanu,* is a custom-built Radon that comes complete with a hot shower. Two-tank boat dives cost $120 including gear; nondivers can come along for the ride for $85. In summer (May–Sept) Bubbles Below offers a three-tank trip for experienced divers only to the "forbidden" island of Niihau, 90 minutes by boat from Kauai. You should be comfortable with vertical drop-offs, huge underwater caverns, possibly choppy surface conditions, and significant currents. You should also be willing to share water space with the resident sharks. The all-day, three-tank trip costs $275, including tanks, weights, dive computer, lunch, drinks, and marine guide.

If you want to snorkel on your own, most dive shops rent snorkel gear for less than $10 a day. They also sell plastic cards with some of the more common reef fish named and pictured so you can identify what you're seeing underwater. **Snorkel Bob's** (4–734 Kuhio Hwy., Kapaa, ☎ 808/823-9433; and 3236 Poipu Rd., Koloa; ☎ 808/742-2206; www.snorkelbob.com) allows you to rent gear on one island (for just $9 a week) and return it on another at no additional charge. Some good snorkel spots are Poipu Beach on the South Side and Kee Beach at the end of the road on the North Shore during summer months only. Lydgate Park on the East Side has a sheltered ocean pool where beginners can practice. But be cautious when you're snorkeling anywhere. Reefs can have dangerous currents even when the water appears calm.

SURFING, WINDSURFING & WATER-SKIING

Kauai's surfing is legendary, and so far, the best breaks still aren't totally jammed with crowds. Locals want to make sure it stays that way, and it's important to understand that you likely won't see too many friendly faces as you paddle out. Be respectful, and don't expect anyone to cut you any slack. Stop in at one of the surf shops in Koloa, Kapaa, or Hanalei to inquire about surf breaks and conditions; you can also rent surf and boogie boards for $5 an hour or $15 to $20 per day.

If you want to learn, you'll find several small schools ready to teach you. Prices range from $60 for a group lesson to $100 for 2 hours of private instruction. At **Titus Kinimaka's Surf School** (☎ 800/662-7055; www.hawaiianschoolofsurfing.com), you'll be taught by the big-wave surfer himself at Hanalei Bay. He guarantees that after one 90-minute lesson ($65), you will be surfing! When you call, you'll be told where to meet.

On the South Side, **Margo Oberg Surfing School** (Poipu Beach; ☎ 808/332-6100 or 808/639-0708; www.surfonkauai.com) is another good place to learn. Oberg (a seven-time world surfing champ) and her staff will work with you on everything from the fundamentals of selecting a board to standing up on a wave. Group lessons (1½ hr.) are $65, semi-private (2–4 people) are $90 for 1½ hours, and private lessons are $125 for 2 hours.

Depending on the conditions, you may see windsurfing and kiteboarding at Shipwreck Beach on the South Side, Kapaa Beach Park on the East Side, and Anini Beach on the North Shore. If you want to try it yourself, **Windsurf Kauai** (Kilauea; ☎ 808/828-6838) is the only game in town. When you call, you'll be told where to meet. It'll cost you $75 for a 3-hour lesson, with equipment, at Anini Beach, or you can rent gear for $25 an hour or $75 per day.

If you still haven't had your fill of watersports, you can go water-skiing on the Wailua River with **Kauai Water Ski & Surf Co.** (4-356 Kuio Hwy., Kapaa; ☎ 808/822-3574), which offers half-hour ($55) and hour-long ($110) outings on weekdays only.

HELICOPTER FLIGHTS

Yes, it is expensive, but it is an experience that you will carry the rest of your life. You will forever be able to close your eyes and feel the sudden weightlessness as the helicopter smoothly left the earth's gravity field and floated effortlessly across the sky. Plus it really is the only way to see two-thirds of the ancient island.

Then the question always comes up: Is it safe? Well, statistically it is safer flying in a helicopter than driving in a car on Kauai. Kauai's helicopter industry has a very successful safety record when you look at the hundreds of thousands of hours versus the handful of accidents. Plus, the operators on Kauai not only meet federal aviation standards for safety but most companies go beyond the requirements to make sure that their equipment is the safest possible.

Let's talk price: This is not the place to pick the cheapest deal available. Here's where I come in: I've selected the best of the best operators; choose from them. And book online, because you can save as much as 37% off.

My second suggestion is to book as soon as you plan your trip (so you will get the dates you want) and to book early in your trip (in case weather forces a cancellation, you still have time to rebook).

The final question that helicopter operators always get is "when is the best time to fly?" The answer is that depends, as weather and conditions are constantly changing. My experience is that I have never had a bad helicopter trip. There is always spectacular scenery, always a view into a remote world, and always something from the trip that stayed in my memory, reminding me why Kauai is such a magical place.

More than a dozen helicopter companies operate on Kauai, which is the statewide hub of the industry. Most of the flights depart from the heliport on Ahukini Road, adjacent to the Lihue Airport. One firm flies out of the Princeville Airport on the North Shore. I advise booking with longtime companies that have years of experience dealing with the tricky winds, fogs, squalls, and mountainous terrain that make flying on Kauai so dangerous. My top pick is **Blue Hawaiian** ★★★ (☎ 800/745-2583; www.bluehawaiian.com); book online for their 55-minute tour of the island in their first-class Eco-Star helicopter for $208 (compared to the rack rate of $241). If Blue Hawaiian is booked, try **Jack Harter Helicopters** (☎ 888/245-2001 or 808/245-3774; www.helicopters-kauai.com), **Island Helicopters** (☎ 800/829-5999 or 808/245-8588; www.islandhelicopters.com), or **Will Squyres Air Kauai** (☎ 888/245-4354 or 808/245-8881; www.helicopters-hawaii.com).

ATTENTION, SHOPPERS!

Kauai has never been known as a shopping mecca, nor has it aspired to be one. That characteristic alone has prompted some prospective tourists to revise their travel plans, although it seems to me there's plenty of shopping to satisfy most visitors. Best of all, many of the stores are delightful, one-of-a-kind boutiques, reflecting the talents and interests of the proprietor.

LIHUE

In spite of that introduction, Kauai does have some big box stores and malls. Fortunately, they're still largely confined to Lihue. The largest and only true regional mall is **Kukui Grove Shopping Center** (3-2600 Kaumualii Hwy., Lihue; ☎ 808/245-7784), where you'll find many of the same fast-food eateries and shops common to Anytown, USA, as well as a fourplex movie cinema and grocery store. Anchor stores include **Sears, Longs Drugs,** and **Macy's,** which carries quality aloha wear for women and men. An especially nice feature of this mall is the **Kukui Grove Exhibition Space** devoted to works by local artists. The juried shows change fairly often and admission to the gallery is free.

Clustered around Kukui Grove are **Home Depot** and **Big Kmart,** both of which are across a large parking lot from **Border's Books, Music & Café**—one of Kauai's most popular stores and hangouts. They have a sizable collection of Hawaiian music and books on various Hawaiiana topics.

Another shopping hot spot among locals is **Hilo Hatties** (3-3252 Kuhio Hwy., Lihue; ☎ 808/245-3404), where the entire store is devoted to lower- and mid-priced aloha wear, including the matching shirt and dress sets that are favored by some couples. You can often find coupons and deals in one of the many free tourism magazines available on-island.

Although these stores provide some of the necessities of life, the only shop worth seeking out in Lihue is the **Kauai Museum Gift Shop** ★ (4428 Rice St.; ☎ 808/246-2470). It's small, but it's an excellent place to find quality goods that are fairly priced, including many handmade and authentic Hawaiian craft items. They carry hand-sewn feather lei hatbands and Niihau shell jewelry, as well as hand-woven lauhala hats, Hawaiiana books, and other distinctive merchandise.

KAPAIA

From Lihue, follow Kuhio Highway for about 2 miles before it dips down to the tiny hamlet of Kapaia, where you can catch the turnoff to Wailua Falls, or stop at **The Kapaia Stichery** ★ (3-3551 Kuhio Hwy.; ☎ 808/245-2281). Located in a restored plantation building with high ceilings, this stand-alone store carries beautiful tropical print fabrics and Hawaiian quilting supplies, as well as top-quality men's aloha shirts and finished Hawaiian quilts, some of them hand-stitched and others machine-sewn.

THE EAST SIDE: WAILUA

In Wailua, you'll find **Bambulei** (Kuhio Hwy. at the intersection with Halelio Rd., Wailua Village; ☎ 808/823-8641), another distinctive store that makes good use of an old plantation-era building to showcase its distressed-wood furniture, women's clothes, and an eclectic assortment of home accessories. It's fun, funky, hip, and pricey, but worth a look. Due to its location on Kuhio Highway, just north of the congested intersection with Halelio Road, it's easiest to slip in and out of here when you're southbound on the highway.

The **Coconut Marketplace** (4-484 Kuhio Hwy., Kapaa; ☎ 808/822-3641) lies kitty-corner to Bambulei, but its mall-style architecture and pedestrian merchandise are so different, it might as well be on another planet. With a number of restaurants and more than three dozen shops, it's the second-largest mall on the island and a magnet for visitors staying in the many Coconut Coast resorts within walking distance.

KAPAA

If you're a die-hard shopper, you'll likely enjoy strolling through the Marketplace, but you'd be better off spending your time and money in north Kapaa, a town that originally served pineapple- and sugar-plantation workers. Small eateries, galleries, and interesting clothing, crafts, and jewelry shops can be found along the half-mile stretch of Kuhio Highway that lies roughly between Ono Family Restaurant and Kojima's Market. Given the steady, slow-moving flow of traffic along the highway, it's easiest to park your car and walk to the different businesses.

My favorite downtown Kapaa store is **Davison's Arts** ★★ (4-1322 Kuhio Hwy., Kapaa; ☎ 808/821-8022; www.davisonarts.com), run by John and Hayley Davison. John's a fine artist with a whimsical, bold style, and Hayley handcrafts furniture and other small pieces from native and local wood. Their work is beautifully displayed in an upbeat, campy gallery that adjoins Kawamoto's, an appliance store that goes back many years. They also sell sumptuous hand-woven rugs and the eclectic, original creations of select local artists. Down the block is **Kela's Glass Gallery** (4-1354 Kuhio Hwy., Kapaa; ☎ 808/822-4527), where the merchandise is exquisite and expensive. If you like glassware, you'll surely find something to tempt you here, and they're masters at shipping their fragile, handmade treasures. Since you're in the neighborhood, stop by **Lightwave Pottery** (961 Kipuni Way, Kapaa; ☎ 808/826-9576; www.lightwavepottery.com), where you can watch potter Dean McRaine work on his functional creations each weekday afternoon between about 1 and 6pm. Take Kipuni Way, the first *mauka* road south of Kapaa Shopping Center, and follow it just past the Kauai Community Federal Credit Union. The studio is on your right; check out the wetlands behind it, where you can often spot endangered Hawaiian water birds.

If you have more practical concerns, you'll find a local Big Save grocery store, post office, self-serve laundry, hardware store, gas station, and a couple of eateries in the **Kapaa Shopping Center** (4-1105 Kuhio Hwy.; ☎ 808/246-0634). Hawaiian Blizzard, the sidewalk shave-ice (the Hawaii version of a snow cone) stand there, is one of Kauai's best. **Business Support Services** (4-1191 Kuhio Hwy., Kapaa; ☎ 808/822-5504) is the place to go when you need to send faxes, ship packages, check e-mail, or download photos from your digital camera. It's just north of a tiny side street that leads to **Cost-U-Less** (4525 Akia Rd., Kapaa; ☎ 808/823-6803), where you'll save money on groceries, especially if you're shopping for a group.

The last hurrah for shopping in Kapaa is **Otsuka's Furniture & Appliances** (4-1624 Kuhio Hwy.; ☎ 808/822-7766), an oceanfront home-furnishings store that caters to visitors with some 20,000 small household items that can be tucked into a suitcase or shipped to your home for free.

THE NORTH SHORE: KILAUEA

For such a tiny town, Kilauea has a surprising number of good stores, perhaps to account for its lack of good restaurants. In any case, they're easy to find, since they're by and large at the **Kong Lung Center** (2484 Keneke St., Kilauea). The most notable is **Kong Lung Co.** (☎ 808/828-1822), a lovely but very expensive emporium set in a historic stone building. It has a selection of quality women's clothing, fine jewelry, and upscale housewares, all of it artistically displayed and absolutely nonessential. More pretty and frivolous merchandise is offered at the **Lotus Gallery of Fine Art** ★ (☎ 808/828-9898). It's owned by a husband-wife team, with the wife designing fine jewelry that's sold alongside crystals and other special treasures in this lovely Asian-influenced gallery. They also have a small outlet in the foyer of the **Beach House Restaurant** (5022 Lawai Rd., Koloa; ☎ 808/742-8649), which focuses on jewelry. **Island Soap & Candle Works** (☎ 808/828-1955) is another worthwhile shop in this small center. You can watch tropical-scented soaps being made and purchase candles and various beauty products.

Across the way, in another small cluster of historic stone buildings, is **Healthy Hut Natural Foods Store** ★★ (4270 Kilauea Lighthouse Rd.; ☎ 808/828-6626; open daily), the cheapest place to buy health foods on Kauai. Although small, it has a good selection. You can also pick up natural foods, alternative and conventional health and beauty products, and a few unique gift items at **North Shore Pharmacy** ★ (2460 Oka St.; ☎ 808/828/1844), which has a very knowledgeable and helpful staff.

If you continue on Kilauea Lighthouse Road, you'll end up at Kilauea Point National Wildlife Refuge, which would be worth a visit even if the **Kilauea Point Natural History Association Bookstore** ★★ (☎ 808/828-0168) weren't so well stocked with natural-history titles, children's coloring books and games, locally made crafts, and various items with a nature theme. All the proceeds benefit the nonprofit association's education and interpretive efforts.

HANALEI

Once you go downhill into Hanalei Valley, you'll find most of the shopping is bunched up in Hanalei's tiny downtown. One exception is **Ola's Hanalei** (☎ 808/826-6937), on Kuhio Highway next to the Hanalei Dolphin restaurant, on the outskirts of town. It has some lovely housewares, art pieces, campy cards, and quality crafts that tend to be pricey. Less expensive and equally interesting is **On the Road to Hanalei** ★ (☎ 808/826-7360), a collection of housewares, clothing, jewelry, and children's games, along with other assorted goodies imported from Indonesia. It's technically part of the **Ching Young Shopping Village,** which fronts Kuhio Highway smack in the middle of Hanalei and has a number of alluring shops. One of my favorites is **Hanalei Video & Music** ★ (Ching Young Village on Kuhio Hwy., Hanalei; ☎ 808/826-9633), where you can buy handmade ukulele, guitars, Hawaiian sheet music, and island-style-music CDs. The **Evolve Love Gallery** (Ching Young Village on Kuhio Hwy., Hanalei; ☎ 808/826-4755) features the work of local artists; and it's worth checking out if you're looking for shell jewelry and unique local crafts. **Village Variety** (Ching Young Village on Kuhio Hwy., Hanalei; ☎ 808/826-6077) has some of the best bargains in Hanalei and an eclectic assortment of merchandise, ranging from film and sunscreen to kitchenware and fishing gear.

THE SOUTH SIDE: KOLOA

In Koloa town itself, check out the locally owned surf shop **Progressive Expressions** (5420 Koloa Rd.; ☎ 808/742-6041). It's been a landmark for more than 30 years, selling custom surfboards, boogie boards, beach gear, and surf clothing. You'll also find a branch of **Island Soap & Candle Works** (5428 Koloa Rd.; ☎ 808/742-1945).

POIPU

Closer to the resorts is **Poipu Shopping Village** (2360 Kiahuna Plantation Rd., Koloa; ☎ 808/742-2831), which has a decent selection of shops and restaurants. The merchandise is skewed toward the youthful surf set, although there are several upscale jewelry stores and art galleries here, too. **Hale Mana Fine Art** ★ (2360 Kiahuna Plantation Dr., Poipu; ☎ 808/742-1027) has unusual and South Pacific–themed products. It's one of my favorite stores on the South Side. The other is **Kebanu Gallery 5** (3440 Poipu Rd., Koloa; ☎ 808/742-2727), which offers a distinctive selection of jewelry, home accessories, and gift items that are handmade and interesting. Both of these shops carry merchandise you won't find elsewhere in Hawaii, although only a few of the items are locally made.

Along Lawai Road, on the western edge of Poipu, lies the **National Tropical Botanical Garden Gift Shop** (Lawai Rd., Poipu; ☎ 808/742-2430), which is stocked with quality botanical-themed merchandise, including books, small art pieces, cards, and housewares. It's right across the street from the Spouting Horn attraction, where a number of vendors have county licenses to hawk their wares.

THE WEST SIDE

You'll find a better selection of locally made products at the **West Kauai Craft Fair,** although you'll have to drive all the way to Waimea to check it out. Vendors—most of them Kauai crafters—set up tables Friday through Sunday in a field on the *makai* side of Kaumualii Highway, across from the West Kauai Technology and Visitor Center. It's a good place to look for Niihau shell jewelry. When you visit Kokee State Park, be certain to stop in at the **Kokee Natural History Museum** ★ (☎ 808/335-9975), a combination gift shop and interpretive center for the park. It has a great selection of books, items handcrafted from native woods and other natural materials, and some special gifts aimed toward nature lovers. You can feel virtuous knowing your purchases benefit the nonprofit organization **Hui O Laka** (☎ 808/335-9975; www.kokee.org), which runs the museum and a number of other programs in Kokee.

Finally, when it's time to leave Kauai, consider picking up some very low-priced fresh flower leis and cut tropical flowers at **Greeters of Hawaii** (Lihue Airport terminal; ☎ 808/245-1679). They're packed in hard-sided containers that make it easy to bring home a special gift or fragrant memento for yourself.

NIGHTLIFE ON KAUAI

Nightlife on Kauai has always been something of a joke, mainly because for so long there wasn't any. Remember, this is a rural island with small, isolated communities, where folks go to bed early and locals are more apt to drink at the beach park, or a friend's carport, than go out.

Still, you can hear live music, dance, knock back a few beers at a sports bar, play pool, throw darts, and occasionally enjoy the performing arts if you feel the need for some post-sundown diversion. Your opportunities to engage in these activities are greatest in Kapaa and Lihue, but you'll find a bit of action in every big resort and small town. In the last 5 years, I've noticed a significant increase in the number of restaurants, lounges, and bars featuring local musicians. You'll most frequently encounter Hawaiian music, but you can also hear Kauai bands performing jazz, rock, and reggae.

LUAUS ON KAUAI

Although I've never been a big fan of commercial luaus because they bear so little resemblance to the real thing, they're fine if viewed solely as entertainment and not as authentic Hawaiian culture. Most luaus have several things in common: a huge spread of food, Polynesian dancing and music, and plenty of strong mai tais. You can expect to dine and watch the show as part of a large group of tourists. Most luaus are fixed in price, generally $68 to $99 for adults, less for children. The luau usually begins at sunset and features Polynesian and Hawaiian entertainment, which can range from lavish affairs with flaming knives or torches being juggled, to performances of ancient hula, missionary-era hula, and modern hula, as well as narration of the stories and legends portrayed by the dances. The food always includes imu-roasted kalua pig, lomi salmon, dried fish, *poke* (raw fish cut into small pieces), *poi* (made from taro), *laulau* (meat, fish, and vegetables wrapped in ti leaves), Hawaiian sweet potato, sautéed vegetables, salad, and the ultimate taste treat, a coconut dessert called haupia. Don't worry; if you've never heard of these items (and can't pronounce them either), most luau will also have more common preparations of fish, chicken, and roast beef, as well as easily recognizable salads and standard desserts like cake.

The mainstay of the feast is the imu, a hot earthen pit in which the pig and other items are cooked. The preparations for the feast actually begin in the morning, when the luau master layers hot stones and banana stalks in the pit to get the temperature up to 400°F. The pig, vegetables, and other items are lowered into the pit and cooked all day. The water in the leaves steams the pig and roasts the meat to a tender texture.

One of the larger commercial luau in the island is **Smith's Tropical Paradise Garden Lu'au,** (in the Tropical Paradise Gardens on the Wailua River; ☎ 808/821-6895 or 808/821-6896), every Monday, Wednesday, and Friday at 5pm (during the popular summer months it's Mon–Fri). Book online to save money: $68 adults (rack racks are $75), juniors ages 7 to 13 years $27 (rack rates are $30), and $17 children 3 to 6 years (rack rates are $19).

Recently the **Sheraton Kauai** (Poipu Beach (☎ 808/742-8200; www.sheratonkauai.com) launched the island's only oceanfront luau. The Surf to Sunset Luau is held on Monday, Wednesday, and Friday, beginning at 6pm with a shell lei greeting and a mai tai. Photos with Poipu Beach serving as the background are offered, and guests can wander among the local artisans who teach lei making, lauhala weaving, and coconut frond weaving. After the feast, and before Pilah's Royal Polynesian Revue begins the entertainment, there is a *pareu* (sarong) fashion show that teaches visitors several techniques for tying this island cloth into a variety of different types of clothing. Cost for adults range from $75 for the buffet dinner and entertainment to $87 for premier seating, table service, and professional photos. Children ages 6 to 12 are $38 and $44.

The luau at the **ResortQuest Kauai Beach at Makaiwa** (650 Aleka Loop, Kapaa; ☎ 808/822-345511; www.resortquesthawaii.com) is Tuesday to Sunday, beginning at 5:30pm with an imu ceremony where the pig is removed from the pit, followed by entertainment featuring ancient and modern hula performances. The cost is $65 for adults, $59 for seniors, $42 for teenagers 13 to 18, $32 for children 3 to 12, and free for children 2 and under.

The **Princeville Resort** puts on a beachside luau called **Pa'ina O' Hanalei** (5520 Kahaku Rd., Princeville; ☎ 800/826-4400 or 808/826-9644; www.princeville.com) Monday and Thursday at 6pm. Under a canopy of stars, a full feast is served and a Polynesian revue performs. The cost is $99 for adults, $90 for seniors, $45 for children 6 to 12.

On the south coast, check out Tihati Production's "Havaiki Nui," in the **Grand Hyatt Kauai Resort & Spa** (1571 Poipu Rd., Poipu (☎ 800/55-HYATT or 808/742-1234; www.kauai-hyatt.com), every Sunday and Thursday. Not only do they have an elaborate buffet but the Polynesian show is very professional. The cost is $75 for adults, $65 for ages 13 to 20, and $40 for children 6 to 12.

THE EAST SIDE

In Lihue, **Rob's Good Time Grill** (Rice Shopping Center, Rice St., Lihue; ☎ 808/246-0311; www.robsgoodtimegrill.net) is a slightly gritty but friendly place that attracts a low-key, unpretentious crowd. It's a rectangular-shaped, rather nondescript establishment in a shopping center where you can eat, drink, sing karaoke, and dance nightly to a DJ mix, and the prices are fairly reasonable. Down by Nawiliwili Harbor, at the Kauai Marriott Resort & Beach Club, is **Duke's Canoe Club Barefoot Bar** (3610 Rice St., Lihue; ☎ 808/246-9599). It's a pleasant, casual spot for a drink and snack, with a great outdoor setting on Kalapaki Bay. It can get noisy because it's usually busy, and the tables are set close together. On Fridays from 4 to 6pm, there's traditional and contemporary Hawaiian music and exotic tropical drinks are just $5.50.

In Kapaa, my favorite places to hear live music are the **Blossoming Lotus Restaurant** (4504 Kukui St., Kapaa; ☎ 808/822-7678; www.blossominglotus.com), which has eclectic entertainment nightly in the dining room, and **Caffe Coco** (4-369 Kuhio Hwy.; ☎ 808/822/7990), where it's fun to order a yummy dessert and/or espresso-bar drink and listen to acoustic music (they have a noteworthy belly-dance show on Wed nights).

In the Coconut Marketplace, the **Hukilau Lanai** (520 Aleka Loop, Kapaa; ☎ 808/822-0600) usually has a Hawaiian trio in the open lounge off the dining room, and there's live Hawaiian entertainment nightly at **Kauai Hula Girl** (4-484 Kuhio Hwy., Kapaa; ☎ 808/822-4422). If you feel like dancing, pop in to the **Tradewinds** (4-484 Kuhio Hwy., Kapaa; ☎ 808/822-1621), which has either a DJ or live music every night, as well as karaoke, video games, and live satellite sports. The Tradewinds, with its South Seas decor and younger crowd, is certainly the liveliest of the three establishments, all of which cater primarily to visitors.

Despite its location next to McDonald's, **Lizard Lounge** (Waipouli Town Center, Kuhio Hwy., Kapaa; ☎ 808/821-2205) is a bar best suited for adults, with a musty smell and scruffy flooring, as well as TVs, dartboards, and a small crowd of gregarious regulars. The food's not too bad and it stays open until 2am.

THE NORTH SHORE

Heading north, **The Landing Pad** (5-3541 Kuhio Hwy., Princeville; ☎ 808/826-9561) is a tiny bar at the Princeville Airport where live music, including reggae on

Wednesday nights, is interspersed with DJ mixes. It's a low-key, inexpensive place to have a drink and dance without getting into any trouble.

Within Princeville proper, you have two choices: **The Living Room at the Princeville Resort** (5520 Ka Haku Rd.; ☎ 808/826-9644) and **Happy Talk Lounge, at Hanalei Bay Resort** (5380 Honoike Rd.; ☎ 808/826-6522). Both are top spots to have a drink and pupu (appetizer) while watching the sunset; however, your tab will be smaller at the Happy Talk, where you'll be listening to live soft jazz and island-style music in a casual, cozy setting. The Living Room is quite elegant and offers excellent live music, but drinks can be very expensive.

In Hanalei, **Tahiti Nui** (5-5134 Kuhio Hwy.; ☎ 808/826-6277) and **Hanalei Gourmet** (5-5161 Kuhio Hwy.; ☎ 808/826-2524; www.hanaleigourmet.com) tend to attract a mix of hard-drinking locals and visitors looking for action. Both places serve food and have live music—nightly at Hanalei Gourmet and on weekends at the Nui, which also has karaoke on Monday nights. The Nui is a funky Polynesian-style place with a long bar and a nice porch; Hanalei Gourmet is darker, smaller, and quieter. They're both right on the main drag, Kuhio Highway, nearly opposite one another.

POIPU

In Poipu, **Stevenson's Library in the Grand Hyatt Regency Kauai Resort and Spa** (1571 Poipu Rd., Koloa; ☎ 808/742-1234) is a quiet place to relax and unwind, with live jazz nightly from 8 to 11pm.

Also in Poipu, **Keoki's Paradise** (in the Poipu Shopping Village, 2360 Kiahuna Plantation Dr. ☎ 808/742-7534) gets going with live music Monday through Friday evenings (call for times). The cafe menu is available from 11am to 11:30pm. Hawaiian, reggae, and contemporary music draw the 21-and-over dancing crowd.

The **Poipu Shopping Village** offers free Tahitian dance performances every Tuesday and Thursday at 5pm in the outdoor courtyard.

Down the street **The Point, at Sheraton Kauai Resort** (2440 Hoonani Rd.; ☎ 808/742-1661), on the water, is the Poipu hotspot for the 20-something crowd, featuring live music Thursday and Saturday with dancing to a range of different artists from contemporary Hawaiian to good ol' rock 'n' roll.

WAIMEA

Waimea Brewing Company (9400 Kaumualii Hwy., Waimea; ☎ 808/338-9733; www.waimeabrewing.com) is a relaxing place to sit outside, enjoy the mountain and ocean views, and try some of this microbrewery's 12 beers—8 of them served on tap. They have other beers and tropical drinks, too, and you can order pupu or a light dinner from the pub menu. On Thursday nights there's good Hawaiian music.

PERFORMING ARTS ON KAUAI

The **Kauai Concert Association** (☎ 808/245-7464) hosts off-island musicians and dance companies touring the state; the season usually runs from the fall through the spring. Their concerts are nearly always scheduled at the Kauai Community College Center for Performing Arts, off Kaumualii Highway, just west of Kukui Grove.

ABCs of Kauai

Area Code All the Hawaiian islands are in the **808** area code.

ATMs/Currency Exchange Your best bet is to change money at the Honolulu Airport before you fly to Kauai, or use traveler's checks. ATMs are widely available and open around the clock at most banks and in many stores.

Business Hours Banks are typically open Monday to Friday from 9am to 4:30pm. Government offices are open weekdays from 8am to 5pm. Most stores are open daily from 9 or 10am to 6pm; some stay open until 9pm.

Car Rentals You'll find car-rental agencies at Lihue Airport. See p. 14.

Emergencies For police, fire department, or ambulance, dial ☎ **911.**

Information The **Kauai Visitors Bureau** (4334 Rice St., Lihue; ☎ **808/245-3971**) is open from 9am to 5pm weekdays.

Medical **Wilcox Memorial Hospital** (3420 Kuhio Hwy., Lihue; ☎ **808/245-1100**) has a 24-hour emergency room, as well as a **walk-in clinic** (☎ **808/245-1500**) Monday through Saturday if you need to see a doctor.

Newspapers *The Garden Island* (50¢; $1.25 on Sun) is published each morning on Kauai and it's widely available in stores and newspaper boxes around the island. Honolulu and mainland newspapers can be purchased at convenience stores and supermarkets.

Pharmacies **Wilcox Memorial Hospital** has a pharmacy, and you can also have prescriptions filled at **North Shore Pharmacy** (2460 Oka St., Kilauea; ☎ **808/828-1844**) and **Longs Drugs** (4-831 Kuhio Hwy., Lihue; ☎ **808/822-4918;** or Kukui Grove Shopping Center, Lihue; ☎ **808/245-8871**).

Police In an emergency, call ☎ **911,** or in non-emergency situations, dial ☎ **808/2411-6711.**

Post Office You'll find post offices in Hanalei, Princeville, Kilauea, Anahola, Kapaa, Lihue, Koloa, Lawai, Hanapepe, Eleele, and Waimea. They each keep different hours, but all are open Monday through Saturday.

Safety Kauai has very little violent crime, so leave your fears at home. But do keep an eye on your possessions, and leave nothing in your rental car.

Transit Info For information regarding the **Kauai Bus,** call ☎ **808/241-6410.**

3 Oahu: The Main E

Though it can be crowded & urban, Oahu's undeniable attractions are hard to resist.

by Jeanette Foster

"OAHU IS SO OVER; KAUAI IS THE PLACE TO GO," SAY CALIFORNIA HIPSTERS.
Well, if you're looking to escape the urban sprawl, they're right. Oahu—aptly known as the Gathering Place—is home to almost a million people. Plus, just less than another half million visit each month. Traffic is a nightmare—and not just in Honolulu. On winter weekends, cars are lined up bumper to bumper "out country," better known as the North Shore, with residents and tourists alike hoping to see big waves.

But Oahu is the most developed of the Hawaiian islands because it has the best of the things that make Hawaii famous—the most accessible, sandy-bottomed beaches; the most consistent, surfer-friendly waves; and easy-to-get-to hikes. Of course, as the home of Pearl Harbor, Oahu also has an irrefutable place in world history and Americans' hearts. As far as Hawaiian history goes, Oahu was the headquarters for the islands' first unifying king—Kamehameha I—and it has remained Hawaii's capital ever since. The major cultural sites reflecting Hawaii's monarchy are all here—Iolani Palace, the Royal Mausoleum, and Queen Emma's Summer Palace.

It's also an exciting time to be on Oahu. Just a decade ago, Honolulu, the island's nerve center, was a provincial town suffering from a severe case of brain drain, with talented locals going off to college on the mainland and not coming back because there were no job opportunities on the island. In the last few years, those people have become disenchanted with places like New York, Los Angeles, and San Francisco, and they've been lured back by their island home. For all its urban development, Oahu still has an island rhythm and its own culture that's evolved from its diversity. New residents from all over the world are choosing to settle here, too.

The result is a bustling island where there's always something to do. Oahu is home to the Hawaii International Film Festival, the Hawaii International Jazz Festival, and the Honolulu Marathon.

Oahu is also more "Hawaiian" than it has been since an 1896 law closed Hawaiian-language schools and mandated that English be the language of instruction in public schools. A cultural renaissance that began in the 1970s is seeing a rip[illegible]e more hula *halau* (troupes) than ever, Hawaiian music is thriving (in 2[illegible]rael Kamakawiwo'ole's album *Iz* became the first Hawaiian album to go platinum), and the art of growing taro is practiced all over the island.

In addition to celebrating its traditions, Honolulu has a famous melting-pot culture—one created from the tastes and traditions of the islands' Japanese, Chinese, Samoan, Korean, and Filipino residents—which adds a cosmopolitan vibe. You'll find a bustling Chinatown next door to a skyscraper-filled business district. There's a kava bar on one corner and just a few doors down a chic, sleek restaurant and bar owned by a Japanese impresario, where people dish over cocktails to the sounds of electronic music. These odd neighbors capture modern Oahu in a nutshell: Simultaneously, it digs into its traditional roots and keeps up with the rest of the world.

DON'T LEAVE OAHU WITHOUT . . .

Swimming in Waimea Bay (or, if it's winter, watching the big waves from the safety of shore). In summer, this wide bowl of water is the ultimate aquamarine saltwater swimming pool. See p. 137.

Swanning around an heiress's estate. Shangri La, the oceanfront home of the late Doris Duke (her father founded Duke University), is a sumptuous spread that defines island chic. It's also an Ali Baba den of Islamic art from around the world. A "playhouse" is the reproduction of a 17th-century royal pavilion in Isfahan, Iran. Opened to the public in 2002, Shangri La quickly became a hot-ticket destination for aesthetes. See p. 149.

Taking a surf lesson. Waikiki Beach's consistent lineup of gently rolling waves are the best in the world for first timers. Hire an instructor (p. 157) from one of the many beach-boy stands on the sand or sign up with a school—but do it at the crack of dawn, because the afternoon crowds are daunting.

Listening to three of the island's best musicians jam. Every Sunday Martin Pahinui, George Kuo, and Aaron Mahi play the best of the great Hawaiian songbook—for free—at the Marriott Beach Resort's Moana Terrace. Sip a passionfruit margarita while you absorb the sweet sounds of expertly played slack-key guitar and tunes such as "Pua Lililehua." See p. 177.

A BRIEF HISTORY

Archaeologists speculate that when Polynesians arrived on the islands aboard oversize outrigger canoes about 1,700 years ago, they settled on Oahu first—in Waimanalo, Kailua, and Kaneohe. The areas' fertile soil and fish-packed bays were perfect for the skilled farmers and fishermen. The remnants of this ancient life are still visible at the Ulupo Heiau (p. 143) in Kailua.

THE 18TH CENTURY

Oahu's early Polynesians were a simple patriarchal society, but by the time Captain James Cook stumbled upon the Hawaiian Islands in 1778, it was a nation of island states ruled by *alii* (chiefs)—and they were skirmishing for archipelago domination. Cook's arrival tipped the scale—with Western weapons. By

1795, guns were the deciding factor in the famous Battle of Nuuanu, in which Kamehameha, from the Big Island, and his armed men, drove the Oahu opposition off the Pali (now a popular tourist stop on the Pali Hwy.). The event paved the way for *alii* Kamehameha to unify the islands, becoming Hawaii's first king. Kamehameha the Great made Waikiki—the home of Oahu's chiefs for hundreds of years—his capital. Waikiki was where royalty liked to play—surfing and lounging—and it's still the island's sun-and-fun playground.

But an even more momentous event led to Oahu becoming the chain's "main" island: the English merchant captain William Brown's "discovery" of 30-foot-deep Honolulu Harbor in 1792 or 1793 (the exact date is unknown). From that point on, Honolulu became the hub of trade and commerce, growing during the whaling and sandalwood booms in the early 1800s. Kamehameha moved the capital from Waikiki to Honolulu in 1805. And 15 years later, shops, bars, and bordellos opened, catering to the crews of visiting ships. The Honolulu area is still Oahu's hub of commerce, dominated by skyscrapers that are home to big banks like First Hawaiian and Bank of Hawaii.

Hawaiians had lived under a *kapu* system, strict societal rules governing how the sexes interacted. For example, women were not allowed to eat with men. Breaking a *kapu* could result in death, but with the arrival of *haoles* (foreigners), the system began to unravel. Just 6 months after Kamehameha died in 1819, it was overthrown.

THE 19TH CENTURY

When the brig *Thaddeus* pulled into Honolulu Harbor in 1820, carrying a boatload of American Protestants from the Foreign Mission School in Connecticut, Hawaii's fate was sealed. Queen Kaahumanu, Kamehameha's wife, was an early convert, championing the missionaries' cause. You can see three of the original buildings of the Sandwich Islands Mission at the **Mission Houses Museum** (p. 147).

Missionaries started schools (the island became known for its high literacy rate), translated the Bible into Hawaiian, and provided health care to native Hawaiians. On the downside, the missionaries forbid all performances of the scandalous hula, they put women in muumuus, banned the Hawaiian language, and discouraged activities they considered frivolous, such as surfing, in effect hobbling Hawaiian culture to create a Puritan society. At the same time, missionaries made inroads into the budding government, amassing power and title to land. Today, Hawaiians are still trying to rebuild that cultural wealth, while the descendants of those missionaries remain some of Oahu's wealthiest residents. Through the reigns of a succession of kings—Kamehamehas II to V, Lunalilo, and Kalakaua—Hawaii became increasingly Westernized, as American interests took more and more control. Whaling boomed and busted, and then came the rise of sugar. By 1852, sugar-plantation owners brought in the first Chinese laborers to work the fields, and the first Japanese arrived in 1868, setting the stage for today's multicultural population. Many of the Asians you see in the streets of Honolulu are the grandchildren and great grandchildren of plantation workers.

In 1887, a group of residents (many of them descendants of Protestant missionaries) formed the Hawaiian League in opposition to King Kalakaua, whom they felt was an irresponsible leader wreaking havoc on the economy and political stability, making private enterprise difficult. The league wrote a constitution that stripped Kalakaua of his authority. The constitution also stripped Hawaiians of their power—they had to make $600 a year and own taxable property worth $3,000 to vote, which meant two-thirds of the native population didn't qualify to elect leaders.

Kalakaua died in 1891 and his sister, Liliuokalani (who was married to an American, John Dominis), became queen. Wanting to restore power to the Hawaiian monarchy and its people, she faced opposition from a group of white men, led by lawyer and missionary descendent Lorrin A. Thurston. On January 14, 1893, Liliuokalani announced to her cabinet ministers her intention to draft a new constitution. Three days later, the Committee of Safety, an annexationist group, overthrew her. On January 31, the American flag was raised over the government building in downtown Honolulu. To this day, Hawaiian activists do not recognize the unconstitutional act—as it was called in a report commissioned by President Grover Cleveland—and hold that Hawaii is still an independent kingdom. In 1898, Hawaii was annexed to the U.S.

EARLY 20TH CENTURY TO TODAY

Very quickly Oahu started playing a big role in the defense of its new parent nation. In 1907, the military established Fort Shafter, and construction on Pearl Harbor started a year later. (Since then, the militarization of Oahu has never stopped. Today the military occupies 25% of the island, from Pearl Harbor to Bellows Field in Waimanalo).

In the early 1900s, the major sugar-plantation companies started consuming each other, consolidating much like today's media conglomerates, until a core group of agencies emerged—Castle & Cooke, Alexander & Baldwin, Theo H. Davies & Co., C. Brewer & Co., and American Factors. The first two are names you still see today. Much of the suburban sprawl of Central Oahu, a short-sighted development project that has caused massive traffic problems and water shortages, was built by Castle & Cooke Homes. They've gone from growing sugar cane to growing subdivisions. The powerful businesses were collectively known as the Big Five, and the white oligarchy ruled Oahu's money and government until the 1950s.

In 1921, the transformation of Waikiki from wetland to real estate subdivisions started; the Royal Hawaiian Hotel went up in 1927; and Oahu's second-largest industry—tourism—was born.

Between the missionary history, the plantation owners' treatment of Asian labor, the iron grip Caucasian businessmen held on the island's economy through the 1950s, and now the buying up of real estate by retirees and flush investors from the mainland, an unspoken tension lingers between Caucasians, Hawaiians, and Asians on Oahu. No matter how integrated the social fabric appears, and how many mixed marriages take place, history still fuels a simmering resentment beneath the surface of our "melting pot." It's not uncommon to see a fight between servicemen and locals break out in bar-fueled areas like Waikiki.

After more than half a century as a U.S. territory, Oahu became the 50th state in 1959. Who didn't want statehood? Opponents included Honolulu power brokers such as wealthy industrialist Walter F. Dillingham (he's the one who drained Waikiki, paving the way for today's hive of hotels) and Lorrin P. Thurston, son of the Lorrin A. Thurston who led the overthrow of Queen Liliuokalani. They worried that the hoi polloi would not elect "the proper class of men," as Gavan Daws writes in *Shoal of Time* (University of Hawaii Press). And they were right. Ninety percent of Hawaiians—many of them former plantation workers, and the sons and daughters of those laborers—voted for statehood, and by the 1960s, Japanese and Chinese leaders such as Inouye were helping lead one of the most forward-thinking state governments in the nation. Being a Democrat became all the rage. The Democratic fervor was sparked by a *haole:* John A. Burns, a former police officer who became Hawaii's second elected governor. Fed up with elite Republicans controlling Honolulu and the rest of the state, the plain-spoken Burns was ready for change, and he groomed a coterie of protégés such as Inouye to lead a new Democratic party that rules to this day. Go to the state capitol while the Legislature is in session (Jan–April) and you'll see a mix of white, Asian, and Polynesian senators and representatives.

HONOLULU TODAY

Now, almost another half decade has gone by, and the new guard is the old guard. Inouye is viewed as a pork-barrel king, voting in the Senate to give the military ever more entree to the islands to keep government dollars coming into the state. At the state capitol in Honolulu, the Democratic party is floundering without any new leadership blood and a Republican is governor.

While Asian-Americans found their power foothold on Oahu, the island was also where the Hawaiian renaissance and sovereignty movement started. The University of Hawaii has established a Hawaiian Studies department, there has been a huge revival of hula, Oahu's first Punana Leo (Hawaiian-language school) opened in 1985, and Hawaiian music now has its own category at the Grammy Awards. Unfortunately, Oahu's last pockets of undeveloped land continue to be eyed by developers, but heightened awareness of what has already slipped away has led to sweet conservationist victories. In January 2006, the City & County of Honolulu stepped up to save Waimea Valley (p. 151), an ancient Hawaiian *ahupuaa* (traditional pie-shaped land division that runs from mountain to sea). Visitors like you will be able to continue to see one of the most beautiful valleys on the island, free of houses.

LAY OF THE LAND

The capital of Hawaii is Honolulu.The City & County of Honolulu covers all of Oahu, which has a population of almost 900,000, while Honolulu proper is home to about 420,000 residents. Made up of neighborhoods stretching from the airport east to Hawaii Kai, this strip of concentrated development snakes up into the valleys along the coast.

WAIKIKI

The tourist hub—famous Waikiki—is a dense warren of luxury hotels and T-shirt shops, low-slung cinderblock apartment buildings, and tour-selling stands. As in any resort area, splendor and seediness go hand in hand. Lots of locals avoid Waikiki because it's so busy and parking can be hard to find. Yet, the area is also a residential place where students, new arrivals, and old-timers alike can still find affordable rents. And with 500-acre Kapiolani Park on its edge, Waikiki is sports-central for a town crazy about the outdoors; on weekends, you'll find people training for the Honolulu marathon, kayaking, paddling, surfing, and playing soccer

Oahu

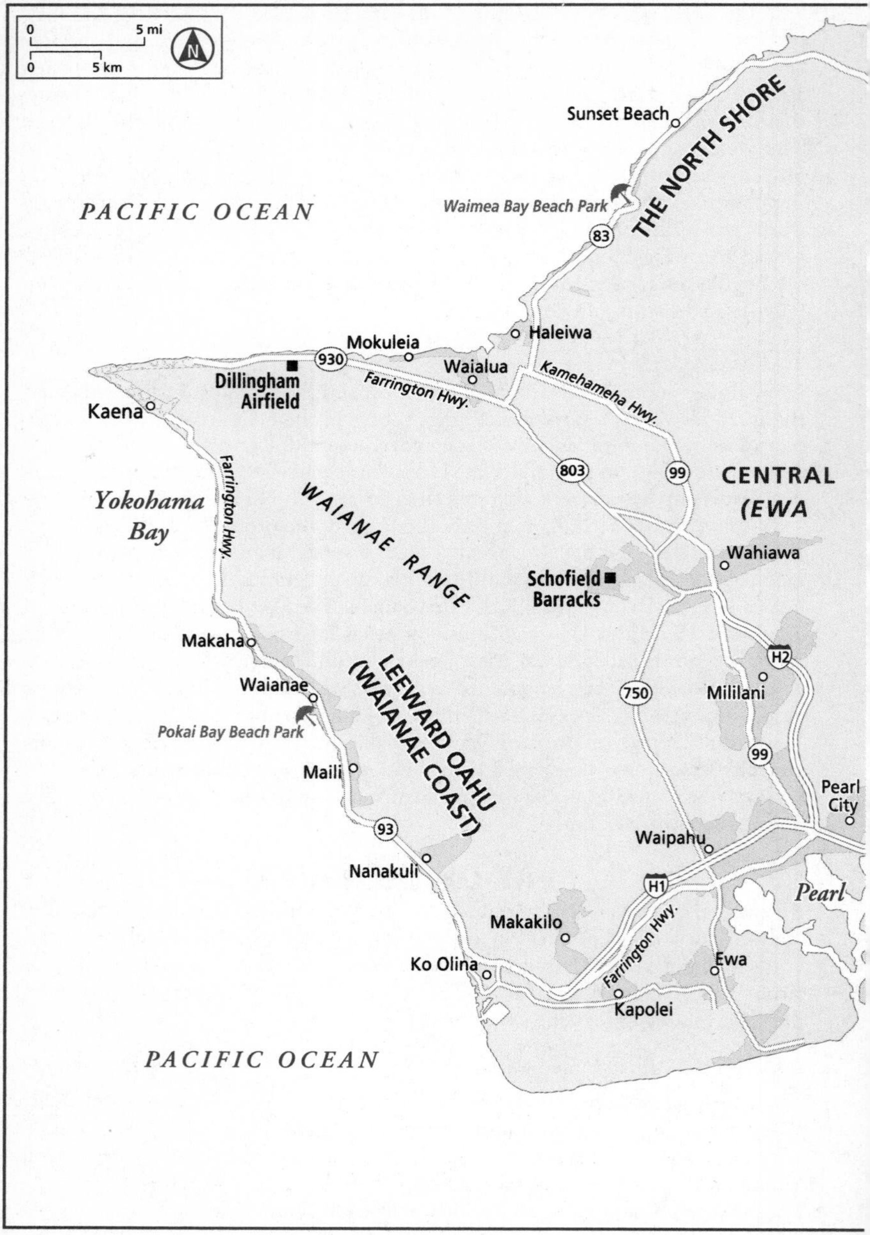
0
5 mi
0
5 km
N
PACIFIC OCEAN
Sunset Beach
THE NORTH SHORE
Waimea Bay Beach Park
83
Haleiwa
Mokuleia
930
Dillingham
Airfield
Waialua
Kamehameha Hwy.
Farrington Hwy.
Kaena
Farrington Hwy.
Yokohama
Bay
WAIANAE RANGE
803
99
CENTRAL
(EWA
Wahiawa
Schofield
Barracks
Makaha
LEEWARD OAHU
(WAIANAE COAST)
Waianae
Pokai Bay Beach Park
H2
Mililani
750
Maili
99
Pearl
City
93
Waipahu
Nanakuli
H1
Pearl
Farrington Hwy.
Makakilo
Ko Olina
Ewa
Kapolei
PACIFIC OCEAN

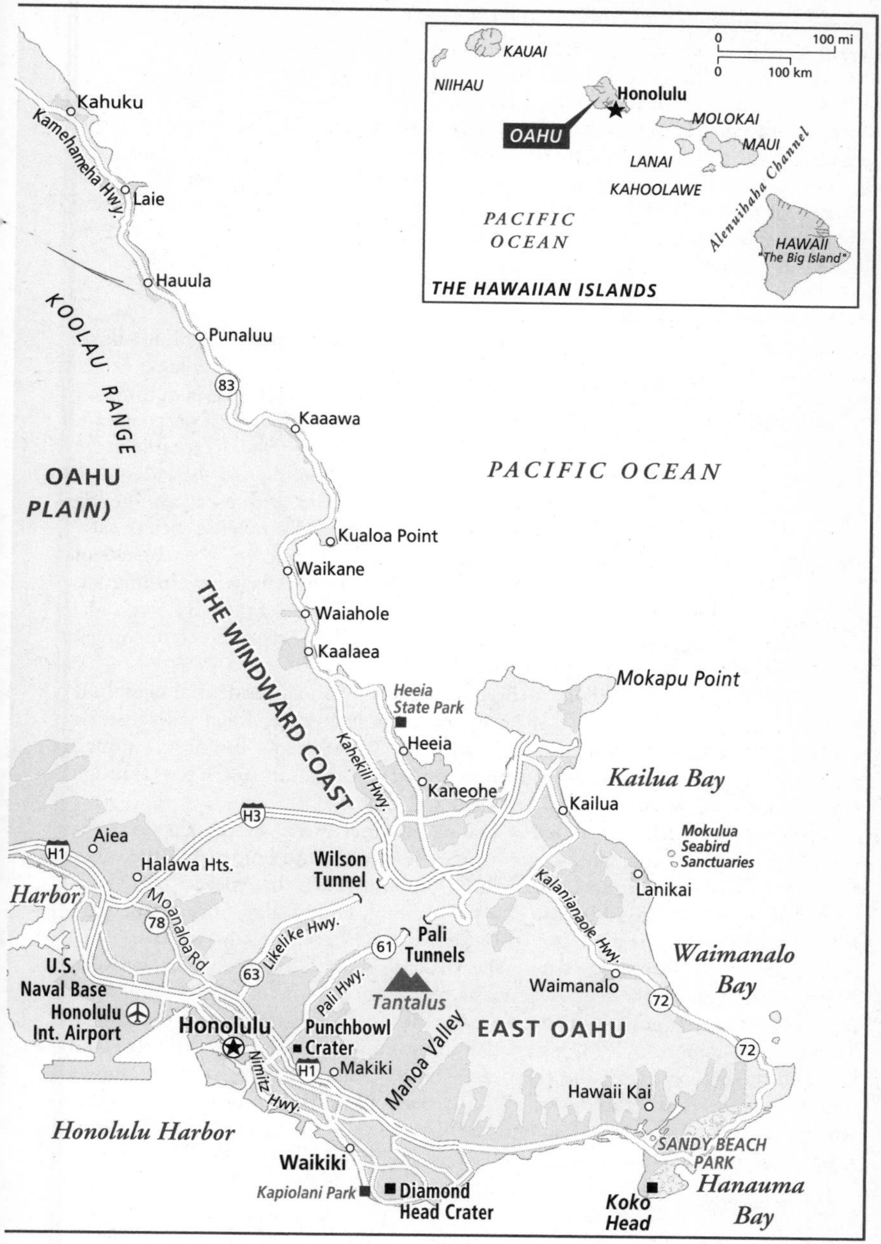

THE HAWAIIAN ISLANDS
KAUAI
NIIHAU
OAHU
Honolulu
MOLOKAI
MAUI
LANAI
KAHOOLAWE
Alenuihaha Channel
PACIFIC OCEAN
HAWAII "The Big Island"
0 100 mi
0 100 km
Kahuku
Kamehameha Hwy.
Laie
Hauula
Punaluu
KOOLAU RANGE
83
Kaaawa
OAHU
PLAIN)
PACIFIC OCEAN
Kualoa Point
Waikane
Waiahole
Kaalaea
THE WINDWARD COAST
Mokapu Point
Heeia State Park
Heeia
Kahekili Hwy.
Kaneohe
Kailua Bay
Kailua
H3
Aiea
H1
Halawa Hts.
Wilson Tunnel
Mokulua Seabird Sanctuaries
Lanikai
Harbor
Moanaloa Rd.
78
Likelike Hwy.
Kalanianaole Hwy.
Pali Tunnels
61
U.S. Naval Base
63
Pali Hwy.
Waimanalo Bay
Waimanalo
Tantalus
Honolulu Int. Airport
Honolulu
Punchbowl Crater
Manoa Valley
EAST OAHU
72
Nimitz Hwy.
H1
Makiki
Hawaii Kai
Honolulu Harbor
SANDY BEACH PARK
Waikiki
Kapiolani Park
Diamond Head Crater
Koko Head
Hanauma Bay

games or lacrosse. For visitors, Waikiki is a good central spot to be for accommodations, nightlife, shopping, beach culture, and public transportation.

The best way to get a feel for the lay of the land, as it once was, is to take the self-guided tour of the **Waikiki Historic Trail** (www.waikikihistorictrail.com). Created by the late historian George Kanahele and local architect Charlie Palumbo, the trail is marked by bronze plaques.

Geared toward designer-hungry Japanese tourists, Waikiki's main drag, Kalakaua Avenue, is packed with upscale shops such as Prada, Yves Saint Laurent, Hermès, Chanel, and Coach. But it's also home to discount T-shirt shops, cheap-ramen stands, and guys who'll take your picture with their parrots on your shoulder.

KAPAHULU

Outside of Waikiki, another hub of activity is downtown, where Honolulu's business and government life is concentrated. Sandwiched between Beretania Street and Nimitz Highway are clusters of high-rises along with open spaces dominated by imposing federal and state buildings. There are also remnants of past Hawaii: Iolani Palace and Kawaiahao Church. Men in aloha shirts (the acceptable attire for office types) and women in light suits walk purposefully on the sidewalks. Keep walking west and the streets take a turn for the seedy, with executives giving way to far less affluent souls—you're in Chinatown. Aside from being the last safe-ish harbor for people down on their luck, low-rise Chinatown, with blocks of pre–World War II buildings huddling together, is a hot enclave where immigrant merchants, gallery owners, and nightclub impresarios work side by side. The neighborhood, a square between Honolulu Harbor, River Street, Beretania Street, and Bethel Street, is fast being gentrified.

Downtown and Waikiki are surrounded by lots of small residential neighborhoods. Nuuanu, just northeast of downtown, is a lush valley filled with historic homes, Queen Emma's Palace, and lots of places of worship—Buddhist temples, a synagogue, and churches that run from Baptist to Unitarian. You'll pass through this area on your way to the Pali Lookout and Kailua.

Heading east, the next valley is Manoa, another green swatch that was the domain of wealthy missionary descendents who built grand homes. On the valley floor are a lot of tract homes built in the 1950s and 1960s that cost $55,000 back then and go for $800,000 today. This sleepy, cool, rainy valley, once a sanctuary for Hawaiian royalty, is now a sought-after neighborhood for new arrivals.

Farther east is Kaimuki, where the main drag of Waialae Avenue between Ninth Avenue and Kokohead Avenue is a restaurant row of cuisines ranging from Japanese to contemporary Mediterranean. In between Kaimuki and the end of Waikiki is Diamond Head, where fabulous homes line a thin strip of land between the extinct crater and the beach (Doris Duke's Shangri La estate, now a museum, is the most fabulous of all). Diamond Head then morphs into Kahala which boasts gaudy mansions alongside old-style wood Hawaiian homes. It's considered the most exclusive neighborhood on the island.

EASTERN OAHU

Acres of suburbs lie east of Honolulu, the most prominent of which is the development Hawaii Kai, started by Henry J. Kaiser in the 1950s. The winding stretch from Hawaii Kai to Waimanalo is where it gets interesting, as this rugged, arid coastline literally undulates. Right past Hawaii Kai is Hanauma Bay, famous for its snorkeling, and then bodysurfing mecca Sandy Beach. This area is known in Hawaiian as Ka Iwi. The road ascends to a lovely lookout point above Makapuu Beach.

Waimanalo is a sleepy little enclave. On the *mauka* (mountain) side of Kalanianaole Highway are farms and plant nurseries, and on the *makai* (ocean) side are homes (many of them vacation rentals; p. 104). Its main features for visitors are the 5-mile-long white-sand stretch of Waimanalo Bay, and, across the street from Bellows Field, the Honolulu Polo Club (season runs June–Oct, with matches held Sun afternoons at 2:30pm).

THE WINDWARD SIDE

While the northeast coast of the island runs from Kahuku Point on the North Shore to Makapuu Point in the south, the "Windward Side" mostly refers to the towns of Kailua and Kaneohe. Originally bedroom communities to Honolulu they're bustling hubs in their own right now, with lots of shops and restaurants. While there are no hotels here, there is a hotbed of small bed-and-breakfasts and rental houses.

The main reason non-Windward residents go to Kailua is for the beach—2½ miles of it. The northeasterly winds make this big bay a mecca for windsurfers (former world champion Robbie Naish, who has a windsurf shop in town, is from here) and kite surfers. Off the coast is Popoia Island, which locals call Flat Island, part of the Hawaii State Seabird Sanctuary. A rich place in precontact days, with fertile taro-growing grounds and fish-filled waters, Kailua was home to powerful chiefs. According to legend, it's the origin of Menehunes—Hawaii's version of elves, or leprechauns, depending on whom you talk to—who busily built *heiau* (temples) and fishponds at night. Only one of a handful of *heiau* remains in Kailua, near Castle Junction at the entrance to Kailua (p. 143).

With the dramatic Koolau Range as a backdrop, Kaneohe is often cloudy and wet compared to sunny Kailua. Kaneohe Bay doesn't have a good swimming beach—this is where fishermen come, taking off in their boats from Heeia Kea Boat Harbor. But the coastline here has interesting cultural features, such as the Heeia fish pond. Ancient Hawaiians encircled natural bays with lava rock, allowing young fish to come and go, but keeping mature fish inside for harvest—it was early aquaculture and kept the people supplied with food.

On the left side of Kaneohe Bay (a military outpost off-limits to civilians) is Kualoa Regional Park, where the water is shallow and reefy, and not great for swimming. Across the highway and offshore is Chinaman's Hat, or Mokolii, a small island and bird preserve.

Heading north along Kamehameha Highway, which requires a leisurely driving pace on this two-lane road, the next inlet is 4,000-acre Kualoa Ranch and Activity Club (p. 165), which includes picturesque Kaaawa Valley, where scenes from *Jurassic Park* and other films were shot. Also quite scenic (but with murky water) is the next inlet, Kahana Bay, across from which is Ahupuaa O Kahana State Park, one of only two publicly owned *ahupuaa,* or Hawaiian land divisions (the other is Waimea Valley on the North Shore). It's like a jungle, dark and shadowy with dense trees and plants.

The little-developed coast continues, dotted by the tiny towns of Punaluu, Hauula, and Laie (home of the **Polynesian Cultural Center,** p. 154). This side of the island ends at Kahuku, a former sugar-plantation town.

CENTRAL OAHU

Two mountain ranges—Waianae and Koolau—run parallel down Oahu. The plain that lies between them is Central Oahu. This area was once covered with pineapple and sugar cane, but as those industries have waned, the fields have made way for subdivisions. Now, Central Oahu is the province of suburban commuters, and what you pass through to get to the North Shore. Driving, take H-1, then H-2, to Wahiawa, down the road from Schofield Barracks. A town that's a mix of plantation-labor descendents and military, Wahiawa has a seedy, low-rise feel, with lots of pawn shops and tattoo parlors. But nearby is also where you'll find the **Kukaniloko birthing stones** (p. 144).

NORTH SHORE

When Honoluluans need a mini-escape, they take a drive to the North Shore on the weekend, what we call the "country." As you approach the coastline, driving on the two-lane road passing through the flat, red-dirt pineapple fields (which won't be there much longer), and see the long stretch of coast appear, your spirit will surge. Sounds corny, but it's true. The North Shore stretches from Kaena Point to Kahuku Point, for roughly 20 miles of famous surf breaks.

You first hit Haleiwa, the North Shore's main town. Although the area has become a millionaire's playground (there's a housing crisis for locals looking for affordable rent, as mainland and foreign investors buy second vacation homes here), Haleiwa has maintained a rural-town feel thanks to its designation as a State Historic, Cultural and Scenic District in 1984.

All along the coast, locals refer to surf spots, beaches, and dive spots as landmarks—Waimea, Shark's Cove, Sunset, and Yokohama.

LEEWARD SIDE

Hot and arid, Oahu's Waianae Coast has no chi-chi shopping centers, lush botanical gardens, or deluxe resorts. As you pass through the towns of Nanakuli, Waianae, and Makaha, you'll see houses surrounded by junked cars and dirt yards. The Leeward side is home to one of the largest Native Hawaiian communities in the state. Almost 20% of the area's population lives at the poverty level, and a growing number of homeless seek refuge on the beaches. But there are also inviting beaches such as Maile and Makaha. So even Waianae is changing—as sort of the last frontier of development, subdivisions are springing up and retirees from the mainland are taking advantage of the lowest prices in town. Also, Waianae's very lack of development is appealing to a new type of tourist looking for an "authentic" Oahu.

GETTING TO & AROUND OAHU

Most major U.S. and many international carriers fly to Honolulu International Airport.

United Airlines (☎ 800/225-5825; www.ual.com) offers the most frequent service from the U.S. mainland. **American Airlines** (☎ 800/433-7300; www.americanair.com) offers flights from Dallas, Chicago, San Francisco, San Jose, Los

Road Warrior

Oahu is a driving island. During the week, the H-1 is bumper to bumper from 7 to 9am as everyone from around the island pours into the city, and then again from 4 to 7pm as everyone goes back home. Here are distances and average drive times to points around the island from Waikiki.

Destination	Miles	Time
Haleiwa	29	60 minutes
Hanauma Bay	11	30 minutes
Honolulu Airport	9	20 minutes
Kailua	14	30 minutes
Laie	34	1 hour
Makaha Beach	36	1 hour
Sunset Beach	37	1 hour
USS *Arizona* Memorial	12	30 minutes
Waikele Premium Outlets	17	40 minutes

Angeles, and St. Louis to Honolulu. **Continental Airlines** (☎ 800/231-0856; www.continental.com) offers the only daily nonstop from the New York area (Newark) to Honolulu. **Delta Air Lines** (☎ 800/221-1212; www.delta.com) flies nonstop from the West Coast and from Houston and Cincinnati. **Hawaiian Airlines** (☎ 800/367-5320; www.hawaiianair.com) offers nonstop flights to Honolulu from several West Coast cities (including new service from San Diego). **Northwest Airlines** (☎ 800/225-2525; www.nwa.com) has a daily nonstop from Detroit to Honolulu.

Airlines serving Hawaii from places other than the U.S. mainland include **Air Canada** (☎ 800/776-3000; www.aircanada.ca); **Air New Zealand** (☎ 0800/737-000 in Auckland, 643/379-5200 in Christchurch, 800/926-7255 in the U.S.; www.airnewzealand.com); **Qantas** (☎ 008/177-767 in Australia, 800/227-4500 in the U.S.; www.qantas.com.au); **Japan Air Lines** (☎ 03/5489-1111 in Tokyo, 800/525-3663 in the U.S.; www.japanair.com); **All Nippon Airways** (ANA) (☎ 03/5489-1212 in Tokyo, 800/235-9262 in the U.S.; www.fly-ana.com); **China Airlines** (☎ 02/715-1212 in Taipei, 800/227-5118 in the U.S.; www.china-airlines.com); **Air Pacific,** serving Fiji, Australia, New Zealand, and the South Pacific (☎ 800/227-4446; www.airpacific.com); **Korean Air** (☎ 02/656-2000 in Seoul, 800/223-1155 on the East Coast, 800/421-8200 on the West Coast, 800/438-5000 from Hawaii; www.koreanair.com); and **Philippine Airlines** (☎ 631/816-6691 in Manila, 800/435-9725 in the U.S.; www.philippineair.com). Locally, **Hawaiian Airlines** (☎ 800/367-5320; www.hawaiianair.com) flies nonstop to Sydney, Tahiti, American Samoa and Manila in the Philippines

Fares to Oahu from the U.S. Mainland vary wildly by time of year. During the week of Christmas, a round-trip ticket can run as high as $1,200; at other times it can drop to as low as $500, depending on where you're departing from and when you're traveling. Hawaiian Air runs frequent sales (it's worthwhile to sign up for their newsletter, which publishes the sale rates), but their reach only extends to a handful of cities on the West Coast. For more information on getting the best air prices to Hawaii, see p. 428.

GETTING TO & FROM THE AIRPORT

Central Honolulu is a 15- to 45-minute ride from the airport, depending on the dreaded traffic situation. If you're staying in the city, there are a few transportation options to choose from. If you've booked accommodations outside of Honolulu, I recommend that you rent a car because there is no convenient public transportation.

If you're headed to Waikiki and you don't want to rent a car, the easiest option is to take a **taxi** (AMPCO Express; ☎ 808/861-8294), which costs about $28, but can go up to $35 depending on your distance from the airport and how heavy the traffic is. Look for the taxi dispatchers on the center median across the street from baggage claim. Or you can prearrange a taxi. For a flat fee of $30, **Star Taxi** (☎ 800/671-2999 or 808/942-STAR) will take up to four passengers from the airport to Waikiki (with no extra charges for baggage); however, you must book in advance. After you've arrived and before you pick up your luggage, re-call Star to make sure that they will be outside waiting for you when your luggage arrives.

To save money, you can take the **Airport Waikiki Express** (☎ 800/831-5541 or 808/539-9400; www.hawaii.gov/dot/airports/hnl/hnl_ground_trans.htm; $9 one way, $15 roundtrip children under 3 free), which will take you to any hotel in Waikiki. From 3am to 10am, buses leave every hour, and after 10am, they leave every 20 to 25 minutes.

Round the Island on TheBus

TheBus is a cheap way to go round the island. For $2, you get one transfer (you have to ask the driver for it), which allows you to get off and look around and get back on the next bus. If you want to make more stops, you'll have to pay $2 every other time. At Ala Moana Center, take the No. 52 Wahiawa–Circle Island bus (it departs every half-hour from 6:30am to 5:16pm, then every hour until 8:15pm) for a clockwise trip that goes to the North Shore, stopping at Haleiwa Beach Park, Turtle Bay Resort, the Polynesian Cultural Center in Laie, Hauula, Kaaawa, and Kahaluu. When the bus reaches Kahaluu, it turns into No. 55 and runs along the Windward Coast to Kaneohe, returning to Ala Moana over the Pali Highway. To do the trip in reverse, take the No. 55 Kaneohe–Circle Isle bus. This can be an especially nice ride if you stop in Haleiwa for dinner and get back on for the return trip through downtown.

For full routes and schedules, visit **www.thebus.org**. There's an online At Your Service Custom Trip Planner, but when the system is overwhelmed, it goes down. Don't fret: You can call ☎ **808/848-5555** and actually speak to a real person. You might have to wait a bit, but you'll eventually get someone to answer route and schedule questions.

The Lingo: Local Directions

In Honolulu, two markers are Diamond Head and Ewa, which stand for east and west. If I'm telling someone to meet me at a restaurant and I say it's on King Street, my friend is likely to ask, "Where on King Street, Diamond Head or Ewa of Keeaumoku Street?" So if someone tells you something is just Diamond Head of something, they're saying it's east, in the direction of the old crater.

The other two markers are the mountains and ocean. If something is in the direction of the mountains, we say "on the *mauka* side." If it's in the direction of the water, we say "on the *makai* side."

Another good shuttle service, **Airport-Island Shuttles** (☎ 800/624-9554 or 808/521-2121; www.shuttleguys.com) will go door-to-door anywhere on the island, good news for those not staying in hotels. A ride to Waikiki is $27 for the first person and an additional $7 for the second person. If you are picked up at the airport between 8pm and 8am, there is an additional $5 charge. The most expensive ride is $90 to Turtle Bay Resort in Kahuku, Hauula, or Laie.

GETTING AROUND OAHU

Honolulu is fairly navigable by public transport, but renting a car will help you make the most of your time if you want to explore the island.

The best deal by far is to book ahead with **www.orbitz.com** because of the deal it has with Dollar Rent-a-Car. Through Orbitz, you can get a compact car from Dollar for as low as $148 per week, which comes out to $21 a day—and that includes taxes and fees. Second cheapest tends to be Enterprise, which charges about $31 a day, with taxes, for a week's use of a compact car. You may also want to try one of the opaque booking engines such as Hotwire and Priceline.com, which sometimes match or even undercut these prices (though you won't know what rental company you're getting until after you pay). Alamo can also be inexpensive but it has a bad habit of overbooking, meaning you might have a 1 to 2 hour wait for a car once you get off the plane. If you can get lower rates with other companies (and most will cost an average of $40 a day with tax) go with them.

All the major renters are located at the airport: **Avis** (☎ 800/321-3712 or 808/843-553 www.avis.com); **Budget** (☎ 800/935-6878; https://rent.drivebudget.com/Home.jsp); **Dollar** (☎ 800/800-4000; www.dollarcar.com); **Enterprise** (☎ 800/325-8007; www.enterprise.com); **Hertz** (☎ 800/654-3011; www.hertz.com); **National** (☎ 800/227-7368; www.nationalcar.com); and **Thrifty** (☎ 800/367-2277; www.thrifty.com).

ACCOMMODATIONS, BOTH STANDARD & NOT

Oahu's hotels are concentrated in Waikiki, where a warren of accommodations run from downscale, two-story, cinderblock cheapies to one of the plushest hotels in the world (the Halekulani). There are lots of comfortable, plain options, big chains (Hilton, Sheraton, Hyatt, Marriott) that aren't cheap, and the famous, historic big three: Moana Surfrider, a Westin; Royal Hawaiian; and Halekulani.

But there's a whole island beyond Honolulu, where hotels are few and vacation rental houses abound. This is the best way to experience island living. For a little more money (and sometimes less, if you go with a more alternative form of accommodations), you can get a feel of real island life away from the madding Waikiki crowd. ***Important note:*** In Hawaii, lodging—including hostels and vacation rentals—is subject to an 11.416% tax, a combination of the 4.166% state tax and 7.25% transient tax. So be sure to factor all of it in when you're budgeting for your vacation.

BED & BREAKFASTS, CONDOS & VACATION RENTALS

Lower-cost B&Bs and vacation-home rental opportunities are sprinkled throughout Honolulu, and the best ones rent through the agencies listed below. Outside of the city, B&Bs are concentrated in Kailua, on the Windward Side of the island. The easiest way to book a room in a home, bed-and-breakfast, private condo, or a whole beachfront house is through an agency. It ensures that the property has been vetted, and you have the option of moving to another lodging, through the agency, at no extra cost, should accommodations not be to your liking upon arrival. However, direct to owner websites, such as Rentalo.com and VRBO.com often have better rates. See below for more on that.

Note: Some unlicensed, and sometimes unmonitored, B&Bs and vacation rentals have popped up in Kailua, prompting a group of residents, annoyed by parked cars and noise, to organize and try to shut down the B&Bs in the neighborhood. In this chapter, I've listed only legal and respected businesses that regulate their guests and are considerate of their neighbors.

To my mind the two most reliable and well-established companies for aboveboard rentals and B&Bs on the island are:

Be Back Hawaii (☎ 877/4-BEBACK, 808/732-6618, or 808/732-2921; www.beback.com): Efficiently run by German travel agent Brigitte Baccus and her husband David, a former art-gallery owner, this agency represents more than 300 properties in Hawaii, about 100 of them on Oahu. The modus operandi here is hands on. "They're turning every doghouse and closet into a vacation rental on this island," sighed David when we last spoke. "So Brigitte and I go out every weekend to inspect rentals and find new ones. We periodically stay the night in the properties we represent because we want to see what it's like from the inside out. That way, we can guarantee that you'll enjoy your stay." The selection runs from luxury beachfront estates in the exclusive neighborhood of Kahala to small studios in often rainy Kaneohe; and from family-friendly homes right on the beach to convenient apartments in Waikiki. With such a wide selection (and this agency really does it all—B&Bs, condos, and vacation-home rentals), rates range all the way from $75 to $500 a night, but the average cost is between $100 and $120. Some properties do take credit cards and some are cash only. Their well-designed website has pictures of most of the properties they represent.

Bed and Breakfast Honolulu (☎ 800/288-4666 or 808/595-7533; www.hawaiibnb.com): For accommodations at the lower end of the price scale, with nightly rates ranging from $55 for a Waikiki studio to $250 for a four-bedroom house in Kailua, Bed and Breakfast Honolulu is the agency to call. It takes bookings for more than 100 modest but nice properties on Oahu (only a few of which are pictured on its website) and states quite candidly that its properties, which tend to be smaller and thus cheaper, are better for couples than families. (This company also doesn't offer the level of personal service that Be Back Hawaii does, but that also keeps their prices lower.) To get a better idea of what they offer, I recently visited a number of the company's properties, including three studio units in a low-rise cinderblock apartment building in Waikiki that may well be the best deals in town (2 nights $78/night, 4 nights $68/night, 5 nights $48/night). Yes, you get what you pay for: a windowless apartment, but one that's spotlessly clean and fully equipped, with a useable kitchen, access to a pool, cable TV, shower, and a fold-out futon couch for far less than you'd pay elsewhere. The condos were just a block from Kuhio Beach. The agency also represents B&Bs all over the island, as well as a handful of full-scale, multibedroom vacation rentals (but as I said before, it specializes in smaller units).

GOING DIRECT TO THE OWNERS

Many people buy apartments, condos, and homes in Waikiki as investments, renting them out to pay the mortgage. In fact, throughout Oahu, there are literally hundreds who directly rent out their apartments, rooms in their homes, or even whole houses to vacationers. Nightly rates at these sorts of properties are quite low compared to hotels—and they usually go down the longer you stay. Factor in the savings on restaurant meals (they all come equipped with kitchens) and you have the makings of a real deal.

Vacation Rentals by Owner (www.vrbo.com) is the foremost clearinghouse of those properties that don't work through agencies. Rentals aren't vetted by VRBO, so there is some risk involved, but for the ones I've checked out—in and outside of Honolulu—the owners turned out to be gracious, on-the-ball hosts and the accommodations matched up with their online listings and photos.

Craig's List (www.craigslist.com) launched its Hawaii section in 2004, and it quickly became another good source for vacation rentals. But unfortunately they do not divide vacation rental and B&B by island; you have to scroll down and either know which island you are looking for or have a keen sense of names of Hawaiian towns to know which islands the towns are located in. You could find a good deal, only to find out that the vacation rental of your dreams is not on Oahu but another island. With digital images included in many of the listings, it's easy to spot ones that are clean and well kept. I have also visited a number of these (many of them are also on www.vrbo.com and rentalo.com) and found that they, too, lived up to the billings posted on the site.

On both websites you can find everything from a $52-a-night Waikiki studio to a three-bedroom beachfront home right on the North Shore's famous Sunset Beach for $500 a night.

There are a few caveats: If you are booking directly with an owner make sure that you have contact information in case there is a problem with the units (like the plumbing goes out at 10 at night, or if your flight is delayed for 4 hours, who will check you in?). And if there are any problems find out if they have a relationship with the plumber, and so on so you won't get stuck with the bill.

Here are two examples of what you can find at these two websites:

"I'm not looking to make a million dollars," says Dawn Rogers, which is why she charges just $79 a night for her 19th-floor corner studio in the big **Pacific**

A Plug for Travel Packages

by Pauline Frommer

Before we get into a discussion of the many hotels on Oahu, I'm going to suggest that travelers who put budget first should read this box and perhaps turn to a travel packager to put together your vacation. Oahu is one of the top destinations in the world for travel packages—by which I mean travel products that bundle together airfare, hotel, and sometimes a rental car at one reasonable price—because it has so many hotel rooms that need to be filled year-round (and those large companies that guarantee this are able to get discounts that you, the individual traveler, could never touch). Though the cheapest of these packages traditionally use mainstream, somewhat dull Waikiki hotels, booking a travel package can result in big savings, in some cases overall prices of $100 a day or less for airfare, rental car, and hotel (not including food and gas). No, you won't have the chicest of lodgings, but you will get a clean, convenient place to stay (with private bathroom), which is fine for those simply using their hotel as a place to crash after long days exploring the island. Packages can also yield savings on pricey, beachfront hotels, so even luxury travelers should consider this route when booking.

Some companies allow travelers to customize their packages, choosing dates of travel, hotels, make of car, and so on. But those who can be more flexible with time and accommodations get the very best deals: ready-made packages that take advantage of seasonal downtime (post-holiday periods offer especially good values) and have fixed dates and hotels.

Your first stop when shopping for a travel package should be California-based **Pleasant Holidays** (☎ 800/742-9244; www.pleasantholidays.com), which has focused on Hawaii since 1962. The prices on its seasonal specials are tough to beat (Pleasant periodically runs the 1-week-in-Hawaii-from-$500-on-up ads in the newspaper). Usually, its deals come with restrictions, such as Wednesday or Thursday departures only. But when you see a great deal, chances are it will soon be gone, so grab it while you can (get on their mailing list and you'll always have a heads-up). It's also

Monarch condo/hotel (444 Niu St., at Ala Wai; ☎ 808/223-0467; hawaiinshine@aol.com). The room is small, but it has a sweeping view of the mountains, the Ala Wai Canal, and a sliver of Waikiki Beach. It comes equipped with a double bed, a small futon for kids, minifridge, coffeemaker, microwave oven, air-conditioning, cable TV, and a phone. You can also use the building's pool and coin-operated laundry facilities. Rogers recommends booking 2 to 3 months in advance, but she sometimes has last-minute openings. Small efficiency lodgings like this are good for the active couple who plans on doing a lot of sightseeing and just needs a home base to sleep.

important to have high-speed Internet access because the Pleasant site is slow, clumsy, and anything but pleasant to use. Nonetheless, they are usually the price leader. As we went to press, I was recently able to find a flight from Los Angeles, plus 7 nights accommodations at the absolutely fine Castle Maile Sky Court in Waikiki for $585 per person during the low season and $656 per person during the high (winter) season, including taxes, and a lei greeting at the airport—an unbeatable price. Also, Pleasant Holidays has the most extensive choice of hotels, due to its partnerships with a long list of companies.

Pleasant rules when it comes to fixed packages, but when it comes to customized packages, the competition moves in. Shop on the Web among the Big Three—**Orbitz** (☎ 877/672-4893; www.orbitz.com), **Travelocity** (☎ 888/709-5983; www.travelocity.com), and **Expedia** (☎ 800/342-8516; www.expedia.com). They all offer good deals and have far more user-friendly websites than Pleasant. For non–West Coast gateways, their prices sometimes beat Pleasant's rates.

You should also see what **Funjet Vacations** (☎ 888/558-6654; www.funjet.com) has to offer. They specialize in hotel-and-air packages, with a wide range of hotels to choose from, without the rental car. The prices always look lower than the other package dealers, but when you add the vehicle cost—and it's hard to get around in Hawaii without a car—its prices are comparable to the competition's.

Other companies that periodically run excellent specials for airfare and hotel (and sometimes car rental) include:

- **Travel Services** (☎ 800/675-4050 or 925/304-5000; www.off2hawaii.com)
- **Panda Travel** (☎ 800/303-6702 or 808/738-3898; www.pandaonline.com)
- **ATA Vacations** (☎ 800/442-8952; www.atavacations.com)
- **United Vacations** (☎ 888/854-3899; www.unitedvacations.com)

In 2005, David and Elle Cholokian redid their **Kaaawa home** (51–346 #B Hauhele St., Kaaawa; ☎ 808/237-8345; vacationinhawaii@yahoo.com) to create two rentals. The lush enclave, at the foot of the majestic Koolau mountain range on a quiet residential street, includes a small (man-made) waterfall trickling into a large fishpond. The back garden is filled with hibiscus bushes and plumeria trees. Guests can choose from a Japanese-style cottage ($660–$780 per week, depending on the dates) with shoji doors and the three-bedroom main house ($150–$250 per night) that's made sexy with Balinese furnishings. Kaaawa is about a 45-minute drive from Honolulu on the Windward Coast, a sleepy area where you can clear your head. If I were flying all the way to Hawaii and wanted to experience real island life, I'd stay here.

WAIKIKI

Unlike other islands where resorts are sprinkled all around, Oahu's hotels are clustered in Waikiki, with only three major resorts—Kohala, Ko Olina, and Turtle Bay Resort—situated outside Honolulu. It may not be the blissed-out, far-from-the-madding-crowd atmosphere for which you yearned, but it's certainly the most convenient, with lots of public transport to destinations outside Honolulu, access to shopping (of course), and the best waves for aspiring surfers. You can find accommodations—from a hostel to one of the best hotels in the world—to fit every budget.

Waikiki used to be riddled with low-slung, Polynesian-themed, super-affordable hotels, the kind where you could imagine Gidget sipping a (virgin) daiquiri poolside. But these 1960s relics have steadily been razed to make way for redevelopment, and now there is just one enclave left: two rows on parallel Beachwalk and Saratoga Road, at the gateway to Waikiki. Here are the best old-school options in the area.

$ I'm a sucker for retro, so I'd choose to stay at the **Kai Aloha** (235 Saratoga Rd.; ☎ 808/923-6723; www.magickhawaii.com/kaialoha; AE, MC, V) even if it didn't have some of the cheapest prices in town. The family-owned three-story hotel celebrated its 50th anniversary in 2006, and its fly-in-amber vibe is what attracts its left-of-center (much of it European) clientele. If you're into chain hotels, you'll think this place is shabby; if you like vintage rattan furniture and hand-carved monkeypod lamps, you'll love it. Sure, the beds are on the soft side and the TVs are on their last cathode ray, but that's could be a good thing or bad thing, depending on your style. All rooms are either a studio or one-bedroom apartment (like a Manhattan railroad apartment) with kitchenette. Studios range from $80 to $90, and one-bedrooms, which have two trundle beds in the living room and two twins in the bedroom, run from $90 to $100. Parking is available across the street for $12 per 24 hours. There's no restaurant in Kai Aloha, but just down the street is the pleasant prix-fixe Italian restaurant **Caffelatte** (339 Saratoga Rd.; ☎ 808/924-1414), where Milan native Laura Proserpio will make you feel at home. Fort DeRussy beach is 2 minutes away. ***Note:*** There is a 3-night minimum stay.

$$–$$$ Behind Kai Aloha on Beachwalk is **The Breakers** ★ (250 Beachwalk; ☎ 808/923-3181; www.breakers-hawaii.com; AE, DC, MC, V), where mainland snowbirds book their rooms months in advance (some of them look like they've been doing it since the place opened in 1955). I love the laid-back island feel and the small, intimate scale. You enter into a courtyard, in the center of which is a blue pool surrounded by a two-story reef of rooms, all done up quasi-Japanese style with faux-shoji sliding doors. The rooms have been modernized, unfortunately, with generic-chain-hotel bedspreads and furniture, but a 1940's tiki vibe still lingers. Rooms are all equipped with kitchenettes, and, of course, the garden apartments opening up to the pool are more expensive. Singles cost $103 to $120, doubles are $125 to $135, garden suites are $165 to $185, and you'll have to tack on $20 for an additional person. There's a snack bar and lounge on-site.

What's the Room Situation Like?

Some 4.2 million visitors arrived on Oahu in 2007. At the same time, the number of hotel rooms on the island decreased nearly 10% as hotel operators convert rooms to timeshares and condos. If that news wasn't bad enough, at the same time, the average room rate on Oahu increased 5.8 % to $162, and rates for 2008 are moving ever upward.

Even with the array of alternative accommodations—B&Bs, home stays, and private condo rentals—sometimes it's impossible to find a room. It's hardest to find a room during the weeks of Thanksgiving, Christmas, and New Year's, but events and conventions can make occupancy rates swell at any time of year. When the Honolulu Marathon occurs in early December, hotels are booked solid. In fact, growing numbers of sports events, ranging from golf tournaments to the Century Bike Ride in September keep Honolulu booked year-round.

The good news is that after years of no hotel growth in Waikiki, a spate of building that started in 2005 will bring hundreds of new rooms to the neighborhood by 2009. The bad news is that if you visit before then, you'll still experience the crunch.

$-$$$$ The locally owned **Queen Kapiolani Hotel** ★★ kids (150 Kapahulu Ave.; ☎ 808/922-4671; www.queenkapiolani.com; AE, DC, DISC, MC, V) is a favorite with *kamaaina* (locals) in town from the neighboring islands. They like the location—at the quieter end of the busy Kalakaua strip, across the street from Kapiolani Park, 2 minutes from the beach, near Starbucks—and the low prices (a standard room with an ocean view is just $90–$103 if you book online). The grand high-ceilinged lobby is hung with chandeliers and portraits of Hawaiian royalty. The rooms are more modest—generic mauve-toned spaces with hideous floral bedspreads—but the beds are firm and the spaces clean. If you can snag a corner oceanview room, you get a breathtaking vista that sweeps from Diamond Head to Ewa. The park and beach proximity make this a good choice for families with active kids. If you want a big full-service hotel, the Queen Kapiolani is the best deal in town. ***Note:*** Parking is $15 a day.

$-$$$$ Remember the opening scene of Hawaii Five-O, with Steve McGarrett standing on a balcony? That's the **Renaissance Waikiki Ilikai Hotel** ★★ (1777 Ala Moana Blvd.; ☎ 800/245-4524 or 808/949-3811; www.ilikaihotel.com; AE, DC, DISC, MC, V). In the 1960s and 1970s, this hotel was the *it* spot, with a hot nightclub and restaurant (Elvis and Mickey Mantle stayed here). It fell out of favor and was looked on as outdated in the 1980s and 1990s, but a huge renovation has given the hotel new life, with a Polynesian-boutique look in the airy lobby outfitted with tasteful rattan furniture. The *Lost* crew stays here when the hit series is filming. Located at the edge of Waikiki, it's closer to Ala Moana Shopping Center than Kuhio Beach. A basic room—crisply outfitted with sleek wood furniture and upholstered armchairs—in the hotel proper starts at $259,

Where to Stay in Waikiki

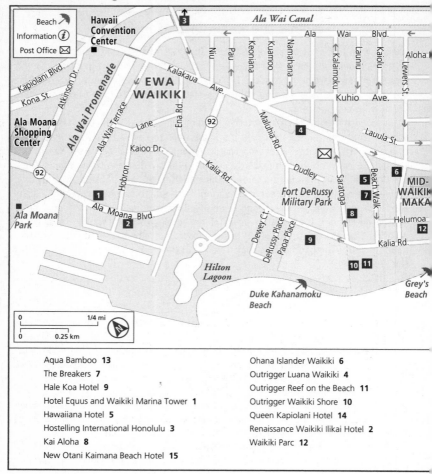

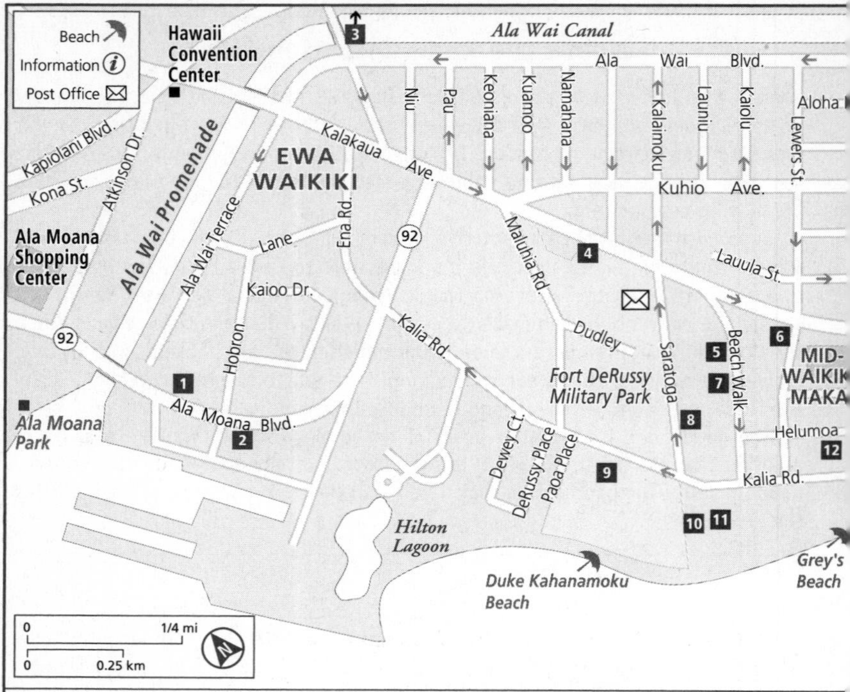

Aqua Bamboo **13**	Ohana Islander Waikiki **6**
The Breakers **7**	Outrigger Luana Waikiki **4**
Hale Koa Hotel **9**	Outrigger Reef on the Beach **11**
Hotel Equus and Waikiki Marina Tower **1**	Outrigger Waikiki Shore **10**
Hawaiiana Hotel **5**	Queen Kapiolani Hotel **14**
Hostelling International Honolulu **3**	Renaissance Waikiki Ilikai Hotel **2**
Kai Aloha **8**	Waikiki Parc **12**
New Otani Kaimana Beach Hotel **15**	

but the Ilikai also has condos, and through a management agency the owners rent out their apartments for rates that range from $50 to $500 depending on the type of room (the furnishings vary greatly) and your dates. To book condos, contact Pat Carsten (☎ 808/271-5957; www.ilikai.com). The Ilikai has one of the best Hawaiian Regional Cuisine restaurants in Waikiki, Canoes, where you can get dishes like kalua-pig quesadillas. ***Note:*** Parking is $25 per day.

$–$$$ If you're traveling with kids and want to be in the thick of things, the **Ohana Islander Waikiki** (kids) (270 Lewers St.; ☎ 800/462-6262 or 808/923-7711; www.ohanahotels.com; AE, DC, MC, V) might be your best pick. Ohana means "family" in Hawaiian, and though these pastel-colored, rather sterile-looking rooms aren't

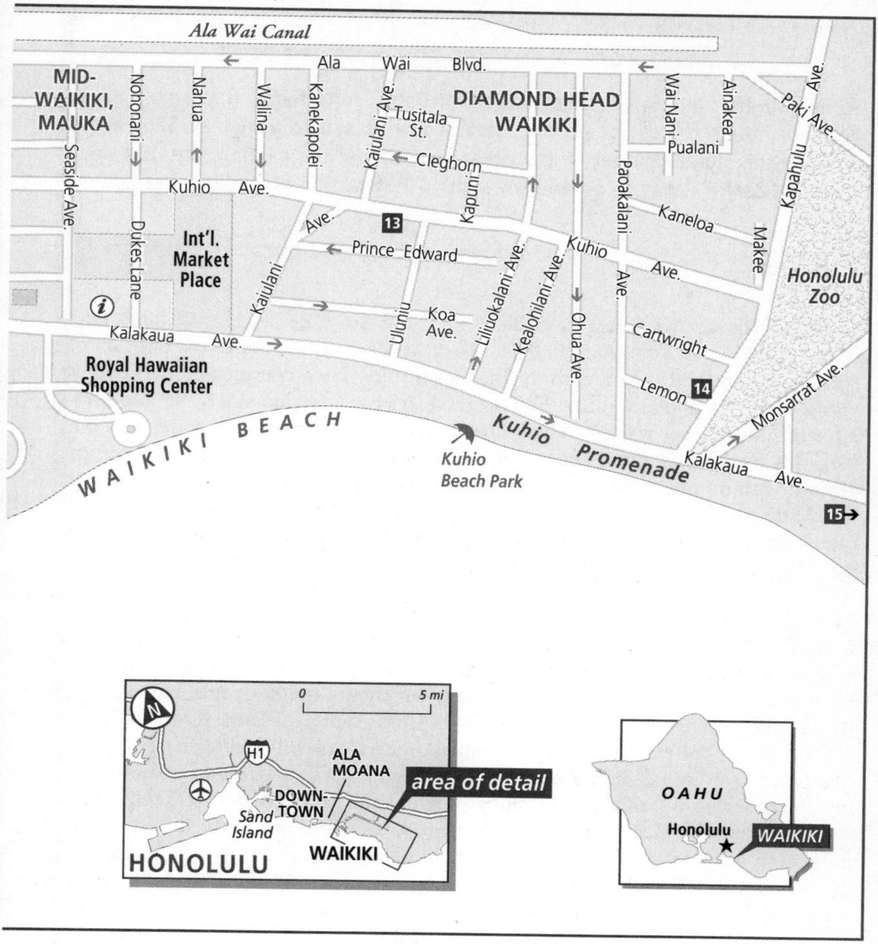

stylish, they've been created with the needs of families in mind. All are spacious enough for extra beds, and every single room in the hotel connects. Even the prices are right for cash-strapped parents: Though the rack rate is $239, nearly constant Web specials offered on the Ohana site can bring the price down to a more modest $99 to $119. As for the area of the hotel, Lewers Street is undergoing a drastic makeover—in 2005, old hotels were demolished to make way for the new Waikiki Beach Walk retail complex. At the entrance to the sparkling new promenade of consumerism is the Islander. If you happen to be in town for a parade, such as the Kamehameha Day Parade held on June 11, book a room on the Diamond Head side of the building—you'll have an amazing bird's-eye view of the procession. ***Note:*** Parking is $18 per day.

Don't Forget to Add the Parking Fees

While you are figuring out your budget for Oahu, don't forget that nearly all of Waikiki's hotels charge for parking, from a low of $15 to a high of $25 (oddly enough, the closer you get to the ocean, the higher the parking rate, like your car could care if it has an ocean view stall). These additional parking fees add up quickly.

$$–$$$$ **Hawaiiana Hotel** (260 Beachwalk; ☎ 808/923-3811; www.hawaiiana hotelatwaikiki.com.com; AE, DC, DISC, MC, V) is the most upscale of the old-school spots, whitewashed into a Fantasy Island gentility. It's a complex of two courtyards, with two pools, and like The Breakers, it's been around since 1955 and has a lot of older repeat visitors. The white, breezy rooms have kitchenettes and big tubs. It's the kind of place where you can mix up your own mai tais and lounge around with no pretension—you can even reserve a grill and host your own poolside barbecue. Rooms run from $125 for a standard that sleeps two to $235 for a one-bedroom suite that can accommodate up to four people. Be sure to include the $15 parking per day in your budget.

$$$–$$$$ The beachfront **New Otani Kaimana Beach Hotel** ★★ (2863 Kalakaua Ave.; ☎ 800/356-8264 or 808/923-1555; www.kaimana.com; AE, DC, DISC, MC, V) is another islander favorite, but at the next level up. The prices may seem steep (standard rooms start at $160, low season), but they're the most reasonable of the beachfront establishments. Across the street from Kapiolani Park, Kaimana is the place to stay if you're looking for some quiet or are sports-minded (or have a sporty family). There are public tennis courts, a jogging path, a workout station, surf breaks, and Honolulu's best swimming beach at the hotel's doorstep. Take a 6am walk up Diamond Head Road to see the sunrise with Molokai in the distance. The hotel even has a bit of history—in the 1800s, *Treasure Island* author Robert Louis Stevenson lounged and wrote beneath the hau trees in what is now the open-air Hau Tree Lanai restaurant (a popular brunch spot). The basic rooms are tiny but well appointed in a mainstream-hotel kind of way. Parking is $18 per day.

$$$–$$$$ For the couple who craves a grown-up getaway, the **Outrigger Luana Waikiki** ★ (2045 Kalakaua Ave.; ☎ 800/688-7444 or 808/955-6000; www.outrigger.com; AE, DC, DISC, MC, V), refurbished and reopened in 2005, is a good option. The studios and one-bedroom condo suites have a clean, executive look—wood headboards, stone floors, and bronze hula-girl lamps—plus kitchenettes or kitchens. Located at the very start of Waikiki, the Luana is about a 10-minute walk from Fort DeRussy Beach (you walk across a park), and if you get an oceanview room, it's great for sunset watching through a picture window. Regular rates are $265 to $485, but if you book online and there are rooms available, you might be able to find a price as low as $159. ***Note:*** Parking is $18 per day. If Outrigger Luana Waikiki is full, you might want to check out the also-recommended **Outrigger Reef** or **Outrigger Waikiki Shore** (both listed on the hotel website, above).

$–$$$$ Oahu's newest minichain is Aqua Hotels & Resorts. In 5 years, hotel veteran Mike Paulin has parlayed his resort management company from one property to five Waikiki "condotels." A local developer converts hotels into condos and Paulin manages the rental aspects for the owners, putting the "tel" into the operation. The best-located property is **Aqua Bamboo** ★★ (2425 Kuhio Ave.; ☎ 866-406-2782; www.aquaresorts.com; AE, DC, DISC, MC, V). Condotel means even the standard rooms ($149) are like really nice apartments (most, but not all, have kitchenettes). Although this might seem like a splurge, if you're looking to spend less than $100 a night, you can save money by cooking. It's also the chicest-looking place in this price range, for travelers who value the appearance of things: rooms are in ivory and black, with deliciously firm beds, soft pillows, and big black tubs. The spa, just opened in 2005, is in a small building beside the pool. Top-notch licensed massage and occupational therapists offer Swedish, lomilomi (traditional Hawaiian-style), and hot-stone-massage treatments, as well as facials and body scrubs (the ginger-honey version makes you feel as smooth as a baby's inner arm). If you book for a week, nights 6 and 7 are free. Check the website for Savy Surfer Web deals, where we got a room for $98 a night during the high season. Unfortunately, parking is $18 per day.

$$$–$$$$ You get glamour for grown-ups at **Waikiki Parc** ★★ (2233 Helumoa Rd.; ☎ 800/422-0450 or 808/921-7272; www.waikikiparc.com; AE, DC, MC, V). The more affordable sister to the Halekulani across the street, the Waikiki Parc is a sleek boutique operation. Rack rates are $205 for a standard room to $275 for a deluxe oceanview room, but if you book online, you'll get the best rate at the time, which can be as low as $175 for a standard room. Recently redesigned and renovated especially for the 20s to 30s crowd, this "hidden" hotel offers lots of bonuses, including a terrific location, just 100 yards from the beach. The compact, beautifully appointed rooms underwent complete renovation in 2006 with

A Second Home for the Brave in Hawaii

The military-owned **Hale Koa Hotel** (2055 Kalia Rd.; ☎ 808/955-0555 or 808/367-6027; www.halekoa.com; AE, DC, DISC, MC, V) in Waikiki has a mission: "To operate a first class hotel and recreation facility at affordable prices for military members and their families." Just down the road from the chi-chi Halekulani, the 66-acre Hale Koa is like any other big chain hotel, with two towers of rooms, a big blue pool, a luau—but for service people only. There's a special icon on the website just for "Operation Iraqi Freedom" reservations. Who qualifies? Active-duty members of all the armed forces, retirees, honorably discharged veterans, public-health staffers, and many more categories (check the website for details). The prices are bargain basement. For enlisted men and women, the rates run from $83 for a standard room to $154 for a deluxe oceanfront room. For retired Department of Defense civilians, the range is $107 to $202. Parking is a deal, too: only $6 per day.

Room-Filling Events

Periodically throughout the year, convention groups descend on Oahu and special events flood the island. In 2006, for example, 10,700 lawyers flew in for the American Bar Association annual meeting; later that year, the Honolulu Marathon brought a whopping 20,000 fit folks to the island. For upcoming events—and consequently times of year to avoid—check the websites of the Hawaii Visitors & Convention Bureau (www.hvcb.org) and the Hawaii Convention Center (www.hawaiiconvention.com).

new, modern, contemporary, Hawaiian-Zen decor. Superfluous furniture was removed to make the rooms look more spacious, and wired Internet access was installed. All rooms have lanais with an ocean, mountain, or city view. Nice extras include adjustable floor-to-ceiling shutters for those who want to sleep in. The Parc features the same level of service that has made the Halekulani famous and offers two excellent restaurants, one of which, Nobu Waikiki, just opened in 2007. Don't forget parking at $20 per day.

NEAR THE ALA MOANA SHOPPING CENTER

$–$$ Mike Daley, godfather of Oahu's polo scene, owns the funky, fun **Hotel Equus and Waikiki Marina Tower** (1696 Ala Moana Blvd.; ☎ 866-406-2782 [8am–4pm Hawaii time]; www.hawaiipolo.com; AE, DC, DISC, MC, V), which explains the polo-tournament trophies and other horsey memorabilia in its rooms. Located between Ala Moana Shopping Center and the beginning of Waikiki, guests have to walk to prime beaches (about 15 min.) and shopping (about 10 min.). But that minor inconvenience is partially why prices are so reasonable—from $94 to $117 for a standard room to $122 for a studio suite. If you book online and are flexible with your dates, you can find some deals. The rooms in the main hotel are a little worn but tropically done up with rattan furniture. The "tower" is actually the adjacent Aqua Marina Hotel, in which the Polo Inn retains its newly renovated suites, which are much nicer than the inn rooms. Sleek, with koa furniture and kitchenettes, they make a nice getaway for a couple. This place is popular with neighbor islanders in town for sports events such as the Honolulu Marathon and who aren't looking for frills (service is on the lackadaisical side). Parking is $18 per day.

MANOA

Cool, green Manoa Valley is one of Honolulu's most sought-after neighborhoods. Staying here gives visitors a taste of real residential life, away from the coast (I don't know anyone who lives in a beachfront home). Good bus lines make the rest of the city easily accessible.

$ Right near the University of Hawaii, and run by the venerable Thelma Akau (her husband started the hostel, Oahu's first, in 1969), **Hostelling International Honolulu** ★ (2323A Seaview Ave.; ☎ 808/946-0591; www.hostelsaloha.com; MC,

V) is a pretty genteel enclave as far as hostels go. Its lanai is filled with native plants and its library houses travel and reference books. It gets adult academic types in addition to the usual collection of international backpackers and college kids. Ultraclean, the hostel has two men's dormitories, three women's dormitories (both have bunk beds with thin mattresses), 2 "couple's rooms," and a communal kitchen. No private bathrooms. Situated in a quiet residential neighborhood, this hostel is the best choice for adults. Right near the bus stop, there are frequent buses to Waikiki and Ala Moana Center. It's also a few bucks cheaper than the Waikiki branch, with dorm rooms going for $18 to $21 a night and the private rooms priced at $46 to $52 for two people. Parking is extremely limited, and on-street parking is impossible. I would not stay here if I had a car.

$–$$$ If your idea of a B&B is one of those historic converted homes in New England, you'll love the **Manoa Valley Inn** (2001 Vancouver Dr.; ☎ 808/947-6019; www.manoavalleyinn.com; MC, V; payment due 30 days prior to arrival). Built as a residence in 1912 by Milton Moore and converted in 1978 to a B&B by T-shirt mogul Rick Ralston (he saved it from demolition), the Victorian Manoa Valley Inn is now owned by 18-year B&B veteran Theresa Wery, who has an eye for antiques (think handsome English four-poster mahogany beds and floral wallpaper). Right near the University of Hawaii, it's in one of Honolulu's most coveted residential neighborhoods. Of the eight rooms, especially pleasant is the light-filled sunroom, with lots of windows looking out on the garden and beyond to Waikiki. Rates are $99 to $120 for a double with a shared bathroom, $140 to $199 for a double with a private bathroom, and $150 for the small but charming stand-alone cottage that sleeps two. The pool is off-limits to guests. Staying here is a more independent experience than at most B&Bs: Guests help themselves to a continental breakfast on the big veranda and can come and go as they please with their own sets of keys. Super-tranquil, Wery calls this inn "a healing place," and I agree with her apt appraisal.

EASTERN OAHU

East of Honolulu you'll find the suburban enclave of Hawaii Kai (with no hotels, many would say the only reason to come here is to eat at the Hawaii Regional Cuisine restaurant Roy's) and bucolic Waimanalo, 15 minutes beyond Hawaii Kai on Kalanianaole Highway. The latter is a quiet little hideaway that's home to lots of Hawaiians, plant nurseries, farms, and a polo field. Houses line the beach, and investors have turned many of them into profitable vacation rentals. Although

Avoid the Chains

A big trend in Hawaii is buying local—to keep dollars on the island, instead of sending them to corporate headquarters on the mainland. So while there are Hyatts and Marriotts on Oahu, I encourage people to patronize locally owned hotels, such as the Queen Kapiolani, owned by developer Bert Kobayashi, and the Ohana and Outrigger hotels, chains owned by the local Kelley family.

there are only a few sundry stores like 7-Eleven, and it can take a while to get into town by bus, the long white-sand beach is a big draw. If urban Honolulu isn't your scene, Waimanalo may be perfect.

$ **J & B's Haven** ★ (909 Kahauloa Place; ☎ 808/396-9462; home.hawaii.rr.com/jnbshaven; cash only), run by a British mother-and-daughter team Barbara and Joan Webb, is set in Hahaione Valley, one of greener parts of the area and offers two of the most sleek and sophisticated B&B rooms on the island. Half of the corner King Room ($90) is floor-to-ceiling windows; plus, the room has a wraparound lanai, a comfy king-size bed, and a microwave oven. The Queen Room ($80) is a little smaller and has no oven. The best thing about being in Hawaii Kai is its proximity to snorkel haven Hanauma Bay and Makapuu Beach (the bay is about a 10-min. uphill drive away). ***Note:*** A 3-night minimum is required or an additional $20 per night fee is added.

$$$$ If you dream about what it's like to actually live in rural Hawaii, rent from **Beach House Hawaii** ★★ (☎ 866/625-6946 or 808/259-7792; www.beachhousehawaii.com; AE, DC, DISC, MC, V), which has 13 properties in Waimanalo. If you're just a couple, this can be a pricey option, but the bigger the group, the bigger the savings. For example, the Sunrise Beach House is $345 a night, so if you have the maximum four people, that comes out to only $57.50 a night. Last-minute bookings can also yield a discount. Young couple Ana Ziegner and Kini Murray own three of the homes and manage the rest for other people.

THE WINDWARD SIDE: KAILUA & LANIKAI

Once a bedroom community to Honolulu, which was largely populated by military families, Kailua is now a thriving town in its own right. Just a 15-minute drive away from Honolulu, over the Pali Highway, this area offers a slow pace and a great beach. Adjacent to Kailua, Lanikai is one of Oahu's most exclusive neighborhoods (Michelle Pfeiffer had a house in the area for 5 years). Multimillion-dollar homes line the white sands on what is arguably one of the island's most beautiful beaches, with calm aquamarine waters full of sea turtles (but there are no public showers or restrooms). ***Note:*** Homes range in price based on size and length of stay, with most of the homes renting for a minimum of a month.

$ From the street, **Sharon's Kailua Serenity Bed & Breakfast** ★ (127 Kakahiaka St., Kailua; ☎ 800/914-2271 or 808/262-5621; www.sharonsserenity.com; MC, V) looks like all the other unremarkable one-story ranch-style houses lining the quiet block. But inside, it's an oasis with a grand terrace and pool overlooking a canal where you might see paddlers skim by in an outrigger canoe. Cheerful hostess Sharon Price runs a professional operation with three homey rooms (all with their own bathroom for $80 each), one big enough to hold a family of four for just $90 a night (although that price is for two, add $20 for each additional person). Have your continental breakfast poolside. And Price is proud to point out that there are no additional cleaning fees, as is the case with many B&Bs. Kailua Beach is a 10-minute walk away. Children under 8 not allowed.

Eastern Oahu & the Windward Coast

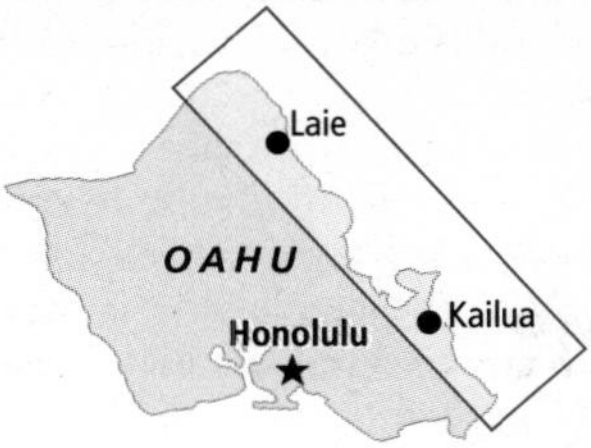

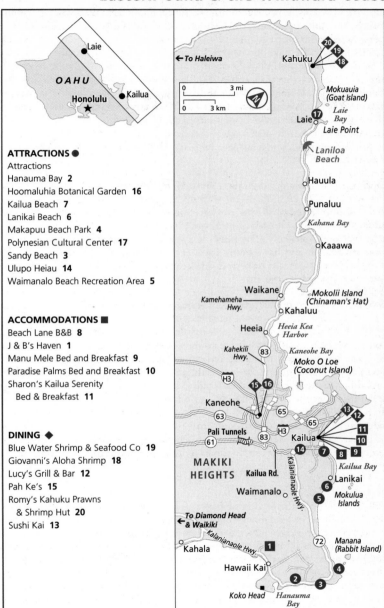

ATTRACTIONS ●

Attractions
Hanauma Bay **2**
Hoomaluhia Botanical Garden **16**
Kailua Beach **7**
Lanikai Beach **6**
Makapuu Beach Park **4**
Polynesian Cultural Center **17**
Sandy Beach **3**
Ulupo Heiau **14**
Waimanalo Beach Recreation Area **5**

ACCOMMODATIONS ■

Beach Lane B&B **8**
J & B's Haven **1**
Manu Mele Bed and Breakfast **9**
Paradise Palms Bed and Breakfast **10**
Sharon's Kailua Serenity
Bed & Breakfast **11**

DINING ◆

Blue Water Shrimp & Seafood Co **19**
Giovanni's Aloha Shrimp **18**
Lucy's Grill & Bar **12**
Pah Ke's **15**
Romy's Kahuku Prawns
& Shrimp Hut **20**
Sushi Kai **13**

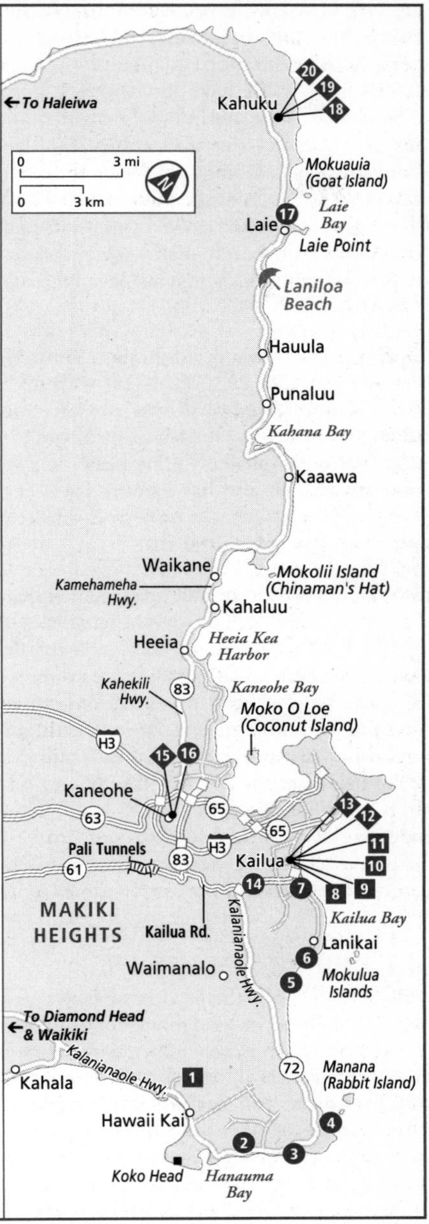

$ Gracious and warm retired couple Jim and Marilyn Warman run **Paradise Palms Bed and Breakfast** (804 Mokapu Rd., Kailua; ☎ 808/254-4234; www.paradisepalmshawaii.com; cash only), the epitome of cozy. The two guest suites ($110 and $120) have kitchenettes, private entrances, and plant-filled lanais. There's a 7-night minimum (3-night minimum with last minute bookings), but no extra charges like a cleaning fee. The house, with a big garden lush with bougainvillea, sits along a canal in the quiet suburb of Kailua, within walking distance of the beach of the same name. The Warmans stock the kitchenettes with 3 days' worth of baked goods, fruit, and juice. The beach is a short walk away and the rooms have beach chairs, towels, mats, and coolers that you can use. A $200 deposit is required, and you pay the balance in full in cash or traveler's checks upon arrival.

$–$$ For a tranquil, adult stay, **Manu Mele Bed and Breakfast** (153 Kailuna Place, Kailua; ☎ 808/262-0016; www.pixi.com/~manumele; cash only) is a good B&B option. The two private-entrance rooms ($100 and $120) are clean, white-tiled, and have a mishmash of furnishings (as well as a two-person max; you can't add kids on a rollaway). The beach is a short walk down a sandy path, and the one-story home also has a lovely patio and pool. You pay in full upon arrival—cash or traveler's checks only. You get breakfast on your first morning there, but you're on your own after that.

$–$$$$ A 2-minute walk from Kailua Beach is **Beach Lane B&B** ★★ (111 Hekili St.; ☎ 808/262-8286; www.beachlane.com; cash only), run by Tonic Bille, who speaks English, German, Danish, Swedish, and Norwegian. With her European sensibility, Beach Lane's rooms are more sleek and spare than Kailua's other B&Bs. You can choose from two-bedroom suites (you can see the beach when you're lying down on the queen-size beds) and an airy studio that has a private entrance and kitchenette. The two rooms are $125 each, with continental breakfast included. The studio goes for $95 to $135 (without breakfast). There is also Beach Lane Cottage, with two bedrooms and two baths and a full kitchen and which rents as a one-bedroom unit ($175–$205) or as a two-bedroom ($195–$250). Bille has stocked the place with beach mats and chairs, towels, body boards, and ice coolers for guests to use. ***Note:*** No matter how long you stay, there is a $40 cleaning fee for the B&B and a $90 cleaning fee for the cottage.

OAHU'S WEST SIDE

$$$–$$$$ The Waianae Coast has always been the "other side" of the island, one not highlighted in guidebooks and not recommended to tourists. But the main reason visitors didn't spend time out there is that there were no accommodations. That changed in 1993 with the arrival of Oahu's biggest resort: **J.W. Marriott Ihilani Resort and Spa at Ko Olina** (Ko Olina Resort, 92-1001 Olani St., Kapolei ☎ 808/679-0079 or 800/228-9290; www.ihilani.com). The Ihilani's pricey, but now tourists in search of an "old Hawaii" (read: no big buildings) come to this area, despite its remote nature. This part of the island is where you can find one of my favorite treks, the beach that was the site of the world's first international surfing contest and world-class golf.

Campgrounds

Camping on Oahu means slim pickings—there are no national parks with campgrounds, but there are state and county options. It has to be said that camping on Oahu can be a bit dodgy. Friends of mine won't even park their cars at hiking trail heads for fear that their cars will be broken into. And tourists may encounter some hostility from local campers, or they could find themselves neighbors to a family filled with aloha and have an amazing time. A thorough listing of campsites can be found at **www.alternative-hawaii.com**. Here are the best (and safest) options:

The most popular campsite is **Malaekahana State Park** (off Kamehameha Hwy., ½ mile north of Laie; $5/campsite/night) on the North Shore. On a secluded bay that has little waves for beginner surfers, the campsite is shrouded in ironwood trees. It's usually windy here, but the campsite nooks are protected. Choose from the state campsite or an adjacent gated campsite run by the nonprofit **Friends of Malaekahana** (P.O. Box 305, Laie, HI 96762; ☎ 808/293-1736; www.alternative-hawaii.com/fom/index.html; $5/person/night)—this area is gated and has a security guard, making it the safest campsite on the island. Each site has a picnic table and fire pit, and there are toilet facilities and hot outdoor showers.

Everyone who grew up here has memories of camping at **Bellows Field Beach Park** (41-043 Kalanianaole Hwy.; free) in Waimanalo. On a 3½-mile-long stretch of white-sand beach lined with ironwood trees, Bellows draws families year-round. It's not exactly secluded—there are 50 campsites at this City & County-run park, and it can get busy. There are bathrooms, outdoor cold showers, and a lifeguard on duty. On windy days, the relentless shore break is good for bodysurfing; on calm days, it's perfect for long swims.

Just down the beach from Bellows is more of the same at the county-run **Waimanalo Bay Recreation Area** (41-043 Aloiloi St., off Kalanianaole Hwy.; free). With only 10 campsites, you'll feel slightly more isolated here, but there's a bathroom facility, lifeguard, picnic tables, and night security.

For a tranquil, green camping experience, try **Hoomaluhia Botanical Garden** (45-680 Luluku Rd.; ☎ 808/233-7323; free), which offers tent camping on Friday, Saturday, and Sunday only. You'll be amid 400 acres of tropical plants and hiking trails, tucked behind residential Kaneohe. Campsites have bathroom facilities. Permits from the botanical garden are free. At the base of the grand Koolau Mountains, it's often overcast. This spot is great for plant lovers who don't have to be at the beach every waking minute (since there's no good beach nearby).

$$–$$$$ For an affordable golf getaway—or just some old-school resort living—**Makaha Golf Club Resort and Hotel** (84–626 Makaha Valley Rd.; ☎ 808/695-9544 or 866/576-6447; www.makaharesort.net; AE, DC, DISC, MC, V) is a good option. Built in 1969 by pioneering local developer Chinn Ho (yes, the character on *Hawaii Five-O* was named after him), this spread, 45 miles from Honolulu, is worn around the edges, but after years of limping along (it actually closed in 1995 then reopened in 2001 when it was bought by Canada-based Fairmont Resorts), it had its best year in decades in 2005 due to partnerships with Internet travel wholesalers, fully booked Waikiki hotels, and reasonable rates. Rack rates are $205 for a standard room to $400 for a parlor suite with kitchen. But searching online booking outfits such as Expedia for the end of May, offer a standard room for $106 and a one bedroom suite for $119; and if you stay a week, 1 night is free, which means it comes out to $99 a night. The area is home to a large percentage of Oahu's native Hawaiians, who are on staff and also are part of a program that brings in artisans and cultural practitioners, so guests can get a real taste of traditional Hawaiian life. Rooms are pleasant, but nothing fancy. The big draw is the par-72 golf course that lies between the towering Waianae Mountain range and the ocean. Golf fee for guests: $80 in the morning, $65 after noon. Makaha Beach is across the road from the entrance to the resort, but it's a long driveway, so a walk takes about 10 minutes.

OAHU'S NORTH SHORE

When locals say "country," they mean the North Shore. Forty year ago, funky beach houses rented for $300 a month. Now rents are more like $2,500 a month, and when the winter waves are up, the traffic is bumper-to-bumper, but a rural feel lingers. To get a taste of Surf City, the North Shore is the place to be. Here, vacation rentals are more plentiful than hotel rooms, and during surfing's Triple Crown season—November to January—it's hard to find any kind of room on the North Shore.

$–$$$$ Surfers on a budget (and that's most of them) make a beeline for **Backpackers Vacation Inn and Plantation Village** ★ (59–788 Kamehameha Hwy.; ☎ 808/638-7838; www.backpackers-hawaii.com; DC, Disc, MC, V). A collection of three big houses (the Beach House, the Main House, and the Brown House) and a cluster of tiny plantation-style cabins, Backpackers offers dorm rooms, private rooms, and studios. You can't beat the location—in the thick of the surf scene—right across from snorkel spot Three Tables Beach, and near Foodland. It's rustic island style, with rattan furniture, marine-life murals, and floral prints. The dorm rooms are really bare-bones, with thin mattresses on bunk beds. Hostel beds are $27 in the Main House and plantation houses, and $30 in the Beach House. Hostellers who stay a week or more get a 10% discount. Private rooms for two in the plantation houses and Brown House (with shared bathrooms) are $62 to $85. Studios in the Beach House have kitchenettes or full kitchens, private bathroom, and TV and go for $120 to $145. The private cabins are a good pick for families or large groups. You can get a two-, three-, or four-bedroom cabin for $162 to $325, all of which have full kitchens. If you plan to come in winter for the big waves, book far in advance.

Camping Permits

For City & County of Honolulu (which is all of Oahu) campsites, you must first obtain a (free) permit at the **Department of Parks and Recreation** (650 S. King St.; ☎ 808/523-4525; www.co.honolulu.hi.us/parks/permits.htm; Mon–Fri 7:45am–4pm). You must apply in person, and each permit covers up to 10 people for a maximum of 5 consecutive nights at any one park.

For state parks, you can apply for permits in writing up to 30 days before the first day of camping through the **Department of Land and Natural Resources** (P.O. Box 621, Honolulu, HI 96809; in person 1151 Punchbowl St.; ☎ 808/587-0300; www.hawaii.gov/dlnr; cash only). Permits are $5 per campsite per night and good for 5 consecutive nights.

$$–$$$$ My condos of choice on the North Shore are the **Ke Iki Beach Bungalows** (66–250 Kamehameha Hwy.; ☎ 866/638-8229 or 808/638-8229; www.keikibeach.com). Owned by an Oregon family and efficiently run by Gregory Gerstenberger, this is a laid-back compound of bungalows and cottages where you can do your own thing. It's right on the wide, white Ke Iki Beach, just down the sand from Banzai Pipeline, and a 10-minute walk to Foodland (the area's main grocery store) and Starbucks. Don't be surprised if you see the likes of six-time world surfing champ Kelly Slater sitting on the curb sipping a latte and chatting on his cellphone. Sitting on the lanai of the second-story, one-bedroom Orchid at night, the sky is a celestial extravaganza of stars. On the beach, you might see a bonfire circled by fishermen as palm fronds rustle in the breeze. The immaculately clean rooms, done up in island style with bamboo furniture, aren't fancy but are equipped with everything you need. Don't feel like cooking? Haleiwa and its restaurants are a 10-minute drive away. In summer the water is lovely for swimming, but in winter the strong currents and waves are for watching only. Ke Iki's units each have a full kitchen, phone, cable TV and BBQ, and, depending on size sleep 2 to 8 people. ***Note:*** If you stay less than 1 week, there is a $50 to $95 cleaning fee.

DINING FOR ALL TASTES

On Oahu, food is a common topic of conversation, whether it's where to get the best lomilomi salmon or who's the hottest up-and-coming chef. And you can eat well here, whether you drop $5 in a shabby Chinatown pho (noodle) shop or $150 at nationally recognized Chef Mavro. The key to finding the best food is getting out of Waikiki—if that's where you're staying. In Honolulu, you'll find clusters of good restaurants in Kaimuki, along Kapahulu Avenue (within walking distance of Waikiki), and in Chinatown. Outside of the city, the pickings are slim, but there are a few highlights. Here are enough choices to keep you eating out every night.

WAIKIKI

The state staple is the "plate lunch"—basically local fast food. It's a paper plate of a main dish, two scoops of rice (the sticky Japanese kind), and a scoop of macaroni

Where to Dine in Waikiki

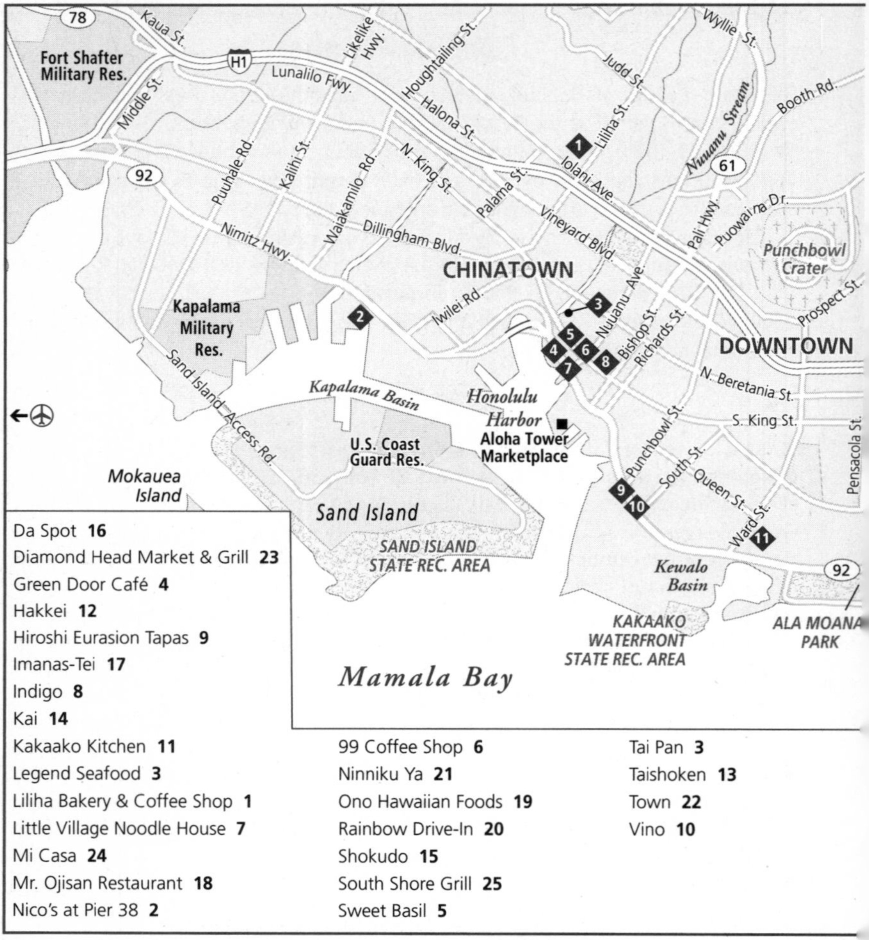

salad. The main dish can be a range of food that reflects Hawaii's cultural mix: Korean barbecued ribs, Japanese chicken katsu (a breaded, fried, and sliced breast), quasi-American hamburger steak (a patty smothered in gravy), or Chinese-influenced sweet-and-sour spareribs. Plate lunches are satisfying the way Southern food is satisfying—comforting and heavy and worth a try.

$ You can find plate-lunch spots all over the island—the biggest local chains are Zippy's and L&L Drive-Inn, but I don't recommend them. As the relentless march of development continues, Oahu's old-school local eateries are slowly being lost, but a classic that's been around since 1961 is one I do recommend. At the **Rainbow Drive-In** (3308 Kanaina Ave., at Kapahulu Ave.; ☎ 808/737-0177; cash only), surfers from nearby Waikiki, construction workers, police officers, and

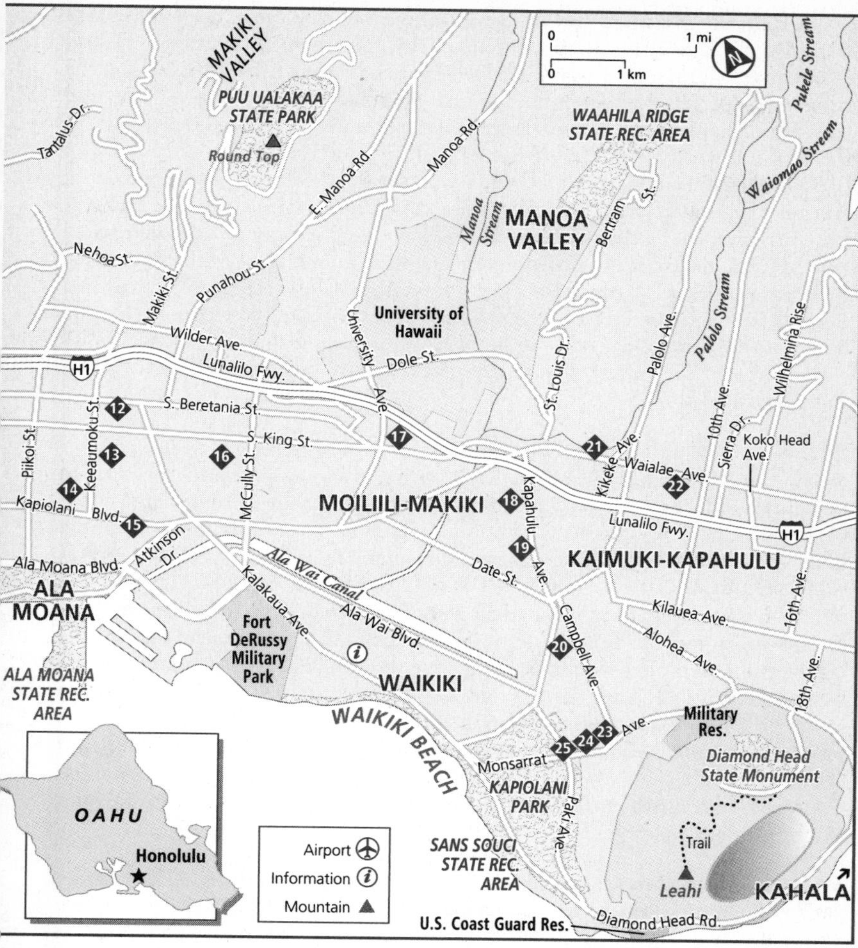

bored teenagers all converge for teriyaki beef plates, barbecued-pork sandwiches, and the famous chili, which is made fresh every morning (though from canned ingredients), all costing under $6.50. Order at one of the two windows, grab a table on the outdoor lanai, and wait until your food appears on the counter. Entrees run $2.50 to $6.50.

$–$$ Over the past couple of years, some chefs and entrepreneurs have reinvented the plate lunch, using fresh ingredients and updated recipes. The two best examples are **Kakaako Kitchen** ★★ (Ward Centre, 1200 Ala Moana Blvd.; ☎ 808/596-7488; MC, V), the casual brainchild of star chef Russell Siu (his upscale spot is 3660 on the Rise in Kaimuki) and **Diamond Head Market & Grill** ★★ (3158 Monsarrat Ave.; ☎ 808/732-0077; AE, DC, DISC, MC, V).

At **Kakaako Kitchen,** you can get plate lunches that range from crab sandwiches to chicken curry, and none of them cost more than $9.50. Better, instead of scoops of white rice, you can have brown rice or a green salad. You order at the counter, the server gives you a number that you place on your table outside, and your Styrofoam box of food is delivered when it's ready. Try their deserts, some of the best in town. Entrees range from $7.25 to $11.

Diamond Head Market & Grill, a gourmet store with prepared food and a takeout plate-lunch counter, is the closest thing in Hawaii to Dean & DeLuca. Enterprising owner Kelvin Ro sells dishes like refreshing jicama salad and roasted rack of lamb, deluxe bento boxes, and his famous scones, along with condiments such as mint-ginger sauce from his cousin Glenn Chu's Heaven & Earth line (Chu is the chef-owner of Indigo). The condiments make great gifts for foodies back home. At the "grill," you can buy fresh-grilled ahi plate lunch for $9.75. It's a favorite stop for surfers after a day of riding the waves at Diamond Head. Entrees cost $5 to $15.

CHINATOWN

$–$$$ Like all Chinatowns, Honolulu's version is a food mecca. It's the place to buy great produce at bargain prices, find sashimi-grade fish at Oahu Market, and, of course, eat well. Of the many dim sum spots in the area, the best two are in the Chinese Cultural Plaza. The undisputed dim sum king is **Legend Seafood** ✪✪✪ (Chinese Cultural Plaza, 100 Beretania St., at River St.; ☎ 808/532-1868; AE, DC, MC, V), a classic, big, open dining hall with white tablecloths and all the familiar dumplings, and prices from $2.40 to $6 an item. What sets Legend apart is the quality—the dumpling dough is just a little thinner and more delicate, and the fresh ingredients pop with flavor. From 10:30am to 2pm, you can flag down carts serving silky *chow fun* (extra wide noodles) hiding sweet scallops or beef, crisp mochi balls stuffed with a rich pork filling, and dumplings of spicy scallions and chewy pine nuts. This restaurant is open for dinner, too, serving good, familiar Cantonese food, with entrees from $9 to $16. It also has a vegetarian dim sum sister next door.

$ At the opposite end of the center, past the herbalists and jewelry shops, is tiny **Tai Pan** (Chinese Cultural Plaza, 100 Beretania St., at River St.; ☎ 808/599-8899; cash only), where it's hard to find a seat at noon (you'll likely share a big round table with a couple of Cantonese-speaking diners) or a server who speaks English. But the good news is that the spot serves dim sum until 4pm. The food is a notch down from Legend's, but everything is a buck or two less; dim sum items are $2.05 to $4.35 here and entrees range from $6 to $9.

$ This neighborhood is also packed with Vietnamese holes in the wall, and my favorite is **99 Coffee Shop** (174 N. King St.; ☎ 808/537-4276; cash only). Besides a steaming bowl of pho (soup with meat of your choice and veggies in an intense, five-spice-scented broth for $7.35), you can get dishes such as "broken rice"—jagged chips of jasmine rice topped with barbecued pork. On a bustling street, 99 Coffee Shop, where most things cost $7 to $8.50 (though a couple of entrees are as high as $9.75) is a nice place to take a break from exploring Chinatown.

$–$$ Perennial local award-winning **Little Village Noodle House** (1133 Smith St.; ☎ 808/545-3008; www.littlevillagehawaii.com; AE, DISC, MC, V) is so popular that last year it expanded into the adjacent building—and there are still lines for dinner after events at nearby Hawaii Theatre and the First Friday gallery walk. Businesspeople, downtown hipsters, and families crowd the restaurant for multiregional Chinese food. Flavors run from mild (steamed catfish in a delicate gingery broth) to pungent (crunchy, sweet-and-spicy pan-fried beef), and the prices range from $6.50 to $13.

$–$$ A newer entry in the Chinatown dining scene are Thai restaurants. Of these, I like **Sweet Basil** (1152A Maunakea St.; ☎ 808/545-5800; cash only) best for its excellent curries—don't miss the short ribs in a thick, rich massaman curry sauce. You don't even need a knife for this long-simmered meat. Office drones beeline for the $9.95 all-you-can-eat buffet, which is good, but the a la carte, cooked-to-order food is better. Sweet Basil is open for lunch Monday through Saturday until 2pm and dinner Friday and Saturday. Entrees are reasonably priced at $5 to $14.

$$$–$$$$ Chinatown is Honolulu's nightlife hot spot, with clubs such as thirtyninehotel and NextDoor bringing in international DJs, and the restaurant that pioneered the scene is **Indigo** ★ (1121 Nuuanu Ave.; ☎ 808/521-2900; DC, DISC, MC, V). In an old brick building, this Eurasian eatery is a warren of rooms and multiple bars filled with Asian antiques. The place has one of the best lunch buffets in town—lots of vegetable dishes along with fish, chicken, and steak—for $18. Lunch entrees range from $20 to $30. Well-spiced dishes, such as beef rendang and duck glazed in a raspberry-hoisin sauce, run from $20 to $30 and feed the dinner crowd. Late at night the place morphs into a nightclub.

IWILEI

$ Young Frenchman Nicolas Chaize opened his plate-lunch spot, **Nico's at Pier 38** ★★ (Pier 38, 1133 N. Nimitz Hwy.; ☎ 808/540-1377; www.nicospier38.com), across a parking lot from the United Fishing Agency—Honolulu's fish auction house. So every day he offers primo island fish that's literally fresh off the boat. You can rub shoulders with fishermen and fish brokers while eating onaga grilled with a lilikoi beurre blanc sauce or calamari salad. Expect top-notch ingredients nicely prepared (Chaize used to work in the kitchen at haute eatery Chef Mavro) at fast-food prices ($8.50 tops). If you're not into seafood, Nico's also serves one of the best burgers in town. Walk around the pier and check out the fishing boats. While Nico's might seem out of the way, it's a 5-minute drive from downtown. Open 6:30am until 5pm Monday to Friday and 2:30pm on Saturday.

DIAMOND HEAD

$ When I don't feel like cooking, I automatically head to **Da Spot** (908 Pumehana St., between Waiola and Algaroba sts.; ☎ 808/941-1313; cash only). It's a grubby storefront in the residential neighborhood known as Moiliili, and you won't find it in any other guidebooks. One of my favorite eateries, I know I am going to get deeply satisfying home cooking here and a lot of aloha from owners Ahmad Ramadan and Ako Kifuji. They make some of the best smoothies in town (21 different types), but it's their daily specials (which run from $6.50–$8) and feature such items as Egyptian chicken heady with cardamom and cinnamon and a rich, red stew of lamb and vegetables—that keep me coming back. The food is a reflection of Ramadan's Egyptian heritage: "I can't cook Japanese food," admits Kifuji with a shrug. You might end up playing with one of the couple's two young children while you wait for your food, which arrives in Styrofoam boxes along with rice and salad, all for about $7. I like to take my dinner over to the park bench at the school kitty-corner to Da Spot.

$–$$ A spate of Mexican *taquerias* opened on Oahu in the past few years, and **Mi Casa** (3046 Monsarrat Ave.; ☎ 808/737-1562; DC, DISC, MC, V), at the foot of Diamond Head, is the best. What makes it stand out is the fact that Spokane transplant Angelica Selvidge (who's originally from Jalisco, Mexico) makes her own corn-flour tortillas. She shapes them thick so they won't fall apart when stuffed with *carne asada* and *picadillo,* and they're as soft as the wheat version. Her husband, Ken, makes the best *carnitas* on the island—he cooks the pork in a skillet rather than frying it in lard. (In fact, in a nod to healthy eating, nothing is fried at Mi Casa.) After rendering the meat in its own juices, Selvidge finishes it off in milk and orange juice, leaving it supermoist and with a subtle tang. Combination plates are reasonably priced at $7.50 to $14. You can take a seat in the bustling cafe (the table in front of the window that looks out on Monsarrat St. is the best) or on the sliver of an outdoor deck. Grab some *cerveza* (beer) from the liquor store across the street.

$ Just up the road is the place to get fresh mahimahi soft tacos. At **South Shore Grill** (3114 Monsarrat Ave.; ☎ 808/734-0229; cash only), Linda Gehring makes everything from scratch. Order your dish as an entree and it comes with an addictive Asian-accented slaw for just $6 to $8.

DOWNTOWN

$ For a truly local experience, stop in at Honolulu's last old-school diner: **Liliha Bakery & Coffee Shop** (515 Kuakini St.; ☎ 808/531-1651; cash only). Known for its sweet Coco Puffs pastries and Chantilly cake, I like to sit at the long Formica counter and order dishes like hamburger steak smothered in gravy along with an orange freeze (this is one of the last places on the island to serve the old-school soda-fountain favorite) or meatloaf (the Tues special) that costs $8.25. Open 24 hours from Tuesday to Sunday, you can spot people (often local bands and post-club revelers) eating oversize pancakes at 1am before heading home. Breakfast ranges from $5.75 to $7.50 and lunch/dinner entrees are $5.95 to $9.

$–$$ Ramen is serious business on Oahu, and my favorite spot for it is the first Honolulu branch of a famous Tokyo spot, **Taishoken** ★ (903 Keeaumoku St.; ☎ 808/955-8860). There are only a few seats in the brightly lit white box where the soba noodles are made fresh daily. Sit at the counter and you can watch the cook toiling over a giant steaming pot. Taishoken is notable for inventing its own style of ramen: Tsukemen, which goes for under $8 a bowl. You get a plateful of noodles that stay firm because they're not sitting in broth, then you dip them in a bowl of soup—either miso or shoyu. I like the faintly sweet tinge of the miso. The most expense entree on the menu is only $12. Big plus: Taishoken is open until 10pm Tuesday to Saturday.

$–$$$ Hawaii's long-intertwined history with Japan means that Japanese cuisine is an integral part of the dining landscape. There's a huge range, from local mom-and-pop saimin shops to a new wave of high-concept contemporary Japanese restaurants opened by Nihon-jin (Japanese nationals). For local Japanese food, I head to **Mr. Ojisan Restaurant** ★ (Kilohana Sq., 1018 Kapahulu Ave.; ☎ 808/735-4455; MC, V), where you can get everything from little *izakaya* (Japanese pub) dishes—such as grilled eggplant and vinegary seafood salad—to big bowls of steaming ramen, to sushi, to complete dinners of pork katsu and unagi. Most dishes are under $12. Rows of shochu and sake bottles emblazoned with regular customers' names line one counter. The clean, spare room and crisply presented food attract the likes of star chef Alan Wong. ***Budget tip:*** Go for lunch when entrees are $8 to $16 versus dinner when entrees are $15 to $22.

$–$$ Oahu has a handful of Hawaiian restaurants—most of them run by Japanese or Chinese families—and they all have their specialties, but dingy **Ono Hawaiian Foods** ★ (726 Kapahulu Ave.; ☎ 808/737-2275; cash only), established more than 4 decades ago, is consistently the all-around best—which is why there's always a line. Inside, weathered photos of local and national celebrities who have eaten here coat the walls. It's rare that an institution keeps up its quality over nearly half a century, but Ono does. The poi is fresh and thick, the *laulau giant* and tasty. This place is also the most Hawaiian—serving dishes such as *naau puaa* (stewed pork intestines) and *opihi* (raw indigenous limpets found only in Hawaii waters). You can eat for under $6, but I'd recommend ordering one of the "special plates"—a-little-bit-of-everything meals that run from $11 to $15. Everything arrives in plastic dishes that look like they're from an elementary school cafeteria circa 1972. Use the poi as a condiment to cut the saltiness of the kalua pig.

$–$$$ Newer, style-conscious spots attract a youthful party crowd. For reliable food in a rock-star setting (Tokyo design star Yasumichi Morita, who did Manhattan hot spot Megu, redid this former cavernous bank space), I head to **Shokudo** ★ (Ala Moana Pacific Center, ground floor, 1585 Kapiolani Blvd.; ☎ 808/941-3701; www.shokudojapanese.com; MC, V). Fresh tofu comes out of the kitchen hourly. It's served plain, in a straw bowl, and the silky globs that you top with salt, green onions, nori, and some dashi have made me rethink soybean curd. If you prefer, you can order it fried in a slightly sweet soy sauce. Hybrid dishes like sukiyaki topped with mashed potatoes (imagine Japanese shepherd's pie) and mochi gratin sound wacky but taste good. Effervescent vodka soda cocktails (honey lemon is my soothing favorite) keep the buzzing crowd lubricated. While most dishes are under $12, you eat them family-style, and as your group keeps ordering, the bill can add up as each entree ranges from $9 to $21.

$–$$$$ Since I can't afford to eat at the better-known Japanese eateries, my sushi joint of choice is **Imanas-Tei** ★★ (2626 S. King St.; ☎ 808/941-2626; cash only). Near the University of Hawaii, this Zen bamboo-paneled haven serves high-quality, edomae-style sushi—dainty one-bite sizes of nigiri. It's still on the pricey side, but for me, cheap and sushi are two words that don't mix. Imanas-Tei also serves small dishes like delectable braised kabocha squash, the crunchiest fried chicken (drizzled with a slightly sweet soy sauce) this side of the Mississippi, and

Fish & Poi

What is Hawaiian food? If you go back to ancient times, the staples of the healthy Hawaiian diet were poi (taro root pounded to a gooey paste), sweet potatoes, fish (raw and cooked), and pork. Salt and mashed kukui nuts were the only seasoning. Dr. Terry Shintani did a study of the traditional Hawaiian diet, which is high in carbohydrates and low in fats, and came up with the book, *The Hawaii Diet* (Atria). Working in the impoverished Hawaiian community in Waianae, on Oahu's west coast, Shintani saw a weight loss of about 11 pounds in obese native Hawaiians who followed the diet for 21 days.

Today, what is called Hawaiian food is an amalgam of traditional food, with Western and Asian influences—seen in dishes like lomilomi salmon (cerviche-style fish dish with a tomato-and-onion salad) and chicken long rice, made with Chinese noodles and ginger. But the centerpiece is still poi, kalua pig (a whole animal traditionally steamed in an imu, or pit), steamed sweet potato, and laulau (pork and fish wrapped in young taro leaves, then steamed).

steaming pots of cook-your-own nabe. Like other izakaya places, individual dishes are cheap, ranging in price from $5 to $24—but they add up (so order carefully). Japanese nationals and locals flock to this place, so expect a wait on the bench outside—the restaurant doesn't take reservations after 7pm.

$$–$$$$ Another style-conscious spot is **Kai** (1427 Makaloa St.; ☎ 808/944-1555; cash only), specializing in the Japanese street food okonomiyaki, a sort of pancake topped with things like squid, pork, and kimchi. You can also get small dishes like daikon long-braised in dashi and a simple, delicious salad of mizuna and egg. Simple, but not cheap, as entrees start at $13 and go up to $29. Kai is right near Ala Moana Shopping Center.

$$–$$$$ Opened in January 2006, **Hakkei** ★★ (1436 Young St., between Kalakaua Ave. and Keeaumoku St.; ☎ 808/944-6688; www.hakkei-honolulu.com; AE, MC, V) is the offshoot of a well-known hot-spring inn in Japan known for its kaiseki cuisine. Instead of haute kaiseki cuisine, Hakkei's specialty is the Japanese comfort food known as oden, a hotpot of *dashi* (broth) dotted with long-simmered vegetables and goodies such as sweet potato wrapped in cabbage leaves. You can go either for a "set" three-course dinner (the $35 option that includes oden is a good way to sample Hakkei's food) or order lots of little dishes a la carte ($9–$15).

KAHALA

$–$$ My favorite Chinatown cheap eats has moved to the Kahala Mall. The **Green Door Café** (Kahala Mall; ☎ 808/533-0606; cash only), is where Betty Pang cooks-to-order pungently spiced Malaysian food. The new location seats 100, a vast improvement over the lime green cubbyhole in Chinatown with just a handful of tables and chairs. The big flavors and small prices keep a core of addicted fans coming back. Order some freshly made *roti* (crepelike flat bread) and dip it in the creamy chicken curry. If you're familiar with the cuisine and your favorite isn't on the handwritten menu, Betty just might make it for you anyway.

KAIMUKI

$–$$$$ The neighborhood of Kaimuki is emerging as a restaurant hub, and one casual spot in particular has pushed Honolulu's dining envelope. Called **Town** ★ (3435 Waialae Ave., Kaimuki; ☎ 808/735-5900; AE, MC, V), it's a sleek, low-key enclave of Mediterranean-leaning food, made with as many naturally grown local ingredients as chef/owner Ted Kenney can get his hands on. The menu changes daily, but some rotating highlights include mussels and cavatelli in a citrusy Cinzano-spiked broth and brined, flattened chicken with bits of torn bread, roasted grapes, and crunchy pancetta. Kenney also reinvents local dishes such as oxtail soup, presenting fall-off-the-bone oxtail smeared with a cilantro-ginger pesto atop creamy risotto dotted with boiled peanuts (a favorite Hawaii snack). ***Budget tip:*** Go for lunch, where entrees are $6 to $15 vs. dinner when entrees jump up to $16 to $28.

Late-Night Eats

Oahu eats early. Most restaurants stop serving dinner at 9:30pm. It used to be that the only place you could get a midnight snack was at the fast-food chain Zippy's. But that's slowly changing. If your flight to Honolulu arrives late and you're starving, there now is help in Waikiki with the newly opened **MAC 24-7** (which stands for Moderan American Cooking, 24 hr. a day, 7 days a week), at the **Hilton Waikiki Prince Kuhio Hotel** (2500 Kuhio Ave., at Liliuokalani Ave.; ☎ 808/921-5564). All day, every day, the menu has everything from breakfast, lunch, and dinner to snacks and desserts (the bar stops pouring drinks between 4–6am for some reason). It's not just for late-night dining; it's also a great place to get picnic lunches during the day. The view from the floor to ceiling windows is of the landscaped gardens in the lobby, the interior design is the new "in" decor—sophisticated but sparse in a Zen mode with splashes of bright color—and the waitstaff is friendly and helpful. The cuisine is hotel coffee shop/diner "comfort" food, reasonably priced for Waikiki ($4–$28, with most entrees in the $11–$16 range), and plenty of it. The portion sizes can feed two and, in some cases, three people (even three hungry people).

Here are a few other eateries that keep night-owl hours:

- **Imanas-Tei:** Monday to Saturday until 11:30pm (p. 127)
- **Mr. Ojisan:** Monday to Thursday until 11:30pm, Friday and Saturday until 1am (p. 127)
- **Shokudo:** Daily until 2am (p. 127)
- **Vino:** Friday and Saturday until 11pm (p. 130)

$$–$$$ Ninniku Ya Garlic Restaurant (3196 Waialae Ave.; ☎ 808/735-0784; AE, DC, DISC, MC, V), also known as the Garlic Restaurant, is an offbeat option—the cozy restaurant is in an old Craftsman bungalow, and inside is a warm woody glow that matches the simple, affordable food (entrees hover in the $16 range), all flavored with garlic by chef-owner Eiyuki Endo. New York steak, tender filet mignon, and tiger prawns cooked with the stinking rose are perfect dishes. But don't miss the four-mushroom pasta and the garlic rice (which can be a meal in itself). Yes, everything has garlic, even the house-made garlic gelato, but it doesn't overpower. Yes, that's garlic gelato—and don't knock it until you try it.

★ **$–$$$$ Vino Italian Tapas and Wine Bar** ★★ (☎ 808/533-4476; AE, DISC, MC, V) is the brainchild of Chuck Furuya, one of only two master sommeliers in Hawaii. Furuya, who's usually in the house, is an Italophile and wine freak who's constantly combing the globe for his latest finds, and he wants to share his knowledge with his customers. He has all kinds of programs, from bringing in famous winemakers such as Roger Dagorn for tastings with patrons to holding his monthly $30 "Chuck's Table" communal dinners for 12—he opens a bottle for each of the three courses and talks wine (he's also a great source for Honolulu restaurant stories; he's pals with all the top chefs). With more than 20 wines by the glass and more than 60 by the bottle, Vino has become the oenophile hangout. The menu is very similar to Vino on Maui, and features tapas, or small plates. I'd recommend any ravioli on the menu, but signature dishes include roasted peppers with grilled foccacia, tender crispy calamari, baby asparagus with quail egg and sage butter gnocchi. Expect to pay about $6.95 for most plates. Don't pass up the house-made gnocchi or the daily pizza. Furuyu has put together an amazing array of wines by the glass, dispensed from a custom-crafted 20-spigot wine Cruvinet. The idea here is to enjoy great wines and be able to taste great Italian food.

$–$$$$ At sister restaurant **Hiroshi Eurasion Tapas** ★★ (Restaurant Row, 500 Ala Moana Blvd.; ☎ 808/524-8466; www.hiroshihawaii.com; AE, DISC, MC, V), the focus is on chef Hiroshi Fukui's legerdemain—he effortlessly combines French technique with Pacific and Asian ingredients, and plays with culinary idioms, making upscale versions of Japanese comfort foods. Order a bunch of small plates ($7.50–$13), or one large plate ($23–$28), and share. A signature dish: the $9.50 tapa plate of kampachi carpaccio perfectly balanced with a generous topping of finely diced ginger, tomato, artisanal tofu, and cilantro.

THE WINDWARD SIDE

$$ Inside the sparely stylish **Sushi Kai** ★ (20 Kainehe St.; ☎ 808/262-5661; AE, MC, V) are round paper hanging lamps, a two-tone paint job of olive drab and ecru, and a stone floor—all of which set a fashionable tone. The around-$10 small-plate Japanese dishes excel, with chef Jason Roldan tweaking traditional formulas to create things like sake-simmered clams boosted with roasted-garlic slivers and garlic butter. The fish variety on the sushi menu is limited but of good quality. Roldan also makes ambitious full-size entrees that can go up in price to $19, but that's for a delicious and worthwhile macadamia-crusted mahimahi in béarnaise sauce. Honoluluans wish Sushi Kai would open a branch in town.

$$–$$$ In Kaneohe, **Pah Ke's** (48–018 Kamehameha Hwy.; ☎ 808/235-4505; AE, DC, MC, V) looks like any other Chinese joint, and is located in an aging strip mall, but owner Raymond Siu makes a lot more than sweet-and-sour pork. Sure, there's the regular Chinese menu, which is good, but Siu has an "other" menu, which includes tasty fusion-type dishes like spinach salad with a citrusy vinaigrette made with kau oranges (from the Big Island), moo shu tofu with goat cheese and hoisin sauce, and sautéed beef with sweet-and-sour sauce. The price is right, too: Entrees range from $10 to $16.

$$–$$$$ Kailua isn't exactly known for its food, but when **Lucy's Grill & Bar** (33 Aulike St.; ☎ 808/230-8188; MC, V) opened in 2001, a reason for Honolulu residents to drive over the Pali was born. Serving what it calls "Euro-local" food, Lucy's Grill & Bar is a TGI Island Bistro, with Hawaiian Regional Cuisine leaning hard toward lots of sweet sauces and oversize portions, which makes it a crowd pleaser—on any given night, this surfboards-on-the-wall place is jammed with Kailua residents. Sugary Mongolian barbecue sauce is slathered on kiawe-grilled baby back ribs; ahi is crusted with pepper and served in a rich beurre blanc sauce. Expect entree prices in the $15 to $30 range. The indoor-outdoor bar is a good place to perch for a passion-fruit margarita and rub elbows with locals. Owner-chef Christian Schneider knows what he's doing—he's the son of Bobbie Lou Schneider, who owns Kailua dining landmark Buzz's Original Steakhouse (which I'm not recommending because I don't go for the teriyaki-steak-and-salad-bar scene).

THE NORTH SHORE

$–$$ For a long time, burgers and burritos were the staples on the North Shore, with everyone stopping in at Haleiwa's well-known **Kua Aina** (1116 Auahi Bay 5; ☎ 808/591-9133; cash only) for big mahimahi sandwiches. But in the past couple of years, things have changed, with young restaurateurs upping the restaurant options. When **Banzai Sushi** ★ (North Shore Market Place, 66–246B Kamehameha Hwy., Haleiwa; ☎ 808/384-4376; MC, V) opened in 2004, it quickly became a hot spot (people like seven-time world-champion surfer Kelly Slater eat here). Run by willowy blonde Brazilian import Alessia Ucelli, who was tired of driving into Honolulu three times a week for her sushi fix, Banzai serves decent sushi—you can get a complete dinner for $19—and a really good ceviche dotted with chunks of tomato and laced with cilantro and shishimi pepper, courtesy of the Brazilian chef. The open-air lanai has conventional tables and chairs and low tables at which you sit on cushions. It's great to sit and sip sake while samba and crickets in the night play.

$ At **Paradise Found Café** (66–443 Kamehameha Hwy., Haleiwa; ☎ 808/637-4540; cash only), owner-cook Chip Sandt uses locally grown organic ingredients to create tasty, filling, and cheap vegetarian food. Tucked in the back of the super-crunchy Celestial Foods health-food store in an old wood building, Paradise Found serves globally inflected food like a peanut-sauce veggie plate and over-stuffed burritos, both of which cost under $8. It's popular with local surfers who like to pop in for the fruity smoothies.

$$ New York transplants Kenny and Peggy Usamanont wanted a change from Manhattan and decided to open **Haleiwa Eats** (66–079 Kamehameha Hwy.;

Shrimp Trucks

Large-scale shrimp farming took hold in Kahuku, on the North Shore, in the early 1990s, and it wasn't long before the first lunch wagons serving freshwater Kahuku-raised shrimp made their appearance. Today, shrimp trucks are one of the area's prime roadside attractions. Bring cash, as most do not take credit cards. **Giovanni's Aloha Shrimp** (Kamehameha Hwy., sometimes in Haleiwa, sometimes in Kahuku; ☎ 808/293-1839; $$), is actually owned by a guy named Troy Nitsche, and is the granddaddy of them all. Opened in 1993 and cited in guidebooks and food magazines ever since, it's repeatedly heralded as the best. In fact, the place is so popular that it needs more shrimp than the Kahuku farms can supply—Giovanni's now gets its shrimp shipped in from Kauai. Carloads of tourists pull up to the graffiti-coated white truck to sit at plastic benches under a tent and eat platefuls of shrimp: fried and coated in garlic (and curiously called scampi), steamed and served with butter and lemon, or on fire with a famous spicy sauce. For $12, you get a dozen shrimp (and two scoops of rice) along with a side of attitude from the girls at the counter that says, "I'm sick of shrimp and tourists."

To me, the whole point of eating at a shrimp truck is to have super-fresh shrimp just plucked from a Kahuku pond. So my favorite is **Romy's Kahuku Prawns & Shrimp Hut** ★ (56–781 Kamehameha Hwy.; ☎ 808/232-2202), a stand set up right in front of Romy Aguinaldo's 31 ponds on 40 acres. During one recent visit, the friendly man at the window told me they were out of prawns, "But we're harvesting some right now." That's how fresh the crustaceans are—firm and ever so slightly sweet, you're guaranteed a naturally good product. Here, you get a half-pound of shrimp or prawns (8–10) for $11.

Joining the fray recently was the **Blue Water Shrimp & Seafood Co.** (just south of Turtle Bay Resort; no phone). Part of the local pizza chain Magoo's, Blue Water is competing with the other trucks by foregoing freshwater shrimp altogether—it serves tiger prawns from the ocean. Deep blue and painted with a cheesy underwater scene, you can't miss the truck. If serving locally raised shrimp wasn't my No. 1 criterion for best shrimp truck, I'd say this spot actually has the best food. Order the "really garlic shrimp" and you get a Styrofoam box filled with shrimp (seven for $11) sautéed in a garlicky chili sauce dotted with capers, along with crunchy slaw, a slice of pineapple, and two scoops of rice. Plus, service here is sunny.

☎ 808/637-4247; AE, DC, MC, V) after a vacation to Oahu. Kenny's mother is a Thai-restaurant veteran and he learned all her recipes, including a crunchy, tangy ginger salad, and sweet-and-tart duck slathered in tamarind sauce. At the casual cafe, with white tile floors and a big statue of a Thai angel, nothing costs more than $14.

$$–$$$ For a nicer meal on the North Shore, try **Lei Lei's** (57–091 Kamehameha Hwy., Kahuku; ☎ 808/293-2662; AE, DC, MC, V) in the Turtle Bay Resort. In winter, during big-surf season, you'll find all the top wave riders here chowing down on American food with some Pacific accents. It's casual but not cheap, with dishes like Dijon-rosemary-rubbed double pork loin chop priced at $21. The fresh island catch of the day, at $24, is always a good choice. Take a seat on the open-air lanai overlooking the golf course.

THE WEST SIDE

$ The eating options are slim on the Waianae Coast, which is the least developed area of the island. But **Hannara's** (86–078 Farrington Hwy., Makaha; ☎ 808/696-6137; MC, V) is a good, no-frills diner, serving big breakfasts of everything from eggs Benedict to fried-rice-stuffed omelets, Hawaiian food, and local plate-lunch items including chicken katsu and what the restaurant claims is the best hamburger steak on the island. And truth be told, the gravy-slathered hamburger patty with two scoops of rice is pretty damn good.

WHY YOU'RE HERE: OAHU'S BEACHES

As Oahu's population grows, the number of people on the beaches increases too. And folks never stop thinking of ways to use the water—surfing, windsurfing, kiteboarding, snorkeling, swimming, strolling, sunning, boating, fishing . . . the list goes on. For more information on what to do at Oahu's beaches, see "Active Oahu" on p. 156.

THE WAIKIKI COAST

Gold-sand **Ala Moana Beach Park** ★★ ("by the sea"), on sunny Mamala Bay, stretches for more than a mile along Honolulu's coast between downtown and Waikiki. It has a man-made beach, created in the 1930s by filling a coral reef with Waianae Coast sand, as well as its own lagoon, yacht harbor, tennis courts, music pavilion, bathhouses, picnic tables, and enough wide-open green spaces to accommodate four million visitors a year. The water is calm, protected by black lava rocks set offshore.

Famous **Waikiki Beach** ★★★, a 1½-mile-long crescent of sand (which used to be imported from Molokai), at the foot of a string of high-rise hotels, is home to the world's longest-running beach party. Despite its small size, Waikiki attracts nearly five million visitors a year.

A string of beaches extend between Sans Souci State Recreational Area, near Diamond Head to the east, and Duke Kahanamoku Beach, in front of the Hilton Hawaiian Village, to the west. Great stretches include **Kuhio Beach,** next to the Moana Surfrider, a Westin; **Grey's Beach,** in front of the Royal Hawaiian Hotel; and **Sans Souci,** in front of the New Otani Kaimana Beach Hotel.

Facilities in Waikiki include showers, lifeguards, restrooms, grills, picnic tables, and pavilions at the Queen's Surf end of the beach (at Kapiolani Park, between the zoo and the aquarium). The best place to park is at Kapiolani Park, near Sans Souci.

Beaches & Outdoor Pursuits on Oahu

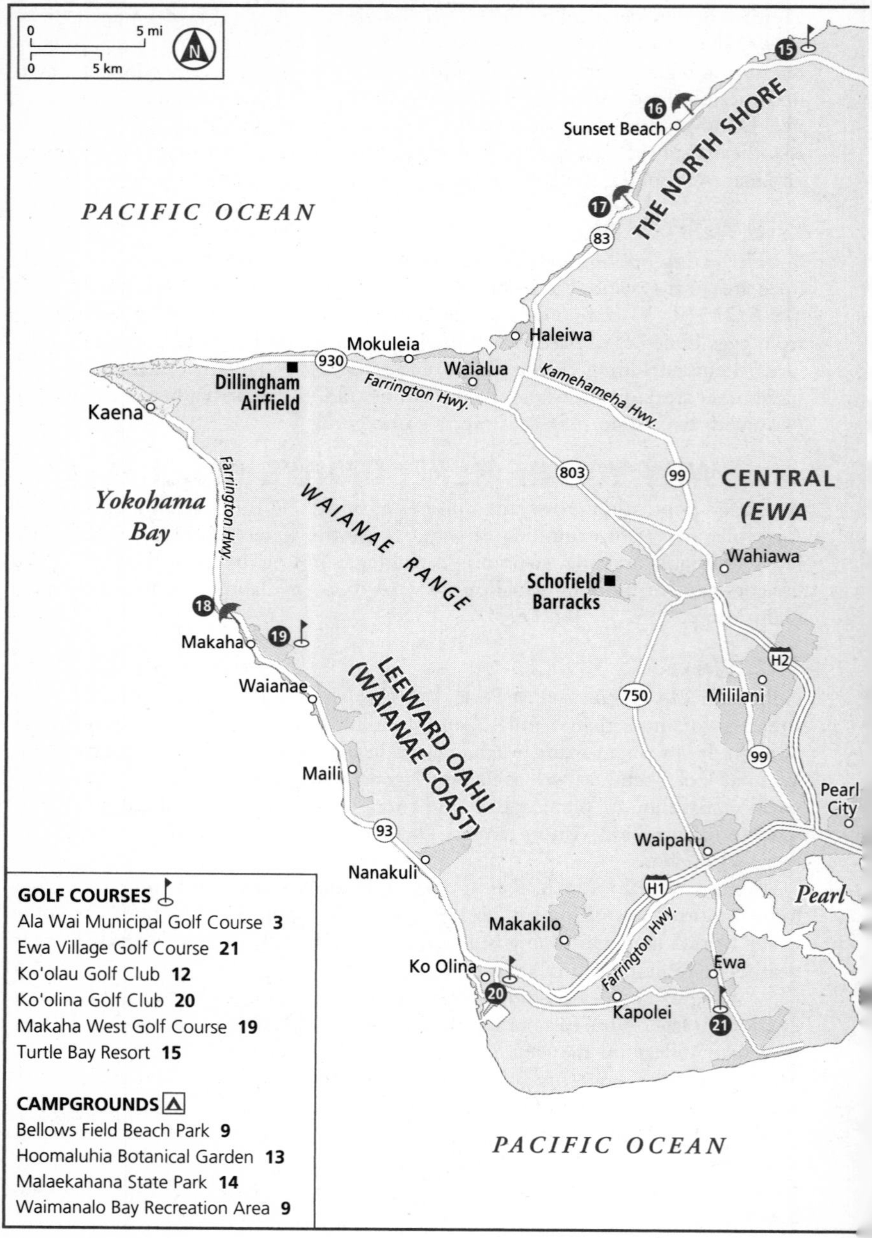

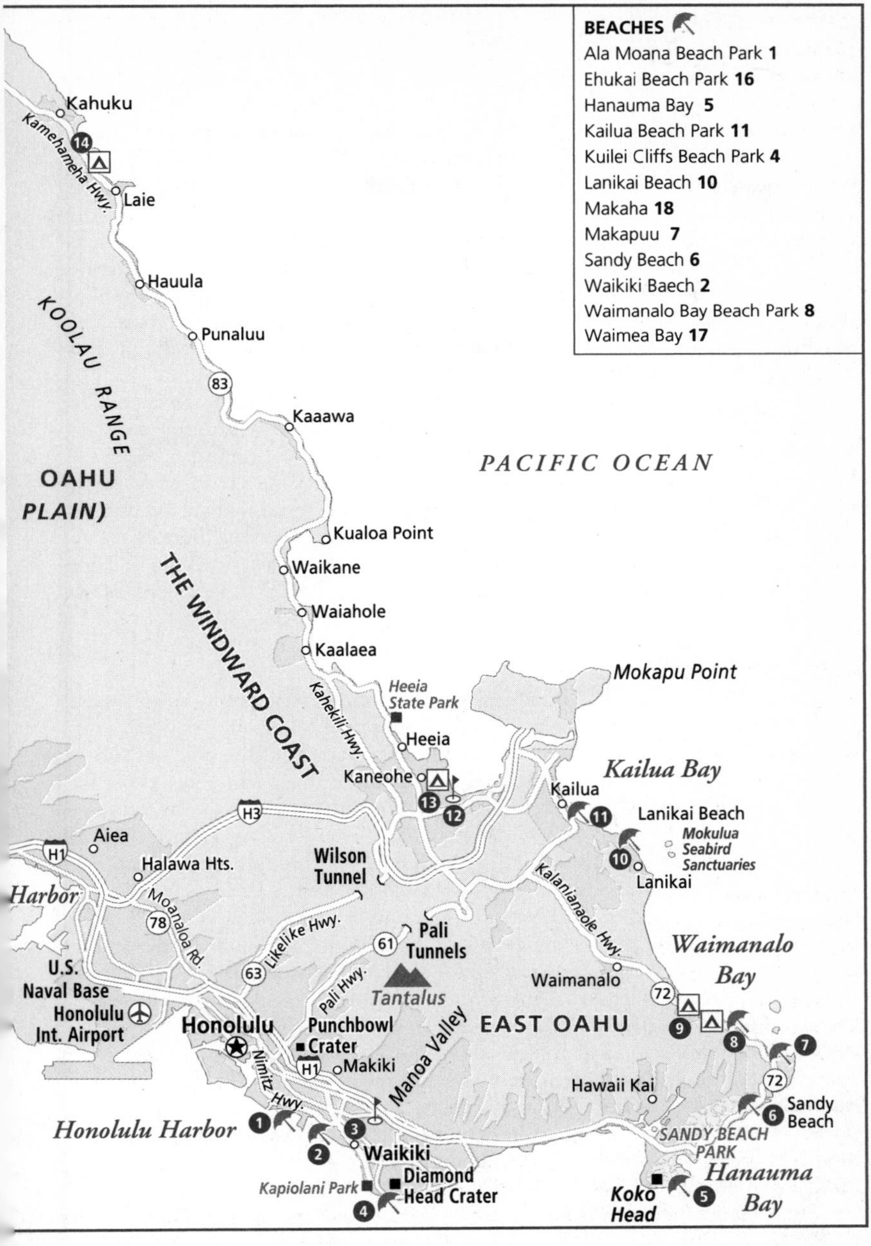
BEACHES
Ala Moana Beach Park 1
Ehukai Beach Park 16
Hanauma Bay 5
Kailua Beach Park 11
Kuilei Cliffs Beach Park 4
Lanikai Beach 10
Makaha 18
Makapuu 7
Sandy Beach 6
Waikiki Baech 2
Waimanalo Bay Beach Park 8
Waimea Bay 17
Kahuku
Kamehameha Hwy.
Laie
Hauula
Punaluu
83
Kaaawa
KOOLAU RANGE
OAHU
PLAIN)
PACIFIC OCEAN
Kualoa Point
Waikane
Waiahole
Kaalaea
THE WINDWARD COAST
Kahekili Hwy.
Heeia State Park
Heeia
Mokapu Point
Kaneohe
Kailua Bay
Kailua
Lanikai Beach
Mokulua Seabird Sanctuaries
Lanikai
H3
Aiea
H1
Halawa Hts.
Harbor
Wilson Tunnel
Moanaloa Rd.
78
Likelike Hwy.
Kalanianaole Hwy.
Pali Tunnels
61
63
U.S. Naval Base
Honolulu Int. Airport
Pali Hwy.
Tantalus
Waimanalo
Waimanalo Bay
72
Honolulu
Punchbowl Crater
Manoa Valley
EAST OAHU
Nimitz Hwy.
Makiki
Hawaii Kai
Honolulu Harbor
Waikiki
Sandy Beach
SANDY BEACH PARK
Hanauma Bay
Kapiolani Park
Diamond Head Crater
Koko Head

EAST OAHU

Oahu's most popular snorkeling spot is **Hanauma Bay** ★★, a volcanic crater with a broken sea wall; its small, curved, 2,000-foot gold-sand beach is packed elbow-to-elbow with people.

Sandy Beach ★ is one of the best bodysurfing beaches on Oahu, but it's also one of the most dangerous. Weak swimmers and children should stay out of the water here; Sandy Beach's heroic lifeguards make more rescues in a year than those at any other beach. Take a look at the flags they post to alert beachgoers to the day's surf: Green means safe, yellow caution, and red indicates very dangerous water conditions. Facilities include restrooms and parking. From Waikiki, drive east on the H-1, which becomes Kalanianaole Highway; proceed past Hawaii Kai, up the hill to Hanauma Bay, past the Halona Blow Hole, and along the coast. The next big, gold, sandy beach you see ahead on the right is Sandy Beach. TheBus no. 22 will also bring you here.

Makapuu Beach Park is a beautiful 1,000-foot-long gold-sand beach cupped in the stark black Koolau cliffs on Oahu's easternmost point. You've probably seen this site featured in TV shows like *Hawaii Five-O* or *Magnum, P.I.* In summer, the ocean here is gentle, and swimming and diving are perfect. But come winter, Makapuu is hit with expert bodysurfers, who come for big, pounding waves that are too dangerous for regular swimmers. Small boards—3 feet or less with no skeg (bottom fin)—are permitted; regular board surfing is banned by state law. Facilities include restrooms, lifeguards, barbecue grills, picnic tables, and parking. To get here, follow Kalanianaole Highway toward Waimanalo, or take TheBus no. 57 or 58.

THE WINDWARD COAST

One of Hawaii's best spots for swimming, the crystal-clear lagoon at gold-sand **Lanikai Beach** is like a giant saltwater swimming pool filled with resident tropical fish and sea turtles. It's a mile long and thin in places, but the sand's as soft as talcum powder. Prevailing onshore trade winds make this an excellent place for sailing and windsurfing. Kayakers often paddle out to the two tiny offshore Mokulua islands, which are seabird sanctuaries. There are no facilities. From Waikiki, take the H-1 to the Pali Highway (Hwy. 61) through the Nuuanu Pali Tunnel to Kailua, where the Pali Highway becomes Kailua Road as it proceeds through town. At Kalaheo Avenue, turn right and follow the coast about 2 miles to Kailua Beach Park; just past it, turn left at the T intersection and drive uphill on Aalapapa Drive, a one-way street that loops back as Mokulua Drive. Park on Mokulua Drive and walk down any of the eight public-access lanes to the shore. Or, take TheBus no. 56 or 57 (Kailua) and transfer to the shuttle bus.

Two-mile-long, wide, and golden, **Kailua Beach** ★★★ has dunes, palm trees, panoramic views, and offshore islets that are home to seabirds. The swimming is excellent. It's also a favorite spot to sail catamarans, bodysurf or windsurf the gentle waves, and paddle a kayak. Water conditions are quite safe, especially at the mouth of Kaelepulu Stream, where toddlers play in the freshwater shallows at the middle of the beach park.

The 35-acre beach park is intersected by a freshwater stream and watched over by lifeguards. Facilities include picnic tables, barbecues, restrooms, a volleyball court, a public boat ramp, free parking, and an open-air cafe. Kailua's new bike path weaves through the park, and windsurfer and kayak rentals are available as well. To get here, take Pali Highway (Hwy. 61) to Kailua, drive through town, turn right on Kalaheo Avenue, and go a mile until you see the beach on your left. Or, take TheBus no. 56 or 57 into Kailua, then the no. 70 shuttle.

Kualoa Regional Park ★★ is on Kaneohe Bay's north shore, at the foot of the spiky Koolau Ridge. This 150-acre coco palm–fringed peninsula is the biggest beach park on the windward side and one of Hawaii's most scenic. Its long, narrow, white-sand beach is ideal for swimming, walking, beachcombing, kite-flying, or just enjoying the natural beauty. The waters are shallow and safe for swimming year-round (lifeguards are on duty). At low tide, you can swim or wade out to Mokolii (also known as Chinaman's Hat), which has a small sandy beach and is a bird preserve. The park is on Kamehameha Highway (Hwy. 83) in Kualoa; you can get here via TheBus no. 55.

THE NORTH SHORE

Malaekahana Bay State Recreation Area ★★, almost a mile-long white crescent, is excellent for swimming. On a weekday you may be the only one here; but should some net fisherman—or kindred soul—intrude upon your delicious privacy, you can swim out to Goat Island (or wade across at low tide) and play Robinson Crusoe. (The islet is a sanctuary for seabirds and turtles; don't chase them.) Facilities include restrooms, barbecue grills, picnic tables, outdoor showers, and parking.

To get here, take Kamehameha Highway (Hwy. 83) 2 miles north of the Polynesian Cultural Center; as you enter the main gate, you'll come upon the wooded beach park. Or you can take TheBus no. 52.

Waimea Beach Park ★★ is a deep, sandy bowl providing gentle summer waves that are excellent for swimming, snorkeling, and bodysurfing. But winter waves pound the narrow bay, sometimes rising to 50 feet high. When the surf's really up, very strong currents and shore breaks sweep the bay—and it seems like everyone on Oahu drives out to Waimea to get a look at the monster waves and those who ride them.

Facilities include lifeguards, restrooms, showers, parking, and nearby restaurants and shops in Haleiwa town. The beach is on Kamehameha Highway (Hwy. 83); from Waikiki, you can take TheBus no. 52.

LEEWARD OAHU/THE WAIANAE COAST

When surf's up here, it's spectacular at **Makaha Beach Park** ★★: Monstrous waves pound the beach. The original home of Hawaii's big-wave surfing championship, surfers today know it as the home of Buffalo's Big Board Surf Classic. Nearly a mile long, this half-moon, gold-sand beach is tucked between 231-foot Lahilahi Point, which locals call Black Rock, and Kepuhi Point, a toe of the Waianae mountain range. Summer is the best time to visit, when the water's safe for swimming. ***A caveat:*** This is a "local" beach; you're welcome, of course, but make sure to be respectful of the beach and the residents.

Facilities include restrooms, lifeguards, and parking. To get here, take the H-1 freeway to the end of the line, where it becomes Farrington Highway (Hwy. 93), and follow it to the beach; or take TheBus no. 51.

Where Farrington Highway (Hwy. 93) ends, the wilderness of **Kaena Point State Park** begins. It's a remote 853-acre coastline park of empty beaches, sand dunes, cliffs, and deep-blue water. This is the last sandy stretch of shore on the northwest coast of Oahu. Sometimes, it's known as Keawalua Beach or Puau Beach, but everybody here calls it **Yokohama Bay** ★, after the Japanese immigrants who came from that port city to work the cane fields and fished along this shoreline. When the surf's calm—mainly in summer—this is a good area for snorkeling, diving, swimming, shore fishing, and picnicking. When surf's up, board- and bodysurfers are out in droves; don't go in the water then unless you're an expert. There are no lifeguards or facilities, except at the park entrance, where there's a restroom and lifeguard stand.

THE TOP SIGHTS & ATTRACTIONS

Aside from its natural beauty, Oahu has international historical significance for its pivotal role in World War II, ancient sites that reveal secrets of traditional Polynesian life, and some remarkable art.

WORLD WAR II SITES

On December 7, 1941, Japanese planes bombed Oahu's Pearl Harbor—home to the U.S.'s Pacific fleet—and 2,280 military and 68 civilians were killed. Eight battleships were destroyed or badly damaged, and as a result the United States plunged into World War II. For many Americans, that "day of infamy" is seared into their memories, but until 1962 there was no appropriate place for them to visit. In that year, an elegant, simple, and highly affecting memorial, designed by architect Alfred Preis, was built over one of the lost ships, the USS *Arizona,* and it has been Oahu's top visitor attraction since the day it opened.

The *Arizona* Memorial ★★★ (1 Arizona Memorial Rd.; ☎ 808/422-0561; www.arizonamemorial.org; 7:30am–5pm, first tour starts at 8am, subsequent tours every 15 min. thereafter, with last tour at 3pm; free) is part of a visitors complex at Pearl Harbor, which is still an active naval station. The small on-site museum and bookstore are always crowded—about 4,500 people stream through here daily, so it's best to go early before the throngs arrive and the heat of the day

Creating a World War II Itinerary

Oahu's three major World War II memorials are clustered at Pearl Harbor, and the Hawaii Army Museum is in Waikiki. At Pearl Harbor, of course, the crown jewel is the *Arizona* Memorial. Right next to it is the USS *Bowfin* Submarine Museum & Park, and the Battleship *Missouri* Memorial, on Ford Island, is a short shuttle ride away. While the *Arizona* is part of the National Park Service and the *Bowfin* and *Missouri* are run by nonprofit organizations, together they make a fascinating whole, and it's possible to see all three in 1 day (although you'll be pretty tired by the end). Do the tour according to the chronology of the war of the Pacific, starting with the *Arizona,* continuing to the *Bowfin,* then the *Missouri,* on whose deck the war ended (about a 6-hr. day of military might). If you have time for just one, it should be the *Arizona* Memorial.

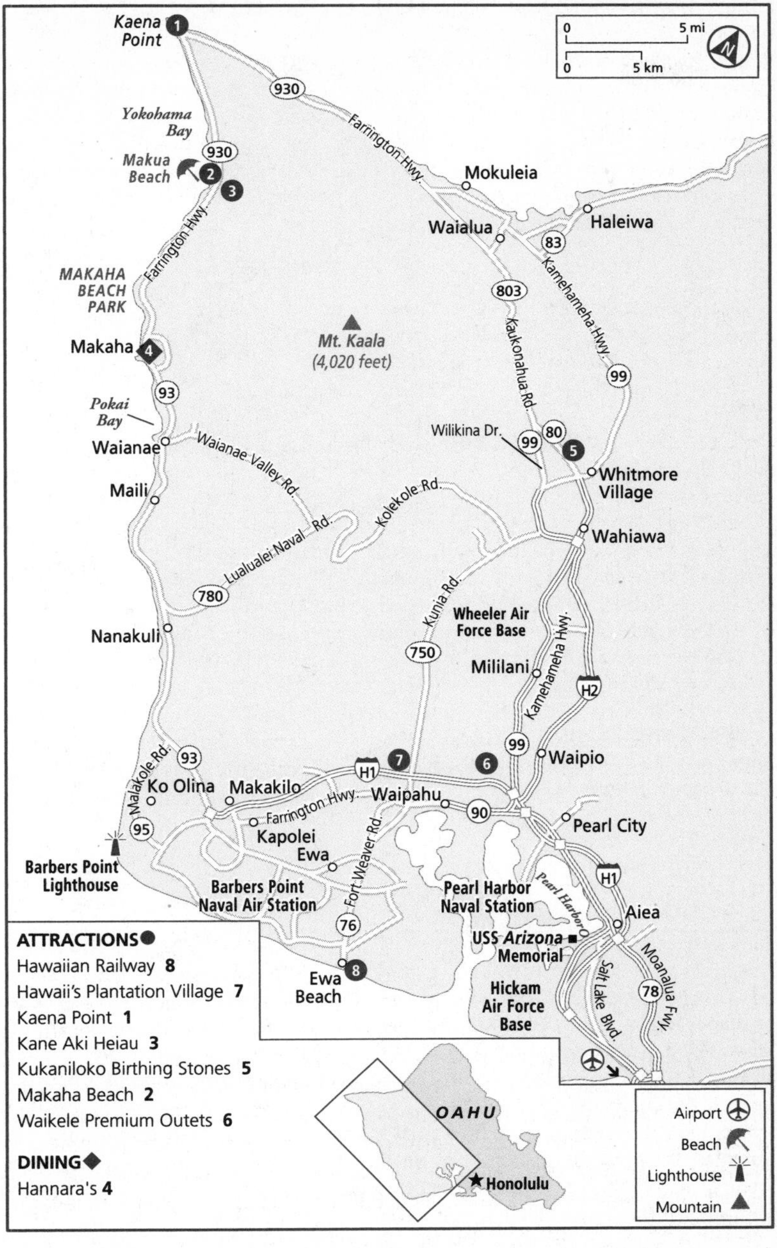

ATTRACTIONS

- Hawaiian Railway **8**
- Hawaii's Plantation Village **7**
- Kaena Point **1**
- Kane Aki Heiau **3**
- Kukaniloko Birthing Stones **5**
- Makaha Beach **2**
- Waikele Premium Outets **6**

DINING

- Hannara's **4**

Downtown & Chinatown

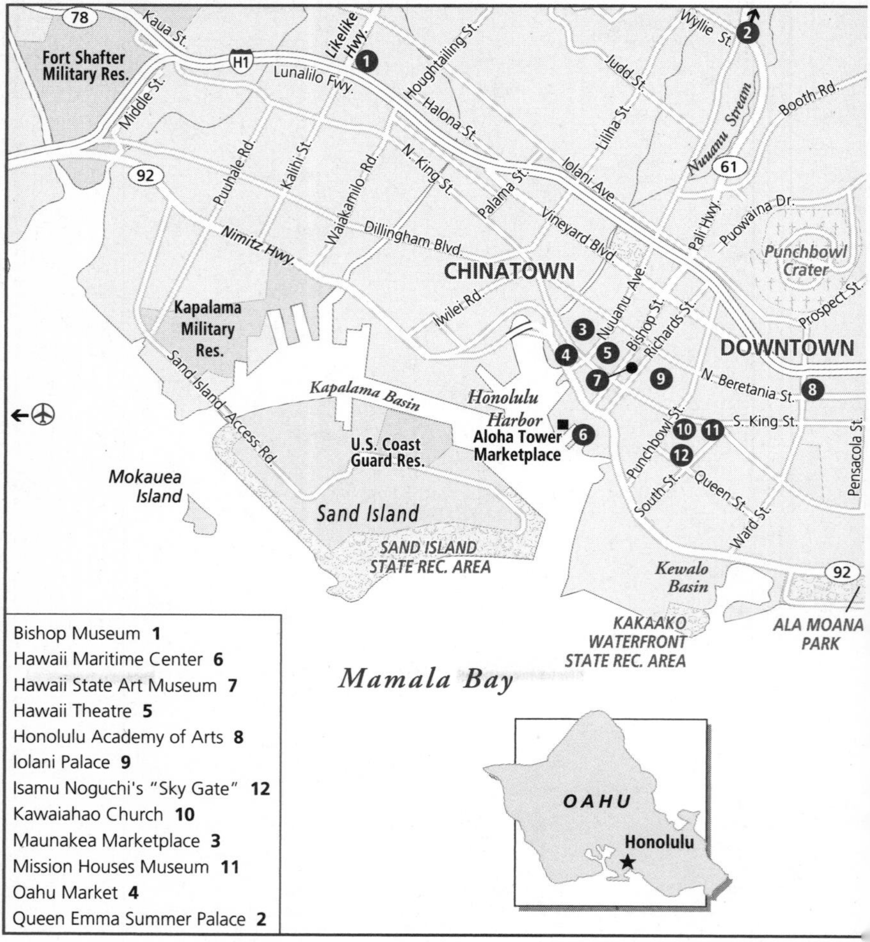

sets in. (Also, leave any kind of bag—purse, fanny pack, backpack, camera bag, or diaper bag—in the car, as security is very strict.) Built in 1980, the visitor center was designed to accommodate 750,000 people a year but today the number is around 1.6 million and the worn structure is sinking. Plans to build a new $27-million building are in the works.

Your short boat trip to the memorial is preceded by a powerful 23-minute documentary that vividly depicts the attack. Emerging from this film to the actual scene of it is highly surreal; and once you get to the *Arizona* Memorial, a visceral reminder of the attack awaits—the water above the USS *Arizona* is shiny with oil that still oozes from the ship. (And the knowledge that down below, in the ship, are the remains of many of the 1,777 crew only heightens emotions.)

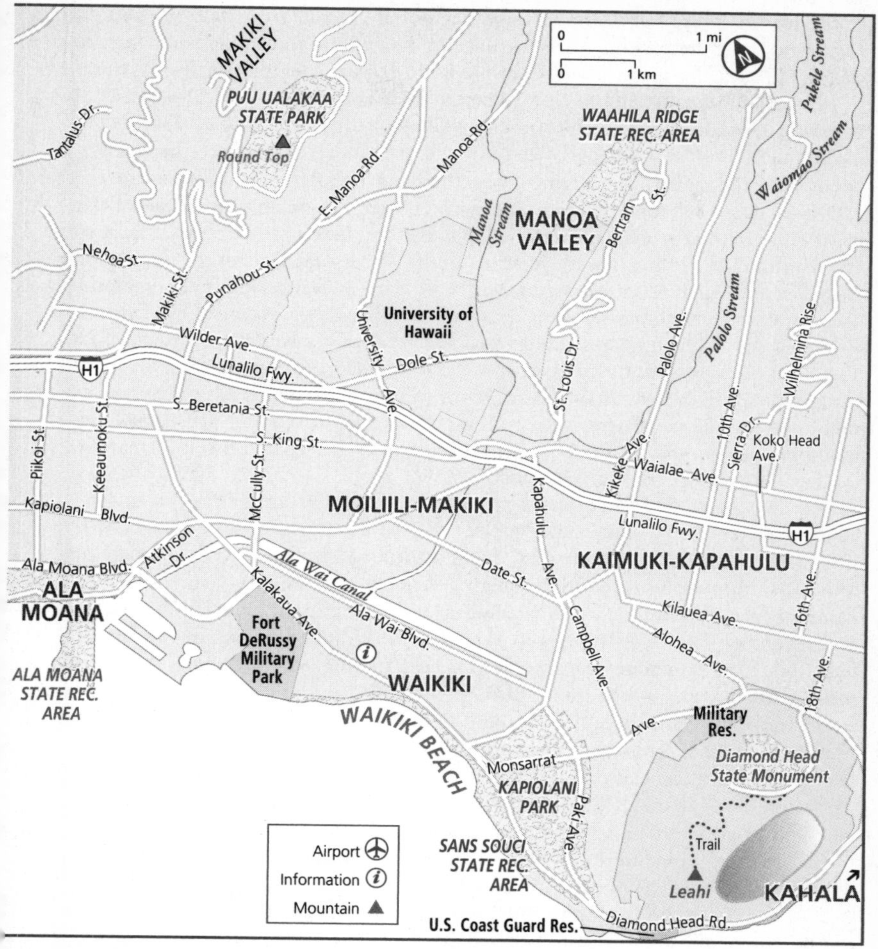

The memorial took on new significance to visitors and locals after the September 11, 2001, terrorist attacks. In fact, many people now visit the memorial on the anniversary of 9/11, when there is a bell ringing and a minute of silence. The flags that fly over the memorial are now sought-after symbols. Tattered by trade winds, the flags are replaced every 6 weeks. They used to be given to a local Boy Scout troop to be burned (a proper flag disposal), but are now requested across the country, and have been given to the National Mall in D.C., and New York City's Police Museum, among others.

An important note on travel directions: Driving to the memorial is tricky. From Honolulu, take H-1 West and exit at USS Arizona/Stadium 15A. Don't take the Pearl Harbor exit. Continue on HI-99 (Kamehameha Hwy.) and turn left at the fourth traffic light onto *Arizona* Memorial Place. At the base of the hill, turn right, and the parking lot is on the left. For public transport, you can take the no. 20 or 42 bus from Waikiki to the USS *Arizona* Memorial Visitor Center.

At the **USS *Bowfin* Submarine Museum & Park** ★ (11 Arizona Memorial Dr.; ☎ 808/423-1341; www.bowfin.org; daily 8am–5pm; $10 adults, $3 children 4-12; children under 4 not permitted for safety reasons), adjacent to the *Arizona* Memorial, the famed submarine is berthed off the park grounds where the 10,000-square-foot museum sits. Submarines were responsible for some of the most effective retaliations against the Japanese, and here you have the chance to crawl around one of the most successful World War II predators of the deep—the USS *Bowfin,* which was nicknamed the "Pearl Harbor Avenger." Experiencing the claustrophobia of submarine life is the draw here—men were stacked like cards in a deck in the sleeping quarters and you'll feel what that meant as you tour; you'll also have the opportunity to peer into the dark chambers of the torpedo room (kids will especially love this). The museum section of the site is less interesting to me, featuring the usual array of paintings, photographs, models, and things that go boom (a C-3 missile). See above for driving instructions and bus information.

The **Battleship *Missouri* Memorial** ★ (Ford Island; ☎ 808/973-2494; www.ussmissouri.com; daily 9am–5pm; $16 for adults, $8 for children ages 4–12 years, children 3 and under are free; for $22 in combination with USS *Bowfin,* Chief's tour $22, Captain's tour $33, Explorer's tour $45) takes you from crushing blow to stunning victory—the "Mighty Mo" is the ship on which Foreign Minister Mamoru Shigemitsu formally surrendered to Gen. Douglas MacArthur on September 2, 1945. Brought to Hawaii in 1998 (after serving in the Persian Gulf War) to complete the Pacific Theater picture, the *Missouri* is now a museum/memorial with exhibits throughout consisting of videos, photographs, audio recordings of people like Admiral Stuart Murray (Mighty Mo's captain at the time of the surrender), and blueprints of the ship. Visitors can explore the teak-wood decks on their own or take the 1-hour Chief's guided tour, but if you're really interested in naval history, I recommend one of two premium tours that take you to areas off-limits to the general public. The 90-minute Captain's tour includes refreshments in the captain's cabin and walks through the officers' quarters, the area where the massive anchors are dropped, and the area housing the big guns. The 90-minute Explorer's tour equips you with flashlights and takes you to the bowels of the ship, into the fire rooms and "Broadway," where the switchboard and analog computers controlled the ship's massive gun turrets—perfect for people who watch the History Channel and love war lore. Both are worthwhile, and kids will love climbing up the ladders and clambering through steel hatches.

Berthed at Ford Island, which is still an active military facility, the *Missouri* is accessible only by shuttle bus from the USS *Bowfin* Submarine Museum & Park (see above), which is also where you buy your tickets.

For hard-core military-history fans only, the **Hawaii Army Museum** (2055 Kalia Rd.; ☎ 808/955-9552; www.hiarmymuseumsoc.org; 10am–4:15pm Tues–Sun; free) is the last of Oahu's sites dedicated to war. Part of the Fort DeRussy Recreation Center, 18 military-controlled acres in Waikiki, the museum is housed in a former R&R center with exhibits that span the ages from ancient Hawaiian warfare to the Vietnam War (and, of course, there's a section on World War II).

ANCIENT OAHU

Sprinkled around the island are the fascinating and often highly mysterious remnants of traditional Hawaiian culture. Because precontact Hawaiians had no written language, Oahu's ancient history is largely speculative. Accounts of traditions and events are pieced together from archaeological studies and fragments of oral history that survived. That's why dates and quantitative data are sketchy. But it's kind of sexy, and appropriate, the way legend mixes with fact in Hawaii. Bear in mind that sites such as *heiau* (temples), are still sacred to Hawaiians. Don't climb on them or take souvenir rocks (remember what happened to the Brady Bunch?).

> *"Nothing had prepared me for Honolulu . . . . All these strange people live close to each other, with different languages and different thoughts; they believe in a different god and they have different values; two passions alone they share, love and hunger. And somehow as you watch them, you have an impression of extraordinary vitality."*
>
> —W. Somerset Maugham, 1921

Towering in importance above all the rest is Oahu's largest remaining sacrificial temple, **Puu O Mahuka Heiau** ★★ (Pupukea Rd.; free), where three of Captain George Vancouver's men, who were sent ashore to fetch fresh water, were sacrificed in 1792. Up on Pupukea, a 300-foot bluff overlooking Waimea Bay, Puu O Mahuka may look like little more than a big rectangular stone wall, but there's no disputing the *mana* (spiritual power) emanating from this sacred site, built in the 1600s and occupying a full 5 acres. This is where the great *kahuna* (high priest) Kaopulupulu presided in the 1770s. In 1779, Kahahana, king of Oahu, didn't trust Kaopulupulu and had him murdered, but before the *kahuna* died, he made his famous prediction that foreigners would conquer Oahu, according to Hawaiian historian George Kanahele. Today the site, a National Historic Monument, is tranquil, with few visitors. Hawaiians still come to drape leis on the rocks as offerings to the gods represented here: Kanaloa, Kane, Ku, and Lono. If you visit in November, come at dusk; you can see the Makalii (Pleiades to Westerners) rise at Kaena Point to the left. The event marks the start of Makahiki—time of harvest and bounty for Hawaiians. Walk to the bottom of the *heiau,* take a short red-dirt trail to the edge and look down at the white crescent of Waimea Bay.

If you're driving: Coming from Haleiwa on Kamehameha Highway, Puu O Mahuka is just a mile past Waimea Bay. Turn right on Pupukea Road (at Foodland), drive ¾ mile up, and make a right on an unmarked, single-lane paved (barely) road that will lead you to the parking lot at the *heiau.* By bus: Take no. 52 to Foodland, and then walk up Pupukea Road.

At **Ulupo Heiau** ★★ (Manu O'o St., Kailua; free) you'll feel like you've stepped back in time—it's hard to believe you're just 15 minutes from downtown Honolulu and 2 miles from Kailua at this serene spot (the name means "night of inspiration"). Archaeologists estimate that Ulupo Heiau was built between A.D. 700 and 800, originally as a temple to agriculture and later as a place to pray for victory in war. The walls of the terraced stone platform reach upwards of 30 feet. Surrounded by mango trees, the *heiau* is one of the oldest in Hawaii, which makes sense because Kailua was one of the first areas in the islands settled by Polynesians. At the bottom of the *heiau* is a *lo'i* (taro patch) where you may see volunteer Bill Fien working the muddy square of land as Hawaiians have for centuries. (If he's on a break, ask him about taro farming and the area's natural springs.) If you have time to wander, a path from the *heiau* leads to the remnants of ancient *lo'i* and, beyond that, Kawainui Marsh, a protected bird habitat.

If you're driving: Take the Pali Highway from Honolulu. After you've passed through the tunnels, take the first left after the second stoplight (Castle Junction) onto Uluoa Street, then turn right on Manu Aloha Street, and right on Manu O'o Street, where you'll see a parking lot and YMCA. The *heiau* is behind the YMCA.

Amidst Central Oahu's pineapple fields and military housing is another of the island's most sacred Hawaiian sites: **Kukaniloko Birthstones State Monument** ★. For 700 years, this is where royalty came to give birth. Hawaiians believed that the stones relieved pain and that the gods blessed children born here. More than 80 rounded lava rocks, their tops crusted with lichen, are clustered on this flat plain, surrounded by thin-trunked coconut and eucalyptus trees. Kukaniloko is worth a stop en route to the North Shore from Honolulu.

If you're driving: Take Kamehameha Highway toward Wahiawa. You'll come to an intersection with California Avenue; ¾ mile past the intersection, at Whitmore Avenue, turn left onto a dirt road. Proceed a quarter mile through the pineapple field until you come to the parking area.

If you go out to Makaha to do the Kaena Point hike or are staying at the Makaha Golf Club Resort & Hotel, I recommend stopping at one final outdoor temple: **Kane Aki Heiau** (Makaha Valley Rd.; ★ 808/695-8174; Tues–Sun 10am–2pm). A smaller *heiau* than the ones mentioned above, Kane Aki Heiau was dedicated to Lono, god of the harvest and fertility. The site has been nicely restored with a grass hut on-site, though since it sits on private land, the *heiau* is open to visitors for only 4 hours a day.

If you're driving: From Honolulu, take H-1 westbound until it turns into Farrington Highway. Turn right on Makaha Valley Road and follow the KANEAKI HEIAU signs.

MUSEUMS OF SCIENCE & CULTURE

From ancient Hawaiian history to cutting-edge contemporary art, Oahu's museums are worth your time. The island's geographical location has resulted in it being a nexus of Polynesian, Asian, and Western art.

I never tire of the **Bishop Museum** ★★★ (1525 Bernice St.; ☎ 808/847-3511; www.bishopmuseum.org; daily 9am–5pm except Christmas; Admission $16 adults, $13 children 4–12 and seniors). It's like the British Museum—filled with irreplaceable cultural and natural artifacts from across the Pacific (it's also one of the foremost research centers on natural history in the region). The museum was the brainchild of Princess Bernice Pauahi Bishop, the half-Caucasian, half-Hawaiian noblewoman who was the last descendant of the royal Kamehameha line. In the late 1800s, she saw that her culture and people were slipping away and wanted to preserve her Hawaiian artifacts and royal family heirlooms. Though she did not live to see that happen—Bishop died in 1884—her husband, Charles Reed Bishop, founded the museum in 1889 in accordance with his wife's will.

Hawaiian History 101

If you want to take a tour and learn about Hawaiian culture, I recommend **Mauka Makai Excursions** (350 Ward Ave.; ☎ 808/255-2206; www.hawaiianecotours.net; $50–$80 adults, $40–$60 children), led by the ebullient Dominic Kealoha Aki. Aki is the real deal—his knowledge of history is extraordinary and he's careful about following Hawaiian protocol such as chanting before entering sacred sites. He'll take you to nooks and crannies, such as a sea cave where you can see petroglyphs that even most locals don't know about. Mauka Makai offers two full-day tours, Legends and Myths of Koolau-poko (includes Ulupo Heiau) and Sacred Sites of Oahu's North Shore (includes Puu O Mahuka Heiau). If you have less time, there's a half-day tour. The fee is worth every penny.

Today the museum bustles with activity like a small college campus, composed of three buildings plus a planetarium, each brimming with exhibits. If you have limited time, head directly to Hawaiian Hall. Set in a dark, hushed 1890s black lava-stone building, this is where you'll find the princess's treasures (along with other pieces collected in the last 125 years)—hundreds of Hawaiian artifacts in glass cases on three tiered levels, in the center of which hangs a model of a sperm whale, a symbol of bygone whaling days (sperm whales are rare in Hawaii waters today). The skilled (and lost) artistry of old Hawaii is seen in the royal capes of gold and red—made from hundreds of thousands of feathers (most of the birds they came from are now extinct). One on view actually draped the shoulders of King Kamehameha I, a figure who looms large in the collective consciousness of Hawaiians. Another distinctive treasure are the *lei niho palaoa,* necklaces made of thin strands of finely braided human hair, that only the highest rank of *alii* (royalty) wore. Also of note are the artifacts from everyday life—stone poi pounders, the island's last grass hut, big wood bowls, and fishhooks carved from bone.

For a bigger Pacific picture, head to the Polynesian Hall, a two-floor gallery of clothing, weapons, tools, and other artifacts from Tonga, Fiji, the Marquesas, and other cultures in Polynesia, Melanesia, and Micronesia. Castle Hall is where traveling exhibitions are housed. The on-site planetarium teaches visitors about Hawaii's skies.

The newest attraction at the Bishop, the **Science Adventure Center** ★, opened in November 2005 to much acclaim. A modern curvilinear building with three levels of interactive exhibits, it's the place to learn about natural Hawaii. One of the most effective exhibits is a high-tech re-creation of Kilauea's active vent called Pu'u O'o, where visitors watch staff throw cinders into a furnace to melt it into lava, which drips out glowing orange. Other displays show how waves form and feature Hawaii's indigenous wildlife.

Seminars and performances: Staff scientists like entomologist Neal Evanhuis and archaeologist Tianlong Jiao are leaders in their fields, constantly discovering new bug species or forming new theories about migration to Hawaii. I like to learn about what they're doing by attending the museum's seminars, talks, and workshops, all listed on the website. In any given week, there's at least one such event scheduled. The museum also features daily hula performances (at 11am and 2pm) and Hawaiian-craft demonstrations.

An offshoot of the Bishop Museum, the **Hawaii Maritime Center** ★★ (kids) (Pier 7, next to Aloha Tower, Honolulu Harbor; ☎ 808/536-6373; www.bishopmuseum.org/exhibits/hmc/hmc.html; daily 8:30am–5pm; $7.50 adults, $4.50 children 6–17) is a 15-minute drive away at Honolulu Harbor, right near where big cruise ships dock. Expertly curated, this complex of a museum and two ships covers the history of everything maritime, from surfing to luxury liners to ancient Hawaiian navigation to whaling. Kids love the giant humpback-whale skeleton suspended from the ceiling of the King Kalakaua Boathouse Museum. The center includes the *Falls of Clyde,* an 1878 four-masted four-rigger ship, the last one of its kind on the planet, which you can explore. Also berthed at the center is the *Hokulea,* the seagoing pride of Oahu. This replica of a traditional double-hulled sailing canoe is what Polynesians sailed across the Pacific Ocean in. But the *Hokulea* isn't always there—captained by local hero Nainoa Thompson, the vessel goes on long-distance trips, navigating by the stars as the ancient Hawaiians did.

PALACES, VILLAGES & OTHER HISTORIC SITES

In less than 100 years, Hawaii's royalty went from living in thatched houses to a palace that had electricity when the White House was still in the dark. At **Iolani Palace** ★ (364 S. King St.; see Downtown & Chinatown map on p. 140; ☎ 808/522-0832; www.iolanipalace.org; Tues–Sat 9am–4pm; prices below; reservations recommended), you see the embodiment of that lavishness and a powerful symbol of a lost sovereign nation—Queen Liliuokalani was held here under house arrest after her overthrow. King Kalakaua had the four-story Italian Renaissance palace built in 1882 to the tune of $360,000, a price that almost bankrupted the government. But Hawaiian royalty didn't stay in it long; 11 years later the U.S. government overthrew the Hawaiian monarchy. A symbol of independence for today's sovereignty movement, this is where activist marches for Hawaiian issues often start. The red-and-gold throne room, holding the royal seats of King Kalakaua and Queen Kapiolani, gives an inkling of the Hawaiian nobles' taste for opulence. You can take the 90-minute guided Grand Tour of the palace (be prepared to put on booties so you don't scuff the shiny wood floors), or explore the Palace Galleries on your own. In the galleries, you'll view the royal jewels, including a crown that was stolen by a guard in the 1890s, but was later recovered and removed from the palace with the other jewels for safekeeping. In 2000 the whole set was reinstalled in the refurbished galleries, back in the palace for the first time in more than 100 years. **Guided Tours** are $20 adults, $5 children 5–17; Audio Tour $12 adults, $5 children ages 5-17; Galleries Tour $6 adults, $3 children 5–17. Combine a visit to Iolani Palace with a stop at the Hawaii State Art Museum across the street.

Queen Emma Summer Palace ★★ (2193 Pali Hwy.; see Downtown & Chinatown map on p. 140; ☎ 808/595-3167; www.daughtersofhawaii.org; daily 9am–4pm; $6 adults, $1 children) is a royal dwelling of a much more modest sort. Honolulu matrons dressed in muumuu—members of the Daughters of Hawaii—maintain (with no state or federal funding) the country getaway of Queen Emma, wife of King Kamehameha IV. The 1848 "palace" is really a seven-room Greek Revival home, but the estate is a lovely stop, and the ladies on duty are always happy to chat—talking with them is a good way to meet people who have deep roots in Hawaii. You can tickle the ivories of the 1865 Dresden piano "if you really know how to play," says the staff. The furnishings—like 19th-century English carved beds and feathered *kahili* (standards)—were taken from all seven of Queen Emma's homes. Walking through the house and around the lush green grounds offers a glimpse into the short-lived era of royal gentility in Hawaii. Follow your visit here with a stop at the Nuuanu Pali (p. 153).

After the gilt of royal heritage at places such as Iolani Palace and the Bishop Museum, **Hawaii's Plantation Village** ★ (94-95 Waipahu St., Waipahu; see Central & Leeward Oahu map on p. 139; ☎ 808/677-0110; www.hawaiiplantationvillage.org; Mon–Sat 10am–3pm; $13 adults, $10 seniors, $5 children 4–11) reveals life on the other end of the economic spectrum. It showcases how plantation workers—hailing from China to Puerto Rico—lived around 1900. Restored and replica camp houses, the plantation store (where laborers spent most of the little cash they made), and community venues such as a sumo ring are set on the 50 acres of the Waipahu Cultural Garden Park. Homes are filled with the tools of daily life donated by local families. The tour is an hour long, and it's worth the time. Afterward, go see the Kukaniloko birthing stones (p. 144).

If you walk toward the water on Richards Street and make a left on King Street, you'll come to **Kawaiahao Church** (at Punchbowl and King sts.; ☎ 808/522-1333). The island's oldest church, completed in 1842, is on the site of the grass thatch house of worship that the first Protestant missionaries built in 1820. Made of giant coral blocks cut from the reef, the church is airy and white inside with wood beams and pews. Hawaiian elite have their weddings here, and services are held in Hawaiian on Sunday at 9am—that's the time to come. At the **Mission Houses Museum** (553 King St., at Kawaiahao St.; ☎ 808/531-0481; www.missionhouses.org; Tues–Sat 10am–4pm; $10 adults, $8 seniors, $6 students), the course of Hawaiian history was changed forever. Protestant missionaries set up their Sandwich Islands Mission here in 1820, and the small cluster of buildings remains. A "living history" museum, houses are set up with period items—dishes on tables, wooden four-poster beds—as if the missionaries were still in residence. The centerpiece of the grounds is the 1821 Frame House, the oldest wood house in the state. The missionaries introduced the written word to Hawaii, and the Printing House is the place where the first Hawaiian-language book—the Bible, of course—was produced. In the coral-block Chamberlain House is an exhibition space where shows featuring traditions such as Hawaiian quilting are installed. Founded in 1920 by the Hawaiian Mission Children's Society, the museum still counts missionary descendents on its board—it's kind of a junior society league.

ART MUSEUMS

You might think a small museum in a smallish city like Honolulu wouldn't be worth a look, but there are surprising gems to be found at the **Honolulu Academy of Arts** ★ (900 Beretania St.; ☎ 808/532-8700; www.honoluluacademy.org; Tues–Sat 10am–4:30pm, Sun 1–5pm; $7 adults, $4 seniors and students, free for kids under 12). It's a no-brainer that an institution in the Pacific would have one of the best Asian collections in the country. For me, the highlight of the collection is the James Michener Collection of Japanese Ukiyo-e prints, which includes that iconic blue swell *The Great Wave off Kanegawa* by woodblock-print master

Katsushika Hokusai. There are also surprising Western masterpieces to be found, like Whistler's 1881 *Arrangement in Black No. 5: Lady Meux,* a seductive portrait of a woman outlined in white ermine, and Gauguin's *Two Nudes on a Tahitian Beach.* The Dole Company hired Georgia O'Keeffe to paint promotional pictures of the islands, and in 1939 the artist spent 4 months in the islands (and refused to paint a pineapple). Four of the paintings she did, such as a lush green study of Maui's Iao Valley, are in the museum's collection and sometimes hang in the contemporary gallery. In an effort to appeal to a younger crowd, the museum brings in shows of cutting-edge artists such as Neo Rauch and hosts the monthly theme party Art After Dark.

The academy was founded in 1927 by Anna Rice Cooke, a daughter of missionaries, who married Charles Montague Cooke, a wealthy son of missionaries. The art-collecting Cooke decided to tear down her grand wooden house and have it rebuilt as a public museum. (She built a new house on Maikiki Heights, which is now the Contemporary Museum.) The result is the handsomest building in town, a stucco hip-roofed island-style building designed by New York architect Bertram Goodhue. The museum has since had additional galleries built. One of the swellest lunch spots in town happens to be the academy's **Pavilion Café**

Riding the Rails

The first time I went to the **Hawaiian Railway** ★ kids (Ewa; see Central & Leeward Oahu map on p. 139; ☎ 808/681-5461; www.hawaiianrailway.com; Sun at 1 and 3pm; $10 adults, $7 children 2–12 and seniors), I was expecting a hokey train ride but ended up getting a completely new view of a part of the island I don't know well and learning a lot about Oahu. The operation is a labor of love by train buffs. "I've realized my dream here," says Corey Hood, who with his family restored a crumbling 1940s Navy box car. A former military staffer, Hood and his cohorts have put their own money into the Hawaiian railway, using the old roadbed that runs from Ewa to Pearl Harbor. Originally built by plantation owner Benjamin Dillingham, the railroad was used to transport sugar to Honolulu. One can't help thinking that if the railway worked in 1900, why can't it be used to ease traffic now? Visitors pile into open-air cars that lumber along at 15 mph across the Ewa coral plain, and you get a great detailed narration of the area's and the railroad's history. In the spring, you can see whales spouting off Kahe Point. After your 90-minute train trip, check out George Joy's model-train operation in a boxcar on the property. Kids love it.

By car: Take H-1 west, exit on 5A Ewa. Stay on Highway 76 south (Ft. Weaver Rd.) for 2½ miles. Turn right at the Tesoro gas station onto Renton Road, and continue for 1½ miles. Turn left onto a small lane, and you'll see the entrance to the Hawaiian Railway on the right, through the chain-link fence. **By bus:** From Waikiki, take 42 Ewa Beach to Waipahu Transit Center, and transfer to 431 Ewa Town Center.

An Heiress's Art-Filled Retreat

Tobacco heiress Doris Duke's **Shangri La** ★★★ (meet at Honolulu Academy of Arts, 900 Beretania St.; ☎ 866/DUKE-TIX or 808/532-8700; www.shangrilahawaii.org; guided visits only, Wed–Sat beginning at 8:30am, 11am, and 1:30pm; adults $25, children under 12 not admitted; closed Sept, Jan 1, July 4, Thanksgiving, and Dec 25) has quickly become one of Oahu's most popular attractions—and deservedly so. Book far in advance for this one; tours sell out and you don't want to miss this over-the-top mansion, which will delight on a number of levels. For good ol'-fashioned lowbrow fun, it affords visitors a peephole into the privileged existence of one of the 20th century's rich and famous heiress: Doris Duke. And for a highbrow kick, you have one of the world's richest (and quirkiest) private collections of Islamic art housed in a stunningly beautiful complex of gardens, libraries, and dining halls, built and added to over the course of more than 60 years.

Opened to the public in 2003, Shangri La was Doris Duke's oceanfront hideaway, which she built in 1937, inspired by her (first) honeymoon: a long tour through India, the Middle East, and Hawaii. She bought 5 acres in what is now a tony residential neighborhood known as Black Point, below Diamond Head. The building's facade is deceptively simple—white plaster walls with ceramic-tiled roof—but when you enter, the sensory overload is palpable. Every nook and cranny of the home has some kind of tile work or art from Spain, Morocco, Tunisia, Egypt, Iran, Iraq, Syria, Turkey, India, Pakistan, Uzbekistan, the Philippines, and China. Knowledgeable volunteer docents take you through each room, explaining the opulent decor and art, and telling amusing anecdotes about the eccentric owner (once good friends with Imelda Marcos), who died in 1993. A highlight is the Damascus Room. In the early 1950s, Duke bought the entire 17th-century interior of a Syrian home and installed it in Shangri La. It's lined with carved, painted, and gilded wood panels, and backlit vitrines hold delicate ceramics.

Asked when Shangri La was completed, Duke's longtime right-hand man, Sri Lankan Johnny Gomez, who still lives in Honolulu, says, "Never was finished, never. There was no such word as finished."

(☎ 808/532-8734), where chef Mike Nevin makes Mediterranean-leaning light bites and nothing costs more than $12. Reservations are a must.

While the Academy of Arts is the old-school art enclave, **The Contemporary Museum** ★ (2411 Makiki Heights Dr.; ☎ 808/562-0232; www.tcmhi.org; adults $5, students $3, free for children 12 and under) has the most exciting art programs in town, bringing in international stars such as Japan's Yoshitomo Nara and street artist Shepard Fairey for extended stays that include lectures at the University of Hawaii and parties at nightclubs. The museum has a collection of almost 2,000

Best Public Sculpture

Across the street from Kawaiahao Church is **Isamu Noguchi's Sky Gate** (see Downtown & Chinatown map on p. 140). Created in 1977, the 24-foot-tall tubular steel tripod, painted matte black, is a viewfinder to the heavens. On a clear night, people lie on the concrete platform under the sculpture and gaze up. Noguchi framed Hawaii's beautiful sky just for us.

works by artists such as Josef Albers, Sam Francis, and Jim Dine, but doesn't have the space to show it off. Its gallery is reserved for exhibitions, some curated in-house, others visiting. Highlight: David Hockney's permanent installation of his sets and costumes for the Ravel opera *L'enfant et les sortileges*—the room where it's housed cocoons you in blue, the walls alive with Hockney's whimsical red-trunked trees and flying creatures. You'll usually see one or more pieces installed in the garden. There's also a popular cafe. The museum's downtown satellite at the **First Hawaiian Bank Center** (999 Bishop St.), open weekdays only, shows works by local artists.

The state has been buying works by local artists since the 1970s, but it wasn't until 2002 that the collection of more than 5,000 pieces had a place to be seen. That's when the **Hawaii State Art Museum** ★ (250 S. Hotel St., at Richards St.; see map of Downtown & Chinatown on p. 140; ☎ 808/586-0900; www.state.hi.us/sfca; free) opened in a palazzo-like building that was once a hotel, a YMCA for servicemen during World War II, and most recently a government office. Hawaii has a rich artistic history, and the semipermanent exhibition "Enriched by Diversity: The Art of Hawaii" has works by Hawaii's most prominent artists, running from the 1930s to the present. I'm mesmerized by the red abstract blur of "Cosmic Alchemy" by Isamu Doi, who led the way for a generation of Japanese-American artists such as Tadashi Sato, Toshiko Takaezu, Satoru Abe, and Harry Tsuchidana (whose work is also in this exhibit). The exhibition also includes Franco Salmoiraghi's portraits of native Hawaiians and Mark Hamasaki and Anne K. Landgraf's politically charged documentation of the controversial building of the H3 freeway. In the show, visitors get a taste of past island life in the photo-realist watercolors by Doug Young—they are a potent nostalgia trip for residents. And it's all free.

NATURAL OAHU

The hike up Honolulu's 750-foot-high iconic natural landmark, which is actually called Leahi by Hawaiians, isn't a pretty one—you walk up a dry, rocky trail in an arid crater—but the view from the top, at the **Diamond Head State Monument** ★, is the payoff. You can see the whole city, from the Hawaii Kai suburb to the east to Pearl Harbor (and beyond) to the west, lying like a snake between shore and mountain. Look out toward the ocean to see the horizon curve faintly and Molokai in the distance. The changing shades of blue as the water deepens are mesmerizing. The view is why the military bought Diamond Head in 1904, and 4 years later built gun emplacements, batteries, and the trail, among other things.

Leahi is a sacred site for Hawaiians—it got its name, which means "brow of the ahi," from Hiiaka, sister of the fire goddess Pele. Kamehameha I had a *heiau* (temple) built at the top.

By 10am it's hot up there, so get an early start, and you'll beat the busloads of tourists, too. The hike is fairly easy, but visitors who aren't fit may struggle up the 271 stairs. The entrance to the park is on the *mauka* side of the crater; to get there from Waikiki, take Kalakaua Avenue toward Kapiolani Park. At the park, make a left onto Monsarrat Avenue, which becomes Diamond Head Road after Campbell Avenue. Continue on Diamond Head Road to the turnoff for the crater. From

A Valley Saved

In early 2006, Oahu residents held their breath while the City & County of Honolulu scrambled to come up with money to save the North Shore's magnificent Waimea Valley from New York investor Christian Wolffer, who wanted to build homes on 1,575 acres of the upper valley. In January, a deal was reached, and everyone breathed a sigh of relief. The valley is an *ahupuaa,* the traditional Hawaiian land division, sort of a pie slice of island that included everything a community needed to live, running from mountain down to ocean. Oahu's high priests called Waimea home for more than 600 years, making it an important spiritual zone. In the 1990s the valley was an adventure park with "jungle rides."

It offers a lush walk into the past. The valley is packed with archaeological sites, including the 600-year-old Hale O Lono, a *heiau* (temple) dedicated to the Hawaiian god Lono, which you'll find to the left of the entrance to the **Waimea Valley** ★★ (kids) (59-854 Kamehameha Hwy.; ☎ 808/638-7766. www.waimeavalley.org.; $10 adults, $5 seniors, $5 children 4–12). The botanical collection has 35 different gardens, including super-rare Hawaiian species such as the endangered Kokia cookie hibiscus. The valley is also home to fauna such as the endangered Hawaiian moorhen; look for a black bird with a red face cruising in the ponds. Walk through the gardens (take the paved paths or dirt trails) and you wind up at 30-foot-high Waimea Falls—bring your bathing suit and you can dive into the cold, murky water. The center offers guided walks and starting in 2008, the Office of Hawaiian Affairs (which took over management of the park) will offer activities focused on "living Hawaiian culture." As we went to press, the new corporation had plans to have authentic hula performances and demonstrations of native Hawaiian crafts. Right across the street from Waimea Bay, you can combine a visit here with a couple of hours at the beach.

Driving directions: From Haleiwa, head west on Kamehameha Highway, turn right at the entrance, right across the street from Waimea Bay. **TheBus:** 52.

Hawaiian Online

Interested in the Hawaiian language? Now online is www.ulukau.org, an electronic Hawaiian library that includes a Hawaiian-English dictionary. Just type in the Hawaiian or English word you want to translate, and get the definition. The site is maintained by the organization Alu Like.

Diamond Head Road, it's a half-mile uphill to the park center. To enter, it costs $5 per car and $1 per person on foot; the park is open from 6am to 6pm. TheBus: no. 22 or 58.

Kapi'olani Park ★ kids, 130 acres at the Diamond Head end of Waikiki, is where Honolulu goes to play. It has public tennis courts (get there early if you don't want to wait a long time), playing fields, an exercise station, a paved jogging path around its perimeter, bathroom facilities, and a bandstand where events such as the annual Ukulele Festival are held. Also in the park is my favorite music venue, the Waikiki Shell, a mini-Hollywood Bowl.

Whether you're a hard-core gardener and really into plants, a hiker, or simply interested in Hawaiian culture and want to see what a swatch of indigenous plant life looks like, stop at **Hoomaluhia Botanical Garden** ★ (45-680 Luluku Rd., Kaneohe; ☎ 808/233-7323; www.co.honolulu.hi.us/parks/hbg/hmbg.htm; Mon–Thurs 9am–4pm; free) on the Windward Side. (***Tip:*** It rains a lot over there, so take an umbrella.) The City & County of Honolulu oversees five botanical gardens, and the biggest is the 400-acre Hoomaluhia Botanical Garden in Kaneohe. Built by the U.S. Army Corps of Engineers as a flood buffer for Kaneohe, the garden, at the foot of the powerful Koolau mountain range, includes a 32-acre lake (you can borrow fishing poles from the visitor center). Divvied up into geographical sections, its trails wind through the flora of the Philippines, Hawaii, Africa, Sri Lanka, India, Polynesia, Melanesia, Malaysia, and tropical America. Volunteers give guided walks at 10am on Saturday and 1pm on Sunday (call to register). The tours are cool—the guides give you the lowdown on kooky plants, such as the lipstick tree, which yields a vibrant red ink, and pluck flowers and fruit for you to inspect and taste. Buy plate lunches in Kaneohe and have a picnic here. The garden also has campsites (p. 119).

If you're driving: From Honolulu, take H-1 to the Pali Hwy. (Hwy. 61); turn left on Kamehameha Hwy. (Hwy. 83); at the fourth light, turn left onto Luluku Road. TheBus: No. 55 or 56 will stop on Kamehameha Hwy.; it's a 2-mile walk to the visitor center.

If you're used to mega Sea Worlds, **The Waikiki Aquarium** ★★★ kids (2777 Kalakaua Ave.; ☎ 808/923-9741; www.waquarium.org; daily 9am–4:30pm; $9 adults, $6 seniors, $4 youths 13–17, $2 kids 5–12) may look small and unassuming on the outside. But in reality, this little aquarium (part of the University of Hawaii) is a must-see research hotbed and the place to find out what's happening in all that water surrounding the island. The indoor-outdoor facility is right on the water, across the street from Kapi'olani Park. Indoors are four darkened galleries of illuminated tanks filled with everything from psychedelic reef fish to the rare chambered nautilus (the Waikiki Aquarium was the first aquarium in the U.S. to successfully breed this living fossil). The latest permanent exhibit is "Ocean Drifters," a living gallery of jellyfish. Outside are a number of other tanks, one holding a notable coral farm—few aquariums can grow coral, and this aquarium raises the stationary animals to send to other aquariums. Marine biologist Syd Kraul developed ways to raise mahimahi in the 1980s and you can see the result in the mahimahi hatchery. The "Edge of the Reef" exhibit re-creates the Oahu shoreline and tide pools. Don't even try to pull kids away from the pool of antic monk seals.

Another top spot for families is the **Nuuanu Pali Lookout** ★★ kids. Kids and grown-ups alike love leaning into the strong winds whipping through the famous cliff called Pali. Locals driving across Pali Highway often make a quick stop here just to catch the view—it's exhilarating. The thousand-foot cliff is where in 1795 Kamehameha I and his men cornered the warriors of Kalanikupule, the chief of Oahu, many of them falling to their deaths. When the old Pali Road to the lookout was built in 1898, workers found 800 skulls at the base of the cliff. Park in the lot and walk to the lookout, where you'll see the Windward Side of the island—Waimanalo, Kailua, and Kaneohe bays—stretched out below, and around you the craggy, fern-covered walls of the Koolau Mountains. The lookout is near the summit of Pali Highway (Hwy. 61); take the Nuuanu Pali Lookout turnoff.

CHINATOWN

The 15 blocks of Chinatown is where Honolulu feels like a real urban-grit city. Teeming with Asian markets run by Hawaii-born merchants and recent immigrants, Chinatown is where you can buy fresh, cheap produce, Chinese antiques, high-quality sashimi, and Hong Kong designer-bag knockoffs.

The first Chinese arrived on two ships in 1788, and the seed of Chinatown was planted. When the first Chinese plantation contract laborers arrived in 1852, the neighborhood really got going. By 1884, there were 5,000 Chinese in Honolulu, and the 25 acres of Chinatown bustled with *tongs* (clubhouses), herb shops, restaurants, temples, and stores. Today, those things are still here, along with some of the hottest nightspots in town.

There are excellent organized walking tours of Chinatown available: For a general tour that covers history and culture, go on the 3-hour guided tours of Chinatown which are offered Tuesdays at 9:30am by the **Chinese Chamber of Commerce** (42 N. King St., second floor; Mon 9:30am; ☎ 808/533-3181; $10). Depending on your guide, you may venture to various culinary places and get to sample the exotic cuisines of Chinatown. The Chinese Chamber cannot guarantee your guide, but if you are more interested in cuisine than in architecture, be sure to make that request when you book your tour.

To explore the area on your own, you can download a free walking map at www.chinatownhi.com that has all the major landmarks and insider spots.

The pride of Chinatown is the restored 1922 **Hawaii Theatre** (1130 Bethel St.; ☎ 808/528-0506; www.hawaiitheatre.com), often called the Carnegie Hall of the Pacific. The grand Beaux Arts building is where you can see everything from top local musicians to visiting acts like the musical Stomp. The Hawaii International Film Festival has its premieres here, too.

Oahu's Famous Tourist Trap

The **Polynesian Cultural Center** (55–370 Kamehameha Hwy., Laie; ☎ 800/ 367-7060 or 808/293-3333; www.polynesia.com; Mon–Sat noon–9pm; $50–$200 adults, $35–$150 kids 3–17) has always reminded me of Disney's saccharine "It's a Small World" boat ride. This one's just of Polynesia and with real, live people. There's a Hawaii section, a Tonga section, a New Zealand section—you get the idea. In these "villages," Polynesians (meant as a generic term since you may get a Hawaiian passing himself off as a Tahitian) do a presentation, perhaps a demo of how to hack open a coconut or how to make traditional tapa cloth, at designated times during the day. From 2:30 to 3pm every day, the Rainbows of Paradise pageant is held, which is actually a flotilla of Astroturf-topped rafts that make their way up a fake, stagnant river bearing a dance troupe from each of the island nations. Their costumes are Hollywood authentic.

As someone from Hawaii, I find the whole affair cheesy and heinous, a Disney-fied Polynesialand. But I will admit that it's for a good cause—owned by the Church of Latter Day Saints, the center is a giant fundraiser for education. The money goes to students attending the adjacent Brigham Young University campus. Most of the Polynesians serving you and dancing for you are Mormon college kids.

You can get packages that include the Alii Luau Feast, a buffet of pallid quasi-Hawaiian food that you share with a couple hundred other people, and the "Horizons: Where the Sea Meets the Sky" show, held in a 2,800-person theater, with fire dancers, hula dancers, and the like. Of course, you'd have a more authentic (and cheaper) Polynesian experience by going to the Bishop Museum (p. 144) and then having dinner at Ono Hawaiian Foods (p. 127) in Kapahulu.

Six blocks away is the bustling open-air **Oahu Market** (the corner of N. King and Kekaulike sts.; ☎ 808/841-6924), where vendors sell caught-that-day fish, roasted pork, and other edibles. Opened in 1922, it's still a major food hub for locals.

Maunakea Marketplace (1120 Maunakea St.; ☎ 808/524-3409) is the other big fresh-food center. In the courtyard are stalls of Chinese trinkets and clothing. Inside, you'll find a food court of stalls selling prepared Singaporean, Vietnamese, Thai, Chinese, Japanese, and Filipino food. When I'm in the neighborhood, I stop for a curry at Malee Thai/Vietnamese Cuisine, or grab a bento box at the adjacent Masa's.

THE OTHER OAHU

As is true of any vacation destination, there can be an invisible "us" and "them" barrier between visitor and resident on Oahu. Here are the insider tips on where the locals go, whether it's shopping at a farmers market or meditating in a Korean Buddhist temple tucked in the back of a valley. Tourists are rarely in sight.

The old Polynesian tradition of drinking *awa* (or *kava,* as it's known in Fiji and in diet supplements) is making a comeback in Honolulu. For example, **Diamond Head Cove Health Bar** (3045 Monsarrat Ave., 808/732-8744; www.diamondhead cove.com)—by day a casual lunch-and-smoothie spot—turns into an *awa* bar and nightly party, once the sun sets. Hawaiian studies students and staff from Hawaiian language schools hang out here, and you can often hear Hawaiian spoken. *Awa,* made from the plant's root and mixed with water, is served in wood bowls. When you go to the counter, you'll be asked if you've ever had *awa* before. If not, the server will tell you that you can't drink *awa* if you've had alcohol (you'll get an upset stomach). The liquid has an earthy flavor and lightly numbs the lips, eventually yielding a floaty feeling after a couple of bowls. You'll understand why the scene is so mellow. People like virtuoso guitarist Makana drop by. Surfboards and art hang on the walls as people perch at the few small tables and at the counter, drinking *awa* from paper bowls and munching on snacks.

For a taste of a backyard *kanikapila*—when musicians get together and jam Hawaiian-style—head to the weekly Sunday jam at the **Koolau Golf Club** (45-550 Kionaole Rd.; ☎ 808/247-7088; www.koolaugolfclub.com; no cover) in Kaneohe. Slack-key guitarist Mike Kaawa is the regular headliner, but he's always joined by old-school legends like ukulele master Eddie Kamae and Analu Aina (who played bass for Israel Kamakawioole). The party happens from 3:30 to 7:30pm. You'll be sitting with real-deal old-timers, eating pupu like poke (cubed ahi in soy sauce) and mochiko chicken (breaded in rice flour and fried) and throwing back the beers.

Jazz also thrives in Honolulu, with young bands finding homes at the hot nightspots. But hard-core fans and musicians go to the **Hawaii Musicians' Union** (949 Kapiolani Blvd., entrance on Waimanu St., second floor; ☎ 808/596-2905; www.livemusicbiz.com/now.htm; $7) on Tuesday at 8pm for its weekly Studio 6 live-music night (call in advance—sometimes the events are cancelled if no musician is scheduled). Here you can hear top local talent such as saxophonist Gabe Baltazar and trumpeter DeShannon Higa play for their peers. It's a no-frills room—it's all about the music.

The visual-arts scene is concentrated in Chinatown, with galleries by established artists such as Pegge Hopper and newcomers like Bethel Street Gallery. In 2003 the community, led by nonprofit group **ARTS at Marks Garage** (1159 Nuuanu Ave.; ☎ 808/521-2903; www.artsatmarks.com; free), banded together to launch First Fridays, a gallery walk that runs from 5 to 9pm on the first Friday of each month. Now hundreds of people roam the blocks, looking at paintings, stopping in at events, shopping (many stores and other businesses stay open for the event), and eating at one of the many restaurants in the area. Want to meet some local creative types? This is the place to go. Walking maps are available at ARTS at Marks Garage.

Hiking is popular on Oahu, which is riddled with valley-to-mountain trails. A good way to go is with the local chapter of the **Sierra Club** (☎ 808/538-6616; www.hi.sierraclub.org; $5), which organizes group hikes led by certified guides who are knowledgeable about local plant life. To go a step further, sign on for a volunteer day project and help restore a trail or clear an area being developed into a park. It's a great way to rub elbows with locals who really care about the island,

and do something for the place you're visiting. Call ahead to sign up for hikes and day projects; you'll find the hike schedule and descriptions on the website.

Honolulu is home to a lot of bad community theater that dredges up old musicals. But we have one saving grace: **Kumu Kahua Theatre** (46 Merchant St.; ☎ 808/536-4441; www.kumukahua.org; $16; ***Budget hint:*** Go Thurs nights for just $13). Its mission is to produce plays by local writers about local life. If a Lee Cataluna play is on stage during your visit, go. The spunky columnist of the *Honolulu Advertiser* writes works that are half humor, half social commentary. Her biggest hit has been *Folks You Meet at Longs.* Longs is the Walgreens of Hawaii, and everyone goes there. The cast of characters—cashiers and customers—will give you a good idea of prototypical Hawaii residents and their foibles. Housed in an 1871 building that was originally a post office—and the first building in the country made with precast concrete block and steel reinforcement—this 100-seat theater sells out fast.

Started in 2003 by local food writer Joan Namkoong and the Hawaii Farm Bureau Federation as a single **Farmers Market at Kapi'olani Community College** (4303 Diamond Head Rd.; www.hfbf.org/FarmersMarketKCC.html; free), across from the entrance to Diamond Head State Monument, the program has been so successful it now has three markets. The main one is still the original, which happens every Saturday from 7:30 to 11am. While I don't expect visitors to stock up on the great organic produce, the market also has food booths and good gifts that you won't find in any department store. Before going on trips, I like to stock up on gifts of Made in Hawaii jams, honey from the Hawaiian Beekeepers' Association, spice rubs from Kaiulani's Spices, and PacifiKool's ginger syrup, made from Big Island ginger. PacifiKool owner Cheryl To also makes fresh ginger ale at her booth, and it's the best I've ever tasted—she's made fans of visitors from Australia to France. The no. 3, 22, and 58 buses stop here. The other markets are in **Kailua** (behind Longs on Kailua Rd.; Thurs 5–7:30pm) and **Mililani** (Mililani High School, 95-1200 Meheula Pkwy.; Sun 8am–noon).

Gregory Pai, a former chief economist for First Hawaiian Bank, is a longtime student of famed Burmese Buddhist monk Sayaew U Kundala. He passes on his teachings at a free Vipassana meditation class every Saturday at the **Mu Ryang Sa Korean temple** (2420 Halelaau Place; ☎ 808/735-4679; gpai@lava.net) in Palolo. The grand, ornate temple alone is worth a visit. The sittings are held in the Memorial Hall, where you'll see a lavish altar and photographs of the dead who have had services there. Pai welcomes beginners and seasoned meditators alike. Pai talks participants through to "the point where you're not constantly editorializing or judging; you are at a point of pure awareness," he says. After an hour, whether you reach epiphany or not, you feel calm and relaxed. And maybe you'll make some enlightened friends. To get to the temple, coming from town on Waialae Avenue, turn left on 10th Avenue, drive all the way to the back of the temple, and turn right on Halelaau Place. Although the sitting is free, a small donation is welcome.

ACTIVE OAHU

There's more to do in Oahu than you may have ever imagined: skydiving, hiking, golfing, you name it. In the pages that follow, I'll discuss the island's outstanding and most rewarding active sports, with tips on how to make the most of your time—and save money, too.

WATERSPORTS

Oahu is surrounded by the largest ocean on earth, and residents make use of it. From night snorkeling at Hanauma Bay to kiteboarding at Kailua Beach, the options are limitless.

THE MOST FAMOUS SPORT: SURFING

Hawaii is synonymous with surfing and Oahu is the best island to learn this sport. The gentlest, most forgiving waves on the planet are at Waikiki (which is also why it's so crowded), and the board's-eye view of the coastline from here is unmatchable. In Honolulu, the easiest (and most crowded) break is **Canoes,** right off Kuhio Beach. But if you're above average in talent, try **Cliffs,** at the base of Diamond Head, where the waves are in the 4-to-6-foot range. Seasoned surfers will want to visit Hawaii in the winter, from December to March, as that's when the North Shore gets its legendary 20-foot-high waves.

Beach stands where you can rent a surfboard ($10/hr. on average) are set up all along Waikiki, from the Hilton Hawaiian Village to Kapiolani Park. If you plan on surfing and renting from a beach stand, don't bring extra cash or credit cards. The beach stands will hold your valuables, but their assistance is at your own risk. With so much traffic on the Waikiki beaches, wallets and valuables can easily "walk off" while you're enjoying the surf.

If you're a beginner, take a surf lesson—for instruction but also for protection against the other clueless people wielding potentially lethal long boards. Most schools schedule 1- to 2-hour classes for beginners. That may not seem like a long time, but until your body is used to paddling out to the waves, an hour can feel like an eternity. Most surf schools guarantee they can get you up and surfing by the end of your session.

Hans Hedemann Surf School ★ (2863 Kalakaua Ave., Waikiki; ☎ 808/924-7778; www.hhsurf.com) is the most professional operation in Waikiki. Run by former 1970s pro surfer Hans Hedemann, this school has three locations: Waikiki, Turtle Bay Resort on the North Shore, and Kohala Resort. Hedemann himself gives private lessons—at $115 for an hour. (He has taught celebrities such as Cameron Diaz and Adam Sandler.) If the expenditure is beyond your budget, go for a $50 1-hour group lesson (maximum four people) with a CPR-certified, seasoned instructor. Teachers start with a brief on-land training exercise (where to position yourself on the board, how to stand up), then you're off to the breaks near Waikiki Aquarium and Natatorium.

Another top academy, the **Hawaiian Fire Surf School** (☎ 888/955-7873 or 808/737-3473; www.hawaiianfire.com), is owned and operated by the Honolulu firefighters. So you know the instructors (all firefighters) are going to put safety first. Towards that end, they transport their clients from Waikiki to a very uncrowded, remote beach in Kalaeloa in West Oahu, where there's little competition for wave space. Two hour group lessons (one teacher for every three students) are $99 for kids and $169 for adults. Expect to spend about 45 minutes on the beach learning the basics and then about 75 minutes in the water.

A third option is Suzy Stewart of **Sunset Suzy** ★★ (☎ 808/781-2692; www.sunsetsuzy.com; $95 for a private lesson, $75 each for group of 3-5 people)—a former stuntwoman on *Baywatch.* (She also appeared in *Blue Crush.*) Stewart specializes in beginners, and offers a bunch of different packages, including a weeklong women's surf camp for $1,450 that includes accommodations (but not airfare). She starts beginners off at gentle Alii Beach Park in Haleiwa, on the North Shore.

Cheapest lessons (about $30 an hour for group lessons, $80 for private lessons) can be had from the local guys who staff the beach-boy **kiosks along Waikiki beach.** The quality of service at these stands varies wildly; some of them are manned by bored, inattentive surf rats who aren't thrilled to be answering tourists' questions all day. Or you might luck out and get an old Hawaiian grandfather who likes nothing better than to get someone to stand up on their board even after 40 years of working on the beach. Ask to speak to your would-be instructor before biting and see what kind of vibe you get.

WINDSURFING

The best place on the island to hone windsurfing skills is Kailua Bay. On any given day, you'll see experts and first-timers gliding over the water. **Hawaiian Water Sports** (354 Hahani St., Kailua; ☎ 808/262-5483; www.hawaiianwatersports.com) offers a free shuttle service from Waikiki hotels when you purchase $75 or more in lessons (the cost of a 2-hour group lesson, when you book online). The pickup is at 9am and they'll have you back between 2 and 6pm. Advanced sailors head to Diamond Head to jump the waves. If you're on the North Shore, Haleiwa Harbor is also a haven for windsurfers.

Unless you're a really serious windsurfer, you're not likely to bring a sail and rig with you on holiday. Not to worry: There are outfits that rent out all the gear you need, from car racks to sails. Here are the two best:

Visitors new to the sport can learn it from Hawaii's oldest windsurfing operation—**Naish Hawaii** (155a Hamakua Dr., Kailua; ☎ 808/262-6068; www.naish.com), owned by former world champion Robbie Naish and his parents. Private lessons are $75 and group lessons are $45 per person. In addition to teaching, Naish has been producing windsurf boards since the early 1980s, and it rents gear, too. Rental prices: $40 for 2 hours or $45 for a full day for beginner-level sail and rig; $45 for a half day or $50 for a full day for intermediate-level sail and rig; $50 for half day or $55 for full day for advanced-level sail and rig.

The other top-flight Kailua operation is **Hawaiian Water Sports** (354 Hahani St., Kailua; ☎ 808/262-5483; www.hawaiianwatersports.com). On the teaching staff are pros Pascal Bronniman and Josh Seymour, world-ranked competitors. Hawaiian Water Sports offers three types of lessons: a 2-hour group lesson for $95 ($75 if you book online) a 2-hour private lesson for $175 ($155 if you book online), and an all-day windsurfing lesson and experience for $299 ($275 if you book online). Beginning lessons start at Kailua Beach Park, while more experienced sailors go to Diamond Head.

Broadcasting the Waves

To find out where the surf's up, call **Surf News Network Surfline** (☎ 808/596-SURF) to get the latest surf conditions.

KITEBOARDING

This relatively new sport—a combination of wakeboarding, windsurfing, and acrobatics—is physically grueling and challenging. Kailua Bay is the epicenter for kiteboarding, as the wind is always blowing there, but the water's fairly calm. Windsurfer Robbie Naish is a recent convert to kiteboarding, and his shop **Naish Hawaii** ★ (155a Hamakua Dr., Kailua; ☎ 808/262-6068; www.naish.com) has become the best outpost for would-be daredevils. As with windsurfing, private lessons are $75 and group lessons $55 per person.

SNORKELING

While Oahu doesn't have the brilliant underwater gardens of waving, multihued soft corals one finds in places such as Indonesia and Fiji, snorkeling is still a great experience. Its clear waters are home to many types of hard corals—white, black, and pink—that harbor reef fish, sea urchins, eels, octopuses, and lots of other sea life. The more remote the spot, the more fish you'll see. If you snorkel on the west shore during the winter months, you can sometimes hear whales singing, too.

Warning: Barracuda and other predatory fish are attracted to shiny objects, so take off your wedding ring, watch, and the like before snorkeling. It doesn't happen often, but barracuda will bite at rings. Fingers included.

If you have only one chance to snorkel, make a beeline for **Hanauma Bay Nature Preserve** ★★★ (7455 Kalaniana'ole Hwy.; ☎ 808/396-4229; www.co.honolulu.hi.us/parks/facility/hanaumabay; Wed–Mon 6am–6pm, Apr–Oct 6am–7pm; $5). More than three million people—visitors and residents, absolute beginners, and seasoned divers—visit the preserve each year. The remnant of a volcanic crater, the crescent of sand here is fronted by a shallow reef that simply teems with sea life. In sandy pockets, you'll spot butterflyfish, damselfish, wrasses, sea turtles (I followed one around last time I went), and other marine life. When you arrive, stop first at the visitor center on the ridge above the beach. After paying, you'll enter a theater to watch a mandatory 10-minute video about Hanauma Bay and how to be an eco-friendly snorkeler (stepping on coral is a no no). The video is shown every 15 minutes and there are informative interactive displays on beach history to browse if you need to wait. Locals tend to bring picnics, but there's a snack bar outside the visitor center. On the beach are full bathroom facilities and a snorkel-rental kiosk ($6 for snorkel kit, $5 for dive lights).

A word of caution: Parking is a problem. Get to the preserve early to find a spot, or you're going to have to park on the road outside and walk to the park—more than a mile each way. One way to avoid the crowds is to go on the second Saturday of each month, when the park is open until 10pm for night dives. The reef is luminous under the beam of your flashlight.

If you're driving from Honolulu: Take H-1 East and it runs into Kalaniana'ole Highway. It's about 10 miles from Waikiki, all through towns, so it can be slow getting there. **By bus:** No. 22 stops right in front of Hanauma Bay.

While Hanauma Bay is the best spot for beginners, and a sort of one-stop shop for a snorkeling experience, a hidden gem is the area just off where the boats are parked on the shore of **Lanikai Beach** (p. 136). The water is crystal clear and the reefs are so close to shore, you don't have to worry about going out too deep before seeing clown fish, eels, and other fish. On the Waianae Coast, the **Makaha** area has some great snorkeling and scuba spots. You can see dolphins at **Makua**

Beach, where there are also a lot of small caves to explore. All three beaches offer free public access, but you'll have to bring your own drinking water and snacks. Restrooms are available at Makaha and Makua, but not at Lanikai.

To rent snorkel gear, try one of the following options:

- **Aloha Dive Shop** (Koko Marina Shopping Center; ☎ 808/395-5922; www.aloha diveshop.com) is the closest dive shop to the underwater park at Hanauma Bay.
- **Snorkel Bob's** ★ kids (700 Kapahulu Ave.; ☎ 808/735-7944; www.snorkel bob.com) is at the edge of Waikiki, on the way to Hanauma Bay. It's a chain with shops all around the islands, so if you're island hopping, you can rent gear on Oahu and drop it off on, say, Maui. Snorkel Bob's has a budget-crunch rental special of $9 a week for snorkel, standard mask, and fins (adults only). Snorkel-rental packages go on up to $44 a week for higher-end gear.
- **Kailua Sailboards & Kayaks** (130 Kailua Rd.; ☎ 808/262-2555; www.kailua sailboards.com), on the Windward Side, charges $48 per week for rentals and leads snorkel trips.
- **Surf-N-Sea** kids (62-595 Kamehameha Hwy., Haleiwa; ☎ 808/637-9887; www. surfnsea.com) is the place to go on the North Shore. You can rent a set of mask, fins, and snorkel for $9.50 a day or $45 a week. Surf-N-Sea also gives 2-hour snorkeling tours for $45 per person, and if you're a family of three or more the cost is $40 per person.

SCUBA DIVING

Oahu has shipwrecks and plane wrecks, plus dolphins and whales, in its waters. It's a superb place for those into wreck diving (you can see the sunken 185-foot minesweeper *Mahi* just south of Waianae) and just as good for those into wildlife spotting (a spectacular area is the Kahuna Canyon, a massive and natural underwater amphitheater, home to dozens of species). Experienced divers will want to head to the Waianae Coast, where whales are abundant during the winter (Dec–Apr). But wherever you end up, you're guaranteed to see something worthwhile; there are more than 200 species that are found only in Hawaiian waters.

Oahu's best dives are offshore, so you're going to want to book a two-tank dive from a dive boat. Of the many companies on the island, my favorite is **Captain Bruce's Hawaii Extreme Comfort Diving** (718 10th Ave.; ☎ 800/535-2487 or 808/ 373-3590; www.captainbruce.com; certified divers not needing equipment $105, certified divers needing equipment $115; both fees include transportation from Waikiki and food). Most scuba and tour businesses follow strict schedules for their dives, but owners Randy and Suzette Farnum determine what sites to dive to by where the best conditions are. They operate on the Waianae Coast, which has lava tubes to swim in, but the real benefit to diving in this area is that you can hear—and see—whales from December through April. For $110, the Farnums will pick you up in Waikiki, feed you on the boat, and show you the best diving on Oahu. Some days, they'll take you to the *Mahi* Shipwreck, a 1942 mine sweeper that went down 24 years ago in about 90 feet of water. Other diving spots are Airplane Canyon, just outside Waianae Harbor, and the Makaha Taverns, where sea turtles congregate. Average visibility is about 80 to 100 feet. On a bad day, it's 50 feet.

A Fishy Guide

Make the most of your snorkeling experience and spend $5 at local snorkel shops for **Franko's Oahu Reef Creatures Guide** or another fish card. Franko's card has pictures of all the fish you can expect to see when you bob your head down, along with the names of the coral, shells, eels, and plants. It's laminated so you can take the card underwater with you.

If you're strapped for time, you can still get some decent diving done right off Waikiki with **Dive Oahu** (1085 Ala Moana Blvd.; ☎ 808/922-3483; www.diveoahu.com; $99–$129). Certified divers will dive the same Corsair shipwreck and reef that the submarine rides tour, going down about 100 feet, where you'll find white-tip reef sharks, an occasional hammerhead, sea turtles, and reef fish. Noncertified divers watch an instructional DVD and take onshore instruction, then head with an instructor to the Turtle Canyon reef about 4 minutes from the shipwreck. They descend about 30 feet by the end of their training. If you don't want to scuba dive but your friend does, you can tag along on the boat and catch some sun for about $35. Dives begin at 8am and return around noon. Afternoon dives go from 1 to 4pm. For a 20% discount, book online

BOATING & WHALE-WATCHING

December to April is humpback-whale season in Hawaii, when the giants migrate down from Alaska to breed and give birth. The whales are a protected species, so tour boats are supposed to stay a couple of hundred yards away, but savvy tour operators kill the engines when they spot humpbacks and let the whales come to them. When they do, it's an experience you'll never forget. The whales don't seem to be bothered by the boats. Sometimes, they'll even brush up against them. Seeing these behemoths surface, blow, breach, or dive, is a true once in a lifetime experience.

Marine biologists are aboard the catamarans of **Sail Hawaii** ★★ (kids) (Waianae Boat Harbor, A11; ☎ 808/306-7273; www.sailhawaii.com), and their expertise makes this tour the most educational of those offered on Oahu. Specializing in whale-watching and snorkel tours, a 4-hour sail that includes snorkeling is a reasonable $105 per person; a 2-hour afternoon reef snorkel is $75. Beyond the expertise of the crew, Sail Hawaii gives its customers more time on the water than average, making this a terrific value.

If you're looking for a smooth ride close to Waikiki, the ***Navatek 1*** (Pier 6, Aloha Tower Marketplace; ☎ 808/973-1311; www.navatek.us) combines whale-watching with lunch for $62 ($31 for children 2–12). Better known for its nighttime "booze cruises," the 380-passenger *Navatek* is a catamaran and the flagship of the Royal Hawaiian Cruises Fleet. An even cheaper quickie cruise is offered by The ***Maita'i* Catamaran** (☎ 808/922-5665; www.leahi.com). The name says it all: These are sunset sails off of Waikiki Beach with plenty of potent potables aboard to enhance the ride ($34 adults, $17 for children 4–12). The boat sets sail at 5pm and stays out till about 6 or 6:30.

Hawaii Nautical (Ko Olina Resort and Marina, 92–1480 Aliinui Dr., Ko Olina; ☎ 808/234-SAIL; www.hawaiinautical.com), not only offers snorkeling cruises, it will allow you to steer the catamaran, after you take one of its 1-day sailing lessons, that is. These range from basic keelboat sailing ($350) to catamaran cruising ($400).

SPORTFISHING

The Big Island's Kona Coast may be Hawaii's sportfishing mecca, but Oahu gets its share of line-fighting fish. Once at Kewalo Basin, I saw four seniors—all women—posing with a 300-pound blue marlin they had reeled in together on their excursion. The charters here may not always get you a marlin, but they always seem to bring back something. The North Shore is where you can reel in yellowfin tuna. Other fish to land: skipjack tuna (aku), mahimahi, and wahoo (ono). Chasing marlins and other big-game fish isn't cheap. Of course, if you happen to land a 350-pound marlin and you're back at the dock taking a photo alongside it, it might feel like a worthy splurge.

Kewalo Basin, between the Honolulu International Airport and Waikiki, is the main location for charter fishing boats on Oahu. From Waikiki, take Kalakaua Ewa (west) beyond Ala Moana Center; Kewalo Basin is on the left, across from Ward Centre. Look for charter boats all in a row in their slips; on lucky days, the captains display the catch of the day in the afternoon. You can also take TheBus no. 19 or 20 (Airport).

The best way to book a sportfishing charter is through the experts; the best booking desk in the state is **Sportfish Hawaii** ★ (☎ 877/388-1376 or 808/396-2607; www.sportfishhawaii.com), which not only books boats on Oahu, but on all islands. These fishing vessels have been inspected and must meet rigorous criteria to guarantee that you will have a great time. Prices range from $812 to $932 for a full-day exclusive charter (you, plus five friends, get the entire boat to yourself); $717 for a half-day exclusive; or from $187 for a full-day share charter

A Dolphin Encounter

Frolicking with Flipper may be one of the all-time biggest dreams for kids (even the grown-up kind). The **Kahala Hotel** (5000 Kahala Ave.; ☎ 808/739-8918; www.dolphinquest.org; $210–$289 ages 11 and up, $175–$275 kids 5–10) features a natural lagoon that's home to six Atlantic bottlenose dolphins. Children and adults, even those not staying at the hotel, can touch and observe the dolphins up close in shallow water, overseen by staff trainers. The 2-hour kids' Quest for Knowledge session also includes feeding reef fish and sting rays. Spending time with Hoku, Liho, and the other dolphins will probably be the highlight of any Oahu trip and is a worthy splurge.

Of course, swimming with dolphins has its critics and supporters. You may want to visit the Whale and Dolphins Conservation Society's website at www.wdcs.org. For more information about responsible travel in general, check out Tread Lightly (www.treadlightly.org) and the International Ecotourism Society (www.ecotourism.org).

(you share the boat with five other people). All but the most gung ho fishermen usually find the half day sufficient.

KAYAKING & CANOEING

Kailua and Lanikai on the windward side are the most exciting spots on the island for paddling. The shallow waters allow you to see all the coral and you can often see turtles popping up their heads and swimming along. If you continue on to the mokuluas, two off-shore islands, you can play on the sandy beach or take a walk around the protected bird sanctuary there. However this itinerary is only recommended to expert paddlers: The waves hit the backside of the mokuluas with amazing force (it's considered the boundary line for the reef that protects the Kailua and Lanikai shores). More than one tourist has been swept out to sea trying to climb the backside.

Beginners should head for the Windward Coast's Kahana Stream. It's like going on a jungle hike, but in placid, calm water, as you head up lush Kahana Valley. Start at Kahana Bay Beach Park and paddle the tranquil water amid a chorus of birds. The upstream trip is less than a mile.

Kayak rental shops are clustered in Kailua, where you can also rent a vessel (single or tandem) right on the beach. One suggestion: Kayaking is more physical than it looks. If you've got weak stomach muscles, pay extra for the back rest; if you're just plain weak in general, get a tandem kayak to share the load. The rental prices below are for standard gear, but shops also offer premium kayaks (at premium prices) for experienced kayakers.

Kailua Sailboards and Kayaks (139 Kailua Rd.; ☎ 808/262-2555; www.kailuasailboards.com) is 1 block from Kailua Beach and offers tours and lessons. A guided, 2-hour tour is $89, while rentals can go from $39 for a single kayak for a half day to $59 for a full-day double (weekly rates are also available). In business since 1982, **Twogood Kayaks & Canoes** ★ (345 Hahani St.; ☎ 808/262-5656; www.twogoodkayaks.com) is a reliable outfit with a seasoned staff. Its rental rates are the same as Kailua Sailboards and Kayaks, but its guided tour to the Mokuluas is $109. The best Kailua deal is found at **Hawaiian Watersports** (354 Hahani St.; ☎ 808/262-5483; www.hawaiianwatersports.com). Its rental prices are the same as the competition, but it includes back rests, which you have to pay extra for elsewhere. And its 4-hour group tours to the mokuluas are only $125 ($105 if you book online).

If you're in Waikiki and want to stay there, you can get outfitted at **Go Bananas** (799 Kapahulu Ave.; ☎ 808/737-9514; www.gobananaskayaks.com), a mile from Waikiki beach. Rentals cost $30 for a single and $45 for a double for the day, and the price includes car racks (because you'll need them—along with a rental car to drive the kayaks to the beach).

SUBMARINE RIDES

With a sub ride, there's no getting wet, no physical activity, and you sit side by side in air-conditioning. It's a wonderful option for those unable to snorkel or scuba as you'll view some of the island's most fascinating underwater sights: man-made reefs, sunken ships and planes, turtles, tons of tropical fish, and sometimes even sharks. The only downside: no bathrooms and it won't be a fun experience for claustrophobes.

The only submarine tour on the island is in Waikiki, with **Atlantis Submarines** (Hilton Hawaiian Village, Alii Tower, next to Tropics Cafe; ☎ 800/548-6262 or 808/973-9811; www.go-atlantis.com). The 1½-hour submarine tour starts at $95 for adults and $48 for kids up to age 12 if you book online.

HOVER WITH THE SHARKS

You're a Discovery Channel addict and want to see sharks with a bona fide shark-crazed captain? Book a trip with the North Shore's **Hawaii Shark Encounters** ★ (Haleiwa Boat Harbor; ☎ 888/349-7888 or 808/356-1800; www.hawaiisharkencounters.com; $105 adults, $70 children under 12) and have your picture taken with Jimmy Hall. On December 29, 2005, Hall was leading a cage-dive expedition when his students started motioning: A great white was swimming by. Hall did the unthinkable and left the cage to film the shark. He felt so comfortable, he touched the 19-footer as it passed. Great whites are a rare sight in Hawaiian waters (you'll most likely see Galapagos and sandbar sharks), but that's proof that you never know what to expect when you're 3 miles out to sea. You'll put on a provided mask and snorkel and be suspended about 10 feet deep in a 6×6-foot Plexiglas-shielded cage—just enough distance to keep you safe from the sharks' jaws. And if you don't see a shark (a rarity), you don't pay. Generally, tours run for about 2 hours and carry about six people on the boat, with all equipment provided.

North Shore Shark Adventures ★★ (Haleiwa; ☎ 808/228-5900; www.hawaiisharkadventures.com; $120, check online for specials as low as $96) is a tad more expensive, but the people working at Hawaii Shark Encounters got their start here, at the oldest shark-viewing operation on Oahu. Surfer, diver, and artist—and experienced boat captain—Joe Pavsek takes clients about 3 miles offshore in 400 feet of water for the 2-hour tours. Passengers put on snorkels and get into the cage while chum is tossed in the water. Soon, reef sharks, Galapagos, maybe even a vicious tiger shark, will circle around you. If you just want to watch from the boat—which is plenty thrilling in itself—the tour costs half-price.

PARASAILING/JET SKIS

You don't have to jump out of a plane or rent a glider or helicopter to get a unique look at Oahu. Instead, you can either go single or tandem parasailing, where you're pulled by a boat and lifted 300 to 800 feet in the air. The boat tows you along as you "fly" quietly above the ocean, viewing dolphins, turtles, and (Dec–Apr) whales. You'll also get an eyeful of Diamond Head, Honolulu, and Waikiki if you leave out of Kewalo Basin, or Hawaii Kai if you leave out of Koko Marina.

Two outfits are recommended. The first is **Hawaiian Parasail** ★ (Kewalo Basin, 1085 Ala Moana Blvd.; ☎ 808/591-1280; www.tombarefoot.com; $46 for 10 min.), which takes you soaring off Waikiki and offers free shuttles from hotels. It also accepts people who use wheelchairs for parasailing (you will be carried onto the boat). Book online for a 10% discount. The other is **Hawaii Water Sports Center** ★ (Koko Marina Shopping Center; ☎ 808/395-3773; www.hawaiiwatersportscenter.com; parasail $59 for 10 min. in air, jet ski $69 for half-hour) is a one-stop shop for boat-related watersports such as parasailing, jet skiing, and wakeboarding. You'll be off the coast of Hawaii Kai—check out the luxurious beachfront homes as you loft in the air or rip the calm waters on your jet ski. **By bus:** no. 58 from Waikiki.

HORSEBACK RIDING

So you want to be a *paniolo* (Hawaiian cowboy)? Put yourself in the stirrups of the **Kualoa Ranch and Activity Club** (Kaaawa; ☎ 808/237-8515; www.kualoa.com; $59 for a 1-hr. ride, $89 for a 2-hr. ride), which owns two of the most spectacular valleys on the island. Single hour trots of the southern half of the 4,000-acre spread offer up delightful views of Chinaman's Hat and an 800-year-old fishpond. But I recommend you pay the extra $30 to go deep into Kaawa Valley, where scenes of *Jurassic Park* were filmed. It's easy to see why, with its rolling hills, stands of hau and hala trees, and guava groves. You'll also ride past World War II bunkers. The ranch offers ATV rides as well (but I prefer the quiet of horseback), and kayaking, and has a shooting range. It combines activities in full- and half-day packages that include a buffet lunch and round-trip transport from Waikiki; package prices range from $94 to $139 for adults and $69 to $79 for children.

Experienced riders will be happily surprised by the quality of horses at **Happy Trails Hawaii** (59-231 Pupukea Rd.; ☎ 808/638-7433; www.happytrailshawaii.com; $62 for a 1-hr. ride, $83 for 2 hr.) on the North Shore. The manager is a polo player, and many of his mounts are impeccably trained, retired, thoroughbred polo ponies. Guides take riders through tropical fruit orchards and rolling green ranchland. Ride time includes a briefing; Happy Trails accepts children 6 and older.

SKATEBOARDING

Grinding the stair railings of a public building isn't legal here, but that doesn't stop the hundreds of kids who find ways to amuse themselves everywhere from a Jiffy Lube parking lot to the roof of Manoa Elementary School. To keep skaters off the streets, the City & County of Honolulu have slowly been building skate parks around the island.

The epicenter of the Hawaiian scene is **Aala Park** (Beretania St., between Aala St. and River St.); with its lips and rails, Aala has the best street course. Exhibitions (pros Stevie Williams, Jack Curtin, Wade Desarmo, and Marcus McBride did a demo on this course in early 2006) and competitions are occasionally held here, but in general you'll find top local skaters hanging around most evenings—the park is lit until 9pm.

Kamiloiki Community Skatepark (7750 Hawaii Kai Dr., Hawaii Kai) has three miniramp bowls. Christian Hosoi has been known to drop by when he's in town.

In Kailua is Keolu Hills Skatepark, designed by Chuck Mitsui, who owns the Kailua skate shop **808 Skate** (354 Hahani St., Kailua; ☎ 808/263-0808; www.808skate.com). You'll find bowls and a street area.

For gear and perhaps hooking up with local skaters, visit **Aala Park Boardshop** (1200 College Walk, at Beretania St.; ☎ 808/585-8538), more commonly known as APB, on the edge of Chinatown. It's conveniently located across the street from the Aala Park skate park.

To find out about events and Oahu skate gossip, visit www.hirollingmedia.com, a local skateboard site run by former sponsored skater Ryan Toyama.

Discounted Golf Online

For last-minute and discount tee times, call **Stand-by Golf** (from Hawaii, call ☎ 888/645-BOOK; www.stand-bygolf.com), which offers discounted and guaranteed tee times for same-day or next-day golfing. You can call between 7am and 11pm Hawaii Standard Time, to book one of the seven semiprivate and resort courses they handle and get a guaranteed tee time for the next day at a 10% to 40% discount.

GOLF

When it comes to golf on Oahu, it's all about choices—there are 39 courses on the island and they range from easy executive links to one that's considered by many to be among the hardest on the planet (Ko'olau Golf Club, below). A couple of things to remember: Oahu has what many local golfers call "microclimates" that make it possible to almost always find a dry golf game; you simply have to be willing to drive. In the rainy winter months, head to the Leeward coast. Courses in Ewa and Makaha don't get nearly as much precipitation as the Koolau mountain range and North Shore courses.

There are also some good deals to be had for this sport of kings. You can expect to pay at least $90 or $100 at the public, semiprivate, and resort courses, but if you're willing to sacrifice well-kept fairways with yardage markers, the municipal courses are a great deal at just $42 a round. Actually, if you can get a tee time at Ala Wai Municipal, you're getting the best value on the island.

Ala Wai Municipal ★★ (404 Kapahulu Ave.; ☎ 808/733-7387 or 808/296-2000; $42 nonresidents) is the crème de la crème of the municipals, the flagship the city pumps its money into, and just a stone's throw from Diamond Head. (Good luck getting a weekend tee time, though—bookings for locals start at 6:30am, 7 days in advance, while nonresidents can book only 3 days in advance, so chances of getting an early-morning time are relegated to the standby list—which is always long.) This is the only municipal with good yardage markers, and the greens rival most on Oahu. It's known not only for its convenient Waikiki location, but for its abundance of long par-3s, at least three over 190 yards, and well-kept greens. Unlike the other municipals, Ala Wai has a great practice facility that's always busy, a beautiful clubhouse and restaurant, and marshals who give you the boot if your group is not keeping up to the group in front—that's how the Ala Wai is able to host more than 90,000 rounds a year, the most of any course in the country. Play fast, or play elsewhere.

Because getting a tee time at Ala Wai is like hitting the lottery, you might try the next best municipal option: **Ewa Village Golf Course** ★ (91-1760 Park Row St., Ewa Beach; ☎ 808/681-0220 or 808/296-2000; $42 nonresidents). There are some dirt patches on all the munis, but Ewa Village typically has consistent greens, better-than-average length, and a good mix of short and long holes. And it's cheap.

With spectacular ocean and mountain views, **Makaha West Golf Club** ★★ (84-626 Makaha Valley Rd., Waianae; ☎ 808/695-9544; $140 weekdays before noon, $95 after noon) is Oahu's underrated gem. The course is always well manicured, the ocean can be seen on most holes, and if you look to the mountain range, you'll almost always see rainbows lapping over each other. If it's raining on other parts of the island, local golfers trek to Makaha. ***Tip:*** Pay attention to where the mountains and ocean are on each putt—the grain on the Bermuda-grass greens pulls *makai* (toward the water). Played from the tips, the West course is one of the island's longest at more than 7,000 yards.

Playing at the **Ko'olau Golf Club** ★★ (45-550 Kionaole Rd., Kaneohe; ☎ 808/236-4653; $135, $99 after noon, $79 after 2pm) is more of a novelty, but you will be able to say you tackled the world's toughest course (as it's named). After you play it, you'll have a few more choice names for it, too. Tucked just below the Koolau mountain range in a rainforest, playing the course feels like being in *Jurassic Park* (in fact, scenes from the film were shot nearby). The par-4, 18th hole plays over two ravines, and if you're playing a skins game, it's not uncommon to offer an extra one for simply making par on the final hole, where the green is also surrounded by sand bunkers. Locals advise golfers to bring at least one ball per handicap number, and even if you're a single-digit handicap, you should bring a dozen balls. Then again, you can always step into the bush at virtually any spot on the course and find someone's lost ball. Because of the course's rainforest location, the high amount of rain makes it cart-path-only year-round.

There aren't too many golfers who aren't willing to shell out the $165 to play the **Arnold Palmer Course at Turtle Bay Resort** ★★★ (57-091 Kamehameha Hwy., Kahuku; ☎ 808/293-8574; $175 for the Palmer course, $155 for the Fazio course). If you can manage to play 36 holes in a day, this is the place to do it. The resort also features the **George Fazio Course.** Both courses have massive, undulating greens. If you really want a challenge, played from the tips, the Palmer course measures over 7,100 yards. When the trade winds are blowing, breaking 80 and even 90 is a heroic feat. Enjoy the course and play from the whites or blues. The cavernous greens and trade winds are enough of a challenge. The front of the Palmer course is more of a links course; the back features more trees.

Not as long as Turtle Bay (and the wind doesn't come into play as much), **Ko Olina Golf Club** ★★★ (92-1220 Aliinui Dr., Kapolei; ☎ 808/676-5300; www.koolinagolf.com; $150, $80 twilight, $110 after noon) offers amenities that are as big a draw as the course itself. In early February, you'll find NFL stars (in town for the Pro Bowl) dotting the fairways. The rest of the time, you'll see some wonderfully set-up holes, including one where you'll pass under a waterfall to get to the next tee. The par-4 18th is a great finishing hole. Big hitters will have to lighten up or risk losing their ball in the pond that's about 280 yards out from the blues. The approach shot is over the water onto a green surrounded by sand bunkers. When you finally sink your putt, the ultragourmet Roy's Restaurant is just a few steps away.

HIKING

With rainforests, waterfalls, streams, cliffs, valleys, and ridges—some right in Honolulu—Oahu is a hiker's paradise. Hitting the trails is a great way to see the island, especially since most paths lead up, ending with spectacular views.

Trail Guides

Want someone else to lead the way? **Oahu Nature Tours** (☎ 808/924-2473; www.oahunaturetours.com) mixes history and botany lessons along with Hawaiian legends into their guided hikes. You'll get a real sense of what you're hiking across.

Important: When you're hiking on Oahu, wear bright clothing, check your cellphone coverage, don a wide-brim hat, bring insect repellant and sun screen, and let friends and family know the route you're taking. Bring a lot of water. Don't think that you can't get lost because it's an island. For maps and detailed descriptions of Oahu's hikes, visit www.hawaiitrails.com, the website of Na Ala Hele, the state's Trail and Access program.

Ten minutes from Waikiki is the Makiki Forest Recreation Area, which has a network of trails I highly recommend for their convenience and variety. The trail head is at the **Hawaii Nature Center** (2131 Makiki Heights; ☎ 808/955-0100; www.hawaiinaturecenter.org), where you'll find a restroom and water fountain. From here, take the Kanealole trail, which connects to the easy 1.1-mile **Makiki Valley Trail** and the .7-mile **Maunalaha Trail** that rises to a dry, forested ridgeline, 500 feet above sea level. If you take the Makiki Valley Trail, you'll make a loop with nine interpretive signs about the forest you're walking through and the medicinal uses of the plants you see. The valley was once home to a thriving Hawaiian community and you'll view remnants of it—a stone wall here, a coffee plant there—as you hike. Cool and dense with trees, these are nifty hikes at any time of day.

If you're driving: On Makiki Street, driving toward the mountain, take a left on Makiki Heights Drive. Proceed about a half-mile. The road makes a sharp left turn, but continue straight, past a row of mailboxes and through a green gate. Continue up the road and park in the gravel parking lot on your left. Proceed up the road on foot; the trail head begins behind the public restroom.

Manoa Falls ★★ is a popular hike in town because it's short (great for families) and leads to a waterfall. If you hike it, pay the $5 to park in Paradise Park (a safer option than parking in the surrounding area; also, if you park anywhere on the fire land beyond Paradise Park, you'll be fined and towed). The **Wili Wili Nui Trail** is a quick trip to the top through a forest reserve filled with guava, mountain apples, and wild ginger. You'll be rewarded with a beautiful view, but be sure to bring bug repellent—the area is filled with mosquitoes; also **call ☎ 808/587-1300 before you set out** to make sure that the trail is open.

One of the locals' favorite hiking spots is the **Makapuu Lighthouse Trail.** It's just 1.4 miles in length and there's no designated parking area, but it's paved to the top, where you get a view of the lighthouse and passing ships. If you bring your binoculars, you should be able to see the show at Sea Life Park and the boogie boarders on Sandy Beach. You're likely to see whales in the winter months and turtles year-round. Park along Kalanianaole Highway (Hwy. 72), head through the gate, and stay on the road.

Long but easy, the 6.8-mile round-trip trail in the **Kaena Point Natural Area Reserve** is a great alternative to the forested mountain hikes. The payoff here is a wild coastline of dunes, where albatross nest during the winter. The trail follows the old bed of a train line that once hauled sugar cane to Honolulu. Go early to beat the heat—the sun is strong out at this westernmost point of Oahu—and take water with you.

If you're driving: Take Kamehameha Highway all the way to the end. Park by the bathroom and lifeguard stand to avoid having your car broken into, and walk to the trail head at the end of the road.

BIKING

Oahu is not a bike-friendly island. Bisected by the HI freeway, it's easy to find yourself in hairy four-way intersections under overpasses. Though there are bike lanes on roads within the city, they aren't respected by local drivers. And there's no getting around the fact that the island is divided by two mountain ranges—that's a lot of uphill roads.

Now that you have our warning, there are a handful of areas that are nice for street cruises—around Kapiolani Park, Waikiki, and Ala Moana Beach Park, for example, all of which have bike lanes that are respected. If you're an avid two-wheeler, check out the great values at **Big Kahuna Rentals** (407 Seaside Ave.; ☎ 888/451-5544 or 808/924-2736; www.bigkahunarentals.com; $20 for 24 hr., $100 per week). Prices include a Giant-brand bike, a city map, locks, and helmets. The staff will point you to the safer areas to ride, including toward Kapiolani Park and into the posh residential neighborhood of Kahala. You can bike up to Diamond Head from Waikiki, spend a few hours hiking up the crater, then bolt back down to your hotel without dealing with heavy traffic congestion.

On the North Shore, **Barnfield's Raging Isle Surf & Cycle** (66-250 Kamehameha Hwy., Bldg. B, Haleiwa; ☎ 808/637-7707) rents mountain bikes starting at $40 a day and has bike racks available for your rental car.

If you like to play in the dirt, there's only one place to go on Oahu: **Bike Hawaii** ★ kids (☎ 877/682-7433; www.bikehawaii.com). Gregarious owner and guide John Alford is a competitive mountain biker and wrote the book *Mountain Biking Hawaii,* a guide to the best spots on six of the Hawaiian Islands. I highly recommend the 6-mile, 3-hour Kaaawa Valley tour. The valley is privately owned by Kualoa Ranch (p. 165), and the only way to see this primeval swath of land is to book a horseback or ATV ride on the ranch, or to mountain-bike with Alford. You don't have to be a rock-hopping expert to take the tour, but if you are, a guide will split off from the beginner group to advanced single-track trails, so everyone

Hiking & Car Thieves

Cars parked near trail heads are targets for thieves. If you drive to a hiking spot, be sure not to leave valuables in the car. Leave your wallet in the hotel safe, and do *not* leave anything of value in the trunk. Thieves can pop open your trunk faster than you can open it with your car key.

The Century Ride

In late September, hundreds of people enter the annual Honolulu Century Ride, which begins and ends at Kapiolani Park. You can ride 25, 50, 75, or 100 miles (the longest stretch goes all the way to Hauula) and it's a great way to see the island. Download an entry form at www.hbl.org. At this same site, you'll find helpful listings of bike-route maps and mountain-biking trails, along with weekly rides and clinics available the rest of the year.

is happy. Besides getting a good ride, you'll explore a World War II bunker (which is now a mini-museum highlighting the films that have been shot in the valley), ride through dense stands of hala, hau, and guava trees (if they're in season, guides might even pick some fruit for you to taste), and learn about the flora and valley history from your knowledgeable guides. To give you an idea of the trail variety, Kaaawa Valley is where the annual 24 Hours of Hell mountain-bike competition is held.

If you prefer a road ride, another excellent tour is the 6-hour Bike & Hike—Alford leases 200 acres of private land in Manoa and his company is the only one that can take people on this 2-mile round-trip hike through lush forest to a waterfall. You'll see brilliant red torch ginger, the remnants of ancient Hawaiian taro patches, and maybe a rare bird or two. From the hike, Bike Hawaii shuttles you to the top of Tantalus and you cruise 5 miles downhill, taking in panoramic city views and a roadside lunch. Both tours cost $96 for adults ($72 for kids 13 and under).

For experienced mountain bikers: You won't find it on their website, but upon request Alford will set up an exclusive "100% Dirt Tour," a guided, hard-core, single-track trail ride.

Bike Hawaii supplies the suspension bikes (good-quality Trek models), helmets, and sandwich lunches, and it picks up riders at a number of Waikiki Hotels. The company also has a tour that includes snorkeling in the mix, and a hike-only option.

SKYDIVING

If you're going to plunge out of a plane, Oahu is one of the best places to do it—from 11,000 to 13,000 feet up, you can see the entire island while sating your inner adrenalin junkie. The instructors are world-class and both local companies have excellent safety records.

That being said, I think the better choice between the two is **Pacific International Skydiving** ★★★ (☎ 808/637-7472; www.pacific-skydiving.com; $298 tandem jump, book online and save an additional $100 off ; must be 18 or older and weigh less than 240 lb.; no scuba diving 24 hr. prior, day advance), which has a newer, more powerful plane (King Air 100) that is quicker and can attain a higher altitude. Pacific International runs $100-off coupons in local tourist publications such as *This Week Oahu,* which is available for free all over the island, from street racks in Waikiki to hotel lobbies.

Skydive Hawaii ★★ (☎ 808/637-9700; www.skydivehawaii.com; $225, book online to save an additional $75; must be 18 or older and weigh less than 200 lb.) gets a lot of traffic in part because it's the first company you hit at the airfield.

Both companies offer tandem jumps for first-timers as well as courses to become a certified skydiver.

If you're driving: From Honolulu, take H-1 West to H-2 North. When H-2 ends, it turns into Highway 803, which you'll take past Schofield Barracks toward Mokuleia. Follow the signs to Waialua, past the blinking light. At the circle drive, stay left and you'll hit Farrington Highway (Hwy. 930). Go 4½ miles to the Dillingham Airfield. Skydive Hawaii is the first building on the left, Pacific Skydiving the third.

HELICOPTER TOURS

There's only one way to see Oahu's hidden gem, a majestic, 1,000-foot waterfall, and that's by helicopter tour. About 10 years ago, 10 hikers died in a mudslide while trekking to the cascade—what we know as Sacred Falls—and the once-popular hiking trail has been off-limits to the public ever since. That's where helicopters come in—they offer the only opportunity to hover over Sacred Falls, deep in Kaaawa Valley. Helicopter tours are the quickest and most scenic way to tour Oahu and other islands. You can look inside Diamond Head Crater, get a bird's-eye view of where the Japanese flew in and bombed Pearl Harbor, and travel across the North Shore, Kaaawa Valley, and every other scenic spot on the island. Most of the tour operations are based out of Turtle Bay Resort's helipad. **Paradise Helicopters** (☎ 808/293-2570; www.paradisecopters.com; $120–$220) and **Mauna Loa Helicopters** (☎ 808/834-6799; www.maunaloahelicopters.com; $135–$240) are both based out of Turtle Bay. The rest of the helicopters are based at the airport. Tours for all helicopter services range from 15 minutes to 2 hours or more. Another solid company, **Makani Kai Helicopters** (☎ 808/834-5813; www.makanikai.com; $325/hr.) often hooks up with incoming cruise-line ships to give their passengers rides.

GLIDER RIDES

Observing the island by glider is the opposite of noisy helicopters; you'll feel like a whisper in the clouds soaring over Oahu, which has wind conditions that make it one of the best places on earth to pilot gliders. **Soar Hawaii** (Dillingham Airfield Gate #2, Rte. 930, Mokuleia; ☎ 808/637-3147; www.soarhawaii.com; $39 for 10 min., $178 for 1 hr.) offers four different glider rides that run from a serene sightseeing tour to an acrobatic stomach-turner with somersaults. The company has six glider planes and two tow planes. Kids must be 11 or older to fly alone. The scenic tour takes you over Mount Kaala, the highest mountain on the island, part of the Waianae range, and the cliffs and breaking surf on the North Shore. On clear days, you can see most of the island, including Pearl Harbor, Diamond Head, and Honolulu.

ATTENTION, SHOPPERS!

For a long time, shopping on Oahu was geared to Japanese tourists, which explains the prevalence of high-end boutiques—including Prada, Yves Saint Laurent, Chanel, and Gucci—along Kalakaua Avenue. Goods from shops like these are a lot cheaper here than in Tokyo and designer-hungry Japanese flock to them, dropping hundreds a pop. Honolulu is also home to the world's largest open-air mall, and 45 minutes away is a big outlet center. When I travel, I like to buy things that speak of the place but aren't made expressly for tourists. That's what I concentrate on here.

MALLS

When it opened in 1959, **Ala Moana Center** (1450 Ala Moana Blvd.; ☎ 808/955-9517; www.alamoana.com) was the biggest shopping center in the nation. Still growing, it's now the largest open-air shopping center in the world, with more than 260 shops and restaurants. If shopping is your hobby, you can easily spend a whole day here, taking a break at the food court (for Hawaiian food, try the Poi Bowl), and strolling from one end to the other. More than 56 million people shuffle through its four levels every year (it's especially crowded in the run-up to the holidays, and parking is nonexistent then). You'll find numerous high-end stores—Neiman Marcus, Prada, Christian Dior, and Armani; mall staples like Gap and Banana Republic; and lots of other usual suspects.

But you can also buy local here. Hawaii's premier maker of koa furniture, jewelry boxes, and other knickknacks is **Martin & MacArthur** (mall level; ☎ 808/941-0074). For high-end ukuleles, where else would you head but **Ukulele House** (mall level; ☎ 808/955-8587). For surf shorts, bathing suits, surf gear, and street wear, there are three Hawaii-based companies with shops in Ala Moana: **Locals Only** (street level; ☎ 808/942-1555), **Island Snow** (mall level; ☎ 808/943-0088), and **Hawaiian Island Creations** (street level; ☎ 808/973-6780). At **Honolulu City Store** (street level; ☎ 808/955-3075), goods are emblazoned with the names of city agencies, such as Honolulu Fire Department T-shirts. **Products of Hawaii, Too** (street level; ☎ 808/949-6866) and **Islands' Best** (street level; ☎ 808/949-5345) sell locally made crafts and foods such as jams, chocolates, and condiments.

For everything Japanese, from Hello Kitty stickers to sake sets, Oahuans head to **Shirokiya** (mall level; ☎ 808/973-9160), where the food department is chockfull of delicious prepared foods. Buy a bento lunch and take it across the street to Ala Moana Beach Park.

Honolulu's two other main shopping hubs are **Ward Centre** (1200 Ala Moana Blvd.; ☎ 808/591-8411) and **Ward Warehouse** (1050 Ala Moana Blvd.; ☎ 808/591-8411)—which are on a more human scale than Ala Moana (and just west of the giant mall on Ala Moana Blvd.). They're part of a complex called Victoria Ward Centers, named after the woman who, with her husband, developed a luxurious 100-acre estate that stretched from Blaisdell Concert Hall to this consumer zone.

Ward Centre features **Welcome to the Islands** (☎ 808/593-2035), which carries locally produced body-care lines, home furnishings, and clothing; a **Borders Books & Music** (☎ 808/591-8995) with a good Hawaiian book section; and the cool Pacific-oriented home-design shop **SoHa** (☎ 808/591-9777).

At Ward Warehouse, former international model **Mamo Howell** (☎ 808/591-2002; www.mamohowell.com) has an eponymous store selling resort-wear designs that run from $40 T-shirts to dramatic full-length floral muumuus for $160.

Mall Time

Ala Moana Center: Open Monday to Saturday 9:30am to 9pm, Sunday 10am to 7pm. From Waikiki, catch TheBus 8, 19, 20, 42, or 58. Buses drop off passengers at the Kona Street Transit Center on the north side of the center. Ala Moana also offers $2 shuttle transportation (look for the Pink Line trolleys) between 10 Waikiki locations. Runs 7 days a week, every 8 minutes. Pickup at Ala Moana Center is at the Ala Moana Boulevard trolley depot. Shuttle stops: Royal Hawaiian Shopping Center, Duke Kahanamoku Statue, Aston Waikiki Beach Hotel, Waikiki Sand Villa Hotel, Ambassador Hotel of Waikiki, Hilton Hawaiian Village, Palms at Waikiki, and Ilikai Hotel (on Ala Moana Blvd., adjacent to Ilikai Hotel).

Ward Warehouse and Ward Centre: Open Monday to Saturday 10am to 9pm, Sunday 10am to 5pm. From Waikiki, you can catch TheBus 19, 20, or 42 from Kuhio Avenue. Other city bus lines that service Victoria Ward Centers are no. 6 (University/Pauoa), nos. 55 and 65 (Kaneohe), and nos. 56 and 57 (Kailua). The Waikiki Trolley (Sightseeing Red Line and Shopping Yellow Line; ☎ 808/593-2822) and Rainbow Trolley (☎ 808/539-9495) stop at the Victoria Ward Centers.

Note: Most shops are closed on Easter Sunday, Thanksgiving Day, and Christmas Day.

Cinnamon Girl (☎ 808/591-6532; www.cinnamongirl.com) specializes in original-print sundresses, tops, and skirts (and lots of mother-daughter match-ups) with dresses running from $59 to $170. The **Nohea Gallery** (☎ 808/591-9001; www.noheagallery.com) features work by local artisans; you can pick up $10 dish towels with Hawaiian prints or hand-turned koa bowls for $200.

In the face of Oahu's high cost of living, residents love bargains. When the **Waikele Premium Outlets** (94–790 Lumiaina St., Waipahu; ☎ 808/676-5656; www.premiumoutlets.com) opened in the 1990s, locals went crazy. And Japanese tourists crowd the trolleys that shuttle from Waikiki to Waikele, a 45-minute drive from Honolulu. I go out there to shop at the Barneys New York outlet once in a while. Otherwise, it's like any other outlet mall on the mainland (with such stores as Coach, Calvin Klein and A/X Armani Exchange). The few Hawaii-based companies represented here include Hawaiian Moon, Local Motion, and Crazy Shirts.

ANTIQUES

On Kapahulu Avenue, drive toward the mountains and on the left you'll spy the **Hawaii Antique Center** (932 Kapahulu Ave.; ☎ 808/734-6222). This no-frills shop carries cool Polynesian design items from Hawaii's prestatehood days. You can find carved monkeypod lamps, vintage posters, glassware, koa, and rattan furniture upholstered with floral bark-cloth fabrics. Prices range from $10 for little collectibles like Primo (a now extinct locally brewed beer) to $2,500 for a set of furniture.

BOOKSTORES

If you're looking for a book on any aspect of Hawaii—nature, history, traditional arts—chances are you'll find it at **Native Books/Na Mea Hawai'i** (Ward Centre, 1050 Ala Moana Blvd.; ☎ 800/887-7751 or 808/597-8967; www.nativebooks hawaii.com). This shop is more than a bookstore. It's like a community center, with free classes in Hawaiian language and lauhala weaving, artist demonstrations, and a weekly concert by top performers in the mini-amphitheater outside the shop. Owner Maile Meyer carries art, handicrafts, jewelry, clothing, and body products that are all made in Hawaii. So, yes, that kukui-nut lei is more expensive than the one you saw at the jewelry stall in Ala Moana, but that's because it was made here, not in the Philippines—discerning eyes can easily see the difference in quality. There's also a branch in the Waikiki Hilton Hawaiian Village (2005 Kalia Rd.; ☎ 808/949-3989).

CLOTHING

Around since 1963, **Tahiti Imports** (1174 Waimanu St.; ☎ 808/591-2929; www.tahitiimports.com) carries fabrics from Tahiti and ones that co-owner Betty Lou Severson designs. You can buy shirts, skirts, and dresses made from the colorful floral cloths. If you're looking for a cool beach wrap, I highly recommend this shop.

Two well-known local artisans teamed up to open **Mango Season** (2636 S. King St.; ☎ 808/949-4355), where you can stock up on made-in-Hawaii gifts—most of them under $30. You'll find T-shirts by Cane Haul Road, which is known for designs that make whimsical design puns out of local sayings and traditions, and clothing by Tutuvi, made from beautiful Polynesian-patterned, hand-screened fabrics, along with lots of other handcrafted items. In the Moiliili neighborhood, Mango Season is on a busy stretch of King Street near the university.

Kapahulu Avenue, on the Diamond Head end of Waikiki, has evolved into an antiques alley. Vintage aloha-shirt collectors gravitate to **Bailey's Antiques and Aloha Shirts** (517 Kapahulu Ave.; ☎ 808/734-7628). People plunk down $5,000 for especially rare shirts, like one from Samoa, but the packed-to-the-rafters store has more affordable finds, like vintage University of Hawaii T-shirts and Polynesian tiki kitsch, and it's a fun place to browse.

Aloha Bling

Hawaii has its own style of gold jewelry, involving floral designs such as earrings in the shape of plumerias and old English lettering on bracelets. Bracelets are especially popular here. One of the best manufacturers of traditional Hawaiian jewelry is **Philip Rickard Honolulu** (Royal Hawaiian Shopping Center, 1st floor Ilima Court, 2201 Kalakaua Ave.; ☎ 808/924-7972; www.philiprickardhonolulu.com). Rickard's bangles caught the eye of pop diva Gwen Stefani, who had her models sport his jewelry in the shows of her design line L.A.M.B.

Enterprising young Oahuans have opened a slew of street-wear shops in the last few years, most of them featuring their own designs, along with name-brand products. Honolulu's cool 20-something guys get their sneakers at **Kicks Hawaii** (1522 Makaloa St., second floor; ☎ 808/941-9191), which specializes in limited-edition and other hard-to-find shoes. There's also an in-house clothing line called Bittersweet. It's 1 block *mauka* of Ala Moana Center. Kicks Hawaii shares its space with **Leilow** (☎ 808/941-9191; www.leilow.com), a brand created by British former pro skater Jules Gayton.

In4mation (Ward Warehouse, 1050 Ala Moana Blvd., ☎ 808/597-1447, and Waikiki Shopping Plaza, 2250 Kalakaua Ave.; ☎ 808/923-0888; www.in4mants.com) sells in-house-designed T-shirts and the latest sneakers and street wear from other companies such as Stussy and Nike.

Former pro skater Rene Mathyssen and clothing designer Keola Rapozo launched **Fitted Hawaii** (1438 Kona St.; ☎ 808/942-3100) last year. Hawaii's exclusive vendor of New Era baseball caps, Fitted sells limited editions of the head gear, made with materials like linen and silk. Also in the lineup are in-house-designed T-shirts that beat the usual tops emblazoned with designs for tourists. The little boutique is just across the street from Ala Moana.

FOOD

Pat's Island Delights (Davies Pacific Center, 841 Bishop St., ☎ 808/536-1414; and Waiau Center, 98–459 Kamehameha Hwy., Pearl City, ☎ 808/484-8808; www.patsislanddelights.com) sells exclusive locally made edible goodies such as chocolates, cookies, and condiments.

NIGHTLIFE ON OAHU

Oahu's nightlife is the most diverse and rich of all the Hawaiian Islands. The tastes of an extremely varied group of revelers shaped it—royalty, wealthy expats, rabble-rousing military, and plantation workers looking to escape harsh reality—so today you have everything available from high-quality opera (a favorite diversion of King Kalakaua) to chic dance clubs to dive bars.

THE PERFORMING ARTS

The **Neal S. Blaisdell Center** (777 Ward Ave., at King St.; ☎ 808/591-2211; www.blaisdellcenter.com) is Honolulu's entertainment complex and an integral part of life on the island. Named after Honolulu's mayor from 1954 to 1968, the center is made up of a concert hall, arena, and exhibition hall. Among the resident companies that play the concert hall regularly are:

- **Honolulu Symphony** (☎ 808/792-2000; www.honolulusymphony.com). This world-class ensemble of skilled musicians has accompanied such important visiting artists as soprano star Renée Fleming and violinist Sarah Chang.
- **The Symphony Pops** (☎ 808/792-2000; www.honolulusymphony.com). The symphony is especially popular under the baton of charismatic composer-singer-saxophonist Matt Catingub. Dear to locals' hearts because he's part Samoan (his mother was jazz vocalist Mavis Rivers), Catingub puts together innovative programs, including bringing in Kenny G in 2008. He also

High-Culture Seasons

Ballet Hawaii: Two productions a year, August and December (the annual Nutcracker). The ballet also brings in visiting companies in October.

Hawaii Opera Theatre: February to March; in July HOT puts on something lighter, such as a Gilbert & Sullivan operetta or a Broadway musical.

Honolulu Symphony: Masterworks season runs from September to November, and from January to May.

Honolulu Symphony Pops: September to December, and March and April.

appeared in the jazz band in George Clooney's *Good Night, and Good Luck.* (Catingub became friends with the actor/director's aunt when she performed her last-ever concert with the Pops—the recording earned a Grammy nomination in 2002.)

- **Hawaii Opera Theatre** (☎ 808/596-7858; www.hawaiiopera.org). Opera has a long history in Hawaii—royalty like King David Kalakaua loved it. Hawaii Opera Theater continues the tradition under the direction of Honolulu-born Henry Akina, who spent 14 years in Berlin, where he founded the Berlin Chamber Opera.
- **Ballet Hawaii** (☎ 808/521-6514; www.ballethawaii.org). It's not the New York City Ballet, but this little company keeps Oahu on point. Each year, it does one ballet (last year was Coppélia), and its annual Nutcracker production, with a visiting dancer doing principal duties.

Big acts like the Eagles and Elton John perform at the **Arena** when they come to town. Comedians Jerry Seinfeld and Lewis Black have also taken its stage.

Officially part of the Blaisdell complex, but in Kapiolani park, the **Waikiki Shell** (2805 Monsarrat Ave., in Kapiolani Park; ☎ 808/527-5400) is home to the annual Cazimero Brothers' May Day/Lei Day concert (see the sidebar "May Day at the Shell," below) and hosts concerts by performers such as Jack Johnson, Snoop Dogg, and Jimmy Buffett. When the moon and stars are out, this amphitheater is the venue that makes locals feel lucky to live in Hawaii.

Its renovation completed in 2004, the 1922 **Hawaii Theatre** (1130 Bethel St., at Pauahi St.; ☎ 808/528-0506; www.hawaiitheatre.com) promptly won the 2005 Award for Outstanding Restoration Project from the League of Historic American Theatres. The Beaux Arts facade now sports a new marquee, emblazoned with the names of upcoming shows—including Menopause the Musical, Kenny Rankin, and Les Ballet Trockadero de Monte Carlo (a famed all-male ballet troupe). In 1984, the dilapidated theater was likely headed for demolition when concerned citizens formed the nonprofit Hawaii Theatre Center to save the structure. Now you can take a weekly "behind the scenes" **guided tour** (Tues 11am–noon; $5), where docents will take you through the theater, its history,

May Day at the Shell

An Oahu tradition—2008 marks its 31st year—is the Cazimero Brothers' **May Day/Lei Day concert at the Waikiki Shell** ★★ (2805 Monsarrat Ave., in Kapiolani Park; ☎ 808/527-5400). Locals prefer to bypass the reserved seating and buy general admission lawn seating, pack up picnics (but no booze allowed), and spread out mats on the expanse of grass (people can get pretty territorial). It's a great night under the stars at this amphitheater. Robert and Roland Cazimero, part of the 1970s Hawaiian music renaissance, sing in their heart-zinging harmonies, and are joined by surprise local-superstar guests such as Amy Hanaialii-Gilliom. The duo is also accompanied by two hula *halau* (schools): Robert's Gentlemen of Na Kamalei and frequent collaborator Leinaala Kalama Heine's Ladies of Na Pualei O Likolehua. If you're in town on May 1, don't miss it. Gates open at 5:30pm, show at 7:30pm.

architecture, artwork, and a demonstration of the mammoth Robert Morton Orchestral Theatre Pipe Organ. Book the guided tour in advance; sometimes it is cancelled due to rehearsals. For an upcoming schedule, visit the website. One caveat: The seats aren't the most comfortable in town.

BEST LOCAL ENTERTAINMENT

To see some of Hawaii's master traditional musicians, go to the Waikiki Beach Marriott Resort & Spa's **Moana Terrace** ★★★ (2552 Kalakaua Ave.; ☎ 808/922-6611). On Sunday nights, George Kuo, Aaron Mahi, and Martin Pahinui take the stage, playing the great Hawaiian songbook. Bassist Mahi led the Royal Hawaiian Band for 25 years, Pahinui is the son of the late, great slack-key guitarist Gabby Pahinui (his voice is a dead ringer for his dad's), and Kuo is a slack-key virtuoso. There's no admission; just sip a passion-fruit margarita and sit on the open-air terrace overlooking Waikiki listening to Hawaiian favorites like "Pua Lililehua" and "Hiilawe." Chances are you'll be sitting among other well-known musicians, such as Eddie Kamae, who come to listen to their friends play and sit in on the jam sessions.

Come to Halekulani's **House Without a Key** ★★ (2199 Kalia Rd., at Lewers St.; ☎ 800/367-2343 or 808/923-2311; www.halekulani.com)—a big lanai anchored by a giant keawe tree—on Monday and Tuesday nights, when the islanders set up their instruments. Leader Alan Akaka is a master steel guitarist who also happens to be the son of U.S. Senator Daniel Akaka and a music teacher at the prestigious Kamehameha Schools. His short histories and explanations teach you a lot about Hawaiian music.

The restaurant **Chai's Island Bistro** ★ (Aloha Tower Marketplace, 1 Aloha Tower Dr., off Ala Moana Blvd.; ☎ 808/585-0011) showcases Hawaii's biggest contemporary-music stars—the Cazimero Brothers, Jerry Santos (he was half of the 1970s duo Olomana; if you want to take home some Hawaiian CDs, buy the band's masterpiece *Like a Seabird on the Wind*), slack-key virtuoso Makana, and opera-trained Amy Hanaialii-Gilliom, among others. The catch is you have to buy dinner (there are zero lounge seats and not many stools at the bar), and entrees run from $26 to $39 (the menu is so-so Hawaiian Regional Cuisine). If you don't feel embarrassed by ordering just a couple of appetizers ($9.95–$12), which is what I do, it's actually not a bad deal.

BARS & CLUBS

Chinatown

For Oahu's night crawlers, Chinatown has supplanted Waikiki as the place to be, with cool clubs clustered on or near Hotel Street.

Artist and impresario Gelareh Khoie partnered with internationally known DJ Harvey to open **thirtyninehotel** ★★ (39 N. Hotel St., between Smith St. and Nuuanu Ave.; ☎ 808/599-2552; www.thirtyninehotel.com; $8 cover). By night, the club hosts live jazz and visiting and resident DJs (my favorite spot is on the outdoor lanai). By day, thirtyninehotel is an art gallery (Tues–Sat noon–6pm), featuring contemporary local artists. The door is unmarked; enter and walk up the stairs to the second floor.

To the right of thirtyninehotel is **NextDoor** ★★ (43 N. Hotel St.; ☎ 808/550-0496; www.whoisnextdoor.com; $10–$20 cover), a lounge-cinema-music venue started by Brazilian filmmaker Sergio Goes and promoters Chris Kahunahana and Miguel Innes. With its exposed brick walls, double-height ceilings, and plush red couches, NextDoor is my favorite place for a night out. DJs and MCs such as Los Angeles's Z-Trip and Myka Nyne, and New York's Ursula 1000, have played here.

To the left of thirtyninehotel is **Bar 35** (35 N. Hotel St.; ☎ 808/537-3535; www.bar35hawaii.com), a swank drinkery with glass-topped tables and exposed brick walls. The bar says it has 110 beers (although it seems like they're out of the one I want every time I go there), along with wine, cocktails, and pizzas—besides a classic margherita pizza (with mozzarella, tomato, and basil), you can get versions with Indian and Thai accents. The crowd here is more mainstream than the previous two venues.

Around the corner from these three venues is **Indigo Eurasian Cuisine** (1121 Nuuanu Ave.; ☎ 808/521-2900; www.indigo-hawaii.com), which spearheaded the Chinatown revival when it opened in 1994. This nightlife minicomplex includes two small bars called the Green Room and the Opium Den, and a restaurant serving Pacific Rim cuisine until 10pm. The space, broken up into little rooms and alcoves in a historic building, later turns into a club with DJs and live music. When street artist Shepard Fairey was in town for a residency at the Contemporary Museum in fall 2005, he manned the turntables here.

Note: There's very little crime in this area, but don't be shocked if you see a couple of down-and-outs smoking ice (crystal methamphetamine) when you exit these places late at night.

For a more sophisticated bar, head to the Halekulani hotel's **Lewers Lounge** (2199 Kalia Rd., at Royal Hawaiian Ave.; ☎ 808/367-2343; www.halekulani.com), where New York star mixologist Dale DeGroff is in residency 1 week a month. As the hotel's director of beverage arts, DeGroff has revamped the cocktail menu and made it the best in town. Classic drinks like Bees Knees and new creations (try

Party Time

On Oahu, clubs are generally open from 7pm to 2am.

the Mai Tai Royale, made with champagne) are created with fresh fruit juices. DeGroff also teaches cocktail-making classes during the week he's in town, which can be a fun detour from your beach routine.

Waikiki

Waikiki is packed with bars and clubs, and many restaurants and other venues host once-a-week parties. Here are some of the best:

Go-go dancers and a sleek crowd of under-30 partiers have made **Fashion 45** (Waikiki Trade Center, second floor, 2255 Kuhio Ave.; ☎ 808/922-4599; www.fashion45hawaii.com; Wed–Fri only; $15 cover) the success that it is. Lounge in the White Room (yes, it's like being in a cloud), on the white leather couches, or freak out on the spacious main room's dance floor. Grab a vodka tonic from one of the many bars sprinkled throughout the club. On Wednesday, women are admitted free before 11pm.

The Sheraton Waikiki's **Hanohano Room** (2255 Kalakaua Ave.; ☎ 808/922-4422), on the 30th floor, has long been a place where older patrons went for a swank supper-club evening, or to sip highballs at the bar looking out at the sweeping view of Waikiki's lights. But in the past couple of years, the aging space has been renovated and a new space called the Cobalt Lounge was added, which is the scene of two parties, one for the young and hip, the other for the young at heart. On the first and third Saturdays of each month is Skyline ($10), a throbbing scenester event that heats up around midnight. On Fridays, 40-to-60-somethings take over for Live Jazz Fridays (9pm–midnight; free), when Oahu's top jazz acts, such as Honolulu Jazz Quartet and trumpeter DeShannon Higa perform. Sip a Blue Ginger martini ($8), then hit the dance floor. Of course, you can drop in at the Cobalt Lounge on any night. Enjoy nightly 5 to 7pm happy-hour drink and appetizer specials ($5–$12).

The granddaddy of Waikiki nightclubs is **Wave Waikiki** (1877 Kalakaua Ave., at Hobron Lane; ☎ 808/941-0424; www.wavewaikiki.com), which turned 25 last year. The club is known for its events: One night is a Girls Gone Wild Ultimate Rush, the next is a Honolulu bartender flair contest. The venue also hosts live bands and brings in DJs. This is where I go for a raucous night of dance abandon. The painting of a snorkeling geisha out front is by well-known local artist Roy Venters.

One of Honolulu's newest venues is **Jazz Minds Art and Café** ★ (1661 Kapiolani Blvd.; ☎ 808/945-0800), a clubby lounge where you can hear some of the island's best jazz bands, such as the Honolulu Jazz Quartet, and top comedians like Andy Bumatai. Sink into plush sofas or perch at the bar and order some pupu; the kitchen turns out well-done platters of local and Korean food.

What's Happening Where?

To find out what DJs are playing, where to catch lounge acts, find the latest local comedy showcase, or just see what movies are playing, pick up the latest issue of *Honolulu Weekly,* Oahu's free alternative newspaper, which you can find in red boxes around the island. Or buy the Friday edition of the *Honolulu Advertiser,* the island's largest daily, which includes a pullout TGIF section filled with complete entertainment listings. Honolulu's other daily, the *Star-Bulletin,* also has a pull-out "What's Happening" section on Friday.

LIVE MUSIC

The acoustics are terrible, but **Pipeline Café** (805 Pohukaina St.; ☎ 808/589-1999; www.pipelinecafe.net) in Kakaako (near the Victoria Ward Centers) nevertheless is the main live-music venue in town, bringing in rock (the Strokes), hip-hop (Pharcyde), comedy (Robert Shimmel), and DJs (Q-Bert). It's a shoebox of a concert space; upstairs are pool tables, electronic dartboards, and a bar. Check out the website for a current lineup.

GAY BARS & CLUBS

The hub of gay Honolulu is 33-year-old **Hula's Bar and Lei Stand** (Waikiki Grand Hotel, 134 Kapahulu Ave., at Kalakaua Ave., second floor; ☎ 808/923-0669; www.hulas.com) in Waikiki. Owned by impresario Jack Law (Wave Waikiki is also his), Hula's was once the best nightspot, period, in the 1970s, when it was in an open-air location. When it was razed to make way for a shopping center, Law moved the club to this second-floor space with a balcony overlooking Kapahulu Avenue and the zoo. It's still packed most nights, with every kind of man lined up around the big rectangular bar. Speedo-clad go-go boys and special events keep the place humming—if you're looking to hook up, this is the place to go. Hula's even hosts a once-a-week outing: Gay Luau Night. For $85, you can board a bus with up to 14 other gay men and go to the Ko Olina Resort luau on Sunday.

The most laid-back gay gathering place is the bar **Angles** (2256 Kuhio Ave., at Seaside Ave., second floor; ☎ 808/926-9766 or info line 808/923-1130), also in Waikiki. People are friendly, and my gay friends like to drop in to sit on the outdoor lanai, have a drink and chat, and maybe shoot a game of pool. Guys in tank tops and shorts perch around the blond-wood, green-topped bar. Angles hosts a catamaran cruise every Sunday—meet at the bar at 11am and ask the bartender for details.

Oahu's drag queens gather at **Fusion** (2260 Kuhio Ave., second floor; ☎ 808/924-2422), Oahu's only after-hours gay nightclub (it's open until 4am), featuring all-male strip revues, the Gender Bender Lip Gloss Revue on Friday, and the Paper Doll Revue on Saturday. The spot is very local—if you want to meet someone born and raised here, Fusion is for you. Cover charge ranges from free to $5.

ABCs of Oahu

ATMs/Currency Exchange ATMs can be found outside banks, in supermarkets, at shopping centers, and in convenience stores such as 7-Eleven. There is a currency-exchange kiosk at the airport. In town, there is a **Travelex Currency Exchange** (1450 Ala Moana Blvd., second floor; ☎ **808/949-2813**). In Waikiki, the **First Hawaiian Bank** (2181 Kalakaua Ave.; ☎ **808/943-4670**) has a currency exchange.

Business Hours Banks are open Monday to Friday from 8:30am to 4pm. Open hours for offices are Monday to Friday 9am to 5pm. Most stores are open Monday to Saturday from 9am to 5pm, but the large shopping centers such as Ala Moana Center and Ward Centre are open 7 days a week, with extended hours.

Doctors/Hospital Honolulu has 11 major hospitals. Two of the best to call if you need medical assistance are **Queens Medical Center** (1301 Punchbowl St.; ☎ **808/538-9011**) and **Kuakini Medical Center** (347 N. Kuakini St.; ☎ **808/536-2236**).

Emergencies For police, fire, or ambulance, call ☎ **911.**

Internet Access There are many Internet cafes in Honolulu. In Waikiki, there's **Caffe Giovannini** (1888 Kalakaua Ave.; ☎ **808/979-2299;** www.caffegiovannini.com), which doubles as an Internet lounge with seven computers. The biggest is **e-topia** (1363 S. Beretania St.; ☎ **808/593-2050;** www.theetopia.com) with 40 computers and a T1 connection.

Pharmacies **Longs Drugs** is where most locals go to get prescriptions filled, and there are locations all over the island, including one in Ala Moana Center (☎ **808/949-4010;** 8am–7pm). In Waikiki, there's a pharmacy in the Ohana Waikiki West Hotel (2330 Kuhio Ave.; ☎ 808/922-5022; 8am–10pm).

Police In an emergency, call ☎ **911.** In non-emergency situations, go to or call the **Honolulu Police Department** (801 S. Beretania St.; ☎ **808/529-3111**).

Post Office Post offices are all over the island and most are open Monday to Friday from 8am to 4:30pm. The main post office is adjacent to the airport. The downtown post office is at 335 Merchant St. (☎ 808/532-1987). The Makiki Post Office (111 Lunalilo St.; ☎ 808/532-5689) is also open Saturday from 8am to 2pm.

Visitor Information Oahu doesn't have a central tourist office to visit in person. But its two tourism offices send printed material by mail and have informative websites; **Hawaii Visitors & Convention Bureau** (2270 Kalakaua Ave.; ☎ **800/464-2924** or 808/923-1811; www.gohawaii.com); and **Oahu Visitors Bureau** (733 Bishop St., suite 1520; ☎ **877/525-6248** or 808/524-0722; www.visit-oahu.com).

4 Molokai: The Real Hawaii

Unspoiled, quiet & rural, the "Friendly Isle" offers a time capsule of old Hawaii.

by Pauline Frommer

HOW TIMES CHANGE.

Had you been making your first visit to Molokai some 120 years ago, you may well have begun the journey in shackles. Most were coming to Molokai then for one reason and one reason alone: quarantine. Diagnosed with Hansen's Disease (known then as leprosy and described by a Hawaiian phrase as "the sickness that is a crime"), you would have been abruptly removed from your family, probably never to see them again, and taken to a hospital in Honolulu. From there, you would have been shipped to the Kalaupapa Peninsula on Molokai, at the time the world's most notorious leper colony. If the waters were rough and the sailors nervous, at the end of the sea journey you might have been unceremoniously dumped into the sea and forced to swim for your life to shore. Once there, you would have to start anew, ill and with very little help, salvaging a shelter and planting crops to survive. Had you been unlucky enough to be among the first settlers to the colony in 1866, you would have had less than a 50% chance of surviving the first 12 months.

For many decades, Molokai and indeed all of Hawaii, was synonymous with leprosy. At the end of the 19th century, clerks at the *New York Times* compiling a yearly index of stories would "leave the entry beneath the heading 'Hawaiian Islands' blank, with the notation 'see Leprosy,'" according to John Tyman, author of the marvelous history *The Colony* (Scribner). At that time, 1 in 30 Hawaiians were thought to be afflicted with the disease (though many were misdiagnosed). Even today, when you say the word "Molokai" most people immediately associate it with the dread disease.

Interestingly, it was the drama and lurid appeal of the colony that first drew tourists to Molokai. Authors Jack London and Robert Louis Stevenson came (and burnished the island's fame with their accounts of the place); later such notables as actors John Wayne, Edward G. Robinson, and even little Shirley Temple made the pilgrimage.

But despite visits by the early glitterati, Molokai never achieved the glamour status of its sister isles. In fact, I'd say this association with leprosy *saved* Molokai from the over-development that has afflicted Oahu and Maui. When you visit today, you see an island that has changed very little over the years. There's not a single traffic light on the entire island, nor are the beaches fronted by innumerable condo developments and hotels (it's not at all unusual to have the beaches here totally to yourself, especially on weekdays). Although its lowlands have been heavily impacted by large-scale agriculture—predominantly pineapple (no longer farmed here)—Molokai's natural interior remains largely uncultivated and intact. The Nature Conservancy manages extensive tracts of native rainforest that are home to numerous rare and endangered species, including plants, birds, and tree snails with beautiful colored shells. Many Molokai residents still follow, at least in part, a subsistence lifestyle dependent on hunting and fishing, and they want to retain access to the mountains and sea.

Which all means that Molokai is *not* the island for everyone. If you want nightlife, tourist luaus, dozens of activities, and fancy restaurants, stay away; you're bound to be disappointed. But for those seeking a true Hawaiian experience—and Molokai has more native Hawaiians than any other island except tiny Niihau—Molokai will be a revelation. I'm talking rugged outdoor experiences, a relaxed pace, a lifestyle that reflects the Hawaiian culture, and plenty of peace and quiet. Most importantly, Molokai is still home to the colony on the Kalaupapa Peninsula (less than 20 residents live there today), and along with Pearl Harbor, I'd count a visit here as one of the most moving experiences in Hawaii.

DON'T LEAVE MOLOKAI WITHOUT . . .

Traversing the cliff down to Kalaupapa Peninsula. Hearing the stories and seeing the sights in this colony for people with Hansen's Disease (formerly known as leprosy) will likely be the most emotionally charged experience of your vacation. See p. 197.

Picking up a loaf of fresh-baked Molokai sweet bread. Hot out of the oven at 10pm from Kanemitsu's Bakery, smeared with cream cheese and jelly—there's no sweeter bedtime treat in all of Hawaii. See p. 193.

Sending a coconut "postcard." Pick your nut, decorate it with flair, and slap postage on it. The pay-off? Giggling relatives and friends when you get home. See p. 195.

Enjoying the beach utterly alone. Not an unusual experience in Molokai, where the beaches are blissfully empty, especially midweek.

A BRIEF HISTORY

by Joan Conrow

Although most people continue to associate Molokai primarily with Kalaupapa (see p. 197 for more of that history), it had a very different reputation in ancient times. Known as Molokai Pule O'o, or Molokai of the potent prayer, it was an island inhabited by powerful kahuna (priests) who were proficient in ancient chants and mystical practices. The chiefs depended on the kahuna to protect the small island from invaders, and the powers of these priests, who reportedly had the ability to pray an opponent to death, were legendary throughout the islands.

Molokai maintained its reputation as a center of mysticism and sorcery until the late 1700s, when it was conquered by Kamehameha as part of his drive to unify all the islands under his rule. Protestant missionaries began to arrive in 1832, but the island remained largely unchanged until 1848, when the Great Mahele provided for the private ownership of land (prior to this time, the concept of private ownership was unknown in Hawaii). Westerners bought some 70,000 acres and turned it into Molokai Ranch.

In 1923 the Libby Corporation introduced pineapple to Molokai. Four years later, Del Monte also opened a large pineapple plantation on the island, and the two companies constructed plantation towns, then imported workers from Japan and the Philippines. This mono-crop agriculture dominated the island's economy and landscape until the early 1980s, when the plantations closed down due to cheap imports of pineapple from Thailand and other countries.

When the Kaluakoi Corporation opened the Molokai Sheraton in the 1970s, on lands it had purchased nearly a decade earlier from the Molokai Ranch, tourism officially arrived. The Kaluakoi Corp. began selling condominiums and homesites adjacent to the resort, but the resort ultimately failed. In 2002 Molokai Ranch bought back the lands and renovated the hotel and part of its golf course.

Although Molokai is just a 20-minute flight from Oahu, its residents have managed to fight plans for luxury homesites, condominiums, and resorts on the west end. Vandals destroyed part of a pipeline that provided the area with water, and residents recently approved a moratorium on tourist development. Because a majority of residents seem to like their rural lifestyle and are committed to its preservation, Molokai now has the reputation of being the last "antidevelopment" island in Hawaii. In the struggle to gain control of this island's destiny, only time will tell if the residents or the developers prevail.

LAY OF THE LAND

As the fifth-largest of the main Hawaiian Islands, Molokai encompasses just 260 square miles (it's just 38 miles long and never more than 10 miles wide). Despite its small size, its diverse landscape ranges from dry pasturelands to lush tropical valleys, oatmeal-colored sand beaches to magnificent sea cliffs (the tallest in the world at 1,600–2,000 ft.). It is made up of two distinct volcanic land masses that create a natural division between the dry west end and the lush east end, with an arid central plain between them.

East Molokai is where you'll find the main town of **Kaunakakai** and the harbor, as well as the bulk of the resident population which number just under 8,000 people. Mile marker 0 sits in the midst of this tiny town, dividing the island in two. It's also known for its scenic, reef-edged coastline dotted with fishponds that were built by the ancient Hawaiians. **West Molokai** includes the slopes of **Mauna Loa** and a rugged, sandy coastline. Much of the land there is privately owned and inaccessible to visitors, unless they're staying on Molokai Ranch.

Central Molokai is dominated by **Hoolehua,** a Hawaiian Homelands settlement area, as well as agricultural lands. Sugar cane and pineapple were once the main crops in this dry and dusty region, but now coffee and macadamia nuts are

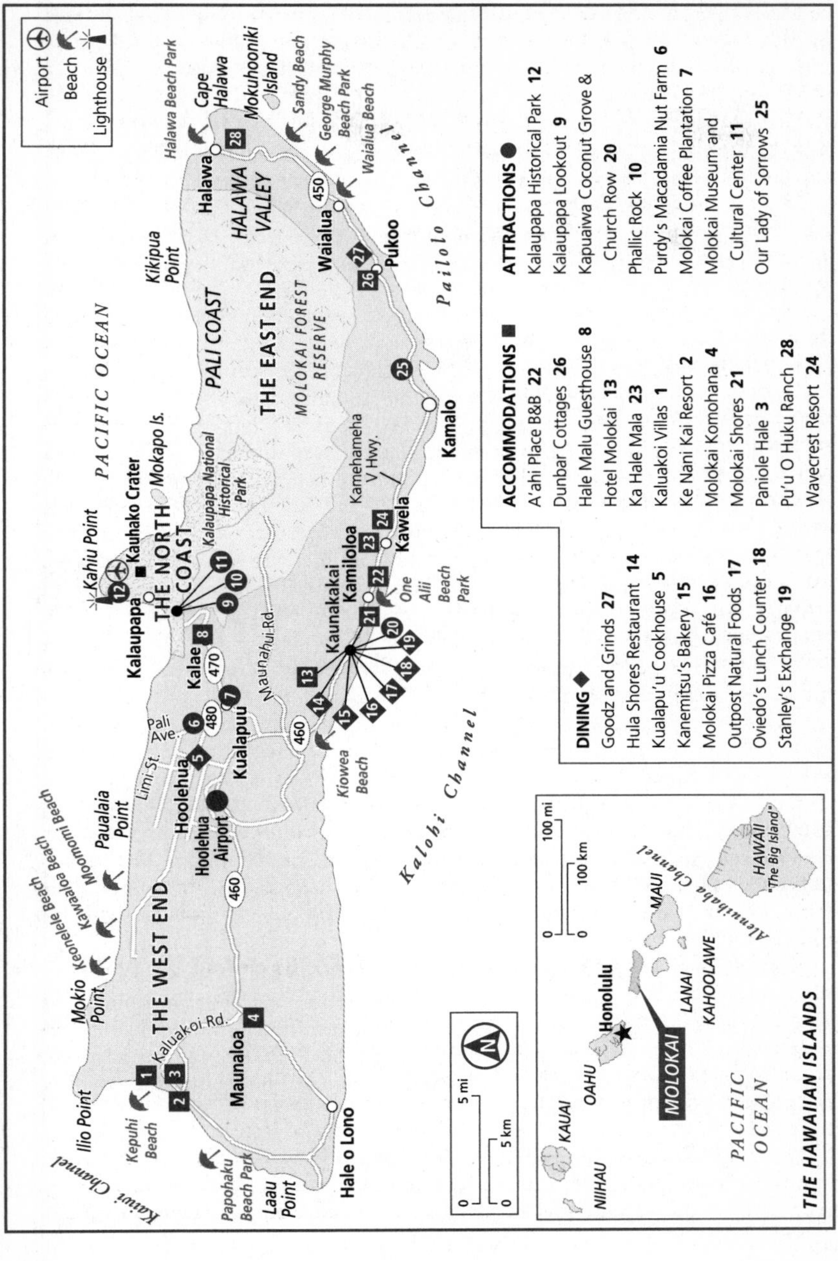
Airport
Beach
Lighthouse
PACIFIC OCEAN
Kaiwi Channel
Kalohi Channel
Pailolo Channel
THE WEST END
THE NORTH COAST
PALI COAST
THE EAST END
HALAWA VALLEY
MOLOKAI FOREST RESERVE
Kalaupapa National Historical Park
Ilio Point
Kepuhi Beach
Papohaku Beach Park
Laau Point
Hale o Lono
Maunaloa
Kaluakoi Rd.
Mokio Point
Keonelele Beach
Kawaaloa Beach
Moomomi Beach
Papaulaia Point
Hoolehua
Hoolehua Airport
Limi St.
Pali Ave.
Kualapuu
Kalae
Maunahui Rd.
Kalaupapa
Kahiu Point
Kauhako Crater
Mokapo Is.
Kiowea Beach
Kaunakakai
Kamiloloa
One Alii Beach Park
Kawela
Kamehameha V Hwy.
Kamalo
Pukoo
Waialua
Waialua Beach
George Murphy Beach Park
Sandy Beach
Mokuhooniki Island
Cape Halawa
Halawa
Halawa Beach Park
Kikipua Point
ACCOMMODATIONS
A'ahi Place B&B 22
Dunbar Cottages 26
Hale Malu Guesthouse 8
Hotel Molokai 13
Ka Hale Mala 23
Kaluakoi Villas 1
Ke Nani Kai Resort 2
Molokai Komohana 4
Molokai Shores 21
Paniole Hale 3
Pu'u O Huku Ranch 28
Wavecrest Resort 24
ATTRACTIONS
Kalaupapa Historical Park 12
Kalaupapa Lookout 9
Kapuaiwa Coconut Grove & Church Row 20
Phallic Rock 10
Purdy's Macadamia Nut Farm 6
Molokai Coffee Plantation 7
Molokai Museum and Cultural Center 11
Our Lady of Sorrows 25
DINING
Goodz and Grinds 27
Hula Shores Restaurant 14
Kualapu'u Cookhouse 5
Kanemitsu's Bakery 15
Molokai Pizza Café 16
Outpost Natural Foods 17
Oviedo's Lunch Counter 18
Stanley's Exchange 19
0 5 mi
0 5 km
THE HAWAIIAN ISLANDS
NIIHAU
KAUAI
OAHU
Honolulu
MOLOKAI
LANAI
KAHOOLAWE
MAUI
HAWAII "The Big Island"
Alenuihaha Channel
PACIFIC OCEAN
0 100 mi
0 100 km

cultivated here. Molokai also plays a major role in producing genetically modified organisms or crops (GMOs). Private companies and universities conduct experimental field trials and grow GMO seed crops in Central Molokai.

GETTING TO & AROUND MOLOKAI

Molokai's **Hoolehua Airport** is easily reached by air from Honolulu or Maui. Daily service is provided by **Island Air** (☎ 800/652-65641; www.islandair.com), **go! Airline** (☎ 888/IFLYGO2; www.iflygo.com), **Pacific Wings** (☎ 800/867-6814; www.pacificwings.com), and **Hawaiian Airlines** (☎ 800/882-8811; www.hawaiianairlines.com), which offer numerous flights throughout the day and currently charge between $53 and $175 for the hop

The **Molokai Ferry** (☎ 866/307-6524; www.molokaiferry.com) provides ferry service between Lahaina (on Maui) and Molokai, with daily morning and evening trips. The 90-minute voyage costs $40 for adults and $20 for children. You can also arrange a number of packages, including a guided tour of the island and a visit to the Kalaupapa Peninsula.

Molokai has no public transportation, so you'll need to rent a car (or at least a bike, see p. 205) to get around the island. Best prices, by far, are offered by a small, local agency called **Island Kine Auto Rental** (☎ 866/527-7368 or 808/553-5242; http://molokai-car-rental.com); it often undercuts the other two by a good 25%. Sure, many of its cars have dings and scratches, but they run fine, and Island Kine offers free airport and ferry pick-up to renters, to boot. If you prefer sticking with a brand-name (and getting a prettier car), try **Budget Rent a Car** (☎ 800/527-7000 or 808/567-6877; www.budget.com) or **Dollar Rent a Car** (☎ 800/800-4000 or 808/567-6877; www.dollar.com). ***Important:*** Make advance reservations for a vehicle as all three companies do occasionally sell out! Also, consider a four-wheel-drive if you expect to off-road it (if you're planning to go to Moomoni, p. 196, for example), but check with your agency first regarding restrictions on this type of driving.

Taxi services are available via **Molokai Off-Road Tours and Taxi** (☎ 808/553-3369; www.molokai.com/offroad.com), which provides service between the airport and Kaunakakai for $7 per person, with a three-person minimum, or **Molokai Outdoors** (☎ 808/553-4477; www.molokai-outdoors.com), which charges a flat fee of $23.

ACCOMMODATIONS, BOTH STANDARD & NOT

Public transportation is non-existent and the sights are spread out on Molokai, so do factor in the cost of a rental car when choosing your hotel. And think long and hard about what type of ambience you're looking for. Though this is a relatively small island, the landscape shifts dramatically from one end to the other, as does the number of available services.

KAUNAKAKAI & CENTRAL MOLOKAI

The dusty town of Kaunakakai and the highlands above it have the advantage of location. No, the beaches in this area aren't prize picks (in fact, many aren't swimmable), but it's an easy drive from this area to the best sands on both the east and the west coasts. And when you base yourself in the center, you have access to what few services Molokai does provide; there simply aren't many banks or supermarkets elsewhere on the island, and only two other eateries, one on each end.

$ That being said, sometimes a bargain trumps all. No, **Hale Malu Guesthouse** ★ (23 Kalama Rd, Kalae; ☎ 808/567-9136; www.halemalu-molokai.com; cash only) isn't in Kaunakakai proper; instead it sits in a residential neighborhood, about a 15-minute drive up in the hills, just a short drive from the start of the path to Kalaupapa (the island's top attraction). But at just $10 to $50 a night are you really going to complain (especially if you've come to Molokai specifically to make the trek to the former leper colony, as so many do)? And this is no dive. Neat as a pin and run with great devotion by German-born Ilima Davis and her husband Richard, coming here is, as the 70-something Ilima says with a chuckle, like going to Grandma's house. "Nobody goes hungry here. If a guest comes in late and the stores are closed, we feed them. And," Davis adds with a twinkle, "sometimes we party with the guests." When I asked what that meant, she explained that occasionally they'll break out a bottle of wine in the evenings. On offer is a cute-as-kittens pentagonal guest cottage for $80 a night. Sleeping up to four, it has a small bedroom with a firm queen-size bed, and a living room with a TV, fridge, daybed and trundle bed beneath. Off the living room, separated just by a curtain (so don't pick this one if you're shy), is a small bathroom with shower. Within the house itself are two guestrooms, which share a bathroom and each go for $50 a night. The Kukui room boasts another good-quality king bed, wicker dressers, and closet. The Lehua room can sleep three (one queen size bed and a twin in here) and like the other rooms is adorned with Davis' watercolors of Molokai and sweet wicker furniture. And in the backyard, Davis has added two "tentalos," really solid greenhouses, comfy, waterproof, and private, set on raised platforms that come with either two twin beds or one double bed, and all linens. It's a step up from camping, but if you want to just camp, that's doable here, too: Davis will supply you with a tent for $25, or you're welcome to pitch your own for $10 a night. Those sleeping in the quiet yard share a teepee-style hot shower (gas heated) and toilet and a BBQ on which they can whip up a meal.

$ Ten bucks cheaper, if a hair grungier, **A'ahi Place B&B** ★ (215 A'ahi St., 2 miles east of Kaukakai; 808/553-8033; www.molokai.com/aahi; cash only) is closer to town and the beach and is a party place several nights a week, when the owner's buddies drop by with their guitars and ukuleles and everyone jams on the lanai. Like most of the B&Bs on island, host Steve lends his guests beach towels and snorkel gear; upping the ante, Steve also willingly lends out golf clubs to visiting duffers. Guests have a choice of four types of accommodations. In the backyard is a grounded mobile home, with a surprisingly spiffy little bedroom inside (the shower's in the room, the toilet and sink through a doorway). In the house proper is a teeny, sky-blue room with two twin beds and a bathroom across the common area plus an enclosed outdoor shower (with views of the ocean) nearby for bathing. These two go for just $40 a night double, $35 single. Next door is a woodsy cottage with a full kitchen, TV and VCR, a bedroom with two double beds (easily sleeping four), and a lanai for kicking back ($75 a night). And upstairs in the main house is a huge apartment, which rents by the week only, for $1,000 total. It can sleep up to six, and since it's where the owner's parents stay for several months a year, it's more cushy than the other offerings (think beds that don't squeak and showers without a trace of mildew) with several TVs, stereo equipment, lots of framed posters on the knotty cedar walls, and plush beds. A small pool was under construction when I last visited; it should be done by the time you're reading this. The owner takes reservations by phone only and books up months in advance, usually with repeat guests. One night free for every seven booked.

$–$$ A third B&B, **Ka Hale Mala** (7 Kamakana Place; ☎ 808/553-9009; http://molokai-bnb.com; cash only) is about 5-miles east of Kaunakakai, up a hill in a quiet, residential cul-de-sac, allowing guests a nice amount of privacy. Hosts Cheryl and Jack Corbiel live upstairs; the basement apartment, with room for four and a full kitchen, is where guests lodge. Looking a bit like a rec-room, with world maps and hats on the walls as the only real decor and well-used furniture, it's nonetheless white glove clean and quite comfortable. The hosts are experts in everything Molokai (Cheryl is a prof at the local community college) and give guests a 1-hour orientation upon arrival, to better help them plan their stay. Another selling point: the fab breakfasts, which are hot, massive, and make good use of the local fruits and produce. Nightly rates are $90 with breakfast, $80 without but including daily maid service, Wi-Fi, and local calls.

$$–$$$$ The only condo complex near Kaunakakai, **Molokai Shores** ★ (kids) (on Rte. 450; contact a rental company on p. 189 to book; www.marcresorts.com; AE, DC, MC, V) is a smart choice for first timers to the island. It's near enough to town to be walkable, but set off from the road sufficiently enough to give it a welcome serenity. Units are individually owned and therefore decorated in a hodgepodge of styles (upkeep can also vary greatly from unit to unit). Still, they're roomy, each boasting an ocean view (the beach is pretty, though too muddy for swimming), and full kitchen. One-bedroom and two-bedroom units are available, and tend to range in price from $95 to $175, though I've seen the rate dip to just $80 a night on VRBO.com. On-site: a pool, putting green, florist, beauty salon, and lots of well-tended grass. If you're sensitive to noise, choose a unit in a room ending in 21 through 34 as these are set away from the highway, and try to stay up on the top floor: The walls are fairly soundproof, but the floors are not, so you'll get a lot of footstep noise if you're below.

$$$–$$$$ When I last visited the island, **Hotel Molokai** (on Rte. 450; ☎ 800/535-0085 or 808/553-5347; www.hotelmolokai.com; AE, DC, MC, V) was in the midst of a major renovation, so I can't say with any certainty what it will look like when done. The manager described the new furnishings as being "Westin-like," if that helps. What I can tell you is that the place has great bones. A collection of groovy '60s-style A-frame buildings, their roofs swooped into Polynesian curves, the resort is right on the water, with a swimming pool and hopping restaurant/bar (p. 194) at its heart. Rooms come in a variety of sizes, from ones large enough to

Renting a Condo on Molokai

Renting a condo ain't rocket science, but it will force you to determine whether price or peace of mind is most important to you. If you're a hardcore budgeteer, simply looking for a place to crash (and cook), then booking directly with condo owners should be your modus operandi. This can easily be done through such sites as VRBO.com, Rentalo.com, or A1 Vacations.com and will save you between $10 and $40 a night, in general, over booking with a local agency. Trouble is, if something goes wrong—you discover the condo is infested with ants, or has a door that won't lock—it's very difficult to get your money back or change units. These types of situations don't happen that often, but when they do, they can be vacation busters.

Booking through an agency gives you a safety net; if you're unhappy with your rental, they'll fix the problem or move you at no additional cost (usually). You will pay slightly more to use an agency, and the cleaning fees often tacked on with condo rentals may also be higher, so be sure to crunch all the numbers before booking. Of the rental agencies specializing in Molokai, I'd recommend:

- **Molokai Vacation Rental** (☎ 800/367-2984; www.molokai-vacation-rental.com), the short term rental arm of real estate agency Swenson Realty. It has in its "stable" over 70 units, and it holds their owners to high standards in terms of decor and amenities. I've also found this agency to have the most plain-spoken staff on Molokai. They are refreshingly open, giving visitors the lowdown (warts and all) on their properties and the island in general.
- **Friendly Isle Realty** (☎ 800/600-4158 or 808/553-3666; www.molokairesorts.com) reps 80 condo units, spread pretty evenly across the island. Because its commission structure is different than the other agencies, its rates and cleaning fees tend to be a hair lower. I didn't find them to be very articulate in discussing the properties they represent, however, so if you're looking for more in the way of service and advice, go with the first company.

hold four (on a queen bed and two singles) and a kitchenette, to much smaller double rooms. Very few have A/C; instead there's latticework cut out at the top of the ceilings to let the trade winds cool the place naturally. Rack rates are high for what you get—up to $229 for an oceanfront kitchenette room, $159 for a standard room—but the hotel discounts heavily through third parties. Try Expedia.com, as it scores a 25% discount here pretty consistently.

EAST END

The greenery is greener and the snorkeling rainbow-colored on this side of the island. Stay east for the sweet little cove beaches that dot the coast and the increasing serenity (or isolation, depending on your point of view) of the island the farther you get from Kanaukakoi.

$$ Set on a picturesque lagoon (visible from most units, but not suitable for swimming) **Wavecrest Resort** (Rte. 450 at mile marker 13; contact a rental agent on p. 189; AE, DC, MC, V) has a definite '70s-vibe to its four-story buildings. When I last visited, I kept imagining Chrissy, Jack, and the rest of the *Three's Company* gang doing their "Hawaiian Vacation" special there. (You know, Chrissy cheating at shuffleboard, while Mr. Roper's scoping out the babes around the pool.) Units are moderate in size, with low-ish popcorn ceilings and lanais big enough for two lounge chairs and about four partiers with umbrellaed drinks. Since these are condos, you never know in advance what the color scheme will be and just how much rattan the owners will stuff into the rooms. But like the other condo developments on the island, units are kept spotless by teams of caring cleaners, and the decor tends to be reflected in the prices (older couches, lower rates). That being said, I've seen condos here range in rates from $95 to $135 for a one-bedroom, and $135 to $155 for two.

$$$ Who doesn't dream of having their own private beach? Well, that's what you get—kinda—at the **Dunbar Cottages** ★ kids (Hwy. 450, past mile marker 18; ☎ 800/673-0520 or 808/558-8153; cash only). Yes, all the beaches in Hawaii are public so anyone would have the right to use the two pocket strands fronting these two cottages. But there's not enough parking to make that really feasible, and so you become pasha of the sands . . . at least for the length of your vacation. Other than that darn nice amenity, these two cottages are wee and simple and somewhat plain, each sporting two bedrooms (one with a king-size bed, and one with two twins), shiny hardwood floors, a useable kitchen, and a comfy "first-apartment" looking living room. The nightly rate of $170 is for up to four in the house (you couldn't fit more comfortably); I'd say the Pauwala house is better for families, as there's an ancient fishpond out front which serves as a buffer for waves, and delivers calm, shallow waters in which the young 'uns can frolic.

$$$–$$$$ **Pu'u O Huku Ranch** ★★ (Hwy. 450, at mile marker 25; ☎ 808/558-8109; www.puuohuku.com; MC, V)—the name means hill of stars—would get three stars from me, if the drive to get to it wasn't so scary. Located between the Halawa Valley and a string of striated sea cliffs, the road here from about mile marker 20 just barely holds two lanes and is as curvy as Pamela Anderson. But once you get here . . . well, the place is knock-down, drop dead gorgeous. A working ranch of 14,000 pristine acres, it has two cottages and one retreat-hotel (11 rooms) on offer, each done up to the nines. I'm talking shiny eucalyptus floors, heavily carved furniture from Indonesia, real kitchens, even top-quality posturepedic mattresses. Both of the cottages start at $140 a night for double occupancy, going up by $20 a night for extra adult guests (kids under 12 stay free). And since one cottage has two bedrooms and the other three, you may well want to bring along some friends. The 11-bedroom unit is meant only for large groups (they get a lot of yoga retreats) because there are no locks on the doors of the individual rooms; renters take the whole shebang at $1,250 a night. On-site is a nice pool, miles of hiking trails, horses for riding (p. 205) and a small store where you can buy the grass-fed beef and organic veggies raised on the ranch. For those seeking seclusion and affordable elegance, this place is it.

WEST SIDE

As with all the Hawaiian islands, the leeward side is the dryer, hotter side, while the windward side gets more rain, and thus more verdant plant life. When you're on the West Side you're on the windward side, which is good news for the vacationer who wants a near-guarantee of sunshine every day. The area is also significantly less populated than the central or eastern slices of the island, which is terrific news for late sleepers for one odd reason: no roosters! Chickens are de rigueur in the residential areas, meaning a piercing, scream-like "cockadoodle do" well before the sun rises (I guess you can tell I fall into the late sleepers' camp).

$ Hands down the classiest looking B&B on the island, the **Molokai Komohana** ★★ (23 Kalama Rd., just before Moana town; ☎ 808/552-2210; MC, V) is just a 5-minute drive to the former Molokai Lodge and a 15-minute drive from some of the nicest beaches of the West End. Two tidy guest rooms, with colorful Hawaiian quilts on the beds, spa robes hung in the closets, and shiny light wood floors welcome visitors. Hot breakfasts are served in an expansive breakfast room filled with tasteful pieces of art picked up in the course of the owners' world travels (they're originally from Michigan). Because the rooms have unattached bathrooms (they're private, but outside the guest rooms), prices are reasonable at $70 to $85 a night.

$$ Ping-Pong tables, tennis courts, washer/dryers in each unit, a heated whirlpool, and one of the largest pools on the island (60 ft.!) make **Ke Nani Kai Resort** ★ kids (in the Kaluakoi Resort development, Kaluakoi Rd., off Hwy. 460; see rental agent box for contact info; www.kenanikai.com; AE, DC, MC, V) a solid pick for traveling families. This condo complex has, hands down, some of the nicest amenities on the island. I wish I could also report that it has beach access or cushy units, but, well, that's what keeps the prices on the more affordable end of the spectrum ($90–$125 for one bedroom, $110–$170 for two bedrooms). Because of lower ceilings (really low on the first-floor units), rooms feel more cramped here than they do at competing condos. As for the look of each: They're individually owned, so it's potluck. Still, the ones I recently visited—and I saw a good half dozen—were well maintained, with suitably tropical furnishings, and quite clean.

$$ Just down the hill, **The Kaluakoi Villas** ★ (in the Kaluakoi Resort development, Kaluakoi Rd., off Hwy. 460; see rental agent box for booking info; www.castleresorts.com; AE, DC, MC, V) suffer from their proximity to the closed and decaying Kaluakoi Resort (these spooky, boarded-up hotel buildings could easily serve as the setting for an Aloha version of *The Shining*). What saves this condo complex are the acres of well-manicured lawns, the picture-perfect white-sand beach down front (good for swimming in summer, surfing in winter), and the darn nice oceanfront pool—a holdover from the days when this was a resort. Second floor units are the ones to pick thanks to their high, sloping ceilings; many have loft beds, a terrific use of the space. Downstairs units feel more cramped, but all are quite tidy and generally well maintained. **Castle Resorts** (☎ 808/552-2721; www.castleresorts.com) manages the majority of the units here, but I've heard complaints about their level of service. Better to go with one of the other rental agencies listed on p. 189 (they tend to have higher standards for decor and amenities, as well). Expect to pay about $105 for a studio, $115 to $135 for a one-bedroom or loft unit—all have ocean views. The other name for this condo complex is "Kepuhi Beach Resort" (you'll likely see two signs and it can be confusing).

$$–$$$ The newest and nicest of the West End condo complexes, **Paniole Hale** ★★★ (Lio Place, next to the Kaluakoi Resort development; see rental agent box for booking info; AE, DC, MC, V) has a Martha Stewart–esque vibe to it. Everything is just so. The grounds are lushly landscaped, the pool a pretty blue tile with a dolphin motif, and the setting ideal, plopped right between a golf course and a delightful white-sand beach (p. 196). Units here are just as nice, featuring 10-foot high glass door and walls, massive lanais (ask for a corner unit as the wraparound porch will double your living space), and cathedral beam ceilings, airy and high. So though they're individually owned and decorated, they all come out quite nice, simply because these lovely Hawaiian Plantation-style structures take the sting out of any missteps in furniture choice. Each has a washer/dryer, too. Oceanfront units cost more than those with ocean views, so expect to pay about $135 for a studio, $150 for a one-bedroom, and $175 for two. If you don't mind a short walk to the beach (and why should you; it's not that far), subtract about 10% from the rates above and if you're visiting between June and September, take off another 10%.

CAMPING

Rural Molokai is the kind of place that invites camping, and you can pitch your tent at four very different campgrounds, although I recommend only two (the other two are located in inconvenient, less pleasant settings). **Palau State Park,** which overlooks the Kalaupapa Peninsula (at the end of Rte. 470), is a cool, forested locale. It has covered pavilions, tables, and restrooms, and you can camp free for a week here with a permit from the **Division of State Parks** (☎ 808/567-6923). For a delightful coastal setting, just off one of Hawaii's longest white-sand beaches, you can't beat **Papohaku Beach Park** (on the island's west end, off Kaluakoi Rd.). It also provides full facilities and is usually as quiet and empty as Palau. Due to strong rip currents, swimming isn't recommended in winter, but this beach is tops for strolling. Campers are limited to 3 consecutive days under a **County Parks and Recreation** (☎ 808/553-3204) permit that costs $3 for adults and 50¢ for kids under 17.

DINING FOR ALL TASTES

If you were to simply look at the menus of Molokai's eateries, you would assume that this agri-island's primary crop was wheat. Seems like most everything on offer here comes either between two slices of bread, slathered on top of dough (as in pizza), or so heavily breaded and fried it might as well be a sandwich. Like many rural communities, the fresh produce, meats, and fish show up at the farmers market, but rarely on the plates of local restaurants. So if you're looking for haute cuisine, or even just healthy cuisine, this ain't the island for you. There are some exceptions (which I've noted below), but for the most part, plan on eating simply on this simple island . . . or cooking it yourself.

IN & AROUND KAUNAKAI

$ Simple, however, doesn't have to mean lacking in flavor. At the **Molokai Pizza Café** ★★ (kids) (Old Wharf Rd., the Kahuna Center; ☎ 808/553-3288; Mon–Thurs 10am–10pm, Fri–Sat 10am–11pm, Sun 11am–10pm; cash only) you'll get darned good pizza—and that assessment comes from a self-confessed NY pizza snob. I'm talking just-gooey-enough cheese, a well-balanced sauce, and a nicely crisped crust. Kids will like the place, too, as it's half restaurant, half arcade—so bring some quarters. Shareable small pizzas start at $11, with individual pies for just $5, and kid's pizzas are $4. Pasta dishes, burgers, sandwiches, and special theme night items (Wed it's Mexican food, Sun prime rib) are also on offer, but they don't hold a candle to the 'za in my opinion. If you're planning to go for lunch, pick up a copy of the free Molokai newspaper first as there's often a coupon there for a $5 full lunch deal.

$ For a cuppa Joe, a glance at the Internet (via free Wi-Fi), and perhaps a free, new paperback book (at the paperback exchange on the back table), head to **Stanley's Exchange** (125 Puali St.; ☎ 808/553-3713; Mon–Fri 7:30am–3:30pm; cash only), Molokai's equivalent of Starbucks. The food's skippable, but the coffee comes in a number of varieties, perfect when you just need a blast of sugary caffeine.

$ Half bakery, half lunch counter, **Kanemitsu's Bakery** ★ (79 Ala Malama St., Kaunakakai; ☎ 808/553-5855; restaurant Wed–Mon 5:30am–noon, bakery Wed–Mon 5:30am–6:30pm and 10pm–midnight; AE, MC, V) is so famous for its Molokai bread that starch fans (and that's most everyone in this state—witness the macaroni salads that come with *everything*) line up for hot bread when it comes out of the oven at 10pm (p. 207). They may be onto something: As bread goes, it's darn good, and comes in an assortment of flavors from onion to apricot-pineapple. The lunch counter isn't quite as successful, serving the thinnest burgers I've ever seen ($2.50), but decent breakfast dishes and sandwiches are cheap (nothing's over $5.50).

$–$$ As much of a culinary tradition as Kanemitsu's, the **Kualapu'u Cookhouse** ★ (102 Farrington Ave., Kualapu'u; ☎ 808/567-9655; Mon 7am–2pm, Tues–Sat 7am–9pm; cash only) started its existence as the cookhouse for workers at the local plantation and is still set in the same rough hewn building, with its tilting plank walls and corrugated tin roof. As a restaurant, it's had its ups and downs over the years, but it's currently on an upswing, serving solid, tasty fare that's a cut above the other plate lunch joints on the island. The food is well seasoned, and the meats used are quality, especially on Thursdays, which is prime rib night ($12). That's also the night when local musicians gather here with their guitars and ukuleles to jam for tips. It's a real party.

$–$$ Noah gathered two of everything. Molokai tends to make do with just one, and in the realm of ethnic foods that's **Oviedo's Lunch Counter** ★ (125 Puali St., Kaunakai; ☎ 808/553-5014; Mon–Fri 10am–5:30pm, Sat–Sun 10am–4pm; cash only), which specializes in garlic-laden Filipino fare. Each heaping plate of food and rice served here costs $9.50 and is, I think, big enough for two to share. You can mix and match on the plate at no extra charge. Tops among their offerings are the unctuously tender adobo pork and the papaya chicken.

$–$$ Molokai's one health food store (yup, just one), **Outpost Natural Foods** (70 Makeana Place; ☎ 808/553-3377; Mon–Thurs 9am–6pm, Fri 9am–4pm, Sat 10am–5pm with lunch service only 10am–3pm; AE, DC, MC, V) has a lunch counter and a picnic table out back with an oh-so-glamorous view of the local Laundromat. It serves up your standard vegetarian fare, without much flair, but at least you won't feel bloated and guilty after a lunch loaded with sprouts, beans, and carrots. Burritos, sandwiches, salads, and different varieties of veggie burgers (taro, tempeh, and so on) make up the menu, with most costing between $3.50 and $6.95. Bring your laptop to siphon off the free Wi-Fi out back.

$$–$$$ For a meal with a view, head to the **The Hula Shores Restaurant** (at the Hotel Molokai, Rte. 450; ☎ 800/367-4500 or 800/272-5275; daily 7am–2pm and 6–9pm; www.hotelmolokai.com; AE, DC, MC, V) . The food will likely be as unmemorable as it is elsewhere on the island, but here you dine on a patio overlooking the beach, and there's often live music to chew to.

EAST END

$–$$ Your best choice because it's, well, your *only* choice on the east side of the island is **Goodz and Grinds** (Rte. 450 at mile marker 16 on Hwy.; Mon–Fri 8am–6pm, Sat–Sun 8am–5pm; DC, MC, V), a lunch counter that cooks up all kinds of comfort food, from burgers to burritos to breakfast plates of eggs, Spam, and rice ($1.65–$5.50, with plate lunches for $7–$8.50). I'm a fan of the mahi burgers, a straightforward but super-fresh filet of fish, grilled, slathered with mayo, and set between slices of lettuce, tomato, and a bun. As you dine, you can check your e-mail as you sit at one of their picnic tables—G&G provides free Wi-Fi to its customers (just ask for the code when you order).

Sometimes You Feel Like a Nut, Sometimes You Post One

Last year, a visiting Scotsman drew an address on a coconut, had it stamped, and sent it home to his family. Its arrival caused such a stir in his small town in the Scottish highlands that it made the local paper. The gentleman then sent the **Hoolehua Post Office** (Puu Pela Ave., Hoolehua off Hwy. 460; ☎ 808/567-6144; Mon–Fri 7:30–11:30am and 12:30–4pm) the article, to add to its collection of thank-you notes, articles, and even posters (from a jazzed kindergarten class) that this tiny post office has been collecting since 1991. That's the year postmen here claim they first tested the "coconut as postcard" theory, and it's been an extremely popular activity ever since. In 2006, approximately 3,000 coconuts were addressed, stamped, and sent from this obscure post office to people across Europe, Asia, Africa, and the Americas.

If you'd like to post your own, simply show up during biz hours (see above), pick a coconut (there are boxes at the ready and free for the taking), and then grab one of the many colored Sharpie pens postal employees provide for those who want to decorate. The average cost to send the coconut within the U.S. is $7.50, though the heavier the nut, the more you'll pay.

WHY YOU'RE HERE: MOLOKAI'S BEACHES

Molokai boasts Hawaii's only continuous barrier reef, which spans 28 miles on the south side. That's good news for scuba divers and snorkelers (and in places, the snorkeling is first rate, particularly if you do it by boat), but bad news for swimmers and surfers, as the reef keeps the waters off the most populated area of the island (from the Kaunakakai area east to about mile marker 22) pretty pond-like. The bottom on this stretch is often muddy, the waters murky and shallow. A string of 62 ancient fishponds and sweet little coves make it picturesque, so if you're more in the mood for wading and sunbathing, you shouldn't mind. Surfers tend to head to the western and far eastern ends of the island, beyond the reef; there are also a few swimmable beaches in those areas as well (waters are calmer in the west in the summer months). ***Warning:*** None of Molokai's beaches have lifeguards, so keep a close eye on your children and consider the depth of the waters as well as your own strengths and weaknesses as a swimmer before taking a dip. Here are my favorite beaches:

On the Western end of the island, the most consistently swimmable and, I think, lovely beach is known as **Dixie Maru Beach** ★★★ (take Kaluakoi Rd. to the end of the pavement) for a 1920s Japanese vessel that foundered on the shoals of the reef here (its name plate was hung at the gate to the beach for many years).

Watch Your Tootsies

Although east-end beaches are sandy along the shoreline, the near-shore waters usually contain coral—which makes for good snorkeling but unpleasant barefoot strolls. Coral is rough and sharp, and it can inflict nasty cuts that tend to fester because the living organisms that comprise coral get into the wound and contribute to infection. *Important:* Wear reef walkers, Japanese fishing tabis, or old sneakers when you're at the beach. And even if you're protected, try not to tread on the reef unnecessarily as it takes just nine tramplings to kill a coral head. And stay out of murky water. The rule of thumb is: If you can't see what's swimming in the water, it won't see you and your toes could get nipped by predatory fish. So stay where the water's clear.

A perfect little horseshoe of multi-colored sands, it offers protected swimming in the cove, and gnarly surfing just beyond the reef—the best of both beachy worlds.

If you're in the mood for strolling, beachcombing, or (in the summer only) swimming, you'll find the golden sands of **Papohaku Beach** ★★ (on Kaluakoi Rd.) enticing. One of the largest beaches in Hawaii at 3 miles long by 300 feet wide, it's backed by a green park with outdoor showers, restrooms, and picnic grounds. This is also a top spot to camp (p. 192).

Just behind the **Paniole Hale Resort** ★ kids (p. 192) is the third beach I'd recommend on this side, mostly for its critter-laden tide pools (they'll keep the younger kids intrigued for hours).

The east end's best swim and snorkel sites are a string of tiny cove beaches from about mile marker 18 to 22 on Highway 450. **Murphy's Beach** ★ kids at marker 20 is arguably the most pleasant of the lot with three picnic tables shaded by ironwood trees, but no bathroom facilities. It's also widely considered to be the best place on the island for offshore snorkeling. Those with kids along may want to head to **Ali'i One Beach** kids (Hwy. 450, 4 miles east of Kaunakakai) for the convenience of bathrooms, showers, and generous parking. Waters here are also quite calm and shallow, making it a favorite among local families on the weekends. I hope that the place gets a make-over soon, though, as the structures here are showing their age.

Finally, those with four-wheel-drive vehicles can head out to the deserted strands of the north side of the island, specifically the idyllic **Moomomi Beaches** ★. Here you'll find the Hawaiian Islands' most extensive sand-dune complex, managed by the **Nature Conservancy** (☎ 808/553-5236; www.nature.org). It's an ecological treasure trove, home to a number of endangered coastal plants (including four that exist only on this beach), and an important breeding ground for sea turtles. Perhaps most interesting are what archaeologists have turned up here: the bones of prehistoric and probably flightless birds, perfectly preserved. Today, Moomoni, which in point of fact comprises three beaches—Keonelele, Kawaaloa, and Moomomi (the last two are the best for swimming)—has a uniquely desolate beauty. It's not hard to imagine it as a place where these ancient sea creatures roamed. To reach this trio, head west out of Hoolehua on Farrington Avenue. The avenue becomes a very rutted and bumpy dirt road, which you'll follow for 2 miles until it forks. Take the right fork another mile to the beach. You can learn more about the area's ecology by contacting the Nature Conservancy (see above).

THE TOP SIGHTS & ATTRACTIONS

I think it says a lot that the **Kalaupapa Historical Park** ★★★ (☎ 808/567-6802; www.nps.gov/kala) inspires legions of travelers each year to fly in for just 1 day, simply to tour the former leper colony. While I'd argue, hard, that Molokai warrants a much longer visit, you cannot do the island justice without touring this wildly scenic, historically overloaded spit of volcanic land. True, most come because it's a lurid thrill to visit a place which has seen so much human tragedy. But even the gawkers come away marveling at how hope blazes forth against all odds, how what was once considered a "living grave" slowly, painfully, transformed into a true community. Perhaps the greatest testament to the power of this peninsula: In 1969, the government ended its policy of quarantining those afflicted with Hansen's Disease (the modern name of leprosy). Despite this, and though they were finally free to leave, the vast majority of patients stayed in Kalaupapa. It was now their home.

Before I discuss how to visit the colony, a bit of history. The colony at Kalaupapa was founded in 1866 in response to several centuries of microbial invasions that decimated the Hawaiian population. In the 2 decades after Captain Cook "discovered" Hawaii, the venereal diseases his crew introduced had killed nearly 10,000 people on Oahu alone. Next came typhoid fever in 1805, which exterminated 5,000 more; influenza in 1848, which killed scores of children; and smallpox in 1853, which slaughtered approximately a fifth of the population living then (an estimated 15,000 dead in 1 year).

So when leprosy first appeared on the scene in the 1840s, the Hawaiian government decided that something extreme needed to be done to stem this most recent, and—with the physical deformity that usually accompanies the disease—most frightening, plague. They chose the Kalaupapa Peninsula as a place of quarantine, reasoning that its towering sea cliffs and rough shoreline formed a natural prison. And then, because the government was strapped for cash but worried of delay, it dropped its first settlers off here in 1866 with little more than the clothes they wore—the settlement as a whole got several sacks of bread and dried meat, the men received a thin wool blanket and either a shovel or an axe, women got just the blanket. For living quarters, they moved into the ruined huts of an abandoned village and for many years, the colony was marked by a high degree of lawlessness and despair. As stories of the brutish conditions spread throughout the

Is It Safe to Visit Kalaupapa?

The short answer is: Yes. Only about 5% of the general population is susceptible to Hansen's Disease and it is thought that to contract it, one must have direct and repeated contact with those suffering from the disease. That type of contact won't occur on a trip of this length (in fact, it's rare to get within 20 ft. of the patients who still live here).

islands, families hid their ill relatives rather than send them to the "living tomb" at Kalaupapa—and so the disease continued to spread.

Conditions began to turn around when a young Belgian priest (and former carpenter) named Father Damien was posted to the island in 1873. He devoted himself to the care of the patients here, enforcing order, planting fruit trees, improving the water supply, and building over 300 small, whitewashed houses (some of which still stand today). Father Damien eventually contracted the disease and died from it. His selfless devotion has prompted a campaign to have him named a Catholic saint. Others, too, cared for the patients, including Mother Marianne Cope and Brother Dutton, who spent more than 44 years here, continuing the work begun by Father Damien. You'll learn all of their stories when you take the tour.

Access to the peninsula is strictly regulated, primarily to protect the residents' privacy, but also the endangered native coastal plant and animal species. Though the disease in not highly contagious (see box, above), no one under 16 is allowed, and all visitors must have permits from the state Department of Health to enter the Kalaupapa settlement. For the general public, these permits are arranged either by **Damien Tours** (808/567-6171) directly (owned and operated by a Kalaupapa resident), **Molokai Mule Ride** (see below), or through **Molokai Fish and Dive** (☎ 808/553-5936; www.molokaifishanddive.com). Along with the permits comes a full tour (which is the only way to visit the peninsula, other than as a resident's guest). The cost is $40. Guides are sometimes former patients, though many who used to lead tours have become infirm in recent years and have imparted their knowledge and stories to the next generation. Nonetheless, you'll hear poignant and compelling firsthand accounts of their lives in Kalaupapa and their experiences with Hansen's disease over the course of the 3-hour bus tour (which makes frequent stops at points of interest).

Getting to the Kalaupapa settlement is an adventure in and of itself. You can arrive one of three ways: by air, by foot, or by mule. I'd recommend the latter. With **Molokai Mule Ride** ★★★ (Hwy. 470 at mile marker 5; ☎ 800/567-7550 or 808/567-6088; www.muleride.com; $165 per person), you'll take a bumpy, awesomely scenic ride down that provides enough of an adrenaline rush to compete with any roller coaster. After the first jolt and glimpse of the sheer drop off to the side, you'll grow to appreciate these sturdy, surefooted animals as they carry you down, and then back up, a narrow, 3-mile trail carved into the face of a 1,600-foot-high cliff that separates the peninsula from the uplands. The ride is offered Monday through Saturday only, leaving the stables at 8am and returning around 3:30pm, including the bus tour. The fee includes a picnic lunch in the primordial-looking setting that provided the background for the films *Jurassic Park 2* and *Jurassic Park 3.* Riders must weigh less than 250 pounds. Be sure to make reservations at least 2 weeks in advance, because only 15 passengers per day can make the trek and the tour fills up quickly.

A cheaper option is to hike the trail and its 26 switchbacks, a strenuous trek that takes about 1½ to 2 hours each way at a pace that allows you to enjoy the view. I'd recommend starting your trek before 8am, so you're not sharing the road with the mules (or dodging their droppings as you trek down; no way to avoid that on the way up though). The path starts just north of the mule stables, off

Highway 470. Hikers, too, must obtain a permit ($40, cash only) and a place on the bus tour before setting off.

If either option seems like too much effort, you can fly to the peninsula from Hoolehua Airport and simply take the ground tour. Flights arrive in Kalaupapa each morning at 9:30am, just in time for the tour (go to Pacific Wing's discount website, www.flypwx.com, for current pricing). Those flying in from Maui should also contact **Pacific Wings** (☎ 888/575-4546 or 808/873-0877; www.flypwx.com) as it's the only reliable airline that has an early enough flight to make the tours. From Oahu, you can take **Island Air** (www.islandair.com) and then change in Molokai for a flight direct to the peninsula. However, if you want to do the hike or mule ride, you'll have to go with Pacific Wings, as it's currently the only one that offers an early enough flight. Since taxi service on Molokai is pricey, I recommend renting a car so that you can spend the afternoon between the end of the tour and your flight out seeing a bit of Molokai. The folks at the Mule Ride can arrange a discounted car rental for their customers.

The final, and I'd venture to say wimpy and not all that exciting, way to see the peninsula is via the **Kalaupapa Lookout** (end of Hwy. 470, free admission), which offers an overview of the large volcanic crater and settlement. Interpretive plaques at the site point out the most significant sights and tell a bit about the history of the peninsula. From this eagle's-eye perch at the tiptop of the cliffs, you'll also see the historic lighthouse, which once had the most powerful beam in the Pacific (it now houses an electric light beacon). The Lookout is in the center of **Palaau State Park** ★ (at the end of Rte. 240), which comprises 234 acres of ironwood and eucalyptus forests at an elevation of 1,600 feet and is worth a visit in its own right. It's a sweet little park that's ideal for a picnic and a stroll beneath the trees. Be sure to take the short walk to **Phallic Rock** (Kauleo Nanahoa), a larger-than-life natural stone representation of the male organ that's been, er, enhanced by human sculptors to assume its ready-for-action pose. (A resident joked with me that they tell male visitors the rock is "size small" in Hawaii.) One of the largest such rocks in the islands, Hawaiian legend says that it is inhabited by Nanahoa, the male fertility god who assumed the current form after a fight with his wife that turned them both to stone. For centuries, women hoping to conceive have come here to leave offerings and camp overnight beside the stone.

CENTRAL MOLOKAI

Bundling together visits to the Lookout (see above) and some of Molokai's farm attractions makes good sense as they're quite near one another, and after the exertion of hiking or riding down the sea cliffs to Kalaupapa you'll be grateful for the free samples generously doled out at these places. In particular, you can munch 'til you're full at family-owned **Purdy's Macadamia Nut Farm** (kids) (Lihipali Ave., off Rte. 480 behind the school in Hoolehua; ☎ 808/567-6601; Tues–Fri 9:30am–3:30pm, Sat 10am–2pm; free). A member of the clan will give you the lowdown on the lifecycle of macadamia trees, which have the remarkable ability to yield fruit year round. Then, you get to crack your own nuts (fun for the kids), and sample both the raw nuts and the more common roasted kinds. The farm uses no insecticides on its 50 trees, and is the only one of its kind on Molokai. And of course, there's a gift shop.

Molokai Coffee Plantation ★ (on Rte. 470 in Kualapuu; ☎ 800/709-BEAN or 808/567-9241; www.molokaicoffee.com; Tues–Fri 9:30am–3:30pm, Sat 10am–2pm) offers a more involved and involving tour, one that stimulates all the senses. You'll taste the coffee berries (they're sweet!), get a noseful of the ambrosial aroma of roasting coffee, and either sore feet or a sore bum from the hour-long tour—by foot or by mule cart (they sure love those mules in Molokai)—of this 500-acre coffee farm. You're also going to learn pretty much everything there is to know about the cultivation and processing of coffee from the wonderfully articulate guides. The mule cart ride is $35 for adults, $10 for kids 5 to 15 (Mon–Fri 8am and 1pm, Sat 8am only), while the guided walking tour is just $20 for adults, $10 for kids (Mon–Fri 10am). Both are pretty neat, but even if you can't make them, it's worth stopping by to pick up a bag of this uniquely smooth coffee (I prefer the all Molokai to the harsher "mule skinner"), or perhaps a "mocha mama" at the snack bar, which is a devilish mix of ice cream and espresso.

If you'd rather learn about farming without setting foot in a field, the **Molokai Museum and Cultural Center** (on Hwy. 470, after mile marker 4; ☎ 808/567-6436; Mon–Sat 10am–2pm; $2.50, $1 for children) memorializes the island's short-lived flirtation with sugar farming. On the grounds is the R.W. Meyer Sugar Mill, built in 1878 and now on the National Register of Historic Places. This low-key facility includes restored sugar-processing equipment and graphics that depict how cane was cultivated and then processed into raw sugar, as well as spectacular photos of the colony on the nearby Kalaupapa Peninsula. Permanent exhibits are supplemented with special festivals and classes.

KANAUKAKAI

I think we in North America and Europe tend to think of important places of state in terms of mansions, courthouses, and palaces. In Hawaii, the wealth of the kings was marked in a more natural manner, and you can still see the might of King Kamehameha V in the **Kapuaiwa Coconut Grove** (Hwy. 460, 1 mile west of Kaunakakai). Planted in 1860, the trees today are giants, soaring as much as 70 feet in the air, set in neat rows (though some have bent out of place over the past century). If you visit, guard your head and your car: The trees are untrimmed and a coconut falling from this height can cause serious damage. Across the street is **Church Row,** a chorus line of denominations (Mormon, Baptist, Jehovah's Witness, and more), set in frill-free chapels of whitewashed wood and crude steeples. Unlike most anyplace I can think of, there are about four times as many churches on Molokai as there are bars.

THE ISLAND'S EAST SIDE

Besides St. Philomena in Kalaupapa, Father Damien built two other churches on Molokai's east side. The older of the two is **Our Lady of Sorrows** (Rte. 450, about 14 miles east of Kaunakakai), originally constructed in 1874, restored in 1966, and still used today. An unpretentious little structure, surrounded by coconut trees, it features fine pen-and-ink drawings depicting the stations of the cross that were imported from Holland. The other is **St. Joseph Catholic Church** (Rte. 450, about 10½ miles east of town), an even tinier chapel—about 16 feet by 30 feet—with a movingly simple wooden altar that was built in 1876 and restored in

Into the Halawa Valley

Sometime around A.D. 650, according to carbon dating of recently uncovered artifacts, the first settlements on Molokai, and some of the first in Hawaii, were founded in the Halawa Valley. A lustrously green dell, its fauna nurtured by two waterfalls and innumerable small streams, it was chosen because it was and is the perfect spot for growing taro, the plant that is a staple, both nutritionally and spiritually, for the Hawaiian people. "Care for the taro and it will care for you. A prophecy tells us that if the taro dies, so will the Hawaiian people," explains Lawrence Aki, who was born in this valley, and returns now to farm taro through his collective and to lead tours here. And remarkable tours they are, because Aki is a master storyteller, weaving together Hawaiian history, myths, and even chants into a tour that feels more like an initiation ritual, capped by a swim under a gloriously picturesque waterfall.

The cost of the tour is high—$75 for adults, $45 for children—but that money goes to support the valley's collective, which is working with local youth and visitors to reintroduce taro into the valley, and thus reclaim a lost way of life. It's also a physically demanding tour, requiring participants hike 4 miles in total, sometimes hopping from one rock to the next over a rushing stream, at other times clambering over fallen tree trunks. But when Aki is leading it, it's one of Molokai's few must do's (make sure Aki is leading the tour; the other guides aren't nearly as compelling).

To book the tour, which occurs once daily (8:30am–2:30pm), contact **Molokai Fish and Dive** (☎ 808/553-5936; www.molokaifishanddive.com).

1995. Outside a perpetually lei-laden metal sculpture of Father Damien greets visitors.

Route 450, where both churches are located, offers the **32-mile coastal drive from Kaunakakai to Halawa Valley** ★★★ that's well known as one of Molokai's scenic treasures. Allow yourself plenty of time to traverse the narrow, winding road, which tightly hugs the eastern coast. In a number of places, the road shrinks down to one lane, and in other spots, a guardrail is all that separates you from a sheer drop off into the sea. A string of ancient fishponds and massive offshore rocks, jutting from the sea, add to the drive's distinctive beauty. The road ends at Halawa Valley, a lush, tropical oasis that fronts a large bay and broad, sandy beach. One of four amphitheater valleys along the north shore, it's only one accessible by car. (See "Into the Halawa Valley," above.)

THE OTHER MOLOKAI

As I said earlier, Molokai is the most "Hawaiian" of the Hawaiian islands, thanks both to its demographics (a larger percentage of native Hawaiians are found here than on Oahu, Maui, Kauai, the Big Island, or Lanai) and the primarily agricultural lifestyle of its inhabitants. Culturally, it's remarkably unvarnished; festivals, music shows, and hula dancing are not "put on" for the tourists; they're simply part island life. If you stumble upon a luau on the beach, it will be one locals are holding to celebrate some special event in their lives; ask nicely, and they might allow you to join the festivities. Should that take more courage than you can muster, here are a few ideas for activities that will plunge you directly into the heart of the Molokai zeitgeist, and allow you to interact in a meaningful way with the friendly folks who inhabit the "Friendly Isle."

One of the best ways to meet people on Molokai is to dance with them. Molokai is widely held to be the birthplace of hula. According to oral tradition, a woman named La'ila'I settled in the Ka'ana region, and soon grew so famous for her dancing that audiences started visiting from other islands. For five generations, her hula was passed down only to her descendents, until one of them, Laka, left Molokai and spread the dance throughout Hawaii. She did so without her family's consent, but apparently all is forgiven: Today Molokai holds one of the largest and most respected hula festivals in the islands, the **Molokai Ka Hula Piko** (3rd weekend in May; ☎ 808/553-3876; www.molokaievents.com). Unlike other fests, where hula is regarded as a competitive sport, with judges pontificating and prizes awarded, here it's all about art and ritual. Some 2,000 people usually attend the 2-day event, held at Papohaku Beach in Kaluakoi, where they attend learned lectures, classes, hula performances, ceremonies in sacred spots, and craft fairs. It's quite a gathering.

Hula is not, of course, practiced just once a year in its birthplace. At the **Mitchel Pauole Community Center** (Ala Malama Ave., right next to the police station in Kaunakakai), classes and rehearsals are held year-round and are open to anyone who wants to watch or participate, even neophytes. "If someone wants to learn our culture it makes us happy," says teacher Moana Dudoit, "it means they love our islands." In fact, these are the only free hula classes held in all the Hawaiian Islands (not counting the non-serious, tourist-oriented kind). Classes for *kapunas* (those 50 and over) are held Tuesdays from 5 to 6pm, for women of all ages on Mondays from 6 to 8pm, and for children on Mondays from 5 to 6pm. And it is a heckuva lot of fun to just try it. When I went, I was lent an appropriate *pahu* skirt (to better accentuate the sway of my clumsy hips—it's harder than it looks!), and then settled into the class, which started slowly, with just a gourd drum keeping time. After absorbing explanations of what the hand movements meant, the singing began, and at the end, we did an entire routine pretty darn quickly, accompanied by live musicians. It was a blast. I was the only visitor that day, and at the end of the class a number of residents came up to inquire where I was from and to chat.

Though it sounds drearily Soviet in concept, touring Molokai's farms is actually a terrifically rewarding way to spend a day. I mentioned the tours at Purdy's Macadamia Nut Farm and Molokai Coffee Plantation (p. 200) earlier in the chapter; they're fun, and will give you an educational overview of how those two crops are grown. But when you book **Rochelle Tempo's Agricultural Tour** (☎ 808/553-8284; www.ohanaconcierge.com), you'll meet the farmers, which brings the experience to another level altogether. Candidly discussing what it takes to coax food from the soil and sea, they lead quirky, involving tours of their farms (and sometimes their homes, too), which cover whatever the participants of the tour are interested in. When I participated, we ended up grilling Mervin Dudoit, who's attempting to bring one of the ancient royal fishponds back to life, about the ways in which the high schoolers who volunteer at the pond are changing their eating habits and learning a more authentically Hawaiian way of life. At the home and hydroponic farm of Kealoha Petier, we discussed the state-of-the-art techniques he's using to "verti-grow" tomatoes, lettuce, herbs, and cucumbers in a limited space and with limited amounts of water. Then we veered off topic, to walk the adobe house he's building (he and his wife currently live in a converted school bus) and to hear about what it's like to live "off the grid," using only wind and solar power for energy. In the course of the tour you will probably also visit a Plumeria farm (and get a fresh lei), the coffee farm, and a salt farm. Though the tour is pricey—$125 per person—part of the proceeds benefit the farms you're visiting and includes your lunch, all transportation (in a comfortable 15-passenger van), and a good 6 hours worth of adventures and conversation. And as Petier said on a quixotically poetic moment of the tour (as we were standing admiring the compost heap, ironically enough): "Being on a farm is good for the soul. It gets you out of the alleys."

Finally, if you have kids, or are of a particularly "crafty" turn of mind, you can learn the art of kite-building at the **Big Wind Kite Factory** (p. 207), from accidental kite-maker Jonathon Socher. "I was out of money and this was idea number 186," explains Socher, a gregarious fellow who has a look that's halfway between Jerry Garcia and Santa Claus. Call in advance and he or his wife Daphne will take you into the workshop and teach you how to create a brightly colored, two-string controllable cloth kite (you'll pay for the materials plus a small bit more for instruction). Those who just show up with kids get a free lesson in simple paper kite making; and then if the store isn't too busy, Socher will take you to the "aeronautical facility" out back (basically the yard) for a quick flying lesson with a couple of the beauties they have for sale.

ACTIVE MOLOKAI

Molokai is best suited to those who can entertain themselves. Although it has plenty of outdoor recreation opportunities, it doesn't have an abundance of companies offering activities, so prices can be high. Here's an assortment of activities, some self-guided and others requiring a tour.

Hiking

Molokai is known for its rugged beauty, especially the four unspoiled valleys on its north coast. Only Halawa, reached at the end of Highway 450, is accessible by automobile. The others—Pelekunu, Wailau, and Waikolu—can be partially viewed by sea, primarily. You can also get a sense of the lush beauty found in these valleys from above at The Nature Conservancy's 2,774-acre **Kamakou Preserve** (808/553-5236; www.nature.org/hawaii), located at an elevation of about 2,700 feet, which is nearly the highest point on the island. This rainforest is home to numerous endemic (found nowhere else) and native plants, and five species of endangered birds. It's also one of the few places in the islands where you're likely to encounter the lovely Kamehameha butterfly. The Nature Conservancy runs regular hikes in the Preserve; see the website above for a schedule.

It's a Bird, It's a Plane, It's . . . Walter Naki

The north side of Molokai is the wild side: An area that once had settlers, but is now only inhabited by a hermit or two, and those who live on the Kalaupapa Peninsula (p. 204). A good 28 waterfalls carve the green valleys here, and at points, the highest sea cliffs in the world loom, casting a long shadow over the waters below. As I mentioned earlier in the chapter, the look of these valleys is so pristine, no, so primordial, that they were used as the setting for the films *Jurassic Park 2* and *Jurassic Park 3*. To see it safely and comprehensively, you need an expert guide, and that's what you'll find in Walter Naki. A former marine studies teacher, who also just happens to be a former surfing champion of Molokai, and who also served 23 years in the National Guard, Walter is, well, Superman. And a darn nice guy. His grandfather lived in the Wailau Valley on the north side, so he knows all its hidden nooks and crannies, from sea caves you'll zoom into aboard his solid Boston Whaler to a swimmable waterfall. Along with north side trips ($100/person for a complete day), Walter also offers snorkeling excursions (p. 206), whale-watching cruises ($50 for 2 hr.), and hunting trips through his company, **Maa Hawaii** (☎ 808/558-8184). The daylong hunts cost $300, and he provides rifles and ammo. Archers pay $200 but must supply their own equipment.

The island's finest hike is the 3-mile path that descends some 1,600 feet into the **Kalaupapa Peninsula.** You'll traverse 26 switchbacks on this well-maintained trail that's also used by mules. It takes at least 90 minutes to make it down, and 2 hours for the return hike—and that's at a fast pace. Allow more time to enjoy the marvelous coastal landscape that's always in view. Since the trail and peninsula are within a National Historic Park, hikers are required to reserve a place on the 4-hour settlement tour (see p. 198)

If you're determined to go off on your own, hike the **Main Forest Road** that travels inland about 20 miles. It's a rough and rutted red dirt road that can be traversed in a four-wheel-drive vehicle, but you'll usually have it all to yourself, especially on weekends. The ground is frequently muddy (and the red clay does not wash out of clothing) beneath a forest canopy of introduced pine, eucalyptus, and native ohia trees. To reach this area, head west on Route 460 from Kaunakakai and turn right at the bridge, just before mile marker 4. You'll pass Homelani Cemetery, where Main Forest Road, also known as Maunahui Road, heads into the mountains. The first part is dry and hilly, but you'll soon be in the forest. If it's dry, drive as far as you comfortably can and park (making sure you don't obstruct the road), then start walking from there. It's also a good mountain-bike trek.

Note: If you wish to hike on your own, pick up maps from the **State Department of Land and Natural Resources** (on Olo Ave., a mile west of Kaunakakai Rd.; 808/533-1745) in Kaunakakai.

Golf

Molokai has one 9-hole course that could be characterized as either charming or primitive, depending on your attitude. It offers 7am tee times, and you can play until sunset. Better yet, the greens fees are cheap compared to the triple-digit prices charged elsewhere in the state. **Ironwood Hills Golf Course** (Kalae Ave., Kualapuu; ☎ 808/567-8000) was built in 1928 for the workers at the Del Monte Plantation. A par-34 course, it's located in the cool hills above the Meyer Sugar Mill at an elevation of 1,200 feet. Heavy winds in some places, and shots that must be driven through small breaks in the treeline in others, make it quite a challenging course. You'll pay just $18 for 9 holes and $25 to play through twice; club and cart rental are available but not food or pro-shop services. It's fairly well maintained but not heavily used.

Tennis

You can play for free on four public courts, all lit for night play. Two are located at Molokai High School in Hoolehua, and another two are at the Kaunakakai Community Center. The Ke Nani Kai and Wavecrest condominium projects also have two courts each, which are restricted to condo guests, who play for free.

Horseback Riding

Those who prefer horseback riding to the mules of the Kalaupapa Peninsula can sign up for trail rides at a working island ranch, called **Puu O Hoku Ranch** (25 miles from Kaunakakai on the east end; ☎ 808/558-8109; http://puuohoku.com). Trail rides take equestrians through open fields to to waterfalls and secluded beaches. Rates are $55 for a 1-hour guided trail ride, $75 for a 2-hour ride, and $15 for each additional hour; service is topnotch as is the scenery. For $120, you can take a half-day ride on a sandy beach.

Bicycling

Quiet and relatively traffic-free, Molokai is an ideal destination for bicycle touring. To rent a good quality cycle, contact **Molokai Bicycle** (80 Mohala St., Kaunakakai; ☎ 800/709-2453 or 808/553-3931; www.bikehawaii.com/molokaibicycle) which is run by a local teacher (he can be difficult to contact so keep trying). He offers well-maintained mountain bikes for $15 to $20 per day or street bikes for $24.

WATERSPORTS

Kayaking

The rough seas around Molokai make kayaking here a specialty sport, recommended only for expert kayakers who have honed their skills elsewhere. If you fall into that category, this can be a highly rewarding paddling area in which you'll see a number of spectacularly beautiful valleys. As I write this, there's only one major company handling kayaking tours, the ubiquitous **Molokai Fish and Dive** (61 Ala Malama, Kaunakakai; ☎ 808/553-5926; www.molokaifishanddive.com). Its early morning trips cost $89 and involve kayaking out to see the sights, a snack, and then a tow back to shore when the waters get rougher. It will no longer rent kayaks as the owners worry solo paddling is too dangerous. However, simple kayak rentals, again only for advanced kayakers, are available through a competing company, **Molokai Outdoors** (☎ 877/553-4477 or www.molokai-outdoors.com) for $26/hour or $113 weekly.

Snorkeling & Scuba Diving

Thanks to Molokai's long and lean fringing reef there are topnotch snorkeling and scuba diving opportunities in the waters around Molokai. And unlike other dive spots in Hawaii, you'll never find yourself surrounded by 200 other floating homo sapiens. Here it's going to be just you and the fish. You can rent snorkel gear for just $9 a day at **Molokai Fish and Dive** (61 Ala Malama, Kaunakakai; ☎ 808/553-5926; www.molokaifishanddive.com) and take it to the bustling reef off the beach at Mile Marker 20 (on the eastern side of the island)—the island's hotspot for shore snorkeling. If you want to snorkel from a boat (and the viewing does improve when you get to the deeper waters at the backside of the reef), book a trip with **Maa Hawaii** ($50 for 2 hr.; ☎ 808/558-8184). Owner Naki knows superb snorkeling spots and takes guests out on a steady Boston Whaler. For scuba diving, the safe choice is **Molokai Fish and Dive,** as it's the only PADI certified dive center on the island. They've pioneered scuba diving here and have found some swell spots, including five blue holes (up to 150 ft. deep) and several awesome spur and groove reef ledges swarming with rainbow-hued fish. Advanced divers should inquire about the turtle rock dive (the rock is home to a colony of monk seals, who you'll swim alongside). Unfortunately, prices are higher than you'll find on neighboring islands for this sport ($135 for a two-tank dive, $275 for three, lessons also available), but that's because so few people are diving here.

Deep-Sea Fishing & Cruises

Several years ago, when two 1,100-pound fish won first prize in a fishing competition on Maui, they weren't caught near Maui, but in the waters off Molokai. The Penguin Banks area, which teems with such game fish as ahi, akui, mahimahi, and marlin, have long been an open secret among the savviest of deep sea fishermen. To try your luck there, you can charter the boats of a number of local companies. There's the **Alyce C** (at the Kaunakakai Harbor, off Kaunakakai Rd.; ☎ 808/558-8377; daily by appointment), a 31-foot fishing boat that goes for $300 for a half day or $400 for a full day, with all gear included. Another option is **Fun Hogs Hawaii** (☎ 08/567-6789; www.molokaifishing.com), which offers 4-hour tours for $428 and 6-hour ones for $555. And if fishing makes you romantic enough to want to tie the knot, you can go out with Captain Clay of **Hallelujah Hou Fishing** (☎ 808/336-1870; www.hallelujahhoufishing.com), a lovely fellow who also happens to be an ordained minister (he performs *lots* of weddings). Unlike the other two, Clay specializes in light tackle fishing around the reefs, and charges rates equivalent to his competition.

All three also offer **sunset cruises** and **whale-watching cruises** (in season) for about $75/person for 2-hour cruises; Walter Naki (p. 204), offers these same sorts of cruises for $50.

ATTENTION, SHOPPERS!

Shopping is not a favorite pastime in Molokai, both due to a shortage of stores and a tendency among residents to embrace a simple, non-materialistic lifestyle. Staples are available at Misakis and Friendly Market Center, the two major grocery stores in Kaunakakai, which are open until 8pm every day except Sunday, when they close at noon. For clothing and every type of beach equipment (surfboards, snorkel gear, and so on, for rent as well as for sale), there's the **Fish and Dive Shop** (61 Ala Malama, Kaunakakai; ☎ 808/553-5926; www.molokaifishand dive.com). A well-stocked drugstore/convenience store, **Molokai Drugs** (in the Kamoi Professional Center, in Kaunakai; ☎ 808/553-5790), doubles as the island's children's bookstore and toy shop (so go here if the kids need indoor entertainment). On Saturdays the main street of town is transformed into a bustling **farmers market** from 6:30am to 2pm. Along with spinach or long beans, you're likely to pick up the local gossip or a new recipe if you stop and browse.

Beyond the basics, my favorite store within Kaunakakai proper is **The Artists & Crafters Guild** ★★ (110 Ala Malama St., Suite 210; ☎ 808/553-8520), a collective of 70 local artists, from painters and sculptors to silk screeners, puzzle makers, jewelers, glass blowers, and others. Each undergoes a rigorous jury process in order to be shown here, ensuring that the goods in the store are of the highest quality. They then pledge a certain number of hours each month to work in the store; a singular pleasure of shopping here is getting to meet the artist whose work you've been admiring.

Cooks will enjoy the unusual sauces and chic cooking implements for sale at **The Bamboo Pantry** (170 Ala Malama St., Kaunakakai; ☎ 808/553-3300; www.bamboopantry.com). And for Hawaiian-style trinkets and gifts, solid quality quilts, bowls, jewelry, and more, look right on the main drag of town for the robin's egg blue store called **Naea's Sunrise Cove** ★ (in Kaunakai).

The only store on Molokai that I'd call addictive—and they know me well there, as I made several passes on my last trip to Molokai—is the **Big Wind Kite Factory & Plantation Gallery** ★★★ (120 Maunaloa Hwy., in Maunaloa; ☎ 808/552-2364). It's an overstuffed, two-sided shop, which catches the kiddies (and whimsical adults) with its boldly patterned kites, all in the most perfectly kite-ish Crayola colors, and the adults with an assortment of unnecessary objects that you'll find, after visiting here, that you just have to have. Jewelry and exotic beads are a strong point—the owners collect unique, ethnic-chic pieces from all over Asia. But there are also the floatiest of silk and cotton island-wear, the largest selection of books on Molokai, pieces of art, cards, games, you name it. And the cheery ex-hippies who run the place will also teach you how to properly fly a kite, if you ask (see p. 203).

NIGHTLIFE ON MOLOKAI

One of the most popular T-shirts sold on Molokai is a simple black one, with a picture of the moon. Beneath that are two words: "Molokai Nightlife." Direct and to the point: There ain't much nightlife on this island, at least in the sense that most people traditionally define the term. But there is a certain alleyway, right off the main drag of Kaunokoi, which gets a crowd well after the sun sets. At 10pm sharp locals and visitors alike head down that alley to an unmarked door where they rap loudly. The door swings open and the fateful question is asked: "Butter, cream cheese, or jelly?" After getting their steamy, hot bread from **Kanemitsu's** (p. 193), slathered with good stuff, folks head to the wharf to talk story over their loaves and admire the stars. I'd say it's a Molokai's nightlife highlight and an experience not to be missed.

More traditional nightlife is available at the bar of the island's major hotel, the **Hotel Molokai** (p. 188), as well as the **Paddler's Inn** (10 Mohala St., Kaunakakai; ☎ 888/632-5642; www.paddlersinnmolokai). Each offers live music several nights a week, though which nights those are shift from season to season. The island also serves up intriguing and ultimately moving "early bird" nightlife. On Fridays from 4 to 6pm at the Hotel Molokai groups of *kapuna* (elders) pull out their ukuleles, their songbooks, and their hula hips to entertain a mix of visitors and locals. The show is of the homegrown variety, with about 16 men and women sitting around a long table, some with their backs to the audience, and simply singing and dancing to one song after another. Occasionally they gently joke with one another, or stop to cheer for whatever sports team is playing on the TV in the corner of the bar, but this all adds to the charm of the evening. It really feels like you've stumbled onto a party and have been warmly welcomed.

ABCs of Molokai

Area Code Like all of Hawaii, Molokai uses the **808** area code.

Business Hours Two full-service banks, each with an ATM, are open weekdays in Kaunakakai from 8:30am to 4:30pm, with extended hours until 6pm on Friday. Government offices are open weekdays from 8am to 5pm. Most stores are open daily from 9 or 10am to 5 or 6pm.

Currency Exchange Change money at the Honolulu Airport before you fly to Molokai, or use traveler's checks.

Emergencies For the police, fire, or ambulance, dial ☎ **911.**

Information The **Molokai Visitors Association** (☎ **800/** or **808/553-3876;** www.molokai-hawaii.com) provides information about visitor services, including maps and brochures.

Medical **Molokai General Hospital** (☎ **808/553-5331**) in Kaunakakai offers 24-hour emergency medical care.

Newspapers The island is served by two local papers, the *Dispatch* (www.molokaidispatch.com) and *Molokai Times* (www.molokaitimes.com), as well as the *Maui News,* the *Honolulu Advertiser,* and the *Honolulu Star-Bulletin.*

Pharmacies You can have prescriptions filled at **Molokai Drugs** (located in the Kamoi Professional Center; ☎ **808/553-5790**) in Kaunakakai.

Police In an emergency, call ☎ **911;** otherwise, dial ☎ **808/553-5355.**

Post Office The main post office, at 120 Ala Malama St. in Kaunakakai, is open weekdays and Saturday mornings.

Safety Molokai is nearly devoid of violent crime, but don't leave valuables in your rental car.

5 Lanai: From Tropical Fruit to Tourism

Get a glimpse of the lifestyles of the rich & famous on this elite, private island.

by Pauline Frommer

LANAI HAS ONLY LIMITED POSSIBILITIES FOR TOURISM. OWNED ALMOST entirely by billionaire David Murdoch, its resorts given over to the Four Seasons to run, it seems far removed from the living culture of the other Hawaiian Islands. Much of the island is still recovering from the hard use it got as Dole's famous "Pineapple Island" for 7 decades. Drive into the interior of the island and you encounter arid plain after arid plain dotted with tiny bits of black plastic (the ground was covered back then with sheets of the stuff to keep the moisture near to the plants roots). The population today is 80% Filipino, another holdover from the plantation days. If you're into nightlife, you'll be disappointed—there literally isn't any of note. Price-wise it's prohibitively expensive. To be blunt: It's more difficult to have a reasonably priced vacation here than it is anywhere else in the Hawaiian Islands. The vast majority of hotel rooms go for over $400 a night, non-hotel rooms are offered illegally (thanks to recent attacks on unlicensed B&Bs and vacation rentals), activities are costlier than usual, and many of Lanai's restaurants charge twice what those on other islands do.

Still, Lanai is a starkly beautiful place with the largest cache of petroglyphs of any of the Hawaiian Isles, and one of the most idyllic beaches in Hawaii. Its hiking opportunities are topnotch, hunters and luxury golfers love it, and it has a serenity that more bustling isles, like Maui and Oahu, lost long ago. So in this chapter, I'm going to try my darndest to give you the tools to afford it. Even if you can't stomach the (largely) high cost of vacationing here, you may want to pop by for a day trip on the ferry and experience this millionaire's private playground for yourself.

DON'T LEAVE LANAI WITHOUT . . .

Rocking out. The so-called "Garden of the Gods" is like an outdoor sculpture gallery of Brancusi-esque boulders and rocks carved by centuries of hard-driving trade winds. Though the road here is primitive, it's worth the trek to see this spectacular moonscape. See p. 218.

Working on your tan. The beach at Manele Bay is quiet, softly sanded, and oh so exclusive. You never have to fight for beach towel space when you're on Lanai.

Conquering the Munro Trail. Like most of the roads on Lanai it's pitted and difficult to navigate, but the views from this ridgeline trail (which you can either hike or drive) are eye candy of the first order, as is the history you'll learn if you go with one of the tours offered by the Lanai Culture and Heritage Center. See p. 219.

A BRIEF HISTORY

Lanai has been used for agriculture since ancient times, long supporting a small population that fished and grew enough taro and sweet potato to meet its needs. But with the arrival of Western missionaries, who bought up most of the island by 1865, Lanai was soon pressed into more productive service as its new owners attempted to raise first sugar, then cattle. These agricultural ventures deforested much of the already arid landscape, causing erosion and the loss of vegetation and natural springs, which worsened the periodic droughts.

New Zealand naturalist George Munro, who came to Lanai in 1911 to run the plantation, spearheaded massive efforts to reverse this trend. To that end, he put into place policies to control feral goats and protect the small remaining native forest. Most importantly, he was Lanai's Johnny Appleseed, but with pine trees, and planted hundreds of moisture-attracting trees throughout Lanai. His mark on the landscape is still evident, particularly in the towering Norfolk pines that give the higher elevation areas a woodsy charm.

Munro proved more adept at reforestation than reviving the ailing plantation, which was forced to sell its extensive holdings. The land was bought and sold several times over the next few years until James Dole purchased it for $1.1 million in 1922.

Like so many other descendants of missionaries, Dole hoped to wrest his fortune from Hawaii's fertile soil. Certain he could succeed where others had failed, Dole launched a massive pineapple cultivation and processing venture that would dominate the island's landscape, economy, and social fabric for the next 70 years. He built Lanai City, the tiny berg that still functions as the island's hub, and

A Haunted Island

Ghosts were once the only inhabitants of Lanai. Or so says Hawaiian legend. According to oral tradition, many generations ago, the *akua ino* (evil ghost) King Pahulu ruled Lanai. He and his followers slaughtered any mortal foolish enough to set foot on the island. Then around A.D. 1400, the son of the ruler of Maui was exiled to Lanai for playing practical jokes. The young prankster Kaulula'au turned his skills to good use and, as the myths tell, tricked the ghosts in various ingenious ways, eventually driving them from the island. Claiming it for his own, the prince returned to Maui and recruited settlers. You'll see their mark, in the form of petroglyphs, rock walls, and *heiau* (temples) scattered across the island. Whether or not the ghosts were real, we know that Lanai was the last settled of all the Hawaiian Isles.

brought in Filipinos to tend his fields and work in the cannery. Under his direction, Lanai became a self-contained company town where nearly every resident worked for the plantation, shopped in its stores, and lived in its housing. Pineapple thrived in the hot, dry conditions, and Dole—whose name is still synonymous with the sweet, prickly-topped fruit—realized his dream of fame and fortune. At its peak, some 18,000 acres were under cultivation, making Lanai the world's largest pineapple plantation.

The dream began to fade as pineapple profits plunged in the 1980s, when Thailand and other Asian nations entered the market with high-quality, low-cost fruit. By then, Dole had been consumed by Castle & Cooke, a major Hawaii conglomerate facing its own economic challenges. It soon became clear that island pineapple could not compete with the lower-priced imports, and the company began scaling back its Lanai operations. Fields were harvested and left fallow, and the work force was steadily reduced, in preparation for shutting down the plantation entirely.

When entrepreneur David Murdoch purchased Castle & Cooke, he decided that the economic focus of the island had to do a 180. Tourism was booming throughout the state, and it was evident that no crop—aside from marijuana—could generate anything close to the revenues possible from land development. So, continuing his predecessor's patriarchal approach to running the island, Murdoch announced that current residents were welcome to stay, so long as they embraced his vision for a new Lanai based not on farm commodities, but a service economy. Although he reportedly liked having his own private island, Murdoch had no plans to make it off limits. He saw no value in following the example set by the Robinson family, which strictly prohibits all access to Niihau and has largely eschewed tourism. Instead, Murdoch laid out the welcome mat and began aggressively marketing the island, whose single, 10-room hotel had hosted relatively few visitors during pineapple's heyday.

Murdoch invested heavily in his development plans, spending more than $350 million to build two luxury hotels, golf courses, and upscale housing in hopes of attracting wealthy visitors who desire the exclusivity and social control that the newly renamed "Private Isle" can provide. When Bill and Melinda Gates were honeymooning on Lanai, Murdoch closed public access to the island's only sandy beach at Manele Bay and hired security forces to keep away paparazzi in a much-publicized demonstration of his willingness to accommodate the special needs of the mega-rich.

Since the 1990 opening of the first resort, the insular, agrarian qualities that once defined Lanai have almost completely disappeared, along with the unique lifestyle they engendered. What the future holds for Lanai is now entirely in the hands of the Four Seasons, the company brought in to manage the resorts, and David Murdoch who has carte blanche to do what he pleases with Lanai . . . and its people.

THE LAY OF THE LAND

Lanai is the sixth-largest Hawaiian Island, encompassing some 140 square miles. Shaped a bit like a kidney bean, it's 13 miles wide and 18 miles long. Lanaihale is the highest peak, rising 3,370 feet above sea level. Dramatic sea cliffs tower 1,500 to 2,000 feet above the Pacific on the island's west side, while the east side is marked by numerous narrow gorges that reach depths of up to 2,000 feet.

Because the power grid on the island is a limited one, the population is centered entirely in tiny Lanai City and the two resort hotels. Those who live elsewhere on the island have their own generators. Lanai City, which sits 1,645 feet above sea level, is a city in name only. More realistically it's a bakers dozen of streets, set in a grid, interrupted by pleasant Dole Park at the center. A farmers market is held in the park on Saturday mornings, and movies are screened under the stars at 7pm on the first Wednesday of the month.

Built by the company, the buildings date from the 1930s and '40s, and are one-story affairs, quaint or shabby looking, depending on your point of view, painted the colors of tropical fruits and flowers. Strands of skyscraper tall Norfolk pines in the center of the town add an odd, but charming, layer of Pacific Northwest mystique to the place.

An abandoned town is set on the northern side of the island along with Shipwreck Beach. Upcountry, but more on the north end, is the famed Garden of the Gods. The Munro Trail traverses the mountainous spine at the center. The Four Seasons beach resort is on the southern side of the airport; the other Four Seasons (and on an island this small, these hotels are major landmarks), called the Lodge at Ko'ele, is right next to Lanai City.

GETTING TO & AROUND LANAI

Lanai can be accessed by air from either Maui or Oahu, or by ferry from Maui only. Water crossings are cheapest and most convenient, and you make these on **Expeditions ferry** (☎ 808/661-3756; www.go-lanai.com; reservations recommended; $25 adult, $20 children ages 2–11). It operates five round-trips daily between Lahaina, Maui, and Manele Bay. The ocean crossing takes only 45 minutes but it can be rough, especially later in the day when the wind picks up. Still, most find adequate compensation in the charm of seeing Maui and the other islands from the water.

Surprisingly, flying is sometimes not much more expensive (though with the closure of Aloha Airlines, prices are on the rise; see p. 429). As we went to press, the oddly named **go! Airline** (☎ 800/637-2910; www.iflygo.com) had been consistently marking down its Maui to Lanai flights to just $29 each way ($49 from Oahu). **Island Air** (☎ 800/652-65641; www.islandair.com), another dependable carrier, offers "Super Special" fares that drop the rate to just $44 from Oahu, or $70 from Maui. Another carrier on this route is **Hawaiian Airlines** (☎ 800/882-8811; www.hawaiianairlines.com), but Hawaiian tends to price at a good $40 to $60 higher on these routes, so my advice would be to search Island Air and go! first. It's also common to see private planes parked at the airport, awaiting their VIP passengers.

GETTING AROUND

Lanai is probably the only island aside from Oahu where you can possibly avoid renting a car. Free shuttle service links the three hotels on the island, and you can hop aboard them to go from town to the beach and back (though they won't get you to hiking areas). That's true even if you're not staying at one of the represented

BEACHES & ATTRACTIONS ●
Cavendish Golf Course 15
The Challenge at Manele 16
Experience at Koele 3
Garden of the Gods 1
The Lanai Culture and
 Heritage Center 12
Lanai Pine Sporting Clays 2
Munro Trail 4

ACCOMMODATIONS ■
Bamboo Gate 5
Dolores Fabrao's House 14
Dreams Come True 13
Hale O Lanai 6
Hotel Lanai 7

DINING ◆
Blue Ginger Café 9
Café 565 10
Lanai Grill 8
Pele's Other Garden 11

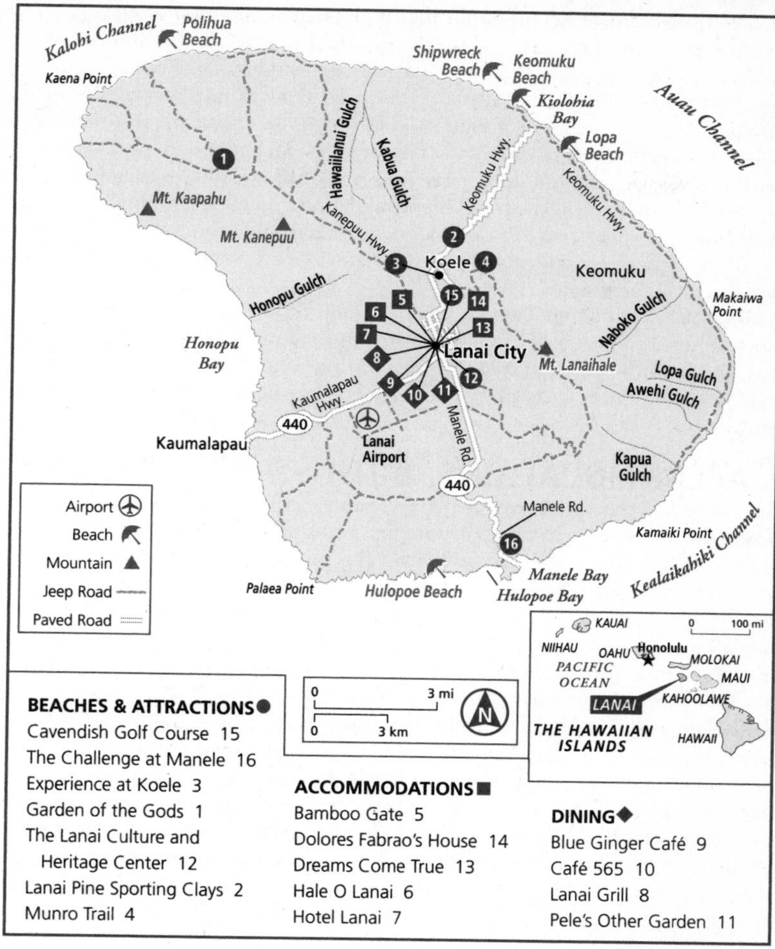

hotels—they don't check for I.D. However, you will have to pay about $10 for the airport shuttle.

If you want to get to Lanai's "outback," you can rent a vehicle at **Lanai City Service Inc.** (1036 Lanai Ave.; ☎ 808/565-7227), the scruffy gas station that doubles as a Dollar-Rent-A-Car outlet. It's wise to reserve a car far, far in advance, as the rental fleet is small and Dollar is the only game in town. A complimentary shuttle service meets customers at the airport and ferry terminal and transports them to the rental office in Lanai City. Expect to pay nearly double the rates charged on the main islands; bargains are virtually nonexistent. Passenger cars run $60 to $80 per day; four-wheel-drive Jeep Wranglers cost about $130. But since passenger cars are restricted to paved roads, you need to resign yourself to getting a Jeep if you want to do any exploring (if you're planning on just staying on the paved roads, you might as well save the cash and simply hop the shuttle). A sign at the rental car agency will alert you of which areas are out of bounds for rental cars. Before venturing off-road, be forewarned that it's not always easy to find your way through the maze of unmarked dirt roads that crisscross the island. Even light rains can make the clay roads slippery and dangerous, so exercise extreme caution while driving and don't push your luck if the weather is sketchy.

Hitchhiking is another option if you're planning to stick mainly to the beaten path, where it's pretty easy to catch a ride during daylight hours. But you may be in for a long wait, or a long walk, if you want to reach some of the more remote beaches or interior sights.

Rabaca's Limousine Service (☎ 808/565-6670; rabaca@aloha.net) offers island tours 24 hours a day in either a stretch limo or four-wheel-drive vehicle—rates are high, however, at $95 an hour, with a 3-hour minimum. Rabaca's also sends a limo to meet every plane and ferry but its prices are off the map (take the shuttles instead).

ACCOMMODATIONS, BOTH STANDARD & NOT

Choosing lodgings on Lanai is a snap simply because you have very, very few options. Unless you're willing to pony up $400-plus a night for a bed (and I'm guessing that you're not since you bought this budget guide), your choices consist of camping, a single hotel, one affordable vacation rental, and under-the-radar B&Bs. There are also some timeshare cottages available at the Manele Bay and Koele Lodge resorts, but unless you're traveling with a large group (and can thus split the costs), the prices are off-putting at $500 or more a night. Still, if you'd like more information on those, contact **Okamoto Realty** (☎ 808/565-7519). All the lodgings in this guide, with the exception of the campground, are located in Lanai City, not at the beach. Book far in advance—they go quickly.

Campers have just one choice on Lanai: **Hulopoe Beach Park,** on the south side of the island. You can pitch your tent on one of six grassy sites near the ocean and enjoy solar-heated showers and modern restroom facilities. Reservations are required, along with a camping permit that costs $5, plus an extra five bucks each camper. Contact the **Lanai Company** (P.O. Box 630310, Lanai City, 96763; ☎ 808/565-3982).

$ One step above camping in terms of the rustic-quality of the accommodations, but many steps higher in the warm and gracious welcome you receive, are the digs at the home of **Dolores Fabrao** ★ (538 Akahi St.; ☎ 808/565-6134; cash only). A local elementary school teacher, who seems to rent out rooms more out of her desire to meet travelers than to make a profit, she has on offer one tiny double ($55/night—it seems to double as a storage room when unoccupied, it's that crammed with stuff) and a converted rec room. The rec room, in the basement, is an unofficial dorm for the hunters who pass through ($25 per bed, up to eight in the room). And when one of those hunting parties is staying in her big room, you may well want to avoid the place as there are only two bathrooms, and these are shared by all. That being said, Dolores is one of the most genuinely friendly, charming people I met in Hawaii, and getting to know her (and taste her marvelous cooking) might be a highlight of your visit.

Legal Issues for Lanai's Accommodations

Except for Lanai's hotels and campground, all other accommodations on the island operate "illegally" (most have been trying to get licensed and haven't been able to successfully navigate the bureaucracy). This despite the fact that they've been in business and paying taxes for years. As we went to press, the mayor of Maui County (which oversees Lanai) was threatening to shut down all unlicensed accommodations, but a lawsuit had temporarily stayed her hand. It's unclear what the future holds, so check carefully with the proprietor in advance of arrival as to the status of these lodgings.

$$–$$$ Set in one of the pastel-hued homes along the main strip of town, **Hale O Lanai** (4th St. and Lanai Ave.; ☎ 808/247-3637; myhawaiibeachfront.com; AE, DC, MC, V) is the vacation rental I mentioned earlier, and it's a cheerful, classic plantation-style home, with shiny oak floors, two tiny bedrooms (one with twins, the other a queen bed), and paintings by a well-respected local artist on the walls. So nothing fancy, but quite pleasant and with such nice amenities as central heating (as it can get chilly), a washer/dryer, and a full kitchen. Rental cost is $125 to $150 a night; it can sleep up to six.

$$–$$$ Just up the road is the much quirkier **Bamboo Gate** (☎ 808/565-9307; www.homeaway.com; MC, V), named for the large Japanese gate out front. Nine rooms in total are on offer here, though the owner often rents them two at a time for extra privacy (the cost is $125 for one, $150 for two), as many lead directly off one another and four share bathrooms. The decor is eclectic, to put it mildly. One might have an African theme with an imitation fur rug on the floor and African statues here and there; another is decorated with Asian fans and furniture; and everywhere are the color-saturated paintings of the owner. No breakfast is provided, but guests have access to the large open kitchen, breakfast nook (if they wish to make their own meals), and massive living room. All rooms have private lanais; rental of the entire house is $1,000 a night.

$$$ The most professional of Lanai's alternative accommodations is **Dreams Come True** ★★ (12th St. and Lanai Ave.; ☎ 800/566-6961 or 808/565-6961; www.dreamscometruelanai.com; AE, MC, V), a comfortable bed-and-breakfast inn. A four-bedroom plantation-style house, built in 1925, it was completely renovated in 2000 to accept guests and now has such nice amenities as whirlpool tubs and skylights. Guests share a large living room, and have use of laundry facilities, a computer, and a modern kitchen (though a custom-prepared breakfast is included). Set on a large lot, amid flowers and fruit trees, guests can watch the sun set from the veranda in back. The common areas are attractively decorated with Indonesian antiques. Rooms are neat and pretty, the beds new, comfortable, and sheathed in home-printed quilts. You can also choose from a variety of room sizes, with some units suitable for four. The entire operation feels fresh and welcoming, and one of the owners, a gourmet chef, will prepare a feast for you in the evenings, for a bit extra. Rooms are $137 a night.

$$$–$$$$ Lanai's first hotel (built in 1923), the **Hotel Lanai** ★ (828 Lanai Ave.; ☎ 800/795-7211 or 808/565-7211; www.hotellanai.com; AE, MC, V) was the 10-room inn where off-island Dole executives would stay when visiting the island, and it still has a pleasantly old-timey ambience. Set back from the road, and surrounded by an expansive lawn and Norfolk pines, it's retained such traditional features as a corrugated iron roof and board-and-batten construction. Not all is ancient, though: It's been remodeled several times over the years, most recently to refurbish the bathrooms and upgrade the furnishings. In keeping with the inn's rustic setting and plantation roots, the rooms are small but comfortable in a country-living way, replete with pineapple shaped lamps, colorful throw rugs on the hardwood floors, and handmade Hawaiian quilts for the beds. A complimentary continental breakfast is served each morning in the dining room paneled in knotty pine and decorated with mounted hunting trophies. Overall, this hotel has an informal, easy ambience. While Hotel Lanai isn't super cheap, it's possible to pay $139 to $159 for these pleasant accommodations; try Sun Islands Hawaii (☎ 808/936-3888; www.sunislandshawaii.com) before booking as it often scores discounts of up to 25%.

DINING FOR ALL TASTES

Although Lanai has a minimal selection of restaurants and cuisines, it does a good job of feeding folks. Meals range from simple to top-notch gourmet, priced accordingly. Most options fall into the budget or super expensive categories, with little in-between. Aside from the dining rooms at the two resorts, all of your choices are in Lanai City.

$–$$$ Consistently good, the **Blue Ginger Café** ★ (409 7th Ave.; ☎ 808/565-6363; daily 6am–8pm; cash only), occupies a restored plantation-style house and serves food that is as down to earth and simple as its surroundings. You'll find standard breakfast fare (most items are under $5) and house-baked pastries on the menu, along with the usual sandwiches, burgers, salads, soups, and plate lunches at prices ranging from $3 to $7.50. At night, the chef branches out into meat-heavy local cuisine, including *kalbi* (Korean-style) ribs, steak, excellent stir-fries, and mixed grill plates, priced $8 to $16. If it's a nice day, the front veranda is an especially pleasant place to dine.

$–$$ Casual fare is also featured at **Café 565** (408 8th St.; ☎ 808/565-6622; Mon–Sat 10am–3pm and 5–8pm; cash only), which takes its name from the Lanai telephone prefix. You'll find a mix of plate lunches and noodle dishes, along with calzones, thin-crust pizzas, soups, salads, and sandwiches, all reasonably priced at $5 to $12. A specialty: the terrifically flavorful portobello "burger" ($6).

$–$$$$ **Pele's Other Garden** ★ (8th and Houston sts.; ☎ 808/565-9628; Mon–Fri 10am–2:30pm and 5–8pm, Sat 5–8pm; AE, DC, MC, V) is a simple deli during the day, but transforms into a cute Italian trattoria come nightfall, complete with tablecloths and candles. Pasta is the dish to pick here, though it is pricey at

$17 to $19 a plate. Still, it's perfectly al dente, well-sauced, and runs the gamut from solid spaghetti and meatballs to an unusual but delicious pasta with smoked salmon and feta cheese. The garlic-happy bruschetta and excellent Caesar salad make good starters.

$$$–$$$$ Celebrated Maui chef Beverly Gannon (of Haile'imaile General Store) has recently taken over the dining room at the Lanai Hotel, and her **Lanai Grill** ★★★ (☎ 808/565-7211; www.hotellanai.com; Wed–Sun 5–9pm; AE, MC, V) is, I think, the most effortlessly classy place to dine on the island (as opposed to the restaurants at the Four Seasons, where the setting is handsome but the food just so-so). This is Lanai, so prices are elevated—main courses start at $25 and go up to $40. But I was perfectly happy making a meal of one of their oversized appetizers and dessert, which left me quite satisfied. Especially recommended are the chicken and Gouda quesadillas in a signature BBQ sauce ($12), the beet salad with Humboldt Fog goat cheese and pecans ($12), and the clams in white wine sauce ($13). Much of the produce used is grown on Lanai.

WHY YOU'RE HERE: LANAI'S BEACHES

Lanai doesn't have a lot of beaches, and, because of strong winds and brisk ocean currents, most of them are better suited to walking and fishing than sunbathing and swimming. That being said, if you're seeking peace and quiet, you'll have plenty of opportunity to find it on the sands here, especially if you have access to the sort of four-wheel-drive vehicle that can reach some of the more remote spots. Be aware that you'll also encounter some of the state's wildest beaches here, which means no houses, no facilities, and generally few people.

At the top of the list is **Hulopoe Beach** ★★★, which lies at the end of Highway 440 (Manele Rd.), about 7 miles south of Lanai City. Actually, this is one of the best beaches in the entire state and possibly the United States (it was so ranked in 1997 by Dr. Stephen Leatherman, aka Doctor Beach). The fine white sand and palm trees are picture perfect, and the water is invariably clean, clear, and temperate at about 70°F (21°C). It's usually calm enough for swimming and the snorkeling is delightful, due to both the excellent visibility and the Bay's status as a Marine Life Conservation District, which limits fishing. It has a grassy day-use area and campground with grill, and showers.

Adjacent **Manele Bay,** an ancient fishing village, is also within the Conservation District and another top choice for snorkeling and diving. Because it serves as an anchorage for tour boats, ferries, and private yachts, it's busier than Hulopoe—and its shoreline is rockier—but it's attractive. Spinner dolphins are frequent visitors at both beaches. Make sure to trek up to nearby "Sweetheart Rock"; the circle of stones on the nearby outcropping is a burial ground. Legend has it a jealous island warrior forced his sweetheart to wait for him in the sea cave here; she drowned when a storm kicked up and he carried her body to the top of this rock before throwing himself over the side.

If you're looking for sand and surf that's off the beaten track, **Shipwreck Beach** ★ fits the bill. It takes some bumpy driving to reach this remote, north shore beach, but that keeps the crowds away. Follow Highway 430 (Keomuku Rd.) north from Lanai City for about 6½ miles until it dead ends, then head west on a very rough road that hugs the shoreline for about a mile before ending at the beach. This 8-mile stretch of coast comprises four separate beaches, each a narrow strip of sand backed by low dunes. Walking and beachcombing are perfect activities to do here, but the waters are usually too rough for safe swimming. Offshore are the remains of a concrete hulled, World War II Liberty Ship. Behind the beach, up the hill and then about 300 feet down in the ravine, is a treasure trove of petroglyphs. (They're delicate, so don't take rubbings.)

Past Shipwreck Beach for another 4 bumpy miles is **Keomuku Beach** ★. Set next to the site of an ancient fishing village, it became the focal point of the failed Maunalei plantation that brought sugar to the island in 1899. At that time, there were some 60 houses and a small railway here in what was called **Keomuku Village,** but all except the islands oldest church (established 1903) and a nearby rock oven have vanished entirely (the wood used in these buildings having been salvaged for other uses). Be sure to stop at the old church, an evocative ruin now. Visitors leave a dollar or two on the shrine, and this goes to support active local churches. This shoreline is good for fishing and beachcombing, but its exposure to trade winds tends to make the water too choppy for pleasant swimming.

Brisk trade winds can also detract from the otherwise idyllic **Polihua Beach,** which boasts 1½ miles of white sand—the longest and widest stretch on the island. It's a gorgeous strand and a good whale-watching spot, but when the prevailing winds are blowing hard, you can expect conditions akin to sandblasting. ***Warning:*** Strong currents make swimming here dangerous. You'll need a four-wheel-drive vehicle to reach this beach, which lies at the end of Polihua Road, accessed from Fraser Street out of Lanai City. There are no facilities.

Four-wheel-drive also is required to traverse any of several rugged dirt roads that branch off Keomuku Road and lead to **Lopa Beach,** a long stretch of white sand fronting coastal waters that are rocky, but shallow enough for kids to safely swim in. It's also popular with pole and throw net fishermen. There are no facilities.

THE TOP SIGHTS & ATTRACTIONS

Lanai's iconic attraction is the so-called **Garden of the Gods** ★★★ (it got that moniker from a European naturalist; native Hawaiians call it *Keahikawelo*). I've always thought a more appropriate name would be "Tantrum of the Gods" as it looks as if some giant being, in a fury, pitched massive boulders and weirdly shaped rocks across the landscape. Of course, it was the pounding trade winds that created this dramatically eroded canyon and continues to shape its pinnacles and buttes. Ancient Hawaiians considered this area sacred. Legend has it that when a war broke out with nearby Molokai, Molokai's high priest sent "death spells" raining down on Lanai from afar. In retaliation, Lanai's chief priest Kavelo came to the highest point here, where he had an unbroken view of all of Molokai. He lit a sacred fire and kept it going day and night, saving the island by boomeranging back the evil prayers.

It's especially beautiful early and late in the day, when the orange clay soil and multi-hued rocks reflect the glow and colors of the rising and setting sun, making them even more vibrant. From Lanai City, take Fraser Street northwest to Polihua Road, which is unpaved. Follow it in a northwesterly direction for 6 miles to the site.

The **Munro Trail** ★★ is Lanai's second most important attraction, an 8-mile track that winds through stands of Norfolk pine and patches of rainforest to the top of Lanaihale Ridge, the island's high point at 3,370 feet. From this vista, you can look down into lush interior gulches and out across the sea, where every Hawaiian island but Kauai is visible on a clear day. You can hike or use a four-wheel-drive vehicle on this rutted, bumpy road, which starts about a mile beyond the Lodge at Koele. Look for the sign along Keomuku Road. Even better, try one of the tours led by staff at the Lanai Culture and Heritage Center (see below). ***Warning:*** Do not attempt the trail after heavy rains; it becomes a dangerous patch of jeep-trapping mud (and with just one tow-truck on the island, you could pay dearly if you got trapped up here).

The breaking news from Lanai is that it now has a small but mighty museum chronicling the history of the island through fascinating, well-explained artifacts, plus video and audio recordings. Set right above Dole Park, **The Lanai Culture and Heritage Center** ★ (Old Dole Building on Lanai Ave.; ☎ 808/565-7117; Mon–Fri 9am–3pm; free) was founded by noted Hawaiian anthropologist Kepa Maly; if he's there (likely), buttonhole him with questions; he's a fascinating fellow. The Center also runs superb tours of the Munro Trail, the Garden of the Gods, and other historically rich areas of the island. Tour prices were in flux when I visited; ask.

THE OTHER LANAI

Although rural Lanai isn't widely known as a focal point for the arts, it's striving to change that through a local arts program called, appropriately enough, the **Lanai Arts Program** (339 7th St.; ☎ 808/565-7503). Offering low-cost classes for residents and visitors alike, it's the closest Lanai has to a community center, except here everyone "communes" as they're painting, silk screening, beading, or trying such unusual techniques as *gyotaku,* the art of using fresh fish to create unique prints on fabric. Classes are taught by local experts, and occasionally by artists from nearby isles. Prices vary greatly. This is the quickest way I know to meet locals and get a pulse on the ever-shifting culture here. Classes are available for children, as well.

ACTIVE LANAI

WATERSPORTS

The clear, clean waters around Lanai are a delight for both snorkelers and divers alike. They turn to **Trilogy Ocean Sports** (☎ 888/628-4800 or 808/565-2387; www.sailtrilogy.com/adventures/lanai), which has an excellent reputation for its guiding services and safety record. It operates in Manale Bay, offering snorkeling, diving, sightseeing, and sailing expeditions on its two catamarans and rigid-bottom inflatable raft. You'll pay $195 for a snorkel/sail to an area known as the "Underwater Cathedral" (you'll understand why once you've seen it); if you go at sunrise, the price drops to $95. One-tank learning dives are $169 including a meal, snacks, gear, and instruction. Experts can do a two-tank dive for $130. Its guided ocean kayaking trips are also quite popular ($125). Whale- and spinner dolphin-watching cruises, while less active, are also less expensive at $75 per person. Kids are usually half-price, and you can save 10% by booking online.

Fishing is another big lure on this rich man's isle. The best outfit for this is **Spinning Dolphin Charters** (☎ 808/565-6613; www.sportfishinglanai.com), though its prices are high at $400 half-day and $800 full with the fee spread between the one to six passengers who sign up. Ahi and aku, two types of tuna, are the most prized catches year-round.

You might also spend your free time on Lanai learning to surf and Nick Palumbo, the former youth champion of Hawaii, is the instructor/owner at **Lanai Surf Safari** (☎ 808/306-9837; www.lanaisurfsafari.com), the only school on the island. His course is expensive (so what else is new; this is Lanai) at $185 per person, but it includes more than just surfing. To get to the gentlest, most consistent waves on the island, Palumbo drives visitors a good 45 minutes from the resorts, giving a fascinating tour along the way and supplying a hearty lunch. Nick's also a lovely, patient guy (hey, I even stood up!) and very good with children (though he doesn't discount for them).

GOLF & TENNIS

For such a small island, Lanai has ample links, with three courses to choose from. The cheapest is **Cavendish Golf Course,** which lies at the end of Nani Street on the outskirts of Lanai City. (Actually, it's free, but donations are requested of nonresidents.) You can play this 9-hole, par-36 course twice to get in 18 holes, and walking through the tall Norfolk pines planted around the course is quite pleasant.

The island's two resorts boast courses that are distinguished by their challenging play and awesome vistas. You'll be treated to stunning views of Molokai and Maui from **Experience at Koele** (☎ 808/565-4653), an uplands course designed by Greg Norman. With four sets of tees ranging from forward to tournament, it suits golfers at all levels of ability. **The Challenge at Manele** (☎ 808/565-2222) follows the coastline near Manele Bay. Designed by Jack Nicklaus, this par-72 course is known for its demanding water hazards: Three holes require tee shots over the ocean. If you're staying at the adjoining hotels, you can golf either course for $190, which includes cart rental, while nonguests pay a whopping $225 plus an additional club rental fee of $50. Savings are tough to come by, but if you hustle, you can play both courses in 1 day and pay just $80 for the second round. And if you come after noon, you can play 9 holes for about half the regular prices at either course.

The two resorts also offer tennis; **Manele Bay** has six unlighted Plexipave courts and **Koele** has three, all of them lit for night play. Court use is complimentary for hotel guests; nonguests pay $25 per hour. Free play is also available from 7am to 8:30pm daily on two tennis courts at Lanai School.

BIKING, HIKING & HORSEBACK RIDING

Lanai has miles of dirt roads with relatively little traffic, making it suitable for cyclists seeking rides that range from easy to strenuous. **Mountain bikes** are available to rent at Hotel Lanai ($25/hr.); guests of Koele Lodge and Manele Bay Hotel can rent road or mountain bikes through their concierge desks ($8/hr., $55/day).

You can comfortably walk or jog on any of the island's roads, but if you want to take a true hike, the **Koloiki Ridge Trail,** a 5-mile trek that starts behind Koele Lodge, is an excellent choice. It meanders through Hulopoe Valley to the Munro Ridge, culminating in expansive views from Koloiki Lookout. A moderately difficult hike that takes about 3 to 4 hours to complete, it's best suited to adults and older children.

If you'd prefer to hike *makai,* rather than *mauka,* you can traverse the 1.5-mile **Fisherman's Trail,** part of an ancient shoreline path that once circled the entire island. It's a mostly level, easy walk that runs from Hulopoe Bay to the Manele Bay Hotel golf course, making it suitable for kids of all ages and out of shape adults.

The most challenging but rewarding hike on the island is, of course, the vista-happy 11-mile **Munro Trail** (see p. 219 for more on that). A lot of it's uphill, though (puff, puff).

The treacherous roads of Lanai are much more palatable on the back of a horse and **The Stables at Koele** (☎ 808/565-4424), which serves both resort guests and the public, offer a number of options for conquering them. They have something for everyone, from 10-minute *keiki* pony rides to 3- and 4-hour trail rides. Prices range from $85 for a 1½-hour jaunt along the Paniolo Trail (up into the ironwood-shaded hills above Koele) to the Mahana Ride (2 hr., $95). Long pants and shoes are required; safety helmets are provided. Bring a jacket; the weather is chilly and rain is frequent. Children must be at least 9 years old and 4 feet tall, and riders cannot weigh more than 250 pounds.

OTHER SPORTS ON LANAI

Lanai is well known for its hunting (and is so isolated it rarely sees the type of protests the other islands do). Axis deer, mouflon sheep, mountain pig, pheasant, and other game birds are the prey; boosters of the sport claim that these creatures, mostly introduced species, are destructive to native flora (and therefore must be "culled"). Muzzleloader muskets, bows and arrows, rifles, and shotguns can be used on public and private lands, provided you have a Hawaii hunting license ($155) and hunting safety card. Contact the state **Department of Natural Resources** (☎ 808/565-7916) for license forms and brochures outlining hunting rules and seasons. The Lanai Company has set aside about ⅔ of the island as a reserve, which it manages for private hunting. It leases the rest to the state for public hunting. The public hunting lands are found in the northwest section of the island, and the state has brochures and maps that denote the public areas.

Guides are highly recommended everywhere, and required if you want to hunt on private lands. Fees run about $750 per day, which includes shipping your trophy home. A separate license ($275 for gun hunter, $50 for archers) is needed to bag game on private land, for which the hunt must be arranged in advance with one of three Lanai Company rangers, a process that can take a bit of time to complete. Call the Lanai Company game management office at ☎ 808/565-3981 for details.

If you want to fire a gun without killing anything (or shoot an arrow peacefully), **Lanai Pine Sporting Clays** (☎ 808/563-4600), located on Keamoku Highway, about a mile north of the Lodge at Koele, will outfit you with all the gear needed to shoot sporting clays from 14 different stations set up around a course. The fee is $145 for 100 targets or $85 for 45 minutes. Skeet shooting with a wobbe trap draws just as many shooters (you pay $8 per box of ammo and 80¢ per target. Trap ranges and an air gun station (my fave, no kickback and appropriate for children) are also available. A Diana-worthy, 12 station archery range rounds out the offerings. Instructions, bows and arrows, and use of facilities will cost you $45; if you bring your own gear, it's $25 to use the course.

ATTENTION, SHOPPERS!

Shopping is limited but fun on Lanai, and surprisingly goes beyond the usual trinket and muumuu stores—though if you're looking for those, you can head to **Gifts with Aloha** (7th and Houston aves.; ☎ 808/565-6589). For example, two of the islands' artists have their own galleries selling paintings and prints filled with palm trees, golden beaches, and brilliantly colored tropical flowers: the **Mike Carroll Gallery** (443 7th St.; ☎ 808/565-7122; www.mikecarrollgallery.com); and **Jordanne Fine Art Studio** (850 Fraser; ☎ 808/563-0088; www.jordanefineart.com).

But my fave, by far, is the **Dis 'N Dat Shop** (418 8th St.; ☎ 808/565-9170; www.disndatshop.com), a fairyland of wind chimes, light catchers, sparkly jewelry, and all sorts of other glittering baubles, hung willy nilly around this small shop (Aladdin's cave probably didn't twinkle this much). It's the perfect place for gift shopping, whether you're into Asian antiques, charm necklaces shaped like flip-flops (their signature item), or handcarved boxwood miniatures. The funnest place on Lanai.

The ABCs of Lanai

Area Code Like all of Hawaii, Lanai uses the **808** area code.

Business Hours Two full-service banks are open in Lanai City from 8:30am to about 3 or 4:30pm weekdays. Government offices are open weekdays from 8am to 5pm. Most stores are open daily from 9 or 10am to 5 or 6pm.

Currency Exchange Your best bet is to change money at the airport in Honolulu or on Maui, before you fly to Lanai, or to use traveler's checks.

Medical **Lanai Community Hospital** (☎ **808/565-6411**) offers 24-hour emergency medical care. Physicians are available during regular business hours at **Lanai Family Health Center** (☎ **808/565-6423**).

Emergencies For the police, fire, or ambulance, dial ☎ **911.**

Information **Destination Lanai** (☎ **800/947-4774** or 808/565-7600; www.visitlanai.net) offers general information about the island. The **Lanai Company** (☎ **808/565-3000**) has free maps, brochures, and other helpful materials.

Newspapers The Lanai Times is published monthly and available all over town.

Pharmacies You can have prescriptions filled at **Lanai Community Hospital** (☎ **808/565-6411**).

Police In an emergency, call ☎ **911;** otherwise, dial ☎ **808/565-6428.**

Post Office A post office is located on Jacaranda Street, adjacent to Dole Park in Lanai City. It's open 9am to 4pm weekdays and 10am to noon on Saturdays.

Safety Lanai is one of the safest destinations in Hawaii, but it's still wise to watch your possessions, and don't leave valuables in your rental car.

6 Maui: Hawaii's Most Celebrated Island

With its small towns & laid-back lifestyle, this beach-lined mountain paradise surpasses Oahu in tourist numbers.

by David Thompson

I'VE KNOWN MAUI SINCE I WAS A KID, AND WE'VE BOTH CHANGED A LOT over the years. I've gotten taller. Maui's gotten more golf courses and more concrete. I'm not always pleased with the direction Maui's taken, and, quite frankly, I sometimes think I'm over her. I think that we've grown so far apart, and we're so different now, that I don't really love her anymore.

Then I get off the plane at Kahului Airport. Instead of indifference or estrangement, I'm struck by the imposing presence of Haleakala volcano, rising smoothly and massively from the sea to 10,023 feet, and beckoning me to the dormant summit. I'm thrilled by the mysterious green folds of the rugged West Maui Mountains, where dark, misty rains alternate with brilliant rainbows. My misgivings about Maui begin to drift away on the trade winds, along with the billowing clouds that float languidly over the island's carpeting of sugar cane. Inevitably I wind up lying half naked along one of Maui's many perfect beaches, watching the shimmering afternoon sun track lazily across the sky while foamy white caps streak the deep blue waters far offshore. And once again I find myself back in Maui's warm embrace, perfectly happy to be there.

DON'T LEAVE MAUI WITHOUT . . .

Rising above it all. Hawaiians named Haleakala "The House of the Sun," and indeed it's the place to go for a sunrise you won't forget. Even if you get up there later, the sublime views and deep sense of calm that prevail on one of the tallest peaks in the Pacific make this a place you still won't forget. See p. 288.

Exploring funky Paia. This quiet plantation town has been reinvented by hippies and windsurfers, who filled it with small shops, eclectic restaurants, and more beautiful people than any town really ought to have. See p. 230.

Spout spotting. Snowbirds aren't the only ones to winter on Maui. From November through April, hundreds of humpback whales come, too. Hop on one of the dozens of whale-watching boats (p. 286), or save the fare and sit at

McGregor Point (p. 286), a prime whale-watching site. Just about any waterfront restaurant in south or west Maui makes for good whale-watching.

Playing budget gourmet. Have a gourmet meal without the gourmet meal prices at Bermudez's Big Wave Café in Kihei. Make it in time for the early-bird special and get two gourmet meals for the price of one. See p. 260.

Tending turtles. Join the researchers from the Hawaii Wildlife Fund and help the next generation of endangered hawksbill sea turtles get a healthy start on life. See p. 294.

Road tripping! The long and winding road to Hana, through a rainforest and past a multitude of waterfalls, is all about the journey. Although the destination is pretty cool, too. See p. 230.

A BRIEF HISTORY

Over the years, Maui has changed. Maui and its closest neighbors—Molokai, Lanai, and Kahoolawe—were all once part of a giant single island, which geologists named Maui Nui, or Big Maui. As Maui Nui aged and sea levels rose, the lowlands slipped beneath the waves, leaving a rough channel between Maui and Molokai to the west, and sheltered waters between Maui, Lanai, and Kahoolawe to the south. Maui will continue changing until it eventually disappears altogether. Hawaiian islands have a well understood life cycle of emergence and subsidence, during which they rise up out of the sea over millions of years, then weather away until they slip back beneath the waves.

Nowadays, during winter, hundreds of whales congregate in the calm waters to mate and calve. Throughout the year, a fleet of commercial pleasure craft takes visitors on snorkeling tours, sunset cocktail cruises, and even submarine rides. The dissolution of Maui Nui has left 120 miles of shoreline along the Maui part of what remains, with more than 80 beaches, including some of the finest in the world.

DISCOVERING MAUI

On the human scale, Maui has been changing since the first Polynesian seafarers landed 1,500 years ago and set about gently altering the landscape. They built with grass, leaf, wood, and stone, and some of their stonework remains intact today. At various sites around the island, you can see skillfully constructed walls, housing foundations, irrigation systems, and other examples of their mortarless masonry. On the road to Hana, you can stop at Piilanihale Heiau, the largest ancient Hawaiian temple in the state. Near Hana and in Makena, you can hike along segments of an ancient stone footpath—the King's Highway—that once circled the island.

Captain Cook never set foot on Maui, but the island's inhabitants certainly knew of him and the fatal falling out he had on the Big Island that ended with his death in 1779. Eight years later, when a French scientific expedition led by Jean Francois de Galaup de La Perouse appeared off the south coast of Maui, hundreds of Hawaiians jumped into canoes and paddled out with pigs, fruit, and fish to trade. The protected cove at the dry, barren foot of Haleakala where La Perouse dropped anchor now bears his name, La Perouse Bay, along with a small monument commemorating his visit as the first by a Westerner to the island. Contact with Western culture profoundly, and often tragically, changed things in Hawaii, but La Perouse Bay remains undeveloped. Go there and you'll find extensive remnants of the villages that La Perouse found, as well as pristine snorkeling waters.

THE TIME OF KAMEHAMEHA

An immediate impact of Western contact was an arms race between the rival chiefs of the various islands—one in which King Kamehameha of the Big Island took an early lead. It was an advantage that helped him become the first chief ever to control all of the islands. When he invaded Maui in 1790, he had something the Maui forces were no match for—muskets and cannons. His men landed on the beach at Kahului, chased Maui's defenders to the back of narrow Iao Valley (today a popular picnic spot), and slaughtered them, sealing his claim to the island.

Of Kamehameha's 21 wives, his favorite was the bright, headstrong Maui girl who became Queen Kaahumanu. After the old king's death in 1819, she sat down to dinner with men, violating a fundamental *kapu* (taboo) that prohibited men and women from eating together, and shattering the elaborate *kapu* system upon which Hawaiian society had been organized. This spelled doom for the ancient gods, and made the job of the Protestant missionaries, who arrived on Maui in 1823, far easier than it might have been. If you make the long, winding drive to the remote town of Hana, you can hike along the water to the cave where Kaahumanu was born.

MISSIONARIES, SUGAR & TOURISM

The missionaries established themselves in Lahaina, the capital of the Hawaiian Kingdom from 1820 until 1845 (at which point it moved to Honolulu). The seminary they established on the hillside above the town has since become a public high school (the oldest school west of the Rocky Mountains). The printing press they built here to publish Hawaiian-language Bibles, textbooks, and newspapers is one of the highlights of a self-guided tour of Lahaina's many historic sites.

The missionaries often clashed with the whalers, who had beat them to Hawaii by a few years, and who, after long months at sea, were as devoted to the flesh as the missionaries were to the spirit. Lahaina was one of their favorite ports. Drunken and frustrated seamen sometimes rampaged in the dusty streets as the town's pious citizenry hid behind the closed shutters and locked doors of the New England–style homes they built. One of these homes, the oldest house on the island, still stands. At this home—what's now the Baldwin Home Museum—missionary doctor Dwight Baldwin ran his practice, shared his faith, and raised his large family. One of his sons went into business with another missionary son, creating a company that grew to become one of the most powerful commercial and political forces in the islands, Alexander & Baldwin, Inc. The company started out producing sugar and expanded into shipping, ranching, and, ultimately, real estate and development. It still produces sugar on Maui today, and the tall smoke stacks visible from all around the central plain belong to its mill. In the shadow of the smokestacks sits a little museum (p. 284), where you can peer into Maui's plantation past and get a sense of how the plantation era and all the new ethnic groups it brought to the islands shaped the Hawaii of today.

Sugar was king on Maui, but no longer. Tourism, once the cocky upstart, has ascended the throne. Population and building booms accompanied the economic transformation. Since 1970, Maui's population has tripled to nearly 130,000 people, not counting the 40,000 visitors on the island on any given day. Along with all the new faces have come traffic jams and sprawling development. Sleepy beach towns that once lined long stretches of the sunny south and west coasts have turned into luxurious resort areas and condominium conurbations. Maui has more condo units put to use as vacation rentals than all the other islands combined, and the dollar-wise will find some of the island's best deals on accommodations among them.

The enormous influx of newcomers who chased their dreams to Maui and never left has given the island its dubious distinction of being the most mainland-like of all the Hawaiian Islands. But local culture—Hawaii's unique amalgamation of Hawaiian ways, Western ways, and the ways of all the ethnic groups that came as plantation labor—still thrives. It just does so in dilution. You can spend a long time on Maui without meeting anyone who was actually born here. The chances that whoever is mixing the mai tai or skippering the tour boat came from California or Minnesota or France are as good as the chances that they're originally from Hawaii.

Before my plane touched down again at Kahului Airport, I thought changes like this one would upset me. But a few days after returning to the island following my long absence, I awoke on the north shore, where the iron-rich volcanic soil colors everything—the sidewalks, the trees, the chickens—a cinder red. And as the sun's first golden light mixed with that indelible color to create the unmistakable hues of a Hawaiian dawn, I realized Maui's true charm. You can't help but love her just as she is.

LAY OF THE LAND

Before anything else, let's first get acquainted with the several distinct parts of Maui and some of its towns.

WEST MAUI

West Maui is the most popular area of the island for visitors (with South Maui a close second). This is where the bustling tourist mecca of Lahaina is, an old New England–style whaling town that's now teeming with T-shirt shops, art galleries, jewelry stores, restaurants, bars, nightlife, historic sites, boat tours, and fun. The only thing Lahaina lacks is enough parking. Farther north is Kaanapali Resort, with 3 miles of golden sand beach and two championship golf courses. Even farther north, a long stretch of beachfront condominiums runs through the former fishing villages of Honokowai, Mahinahina, Kahana, and Napili (Napili is where the best beach and most desirable—though not necessarily the most expensive—condos are). Surrounded by pineapple fields at the end of the line is the Kapalua Resort, domain of two exclusive hotels and some swanky, phenomenally pricey vacation-rental homes and condos.

The Valley Isle

Maui's nickname, "The Valley Isle," is derived from the 7-mile-wide isthmus between the West Maui Mountains and Haleakala.

CENTRAL MAUI

Sugar cane covers much of the broad central plain between Haleakala and the West Maui Mountains, the two volcanoes that constitute Maui. Three highways connecting the north shore to the south traverse the plain. The twin cities of Wailuku and Kahului occupy the north part of the plain. Although they butt up against each other and have no distinguishable boundary, they have distinct characters. Wailuku, the seat of county government, has an old, hilly downtown. Kahului, the younger city, has long since eclipsed Wailuku as the island's commercial center. It was created in the 1950s by Alexander & Baldwin as a suburban "Dream City" where the company's plantation workers could own their own homes. Now it has the major airport and the island's only deep draft harbor, as well as shopping malls, box stores, and strip development reminiscent of many places on the mainland.

SOUTH MAUI

South Maui's coastline runs from north to south along the warmest, driest part of the island. At the southernmost end, in Makena, the paved road passes through the Ahihi-Kinau Natural Area Reserve, where Haleakala's last eruption poured down the mountain into the sea. The road dead-ends at pristine La Perouse Bay, where Maui's contact with the Western world began.

To the north, the side-by-side Makena and Wailea resorts have five championship golf courses and six luxury hotels between the two of them, as well as some exceptionally nice beaches. Though the beaches might seem like the private domains of the hotels, they belong to the public, as do all of Hawaii's beaches.

Wailea's manicured green landscaping gives way abruptly to the more disorderly and democratic landscape of Kihei, which is a long wall of beachfront condominiums and a series of shopping complexes. Kihei is where much of the action is—the mai tais, the dancing, the bargain sushi. It also happens to be where some of the best deals on accommodations, especially in condos, are found.

A large wetlands area called the Kealia Pond National Wildlife Refuge separates Kihei from the small community of Maalaea to the north. Maalaea features a small boat harbor with a fleet of tour boats, a beachfront condominium community, a world-class aquarium, a few shops and restaurants, a miniature golf course, and the strongest winds on the island.

UPCOUNTRY

The high, cool slopes of Haleakala comprise the region known as upcountry Maui—a world of forestland, farmland, ranchland, and small communities. Makawao, one of the larger small communities, has a two-street downtown that

Maui Attractions & Outdoor Activities

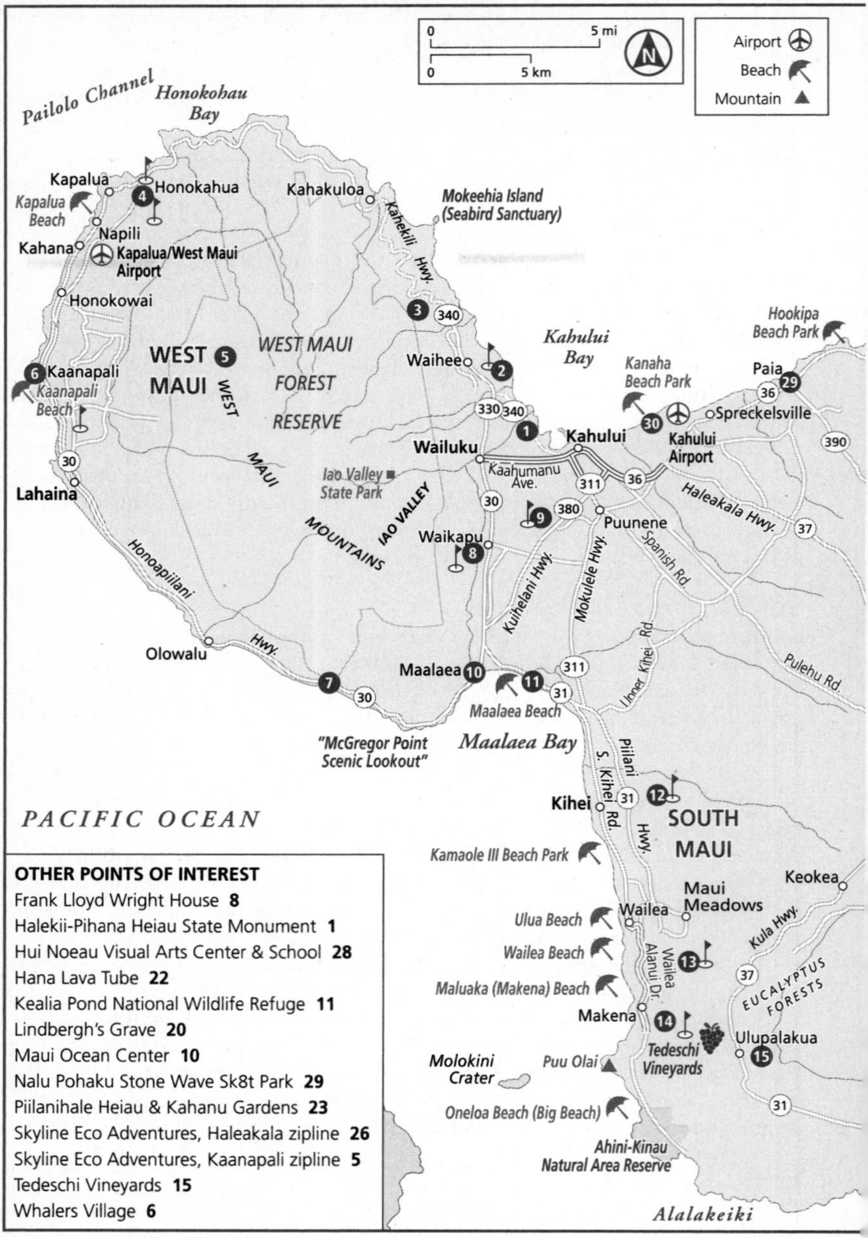
0
5 mi
0
5 km
N
Airport
Beach
Mountain
Pailolo Channel
Honokohau Bay
Kapalua
Kapalua Beach
Honokahua
Napili
Kahana
Kapalua/West Maui Airport
Honokowai
Kahakuloa
Kahekili Hwy.
Mokeehia Island (Seabird Sanctuary)
340
WEST MAUI
WEST MAUI FOREST RESERVE
WEST MAUI MOUNTAINS
Kaanapali
Kaanapali Beach
Waihee
Kahului Bay
Kanaha Beach Park
Hookipa Beach Park
Paia
36
Spreckelsville
330
340
Kahului
Kahului Airport
390
Wailuku
Kaahumanu Ave.
311
36
Haleakala Hwy.
30
Lahaina
Iao Valley State Park
IAO VALLEY
380
Puunene
Spanish Rd.
37
Waikapu
Kuihelani Hwy.
Mokulele Hwy.
Honoapiilani Hwy.
Olowalu
Upper Kihei Rd.
Pulehu Rd.
Maalaea
311
31
Maalaea Beach
30
"McGregor Point Scenic Lookout"
Maalaea Bay
Piilani Hwy.
S. Kihei Rd.
Kihei
31
SOUTH MAUI
PACIFIC OCEAN
Kamaole III Beach Park
Keokea
Maui Meadows
Wailea
Ulua Beach
Kula Hwy.
Wailea Beach
Wailea Alanui Dr.
37
EUCALYPTUS FORESTS
Maluaka (Makena) Beach
Makena
Tedeschi Vineyards
Ulupalakua
Molokini Crater
Puu Olai
31
Oneloa Beach (Big Beach)
Ahini-Kinau Natural Area Reserve
Alalakeiki
OTHER POINTS OF INTEREST
Frank Lloyd Wright House 8
Halekii-Pihana Heiau State Monument 1
Hui Noeau Visual Arts Center & School 28
Hana Lava Tube 22
Kealia Pond National Wildlife Refuge 11
Lindbergh's Grave 20
Maui Ocean Center 10
Nalu Pohaku Stone Wave Sk8t Park 29
Piilanihale Heiau & Kahanu Gardens 23
Skyline Eco Adventures, Haleakala zipline 26
Skyline Eco Adventures, Kaanapali zipline 5
Tedeschi Vineyards 15
Whalers Village 6

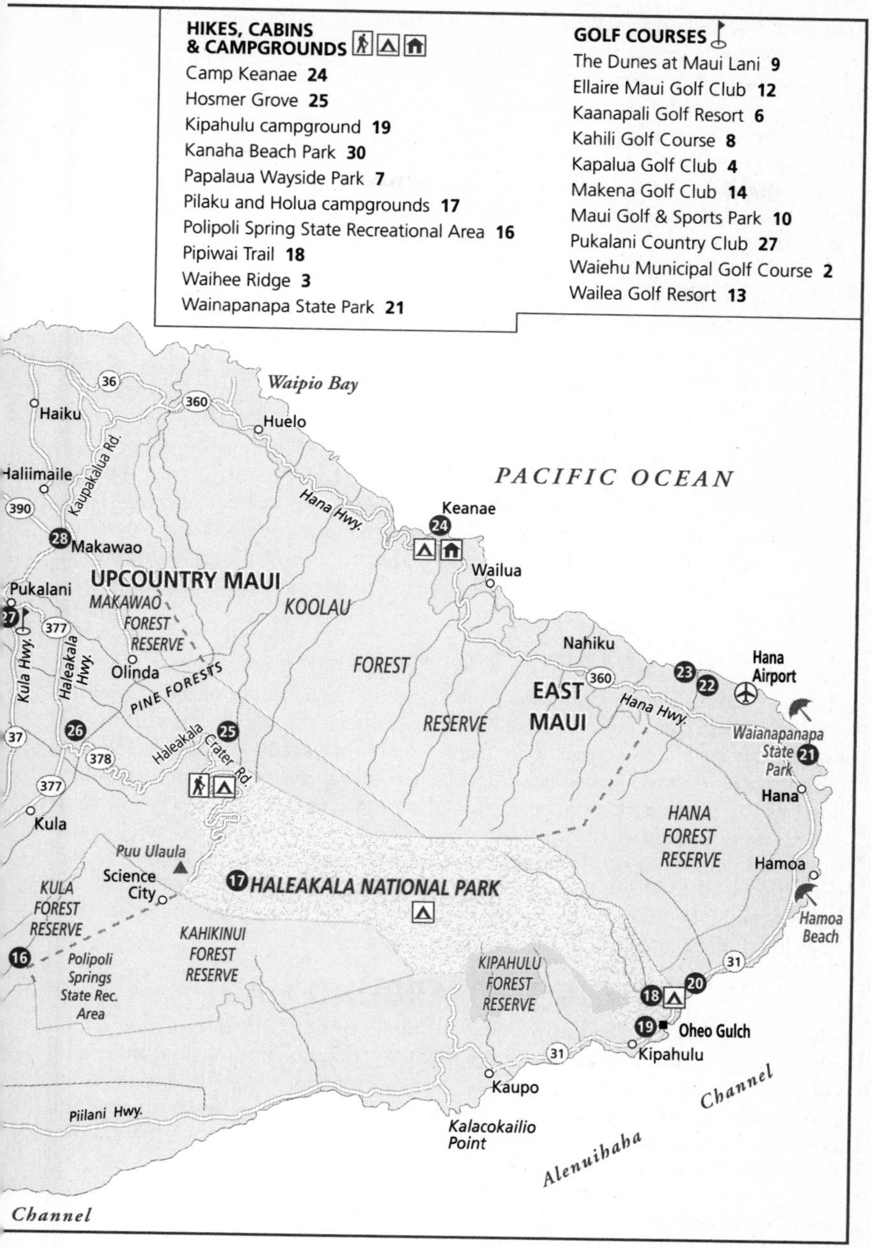
HIKES, CABINS & CAMPGROUNDS
Camp Keanae 24
Hosmer Grove 25
Kipahulu campground 19
Kanaha Beach Park 30
Papalaua Wayside Park 7
Pilaku and Holua campgrounds 17
Polipoli Spring State Recreational Area 16
Pipiwai Trail 18
Waihee Ridge 3
Wainapanapa State Park 21
GOLF COURSES
The Dunes at Maui Lani 9
Ellaire Maui Golf Club 12
Kaanapali Golf Resort 6
Kahili Golf Course 8
Kapalua Golf Club 4
Makena Golf Club 14
Maui Golf & Sports Park 10
Pukalani Country Club 27
Waiehu Municipal Golf Course 2
Wailea Golf Resort 13
Waipio Bay
Haiku
Huelo
Haliimaile
Kaupakalua Rd.
Hana Hwy.
PACIFIC OCEAN
Keanae
Wailua
Makawao
UPCOUNTRY MAUI
Pukalani
MAKAWAO FOREST RESERVE
KOOLAU
FOREST
RESERVE
Nahiku
EAST MAUI
Hana Airport
Kula Hwy.
Haleakala Hwy.
Olinda
PINE FORESTS
Haleakala Crater Rd.
Waianapanapa State Park
Hana
Kula
Puu Ulaula
Science City
HANA FOREST RESERVE
Hamoa
HALEAKALA NATIONAL PARK
Hamoa Beach
KULA FOREST RESERVE
KAHIKINUI FOREST RESERVE
Polipoli Springs State Rec. Area
KIPAHULU FOREST RESERVE
Oheo Gulch
Kipahulu
Kaupo
Piilani Hwy.
Kalacokailio Point
Alenuihaha Channel
Channel

was once solely about cowboys. Now it's all about cowboys, sushi, and yoga, with a bunch of art galleries thrown in. The steep road to the summit of Haleakala cuts through the rich upcountry farming area known as Kula, where Maui onions, Kula greens, orchids, carnations, and otherworldly flowers called protea all thrive. Polipoli Springs State Recreation Area has camping, hiking, mountain biking, and mist-filled conifer forests reminiscent of Northern California. Several ranches offer horseback riding, and one entrepreneur has strung steel cables across a deep gulch in a eucalyptus forest and offers zipline rides along them (see Skyline Eco Adventures on p. 310).

PAIA & HAIKU

Paia, on the island's north shore, was fading as a sugar mill town in the 1960s and 1970s when the hippies arrived. They were joined in the 1980s by windsurfers who had discovered the blustery, wave-jumping fun they could have at nearby Hookipa Beach Park, now known as "the Windsurfing Capital of the World." With its new blood, the old plantation town remade itself as the hippest, funkiest little town on the island, filled with great restaurants, unique boutiques, hard bodies, and the best health-food store on Maui—Mana Foods (p. 266). Haiku, another old plantation community, is 10 minutes away. Its center of things is an old cannery that's been transformed into a shopping area, with a fancy yoga studio, a few restaurants, and a bike-rental shop that offers downhill rides from high up Haleakala to the coast. Most of the rest of Haiku is tucked away in the boonies, out of sight.

HANA & THE ROAD TO IT

Hana is 3 hours and a world away from Kahului. An heirloom of old Hawaii, it has the highest concentration of native Hawaiians on the island. For visitors, it's the journey to Hana—rather than Hana itself—that draws you there. The 54-mile drive along the narrow, winding Hana Highway runs along the lush, cliff-lined windward side of the island, through rainforest, and past taro farms, fruit stands, *heiau* (temples), and a multitude of waterfalls. Beyond Hana, you'll reach the Kipahulu section of Haleakala National Park, one of the panhandles of the park that descends from the summit to the coast. Here is where you'll find the magnificent Oheo Gulch, with its series of waterfalls and swimming spots that step down through steep rainforest terrain to the sea.

GETTING TO & AROUND MAUI

Most flights to Maui land at Kahului Airport, on the north side of the island. Major airlines offer nonstop or direct flights to Kahului from several mainland cities. International flights get only as close as Honolulu (with the exception of two Canadian flights). In addition to the main airport, there's a small airport with interisland service on West Maui, and there's a commuter airport with some inter-island flights in Hana.

INTERISLAND TRAVEL

Interisland air travel is currently dominated by two players, Hawaiian Airlines and a newcomer called **go!** (☎ 888/IFLYGO2; www.iflygo.com). In the past, over-the-counter fares for flights between Honolulu and Kahului cost about $100 one-way.

Finally, Ferry Service

The latest way to island hop in Hawaii is actually a throwback to the original way to island hop—by boat. After surmounting a series of legal, political, and environmental hurdles that threatened to sink it, the **Hawaii Superferry** (☎ 877/443-3779; www.hawaiisuperferry.com) began offering service between Oahu, Maui, and Kauai at the tail end of 2007. The adult fare is about $51 during off-peak days, and $61 during peak days, but a varying fuel surcharge (37% at press time) jacks the price up considerably. You may find cheaper airline tickets, but traveling to and from Maui by sea will give you a fresh perspective on Hawaii. For more on ferry service, go to p. 430.

Since go! entered the market in the summer of 2006, it's been waging a marvelous price war by offering interisland fares as low as $19, forcing the other airlines to follow suit. Unfortunately, with Aloha Airlines now out of the picture, seats are scarce, and prices are expected to increase accordingly. Before making any plans that involve interisland travel, read the box on p. 430.

If you can't snag a seat with Hawaiian Airlines or go! for a reasonable price, your next best bet for saving some money will be to go with one of the island's three smaller carriers. Their fares typically start around $69, with some online discounts. **Pacific Wings** (☎ 888/575-4546 or 808/873-0877; www.pacificwings.com) has nine-passenger aircraft flying between Maui and Honolulu, the Big Island, and Lanai. **Island Air** (☎ 808/877-5755; www.islandair.com) flies direct from Kahului to Hilo and Kona on the Big Island, as well as to Molokai, Honolulu, and Kauai. Its prop-driven planes carry 37 passengers. **Mokulele Flight Service** (☎ 866/260-7070; www.mokulele.com) flies from Maui to the Big Island, Lanai, and Molokai in its nine-passenger aircraft. Lower Internet rates are often available.

For more details on how to find low airfares, see p. 428.

GETTING AROUND

Maui's limited public transportation system is not a good way for visitors to get to and from the airport or around Maui. Service is limited to Central, West, and South Maui; it takes forever; and there's no bus stop at the airport. You're better off with a rental car. If you're hell-bent on riding the bus, you should know this: The bus doesn't run on Sunday; no surfboards, boogie boards, or bicycles are allowed; no change is made; and no transfers are given. For more information on Maui's **buses,** call ☎ 808/871-4383 or go to www.mauicounty.gov/bus.

Car-rental rates on Maui, like everywhere, fluctuate with supply, demand, and the season. If you avoid the high seasons and get lucky, you may get an economy car for less than $200 per week, including all taxes and fees. If you hit the island when rates are high, you could end up paying twice that. All the big national chains and some local ones are here and I have to say, I see little difference in their

Rush Hour

Rush-hour traffic on Maui runs from 6 to 9am and 3 to 6pm. If possible, time your arrival to avoid it.

pricing. You may however, be able to get a good deal "bidding blind" (on a service such as Priceline.com). My advice: go to a good search engine such as Sidestep.com to find out what car rental prices are like during your stay and then slice 15% off that rate in a Priceline.com bid. If you get it, so much the better. If you don't you can always book in a more traditional fashion.

If you're not renting a car, and you don't want to fork out the taxi fare, try the **Executive Airport Shuttle** ★★★ (☎ 800/833-2303 or 808/669-2300; www.mauishuttle.com), which will carry you to your hotel, condo, bed-and-breakfast, friend's house, or wherever for less than cab fare (which clocks in at $2/mile, so unless you're only traveling a short distance, you'll do better with the shuttle). It serves most of the island, from upcountry to West Maui, and offers huge discounts for parties of two. From Kahului Airport to Kihei, it costs about $28 for one and just $30 for two (a taxi would cost about $40); from the airport to Lahaina, it costs $39 for one and $45 for two (taxi: $55); to Paia, it costs about $20 for one and $22 for two (and here the cab fare would be the same). Reservations are required. If you try to book something after you arrive, you'll probably have to wait a couple of hours. It operates from 5am to 10pm.

SpeediShuttle (☎ 877/242-5777 or 808/242-7777; www.speedishuttle.com), Maui's other big airport-shuttle firm, doesn't have the steep discounts for two passengers that Executive Airport Shuttle does. But if Executive Airport Shuttle won't have you, you can count on SpeediShuttle to get from the airport to Kihei for about $28 per person, and to Lahaina for about $46 per person. It doesn't serve Paia, Hana, or upcountry. Reservations required. Hours are from 7am to 10pm, and there's a 10% discount on round-trips.

ACCOMMODATIONS, BOTH STANDARD & NOT

by Pauline Frommer & David Thompson

With the average price of a hotel room in Maui hovering around $270 per night, the Valley Isle can seem downright unfriendly to budget travelers. But don't be discouraged. Maui has Hawaii's highest concentration of outrageously expensive resort hotels and that skews the average. An ample selection of smaller resorts and hotels, plus B&Bs, vacation rentals, and campgrounds (free in some cases!) are available to the cash-conscious traveler. Perhaps most importantly, Maui is literally crawling with condos and the "let's make a deal" nature of the pricing on those is manna to budgeters. For tips on condo savings, head to p. 244; you'll find a number of condo options listed below geographically, as well.

Note: When looking at room rates in this chapter, don't forget to add Hawaii's 11.42% accommodations tax to the total.

Seasons of Savings

During the low seasons of spring and fall (minus Thanksgiving), you'll typically pay 10% to 20% less for a room or condo than during the rest of the year. This is when budget travelers should strike. Not only will you find better deals on accommodations, you'll discover a more relaxed Maui altogether.

February is the most popular month on Maui, though January and the two months that follow it will also be crowded and pricey. The upsurge in family travel in June, July, and especially August make summer high season, as well. And as with most every other resort destination in the U.S., holiday travel (Thanksgiving, Christmas, and New Years) should also be considered peak.

To complicate things, each individual property or rental agency determines if and precisely when it will have a high season. Some add a third tier of rates during "shoulder seasons" between high and low seasons, and some celebrate the holidays by adding restrictions (like 1-week minimums). We've noted the good eggs (those that keep their rates constant year round) below.

WEST MAUI: IN & NEAR LAHAINA

What's it like to stay in Lahaina? The city is like Waikiki with a height ordinance and a sense of history. Both places are party towns swarming with tourists looking for a good time. But where Waikiki sprouted modernist high-rises to form a network of deep concrete canyons, Lahaina stuck close to the ground and retained some of the 19th-century charm of it's rowdy whaling years. You stay here if you want to be in the center of the action, and don't mind the lack of swimmable water nearby (only half the listings below come with pool or beach access; for that see our selections in the rest of the chapter).

$ The cheapest option in the area is West Maui's only hostel, **Patey's Place** (761 Wainee St.; ☎ 808/667-0999; cash only), which is such a friendly, low key place that it attracts travelers from all walks of life. When I was there last, I came upon a dreadlocked family with their two toddlers, two happy go lucky seniors, and a slew of surfer dudes and dudettes returning wearily from the beach. Part of the reason for the mellow ambience is a strict "no drugs or alcohol" policy, which pertains even when the hostel throws its weekly cookout. As for the rooms, they're spare in the extreme, the dorm rooms ($25/night) with mural-laden cement floors and metal bunk beds; the private rooms $80/double with a private bathroom, $60 without) consisting solely of a bed in a whitewashed room, a rickety dresser, but no niceties like bedskirts, closets, or rugs. Still, the rooms were darn tidy (if worn) and the communal kitchen may well be the cleanest I've ever seen at a hostel. And oddly enough, the rooms without bathrooms are in the new addition, so they're

Where to Stay & Dine on Maui

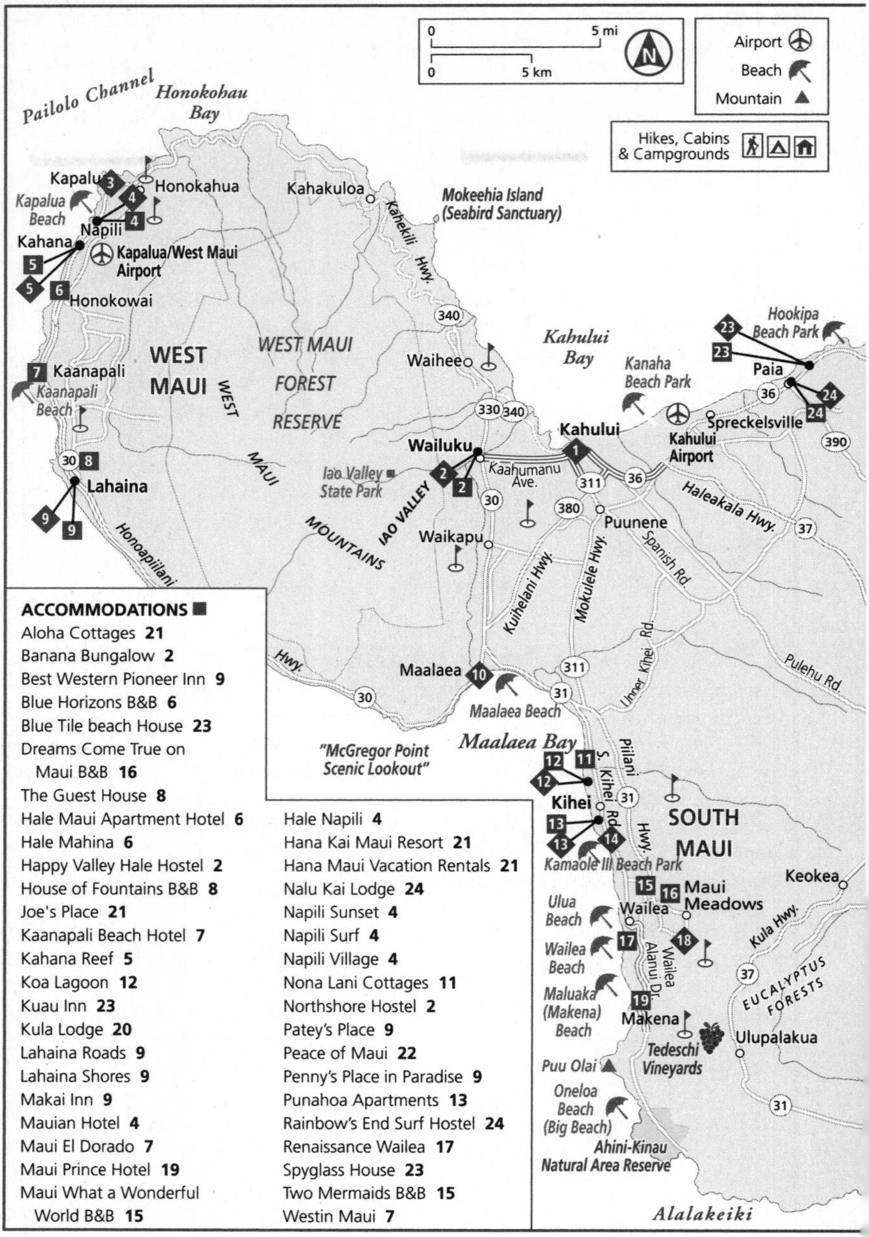

ACCOMMODATIONS ■

Aloha Cottages **21**
Banana Bungalow **2**
Best Western Pioneer Inn **9**
Blue Horizons B&B **6**
Blue Tile beach House **23**
Dreams Come True on Maui B&B **16**
The Guest House **8**
Hale Maui Apartment Hotel **6**
Hale Mahina **6**
Happy Valley Hale Hostel **2**
House of Fountains B&B **8**
Joe's Place **21**
Kaanapali Beach Hotel **7**
Kahana Reef **5**
Koa Lagoon **12**
Kuau Inn **23**
Kula Lodge **20**
Lahaina Roads **9**
Lahaina Shores **9**
Makai Inn **9**
Mauian Hotel **4**
Maui El Dorado **7**
Maui Prince Hotel **19**
Maui What a Wonderful World B&B **15**
Hale Napili **4**
Hana Kai Maui Resort **21**
Hana Maui Vacation Rentals **21**
Nalu Kai Lodge **24**
Napili Sunset **4**
Napili Surf **4**
Napili Village **4**
Nona Lani Cottages **11**
Northshore Hostel **2**
Patey's Place **9**
Peace of Maui **22**
Penny's Place in Paradise **9**
Punahoa Apartments **13**
Rainbow's End Surf Hostel **24**
Renaissance Wailea **17**
Spyglass House **23**
Two Mermaids B&B **15**
Westin Maui **7**

DINING ◆

A Saigon Café **2**
Aloha Mix Plate **9**
Amigo's **12**
Bermudez Big Wave Café **12**
Buzz's Wharf **10**
Bada Bing **13**
Cafe Des Ami **24**
Cafe Marc Aurel **2**
Charley's Restaurant **24**
Da Kitchen, Kihei **14**
Da Kitchen, Kahului **1**
Down to Earth Natural Foods **1**
Flatbread Company **24**
The Gazebo **4**
Jawz **12**
Kau Kau Corner Food Court **1**
Lahaina Grill **9**
Mama's Fishhouse **24**
Mana Foods **24**
Manana Garage **1**
Maui Brewing Company **5**
Maui Swap Meet **1**
Maui Tacos, Lahaina **9**
Maui Tacos, Kamaole Beach Center Kihei **14**
Maui Tacos, Piilani Shopping Center, Kihei **14**
Maui Tacos, Napili Plaza, Napili **4**
Maui Tacos, Kahului **1**
Mulligan's on the Blue **18**
Paia Fishmarket **24**
Pene Pasta **9**
Saigon Seafood **9**
Sam Sato's **2**
South Shore Tiki Lounge **13**
Sports Page Grill & Bar **14**
Seascape Maalaea Restaurant **10**
Stella Blues Café **12**
Sansei Seafood Restraurant and Sushi Bar, Kihai **13**
Sansei Seafood Restaurant and Sushi Bar—Kapalua **3**
Thai Chef **9**
Vietnamese Cuisine **12**

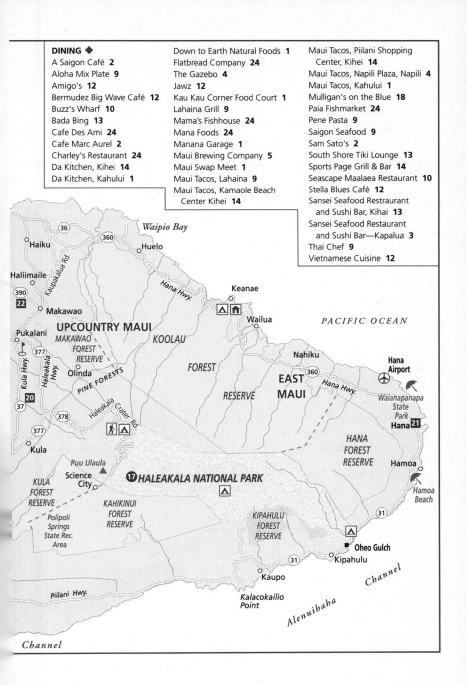

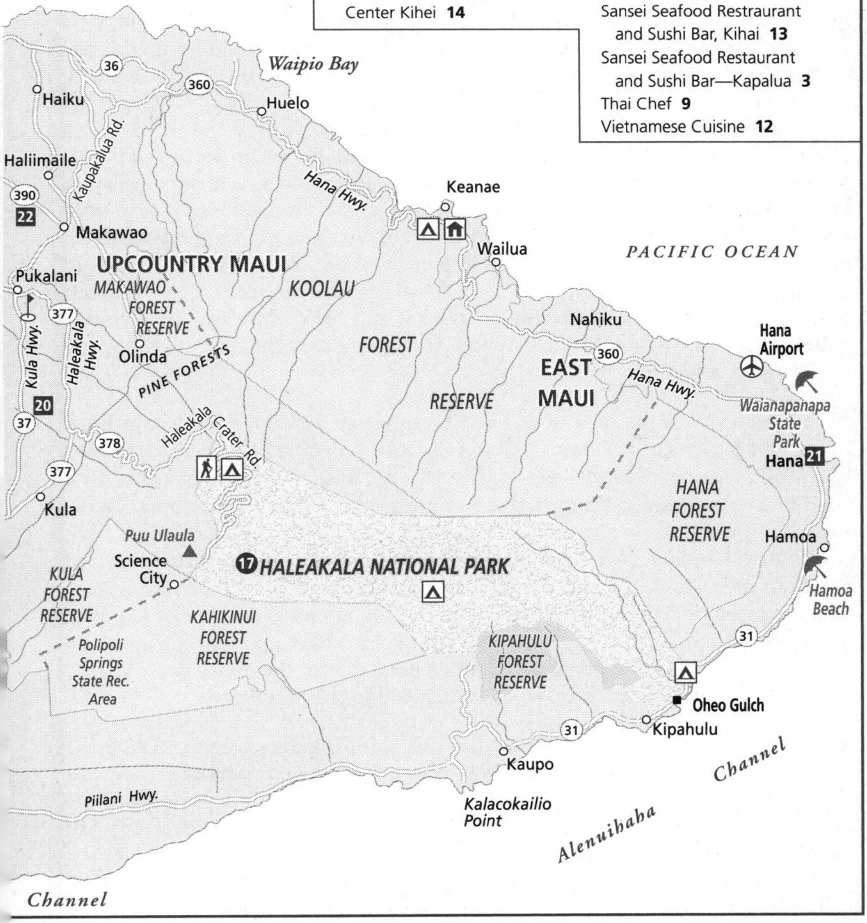

more aesthetically pleasing and a hair larger than those with private facilities, featuring shiny wood floors, nice pieces of artwork and a large, condo-like living room/kitchen shared by just three rooms. Go figure.

$$ Patey's (see above) is fine for those who don't mind bare bones, but the one hotel in Lahaina that truly makes my budget-loving heart go pitter-pat is **The Makai Inn** ★★★ (1415 Front St.; ☎ 808/662-3200 or 808/870-9004; www.makaiinn.net; AE, MC, V), though you won't believe me as you drive up to it, because it looks like a Hawaiian version of the Bates Motel from the outside. Inside, however, it's a gem: a '50s motel restored with loving care, lots of Crayola-colored paint, and a good dollop of wit. You see, it was owner Suzy Duro's goal to make it feel like home to her visitors. So she decorated each room differently, filling them with books, cheerful knick-knacks (like pillows shaped like lobsters or with the words "Where the Heck is Mr. Right?" hand-stitched on them), rattan furniture, and fully useable kitchens. You won't find phones or TVs in them, but you will find Monopoly, Scrabble and chess. Rates range from $100 to $120 for a one-bedroom (prices vary by view and whether the unit has A/C), up to $175 for a massive two bedroom. Top and bottom floors are set around a U-shaped courtyard, with a tenderly kept tropical garden and a teeming population of birds in it. Most rooms have swell ocean views, and though it's too far to walk from here into the center of town, you can easily stroll to the Cannery Mall. All in all, it's the type of low-rent, picture perfect place where you could hole up indefinitely, content to play games, watch whales, and wonder when the secret beach will emerge. (During certain low tides, a miniature white sand beach materializes at the base of the Makai's seawall, though most of the time it's just a seawall without a beach.)

$$ Directly across the road from The Makai (see above), is a sweet 4-unit B&B called **Penny's Place in Paradise** ★ (1440 Front St.; ☎ 877/431-1235 or 808/661-1068; www.pennysplace.net; AE, DC, MC, V). Run, as you might guess, by a good-hearted gal named Penny, it doesn't have a view of much of anything but the road, but it makes up for it with good rates ($98–$122, depending on room size), good eats (including a breakfast of freshly baked fruit breads and fruits plucked from the trees out back) and the good conscience you'll have after staying here (this is a green operation, with solar power heating the water and lots of recycling going on). Rooms are B&B quaint, with antique bedstands, pretty wallpaper, and the like. And though the porch gets a lot of street noises, the rooms don't, thanks to very careful insulation. Free Wi-Fi is included in the nightly rate.

$–$$$$ Unlike other parts of Maui, Lahaina isn't exploding with condos, but it does have two value-laden ones for those who prefer an apartment-style stay. Just a short stroll from the downtown area, but on its own sand beach (it's the only lodging in Lahaina with that perk), the **Lahaina Shores** ★ (475 Front St.; ☎ 800/642-6284 or 808/661-4835; www.lahainashores.com; AE, DC, MC, V) is a place with very few nasty surprises. That's because, though the units are individually owned, the management company has strict guidelines for what each unit must contain, and gives the owners a choice of four furniture packages for the decor (they're all beachy, of course, but done in muted colors). So you know

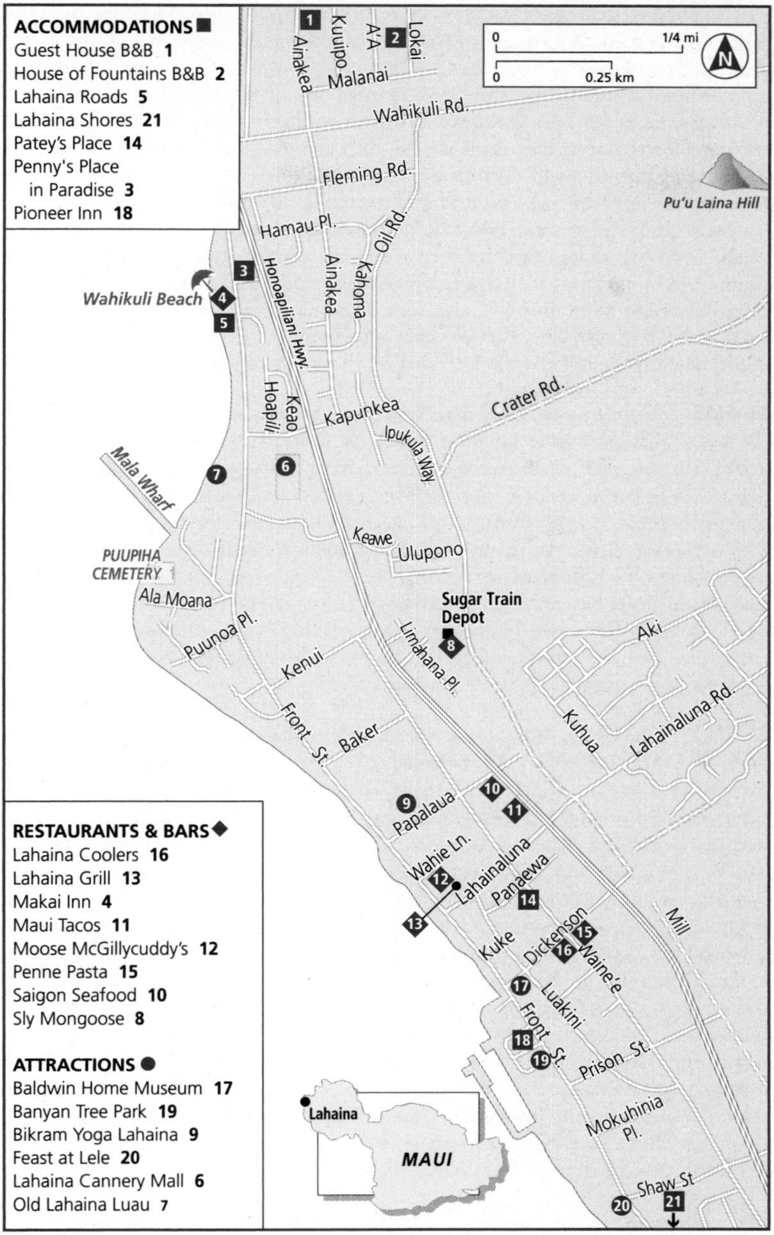
ACCOMMODATIONS
Guest House B&B 1
House of Fountains B&B 2
Lahaina Roads 5
Lahaina Shores 21
Patey's Place 14
Penny's Place in Paradise 3
Pioneer Inn 18
RESTAURANTS & BARS
Lahaina Coolers 16
Lahaina Grill 13
Makai Inn 4
Maui Tacos 11
Moose McGillycuddy's 12
Penne Pasta 15
Saigon Seafood 10
Sly Mongoose 8
ATTRACTIONS
Baldwin Home Museum 17
Banyan Tree Park 19
Bikram Yoga Lahaina 9
Feast at Lele 20
Lahaina Cannery Mall 6
Old Lahaina Luau 7
0
1/4 mi
0
0.25 km
N
Ainakea
Kuuipo
A'A
Lokai
Malanai
Wahikuli Rd.
Fleming Rd.
Pu'u Laina Hill
Hamau Pl.
Oil Rd.
Honoapiiliani Hwy.
Ainakea
Kahoma
Wahikuli Beach
Hoapili
Keao
Kapunkea
Crater Rd.
Ipukula Way
Mala Wharf
Keawe
Ulupono
PUUPIHA CEMETERY
Ala Moana
Sugar Train Depot
Puunoa Pl.
Kenui
Limahana Pl.
Aki
Front St.
Baker
Kuhua
Lahainaluna Rd.
Papalaua
Wahie Ln.
Lahainaluna
Panaewa
Mill
Kuke
Dickenson
Waine'e
Luakini
Front St.
Prison St.
Lahaina
Mokuhinia Pl.
MAUI
Shaw St

you're going to get a microwave, a VCR, and a fully equipped kitchen, in a room where the furniture is no more than 4 years old (and sometimes newer). More than likely you'll be in a spacious studio (550 sq. ft.), as 90% of the units are studios, though it might be set up for a family with a queen size bed, a single, and a pull-out couch; for honeymooners with a single king-size bed; or for night owls who prefer to pretend they don't sleep—they can chose the units with the Murphy bed tucked into the wall. Downsides? Since the owners want to keep their maintenance fees low, the hallways and lobby are overdue for a makeover and can be a bit dreary, but the grounds are well kept, as is the small on-site pool. About 80% of the units are represented by the on-site management company (see above for phone) and they tend to charge between $160 and $200 per night total (no additional cleaning fees). But I've also seen Lahaina Shores on direct to owner sites such as VRBO.com and Rentalo.com and there it's a free for all, meaning you could pay anywhere between $85 and $165 a night for these very same units.

$$–$$$$ Without a beach and set on the north side of town, a farther walk into the heart of it all, condo **Lahaina Roads** ★ (1403 Front St.; see box, p. 242 to book) has one great perk: All of its rooms have heart-stopping ocean views, with private lanais overlooking the nice-size pool (at Lahaina Shores, above, the cheaper rooms face the mountains). A mix of year-round residents and tourists stay here, and units tend to be well-maintained, though they can vary greatly in looks. Chase 'N Rainbows, a topnotch rental agent (see box, p. 242) reps a large number of units here, charging between $125 and $175 for a one-bedroom, and $185 to $305 for a two bedroom, and enforcing strict standards on decor and amenities. But you could also go the "book with the owner" route and pay similar rates to what you'd get at the Lahaina Shores (see above).

$$–$$$$ One of the most unusual choices in Lahaina is the **House of Fountains B&B** ★ (1579 Lokia St.; ☎ 808/667-2121; www.alohahouse.com; MC, V). Its owners are German and Hawaiian, its aesthetic is National Geographic, and its prices are all over the map. You could pay $130 for a smaller room during a slow period, or up $180 at peak season for a suite. Still, when you hit it right, this B&B can be a winner, and will certainly be an experience. The living room, where sumptuous hot breakfasts are served, doubles as a private museum, with artifacts from all over the Polynesian triangle (including a massive outrigger canoe). Owner Don Natay is a participant in the Hawaiian revivalist group Na Koa Kau I Ka Meheu O na Kupuna ("Warriors Who Walk in the Footsteps of our Ancestors") and he's got some mean-looking weaponry on display, such as his sharks-teeth war club. Rooms are just as funky looking with handmade koa wood furnishings, small fridges, and oddly colored, hand-sponged walls (think puce, mustard, or lavender). That being said, the beds are comfortable (and all queen-size), the guests fun to hang with (most come from Europe), and there's a lovely pool out back. Guests get their own kitchen to share, along with videos and DVDs to play in their rooms. Three-night minimum stay, maid service daily.

$$$ Drenched in color and loaded with amenities, **The Guest House** ★★ (1620 Ainakea Rd.; ☎ 800/621-8942 or 808/661-8085; www.mauiguesthouse.com; MC, V) is the romantics' affordable choice in Lahaina. A lovely stained glass window

Napili-Kapalua

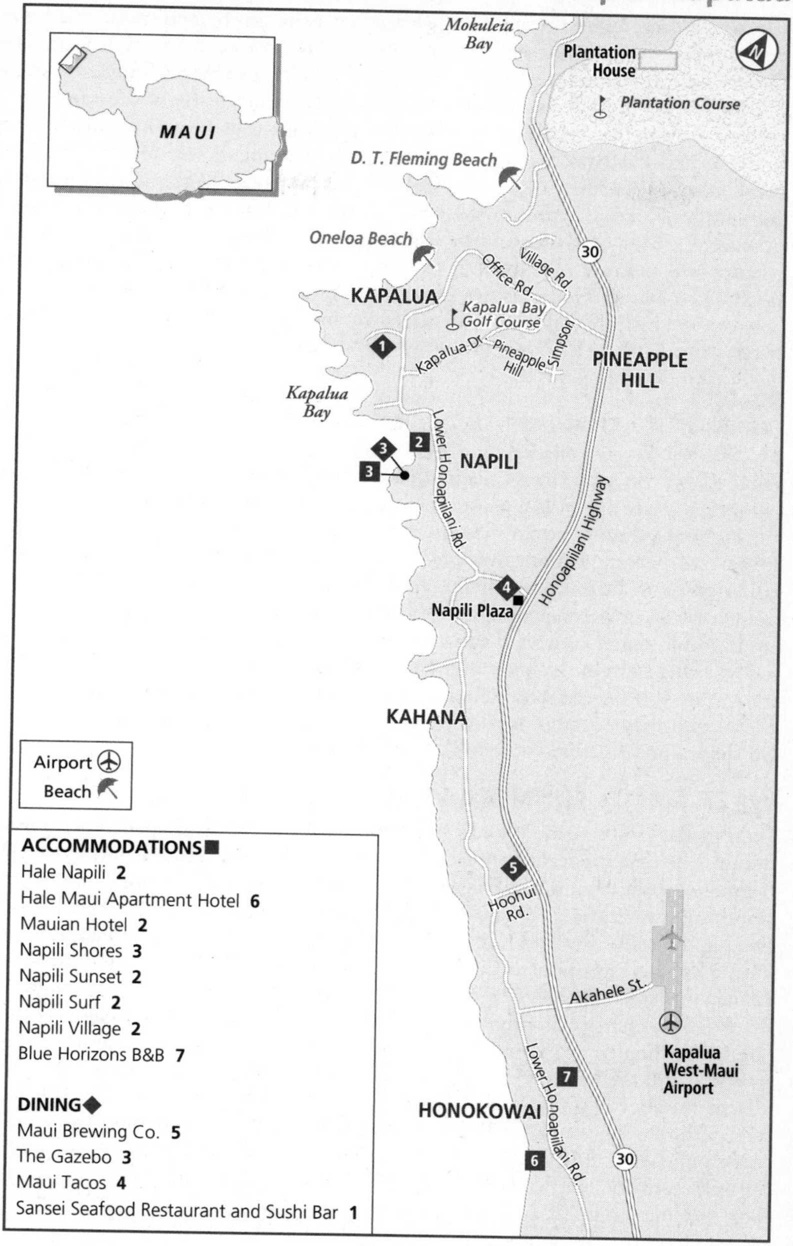
Mokuleia Bay
Plantation House
Plantation Course
MAUI
D. T. Fleming Beach
Oneloa Beach
30
Village Rd.
Office Rd.
KAPALUA
Kapalua Bay Golf Course
Kapalua Dr.
Pineapple Hill
Simpson
PINEAPPLE HILL
Kapalua Bay
Lower Honoapiilani Rd.
NAPILI
Honoapiilani Highway
Napili Plaza
KAHANA
Airport
Beach
Hoohui Rd.
Akahele St.
Kapalua West-Maui Airport
HONOKOWAI
Lower Honoapiilani Rd.
30
ACCOMMODATIONS
Hale Napili 2
Hale Maui Apartment Hotel 6
Mauian Hotel 2
Napili Shores 3
Napili Sunset 2
Napili Surf 2
Napili Village 2
Blue Horizons B&B 7
DINING
Maui Brewing Co. 5
The Gazebo 3
Maui Tacos 4
Sansei Seafood Restaurant and Sushi Bar 1

(or two) fills each guest room with jewel-toned light, all the better to bathe by in your private, full-size hot tub (set on a private lanai). One room even features a kitschy billowing torch nightlight set into an alcove, for those who want to play out "virgins being fed to the volcano"–type fantasies, I guess. Other amenities include full kitchen privileges, free Wi-Fi and phone calls (even long distance in the U.S. and Canada), a usable laundry room, daily maid service, oversized hot breakfasts, high quality mattresses, 42-inch plasma screen TVs, and the option to get your scuba certification in the pool out front or book diving expeditions (or other adventures) at a discount through the owner's company Trinity Tours (same contact info as above). All in all, it's an impressive level of service for a four-room B&B. The Guest House is set in a hilly, residential neighborhood, halfway between the historic center of Lahaina Town and the beaches of Kaanapali. Rates range from $149 to $169 a night, year round.

$$$–$$$$ In the heart of the historic district, the **Best Western Pioneer Inn** ★ (650 Wharf St.; ☎ 800/457-5457 or 808/661-3636; www.pioneerinn-maui.com; AE, DC, MC, V) is furnished as if the calendar still read 1901 (the year the Inn debuted on this, the town's main square). Solid wood furniture, white washed wooden wainscoting, and a plantation-style row of expansive wooden balconies—the Pioneer is dignity personified. In its quiet interior courtyard, that is. Make the mistake of picking a room overlooking rowdy Front Street, however, and you're either going to be happily reliving your frat days or miserably up until the wee hours, listing to other people party way too hearty. If you can snag one of the comfortable, quiet courtyard-facing rooms, it's a good pick for the traveler who enjoys being right in the heart of town (no rental car necessary). But skip it if they try to put you on the street. As for pricing, I've seen it range from $135 up to $190, with the best rates usually going to such outside discounters as Hotels.com (so shop around before you book). Small pool on-site.

WEST MAUI: FROM KAANAPALI TO KAPALUA

Built in the 1960s at the island's westernmost point, the Kaanapali Beach Resort became the first master-planned community resort in the United States. A lovely, 3-mile-long white sand beach is what tempted the original developers, and it continues to draw travelers today. Although it's not as exclusive as the island's other two big resorts Wailea and Kapalua, budget travelers will find slim pickings in this area. The one exception to that, oddly enough, may be the **Westin Maui** (2365 Kaanapali Pkwy; ☎ 888/625-4949 or 808/667-2525; www.westinmaui.com; AE, DC, MC, V) which apparently has been doing brisk business with Priceline.com of late. According to the users of the website BiddingforTravel.com—a site where travelers spill the beans on how much they bid on Priceline and what they got—a large number of guests have been bidding $125 for Kaanapali and ending up here. Who'd have thunk it? This is a positively swank resort, with a fantasy pool playground out front, outrageously expensive art on the walls, and a newly built $5-million dollar spa. So, if you're up for a bit of suspense, go ahead and try your luck bidding blind (if you get something else though, always a possibility on Priceline, don't write us angry letters).

If that's too iffy a proposition for you, head to the gentle 10-mile stretch of coastline north of Kaanapali, a top spot to hunt for deals. In towns named for the

Hana

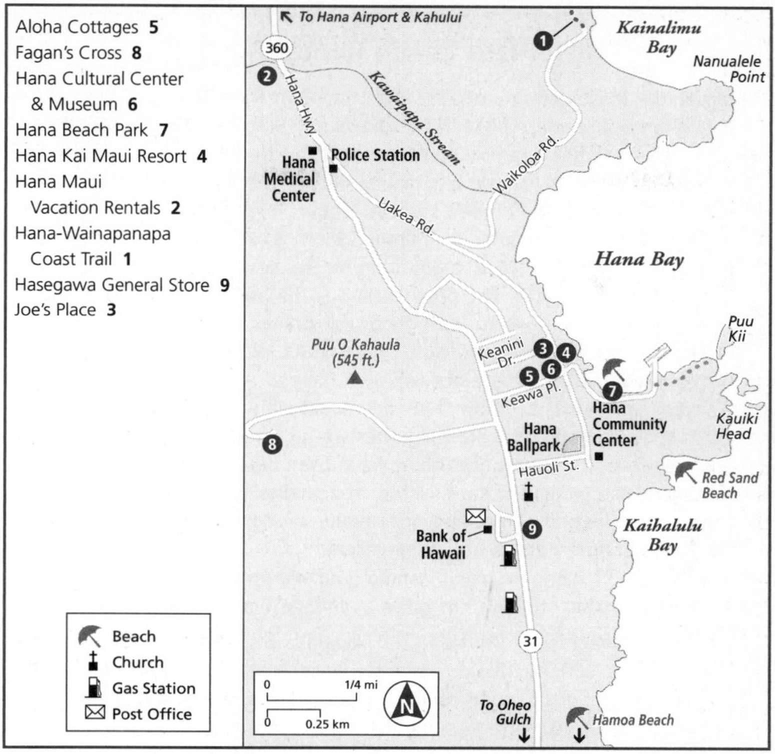

string of fishing villages that once graced this stretch—Honokowai, Mahinahina, Kahana, Napili, and Kapalua—are one condo complex after the other, high- and low-rises, with high and low prices. Among all the condos, you'll find a few shopping plazas and a number of beaches. Only a few of these beaches are as good for swimming as those of Kaanapali, but it's an easy hop from these cheaper condos to the sands of exclusive Kaanapali (and as in the rest of Hawaii, the beaches are publicly owned, so bathe away without worry).

$$–$$$ The pick of the litter in the Honokowai area is **Hale Maui Apartment Hotel** ★★ kids (3711 Lower Honoapiilani Rd.; ☎ 808/669-6312; www.halemaui.com; MC, V), which offers the only swimmable beach along this stretch, a wee little white sand cove, marvelously private. Affordable, cheery, large one-bedrooms are the other big lure. Measuring in at a good 500-plus square feet, they're bigger than what you get at many of the more expensive surrounding condos, and yet cost just $115 a night, even in high season, if you stay for a week, or between $125 and $145 a night for shorter stays. Additional guests over two are charged $15/night, but the bend-over-backwards Zimmerman family, who own this two-story complex, have been known to waive that fee for families—or anyone who asks, for that matter. They're a delightfully gregarious, friendly bunch who

West Maui Condo Rental Agencies

By far the most upfront, expert, and just plain friendly of the West Maui condo rental agencies **Chase 'N Rainbows** (☎ 800/367-6092; www.chasenrainbows.com) has been in business for 25 years and thrives because of its pool of satisfied, repeat customers. Part of the reason they keep coming back are Chase 'N Rainbow's prices: About 75% of their units are in the budget range, with studios averaging $95 to $145 a night and one-bedrooms for $110 to $165 a night (varying by season). Cleaning fees are included in those rates. The other reason is the high standards they maintain. "The carpets have to look good, the drapes have to look good, the linens must be in good condition, or we won't represent the condo," says owner Mindy Miller. "The units will also have all the cookware you need. We want our guests to know that they could whip up a Thanksgiving dinner if they wanted." If something goes wrong, they have a 24-hour emergency number for guests (and there have been cases when clients of other management companies have called, too, being unable to contact their own companies). If something goes really wrong, they'll happily move a guest at no extra cost. A classy operation.

If Chase 'N Rainbows can't handle your request, two other companies are also available (though not quite as highly recommended):

- **Maui Beachfront Rentals** (256 Papalaua St., Lahaina; ☎ 888/661-7200 or 808/661-3500; www.mauibeachfront.com) has condo units in 15 west Maui condo complexes, with 1-week rates starting at $125 a night. It also offers online discounts with Avis.
- **Maui Lodging** (3636 L. Honoapiilani Rd., Honokowai; ☎ 800/487-6002 or 808/669-0089; www.mauilodging.com) offers a better than usual Web experience, with virtual tours of many properties. It handles units throughout the west end of the island.

welcome each guest with a Maui pineapple. As for the rooms, they were all fully renovated in 2007 in a sensible, easy-to-clean palate of tans, deep reds, and yellows (think straightforward tile floors, pre-fab furniture, and pull-out couches); some have a touch of style with shoji screens separating the rooms. All come with fully equipped kitchens and lanais. No phones, no pool, some rooms have only fan, no maid service, but no cleaning fee, either.

$$–$$$ Quiet, simple, and sensibly priced **Kahana Reef** (4471 Lower Honoapiilani Hwy.; see box, above, to book) is an older condo complex located between Kaanapali and Napili on a serene stretch of ocean. There's no beach, its look is dated, the bathrooms are tiny, and the pool ain't grand, but from your lanai you can pitch a stone and have it hit the ocean. In the winter months, the whale views are stellar. As with other condos, there's going to be a lot of variety when it comes to furnishings and upkeep, but because this place is relatively off-the-beaten track, I've

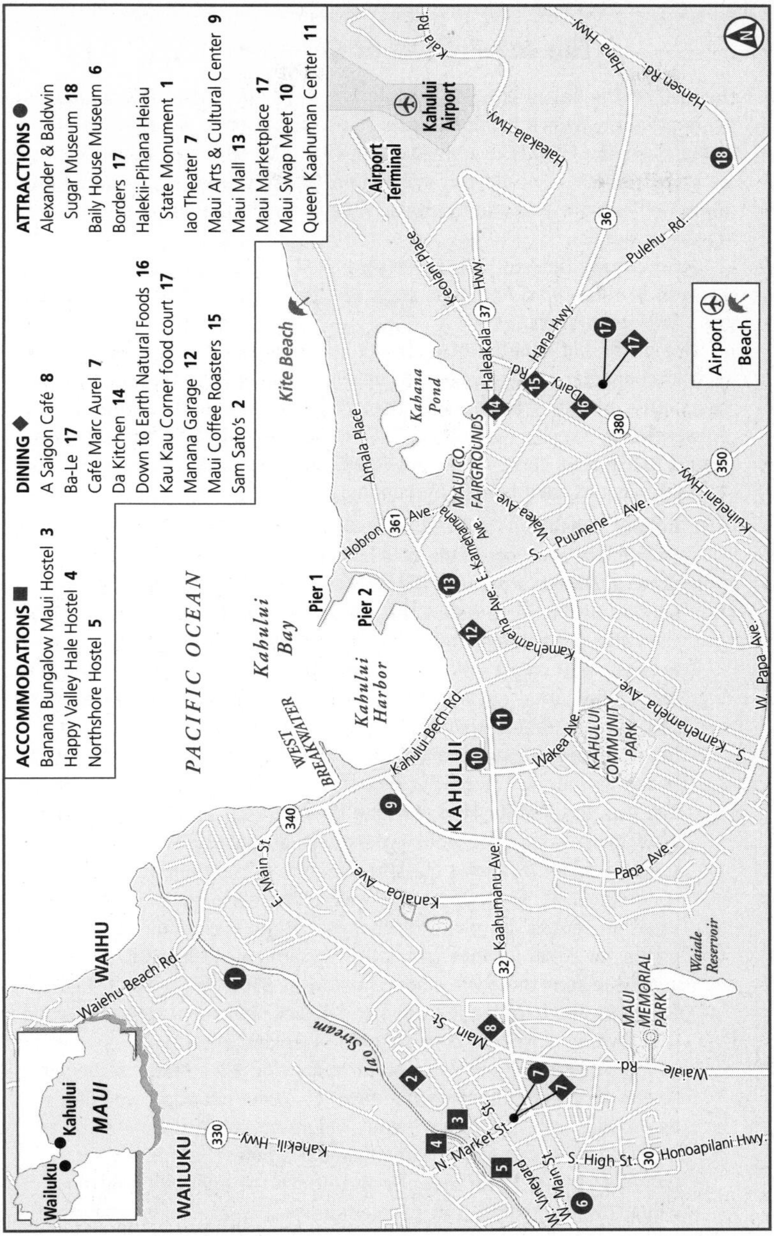
ACCOMMODATIONS
Banana Bungalow Maui Hostel 3
Happy Valley Hale Hostel 4
Northshore Hostel 5
DINING
A Saigon Café 8
Ba-Le 17
Café Marc Aurel 7
Da Kitchen 14
Down to Earth Natural Foods 16
Kau Kau Corner food court 17
Manana Garage 12
Maui Coffee Roasters 15
Sam Sato's 2
ATTRACTIONS
Alexander & Baldwin Sugar Museum 18
Baily House Museum 6
Borders 17
Halekii-Pihana Heiau State Monument 1
Iao Theater 7
Maui Arts & Cultural Center 9
Maui Mall 13
Maui Marketplace 17
Maui Swap Meet 10
Queen Kaahuman Center 11
PACIFIC OCEAN
Kahului Bay
Kahului Harbor
WEST BREAKWATER
Pier 1
Pier 2
Kite Beach
Kahana Pond
MAUI CO. FAIRGROUNDS
Kahului Airport
Airport Terminal
KAHULUI
WAILUKU
WAIHU
KAHULUI COMMUNITY PARK
MAUI MEMORIAL PARK
Waiale Reservoir
Iao Stream
Waiehu Beach Rd.
Kahekili Hwy.
N. Market St.
Main St.
W. Main St.
Vineyard
S. High St.
Honoapiilani Hwy.
Waiale Rd.
Kaahumanu Ave.
Kanaloa Ave.
E. Main St.
Papa Ave.
W. Papa Ave.
Kahului Bech Rd.
Wakea Ave.
Kamehameha Ave.
S. Kamehameha Ave.
E. Kamehameha Ave.
S. Puunene Ave.
Hobron Ave.
Amala Place
Kuihelani Hwy.
Dairy Rd.
Hana Hwy.
Haleakala Hwy.
Keolani Place
Pulehu Rd.
Hansen Rd.
Kala Rd.
Airport
Beach
Wailuku
Kahului
MAUI
N

The Ins & Outs of Condo Rentals

Instead of The Valley Isle, Maui could be called The Condo Isle. It has put more privately owned condominiums to use as vacation rentals than all the other Hawaiian islands combined. More than 100 of these "condo hotels," as state tourism officials call them, line Maui's shores, with some 7,000 units dedicated to vacation rentals. That rivals the 8,000 rooms in Maui's 31 major hotels.

Maui condos tend to be moderately priced, with weekly rates averaging $100 to $250 a night. Minimum stays of 3 days are common and rates also drop for longer stays.

One of the big benefits of renting a condo is that it will have a kitchen or a kitchenette, allowing you to cook for yourself and reduce your food costs. One of the drawbacks is that Maui condos don't always include housekeeping service (though all of the Napili condos reviewed here are among those that come with housekeeping, at no extra charge).

Best ways to save money on condos:

- **Go Off Season:** As with hotel rooms, you'll pay much less when the crowds are elsewhere (see p. 233 for more on the seasons).
- **Take a *Mauka* Room or Go for the Greens:** The least expensive condo units tend to be on the *mauka* sides of their buildings, rather than the *makai* sides. You won't get an ocean view there, but in Kihei at least, you might wake up looking at Haleakala, before it draws up its midday cloud cover. Traffic noise could be the tradeoff. But you can ask the rental agency how far back the condo is set from the highway before you commit. In resort areas, look away from the beach and along the golf courses for the best deals.
- **Cut Out the Middle Man:** Dealing directly with the condo owner can yield lower rates than booking through an agency. Owners often list their units in the Sunday classified section of the Maui News. They also congregate at www.vbro.com, www.rental.com, and evrentals.com, vacation rentals by owner exchanges. High season direct by owner prices for Kihei condos generally run around $150. But sometimes you'll see something dirt-cheap (as low as $50 a night Apr 1–Dec 15). The downside to going it alone? No fallback plan should there be something wrong with your condo. Rental agencies will usually move you if you're dissatisfied and will pop in to fix clogged toilets, misbehaving screen doors, and the like. In a direct to owner situation, you may well be on your own, so always inquire before you book if there's someone in the vicinity you can call upon should problems occur.
- **Consider Travel Insurance:** Because both the agencies and the individual owners require full payment several weeks to several months in advance of stay—and reserve the right to hold onto said payment if they're unable to re-rent their properties—many folks buy travel insurance as a backup, in case they have to cancel at the last minute.

seen prices drop to just $125 from the rental agents for a studio and as low as $110 per night on VRBO.com. One-bedrooms are also available for similarly reasonable rates.

$$$ Among the many, many condo options in this area, I like the **Hale Mahina** ★ (3875 Lower Honoapiilani Hwy.; see box, p. 242 to book) quite a bit. Though it's as drearily blocky-looking from the front as most of the other condos in the area, everything else about it is a cut above. Property managers Larry and Lynn keep the landscaping lush and colorful, the pool is about twice as large as what you'll find at most other condos, and here, there's not just a seawall fronting the ocean but a nifty little swimmable beach. Though decor varies greatly from unit to unit (all are privately owned) the design of the units is far from cookie cutter: All units are on two levels and have semi-enclosed kitchens and roomy lanais, making them delightfully airy. Did I mention there's also a hot tub? As for pricing, I've seen it range from $140 all the way up to $260 (depending on unit amenities and time of year) for a one-bedroom, about $40 more a night for a two-bedroom. One warning: Units are not accessible for those in wheelchairs.

$$$–$$$$ A final suggestion for those looking to have a more resort-like experience in this area: the **Maui Eldorado** (kids) (2661 Kekaa Dr., Kaanapali; ☎ 888/339-8585 or 808/661-0021; www.outrigger.com or www.mauieldorado.com; AE, MC, V) and **Kaanapali Beach Hotel** ★★ (2525 Kaanapali Pkwy.; ☎ 800/262-8450 or 808/661-0011; www.kbhmaui.com; AE, DC, MC, V) offer everything you'd want in a beach getaway—multiple pools, extensive grounds, golf and pretty beaches—but since both are seriously in bed with the major discounters, you can often get big discounts on pricing. I've seen rates dip down to about $165, though usually you'll pay between $185 and $205 from the rate-slashers. Of the two, the Kaanapali Beach Hotel is nicer (the Eldorado property has as much charm as an office park), featuring rambling grounds lush with palms, plumeria and other blossoming shrubs, and a staff that undergoes mandatory Hawaiian cultural training four times a year (so they know their stuff!).

NAPILI & ITS APPEAL

Good deals are scattered throughout West Maui's world of condominiums, but for those who want to roll out of bed and into the surf, Napili may have an edge. With a few exceptions (see above), the beaches north of Kaanapali have reefs just offshore that tend to slice up the toes of swimmers. Napili Beach (p. 272) is different. It's a broad sandy crescent protected by rocky headlands at either end, with no coral around to accidentally kick. It's widely regarded as one of Maui's best beaches, as is another spot on the other side of the north point, Kapalua Beach (p. 273).

$$–$$$ Behind the Napili Beach is an inviting cluster of low-rise vacation rental condominiums, built mostly in the 1960s under a height ordinance that kept them all beneath the tops of the palm trees. Of these, I think that the **Napili Sunset** (46 Hui Dr.; ☎ 800/447-9229 or 808/669-8083; AE, DC, MC, V), **Napili Surf** ★ (kids) (50 Napili P.; ☎ 800/541-0638; cash only) and the **Hale Napili** ★ (65 Hui Dr.; ☎ 800/245-2266 or 808/669-6184; www.halenapilimaui.com; AE, DC, MC, V) offer the best value. The three have much in common, being condos,

B&B Lane

In Maui county, B&Bs are not supposed to cluster together by law. However, the following two were established before the law was. And if you really want a B&B stay, but can't get room at one of these, they should be able to direct you to two other lovely if sadly unlicensed B&Bs in the nearby vicinity.

First up is **Maui What a Wonderful World B&B** ★★ (2828 Umalu Place off Keonakai St.; ☎ 800/943-5804 or 808/879-9103; AE, MC, V), a striking, contemporary pole house, with a massive lanai about twice as big as the studio apartment I lived in when I got out of college. That's where you eat your sinfully caloric breakfast come mornings (sometimes eggs Benedict, sometimes waffles studded with chocolate and slathered with whipped cream), and chat with the gregarious hostess, Eva Tantillo, who has a delightful way of getting all the guests involved in the conversation. The four rooms here ($99, $120, and $135, priced by size) are more like mini-apartments, with fully usable kitchens, TVs with DVDs (there's a complete video and book library to borrow from), and cushy sofas for relaxing. The largest two are actual one-bedrooms, and lovely ones at that, with handsome bamboo furniture and art on the walls. My only quibble, and the reason this one gets two stars, while the other gets three, is that footstep noise from the main house above can be loud in the guest rooms. If you're a late sleeper, bring earplugs.

Just up the block is the delightful **Two Mermaids B&B** ★★★ (2840 Umalu Place off Keonakai St; ☎ 800/598-9550 or 808/874-8687; MC, V). At too many places to cover on Maui, the folks planning "tropical decor" for their properties have gone with a pineapple theme, filling their rooms with drab brown pineapples on sheets, couches, you name it, perhaps adding a touch of yellow here and there to break up the monotony. But at the Two Mermaids, partners Juddee and Diana looked out at the brilliant sunshine, the lush jewel tones of their garden, the glistening aqua of the ocean, and decided—rightly—that tropical decor meant a riot of color. And so they created what may be one of the most cheerful B&Bs anywhere: an undersea theme with fish murals and Nemo-ish pillows on the bed bringing forth a happy giggle in one room, and more of a starburst theme in the other. They also have an eye for amenities such as a synthetic feather bed on top of the mattresses (cushy but not sweaty); baskets of fruits and home-baked breads delivered daily to your door for breakfast; and acoustic guitars in each room, just in case you have the need to strum. Local calls are free, as is Wi-Fi, and there are fresh flowers in each room upon arrival. The Ocean Ohana room ($140/night) has a private Jacuzzi; the poolside studio suite ($115) is off the pool. Both have private entrances and both can be expanded to fit an extra guest or two in extra rooms off the main one (which aren't rented unless there's a group).

built on the beach, in the same era, with their landscaping dotted by small, kidney-shaped pools and shuffleboard courts. But there are some important differences. The **Napili Surf** seems to be the most discount happy. It's always having sales, and I've seen its rates for garden view studios drop to just $98 a night (though usually they'll range between $116–$163). The Surf also has the most generous policy on number of guests to a condo: They'll allow up to three in a studio, and up to five in the larger one-bedrooms (up to four in the smaller ones) at no additional cost, making this a stellar choice for larger groups and families. Free Wi-Fi is available throughout the property. The **Hale Napili** has no pool and no seasonal fluctuations in price: Its 18 units go for $195 for ocean views and $145 for garden views, year round (children under 12 are free; additional adults $10 each). It's greatest asset is manager Patti Sharp, a dynamo in a mumu who keeps the condos gleaming, and is always ready with advice on which tours to pick, restaurants to choose, you name it. She's probably the main reason the Hale Napili gets so many repeat guests (so book early). What distinguishes the **Napili Sunset** is its smart use of the space. Its studio units ($140/night, sometimes $115 with Internet specials) all have Murphy beds, and a number of its one-bedrooms ($295) have loft spaces in addition to the bedroom, turning them into de facto two-bedrooms (at less money). My only quibble with the Sunset is the staff, which is lacking in "Aloha Spirit," to put it mildly. As for what the units look like in these three: Your guess is as good as mine. Each has a different owner, so I've seen some that looked like something out of a very nice nursing home, while others have been downright chic, with quality furniture, nice built-ins, and fine art on the walls.

$$ Remember that tip I gave on p. 244 about staying a few blocks away from the beach in order to save big bucks? That's the guiding principal at **Napili Village** ★★ (5425 Lower Honoapiilani Rd.; ☎ 800/336-2185 or 808/669-6228; www.napilivillage.com), a 28 unit condo complex—5 one-bedrooms, the rest studios—that sits just behind the beachfront condos and thus consistently charges a good 20% less than they do (about $119–$129 during low season and $139–$149 high; price varies by view). Despite the fact that you have to walk about, oh, 2 minutes to get to the sands, it's a darn nice place. Its two-story building is clustered around a courtyard filled with palm, plumeria, and banana trees; a swimming pool usually filled with kids; and a well-used barbecue. Though it's a condo, all rooms are decorated in the same way with dignified hunter green bedspreads, quality beds, fully equipped kitchens, and sound machines (to keep at bay the noises from the nearby road; that's a clue though, that if you're a light sleeper you might want to bring earplugs). I also really like the staff. The two Tongan housekeepers here, who embody the laid-back ambience of the place, chat in their native tongue while they work—or they just stop working altogether, sit down, and chat with the guests in English.

$$ Just outside of Napili, but an easy drive away, the **Blue Horizons B&B** ★★ kids (3894 Mahinahina St. in Kahana; ☎ 800/669-1948 or 808/669-1965; www.bluehorizonsmaui.com; AE, DC, MC, V) is an expansive, woodsy mini-manse set on a hill, with four rental rooms total, ranging in price from $109 to $149 (the suites), year round. It's an unusually handsome place, with a massive lanai out front offering lovely sea views, shiny wood floors, free Wi-Fi, and highly loungable furnishings.

Each of the rooms has a mini-kitchenette, though guests can also use the regular kitchen (and a washer/dryer, too!). Out front is a lap-pool and a barbecue; inside is a huge video library of good stuff to watch in your room in air-conditioned comfort. The only drawback—and it ain't much of one in this day and age—is the lack of phones in the rooms. Since two of the units are suites, with separate living areas, this would be a good choice for families.

$$–$$$ Shuffleboard is a fixture at many Hawaiian resorts, but no shuffleboard course seems to hold such a place of honor as the one at **The Mauian Hotel** ★★ (5441 Lower Honoapiilani Rd.; ☎ 800/367-5034 or 808/669-6205; www.mauian.com; AE, DC, MC, V). Larger than usual, set in the center of this horseshoe shaped cluster of two-story buildings, it grounds the Mauian squarely in the 1950s, which is when this resort was built. And in many ways, it feels as if time did stop well before the Age of Aquarius here. The studio units are cozy affairs, with all wood paneling, bamboo furniture, and framed Hawaiiana prints. Instead of windows, each has a screen wall at the front, with wooden shutters for privacy. Usable kitchenettes parallel the bathrooms. People tend to come here in groups, and they settle into chatting clusters on Napili's lovely white sand beach out front, around the BBQ grills or small pool, or on the well-manicured lawn. Adding to the genial atmosphere is the complimentary continental breakfast served daily in the common room (this is also where folks gather to watch TV or free movies as there are no TV's in the guest rooms), as well as a weekly mai tai and pupu party. Rates are all over the map. Hit the website at the right time and you may find studios for $115 or $130 a night; you're more likely to pay about $160 for a garden view room, up to $240 for a view of the beach (but since you're peering through a screen and slats, I don't think it makes sense to upgrade). A very sweet, happy place to vacation.

SOUTH MAUI: KIHEI

During a development boom that began in the 1970s, the small, sleepy beachfront community of Kihei grew into a sprawling land of condos and shopping plazas, about 6 miles long and 1 mile deep. It stretches along the sunniest, driest part of the island, and it's got some great beaches and views. Unfortunately, it's also got box stores, endless strip malls, and traffic. Lots of traffic. It's not a vista that naturally springs to mind when the words "tropical paradise" are mentioned, but the sheer number of condos in this area keeps it affordable. For dollarwise travelers, therefore, Kihei may be their best choice on the island.

$–$$ Case in point: the **Nona Lani Cottages** (455 S. Kihei Rd.; ☎ 800/733-2688 or 808/879-2497; www.nonalanicottages.com; cash only). One of the

Watch the Numbers

Most of the condo developments are located along South Kihei Road. Those with even numbered addresses are on the beach side, and some right smack on the sands. Those with odd numbers will be across the crowded boulevard. However, you're repaid for the daily 5-minute walk to the beach with prices a good 25% lower.

South Maui Condo Vacation Rental Agencies

A handful of agencies handle the bulk of Kihei's condo rentals. To the prices they quote, add a reservation fee of around $25 to your tab. Those with the lowest rates include:

- **Kihei Maui Vacations** (2395 S. Kihei Rd., Ste. 206; ☎ 800/541-6284 or 808/879-7581; www.kmvmaui.com) has units in 60 condo complexes throughout south Maui. Weekly rates start at about $100, but its online specials sometimes drop the nightly price to $75, off season.
- **Maui Resort Vacation Rentals** (1993 S. Kihei Rd., unit 210, ☎ 800/441-3187 or 808/879-5973; www.mauiersort4u.com) has units in about 20 condo complexes in south and west Maui, with weekly rates starting at $97.
- **AA Oceanfront Condominium Rentals** (1279 S. Kihei Rd., Ste. 107; ☎ 800/448-6004 or 808/879-7288; www.aaoceanfront.com) like its competitor above offers 20 south Maui condos, but its weekly rates start at $95.

pioneering properties in Kihei, this complex was constructed in 1972 and doesn't seem to have changed much since. Wee wooden cabins, with full kitchens, bedrooms, and living rooms crammed into an area the size of about two midsize cars placed side-by-side, they're not for everyone. But if you have a kitschy sensibility, and like waking up to posters of horses and sunsets in the a.m., you may just like this place. You'll certainly get a good night's sleep here: The friendly Kong family, who run the place, have put their money into the mattresses, which are quality pillowtops. No phone or Internet will distract your rest (none of the units have either). The motel-like units in the back are larger and slightly more modern in their decor, with koa wood furnishings and plush carpets, but they don't have kitchens. For either, you'll pay between $75 and $105 a night, a good, old-fashioned rate. The Nona Lani has no beach, but there's a lovely and usually deserted beach across the busy road out front. Because of that road, request a cottage toward the back of the property (cuts down on noise). The cottages are about a 10-minute drive from the heart of Kihei.

Closer to the heart of Kihei, but still wonderfully removed from the maelstrom of South Kihei Drive, the **Punahoa Apartments** ★ (2142 Iliili Rd.; ☎ 800/564-4380 or 808/879-2720; www.punahoabeach.com; AE, DC, MC, V) have a sensuous feeling of isolation to them. Set off an untrafficked road, next to a lovely beach that only gung-ho surfers and turtles seem to use regularly, this tiny apartment building (just 18 units) attracts quiet types who just want to get away from it all, and actually have managed to find a way to do that here, in the most bustling area of bustling Maui. Units themselves are pretty standard in both looks and size (studios run about 560 sq. ft., one-bedrooms 568, two-bedrooms 896) but all have oceanfront lanais and come unusually well-stocked with such items as rice cookers, extra spatulas, and full complements of condiments. Free tennis courts are a short

Lodging Limbo

As we go to press on this edition of *Pauline Frommer's Hawaii,* a number of the B&Bs and vacation rentals on this island, Lanai, and Molokai are engaged in a serious battle for their existence. No, it's not that they don't have enough customers to keep afloat. Actually, the opposite is true. But after promising to reform the licensing system in Maui County, the Mayor's office has instead cracked down on all unlicensed B&Bs and vacation rentals, threatening them with fines of $1,000 a day. New licensing has been suspended.

Since about 80% of the vacation rentals and B&Bs in Maui are unlicensed, this could lead to a serious lodging crunch for visitors. At this stage, legal battles are being waged by the local Vacation Home Rental Associations as well as the B&B Association and it's unclear what the outcome will be. But when calling a B&B, it's the better part of wisdom to inquire as to whether they've been licensed, as you don't want to show up in Hawaii and find that your lodging has been shuttered.

Every lodging in this chapter, with the one exception of Dreams Come True B&B (p. 252), was licensed when we visited in late 2007. Dreams Come True was in the midst of the process, so we're hoping it will be successful in becoming licensed.

Please note that this new regulation does *not* affect condos.

stroll down the road. The manager works as a diving instructor in his spare time and can fills guests in on all the hidden, local spots for snorkeling (ask him to direct you to "the fishbowl"). How are the prices? Usually reasonable, with studios going for just $116 to $150, depending on the season (one-bedrooms are about $40 more; for two-bedroom units add a total of $80 to the studio costs).

Another fave among the condos of Kihei is the **Koa Lagoon** ★★ (800 S. Kihei Rd.; ☎ 800/367-8030 or 808/379-3002; www.koalagoon.com; AE, DC, MC, V)—say that five times fast! The key to its success is attentive management. Bello Realty is charged with the upkeep of the place, has an office on-site, and ends up handling about 70% of the bookings for the individually owned units here (of which there are 42, though 10 are used by full-time residents). So staff are constantly in and out of the apartments, enforcing standards among owners (27 in. or larger TV's required! Fine quality blenders mandatory!); and expertly handling questions from would-be renters. Beside the fine upkeep—which extends to the sweeping expanse of lawn out front (perfect for weddings) and the serviceable pool—the units themselves are well laid out, relatively large (at 670–990 sq. ft., plus 170 sq.-ft. balconies), light and airy, and all face the historic fishponds out front (if you get tired of the pool, the fishpond is swell for calm water swimming, too). Seasonal pricing applies, ranging from $140 to $170 a night for a one-bedroom, $140 to $170 for two, with no cleaning fees.

SOUTH MAUI: WAILEA

The sunny, bustling, condo-thick strip of development that is Kihei comes to an abrupt and elegant end where Wailea begins. Opulent resort hotels, championship golf courses, and posh condominiums thrive on this otherwise parched leeward shore (with the help of five million gallons of water per day). This is a land of $15 mai tais and well-heeled guests so pampered that at one hotel they have a swim-in elevator to carry them to the top of a waterslide. It's a great place to visit (the beaches here are open to the public, and they're exceptionally nice), but it's a difficult place for the budget-minded traveler to save on accommodations. Rack rates for hotels start at around $370 and then begin to soar. Nonetheless, there are two ways to sneak your way into this lap of luxury.

Stop Reading this Chapter & Just Book a Package!

by Pauline Frommer

There's not only safety in numbers . . . but discounts, too. The large air/hotel packagers, those companies that bundle these two vacation elements together (sometimes adding tours, car rental, and more) have bigger buying power than you and I. That's because they work intensely with dozens of Hawaiian hotels, and because they can promise to supply them visitors year round. So the package prices they supply usually—not always, but usually—will beat what individuals can get. Here's an example: In January of 2007 it was possible to buy airfare from L.A. to Maui and 5 nights in a hotel for just $555. In fall, the discounts were even deeper, with 5 nights dropping to $439 on certain dates. Discounted rates from other cities were available for a reasonable add-on fare.

Both of those deals are from the Big Kahuna in Hawaiian air/hotel packages, **Pleasant Holidays** (☎ 800/742-9244 or www.pleasantholidays.com) but there are other big players in this market, too:

- **Panda Travel** (☎ 800/303-6702 or www.pandaonline.com)
- **American Airlines Vacations** (☎ 800/321-212 or www.aavacations.com)
- **Expedia** (www.expedia.com)
- **Hawaii-Aloha.com** (☎ 800/843-8771)
- **United Vacations** (☎ 888/854-3899 or www.unitedvacations.com)

Be sure you do the math fully before booking a package. Remember: They're always based on double occupancy. So add together both you and your partner's prices, find out what the airfare would likely be (go to a search engine such as Farechase.com for that), and then check to see if your hotel payment is still a savings.

Because these packages are geared toward couples, they usually don't represent a savings for solo travelers.

$$ The first is to stay at the **Dreams Come True on Maui B&B** ★ (3259 Akala Dr.; ☎ 877/782-9628 or 808/879-7099; www.dreamscometrueonmaui.com; MC, V), set in a residential community in the hills right above Wailea. It's another one of those "tell us what you want and we'll provide it free and with a big grin" B&Bs where guests are welcome to help themselves to boogie boards, snorkel gear, videos (which can be projected on an 8-foot-wide screen in the living room), books, and more during the course of their stay. There's even an outdoor kitchen for the two guest rooms to share, compete with stove and fridge. Each evening, the host hangs a breakfast menu on the door of the two smallish but shiny clean and light-filled rooms—hey, almost room service! Another nice perk: a lovely aviary and koi pond out back. And prices are a third of what you'd pay on the beach down below, starting at $85 in low season, $99 high for the smaller unit, and $95/$109 for the ocean suite with king-size bed.

$$$$ The second option is to "bid blind" on the Internet. And that's actually not such a risk when it comes to the Wailea/Makena area, as all the resorts in this area are super sniffy, loaded with amenities, and set on the long string of pretty cove beaches that front all the resorts in this area. Surfing the website "Bidding for Travel"—it's the place folks go to brag about what they got on Priceline.com with their blind bids, and how much they paid—I found that the **Maui Prince Hotel** ★★ (5400 Makena Alanui; ☎ 800/321-6284 or 808/874-1111; www.mauiprincehotel.com; AE, DC, MC, V) was most often on the auction block, with lucky gamblers getting it for $170 to $200 per night. So I decided to visit and see for myself why it was on secret blue tag special. Here's the scoop: It's a luxurious and massive high-rise, with Edenic gardens in the center of its huge atrium and more out front. Costly shops, bars, and restaurants pop up every 200 feet—or so it feels—in the public areas, and the beach is a beaut'. Two swimming pools (one for adults, one for kids), six Plexipave tennis courts, and 36 holes of golf—designed by the famed Robert Trent Jones—round out the offerings. But once you get to the rooms . . . well, there's a scuff mark on the wall here, perhaps a frayed lampshade there. Not outrageously bad—heck, the duvets here are as soft as a toddler's tushy—but symptomatic of a place that's slipping a bit, especially when compared to its swank neighbors. Its location, far from the action at the end of a long road, may also be leading to these periodic specials.

The other Priceline fave (at least from my research on BiddingforTravel.com), was the **Renaissance Wailea** ★★ (3550 Wailea Alanui Dr.; ☎ 800/9-WAILEA or 808/879-4900; AE, DC, MC, V) which is every bit as plush as the Maui Prince—lovely beach, two swimming pools, access to nearby tennis courts and golf courses, multiple shops, restaurants and bars on-site, spa, children's program—but smaller with more of a boutiquey feel. It, too, was coming up in the $170 to $200 range on Bidding for Travel.com, which is bargain basement in Wailea.

UPCOUNTRY

The shoreline isn't the only place to stay on Maui. The serene mountain air and phenomenal views you'll find on Haleakala's upper western slopes make upcountry an appealing region, too.

$ It can certainly be appealing in terms of price. At **Peace of Maui** ★★ (1290 Hailiimaile Rd., Hailiimaile; halfway between Paia and Makawao; ☎ 888/475-5045 or 808/572-5045; www.peaceofmaui.com; AE, DISC, MC, V), for example, a large bed in an admittedly tiny room is just $55. The rate is the same in each of the six bedrooms on the ground level of a big cedar home in the country, with a family living upstairs. You share the kitchen, three bathrooms, the living room, and a high-speed Internet connection with the other guests. In addition, you can rent a beautiful two-bedroom cottage, with a panoramic view, for $120 a night. At about 1,000 feet, it feels like you're above it all here, yet you're still only half an hour from the airport and 10 minutes from the beach.

$$–$$$$ Farther above it all are the five charming chalets of the **Kula Lodge** (152000 Haleakala Hwy.; ☎ 800/233-1535 or 808/878-1535; www.kulalodge.com; AE, DISC, MC, V). At 3,200 feet, the lodge is a third of the way up Haleakala. Stay there and you'll have a big leg up on the early morning journey to the summit to see the sunrise. Surrounded by green ranchlands, the lodge's 3-acre grounds are filled with jacaranda trees, eucalyptus, and pathways lined with enormous protea flowers. Dinner at the lodge's fine-dinning restaurant is a splurge, but breakfast and lunch aren't bad at all. Take one look at the terraced garden dinning area with its panoramic view from the north shore to the south, and you'll want to have at least one meal there. The chalets aren't glitzy, but they're all roomy, comfy, and have four-poster queen beds. The four most expensive range from $165 to $195 in the summer and winter high seasons, but you can get the fifth one for $135. (In the low seasons, rates range from $125 to $185.) The budget chalet doesn't have the cozy gas fireplaces, the lofts where you can stash the kids, or the astonishing views that the others have, but it's just as tranquil and enjoys the same cool night air that makes sleeping in upcountry so delightful. If you stay at the lodge, get back there for the sunset. When you're there watching the blazing Hawaiian sun fall toward the sea, while the whole of Central and West Maui is bathed in gold at your feet, you'll feel on top of a peaceful and beautiful world.

THE NORTH SHORE: PAIA

Fifteen minutes east of Kahului Airport funky little Paia is a former sugar-mill town transfigured by hippies, windsurfing, and tourism into a colorful international crossroads with great restaurants and shopping. It's a place with all sorts of budget accommodations ideal for those who thrive on "shabby chic."

$ Just outside of town and cheap as can be is **Rainbow's End Surf Hostel** ★★ (221 Baldwin Ave., Paia; ☎ 808/579-9057; www.mauigateway.com/~riki; cash, travelers check, or money order only). It's one of two Paia hostels, and the nicer one by far. Beds in the dorm rooms go for $25, including tax, while private rooms with their own shared bathroom and kitchen range from $55 to $65 (discounts for extended stays). The young family that owns Rainbow's End lives downstairs, and they won't abide drinkers, druggies, or noisy guests, all of whom are summarily sent to the town's other hostel—which I wouldn't recommend unless you get booted from here.

$$ At the edge of a sugarcane field about a mile beyond town, there's a low-keyed bed-and-breakfast in a classic two-story plantation-style home called the **Kuau Inn** ★★★ (676 Hana Hwy.; ☎ 808/579-6046; www.kuauinn.com; cash, check, or travelers check only). The Chinese dentist who built the house in 1928

Won't You Take Me to Hostel Town?

Wailuku is where the business of island government takes place. Massive malls on the outskirts of nearby Kahului have supplanted the downtown shopping districts, and except for the sunshine and palm trees Wailuku has the downtrodden demeanor of Manchester in the UK or Detroit in Michigan.

But its lack of touristic appeal has made it quite an appealing spot for hostel owners, drawn here by the low rents and tolerant neighbors. For travelers, Wailuku is centrally located, and therefore not a bad spot to commute from to all parts of the island (though truthfully you're not going to want to spend all that much time in Wailuku itself).

Wailuku's three hostels are:

- **Banana Bungalow** (310 N. Market St.; ☎ 800/8HOSTEL or 808/244-5090; www.mauihostel.com; AE, MC, V): A party hearty atmosphere and very hard beds don't translate into a good night's sleep. But that doesn't seem to be the point of staying in this former potato processing factory; this place is more about socializing than snoozing. And people do that at the weekly parties, at the pool and foozball tables, and at the picnic tables and hot tub out back. The big perk is that if you stay here, you can take part in the daily free tours to Hana and Haleakala and the other touristic hotspots around the island. Dorm beds are $27 a night (no one under 18 allowed in the dorms, though kids can stay in the rooms); a private single is $54; private double $65; triple $76. Serious surfers (you have to prove you're riding the waves daily) are eligible for discounts. Free Wi-Fi.
- **Northshore Hostel** (2080 W. Vineyard St.; ☎ 866/946-7835 or 808/986-8095; www.northshorehostel.com; AE, MC, V): If you're over 30—or simply you want calmer, cleaner digs—you'll consider this newly renovated and actually pretty spiffy hostel. Up a staircase, down an alley off a less iffy street than the one Banana and Happy Vale are on, it charges $25 for a night in a dorm bed and just $50 for a double private room, with such nice touches as flouncy curtains and pretty comforters. Wi-Fi is free here, the staff is quite attentive, and there's a TV in the common area. Children 12 and over only; some shuttle services to local events and the airport.
- **Happy Valley Hale Hostel** (332 Alahee Dr.; ☎ 808/870-9100; www.nonalanicottages.com/hvhale.htm; cash only): Character-free but extremely quiet and tidy (the owners are very proud of the fact that they won the title of "cleanest hostel bathrooms in Hawaii" from another reviewer), Happy Vale is marginally the most expensive of the three at $29 for a dorm bed and $69 for a private double. I don't think it's as nice as the Northshore, but if that's full this is a decent second choice (for those who don't want the full tilt festivity of Banana).

couldn't have been very tall, because the ceiling comes down so low over the stairwell you have to duck to get by. But there's plenty of headroom in the rest of the house, which is airy, uncluttered, and spotlessly clean. You get a real sense of the casual, simple elegance of Old Hawaii. High quality linens and handmade, floral-print duvets cover the beds in the four guest rooms. Rooms go for a very reasonable $100 per night, which includes a make-your-own breakfast in a kitchen well stocked with food. The rooms share two indoor baths, and one two-person outdoor shower lined with polished travertine. There's an outdoor party lanai, and the backyard is ringed with fruit trees and has plenty of room for croquet. Across the street is a mom-and-pop country store, and a short stroll down the highway brings you to the acclaimed Mama's Fish House (p. 267). A short hop farther down the road is Hookipa Beach Park, the Windsurfing Capital of the World. Word is out among foreign windsurfers about the inn's proximity to Hookipa, so don't be surprised if the other guests can't stop talking about aerofoils and cambered sails in Swedish, French, or Czech.

$$ Wedged between the storefronts of downtown Paia and the sea is a tightly packed little neighborhood filled with roosters, dead-end lanes, and metal-roofs. Hidden behind a bamboo fence along one of these lanes is a boutique budget hotel where you can hide away on Maui's North Shore right in the thick of it all, **The Nalu Kai Lodge** ★★ (☎ 808/385-4344; www.nalukailodge.com; AE, DISC MC, V). This obscure little place has eight teeny yet artfully decorated rooms, stripped down to the bare essentials: a double bed or a pair of twins, an end table and reading lamp, a beefy ceiling fan, and a private bath with a big walk-in shower and a colorful river-rock floor. Rooms go for $125 a night with a two-night minimum, but the price drops to $115 a night if you stay a week. If you need more space, there's a roomy one-bedroom apartment with full kitchen and Japanese stone hot bath that you can have for $165. The lodge's courtyard features a faux lava rock waterfall, a hammock with room for two, and a thatched-roof BYOB bar where you cook on a barbecue and swap rumors with the other guests. At night the tiki torches are fired, the year-round Christmas lights get plugged in, and the courtyard is filled with a warmly romantic tropical glow. Nice touches like the bag of macadamia nuts you'll find on your bed, the beach towels, the free Wi-Fi, and lockers where you can safely stash your surfboards, tell you the Nalu Kai genuinely cares about you and the other guests. The only drawbacks are the lack of parking—there aren't enough spaces for all the rooms—and the late-night nightclub noise from nearby Jacques (p. 329). Try to get room no. 7 or no. 8. They're the quietest and have peek-a-boo ocean views.

$$–$$$ Another affordable, and more romantic, option, the **Spyglass House** (367 Hana Hwy.; ☎ 800/475-6695 or 808/579-8608; www.spyglassmaui.com; AE, MC, V) is perched on a low sea cliff a short drive north of town. It's a vintage 1970s Northern California–style beach house, with high ceilings, hardwood floors, stained-glass windows, and a weathered wood exterior. In an adjacent cottage, small rooms with shared bathrooms go for $110; larger rooms with their own bathrooms in the cottage and the main house range from $140 to $150. Couples who've come to Maui to act like romantic fools do well here; there are plenty of private places along the cliff where they can gaze into each other's eyes.

$$–$$$$ The owners of Spyglass House also run **Blue Tile Beach House** (459 Hana Hwy., Paia; ☎ 888/579-6446 or 808/579-6446; www.beachvacationmaui.com; AE, MC, V), a short drive farther north. This hulking Mediterranean-style structure stands on a sandy cove with decent summer snorkeling and wicked winter surf. Rates start at $90 for a clean, basic room and run to $250 for an oceanfront suite. Both houses have kitchens, where you can help yourself to the coffee, bagels, yogurt, and fruit. Both Blue Tile Beach House and Spyglass House add $30 to the nightly bill for stays of less than 3 days.

HANA

Too many visitors drive the arduous winding road to Hana, look around a bit, and drive back in the same day. A better way to experience Hana is to stay in the area for a night or two, and there are plenty of affordable places to do that.

$ **Joe's Place** (4870 Uakea Rd.; ☎ 808/248-7033; www.joesrentals.com; MC, V) is where shoestring travelers can lodge and share beaches with the millionaires who stay nearby at the Hotel Hana Maui (see below). Joe's has eight bare-bones rooms starting at $50 and peaking at $60. They're laden with old furniture, worn carpets, and bare walls. In the common areas are a group kitchen and a dispiriting television room. But, on the positive side, it's all white-glove clean. Otherwise, it's got no real amenities, unless you count the Coke machine.

$ For a little more space, you might want to consider the small vacation rentals run by two local families. At the end of the street and around the corner from Joe's, lifelong Hana residents Fusae Nakamura and her husband, Zenzo, operate **Aloha Cottages** ★ (73 Keawa Place; ☎ 808/248-8420; cash only). Made up of five units, located beside the Nakamura's home, each has clean, simple but pleasant redwood interiors. A studio equipped with fridge and hot plate rents for $65, while the two- and three-bedroom apartments with full kitchens run from $90 to $100. None of the rooms have phones, and only some have televisions. Try to snag no. 3, which has two bedrooms and the best view. **Hana Maui Vacation Rentals** (4176 Hana Hwy.; ☎ 800/991-2422 or 808/248-8087; www.maui-hana.com: cash, travelers check, or money order only) is set in small building alongside the home of the owners. Inside are three frill-free vacation rentals: two rooms with microwaves and coffeemakers for $85, and one with a kitchen for $95. The rates include tax and two people, with $20 per extra head. These are simple, comfortable places with dogs and kids around and perfect for folks who just want to bunk down and perhaps prepare an easy meal.

$$$–$$$$ Across the street from Joe's Place (see above), you'll find the **Hana Kai Maui Resort** ★ (1533 Uakea Rd. Hana; ☎ 800/346-2772 or 808/248-8426; www.hanakai.com; MC, V), an attractive, three-story condo complex that feels like an upscale motel, nestled against a rocky black-sand beach where the local surfer kids shred the wild shore break. Studios start at $167 and one-bedrooms start at $190, with discounts for longer stays. None of the simple, peaceful rooms have televisions, but all have lanais and are within earshot of the crashing waves. This is a romantic place in a beautiful setting, great for couples looking for a tropical splurge far from the crowds.

CAMPING

You'll find Maui's very best deal on accommodations at one of the island's most popular visitor attractions, **Haleakala National Park** (☎ 808/572-4459; free with $10 entry fee). The park has two drive-up campgrounds and three wilderness campgrounds where you can stay for free. No permits are needed to stay at either the Hosmer Grove campground, near the park entrance at 7,000 feet, or at the Kipahulu campground, near Oheo Gulch, on Maui's far east side, 10 miles past Hana. You simply drive up, and, if there's room, pitch a tent.

Inside Haleakala Crater, there are two wilderness campsites, the Pilaku and Holua campgrounds. For these, you need to get a permit from the Park Headquarters Visitor Center, near the park entrance. They're issued on a first-come, first-served basis—so if your heart's set on wilderness camping, come early. In addition to the tent sites, there's a primitive cabin at each campground, plus a third cabin in the crater at Kapalaoa. These rent for $75 per night, with guests applying at least 2 months in advance through a lottery system (occasionally there are last-minute cancellations and the cabins are up for grabs—call the park to inquire). Water in the crater must be treated before drinking, and no fires are allowed, so a portable cookstove would come in handy. Also note that weather in the crater can change suddenly—from sunny to torrential rain, or from warm to freezing cold—so pack accordingly.

Stays at all of these places are limited to 3 nights per month. And while the campgrounds themselves are free, there is a $10 park entry fee, which is good for a week.

Once you've exhausted your stay at Haleakala National Park, you can jump to either of the two Maui state parks with campgrounds, where the cost to camp goes up to $5 per night. One campground is high on the slopes of Haleakala, at **Polipoli Spring State Recreation Area,** which is typically sunny in the morning and socked in with clouds in the afternoon, and which has miles of great hiking trails. The other is on the coast at **Wainapanapa State Park,** just outside of Hana. It has a black-sand beach and is surrounded by ancient Hawaiian sites. Permits are needed to camp at either place. To get them, contact the **Division of State Parks** (54 S. High St., Wailuku, HI 96793; ☎ 808/985-8109; www.hawaii.gov/dlnr/dsp). Both campgrounds have cabins, but they're hard to get reservations for, and they're both kind of grungy. If I were you, I'd stick with tent camping here.

You can also camp at two county parks: **Kanaha Beach Park** near Kahului, and **Papalaua Wayside Park** on the way to Lahaina. These are the least desirable public campgrounds. Kanaha, which is at a popular windsurfing beach, is under the flight path for Kahului Airport. Papalaua Wayside sits along busy Honoapiilani Highway, between Maalaea and Lahaina, so there's a lot of traffic noise. Both sites book up quickly, and you need to make reservations well in advance. Campsites cost $3 per night, and there's a 3-night maximum per month. Contact **Maui County Parks and Recreation Department** (1580-C Kaahumanu Ave., Wailuku; ☎ 808/661-4685; www.mauimapp.com).

My favorite campground is perched on a bluff above a peninsula covered with taro patches, halfway to Hana. **Camp Keanae** ★★ (13-375 Hana Hwy., between mile markers 11 and 12, Keanae; ☎ 808/248-8355; www.mauiymca.org/campk.htm) has tent sites for $17 per person or $35 per family, and if you haven't got a tent, you can grab one of the bunks in the dormitories for the same price (bring your own bedding). If your tent leaks and you want to curl up in a dry bunk, you can switch—at no charge.

Camp Keanae has a splendid view of the rugged northeast coastline, and a sprawling, rolling grassy area, with all sorts of nooks and crannies where you can pitch a tent away from the wind. Amenities include fire pits, a basketball court with a hardwood floor, and showers. There's also a duplex cottage with two one-bedroom units that sleep up to four apiece, for $125 per night. They include kitchenettes and share a wraparound lanai and gas grill, so one of you can cook while the others direct from their chaise longues. Ordinarily, serenity prevails. But, now and then, a soccer camp or an African dance group or a Taiko drumming festival shows up. And in that case, I wouldn't call it peaceful. Call ahead to check the schedule.

DINING FOR ALL TASTES

Maui has a thriving, competitive restaurant scene that offers something for everyone. From the most exclusive five-star dining rooms to the lowliest roadside lunch wagon, high standards prevail. Here are some of the best options—from deals to a few choice splurges, and with many excellent meals in between.

SOUTH MAUI: KIHEI/WAILEA

$–$$ Tucked away in the Lipoa Center shopping plaza on a side street off South Kihei Road, is perhaps the most authentic Mexican restaurant on Maui. **Amigo's** (41 E. Lipoa St.; ☎ 808/879-9952; 9am–9pm daily; AE, DC, DISC, MC, V) serves hot, tasty, cheesy dinners for under $9, and breakfast for under $7. This place does a bustling takeout business, though there are a few tables, too. In the mornings, the huevos rancheros ($6.50) are especially good. If you're convinced that nothing allays a hangover quite like slow-cooked, spicy menudo (traditional Mexican soup), they've got it here on Saturday and Sunday—when it's in high demand.

$$ Without a doubt, the best place in south Maui to find a paper plate piled with more food than one person should probably eat all at once, for under $10, is **Da Kitchen** ★ (kids) (Rainbow Mall, 2439 S. Kihei Rd.; ☎ 808/875-7782; also in Kahului at 425 Koloa St., Kahului, ☎ 808/871-7782; 9am–9pm daily; AE, DC, DISC, MC, V). Portions here are so large, two people can generally split a meal and not leave hungry. Local people love the place, and countless visitors have taken their first baby steps into the high-fat, high-protein, and high-carbohydrate world of Hawaiian food here. At Da Kitchen, as with all bona fide local-style eateries in Hawaii, "salad" means macaroni salad. If you want a salad made with lettuce, you must say "green salad." As if the large servings weren't already large enough, the Kihei location has the Big Braddah Combo ($8.75), which gives you two entrees

---

Finding Your Place To Eat

The restaurants in the following sections can be found on the maps starting on p. 234.

Kihei Tiki Culture

Tiki bars are to Hawaiian culture what a bag of goldfish crackers is to a pod of wild spinner dolphins. One is real. The other isn't even close. Still, it's possible to appreciate both goldfish crackers and wild dolphins for what they're worth. While tiki bars may lack authenticity, they can be fun. The **South Shore Tiki Lounge** (1913 S. Kihei Rd., Kihei Kalama Village; ☎ 808/874-6444; 11am–10pm daily, pizza until midnight; AE, MC, V; $-$$) comes complete with all the trimmings you'd expect: bamboo paneling, flaming torches, a black-velvet Elvis, and genuine puffer-fish lampshades over the bar. It's also got tasty grilled sausage sandwiches ($7); burgers ($10); 16-inch pizzas with thin, crispy New York–style crusts (starting at $16); and, of course, those crazy drinks with the little umbrellas and pineapple spears in them ($8).

(choice of teriyaki chicken, teriyaki beef, katsu, and kalua pork). If that's not enough, there's the Sumotori Combo ($9.75), in which you get three. If you have access to a fridge, you can buy a Sumotori Combo and live off of it, more or less, for 2 or 3 days. The Kahului location doesn't do combo plates, but it has something Kihei doesn't: child-size portions ($4.75).

$$ For a lunch or dinner under $10, more sports on television than anybody can keep up with, and a huge selection of beer, check out **The Sports Page Grill & Bar** (2411 S. Kihei Rd., Kamaole Beach Center; ☎ 808/879-0602; kitchen open daily 11am–10pm; AE, DISC, MC, V). The burgers and sandwiches are tasty, and the plate lunches hit the spot (but don't waste your time with the sorry green salads). In addition to the grub, there are pool tables, secondhand smoke, and a friendly neighborhood-pub vibe that makes you want to hang out longer than you probably should in a smoky place.

$$ A place guileless enough to name itself **Vietnamese Cuisine** ★★ (The Azeka Place I, 1280 S. Kihei Rd.; ☎ 808/875-2088; 10am–9:30pm daily; AE, MC, V) is hard not to like before you even get inside. Eat here and you'll like it even more as the food is intensely flavorful. Try the bahn hoi, a Vietnamese burrito filled with beef, chicken, shrimp, or pork; wrapped in rice paper; and garnished with basil, mint, cucumber, romaine lettuce, and bean sprouts, along with vermicelli cake noodles, pickled carrots, and daikons ($13). If that seems too light, try one of the "claypot specialties," catfish or—better yet—mahimahi, braised with black-pepper sauce and simmered in the same clay pot it's served in ($13). Adventurous eaters will love the lemon beef: Nearly raw and almost pickled, it will leave your mouth buzzing. There's a decent vegetarian menu here, too, and often a full house.

Early Bird Gourmet

Raul Bermudez worked as an executive chef at top-end restaurants in Maui's tony resorts for years before bringing his take on Hawaii's regional cuisine down off the mountain and putting it back on the vinyl tablecloths of The People, where it all began. He left the polished crystal and high prices behind, but his deft presentations of blackened ahi, pan-seared opakapaka, and macadamia-nut-crusted onaga (market price on all, which is around $24) stuck with him. At his restaurant, **Bermudez's Big Wave Café** ★★★ (1215 S. Kihei Rd., at the Longs Drugs Kihei Center; ☎ 808/891-8688; 7:30am–9pm daily; D, MC, V; **$$–$$$$**), you can sit outdoors under broad awnings and watch the traffic go by, or indoors under a vaulted ceiling and watch surf videos. Go between 5 and 6pm for the early-bird special, when you can get two dinners for the price of one.

$–$$ **Jawz** (1279 S. Kihei Rd., Azeka Shopping Center; ☎ 808/874-TACO; 11am–9pm daily; AE, DISC, MC, V) started out as a one of the Makena Beach roadside food trucks, but it grew up and got a lease in a shopping plaza. Now it has walls, windows, tables, a commercial kitchen, and a comprehensive salsa bar where you can pile olives, cilantro, jalapenos, an avocado-and-sour-cream mixture, and all sorts of sauces and salsas onto your ahi, ono, or mahimahi tacos. The basic taco ($5.25 with refried or black beans, $6.50 with mahimahi)—heaped with shredded lettuce, cheese, and a delightful house sauce—brims with potential; what you do with it at the salsa bar determines the mark it will make in this world. If you find yourself at a complete loss for where to begin, I recommend a light treatment with the roasted habanera pepper, pineapple, and carrot salsa. Follow up with a robust overlay of the smoky chipotle-pepper hot sauce and then go with your instincts from there.

$$ For hungry Makena beachgoers and visitors to La Perouse Bay, there's a selection of roadside food vendors along Makena Alanui Road. Just be prepared: They all charge more than you'd expect to pay for roadside food. My favorite is **The Shrimp Trap** (parks near Big Beach's north parking lot; cash only), where you can get a small mountain of shrimp scampi on rice, heavy with garlic, for $10. It may not be the best car food, especially if you're the driver, but it is buttery bliss. I appreciate the owner's candor in naming his truck as he did. He considered both The Shrimp King and The Shrimp Master before settling on The Shrimp Trap, reasoning in pidgin English, "I just going trap 'em"—as in the passing motorists. Watching the brake lights of car after car go on after whizzing through his invisible garlicky snare, I'd say his plan unfolded perfectly.

$$$–$$$$ I have to admit, I found something a little unseemly at first about an ocean aquarium running a seafood restaurant right next door. But that's no reason to overlook the Maui Ocean Center's **Seascape Maalaea Restaurant** (kids) (192 Maalaea Rd., The Harbor Shops at Maalaea; ☎ 808/270-7043; lunch only, 11am–3:30pm; DC, DISC, MC, V). It has a good selection of reasonably priced pastas, seafood entrees, and seafood pastas, plus a kids' menu and prices lower

A Gourmet Chef for the Masses

A few years ago the celebrated island chef Mark Ellman, one of the dozen chefs credited with creating the multicultural culinary fusion known as Hawaii Regional Cuisine, stepped away from his gleaming kitchen at a tony Maui resort and reinvented himself as the island's patron saint of practical eaters. Reaching into his bag of organic, whole-grain, locally produced ingredients, he pulled out a chain of healthy, dirt-cheap Mexican restaurants that he named **Maui Tacos** ★★ (multiple locations: Lahaina Sq., Lahaina, ☎ 808/661-8883; Kamaole Beach Center, Kihei, ☎ 808/ 8795005; Piilani Shopping Center, Kihei, ☎ 808/875-9340; Napili Plaza, Napili, ☎ 808/665-0222; Kaahumanu Center, Kahului, ☎ 808/871-7726; Mon–Sat 9am–9pm, Sun 9am–8pm; AE, DISC, DC, MC, V). If the oily shadow of bad cholesterol has kept you from enjoying a good chimichanga for way too long, go to Maui Tacos. A big, crunchy, trans-fat free potato chimichanga will set you back just $6. What the place is best known for, though, are its $4 fish tacos, which are light and delish, too, and which can be customized at a well-stocked condiment bar.

Next, Ellman turned to Italian, opening **Penne Pasta** ★★★ (180 Dickenson St., near Front St.; ☎ 808/661-6633; Mon–Fri 11am–9:30pm, Sat 5–9:30pm, Sun 5–9pm; AE, DISC, MC, V) in a pleasant, pastel-colored space on a side street in Old Lahaina. I nearly wept with joy the first time I stood at the counter there studying the menu. Finally I'd found a place in Hawaii where you can get a plate of linguine pesto for just $7.95—with a delightful selection of reasonably priced beer and wine, to boot. If you want to splurge, you can add a chicken breast or garlic ahi to any pasta for an extra $4.95. If you really want to splurge, you can get one of the weekly specials (lamb osso bucco Wed, lasagna Thurs, and so on) for about $17. If I lived in Lahaina, I'd eat there all the time.

than other joints on the harbor, such as Buzz's Wharf and The Waterfront (see below). Seascape's en plein air dining room opens only for lunch, and the seafood salad ($16) seems as well stocked as the 750,000-gallon main tank next door. If you question the propriety of an aquarium getting into the seafood business, the waitstaff will tell you that they don't serve anything on the "avoid list" of the Monterey Bay Aquarium, which eschews threatened species and seafood caught in environmentally unsound ways. Furthermore, they don't cook anything raised next door.

$$–$$$ For family-style Italian, try **Bada Bing** (1945 S. Kihei Rd.; ☎ 808/875-0188; 11am–10pm daily; DISC, MC, V), a Frank Sinatra–themed pasta place. The signature entree is "One Big Meatball," a comically portioned half-pound whopper in marinara sauce for $12. If that's too much for you, the steaks, pastas, burgers, and submarine sandwiches come in more manageable sizes.

$$–$$$$ A golf-course restaurant in an exclusive resort isn't necessarily where you'd expect to find the highest concentration of Irish in the North Pacific. Yet there they are, on student visas, serving shepherd's pie, pouring Guinness stout, and scrubbing the corn beef and cabbage off the bottom of pans. Irish-run and -owned **Mulligan's on the Blue** (100 Kaukahi St., on the Wailea Blue golf course; ☎ 808/874-1131; www.mulligansontheblue.com; kitchen open 8am–9pm, sometimes 10pm, daily; DISC, MC, V) has an ocean view, live music every night, and delightfully low prices compared to the other restaurants in tony Wailea. The Irish food is the best you'll find for thousands of miles around. Try the corned beef and Kula cabbage ($16), the bangers and mash ($14), or a hearty bowl of Irish stew ($14).

$$$–$$$$ After following the Grateful Dead for several years, the owners of **Stella Blues Cafe** (1279 S. Kihei Rd.; Azeka Mauka; ☎ 808/874-3779; 7:30am–10pm daily; AE, DISC, D, MC, V) settled on Maui and opened up a restaurant in Kihei, adorning the walls with Grateful Dead memorabilia and the menu with references that might go over the heads of all but true Deadheads (Sunshine Daydream Seafood Stew, $22; Mama Tried Meatloaf, $17). They've got creative food, a cheerful staff, pizzas, pastas, steaks, vegetarian entrees, and decorative green concrete countertops at the lively bar. This is the only place in Kihei where you can get a tofu scramble in the morning ($8.95). The veggie lasagna ($16) in the evening is delicious.

$$$–$$$$ Apart from the fantastic harborside location in which it's served—and the outstanding prawns—don't expect much more than standard steak-and-seafood fare at **Buzz's Wharf** (Maalaea Harbor; ☎ 808/244-5426; 11am–9pm

A Fine-Dining Splurge with a Half-Price Option

Lahaina Grill ★★★ (kids) (127 Lahainaluna Rd., Lahaina; ☎ 808/667-5117; www.lahainagrill.com; 6–10pm daily; AE, DISC, MC, V) is at the apex of Maui's fine-dining world. Its impeccably attuned waitstaff, soft warm lighting, enormous desert-toned paintings, and an exquisite New American menu collaborate beneath the pressed-tin ceilings of a historic Lahaina building to form a restaurant that consistently wins accolades from leading gourmet magazines. Year after year the readers of *Honolulu Magazine* vote Lahaina Grill the best restaurant on Maui. "The Kalua duck ($29) was so rich and smooth that if I could walk on water, I'd walk to Lahaina to eat it again," wrote the editor, an estimable gourmand. Dinner here is a splurge, to be sure, but with the recent addition of a demi-menu, you can now sit at the bar and enjoy very large half portions for about half the price. There's one trick though—you have to know to ask about the demi-menu (and it's not offered during the winter high season). Try the exquisite Kona coffee–roasted rack of lamb, with a light coffee-cabernet demiglaze ($39; or demi-menu $20), or the outstanding tequila shrimp and firecracker rice, with Southwestern herbs and spices and butter flavored with tequila ($33; or demi-menu $19). There's also a kids' menu with, among other things, beef kabobs ($12).

Flea Market Maui-Style

If you're staying in one of Maui's many condos, you can stock your kitchen with fresh island-grown produce from the farmers market at the **Maui Swap Meet** (Maui Community College, 310 W. Kaahumanu Hwy.; ☎ 808/877-3100; 7am–noon; admission 50¢) every Saturday. Fruits and vegetables are delightfully inexpensive. For $10 to $15, you can load up on enough mangoes, papayas, sweet corn, string beans, limes, sweet potatoes, spinach, lettuce, and so forth to last for quite some time. Most fun, if you get hungry while shopping, there are plenty of food vendors from which to snack.

daily; AE, MC, V). The prawns come from a saltwater prawn farm in faraway New Caledonia, which is owned by the family that owns the restaurant. Don't come here for dinner, come for an afternoon beer and the Coconut Panko Fried Shrimp ($15)—which isn't really a shrimp dish; all of the shrimp dishes here actually feature prawns. Another one of those faux shrimp dishes are the half-dozen prawns baked in dry vermouth, dill, and a tiny bit of Parmesan ($29) served at dinner—pricey, yes, but they come out tasting like little lobsters.

$$$–$$$$ The early-bird special at **Sansei Seafood Restaurant and Sushi Bar** ★ (1881 S. Kihei Rd., Kihei Town Center; ☎ 808/879-0004; 5:30–10pm Sun–Wed, 5:30–2am Thurs–Sat; AE, DISC, MC, V) slices 25% off all dinners and sushi from 5:30 to 6pm Tuesday through Saturday, and 50% off dinners and sushi from 5 to 6pm Sunday and Monday. The late-night special is even better—50% off sushi and appetizers from 10pm to 1am Thursday, Friday, and Saturday. Beware: Sansei is always mobbed, but the crowd is especially thick during the half-off hours. The late-night specials coincide with laser karaoke night, which is way more fun than you'd expect. The entrees here reflect a firm Japanese influence over Pacific Rim cuisine. The sushi is traditional sushi, except for the house specials, such as the mango crab-salad handroll ($7.95), made with mangoes, blue crab, Kula greens, and a delicious spicy Thai vinaigrette. There are two Sansei restaurants on Maui (and one on Oahu). The Kihei location, a central nightlife hub, is always packed, and reservations are strongly advised. The Kapalua location (The Shops at Kapalua; 115 Bay Dr.; Kapalua; ☎ 808/669-6286) is a little mellower. The Kapalua late-night specials occur from 10pm to 1am Thursday and Friday; the early-bird specials are the same as Kihei's.

WEST MAUI

$–$$ Aloha Mix Plate ★★★ (1285 Front St.; ☎ 808/661-3322; 10:30am–10pm daily; MC, V) is almost too good to be true. It's got an oceanfront location, authentic local cuisine, an open-air bar serving Nutty Mangos and Sassy Wahines, and prices that will make your wallet fall madly in love. The vibe is genuine laid-back Hawaiian, while the seating is entirely outdoors, beneath big shade trees and canvas tarps and umbrellas. Just offshore, sailboats in Lahaina Roads bob at anchor. Around sunset you can hear live Hawaiian music spilling over the lava rock wall separating the restaurant from its neighbor, Old Lahaina Luau (p. 324). If you've never had Hawaiian food before, Aloha Mix Plate is an excellent place to get initiated. The kalua pork, poi, and lau lau are just as good as you'd get if you were at the neighboring luau (the same owners run both places). Plate lunches are Mix Plate's other specialty. They feature island favorites such as Japanese shoyu chicken, Chinese roast duck, and Korean kalbi ribs—and they can be huge. I say "can be" because there are three sizes: mini, regular, and jumbo. Mini plates start at a mere $3.95, while jumbos start at $7.50. At those prices, you can afford to linger after dinner to enjoy the million-dollar view and the $5 drink specials.

$–$$ A block off of Lahaina's busy Front Street, don't miss an easily overlooked place called **Saigon Seafood** (888 Wainee St., at corner of Papalaua, kitty-corner from Hilo Hatties; ☎ 808/661-9955; 10am–9:30pm, Sun 10am–8:30pm; MC, V). This humble little Chinese and Vietnamese restaurant is worth noting because its dishes are both delicious and priced mostly under $10. An extensive menu covers all the bases, from a generous serving of beef broccoli for $8.50 to a big bowl of pho (Vietnamese soup) with thin slices of rare steak cooking in the steaming broth for $7.75. The indoor seating is limited, and the outdoor seating is right along a busy road, so takeout is a good move here.

$$ If you have to wait in line for breakfast, it's nice to have whales to watch. **The Gazebo** ★★★ (5315 L. Honoapiilani Rd., at Napili Shores; ☎ 808/669-5621; 7:30am–2pm daily; MC, V) is so popular among the condo dwellers of the Napili area that you're almost guaranteed a wait in line, at least for breakfast, but it's worth it. With sweeping views across the channels between Maui, Molokai, and Lanai, you can't help but spot whales frolicking offshore in the winter, whether you're in line or seated inside. The Gazebo's open for breakfast and lunch only, and nothing's priced higher than $10.25. Even outside of whale season, the macadamia-nut pancakes are worth some patience.

$$ Whenever I have a chance to talk to restaurant people on Maui, I ask where they like to eat. More often than not, they mention **Thai Chef** ★★★ (Old Lahaina Center, 880 Front St.; ☎ 808/667-2814; 11am–2pm and 5pm–closing, Mon–Fri; DC, DISC, MC, V). When I went to see what the fuss was about, three grinning diners who were leaving stopped me at the door, congratulated me on my fine taste in restaurants, raved about the meal they had just had, and strongly recommended the Thai beef steak. They were right—exquisitely thin slices of beef grilled with a tangy Thai sauce and sprinkled with sesame seeds and green onions ($9.95) is a dish worth raving about. But everything else here is delicious, too—the pad Thai, pan-fried with sweet peanut sauce ($9.95); the Evil Prince, with chicken, bamboo shoots, basil, coconut milk, and red curry, served over shredded cabbage ($9.95); the Pineapple Fried Rice with shrimp, egg, onion, peas, carrots, and pineapple ($9.95); and the garlic squid, with carrots, onions, and bell peppers ($11). And, helping to keep the tab down, it's BYOB (beer and wine are okay; no corkage fee). If my dining companion and I hadn't stayed past closing, we too would have congratulated anyone we met on their way in on their fine taste in restaurants.

$$–$$$$ North of Lahaina, the **Maui Brewing Co.** (4405 Honoapiilani Hwy., Kahana Gateway Center; ☎ 808/669-3474; www.mauibrewingco.com; 11am–9m daily, with a pub menu until midnight; AE, DISC, MC, V) is a microbrewery with a dimly lit, cool, sports-bar interior. It offers six regular beers on tap and a rotating roster of seasonal picks. Try the Double Overhead IPA if it's on tap (p. 328). Although it's a rotisserie—with chicken, ribs, and prime rib roasted over a kiawe-wood fire—they also manage to produce a credible veggie lasagna ($19). Burgers are cheaper ($13).

KAHULUI/WAILUKU

$ The best place in Wailuku to drink coffee in the morning is also the best place to drink wine in the evening: **Café Marc Aurel** (28 N. Market St., Wailuku; ☎ 808/244-0852). Along with the coffee, you'll find delicious bagels and pastries. With wine, you can enjoy gourmet cheeses, desserts, live music, poetry readings, and belly dancing (p. 330). Between the hours of coffee and wine, 8-inch cheese pizzas, bagels, and other things are served for lunch. In neighboring Kahului, in addition to the omnipresent Starbucks Coffee (multiple locations), you'll find Maui Coffee Roasters (444 Hana Hwy.; ☎ 808/877-2877). It's a nice place to enjoy a fresh pastry or bagel, the newspaper, and the euphoric aroma of roasting coffee. They roast and blend Kona coffee here with beans from around the world. Be sure to pay homage at the shrine for Our Lady of the Eternal Double Latte by the restrooms.

$ Maui's most beloved noodle house, **Sam Sato's** (1750 Wili Pa Loop; ☎ 808/244-7124; 7am–2pm Sun–Fri; cash only) is a great place to go for a cheap breakfast and lunches of saimin, chow fun, or dry noodles (everything's under $8). If the noodles aren't speaking to you, you can get barbecued meat sticks, served with two scoops of rice and macaroni salad—the ubiquitous local side dish. Or you can skip the sides and just chow down on the meat sticks for a buck apiece! For an exotic dessert, try the manju, a flaky orbed pastry filled with sweetened lima and adzuki beans. It tastes better than it sounds. Just breakfast and lunch here, unfortunately.

$ For picnic fixings or a light lunch, **Down to Earth Natural Foods** (305 Dairy Rd., Kahului; ☎ 808/877-2661; 7am–9pm Mon–Sat, 8am–8pm Sun; AE, DISC, MC, V) is the best bet in Kahului. You can buy healthy sandwiches and wraps, soups, and smoothies; or choose from the $7.59-per-pound salad-and-hot-food bar.

$–$$ Directly across the highway from Down to Earth, at the Maui Marketplace, you'll find the **Kau Kau Corner Food Court** (270 Dairy Rd.; 9am–9pm Mon–Sat, 9am–7pm Sun) with a host of cheap, good places to eat. My favorite is **Ba-Le** ★ (☎ 808/877-2400; also at Lahaina Cannery Mall; ☎ 808/661-5566), where Vietnam's French colonial influence merges with the American fast-food experience, colored by Hawaii Regional Cuisine. Rice noodles and baguettes stand side by side at Ba-Le. Tofu and lettuce on a croissant may not sound very exciting, but Ba-Le's croissant vegetable sandwich quickly endears itself to you. Better yet, it costs just $3.75. For dessert, try the taro tapioca pudding ($1.65). Weird, but delicious.

$–$$ **A Saigon Cafe** ★★★ (1792 Main St., Wailuku, just over the bridge from Kahului; ☎ 808/243-9560; Mon–Sat 10am–9:30pm, Sun 10am–8:30pm; MC, V) is another fantastic Vietnamese place, and one without Ba-Le's shopping-mall ambience. No signage announces its existence, but the steady stream of customers coming and going tips you off. Follow them inside and you'll find a place bustling as waiters whisk trays with heaps of noodles, crispy shrimp, and baked chicken from the kitchen to tables and booths filled with regulars who know they're in for something good. When not harried, the Vietnamese, Laotian, and Cambodian waitstaff can be hilarious. Our waiter, sporting a deluxe Elvis pompadour, plucked a cellphone off our table and launched into a mock wrong-number conversation. You can't go wrong with anything on the menu here, but I'm particularly enamored of the *goi du du* ($7.50), green papaya salad with sweet-and-sour garlic dressing.

THE NORTH SHORE: PAIA

$ It's no surprise that funky Paia, center of health consciousness and body culture that it is, has the best health-food store on the island, **Mana Foods** ★★ (46 Baldwin Ave.; ☎ 808/579-8078; 8:30am–8:30pm daily; AE, DISC, MC, V). You can stock up on whole-grain, organic, locally grown everything here. You'll also find the island's best hot bar, salad bar, and deli in the back ($6.19 per pound for both hot and cold bar). If you're looking to load the rental car up on healthful snacks, this is the place to do it. And if you're shopping for a fancier occasion (maybe a special picnic), you'll also find gourmet chocolates, gourmet cheeses, and intriguing crackers.

$–$$ You know that the places where local cops eat in the morning are good bets for breakfast, and Paia cops like **Charley's Restaurant** (142 Hana Hwy., Paia; ☎ 808/579-9453; 7am–10pm daily; AE, DISC, MC, V). So do other folks—including windsurfers, celebrities, Hana-bound tourists, and just about everybody else in town. Try the eggs Benedict ($9.50) or better yet, the ono Benedict ($12). Another good choice is the enormous single buttermilk pancake ($3.75), which overlaps the edges of its plate and has a diameter nearly as large as Willie Nelson's gold records, which you'll find hanging on the wall of the bar in the back. Willie lives on the north shore, and this is one of his haunts, not to mention a great place for north-shore nightlife. Lunches feature burgers, calzones, and pizza, while dinners include grilled steak and fish. But breakfast is the best.

$–$$ **Café Des Ami** (42 Baldwin Ave.; ☎ 808/579-6323; daily 8:30am–8:30pm; MC, V) is a colorful, laid-back hole in the wall specializing in the unusual combination of crepes and curries. I'm talking avocado crepes with apple and black pepper (no really, it's good; $9.25), or curried mahimahi with tomato, yogurt, and cilantro ($16). Go, eat, and prepare to feel happy and healthy.

$$–$$$ On a corner at Paia's main intersection, the **Paia Fishmarket** ★★ (100 Hana Hwy., corner of Baldwin Ave; ☎ 808/579-8030; daily 11am–9:30pm; DISC, DC, MC, V) serves excellent, affordable seafood in a range of price levels; you could get a single, filling fish taco for $9.95 or an even more filling seafood pasta in cream sauce for $17. The kitchen knows how to do fish and chips ($13), too.

A Semi Splurge & a Real Splurge

Yes, you came to Maui probably for fun in the sun, but your tongue deserves a vacation, too. At these two increasingly famous restaurants you taste the best in island cuisine. And at the first one you may get to do it at a discount.

That's because **Manana Garage** (33 Lono Ave., Kahului; ☎ 808/873-0220; 11am–9pm daily; AE, D, DISC, MC, V; $$$–$$$$), which serves Latin American fare with Pacific overtones, consistently offers great specials that change monthly (when I was here, they were offering 50% off all entrees between 5–6pm), so you shouldn't rule it out because it's got four dollar signs. Such dishes as citrus-jalapeno glazed salmon with black-bean sauce ($20), or the fresh-fish chimichanga with wasabi sour cream and roasted tomatillo sauce ($18) showcase the terrific creativity of the chef, and make it a good choice for a special occasion. There's also live music on Friday from 6 to 9pm, and $3 margarita specials on Thursday.

Of course, the unbeatable special occasion restaurant on the island is **Mama's Fish House** ★★★ (799 Poho Place, just east of Paia; ☎ 808/579-8488; www.mamasfishhouse.com; 11am–9pm daily; AE, DISC, DC, MC, V; $$$$) and I include it here, despite the prices. If you care about food, this is one splurge you must make. Nestled in a cozy white-sand cove behind a rustling palm grove, Mama's is imbued with an elegant yet casual South Seas castaway vibe that's so hokey it's chic. The executive chef, Perry Bateman, is a local who, as a teenager, began working in the salad pantry here and rose to the top of what's widely regarded as one of the best seafood restaurants in Hawaii. As inspiring as his career path is, his work with roasted kukui nut, paholo fern, organic Maui veggies, and super-fresh seafood is even more so. Mama's gets its fish directly from a small bunch of local fishermen, who put their boats in at nearby Maliko Bay and pull up to Mama's back door with their fresh catch on their way home. The menu gives them credit. On a recent visit, I was sorely tempted by the ahi, caught by Kris Sakamoto in the Alenuihaha Channel near the Big Island, seared with pepper, and then served with a mushroom brandy sauce ($39). Then I tilted toward the ono, caught by Harry Furomoto while trolling near Kahoolawe, and served with caramelized Maui onion and Olinda avocado ($36). In the end, I chose the mahimahi, baked in a macadamia-nut crust, stuffed with lobster, crab, and onion ($54), and caught by Amando Baula along Maui's north shore, somewhere outside the window.

(Lunch prices are lower.) Order at the counter, then try to find a seat at the usually crowded family-style tables where everybody eats together. This is, by the way, an actual fish market.

$$–$$$ Every cool surf town worth its sea salt has a casual, organic eatery doubling as a community gathering place. In Paia, that niche is filled by **The Flatbread Company** ★ (89 Hana Hwy.; 808/579-8989; 11:30am–10pm Sun–Thurs, 11:30am–11pm Fri–Sat; AE, MC, V). Neighbors kick back with neighbors in a breezy dinning room adorned with surfer art and dominated by a wood-fired oven made of lava rock and clay. Organic white flour goes into all the crusts, which are slathered with organic tomato sauce ladled from a cauldron, then sprinkled with whole-milk mozzarella and imported Italian Parmesan cheeses. Toppings include homemade, nitrate-free sausage, goat cheese chevre from a farm high up the slopes of Haleakala, and kalua pork made with the help of free-range pigs. Tuesday night is Community Night, when a few bucks from each pizza goes to a worthwhile local cause. Twelve-inch pies start at $9.50; 16-inchers start at $16.

WHY YOU'RE HERE: MAUI'S BEACHES

The problem with Maui's beaches is that there are so many of them, and they're so beautiful and varied, that it's hard to figure out where to begin. There are fine white-sand concourses stretching for miles along aquamarine waters, and there are sheltered golden crescents nestled between rocky points. There are salt-and-pepper piles of sun-bleached coral and jet-black lava rock tumbled smooth in the shorebreak, there are steep pockets of black sand plunging into the cobalt blue sea, and there's even a deeply hued red-sand beach nourished by an eroding volcanic cinder cone.

There are beaches where everybody wears bathing suits, and there are beaches where nobody does. There are beaches for windsurfers, kiteboarders, and skimboarders; and there are beaches for nothing but sunbathing. There are beaches where the waves challenge the world's best surfers, and there are beaches where beginners can paddle into the breakers without getting killed. There are beaches with paved parking lots, restrooms, and showers, and there are beaches where dirt parking lots and outhouses would be an upgrade. There are beaches with great snorkeling and multitudes of fish, and there are beaches where your own feet are the only things you'll see with fins. There are beaches with sidewalks you can rollerblade along, and there are beaches that only the most diehard beach-goers will ever see, including a particular unmarked beach in Hana at the end of a crumbling cliffside trail so perilous it forces you to ask yourself, "How badly do I really want to go to the beach?"

So where to begin? We may as well start where the coastal highway ends and where contact between Maui's native Hawaiian population and the Western world began, at La Perouse Bay. From there we'll move clockwise along the island's 120-mile coastline, stopping at the very best beaches along the way.

SOUTH MAUI

You won't find soft sand or good swimming at **La Perouse Bay** ★, but you will find a fantastic place to snorkel, dive, and kayak—if the seas are calm. When the south swells hit, a couple of gnarly surf spots light up, and it's fun to lounge on

Finding Your Place in the Sun

The beaches in the following sections can be found on the maps starting on p. 228.

Shark Attack 101

The risk of getting attacked by a shark while on vacation in Hawaii is slim. Millions of people take to the water every year, and sharks, on average, bite just four of them. Victims usually survive. Drownings, on the other hand, take about 60 lives in Hawaii annually. Still, you can further minimize the risk of shark attacks by heeding the advice of the State of Hawaii Shark Task Force (yes, there is such a thing):

- Don't swim alone.
- Avoid swimming at dusk.
- Don't swim with bleeding wounds.
- Avoid murky water.
- Swim in guarded areas.
- Don't wear bright jewelry or high-contrasting colors.
- Refrain from excessive splashing.
- Be alert if turtles and fish are fleeing the area.
- Remove speared fish from the water.
- Don't swim if sharks are known to be present.

the heaps of smooth coral and lava rock near the point, watching the action. (Beware: The waves here are for experienced surfers only.)

In 1786, French navigator Jean Francois de Galaup de La Perouse anchored his two frigates in this bay and introduced himself to the villagers of Keoneoio, becoming the first known Westerner to visit Maui. Extensive remnants of Keoneoio can still be found (p. 277), and the 15-minute hike to the point passes house foundations and walls, a canoe *hale,* and a *heiau,* as well as several small pocket beaches that feel private and wild. This is one of Maui's four marine reserves, and taking anything but pictures and memories is forbidden. It's also raw, undeveloped land, so bring drinking water.

About 2½ miles north of La Perouse Bay is the 165-acre **Makena State Park,** which has three beaches that bear more than three names. **Big Beach** ★★★ is a broad expanse of fine white sand that stretches nearly a mile along turquoise and azure waters. The sea remains calm here most of the time, but it occasionally kicks up a mean shore break, to the delight of bodysurfers. Like La Perouse Bay, Big Beach is part of the last undeveloped stretch of south Maui. Its two parking lots—one at either end—have portable toilets but no running water. ***Important:*** It's very hot and dry here, so remember to bring something to drink.

Although Big Beach is one of the most popular beaches on the island, it can handle a huge crowd without feeling crowded. The parking lots are another matter, and when they fill up, people park along the road between them and cut to the beach through the kiawe forest (taking care not to puncture their feet on the thorns). The Hawaiian name for Big Beach is Oneloa, meaning "long sand," a name this beach shares with an Oneloa Beach in West Maui. Big Beach is also commonly called Makena Beach, a name it shares with two other Makena beaches north of here. Big

Enjoy a Six-Pack at Sunset

Maui County has no open-container law preventing you from drinking in county beach parks. You can crack open a beer or uncork a bottle of wine without fear of getting ticketed. Just be sure you're actually in a county beach park.

Makena is yet another name, and I think a good one. Of all the food vendors who park their rigs along the road, The Shrimp Trap (p. 260) is my favorite.

The lava-rock promontory at Big Beach's north end separates it from **Little Beach** ★★★ (for the best access, park in Big Beach's north parking lot). Scale the rocks and you'll find a secluded sandy cove, as well as naked people, usually lots of them. Little Beach is Maui's foremost nude beach. It has fine swimming, occasional bodysurfing, good snorkeling, and precious little shade. On Sunday, as the sun descends upon the horizon, Little Beach's pagan heart beats to the accompaniment of a drum circle, fire spinners, and a crowd of chanting, twirling, patchouli-burning, and thoroughly tanned old hippies and nouveau tribalists (p. 298). The authorities generally turn a blind eye to the nudity, which isn't legal, but Makena State Park closes at 9pm, and that's strictly enforced. Little Beach is often referred to as Little Makena, and sometimes as Pu'u Olai Beach in honor of the 360-foot-tall cinder cone at its north end.

North of Little Beach, on the other side of the cinder cone, is a broad, mellow strip of white sand called **Maluaka Beach** ★. It fronts the Maui Prince Hotel—a ritzy Japanese-built place and the sole hotel in the exclusive Makena resort. Maluaka has good swimming along its gently sloping sandy shore, lots of fish and turtles among the rocks, coral on each side, and a great shade tree hanging over its southern end. Commercial dive boats anchor offshore for turtle-watching. Some come to dive the World War II–era U.S. Army halftrack and tank permanently parked on the bottom at around 60 feet.

Farther north the extravagant hotels and plush condominiums of Wailea Resort share a string of five golden crescent beaches separated by rocky points. Some of these beaches seem like the private domains of the hotels, but they're not. In Hawaii, the public has the right to any beach. A 1½-mile coastal trail links the Wailea beaches and offers a nice stroll through the resort. **Polo Beach** sits at the south end of the trail, backed by low sand dunes, a high-rise condominium, and the misplaced Moorish architecture of the Kea Lani hotel (turrets, cupolas, and all). The beach offers good swimming most of the time, plus tide pools at the south end, during low tide, at any rate, and good snorkeling on the points. You can snorkel around the north point to the broader, **Wailea Beach,** swarming with guests from the Four Seasons and the Grand Wailea hotels encamped in their hooded beach chairs like half-naked pioneers in miniature Conestoga wagons. It has great swimming and occasional bodysurfing, but not the best snorkeling.

Next are the **Ulua** and **Mokapu** beaches, conjoined twins connected at a stubby rocky point. The point offers great snorkeling and is a popular spot for shore diving. The Wailea Marriott overlooks Ulua, and the Renaissance Wailea Beach Resort stands behind Mokapu. The twin beaches share a public parking lot behind the point, along with restrooms and showers. The coastal trail ends at

Keawakapu Beach ★★, a long, beautiful, and largely ignored beach fronting luxury condos and some very expensive homes. The resort crowd tends to congregate on the first four beaches (or it sticks around the swimming pools and never makes it to the beach at all), leaving Keawakapu Beach relatively unpopulated. I love playing here in the small waves and then stretching out on the sand to dry in the sun, staring across the windy channel at the offshore islands of Molokini and Kahoolawe framed between my knees.

A more democratic group of beaches lies farther up the coast, at the south end of sprawling Kihei. This trio of Roman-numeraled county beach parks, **Kamaole I, Kamaole II,** and **Kamaole III,** draws multitudes of locals and visitors. As with the Wailea beaches, rocky points separate the three Kams, as they're called. All have showers, restrooms, lifeguards, and barbecues. Kam I has beach volleyball. Kam I and II have bodysurfing. Kam III has the most parking, the biggest grassy area, a playground, and something about it that bocce ball players can't resist. Kamaole literally means "without children," which is funny, since kids are everywhere.

WEST MAUI

Drive around Papawai Point, past the rugged, dry cliffs known as Pali A'alaalaua, and after popping out of the only tunnel on the island, you'll come to a long stretch of classic Hawaiian beaches that runs for 7 miles along Honoapiilani Highway—all the way to Lahaina. You can pull off the road almost anywhere along here and find a nice place to cool your heels, if not actually swim. Coral flourishes near shore, making for good snorkeling and creating so many surf breaks that the whole area has become known as Thousand Peaks. To find the beginners' surf spots, just look for the breaks where tourists are on long boards. They don't look like the other surfers, so they should be easy to spot. One of the best snorkel grounds is called **Coral Gardens** (at the first unpaved pullout after the tunnel, between mile markers 10 and 11), a fertile patch of reef abounding in fish, eels, and turtles. Of the four roadside beach parks you'll pass, the nicest is **Launiopoko Beach Park** (near mile marker 18), which provides shade, showers, restrooms, plenty of parking, a broad grassy area, picnic tables, barbecues, a wading pond for children, and nice surfable waves, although not much sand.

About halfway to Lahaina, before you reach Launiopoko, the highway briefly recedes from the sea as you pass through the tiny community of Olowalu. At **Olowalu Beach** (turn on the dirt road across from the French restaurant, near mile marker 15), you'll find outstanding snorkeling when the ocean is calm. Check out the "Turtle Cleaning Station," a spot where turtles congregate to have a small hungry fish called a cleaner wrasse nibble algae from their shells, about 225 feet offshore. When a swell is running, you'll find outstanding surfing, but it's for expert surfers only. And, all year long, you'll find signs that say: WARNING. SHARKS MAY BE PRESENT. SHARK BITES HAVE OCCURRED IN THIS AREA. They were posted in 2002 following the third shark attack here in 12 years, one of them fatal. Even if you're not inclined to go in the water, Olowalu is worth a stop. It has the remains of an old sugar mill to explore, ancient petroglyphs nearby, and quiet places to sit in the shade, look for dorsal fins, and brood on Olowalu's history of blood in the water. In addition to the shark attacks, this was the site of an infamous massacre in 1790, in which an American merchant ship, to avenge the death of a sailor, opened fire on several hundred innocent Hawaiians who paddled out in canoes to trade.

Car Break-Ins

Car break-ins are a perennial problem at beaches throughout Hawaii, and Maui's no exception. Rental cars are prime targets. Hiding valuables under the seat, in the visor, or in the trunk will not protect them. The thieves just assume you've done this and break in anyway. The best strategy is to leave the car unlocked with nothing in it.

Along the Lahaina shoreline, you'll find a small boat harbor, a seawall, and plenty of beachfront with near-shore reefs that can lacerate your toes. For a better place to take a dip, head north of town to the world-renowned **Kaanapali Beach,** which fronts the six grand hotels of the Kaanapali resort. A paved walkway runs from Hanaka'o'o along Kaanapali Beach for more than a mile, past beachside bars, restaurants, and concessionaires offering catamaran rides, parasailing trips, surf lessons, and beach-gear rentals. Kaanapali Beach continues on, but the walkway ends at **Black Rock,** which teems with fish and tourists and has a reputation as one of Maui's best snorkeling spots.

The ancient Hawaiians called Black Rock Pu'u Keka'a and knew it as a "souls leap," a place where the spirit of a dying person would come to cross into the afterlife. This spot may have once served the ethereal, but the stretch of beach just south of it clearly belongs to the corporeal. Dubbed **"Dig Me Beach"** for its intense concentration of taut, tanned, flaunted flesh, this is a celebrated place to see and be seen. It's less crowded north of Black Rock.

The north section of Kaanapali Beach is sometimes referred to as **Kahekili Beach.** This beach has heaped up accolades over the years, including a 2003 ranking as "America's Best Beach" by "Dr. Beach," aka Stephen Leatherman, the beach-ranking coastal expert and professor at Florida International University in Miami, who's dedicated to promoting the balance between environmental quality and recreational use of the nation's beaches. Shortly after the award, strange sea conditions began eroding the sand, taking away America's Best Beach and panicking the hotels. But eventually, the beach returned on its own.

If you don't want to walk up to Kaanapali Beach from Hanaka'o'o Beach Park, try the more convenient parking lot at Whalers Village shopping center, next to The Westin Maui hotel. It has a few free beach parking spots if you know to ask the parking attendant about them; otherwise, you can buy something at the shopping center and get validation, or just pay to park ($3 per hour, $25 per day). There's also a small public parking area next to the public path leading to the beach along the north side of the Kaanapali Beach Hotel, but it fills up fast. The fourth option is to park at the quiet, north end of Kaanapali Beach, at **Kahekili Beach Park.**

Near-shore reefs along the 3 miles of coast north of Kaanapali Beach make swimming conditions poor, with a few exceptions. Nonetheless, the beaches are beautiful, great for sunbathing, and well used by the area's profusion of condo dwellers. The swimming situation changes at Napili Bay, at the start of a 3-mile coastline with five of Maui's best beaches on it. It starts with **Napili Beach** ★★★, a perfect, broad crescent of sand that's well protected by two rocky points, with great waters for swimming and gentle waves for frolicking, although every once in a while a big swell finds its way in and roughs things up. Visitors staying in the pricey Napili Kai Beach Resort on the north point, or in the cluster of more affordable low-rise condominiums behind the beach, make up the majority of Napili's beach-going populace. A lively, happy vibe prevails here, with footballs flying, sunscreen flowing, and whole families lying in the sand, letting the waves roll them up and down the beach like logs. There's not much public parking along the access road, Napili Place, but you might get lucky. The Napili Kai Beach Resort has a nice little outdoor bar with $7 mai tais, where you can sit without your shirt or shoes and still get service.

Around the north point lies another perfect crescent of sand, **Kapalua Beach** ★★. It's a bit smaller than Napili Beach, and even better protected from wind and swells. It has more coral and better snorkeling, and it has public restrooms and showers, which Napili Beach lacks. In 1991 this beach won Dr. Beach's very first America's Best Beach award, an honor the beach commemorates with a plaque near the showers. The Kapalua Bay Hotel Resort fronts the beach and supplies it with a steady crowd of sunbathers, swimmers, snorkelers, and kayakers. The hotel offers a convenient place to get an expensive lunch. There's also great whale-watching from the points, and that's free.

THE NORTH SHORE

The best Hawaiian island for windsurfing is Maui, and the Maui beach where you can learn how to do it is **Kanaha Beach Park** (kids), a 40-acre county park near Kahului airport with lifeguards, volleyball, canoe clubs, and camping (p. 257). Many of the island's windsurfing shops conduct classes here (p. 301). The winds are steady and strong, but not too strong, and they blow onshore, so if you completely screw up out there, at least you'll drift in the right direction. A far-offshore reef (on which experienced windsurfers like to jump waves) shelters the inside waters, leaving calm conditions for beginners. It's also shallow here, making it good for young kids. High-flying kiteboarders (it's not uncommon for them to soar 200 ft. above the waves) used to launch from here until the Federal Aviation Administration (FAA) clamped down after too many of them violated the no-fly zone around the airport's flight path. Now, through a compromise worked out between the FAA and the Hawaii Kiteboarding Association, kiteboarders launch from Kaa Point, just west of Kahana. The spot has been dubbed, logically enough, **Kite Beach** (from Kanaha, follow Amala Place toward Kahului), and it's the best place to watch this new extreme sport.

Farther down Hana Highway, you'll come to the north shore's most popular all-around beach, **H. A. Baldwin Park.** It's a well-used community beach park, near the funky town of Paia, featuring a soccer field, softball backstop, and a big pavilion where a celebration of some sort always seems underway. The beach is long and broad, with plenty of places to get away from the crowd. The bottom drops off quickly, making for good bodysurfing, but the waters can become rough and dangerous. There are lifeguards at the Paia end. It can be windy here, especially in the afternoon, when the strong gusts thwarted my attempts to read the newspaper. The park was named for Harry Baldwin, grandson of the missionary whose Lahaina home has become a museum (p. 279), and whose offspring became predominate members of Maui's sugar aristocracy.

Farther east on the Hana Highway, you'll come to **Hookipa Beach Park** ★ (2 miles past Paia), the preeminent sailboarding beach in Hawaii. It's also Maui's

Tow-in Surfing at Jaws

The wave at Jaws, aka Peahi, rose to fame with the birth of tow-in surfing in the 1990s. It breaks far offshore and only on the largest winter swells. The chances it will break while you're visiting Maui aren't good. But if you hit it right, and you happen to have four-wheel-drive, you might get to see it for yourself. (Bring binoculars, though—it breaks way out.) The cliffs where people watch from aren't easy to get to, and you have to cut across privately owned agricultural land to get there. Keep in mind that if people trash the place, the pineapple company that owns it might put up a gate. To get here from Paia, drive east on Hana Highway (Hwy. 36) to Hahana Road, between mile markers 13 and 14, on the left. Bear left at the fork in the road and continue to the end of the pavement, then continue on the dirt road along the gulch until you reach the coast. There's no beach here, but you'll feel safer up on the cliffs anyway.

most consistent surf break, with waves year-round, and monstrous ones in winter. When gusting winds turn the waves to slop, the sailboarders get Hookipa all to themselves. When the winds are light or dead, surfers savor the glassy conditions, while sailboarders tend to neglected areas of their lives ashore, or mope on the beach. Most of the time, though, both sailboarders and surfers are out, and they've had to learn to get along. The swimming is terrible here, but there's nowhere better to get the flavor of Maui's surf-and-wind-stoked beach culture. Hookipa has a narrow sandy beach with many rocks, a pavilion, showers, restrooms, lifeguards, and two parking lots. It's good form to park in the upper lot and leave the lower spaces for the surfers, sailboarders, and all their gear. Plus, the upper lot offers a better vantage point for watching the action at sea.

The arduous winding road to Hana passes waterfall after waterfall, but you won't find a decent beach to sit on until you reach **Wainapanapa State Park,** right before Hana. A small, steep, black-sand beach here plunges into deep sparkling waters so blue they're practically black sometimes. This beach can be treacherous for swimmers, but it's a great place to explore, situated as it is on a jagged a'a lava coastline. During calm days, a small cave at one end demands investigation. Duck through the low entrance and you'll find a chamber with a ceiling high enough to stand upright beneath, with waves rolling in through a second entrance open to the sea. Along the rugged shore, you'll find sea stacks, a blow hole, a stone arch, and colonies of seabirds. There's also a native hala forest, a Hawaiian burial ground, a legendary water-filled cave, a *heiau,* and an ancient coastal trail that leads to Hana, plus campgrounds and cabins (p. 257). A strong sense of old Hawaii hangs over this place, something that's not so common in modern Hawaii anymore.

In Hana itself, along Hana Bay and at the base of a 390-foot-tall red cinder cone called Kauiki Hill, local kids love to swim at **Hana Beach Park.** You'll also find **Maui Ocean Activities** (☎ 808/667-2001) here, an outfit renting kayaks and offering surf lessons and snorkel tours (p. 305). There's a far more exotic—and hard to reach—place to swim on the other side of Kauiki Hill, where a large section of the cone collapsed and created **Kaihalulu Beach,** or simply Red Sand Beach (the trail begins at the end of Uakea Rd.). Loose cinders make it easy to lose your footing on the steep, treacherous trail. (Some unlucky beachgoers have been seriously injured and even killed along it, so please be careful.) It takes about 15 minutes to hike. If you make it to the end, you'll find a secluded little cove with vibrant red sand and a jagged wall of lava sheltering the beach from the surf's direct hits. Kaihalulu means "roaring sea," and it's wise to take heed; even the protected water here can churn restlessly. The trail crosses private property belonging to the Hotel Hana Maui, and one confused sign at the trail head sends a mixed message: NO TRESPASSING AND USE AT YOUR OWN RISK. If the trail is muddy, don't risk it. Otherwise, you should still walk cautiously and leave your modesty behind: Owing to Red Sand Beach's seclusion, charm, and tradition, swimsuits routinely come off here.

THE TOP SIGHTS & ATTRACTIONS

The sights and attractions of Maui fall into several distinct categories.

ANCIENT MAUI

Although far too many ancient Hawaiian archaeological sites have been lost to cities, hotels, and houses, many physical traces of ancient Hawaii remain. Some of the most enduring are the rock temple foundations of *heiau,* ancient Hawaiian places of worship and sacrifice. *Heiau* were numerous and dedicated to a variety of purposes—fishing, agriculture, fertility, surfing, rain. A few were built especially for human sacrifice. Kahuna, the priests who mediated affairs between the mortal world and the gods, tended them all.

Maui has the largest and most impressive surviving *heiau* in the entire island chain, **Piilanihale Heiau** ★★. Built in the 16th century by King Piilani (who also built the King's Hwy., a coastal trail that once circled the island), this massive seaside war temple on the Hana coast stands 50 feet high in places and covers an area as large as two football fields. Try to imagine it adorned with wooden fencing and thatched *hales*—features that didn't survive but that would have been found when the *heiau* was in use. Jungle swallowed the site until the 1970s, helping to keep its existence secret from all but a handful of Native Hawaiians. The ethno-botanical **Kahanu Gardens** (a half mile down Ulaino Rd., off Hana Hwy. near mile marker 31; ☎ 808/248-8912; Mon–Fri 10am–2pm; $10 adults, free for children 12 and under), part of the National Tropical Botanical Gardens, has since grown up around the *heiau.* You can take a wonderful self-guided tour of the whole place, which is filled with tropical plants that include 130 cultivars of the breadfruit tree. Stream flooding periodically closes the gardens, so call ahead to be sure it's open.

Two more easily accessible *heiau* sit on a hilltop near Wailuku, with a sweeping view of central Maui and Kahului Bay. One of the twin temples at **Halekii-Pihana**

Finding Places to See & Go

The sights & attractions in the following sections can be found on the maps starting on p. 228.

> ### Human Sacrifice
>
> According to mid-19th-century Hawaiian writer Samuel Kamakau, a typical human sacrifice went something like this: After the victim was killed, the corpse was reddened over a fire, then placed face down with the right arm wrapped around a pig and the left hand holding a bunch of bananas. A high chief used a ceremonial hook to pierce the mouth, then recited a chant offering the sacrifice to the gods. Afterward, those assembled listened carefully for the sound of a bird, a rat, or a lizard—the gods' acknowledgement that the sacrifice had been accepted.

Heiau State Monument (at the end of Hea Place off Kuhio Place from Waiehu Beach Rd.; 8am–7pm; free) was dedicated to human sacrifice—though not just any human sacrifice. You had to be *alii* (royalty) of the purest lineage to be sacrificed here. The last sacrifice is believed to have been performed by Kamehameha in 1790, to honor his war god after he vanquished Maui's army. (Kamehameha had wanted a high Maui chieftess who had offended him at Kaupo at the center of the ceremony; he sent for her, but her foster sister arrived instead and took her place.) When you're looking around, keep in mind that this isn't a pristine archaeological site. One of Kamehameha's widows, Queen Kaahumanu, had one of the *heiau* demolished after she converted to Christianity. A road and a waterline later cut through the site, and a bunker was built here during World War II to defend the island against a possible Japanese attack. In 1958 the Maui Historical Society reassembled the demolished *heiau* and restored the other as best it could.

Deeply cut into the West Maui Mountains behind Wailuku, **Iao Valley State Park** (end of Ian Valley Rd.) has an inviting network of paths for strolling and picnicking. A lively stream cascades through the valley and an enormous 2,250-foot felty-green basalt pillar, the Iao Needle, rivets everyone's attention. The tranquillity of the place belies its bloody history. This is where Kamehameha, during his drive to conquer the island chain, smashed Maui's army in 1790. The bodies of so many Maui warriors ended up in the stream that the battle was named Kepaniwai, "the damming of the waters." Maui's defenders may have been motivated in their fight to the death by a prophesy warning that if an enemy succeeded in entering Iao Valley, where generations of *alii* were buried, the Maui kingdom would fall and its way of life would end—which is exactly what happened.

MAUI'S NATURAL WONDERS

In contrast to the misty green interior of Iao Valley, the south shore's **Ahihi-Kinau Natural Area Preserve** is a dry, desolate, largely barren landscape where lava poured into the sea during Haleakala's last eruption. (Most sources give the date as 1790, but recent radiocarbon dating puts the last eruption between the years 1480 and 1600.) The preserve—where taking fish, rocks, sand, or any other part of the natural world is prohibited—includes some of **La Perouse Bay,** where the first known Westerners (the French in this case) appeared on Maui. Jean Francois de Galaup de La Perouse and his crews anchored two frigates here one night in

1786 before sailing on and ultimately disappearing with all hands (their fate was a mystery until 2005, when divers found evidence that the expedition ran aground in the South Pacific on a reef off the Solomon Islands). A coastal trail along the shore of La Perouse Bay cuts through the extensive remains of the **Hawaiian fishing village of Keoneoio.** From the trail (from which you should not stray), you can see numerous stone walls, housing and canoe-shed foundations, a *heiau,* a fishing shrine, and grinding depressions. The snorkeling is fantastic here when waters are calm. And the inaccessible island of Kahoolawe looms 7 miles offshore.

MAUI'S CULTURE & HISTORY

An excellent and more budget-oriented way to learn about Hawaii from Hawaiians, and to paddle a canoe while you're at it, is with the 2-hour tour offered by the Hawaiian cultural group **Maui Nui O Kama** ★★ (Kealia Park on North Kihei Rd., next to Kealia condominium; ☎ 808/242-8536 or 808/276-7219; daily 7:30–9:30am; $40 donation). The tour begins with a Hawaiian chant, followed by an overview of the sacred names of the various components of a canoe, which is followed by paddling instruction. Then you board one of three canoes and paddle off to the wetlands, where you hop out to explore. Next you paddle out to investigate a coral reef (jokingly known as "the Hawaiian fridge" for its abundance of readily accessible seafood). Along the way your guide covers a variety of topics, including native species and ecosystems, the *ahupuaa* land-use system, how Hawaiians fished and farmed by the lunar calendar, and how invading forces could tell a weak chief from a strong one by the condition of his fishponds (and thereby determine the strength of the resistance they could expect at a particular locale). Call for reservations.

You'll find a unique collection of ancient Hawaiian artifacts in Hana at the **Hana Cultural Center and Museum** (4974 Uakea Rd.; ☎ 808/248-8622; Mon–Fri

Maui's Closest Neighbors

From South Maui, two neighbor islands dominate the horizon. The one on the right is Lanai (see chapter 5), which was once dedicated to pineapple cultivation and is now home to posh resorts. The dry dome-shaped island to the left is Kahoolawe. From World War II until 1990, the U.S. Navy used this uninhabited island as a bombing range for aircraft and ships, giving the island its former nickname, the Target Island. During the 1970s, Kahoolawe became a rallying point for Native Hawaiian activists, who wanted the bombing stopped and the land restored. Protests, arrests, lawsuits, and the death of two activists lost at sea while trying to paddle surfboards to the island followed. Finally, in 1990, the military stopped bombing and began cleaning up unexploded ordnance. In 1993, the island was conveyed to the state, and restoration work has continued since then. State law limits use of the island to noncommercial cultural, scientific, and educational purposes.

A Hawaiian Cultural Immersion & All-You-Can-Eat Buffet

Hoomanao ★★★ (kids) (1251 Front St., Old Lahaina Luau grounds, across from Cannery Mall; ☎ 800/248-5828 or 808/667-1998; www.oldlahainaluau.com; Wed and Fri 8:30–11:30am; $69 adults, $49 children 12 and under) is part luau, part breakfast buffet, and part hands-on trip through Hawaiian history and culture. After a hula and a breakfast including kalua pig, scrambled eggs, and coffee, you move through three stations, or kulana. In the hula kulana, you see how the dance was more to early Hawaiians than simple entertainment. It recorded genealogies, chronicled history, and honored gods, as well as titillated. You can learn a few hula moves if you like, or just keep time with a gourd or rattle. In the warfare kulana, you learn about the nature of battle in Hawaiian society, and you get to examine reproductions of ancient Hawaiian weapons such as clubs, shark-tooth daggers, slingshots, and spears (which you're invited to throw). In the third kulana, you explore the native Hawaiian land-use system, the *ahupuaa* (so named because the district boundaries were marked by piles of stone, *ahu,* topped by the heads of pigs, *puaa*). Here you'll see how Hawaiians fished using throw nets, created tapa cloth by pounding bark, and made poi by pounding taro root (and you'll get a chance to try your hand at each of these). This program is a fun and filling (thanks to the all-you-can-eat buffet) way to learn about ancient Hawaii. The unusual hands-on activities can captivate even the most ardent history-hating kid.

10am–4pm; $3 admission, free 12 and younger). The everyday nature of many of the items—a grater for shredding coconut, brooms made from the spines of palm fronds, a hooked lomilomi stick that people used to massage their own backs—helps to bridge the distance from ancient times to ours. On the grounds, you'll also find excellent examples of various Hawaiian *hales* (houses)—a living *hale,* a meeting *hale,* a cooking *hale,* a menstrual *hale*—plus the tiny **Hana District Police Station, Courthouse,** and **Jail.** The old jail, basically a wooden shed with a heavy door, has been decommissioned. But a judge still drives from Wailuku to hear cases at a desk in the pint-size courthouse, which does double duty as the police station, on the first Tuesday of every month.

Maui's best collection of Native Hawaiian artifacts resides in an old missionary home in Wailuku, the **Bailey House Museum** ★★★ (2375-A Main St.; ☎ 808/244-3326; www.mauimuseum.org; Mon–Sat 9am–4pm; $5 adults, $4 seniors, $1 children 7–12, free for children 6 and under). It also boasts an extensive collection of missionary-era artifacts and furnishings, as well as the beautiful oil paintings of Edward Bailey, a missionary teacher whose landscapes provide a surprising documentary record of Maui in transition from 1866 to 1896. Notice the Western-style buildings outnumbering traditional Hawaiian shelters in many of his canvases. The museum grounds abound in native plants.

Walking Tour: A Missionaries & Whalers Walking Tour of Historic Lahaina

Start: The Richards House site, across Front Street from the Pioneer Inn, in the heart of historic Lahaina.
Finish: Hale Pai, at the end of Lahainaluna Road.
Best Time: Morning.
Worst Time: Heat of the day.

The **Lahaina Restoration Foundation** (☎ 808/661-3262), a nonprofit group responsible for saving and now managing much of historic Lahaina, publishes a pamphlet called "Lahaina O Moolelo: A walking tour of historic and cultural sites in Lahaina, First Capitol of the Kingdom of Hawaii" (available at the Baldwin Home Museum and many other historic sites around town; free). It has a map, two recommended walking tours (one takes 30 min., the other 1½ hr.), and descriptions of 30 sites—more than most people get around to seeing. But if you aren't inclined to do the whole thing, just head straight for the highlights:

1 The Richards House site

The walking-tour brochure describes this as the homesite of a missionary, the Rev. William Richards, but today you'll find a pleasant little park in its place. This tranquil place is a good spot to duck into, out of the stream of tourists marching up and down Front Street. You can just sit in the cool shade of a palm tree, stare out upon Lahaina's sparkling waters, and reflect on history. Consider this: Angry whalers once maneuvered their ship just offshore and fired insults and cannonballs at this spot. They did this after Richards, Lahaina's first Protestant missionary, persuaded the Hawaiian *alii* to prohibit women from visiting ships. This house survived the cannonade, but has been lost to time.

Next door is:

2 The Baldwin Home Museum ★★

This stately old missionary home (and the oldest Western-style structure on Maui) has a role similar to the Bailey House Museum in Wailuku. Within its 3-foot-thick walls of lava rock and coral block, missionary doctor Dwight Baldwin treated ailing Hawaiians, raised six baby Baldwins, and inadvertently started one of Hawaii's most powerful commercial dynasties. As a museum, located in the tourist-thick heart of Lahaina, it has all sorts of furnishings and artifacts from the missionary era, as well as kindly volunteers who turn into deep wells of history if given the chance. Check out the trellises behind the house; the grapes that Mother Baldwin planted still grow on them. (The museum is open daily 10am–4pm. $3 adults, $2 seniors, $5 families.) For more information, call ☎ 808/661-3262 or go to www.lahainarestoration.org.

Next door to the Baldwin Home, on the corner of Front St. and Dickenson St., is:

3 The Masters' Reading Room

This was an old missionary storehouse that was rededicated as a hangout for ships' officers, filled with newspapers,

Lahaina Walking Tour

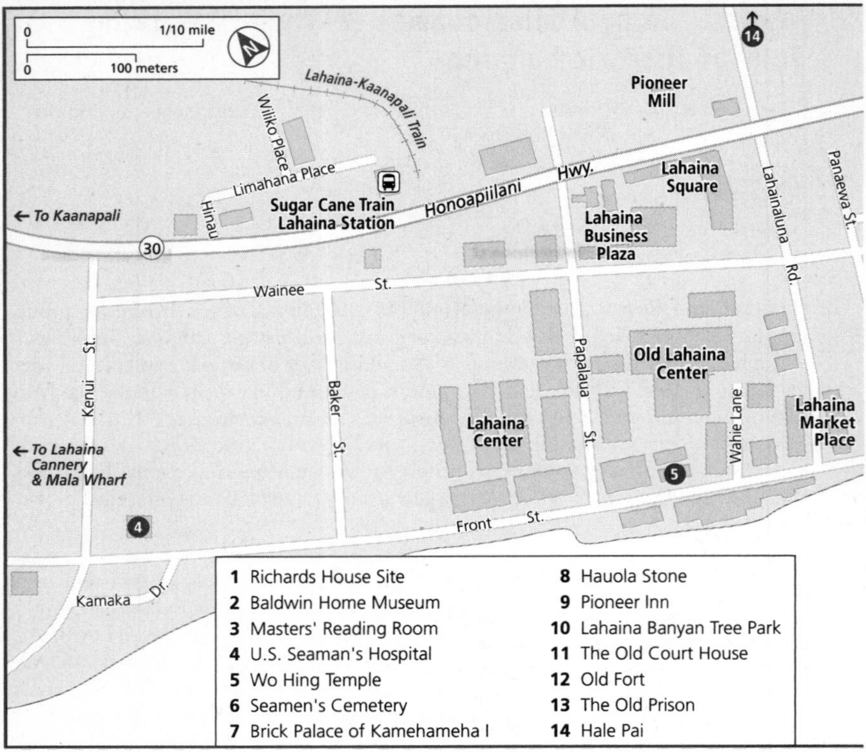

Bibles, and other wholesome reading material. With the Baldwins dwelling right next door, you know the masters couldn't have gotten too rowdy here. For that, they might have gone down the street to site no. 4.

About a half-mile north on Front St. (you're forgiven if you decide to drive) is the:

❹ U.S. Seaman's Hospital

This site at 1024 Front St. was built as an inn by King Kamehameha III for visiting seamen, and it was also one of his favorite places to drink, gamble, and spend time with his beloved sister, Nahienaena. To the horror of the missionaries, he was romantically involved with her (an ancient practice among the *alii* that had yet to die out). The U.S. government leased the inn from the king in 1844 for use as a seamen's hospital, and that's how the building is known today, as the U.S. Seaman's Hospital. Today it houses a television production company, so, unfortunately, you can see it only from the outside.

On your way to or from the Seaman's Hospital, you'll pass 858 Front St., which is the entrance to:

❺ The Wo Hing Temple ★

Built in the early 20th century by Chinese immigrants, under the auspices of the Chee Kung Tong, sort of the Chinese version of the Masons, the

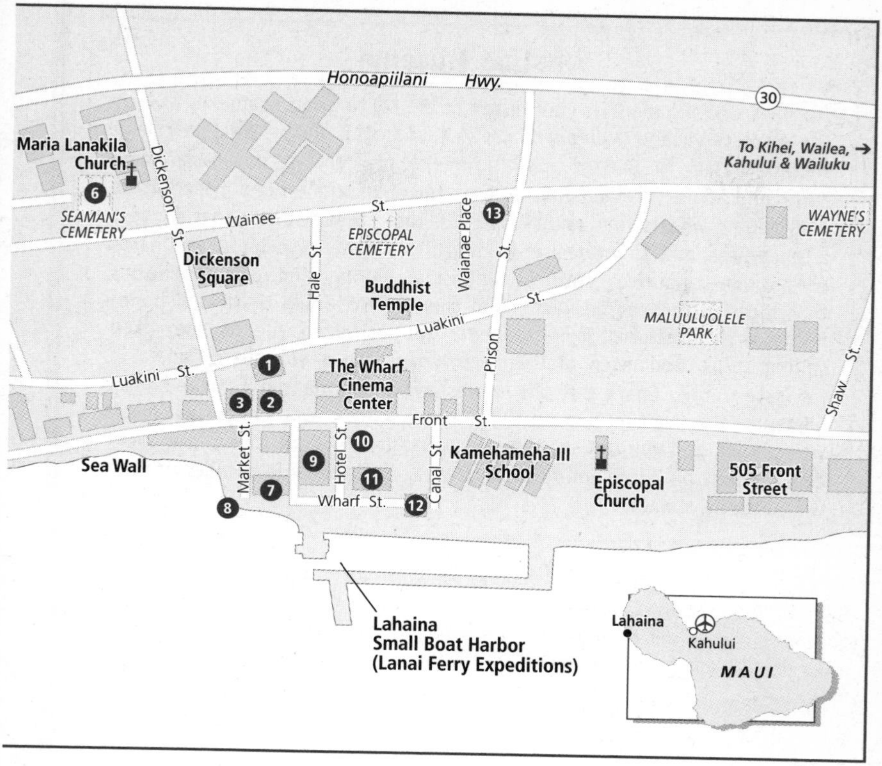

Wo Hing Temple place (☎ 808/661-3262; daily 10am–4pm; $1 admission) was originally designed as a fraternal meeting hall and social club. By the 1940s, though, most Chinese had moved from Maui to Honolulu, where the business opportunities were better, and the building became a home for Chinese old folks. There's a Taoist altar upstairs and a few interesting artifacts in the main building, but the real attraction is in the cookhouse next door, and it has nothing to do with Chinese immigrants or food. In the cookhouse, amid the enormous woks and other early-19th-century cooking implements, is a big-screen TV continuously showing rare movies of Hawaii shot by Thomas Alva Edison between 1898 and 1906. You'll see Honolulu street scenes (including an extended shot taken from a moving street car), Honolulu Harbor in the days when it was still filled with tall ships, and Hawaiians on horseback all dressed up, bedecked in leis and riding off to a big luau. In a long pan across Waikiki Beach, watch for a sloped-shoulder older guy walking toward the camera in coat and a straw boater—that's Edison's cameo shot. The cookhouse is a quiet, shady place where you can not only find respite from the hustle and bustle of modern Lahaina, but also come away with a strong impression of old Hawaii.

Whaling Museum

If Maui's whaling era stirs your imagination, try to go to Kaanapali to visit the **Whalers Village Museum** ★ (2435 Kaanapali Pkwy., at Whalers Village shopping area; ☎ 808/661-5992; 9am–10pm; free). It showcases some surprising artifacts—including an assortment of whale-bone pie crimpers and jagging wheels that sailors made for their sweethearts—that suggest a tenderness, and an interest in baking, that's rarely associated with hardened whalers. Nautical, political, whimsical, gloomy, and romantic themes that recur in their scrimshaw (hand carvings on whale teeth and bone) reflect their loneliness, joys, interests, and obsessions. Clearly, they liked sailing ships, and much of their scrimshaw dwells on square-riggers in intricate detail. Check out the scrimshaw of Alwida the Female Pirate. Somehow the museum dug up the original source from which this image was copied, and you can see the print version of Alwida, found in a 19th-century book on Dutch and Norman pirates, displayed side by side with the whale-tooth version.

Turn off Front St. onto Lahainaluna Rd., and make a right onto Wainee, where you'll come to:

6 The Seamen's Cemetery

Some of the patients who didn't do well at the U.S. Seaman's Hospital, or who died at sea before reaching Lahaina, lay at rest here. They include a cousin of Herman Melville, as well as one of Melville's shipmates (felled by a "disreputable disease"). Only a few marked graves remain.

Make your way back to the Baldwin Home, cross Front St., and walk down the lane toward the harbor, where you'll find a depression in the ground known as:

7 The Brick Palace of Kamehameha I site

Like the Richards House, Kamehameha's Brick Palace is another place on the official walking tour that isn't actually there, though in this case, its outline remains. Kamehameha was fascinated with the idea of Western-style buildings. When two British ex-convicts found their way to Hawaii after doing time in Australia, Kamehameha had them build a two-story, 20-by-40-foot palace, sometime between 1798 and 1802. The king used the building to welcome the earliest sea captains who found their way to Maui. He tried to give the palace to his favorite wife, Queen Kaahumanu, but she wasn't as enamored of brick-and-mortar as her husband and wouldn't stay there. Later, the building served as a warehouse and a meetinghouse, until it collapsed about 70 years after it went up. The footprint of the building was unearthed in the 1960s and lined with brick and concrete, which is what you see today.

A few steps away from the palace and over the seawall in the ocean, you'll find:

8 The Hauola Stone

It's the boulder with a vague similarity to a couch. It was used as a birthing stone for *alii* and probably for healing as well. Such stones exist all over Hawaii, but most of them have been forgotten. The memory of this one, thanks to its central location, endures.

The big green building beside you, on the corner of Wharf and Hotel sts., is:

9 The Pioneer Inn

This is the oldest hotel in Hawaii. The original structure, facing the harbor, was built in 1901. A large addition, built in the same style as the original, dates to 1965. The rooms in the old section are now used as apartments for the hotel staff—they're too dilapidated for guests—but the front desk, bar, and restaurant still inhabit the original structure. The Pioneer Inn is the only site on the historic walking tour that serves alcohol (if you need a short break, grab a beer in the bar and join the colorful mix of visitors and townies that frequent the place). Through much of the 20th century, the Pioneer Inn was at the center of Maui partying and debauchery. Today it's a Best Western property, and, for better or for worse, it has shaken much of its seediness. For a taste of how things used to be, check it out at Halloween, when Lahaina thinks it's New Orleans during Mardi Gras, and the old hotel sits once again in the middle of the ribald merriment. Call ☎ 808/661-3636 to get more information.

Across Wharf St. from the Pioneer Inn is:

10 Lahaina Banyan Tree Park

By 1873, the Protestant missionaries had finished their work, their children had become sugar barons and other prosperous citizens, and a golden anniversary was at hand. To mark the half-century that had passed since missionaries first arrived on Maui in 1823, Lahaina's sheriff planted an 8-foot-tall Indian banyan tree at a gathering spot by the water. It grew to fill ⅔ of an acre and serves as the psychic and arboreal center of town: Lahaina Banyan Tree Park.

Between the park and Lahaina Harbor sits:

11 The Old Courthouse

Originally used as a courthouse, a customshouse, a post office, the tax collector's office, and for all sorts of other civic purposes, this building now houses an art gallery, a visitor center, a gift shop, a nice whaling museum (where you can see the enormous ear bone of a sperm whale and great examples of 19th-century scrimshaw), and—this is worth a mental note—public restrooms.

On either side of the courthouse are the remains of:

12 The Old Fort

After the attack on the Reverend Richards's house, the Hawaiian government built a waterfront fort to answer, or better yet deter, rogue seamen should they feel moved to attack the town again. It was built from coral blocks removed from the ocean where the harbor is now. In reality, seamen laughed at the old fort, which seemed more suited for show than cannon battles. Mostly it was used as a prison. After the original was dismantled in the 1850s, its pieces were carted a few blocks away and reassembled into a more substantial prison. In the 1970s, using original coral blocks the county scrounged up somewhere, a replica of two corners of the old fort were built here, and that's what passes as the old fort today.

Walk down Prison St. to the corner of Wainee St., and you'll find:

13 The Old Prison ★★★

This sprawling 19th-century detention center, known as Hale Paahao or "Stuck-in-Irons House," takes up a whole block.

A wood-frame stockade at the center of the grounds has the tiny cot-size cells where prisoners, mostly seamen, served time for such offenses as reckless horseback riding, Sabbath violating, and drunkenness. Prisoners convicted of more serious offenses were shipped off to Honolulu.

14 Hale Pai

This is one point of interest on the historic walking tour that's too far from town to walk to. It's the printing shop the missionaries built at Lahainaluna Seminary. The seminary, founded in 1831 on a mountainside high above town, is now a public high school (Lahaina Luna High School campus, at the end of Lahainaluna Road; ☎ 808/667-7040; Mon–Fri 10am–4pm), and one with the distinction of being the oldest educational institution west of the Rockies. Inside the printing house, you'll find a replica of the original press along with examples of the thousands of Hawaiian-language Bibles, maps, textbooks, histories, children's readers, newspapers, laws, and whatnot the press churned out. The seminary's students were hired to work the press, so not only were they reading their lessons, they were printing them. Located 700 feet above Lahaina, the seminary was a safe distance from the licentious influence of the whaling port below, and Hale Pai is worth a visit for the view alone. But seeing the examples of the material created here is worth the visit, too. In one richly illustrated book called *Ka Olelo no ka Holoholona o Ka Honua,* or, *Explanation of the Beasts of the Earth,* you discover that kangaroo translates into Hawaiian as "kanegaroo" and reindeer becomes "reinadia." You also see that the missionaries work in Hawaii involved more than just thumping the Bible and suppressing the hula.

MAUI'S PLANTATIONS

Alexander & Baldwin Sugar Museum ★ (3957 Hansen Rd., Puunene, about 10 min. from the main airport; ☎ 808/871-8058; www.sugarmuseum.com; Mon–Sat 9:30am–4:30pm, but call to confirm seasonal hours; $5 adult, $2 children 6–17) is a proud, simple, enthusiastic monument to an industry that shaped and once dominated Maui. Occupying the former home of a plantation superintendent, the museum traces the spectacular feats of 19th-century engineering that brought water from east Maui rainforests to the arid isthmus, where most of the cane was planted. The museum also documents the technological twists and turns of extracting sugar from cane, and it pays tribute to the Chinese, Japanese, Portuguese, Filipino, and other immigrants who came to work in the fields and mills, and who forever altered Hawaii's racial and cultural mix. (I especially like the exhibit depicting one of the favorite pastimes of plantation workers—cock fights. When you look at the razor-sharp gaffes on the feet of the two birds frozen in taxidermic battle, it's not hard to imagine feathers flying in a real fight.) The museum is easy enough to find, located as it is outside of Kahului in the shadow of the sugar mill's towering smokestacks, which you can see from miles away.

Plantation life was kind of slow, and as theme parks go, so is the **Maui Tropical Plantation** (kids) (1670 Honoapiilani Hwy., Waikapu; ☎ 800/451-6805 or 808/244-7643; daily 9am–5pm). But if you're interested in agriculture, you would like to learn more about Hawaii's big mono-crops (sugarcane and pineapples), and you like spider monkeys, this 60-acre celebration of the plantation days is worth a stop. You can look around on your own for free, but it's better to take the narrated 40-minute tram ride ($11 adults, $4 kids ages 3–12) through pineapple and cane fields and a papaya orchard. Characters in plantation garb husk coconuts and demonstrate lei making. There's also a nice gift shop and a little restaurant, where comical spider monkeys keep the mood light.

MAUI'S ARCHITECTURE & ART

If you're in the neighborhood of the Maui Tropical Plantation, take a look at the nearby **Frank Lloyd Wright–designed clubhouse** (at the King Kamehameha Golf Club, 2500 Honoapiilani Hwy.; ☎ 808/244-2011). Wright didn't design the building for golfers, and he couldn't have known it would end up in Hawaii—but here it is. The Pennsylvania family it was designed for never built it. Movie star Marilyn Monroe and her literary husband, Arthur Miller, bought the plans with the intention of building the house in Connecticut, but they split up before getting to it. The Japanese billionaire who built this golf course bought the design and built what has become the only Frank Lloyd Wright–designed building in Hawaii. Wright, a genius at designing in harmony with nature, would have been aghast at how the clubhouse clashes with the landscape.

Before you get to Maui, I'd suggest that you go online and find out what will be happening when you're in the area at **Hui Noeau Visual Arts Center** (2841 Baldwin Ave., Makawao; ☎ 808/572-6560; www.huinoeau.com; daily 10am–4pm; free but donations welcome). A Mediterranean-style plantation mansion (built by those Baldwins again) on the green upcountry hills outside of Makawao, Hui Noeau gets six to eight outstanding art exhibits a year. I saw one called "Wood Skin Ink," which explored the close and colorful relationship between Japanese woodblock carvers, painters, and tattoo artists. Hui Noeau also has regularly scheduled talks by visiting artists, as well as an ongoing series of classes and 1-day workshops (p. 299), which the grounds have been modified to accommodate. The old horse stable, for instance, is now the ceramics studio; the carriage house has become the print studio; and adjoining spaces have been turned into woodworking and jewelry studios.

To see one of the finest permanent art collections on Maui, head to the **Grand Wailea Resort, Hotel & Spa** ★★ (3860 Wailea Alanui Dr., Wailea). The Japanese billionaire who built the place has put much of his personal collection on display here, including works by Pablo Picasso, Andy Warhol, Fernand Leger, and Fernando Botero, as well as Hawaii artists like Herb Kane. You don't have to be a hotel guest to view the collection, and there's no charge. But if you want to park here, you have to surrender your car to the valet, and that traditionally involves a tip upon its return. Of course, you can also park for free at one of the public beach-access parking lots between hotels—look for the county's blue beach-access signs—and walk along the shore to the Grand Wailea. Once you get there, go to the concierge desk and ask for the Art Directory, a free guide to all of the works on display. You won't have any trouble finding Botero's bronze sculptures. Botero clearly likes women—large, languorous, nude women—and you'll see several of them lounging around the main courtyard, surrounding the Botero Bar. Botero's *Woman Smoking a Cigarette,* (she lies on her stomach puffing away, one foot daintily lifted) is the size of a midget submarine. Be sure to step into the bar's pavilion and look up at the ceiling, where you'll see Douglas Riseborough's marvelous merging of classical Italian *trompe l'oeil* with Polynesian characters and themes. In the hotel's **NaPua Gallery** (☎ 808/874-0510 or 800/800-6554; www.napuagallery.com), you'll find 13 of Warhol's Marilyn Monroes and a set of 18 original Picasso lithographs in which two classic figurative nudes grow increasingly Picasso-like, the artist's study of his own evolution from realism to abstractionism.

MAUI'S OCEAN, SHORE & SEA LIFE

At press time, the U.S. Fish and Wildlife Service (www.fws.gov) had yet to open its new 2,200-foot-long boardwalk through the **Kealia Pond National Wildlife Refuge** (along North Kihei Rd., between Kihei and Maalaea; ☎ 808/875-1582). But once the boardwalk is opened (hopefully by the time you arrive), it will be

Whale Season

If you visit Maui from November through May, you'll be vacationing with the humpback whales that come here to procreate after spending the summer up north fattening themselves on Alaskan krill. They appear in waters off all the Hawaiian Islands, but they favor Maui's protected south and west shores. The early arrivals show up before Thanksgiving, the whole crowd turns out in February and March, and the die-hards hang around until spring. If you're here during peak season, you can't miss them—they're easily spotted from the shore. But prime viewing locations include **McGregor Point,** off Honoapiilani Highway between Maalaea and Lahaina, at mile marker 9. Farther toward Lahaina, pull off anywhere along the Honoapiilani Highway after it drops down from the cliffs and you can watch them from your car. And, really, any oceanfront restaurant or bar on the south or west sides will be a good whale-watching post in peak season.

The other option is to get out on the water. Almost every tour boat on Maui takes people whale-watching, with prices ranging from $20 to $100. I like the 2-hour, $23 tours offered by the **Pacific Whale Foundation** (300 Maalaea Rd., Ste. 211, at The Harbor Shops at Maalaea; ☎ 808/249-8811; www.pacificwhale.org), a nonprofit conservation group that supports its work through whale- and dolphin-watching tours, snorkel trips, and sunset cruises.

Early or late in the season, it's possible to get "skunked," where you don't see any whales at all. Some boats will refund your money or give you tickets for another tour if a skunking occurs. A better situation is to get "mugged," where whales surround your boat, which is then prohibited by law from moving. If you get mugged by a "competition pod," you're floating among a group of amorous males competing for the interest of a female. They slap their flukes, smash their heads into one another, dive deeply, ascend rapidly, burst out of the water, and land with enormous splashes. The female may or may not notice, but everyone on the boat will.

Shark Diving & the Secret Sex Lives of Coral

If you're a certified scuba diver and yearn to swim with sharks—safely—the **Maui Ocean Center** (☎ 808/270-7075; reservations required) will let you dive in its shark-filled main tank on Monday, Wednesday, and Friday mornings at 8:30am. The $199 fee includes a tank, weights, and admission for one nondiving guest, so you've got someone to take pictures of your adventure. Though some 20 sharks live in the tank, they're too well fed to pose a threat to scuba divers.

Once each summer, a few days before the new moon in June or July, rice coral all over Hawaii reproduces in one simultaneous, ocean-wide, hermaphroditic blowout. Rice coral releases its own sperm and eggs together to mix in the ocean currents, and scientists can pinpoint—to the hour—when this will happen. That evening, the Maui Ocean Center throws "The Coral Spawning Spectacle" party, where wine and cheese are served while guests await the big moment. If you can't make it for the real thing, check out the video, "The Secret Sex Lives of Coral," playing in a dark corner of the Shallow Reef exhibit, loaded with highlights.

worth a stroll along—especially in the winter. (The delay is due to several problems; among other things, the contractor used nails rather than screws on the recycled planking material, and boards were popping up right and left).

Kealia Pond is a 691-acre saltwater marsh and bird sanctuary, which attracts 30 species of waterfowl and shorebirds, including the endangered Hawaiian stilts, Hawaiian coots, ducks, egrets, herons, sanderlings, ruddy turnstones, wandering tattlers, and the Pacific golden plover, which shows up every winter after a 2,500-mile flight from Alaska. During summer the water levels drop and the pond may completely dry out, revealing why the Hawaiians called the area Kealia, or "salt-encrusted place." The dropping water levels also create an incomparable stench. The Hawaiians used this marsh as a salt pan as well as a fishpond.

Hawaiians stocked their fishponds by building gates to the ocean wide enough for juvenile fish to enter but too narrow for fully grown fish to get back through. You can see a full-scale working model of this, complete with fish, in the "Hawaiians & the Sea" exhibit at the **Maui Ocean Center** ★★★ (192 Maalaea Rd., The Harbor Shops at Maalaea; ☎ 808/270-7000; www.mauioceancenter.com; daily 9am–5pm, open until 6pm July–Aug; $20 adults, $17 seniors, $13 children 3–12, $13 military). This $20-million state-of-the-art aquarium is packed with marine life from Hawaiian waters, and it's definitely worth a visit.

The main attraction is an enormous 750,000-gallon tank filled with sharks, sting rays, thousands of fish, and, at regular intervals, divers who have communications equipment in their face masks so they can field questions from the crowd of visitors peering at them from outside the tank, as they hand-feed the sharks and rays. The outdoor exhibits include turtles, tide pools, and hammerhead sharks. The indoor exhibits organize marine life by depth: the shallow reef (0–30 ft.), midreef (30–60 ft.), and deep reef (60 ft. and beyond). Some of the creatures here are downright bizarre. I can't get over the garden eels; they burrow in clusters, never entirely leave their holes, but emerge enough to sway together in the current like tallgrass—or some uncanny grass/eel hybrid. So skittish are they, you have to view them through one-way glass. If they knew you were watching, they wouldn't come out.

I appreciate this aquarium's natural approach to displaying sea life. You won't find any killer whales trained to jump through hoops or seals trained to balance balls on their noses, but you will find naturalists trained to share facts like this: 80% of the reefs in the United States are in Hawaii; and Hawaii's state fish used to be the humuhumunukunukuapuaa (the triggerfish), but the designation expired and now Hawaii doesn't have a state fish.

Tip 1: The indoor exhibits are dark and cool and usually packed after 10:30am. To avoid the crowd, get here when the place opens at 9am. Also, avoid rainy days. When it rains, the ordinary attendance of 1,500 visitors per day doubles. ***Tip 2:*** The line to get in can take a while to get through. If you book online, you can skip the wait and walk right in. The only catch with online ticketing is that it requires an advance purchase of 3 days.

MAUI'S UNBELIEVABLE DRIVING TOURS

For visitors with cars, the island offers some remarkable and memorable drives.

Visiting the House of the Sun: Haleakala National Park ★★★

At the summit of Haleakala, you might find dazzling sunshine throwing crisp shadows across an otherworldly landscape while illuminating a god's-eye view of the Earth. Or you might find dark rains, frigid air, overpowering winds, and thick cloud cover. In either case, you'll encounter hundreds of tourists gathered atop this volcanic peak towering 10,023 feet above the Pacific because it's the foremost visitor attraction on Maui. Despite the masses, the summit experience can be intensely personal and moving—especially if the weather cooperates. This is one site you absolutely must see (unless a doctor advises against it—the National Park Service recommends that pregnant women, people with respiratory problems or heart conditions, or young children get a medical opinion before venturing to the top).

Ancient Hawaiians gave this mountain its name, which means "The House of the Sun," and they considered it especially sacred. In legend, they told of how the demigod Maui lassoed the sun here and beat it with a club in order to slow its trip across the sky and to give his mother longer days to dry her tapa cloth. Geologists tell of how Haleakala first emerged from the sea about a million years ago, growing taller and taller through a half-million years of continuous eruption, then shifting to its current mode of sporadic flows. The date of the last eruption is widely given as 1790. However, a recent radiocarbon study suggests it actually occurred sometime between 1480 and 1600. (Most literature on the subject, including what the National Park Service itself distributes, has yet to catch up with the science.) In any case, Haleakala is a dormant volcano, not an extinct one, and it is expected to go off again—someday.

At the top of Haleakala is a giant hole, 3,300 feet deep and 21 miles around, that was formed by erosion. The mountain once stood several thousand feet higher than it does now, but weather, gravity, and possibly glaciers brought it down a few notches and formed this enormous depression. Though it's actually a valley, in common usage it's become a crater.

Haleakala's summit sits along the crater rim. Most visitors are content to venture there and then turn around. A hardy and well-prepared subset strikes off on hiking trips around the crater floor, or sometimes through Kaupo Gap—one of two huge openings in the rim—and down the side of the mountain to the coast (p. 309). Others take a mule or horse and ride into the crater and back (p. 310). In the afternoon, clouds rising as the day warms typically pour in through the gaps and fill the crater like a giant bowl of cotton. As the day cools, the clouds spill out of the gaps and the crater drains.

If you can get up early enough, you should visit the summit for sunrise. The best time to do this is soon after you arrive on Maui, before your biological clock catches up with the later time zone you're in. It will be easier then to get moving around 3:30am, which is about when you'll need to leave to beat the sun. From Kihei, it takes about 2 hours to drive to the summit. If you can't make it for sunrise, the sunset on Haleakala isn't bad either. For a weather forecast and sunrise or sunset times, call the **National Weather Service** (☎ 808/877-5111). The *Maui News* also publishes sunrise and sunset times.

The summit is generally 30°F cooler than the coast, and it can drop to around freezing. When the weather turns cold, as it is prone to do, the underdressed huddle together, teeth a-chattering (you, of course, had the foresight to layer).

It's a steep drive to the top, up what's considered the steepest ascending road in the world—it climbs 10,000 feet in just 38 miles. Entry into Haleakala National Park costs $10 per car, and if you save the easy-to-lose receipt, you can come back and visit the Kipahulu section of the park (a long drive from the summit entrance, past Hana), without paying again. The entry fee is good for a week.

The first point of interest you'll pass, down a short spur road just inside the park gate, is **Hosmer Grove** ★, an old experimental forest planted with visions of a forest industry that never caught on. There's a short nature walk here, good for car-weary kids and adults alike.

Next, you'll come to the **Park Headquarters Visitor Center** (open 8am–4pm) located at 7,000 feet. I recommend stopping here for 15 or 20 minutes or so to get acclimated to the altitude. Nothing spoils a visit to the heavens quite like the nausea, lethargy, and headaches of altitude sickness. At Park Headquarters, are a gift shop, exhibits on how Haleakala formed, and outside, lots of nene, the endangered native geese that frequent the area.

At 8,000 feet, halfway from Park Headquarters to the top, is **Leleiwi Overlook** ★, one of the better lookouts along the way. With a short walk, it offers your first view of the crater. Sometimes, in the late afternoon, a bizarre optical phenomenon occurs here, the Brocken Specter, in which you see a reflection of yourself, surrounded by a rainbow, in the clouds filling the crater below you.

At 9,000 feet, you'll pass **Kalahaku Overlook,** but you can't pull out here until you're descending the mountain. This is a good place to get a look at the exotic silversword, a globe-shaped plant with rigid silver leaves, found only on Hawaii's three tallest volcanic peaks.

At 9,740 feet, very near the summit, is a big parking lot and the **Haleakala Visitor Center.** You're essentially at the top now. The visitor center is perched on the carter rim, stocked with postcards and books, and manned by a friendly ranger. This is a popular vantage point for catching the sunrise or sunset. For some solitude, make the short climb up to the top of Pa Kaoao, aka White Peak, standing beside the parking lot. Or walk a short way into the crater down Sliding Sands Trail, but watch your footing—it wasn't given its name for nothing.

To reach the actual summit, keep driving—at the very top of the mountain, there's a parking lot in the shallow bowl of a cinder cone just beneath the **Puu Ulaula Overlook.** This overlook, a glass-enclosed building open 24 hours, sits at the very uppermost part of the mountain. Naturalists here give 10-minute orientations daily, at 11am, 11:30am, and 12:30pm.

Warning: As you drive back down, use low gear so you don't ride the brakes and burn them out.

HANA & THE ROAD TO HANA

If you can stay a night or two in Hana, rather than making the arduous drive out and back in the same day, you should. This sleepy little Hawaiian community on Maui's far east side, with its rolling green hills, deep blue sea, and apparent absence of anything whatsoever to do, reveals itself only to those who take time with it. That's one reason to stay. The other is that a good part of Hana's appeal lies not in what you might find there, but in the ride it takes to get there, and the more unhurried the ride the better. An overnight stay can make the difference between a leisurely trip through the thick rainforest and a long, tiring one. It's only 54 miles from Kahului to Hana, but the four dozen one-lane bridges, the 10-to-15-mph speed limits, the hundreds of switchbacks, and the long caravans of rental cars slowing down for every waterfall draw out the distance.

The Hana Highway begins at **Kahului,** and it starts out widely, well paved, and well graded—but that all changes. The road is still good as it passes through the colorful little north shore town of **Paia** ★, well worth a stop for breakfast (by the way, you should leave early), and your last chance for gas (fill the tank before you go). Just beyond Paia, the road passes **Hookipa Beach Park,** the Windsurfing Capital of the World. The windsurfers don't usually show up in the morning, before the winds pick up, but Hookipa has good surf, too, and surfers live for early-morning glass. Hookipa has an upper and a lower parking lot; the upper one gets you out on the point, where you'll get the best view of the action in the water.

At mile marker 16 the road is still good, but some navigational confusion sets in. Hana Highway remains Hana Highway, but as a numbered highway it changes from Highway 36 to Highway 360, and the mile markers restart at zero. About 3 miles later the straight road crunches up like an accordion. But before the curves begin, after mile marker 2, you'll pass a pullout on the right filled with parked cars and possibly hippies selling fruits, along with arts and crafts. This is **Twin Falls.** The falls are on private property, and they're not a sanctioned tourist site, but the

Adjusting Waterfall Expectations in Droughts

It almost always rains along the lush northeastern side of the island that the Hana Highway traverses, but occasionally the weather goes dry. When it does, the larger falls may slow to trickles and smaller falls may dry up entirely. By the same token, when it pours, the falls can gush like nothing you've ever seen.

owners (you should drop a buck in their donation box) tolerate the hundreds of daily trespassers and let the hippies do their business. The walk to the first fall takes about 10 minutes, and the second fall takes about 15 minutes. If it's been raining heavily, don't go—the streams you have to negotiate will be swollen and dangerous (that goes for walks along all streams in Hawaii). If you've never seen a waterfall, the Twin Falls are nice enough, but bigger and better falls await down the highway.

Between mile markers 9 and 10, is a pullout on the right with a sign reading KOOLAU FOREST RESERVE. Stop here and stretch your legs on the **Waikamoi Ridge Trail** ★ kids, where there's a short, invigorating loop, good for kids, through a forest of eucalyptus, bamboo, and ginger. If you heed the sign that says QUIET, TREES AT WORK, you may hear the enchanting music the wind plays on the scimitar-shaped leaves of the eucalyptus. You may also hear the distant laughter and cries of people swimming in cold waterfall pools at **Waikamoi Stream,** about a mile down the road. Go there and you'll find a small waterfall just off the highway, and a larger one if you hike upstream a bit. If there's no roadside parking when you get there (this is a popular spot), just keep driving. There are plenty of other falls ahead.

Right past mile marker 12 is **Kaumahina State Wayside Park,** which has picnic pavilions, restrooms, and a great view up the coast to Keanae Peninsula. At mile marker 17, you'll come to the bluffs above Keanae Peninsula, where you'll also find **YMCA Camp Keanae** (which offers a campsite or a dormitory bunk for $17 per night; see p. 257). Just around the bend from the camp, you'll hit **Keanae Arboretum,** a free, somewhat ratty botanical garden with lots of native plants and some nice trails to stretch your legs on. The road down to **Keanae Peninsula** comes up right after the arboretum. On the peninsula, there's an age-old Hawaiian community, with a patchwork quilt of taro fields, swaying palms, and a church built of lava rock and coral mortar in 1860. It's one of the few old churches around that's usually left unlocked, and it makes a nice stop. Just keep in mind that this is a quiet rural community, not really a tourist attraction, so be on your best behavior. And if there's a church service in session, don't go in unless you're prepared to stay for the whole thing. If you don't want to take the time venturing onto the peninsula, you can get a bird's-eye view of the community and church from **Keanae Overlook,** just down the road.

Between mile markers 20 and 21, you'll come to **Wailua Overlook.** It peers out over the tiny settlement of Wailua, which has two churches: **St. Gabriel's,** the pink one, and the **"Coral Miracle Church,"** the white and blue one. The legend behind the latter goes like this: In 1860, the men of Wailua were diving for coral to build the church. The coral was in deep water, harvesting it was difficult, and the construction was barely crawling along. Then a freak storm came up and deposited a massive amount of coral onshore, more than enough to finish the church. When construction was complete, another freak storm came and reclaimed the leftovers.

Two great waterfall stops come up next: Just past mile marker 21, is **Waikane Falls,** one of the more voluminous waterfalls along the Hana Highway, and a triple cascade at that. Between mile markers 22 and 23, there's **Puu Kaa State Wayside Park,** which also has a roaring falls, plus a swimming hole and a picnic area.

The Subterranean Hana Coast

Maui Lava Tube ★★★ (turn left on Ulaino Rd., just after mile marker 31; ☎ 808/248-7308; www.mauicave.com; 10:30am–3:30pm Mon–Sat, and sometimes Sun) is one of the most extraordinary natural wonders on the road to Hana. Hawaii has hundreds of lava tubes, former underground expressways for fast-rushing molten lava, but only a few are accessible. This is not only the largest in the state, it's the 18th-largest cavern system in the world. For a reasonable $12 the owner, an enthusiastic spelunker, will outfit you with a hardhat, headlamp, and a giant flashlight and turn you loose in the cave on a self-guided tour, which you can do in about 40 minutes. The cave contains a series of chambers and passageways, with the ceiling height varying from 100 feet to 5 feet. The largest chamber is half the size of a football field. Along with all the stalactites and stalagmites are natural features named as if this were a ski run: Bowling Alley, Nina's Bypass, Little Buddha, Claustrophobia Check, Deadend Chimney. The route is well-marked, so you don't need to worry about disappearing into the bowels of the earth never to return. Bring something warm to wear, as temperatures inside the cave run from 64°F to 74°F (18°C–23°C). When you're inside, turn off your lights and see what it's like to sit in pure darkness.

Farther down Ulaino Road from Kaeleku Caverns, you'll find **Piilanihale Heiau and Kahanu Gardens** ★★ (Ulaino Rd., near mile marker 31 on the Hana Hwy.; ☎ 808/248-8912; Mon–Fri 10am–2pm; $10 adults, free for ages 12 and under). These ethno-botanical gardens surround the largest ancient Hawaiian temple in the state (p. 275).

Shortly before you roll into Hana, just after mile marker 32, you'll come to the turn for **Wainapanapa State Park** (p. 257), a 120-acre park with one of Maui's rare black-sand beaches, set in the back of a deep, protected cove. Wainapanapa's got all sorts of other attractions, as well, including several ancient Hawaiian sites, such as an old graveyard, a segment of the King's Trail (you can hike from here to Hana; see p. 308), and a swim-in lava tube with a periodic bloom of tiny red crustaceans and a curious legend attached (a plaque on-site tells the story, which I won't spoil for you).

Hana ★ is the kind of place that some people love and others hate. It's one of the most Hawaiian places on Maui, and if you're just blasting through in a car, you will always remember it as an utter backwater. But if you take some time there, you'll find there's much to see and do, including snorkeling in **Hana Bay,** or—if you're willing to risk the treacherous hike—lounging around on clothing-optional **Red Sand Beach** (p. 275). You can walk along the base of Kauiki Hill, out past Hana's crumbling old concrete pier, and visit the cave where Queen Kaahumanu, who shattered the ancient *kapu* system, was born.

Other top activities in Hana: the 2-hour kayak and snorkel tour of a reef off Kauiki Hill, offered by **Hana-Maui Sea Sports** (☎ 808/248-7711; gears up at 11am, returns by 2pm; $120). This tiny town also has a museum, the **Hana Cultural Center and Museum** ★ (497 Uakea Rd.; ☎ 808/248-8622; Mon–Fri

10am–4pm) which explores what daily life was like for Native Hawaiians for centuries before Western contact. Many enjoy the 3-mile hike to **Fagan's Cross** (p. 308), on a lovely hill overlooking the whole town and much of the coast.

Spend a night or two in **Hana** (see p. 256 for lodgings), approach the place in the right spirit, and you may discover that, backwater or not, it's one of the most interesting places on Maui. If you can't take me up on my good advice and you just tear through town, at least do what everybody else does: Stop at **Hasegawa General Store** (5165 Hana Hwy.; ☎ 808/248-8231) for snacks and an "I Survived the Road to Hana" T-shirt.

Ten miles beyond Hana is the Kipahulu section of **Haleakala National Park** (☎ 808/248-7375 for ranger station), one of the doglegs of the park stretching from the summit to the sea. There's no summit access from here, except by foot—and it's a long overnight hike uphill. What draws people here is **Oheo Gulch** and its spectacular series of waterfalls and pools, stepping down, one after another, through a steeply sloped rainforest to the sea. Sometimes the cold, clear mountain water cascading from one pool to the next makes for fantastic swimming. Other times, the pools turn into treacherous muddy torrents that have washed swimmers out to sea. Upslope, the mountain gets more than 300 inches of rain per year, and flash flooding is common. When dangerous weather looms, park rangers shut down the swimming. The other attraction in this part of the park is the hike on **Pipiwai Trail** ★, which passes several waterfalls before getting to the 400-foot **Waimoku Falls.** There's a $10-per-car park entrance fee at Kipalulu, which you'll pay when you try to park. But if you've been up to the summit of Haleakala in the past week, and you saved your receipt, you won't have to pay.

A mile past Oheo Gulch, visit the **grave of Charles Lindbergh,** first aviator to fly across the Atlantic Ocean. He retired to Hana, died there in 1974, and is buried at **Palapala Hoomau Congregational Church** (turn left on the road with the sign for the church, just after mile marker 41). From the aeronautic insignia and other little tributes left at his simple, Hawaiian-style grave, it's clear the spot has become a shrine of sorts for modern aviators. It's also a nice place for a picnic.

Most visitors, if they make it this far, turn back at this point and retrace their tracks along the Hana Highway. You can keep going around the backside of Haleakala, but the road has several unpaved sections, the first one of which will void most rental-car contracts, meaning if you break down, you're not entitled to a tow truck. If you go anyway, you'll find a dry, desolately beautiful stretch of coast that most Maui visitors don't see. ***Beware:*** During heavy rains, this road sometimes washes out. Check with the Maui County's recorded message on road conditions (☎ 808/986-1200 ext. 2).

THE OTHER MAUI

If you're curious about the aspects of Maui that visitors rarely encounter, the Maui that locals know and love, this is the section for you. The bulk of visitors tend to cover all of the same ground, see all of the same sites, and do all of the same things in a Maui that has been created especially for them. A separate but parallel Maui exists, where the island's residents live, work, and play—where they train for outrigger canoe races on glassy morning seas, grease up their pompadours and bowl the evening away, and hunt for wild pigs with knives and dogs. As a visitor, a slight effort on your part can yield new insights and possibly new friends.

VOLUNTOURISM

Trading your beach mat for gardening gloves and hand tools—at least for a few hours—is a surefire way to find a deeper connection to Maui than the typical tourist gets anywhere near. You hear people in Hawaii talking all the time about the importance of giving back to the *aina,* or the land, and as it happens, the *aina* of Maui is rife with opportunities to do just that. Every week local residents volunteer to help root out invasive species, restore native vegetation, protect Native Hawaiian cultural sites, clean up beaches, and protect marine life. They would love it if you joined them, and you see who really cares about Maui, meet local experts, and possibly get into parts of the island ordinarily closed to visitors. Perhaps you and a machete-wielding cadre of weekend warriors from a local bank will liberate a native forest from the stranglehold of the India rubber vine. Or maybe you and a spirited group of Kihei condo dwellers will deploy along a beloved coastal trail to keep it neat and clean. Whatever the case, bring your own water and snacks, and get ready to get down and dirty with the *aina.*

To quickly figure out what's on the volunteer calendar when you're on Maui, check with the **Pacific Whale Foundation** (☎ 808/249-8811; www.pacificwhale.org), which acts as a sort of "voluntourism" clearinghouse.

In addition to the seasonal calls for volunteers, there are standing opportunities to get involved that look like this:

Mondays: Join the **South Maui Volunteers** (☎ 808/874-9374; www.hoalohaaina.com) as they hit the Hoaloha'aina oceanside trail for their weekly

Tending Turtles

Volunteer a day or night with researchers from the **Hawaii Wildlife Fund** (☎ 808/575-2046; www.wildhawaii.org) and, perhaps, you'll get to see the hatching of a baby hawksbill turtle, the rarest turtle in the Pacific. Most of Hawaii's tiny population of nesting hawksbills (just 5–15 of them reproduce in a given year) prefer to lay their eggs on the Big Island's remote black-sand beaches, but a few favor Maui's powdery white-sand beaches. Dogs, cats, birds, mongoose, crabs, and even the misplaced steps of people threaten the nests, and traffic along the coastal highway threatens hawksbill mothers and hatchlings alike. In the 1990s, two egg-laden females and numerous hatchlings were killed by cars after straying onto North Kihei Road. Volunteer with the Hawaii Wildlife Fund and you may get to monitor the beach for nesting females, sit watch over their sandy clutches of eggs, or make sure the hatchlings reach the sea safely. If the hawksbills aren't nesting (nesting season runs from Apr–Nov), the more common green sea turtles may be, and volunteers keep watch over them, too. Throughout the year, endangered Hawaiian monk seals occasionally turn up on popular beaches to sleep in the sun after a night of hunting; Wildlife Fund volunteers make sure nobody disturbs their slumber. Call in advance with your travel plans. Donations are welcome.

A Hog-Wild Splurge

For an entirely different way to help the environment—and have a wild, bloody, quintessentially local experience at the same time—you can go on a pig hunt. The first Polynesians to settle in Hawaii brought pigs with them aboard their ocean-voyaging canoes. The Polynesian pigs have since mixed with Eurasian boars, creating a lean, black-tusked, ridge-backed feral breed that runs amok through Hawaii's forests. Their rooting damages native plants and creates breeding grounds for mosquitoes, which carry diseases that threaten native birds.

Local residents have been hunting these little terrors for generations, with the full support of the state and environmental groups like the Sierra Club, which endorses Hawaii's no-bag-limit open season on pigs. Hawaii's pig hunters prefer taking their quarry with dogs and knives, which leaves the pork in better shape than bullets do. The dogs bay the pig, and the hunters finish off the job by hand, with rifles for backup.

Maui Hunting Safari (☎ 808/573-8426; www.mauihuntingsafari.com) will take you pig hunting from sunrise to sunset for $875—not a bad deal for a guided hunt. The fee includes lunch, dogs, and your weapon of choice. If slitting a pig's jugular is too much, you can shoot it and nobody in attendance will think less of you. Up to three guests can go on the hunt, and parents hunting with kids get a 50% discount for the kids. The fee doesn't include the Hawaii State hunters license you need, which costs $105, and which Maui Hunting Safari is authorized to issue, provided you've brought your hunter's safety card from home. For information on licenses and other hunting-related matters in Hawaii, contact the **Department of Land & Natural Resources, Division of Forestry & Wildlife** (☎ 808/587-0166; www.hawaii.gov/dlnr/IdxHunting.htm).

maintenance party. Volunteers pick up litter, pull up the non-native species, prune kiawe trees, and in general leave the trail even more beautiful than they found it—and it's pretty beautiful to begin with. Meet at the Kihei boat ramp at 7:30am and work until 9am.

Tuesdays: Kanaha Beach Park is frequented by windsurfers, kiteboarders, fishermen, divers, sun seekers, and park beautification volunteers with the **Community Work Day Program** (☎ 808/877-2524 on Maui, or 888/592-2522; www.cwdhawaii.org). The park includes a beautiful stretch of white sand beach and some of the last remaining wetlands and sand dunes on the north shore, making it a stronghold for native plants and animals. Volunteers keep it all beautiful by attacking invasive species, planting native plants, and picking up trash. Meet at the park at 9am and work until noon. Bring your swimsuit so you can take a dip afterward.

Fridays: Once slated to become a golf resort, a spectacular 277-acre piece of coastline was saved from development by the **Maui Coastal Land Trust**

(☎ 808/244-5263; www.mauicoastallandtrust.org), which is restoring ancient Hawaiian fish ponds and taro patches there with the help of volunteers. Brush clearers, weed whackers, and invasive species removers are needed. Meet at the trust offices, 2371 W. Vineyard St., in Wailuku, at 7:45am and work until noon.

Saturdays: Lush Honokowai Valley was once filled with a series of terraced agricultural fields where farmers grew taro in ancient times. The valley is off-limits to the public today, but you can gain entry by joining in the on-going effort to stabilize archaeological sites there and replant native species. Meet at 9am in front of the North Sugarcane Train Station on Puukoli Road, in Kaanapali. Work until 2:30pm or so. Call the **Pacific Whale Foundation** (☎ 808/249-8811) to sign up.

Every third Sunday: Pacific Whale Foundation leads volunteers to Hosmer Grove in Haleakala National Park to take out invasive pine trees or play gardener in the park's native species nursery. Meet at the Pacific Whale Foundation's Ocean Store in Maalaea at 7:30am, and catch a lift to the park from there. The program wraps at 2pm, and includes time off for a short hike through Hosmer Grove.

MEETING THE PEOPLE OF MAUI

As in most places where tourists outnumber the locals, there are nooks and crannies where the locals go for a bit of their own space. Encroaching on these areas, however, is not verboten. Most Maui residents will welcome anyone imaginative and adventurous enough to venture into Maui's only bowling alley, **Maui Bowling Center** (1976 Vineyard St., Wailuku; ☎ 808/244-4596; open to the public Mon–Fri noon–4:30pm; $2.50 per game, $1 for shoe rental). Not only will you find yourself at the clamorous heart of a very local scene, you'll also find a window into half a century of island leisure life. With a few exceptions, such as the vintage 1980s video games (including Pacman and Ms. Pacman), this tiny 10-lane bowling alley has remained unchanged since it opened in the 1950s (as have some of the hairstyles). If pool is your game, **Family Billiards** (199 Dairy Rd., Kahului; ☎ 808/871-9313; daily 11am–1am; $4.10 per person per table) has a bustling local scene with 14 pool tables, as well as darts, video games, and one-of-a-kind "Family Billiards, Kahului, Maui" T-shirts, for $15. And if you've ever wondered what hula dancers do after work, you can find out for yourself at **Compadres Bar & Grill** (Lahaina Cannery Mall, 1221 Honoapiilani Hwy., Lahaina; ☎ 808/661-7189). That's where the young men and women who perform at the Old Lahaina Luau (p. 324), located just across the street, gather each night around 9:30pm to unwind after the luau wraps up. They all tend to be as friendly and approachable as they are when they're getting paid to be that way.

If you enjoy country fairs—and who doesn't?—**Maui County Fair** (War Memorial Complex, Wailuku; ☎ 808/270-7626; www.visitmaui.com) is a great place to talk turkey (or horticulture, or cattle) with the locals. It usually takes place in the last week of September or the first one in October. The same deep-fat fried hot dogs and cotton candy you'll find at mainland fairs sell side by side with local favorites like kalua pig, chow fun, and Portuguese bean soup. You'll see the same livestock and agricultural displays you'd find at mainland fairs, along with local horticultural exhibits featuring anthirium, orchids, and bonsai trees.

Community Radio

Tune in to Manao Radio (91.5 FM) for eclectic shows by volunteer DJs who love music but hate commercial radio, and may or may not have announcing skills. This low-powered community broadcaster has no reception on the farthest-flung parts of the island, like Hana, but with a high-speed Internet connection, you can listen to it anywhere in the world through www.manaoradio.com.

LOCAL SPORTS

If you're up for a workout and you're curious about outrigger canoes—the sleek watercraft of ancient Hawaii, built nowadays with modern lightweight materials so they go faster than ever—you can sometimes get a slot paddling with the **Kihei Canoe Club** (meets on the beach around 7:15am, next to the Kihei Beach condominium, south end of North Kihei Rd.; ☎ 808/879-5505; www.kiheicanoeclub.com). When it's not training for races, the club accommodates visitors who drop in during its Tuesday and Thursday morning recreational paddling sessions. A $25 donation is appreciated, and the chances of getting to paddle are hit-or-miss, depending on how many other drop-ins appear and how many experienced steersmen and strokers show up to accommodate them. The canoes hold six, including one steersman and at least one, but sometimes two, experienced strokers. Even if you don't get out on the water, this is still a good place to meet Maui residents with a passion for the sea and impressive upper body strength.

For those with an equine bent of mind, the **Maui Polo Club** (☎ 808/877-7744; www.mauipoloclub.com) takes to the fields every Sunday at 1:30pm in the spring and fall. Hawaii's *paniolo* have been riding here since before old Mexico's northern reaches became the new American West, and the level of horsemanship in the islands is high. That, combined with the aristocratic tendencies of the handful of families owning Maui's vast ranches, has resulted in a flourishing polo scene. From April through June, players compete in a small arena with wooden sideboards at the **Manduke Baldwin Polo Field on Haleakala Ranch** (Haleakala Hwy., just past King Kekaulike High School, on the left). From September through November, full-scale games are held at the **Olinda Polo Field** (a mile up Olinda Rd. from Makawao). Admission is $5, and gates open at 12:30am. A big Hawaiian-style party often follows the matches. During the Oskie Rice Memorial Tournament, held each Memorial Day, and during the High Goal Benefit, on the last Sunday of October, Maui riders pit their considerable skills against players from Argentina, Australia, England, New Zealand, and South Africa.

Another place to find horse people is at a Maui rodeo. With its deep *paniolo* heritage and dozens of working cattle ranches, Maui has no shortage of talented riders. The big event of the year is the **4th of July Makawao Rodeo** (Oskie Rice Memorial Arena, Makawao) organized by the Maui Roping Club. It draws top cowboys and cowgirls from throughout the state and the mainland for barrel racing, calf roping, bull and bronco busting, and all the other fixings of a good rodeo, including a big *paniolo* parade through the two false-fronted main streets of Makawao. Other big events include the **Oskie Rice Memorial Rodeo,** held the weekend after Labor Day, and the **Cancer Benefit Rodeo,** held in April. Some of the local high schools also hold rodeos. Check the events calendar in the weekly newspaper Maui Time for specifics.

MAUI-STYLE WORSHIP

Believe it or not, Maui has become a major outpost for Tibetan Buddhism, as you'll see when you visit the **Maui Dharma Center** (81 Baldwin Ave., Paia; www.mauidharmacenter.org). The prayer flags and Tibetan stupa out front, which looks a little like a big concrete wedding cake, tells you that the Hawaiian-style plantation home on the grounds is no ordinary Maui residence. It's actually a temple. It looks plain enough on the outside, but duck in and it's pure Himalayan rococo, all gilded Buddhas, silk tonkas, brocaded lanterns, and ornate prayer cushions, plus a couple of big, fat, sleepy temple cats. You're welcome to come by to meditate and pray daily between 6:30 and 7:30am and from 5 to 6pm, and on Thursday and Sunday from 10am to noon. The soft-spoken young Tibetan in silken robes you'll probably see running around is the resident monk, Lama Gyatsen.

For a more American style of worship, with a Hawaiian twist, attend a Sunday service at **Keawalai Congregational Church** (5300 Makena Rd., Makena; ☎ 808/879-5557; www.keawalai.org; services at 7:30 and 10am). Rev. Kealahou Alika conducts the service in both English and Hawaiian, which is fitting as Hawaiians themselves (not missionaries) founded this church in 1832. They started out with a grass hut. The building that stands today, with 3-foot-thick lava-rock walls, was built in 1855. This beautiful seaside church in sunny Makena has an old Hawaiian graveyard with headstones bearing ceramic photos of some of the members of congregations past.

For a taste of Maui's latter day pagan life, head for the biggest beach party on the island—the **Sunday drum circle at Little Beach** (p. 270). A crowded nude beach by day, Little Beach is the sight of a weekly gathering of nouveau tribalists and general party animals who come to celebrate the sunset each Sunday. There are drummers, didgeridoo blowers, cow-bell ringers, rattle shakers, fire spinners, herb burners, ecstatic dancers, rainbow-colored flag wavers, and devotees of Ra, Shiva, Shakti, Sura, Gaia, the Green Man, Mother Earth, Apollo, Aphrodite, Venus, Daphne, and God-only-knows who else. As you can imagine, it's a do-your-own-thing kind of happening. Just be sure to get back to your car and on the road before the county locks the gate on the parking lot at 9pm.

INTELLECTUAL & ARTISTIC MAUI

Earning a living as an artist on Maui is a dream dreamed in office cubicles everywhere. For the painters, sculptors, wood carvers and other Maui artists who actually do earn their bread through their artwork, that dream is simply life. To meet some of this creative elite, just walk around downtown Lahaina any Friday night between 6:30pm and 9:30pm. That's when the town's many galleries stay open late, bring in musicians, serve free wine and pupu, and show off their talent. It's called **"Friday Night is Art Night"** ★★★ (☎ 808/661-6284), lest you forget when to go. A map of the participating galleries is available at any of the galleries or at the Lahaina Visitors Center in the Old Lahaina Courthouse building at

Banyan Tree Park. But it's easy enough to just stroll down Front Street and discover the places all by yourself. Don't be shy. Grab a glass of chardonnay and a bit of brie, and chat with some of the island's artistic commercial aces. It's not often you get to compare dreams to reality, and if you discover any escapees from Cubicle Row, all the better.

If you're more interested in developing your own art skills, you should know that **Hui Noeau Visual Arts Center & School** (2841 Baldwin Ave., Makawao; ☎ 808/572-6560; www.huinoeau.com) holds periodic 1-day art workshops. The topics and instructors change all the time. Past classes have dealt with subjects such as making your own pigments and dyes, painting with watercolors, making beads from precious metal clay, travel sketching, silk painting, glass fusing, and restoring old photographs using Adobe PhotoShop. The cost varies depending on your instructor and the materials needed. Each month, Hui Noeau also offers family classes, for artists ages 4 and up. Call or check the website for details.

For more left-brain-oriented, spoken-word presentations, check out the **AstroTalk Maui public lecture series** (contact Gary Fujihara in Hilo at ☎ 808/932-2328, long distance from Maui; www.ifa.hawaii.edu/hilo). Similar to the original AstroTalk series held on the Big Island (p. 399), AstroTalk Maui features preeminent space scientists drawn to Hawaii by some of the earth's best astronomical observatories, such as the Faulkes Telescope atop Haleakala. The lectures, held at Maui Community College, are aimed at the general public, which means they're scientific but not overly so. In a recent lecture, titled "The Hitchhikers Guide to the End of Everything," prominent researchers from the University of Hawaii Institute for Astronomy covered killer asteroids, exploding stars, colliding galaxies, and other substantive research topics.

Time your trip to Maui right, and you can join the monthly gathering of nouveau beatniks, hip-hoppers, artists, activists, agitators, instigators, and other aficionados of spoken-word poetry known as **Maui Slam** (www.mauislam.com). The Slam takes poetry out of English class and puts it into Maui's cafes and nightclubs, sometimes throwing in a DJ, and always putting up a $100 prize for the best poet. The winner is determined by a panel of judges randomly selected from the audience. Select two or three of the best works from your collection, take the stage, and you'll get 3 minutes to wow the crowd. The venue changes all the time, so check the website for particulars.

On Monday evenings at 7pm, the poetry slammers convene at **Café Marc Aurel** (28 N. Market St.; ☎ 808/244-0852; www.cafemarcaurel.com; p. 330) for Open Mic Night. Anyone 18 or older is welcome to take the stage, recite verse, bust rhymes, do stand-up comedy, play a ukulele, or whatever. You won't win any cash, but you might earn a heartfelt round of applause.

ACTIVE MAUI

The number of activities Maui visitors have to choose from can be overwhelming. If you stand in front of one of the giant racks stuffed with flyers, brochures, and handbills about the many things to do, you may feel driven to lay on the beach and do nothing at all. That's not a bad response, and it's something you should certainly do anyway. But if you don't want to spend all your time resting in the sand, here are some suggestions:

Activity Discounters: If It Looks Too Good to be True . . .

Maui is thick with businesses peddling discounts on surf lessons, snorkel tours, luaus, and every other vacation activity. The savings can range from a few bucks to 50% or more. With the bigger discounts, there's almost always a big catch, and it usually involves real estate. Nearly all of the activities discounters deal in condominium timeshares and use the discounts as bait. You go in to find out about the $20 kayak tour, and you come out with visions of owning a beachfront condominium on Maui for 1 week a year for the rest of your life. My gripe about this is that unsuspecting visitors spend a lot of time in these places comparing tour boats, horseback rides, and whatnot before discovering that they must attend a 90-minute timeshare presentation in order to get the big discount. Even then, they may not qualify financially.

But now that you know the game, you can save yourself time by asking for the discounts without the strings attached. They've got those, too. My favorite discounter is the oddball that doesn't deal in timeshares: **Tom Barefoot's Cashback Tours** ★ (834 Front St., Lahaina; ☎ 888/222-3601; www.tombarefoot.com). The discounts are usually modest, many around 5%, but they can go as high as 20%. Go online to check out all the deals, then call the toll-free number with questions. The website is a great place to compare activities and shop around.

SURFING LESSONS

Surfing is one of the most inexpensive ways to have fun ever devised, as thousands of flat-broke surfers all over Hawaii can attest. If you have a surfboard, a bathing suit, and a ride to the beach, you're on. Any kook can paddle into small waves and start learning, but if you've never surfed before, I strongly advise you to get some instruction. A lesson not only cuts down on the time you'll spend floundering around in the soup trying to figure things out, it will enhance both your safety and that of everyone in the water around you. After all, getting smacked in the head with a heavy board, or worse, accidentally smacking someone else with it, can drain a lot of the fun from the sport.

Most surf schools guarantee that they'll have you surfing—or at least standing momentarily on a board propelled by a wave—with one lesson. From there, it's all about practice, sunscreen, and upper body strength.

Maui has nearly two dozen surf schools, including the reputable **Royal Hawaiian Surf Academy** (117 Prison St., Lahaina; ☎ 808/276-7873; www.royalhawaiiansurfacademy.com), source of employment for the surf instructors featured in the short-lived MTV reality show "Living Lahaina." A 2-hour group lesson costs $60. Other surf schools include **Hawaiian Ultimate Adventures** (4242-L Honoapiilani Rd., Lahaina; ☎ 808/669-3720; www.mauifuntours.com), which has group lessons for $55, and **Maui WaveRiders** (meets at 1975 S. Kihei

Rd., Kihei, and 133 Prison St., Lahaina; ☎ 808/875-4761; www.mauiwaveriders.com), which offers group lessons for $60 (and kids' lessons for $50). Maui WaveRiders lets its students keep their boards all day to continue practicing when the lesson's over. Both schools, along with the Royal Hawaiian Surf Academy, conduct classes on the reef near the Lahaina Breakwall, and students wear rubber booties so they don't slice up their feet. Maui WaveRiders also holds classes in Kihei in the very gentle waves at Kalama Beach Park.

Most surfing lessons last 2 hours, which is about how long most people's arms last, if that. Schools also offer private lessons, for around $100, but I think it's better to put the extra money into renting a board and practicing on your own. Board rentals run around $25 per day or $85 per week. Most of the schools rent boards, or you can find a good selection of rental shops such as **Boss Frog's** (150 Lahainaluna Rd.; Lahaina, and other locations; ☎ 888/700-3764 or 808/661-3333) and **Local Motion** (1295 Front St.; Lahaina, and other locations; ☎ 808/661-7873).

WINDSURFING LESSONS

Maui has great surfing, but it's even more renowned for its windsurfing. The island's geographic design, in cooperation with the prevailing northeast trade winds, produce wind conditions that have made the north shore a world-famous windsurfing destination. What happens is that the trade winds stack up against 10,023-foot Haleakala and accelerate as they find their way around it. A 15-knot wind at sea will typically whip across Maui's north shore at 25 knots, and a 25-knot sea breeze will blast by at 35 knots. Summer, fall, and spring are best for dependable wind. North Pacific storm systems can screw things up in the winter.

Kahana Beach Park on the north shore appeals to both seasoned windsurfers and raw neophytes alike. A distant offshore reef gives skilled sailors plenty of waves to jump, while sheltering the inside waters for beginners. An Oahu windsurfer named Alan Cadiz skipped college in the 1980s to turn pro, won several world titles, didn't know what to do afterward, fell into teaching, and now runs the foremost windsurfing school on the island, **Hawaiian Sailboarding Techniques** (425 Koloa St., within Hi-Tech Surf Sports, Kahului; ☎ 800/YOU-JIBE or 808/871-5423; www.hstwindsurfing.com). His 2½-hour introductory classes

Best Surf Spots for Beginners

Lahaina Breakwall (directly in front of Lahaina Harbor) If the south side of the island is getting any surf at all (south swells come in the summer), this spot will pick it up. The outer break is filled with rippers; the inside break is perfect for beginners.

Launiopoko Beach Park (mile marker 18, Honoapiilani Hwy.) Gentle waves and lots of parking, plus showers and a restroom.

The Cove (South Kihei Rd. just south of Kalama Park) Kihei doesn't get much surf, but this spot gets mushy, easy waves fairly consistently.

meet Monday through Saturday at 9am at Kanaha (call ahead). A class costs $79 and includes all gear. Private lessons start at $105 an hour, but don't include gear. Show this book to Alan Cadiz at Hawaiian Sailboarding Techniques (p. 301) and he'll knock 10% off the cost of his introductory windsurfing class for you.

Introductory windsurfing students start out on large, stable boards with small, manageable sails. Even so, the windsurfing learning curve is steeper and more daunting than the one beginning surfers face. Three factors suggest whether or not you might have the knack: 1) If you can sail a boat; 2) if you've mastered other board sports, such as skateboarding, snowboarding, or wakeboarding; and 3) if you're a kid. Kids pick up windsurfing quicker than anyone, especially when they're learning with other kids. A great kids program is the series of 3-day summer camps put on by **Maui Sports Unlimited** ★ kids (☎ 808/280-7060; http://mauisportsunlimited.com). These camps are held every week, through the summer, on Wednesday, Thursday, and Friday from 9am to noon at Kanaha Beach Park. Rash guards, snacks, and equipment are included in the $150 tuition. For an extra $20, there's aftercare until 3:30pm, featuring arts and crafts, hikes, games, and plenty of shade. By the end of camp, most kids can sail out toward the reef, turn 180 degrees, and return to exactly where they started from. It's the rare adult without sailing or boarding experience who can match that. The company also offers adult private windsurfing and surfing lessons for $55 per hour.

SKATEBOARDING IN MAUI

If you skateboard, or have kids who do, consider packing your board, because Maui has three skate parks. The least attractive of the three is the **Keopuolani Skatepark** (at Keopuolani Park, Kahului; open weekdays 2pm–dark, weekends 11am–dark; no charge; helmets required). It has a big wooden half-pipe and an old-fashioned, not particularly inspired concrete street course with ledges, banks, and rails. The better place to skate in Kihei is the **Kalama Skatepark** (at Kalama Park, Kihei; open daily 7am–9:30pm), which features a wooden half-pipe and a fun mix of wooden ramps and concrete banks, as well as a concrete bowl. But the best skate park on the island is the newest one, set on a beautiful north-shore beach in Paia, the **Nalu Pohaku Stone Wave Sk8park** (at the Paia Youth & Cultural Center, Hana Hwy., just west of town; ☎ 808/579-8354; open Tues 3–7pm, Thurs–Sat 3–10pm; $5 admission). It features a series of concrete bowls from 3 to 8 feet deep, and a happy generation of kids whose summers follow a simple schedule: surf, skate, eat, sleep, start over.

SNORKELING IN MAUI

Like surfing, snorkeling is some of the cheapest and purest fun you can have in Maui. Get hold of a good-fitting mask, snorkel, and pair of fins and you've got all

Can I Rent a Kiteboard?

Nope. Nobody rents kiteboarding gear on Maui. You have to buy your own. New gear runs from $1,000 to $2,500. You can save on used gear, and you'll find as much of it on Maui as anywhere.

A Kiteboarding Splurge

Learning the fundamentals of kiteboarding costs more in both time and money than learning how to windsurf or surf. The gear's expensive and the learning curve's steeper even than in windsurfing, but kiteboarding instructors swear that they can teach anyone with dedication, swimming ability, and hand-eye coordination. Just remember: You can't dabble in kiteboarding. You have to commit to it. Some people come to Maui explicitly to learn kiteboarding. For the rest, it's best to just watch.

The **Kitesurfing School of Maui** (22 Hana Hwy., Kahului; ☎ 808/873-0015; www.ksmaui.com), founded in 1999, is the oldest kiteboarding school in the United States. It offers 4-hour private introductory lessons for $290. The first half of the class is spent on the beach, learning to control the kite. Then the class moves into the water, where it usually becomes apparent that the kite's still in charge. According to the school's owner, Martin Kirk, a good athlete needs about 2 to 3 days of instruction—on average—before getting any good boarding time in. The fewer your athletic gifts, the longer it will take. Longer courses, ranging from 2 to 5 days, range in price from $490 to $975. Students can apply 30% of the cost of their lessons to the purchase of new gear.

Maui's other big kiteboarding school is run by **Action Sports Maui** (415A Dairy Rd., Kahului; ☎ 808/871-5857; www.actionsportsmaui.com). Here, an introductory class costs $240 for a 3½-hour lesson, one on one. Longer courses range from a 3-day course for $625 to a 10-day fast-track into the sport for $1,795. If you're serious about going from a novice who can't kiteboard to a novice with some skills, the 10-day class will get you there. Some of the windsurfing schools also offer kiteboarding instruction, including **Alan Cadiz's Hawaiian Sailboarding Techniques** (p. 301), which offers a one-on-one 3-hour beginners' class for $225.

you need to pleasantly spend hours acquainting yourself with Maui's marine environs and their inhabitants. You can rent snorkeling equipment at most dive shops or beach-gear suppliers. **Boss Frog's** (150 Lahainaluna Rd., Lahaina, and other locations; ☎ 888/700-3764 or 808/661-3333) rents mask-snorkel-fins sets for $5 per day or $20 per week. If you want the gear for more than a week, consider buying your own. At **Wal-Mart** (1011 Pakaula St., Kahului; ☎ 808/871-7820), you can get a full set of snorkeling gear for about $35.

Scores of boats at Lahaina and Maalaea offer trips to offshore snorkeling and dive spots. I recommend **Molokini Crater,** a barren half-moon of an island where you'll see thousands of fish in waters with 150-foot visibility. The back wall of the crater plunges straight down 300 feet, and it's a popular, although sharky, scuba-diving area. The protected bay inside the crater is shallower and filled with coral and fish. Snorkeling there is one of the most popular activities on Maui. The state has issued permits for 40 boats to run Molokini tours, and some of them carry up to 150 passengers—which means that the schools of snorkelers can sometimes rival the fish populations. Rates vary, but generally run about $80 for a full-day tour, typically including Molokini and a second stop at a turtle-watching spot. Molokini is best in the morning. Strong afternoon winds reduce visibility, make mooring a rocky affair, and can blow snorkelers out to sea. Some boats offer discounted rates as low as $30 for afternoon tours to two sites including Molokini. The catch is the weather rarely permits snorkeling in Molokini in the afternoon, so the boats skip ahead to the second site.

Maui Dive Shop ★★ (1455 S. Kihei Rd., Kihei; ☎ 800/542-3483 or 808/875-0333; www.mauidiveshop.com) offers a Molokini trip that has the most rock-bottom morning rates: $50 for adults and $45 for kids from 4 to 12. These 3-hour tours use small boats launched from a boat ramp in Kihei, closer to Molokini than the harbors from which the other tour boats leave. You forgo the lunch buffet, live music, and bars that accompany some of the 150-passenger vessels, but you get to Molokini quicker, earlier, and with just two dozen other snorkelers, rather than 12 dozen. You also get a turtle-watching stop on your way back.

If that still sounds a bit pricey, don't worry: Maui's near-shore waters have hundreds of great snorkeling spots that you can explore without cash or credit. They include:

- **Kapalua Beach in Kapalua,** where there's easy ocean entry from a sandy beach, lots of coral near shore, and lava-rock promontories enclosing it all.
- **Black Rock in Kaanapali,** a lava-rock promontory teeming with fish that expect to be fed, and a somewhat secluded cove halfway to the other side, that surprisingly few people explore.
- **Kamaole III Beach Park,** right in the heart of Kihei town.
- **Olowalu near Lahaina,** which features "a turtle cleaning station," where green sea turtles lay on the bottom and let the cleaner wrasse fish nibble the algae off their shells (but this one's known for sharks).
- **La Perouse Bay at the end of the road in Makena,** an undeveloped natural area reserve and site where lava from Haleakala's most recent eruption reached the sea, and where the arid landscape keeps the waters crystal clear.
- **Coral Gardens,** a fertile patch of reef abounding in fish, eels, turtles, and so forth, on the way to Lahaina.

KAYAK & SNORKELING TOURS

Another common snorkeling option is to do a kayak-and-snorkel tour. Many kayak operators also offer whale-watching tours between December and April. There are all sorts of kayak tour companies to choose from, and rates vary widely, so it pays to shop around. My favorite is **Makena Kayak** (kids) (☎ 877/879-8426 or 808/879-8426; www.makenakayaks.net), a Native Hawaiian–owned and operated firm that won't take out more than six people at a time. It charges $55 for a 2½-hour kayak-and-snorkel tour. The two morning tours leave from Makena Landing in south Maui at 7:30am and 8am. Makena Kayak welcomes kids, but if you'd rather not have someone else's kids slowing down the group (you travel at the

A Mask that Fits

The key to happy snorkeling isn't how expensive your gear is, it's how well your mask fits. If the mask leaks water, misery will flow in, too. ***Tip:*** To check the seal of a mask, press it lightly against your face and inhale through your nose. If the vacuum this action creates holds the mask in place, the seal is good. If not, keep testing masks until you find one that stays. ***Remember:*** A $12 mask could fit better than a $90 one.

speed of the slowest paddler), let your preference be known and you'll be scheduled with grown-ups only. For experienced kayakers, there's a 4-hour paddle-and-snorkel trip, with sandwiches, for $85.

Big Kahuna Adventures (☎ 877/747-2875 or 808/875-6398; www.bigkahuna adventures.com) offers 2½-hour kayak-and-snorkeling tours for $69 per person. Big Kahuna also rents kayaks for $40 to $60 per day.

Maui Kayaks (135 Hale Kuai St., Kihei; ☎ 866/771-6284 or 808/874-4000; www.mauikayaks.com) offers various kayak-and-snorkel tours, including its signature tour of the Wailea-Makena area, on which you see great coastline, underwater life, and celebrity homes. A 3-hour tour costs $69. Maui Kayaks also rents boats for $40 to $50 per day.

KAYAK & SAILBOAT RENTALS

Paying for a kayak tour when you can rent your own seems like an unnecessary expense. But one of the benefits of a guided tour is that the guide will keep you out of trouble. Independent kayakers periodically run into rough waters in Hawaii and need to be rescued. If you have any doubt at all about your abilities, a tour is the way to go. Due to the liability concerns, a surprisingly small number of companies on Maui rent kayaks.

In addition to the two kayak companies I just mentioned, you'll also find boats for rent from **Maui Ocean Activities** (on and the beach in front of the Grand Wailea; ☎ 808/667-2001; www.mauiwatersports.com/moahome.html). It rents kayaks for $15 per hour for singles, $24 per hour for tandems, and $10 for each additional hour. If you'd prefer sailing over paddling, the company also rents catamarans from the same beaches. A 14-foot Hobie Cat goes for $55 for 1 hour, $135 for 3 hours, and $195 for 5 hours.

JET-SKIING

Personally, I find jet skis obnoxious. Quiet, nonpolluting kayaks are a much better way to get out on the water and see the ocean. But if your heart is set on tearing up the ocean with a jet ski, head to **Jet Ski Hawaii** (in front of Whalers Village at Kaanapali Beach; ☎ 808/667-2001; $95/hour, $65 for half-hour). The company shares office space, a phone number, and owners with Maui Ocean Activities, which rents kayaks. Those who rent before 10am get a $10 discount.

A Free Underwater Guide

Maui Dive Shop (1455 S. Kihei Rd., Kihei, and other locations; ☎ 808/879-3388; www.mauidiveshop.com) has a complimentary dive guide, with maps and descriptions of the island's most popular snorkeling and dive spots, as well as a handy field guide to 47 Hawaiian reef fish plus a zebra moray eel, a snowflake moray eel, and a couple of sea urchins.

PARASAILING

Another way to get out on the water, and high above it at the same time, is to parasail. All day during the spring, summer, and fall, speedboats ply the waters of west Hawaii, unspooling lines attached to tourists attached to parachutes, then reeling them back in. Traveling either solo or tandem, parasailers can reach heights of up to 900 feet, with no skill required on their part whatsoever. A bag of potatoes could do it. A basic ride lasts just 7 to 10 minutes, but it seems longer when you're up there.

Maui has two other parasail operators. **UFO Parasail Maui** (☎ 808/661-7836) uses inflatable boats to shuttle passengers to its speedboats waiting off Kaanapali Beach in front of the Hyatt. It charges $65 for a 7-minute ride that hits 400 feet, and $75 for a 10-minute ride that hits 800 feet, including tax. If you take the 8am early-bird flight, you'll save $5. **West Maui Parasail** (☎ 808/661-4060) charges $62 for its 400-foot ride, and $70 for its 800-foot ride, both lasting from 8 to 10 minutes. Its early-bird special knocks $7 off of flights during its 8am and 8:30am trips. It leaves from Slip 15 at Lahaina Harbor. Both parasailing operations require reservations.

PARAGLIDING

To scratch the itch for flight in a more unique way than parasailing, consider foot-launched aviation. **Proflyght Paragliding** ★ (☎ 808/874-5433; www.paraglide hawaii.com) offers an introductory lesson in paragliding that includes a tandem flight with the instructor. The flight starts at 6,500 feet in Polipoli Spring State Recreation Area, on the steep slopes of Haleakala, where you and the instructor, strapped snuggly together in your paragliding harness, wait for an updraft to stand the paraglider's wing up in the air. Then you both take off running as fast as you can down a wickedly steep slope, and . . . you simply fly away. The flight lasts from 12 to 15 minutes, descends 3,000 feet, and costs $175. There's a budget option, too: For $75 you start lower up the slope and descend just 1,000 feet in a flight that lasts 3 to 5 minutes. You might think that paragliding is an adrenaline rush, but it's actually more of an endorphin high that results in a sense of well-being that can last all day. Proflyght owner Dexter Binder calls this effect "The Perma-grin."

HIKING

Hiking is the land-based equal of snorkeling on Maui. Not only can a good day of hiking be a cheap day of fun, you'll feel more in touch with the island after

The Tourist Submarine

Another way to visit the deep, but without getting wet, is with **Atlantis Submarines** ★★ (kids) (650 Wharf St., at the Pioneer Inn, Lahaina; ☎ 800/548-6262 or 808/667-2224; www.atlantissubmarines.com). The company's 48-passenger sub, which has two rows of bench seating to give everyone a big porthole view, dives to 130 feet and spends 45 minutes underwater. (The whole tour lasts 1 hr. 45 min.) At 95 feet the sub stops for a visit to a sunken steel-hull schooner that was docked for years at Lahaina harbor and used as a whaling museum, until rust got the better of it. Even if you're a seasoned scuba diver, riding around in what's essentially an underwater tourist tram is something you shouldn't miss—a memorable splurge at $89 for adults and $45 for kids 12 and younger. (***Tip:*** Book online to get 10% off.) You'll typically see lots of fish and coral, and whatever else happens to be in the vicinity when you submerge—sharks, eagle rays, and even, Atlantis claims, the occasional whale. There's no age limit for kids, but there's a 3-foot minimum height requirement, and all passengers must be able to descend a nearly vertical ladder, then get back up it.

wandering on it a bit. Rising from sea level to 10,023 feet, Maui has plenty of varied hiking terrain, from the raw, lava desert along the coast at La Perouse Bay, to the cloud forests, pastures, and stands of redwood in upcountry Maui, to the alien landscape inside of Haleakala crater.

Several companies offer guided hikes to waterfalls, through rainforests, and around the Haleakala's crater. They charge between $60 and $160 for the experience, but frankly, I don't see any reason to spend money for something you can do on your own, just as well, for free. The hiking companies would argue that they can take you to secluded waterfalls on private land that you couldn't reach by yourself. Fair enough, but Maui has no shortage of waterfalls with public access, including many that you might have all to yourself if you hike far enough, arrive early enough, or simply get lucky.

If you do want a guided hike, go with the **National Park Service** (for reservations, call ☎ 808/572-4459), which leads regular hikes through the cloud forest at Waikomoi Preserve—for free (plus the $10 park entrance fee). The hikes begin every Monday and Thursday at 8:45am from Hosmer Grover, just inside the Crater Road entrance to Haleakala National Park. This moderately difficult 3-hour, 3-mile round-trip hike takes you through part of east Hawaii's vast rainforest watershed that supplies much of the island's drinking water, and supports some of Hawaii's rarest native plants, birds, and creepy-crawly things. You can't do Waikomoi on your own—the preserve is off-limits to the public except on guided expeditions like this one. But this hike isn't for everyone. Waikomoi's native trees are scrubby, and its views are nonexistent. It takes patience to understand what the landscape has to offer—unless you're a birder or a botanist, in which case, you'll get it immediately.

Jet Skis, Speedboats & Whales

Jet skis, speed boats, and all other "thrill craft" are banned from Maui's whale-breeding waters from mid-December to mid-May. If someone tells you they saw whales while parasailing, they're lying.

For an easy hike that you can do on your own or with kids, go to **Hosmer Grove** (kids) in Haleakala National Park. It features an easy half-hour nature walk through an experimental forest of several different temperate-zone varieties of trees mostly planted in 1910 by Ralph Hosmer, aka "Hawaii's Father of Forestry," who had visions of a Hawaiian timber industry in mind. To Hosmer's disappointment, none of the trees turned out to be viable timber species in Hawaii, but his failed experiment had a happy unintended consequence—lovely woods to walk through.

Most of the 30 miles of hiking trails in Haleakala National Park aren't nearly as tame as the trail in Hosmer Grove. Haleakala's crater (which is actually a valley with a collection of genuine craters inside it, but the common usage permits its misidentification) has a network of demanding trails, accessed from two summit area trail heads.

Halemauu Trail ★★★ starts at 7,990 feet and descends to the crater floor at 6,600 feet. For a fairly easy hike, just do the first mile, which takes you down 400 feet, through several ecosystems, to the crater rim. That's about a 2-hour round-trip. If you go all the way to the crater floor, 4 miles away through steep switchbacks, the round-trip takes about 5 hours.

Sliding Sands Trail ★★★ starts at 9,800 feet and descends 3,000 feet on loose cinder to the crater floor. For the best daylong hike, park at Halemauu Trail, hitchhike to the summit (it's legal in the park), descend into the crater on Sliding Sands Trail, and hike back out of it on Halemauu Trail. Allow 6 to 8 hours.

For a strenuous and spectacular climb up the West Maui Mountains, hike **Waihee Ridge** (from Kahekili Hwy., turn *mauka* at Maluhia; turn left at the sign that reads BOY SCOUT CAMP MALUHIA; the trail begins here). The ridgeline trail ascends from 1,000 feet to 2,563 feet. The higher you climb, the more native the forest becomes, which creates the effect of climbing backward in time. At the top you'll find a picnic table. On a clear day, you can see into West Maui's most remote valleys. On an extremely clear day, you can see Pu'u Kukui, the highest point in the West Maui Mountains and one of the rainiest spots on earth. Expect to spend about 3 to 4 hours hiking up and back.

Between Hana and Wainapanapa State Park runs a 6-mile trail, a remnant of the ancient Hawaiian King's Highway, built 400 years ago by Chief Piilani. The **Hana-Wainapanapa Coast Trail** (park at Wainapanapa State Park) is flat but somewhat challenging for the rocky terrain it traverses. It will take you past a *heiau* and other remnants of ancient Hawaii, as well as a stretch of enchanting coastline along low cliffs lined with inlets, caves, rock bridges, and a blowhole. It gets hot on the lava during midday, so go earlier or later.

In Hana I enjoy the 3-mile hike to **Fagan's Cross**, a lava-rock monument to the wealthy San Francisco industrialist Paul Fagan. In the 1940s, Fagan founded

Hana Ranch and brought 300 Hereford cattle in to graze on it. He also founded the Hotel Hana-Maui and brought his millionaire friends to stay at it. Then he created a baseball diamond and brought his minor-league baseball team, the San Francisco Seals, to play on it. All his creations are still there. To reach the cross, cut through the cow pasture across from the Hotel Hana-Maui. It's private property, but the landowner allows access, unless the field is filled with cattle. In that case, find another hike. The hill is steep, but there's a big payoff at the top: a sweeping view of the Hana coastline.

Beyond Hana, above the scenic Oheo Gulch, a popular swimming spot (when not closed by flash-flood conditions), you'll find one of Maui's most popular hikes, the **Pipiwai Trail** (10 miles past Hana, parking lot just after mile marker 42; for trail conditions, call the Kipahulu Ranger Station, ☎ 808/248-7375). It's about a 3-hour round-trip tour along Pipiwai Stream, passing several waterfalls, threading bamboo and guava forests, and ending at spectacular 400-foot Waimoku Falls. Along the way, you'll see an old derrick once used to convey sugar cane across the gulch, and 181-foot Makahiku Falls. You'll also pass the Infinity Pool, a swimming spot at the top of a 200-foot cascade. (Don't even think about getting in if waters are running high or if flash flooding might occur.) This trail is in the Kipahulu section of Haleakala National Park, a finger of federal parkland that reaches down from the summit to the sea. There's a $10 park entrance fee, unless you've already been to the top and kept your pass.

More hiking can be found 6,000 feet up the western slope of Haleakala at the **Polipoli Springs State Recreation Area.** An extensive trail system here runs through forests of redwood, eucalyptus, swamp mahogany, and other unlikely species planted during the Great Depression by the Civilian Conservation Corps (CCC). These hikes are worth the effort it takes to reach them. The trail heads begin at the campgrounds. Start out on the Plum Trail, and do the 5-mile loop, which winds through the woods, past an old CCC cabin, and partly along Haleakala Ridge—the volcano's majestic crest line that runs from the summit to the sea. Along the way are sweeping views of Kahoolawe, Lanai, Molokai, and West Maui. Most afternoons, though, the clouds set in, obliterating the views and creating damp, chilly woods that some find mysteriously alluring and others find overwhelmingly lonely. I think it's best to hike here in the early morning, then go spend the afternoon on a sunny beach. It can get really cold here, but there aren't any mosquitoes. Only half of the 10-mile road through the park to the trail heads is paved; the rest of the road is graded dirt and gravel, and, unless you've rented a four-wheel-drive vehicle, you'll probably nullify your rental contract by driving here and free the car-rental agency from its obligation to send a tow truck for you if things go wrong.

Pick Up a Maui Trail Guide

The best resource for finding hiking trails on Maui is *Maui Trailblazer: Where to Hike, Snorkel, Paddle, Surf, Drive,* by Jerry and Janine Sprout. It features more than 100 hikes, with good maps. The watersports sections are good, too.

Prepare Yourself for the Mountain

If you're hiking into Haleakala's crater, bring food, water, sunscreen, warm clothing, and rain gear. The weather can change suddenly and extremely at the summit, where it sometimes snows. Go ready for the worst. Don't tempt the mountain by showing up unprepared.

THE ZIPLINE

For a peaceful walk through an old upcountry eucalyptus forest, punctuated by moments of adrenaline-laced fun—or screaming terror, depending on your idea of a good time—try the zipline trail of **Skyline Eco Adventures** ★★★ (about 2½ miles up Crater Rd.; ☎ 808/878-8400; www.skylinehawaii.com). Five ziplines run back and forth across a deep, intimidating ravine, with each line growing progressively longer and faster. (A zipline is a steel cable you "zip" across, thanks to gravity and a harness.) There's also a bouncy suspended bridge you must cross at one point along the way. It's a low-tech thrill ride led by enthusiastic young zipline guides who make it an "eco-adventure" by giving short talks on natural history between rides. Each zipline run has the name of a native Hawaiian bird species. The first was named for the Hawaiian crow, the alala, because alala means "scream" in Hawaiian, and that's what people do the first time they step into thin air off a wooden platform perched on the edge of a rugged gulch and zip off to the other side. The whole tour takes between 1½ and 2 hours and costs $79 per person. You can save 15% by booking online, and there's no good reason not to, since reservations are required and they typically book up a week in advance. Riders must be at least 10 years old and weigh between 80 and 260 pounds. The company has a second, longer zipline course in the hills above Kaanapali, but it's more expensive—$150.

HORSEBACK RIDING

About a dozen outfits on Maui offer horseback-riding tours. One of the most unusual and popular experiences is offered by **Pony Express Tours** ★★★ (2½ miles up Crater Rd., next to Skyline Eco Adventures; ☎ 808/667-2200; www.ponyexpresstours.com). This tour takes riders from the rim of Haleakala to the crater floor 3,200 feet below. The 4-hour ride, which includes a lunch of croissant sandwiches served deep inside the crater, begins at 8:30am and costs $175 (not including the $10 park entrance fee). Pony Express also leads rides around Haleakala Ranch, on the lower, 4,000-foot slopes of the volcano. They range from a 1½-hour ride for $90 to a 2-hour ride for $105. You'll save 10% on all rides if you book online.

Piiholo Ranch (at the end of Waiahiwi Rd., Makawao; ☎ 808/357-5544; www.piiholo.com; $120 for 2 hr.) offers another good horseback ride on the lower slopes of Haleakala, at about 2,000 feet, in small groups of six riders. You pass through pastures and in and out of eucalyptus, ohia, and koa forests, with stunning views of West Maui and the surrounding Pacific along the way. The countryside is stunning, but be sure you're completely candid about how much horseback-riding experience you have. While signing in, in a moment of hubris, I checked a box that said I had some experience with horses, when in fact I should have checked the box that said I had none. The horse I was assigned, Frank, made me pay for my little white lie for 2 solid hours.

BIKING ON MAUI

You may have heard of Maui's long downhill bike tours from the summit of Haleakala to the sea. Well, don't get your hopes up. They've been abolished. There were too many serious wipeouts and deaths over the years. In 2007, after one poor rider rode head first into on oncoming van and died, the National Park Service yanked the tour operators' permits. Nevertheless, a couple of the companies offer abbreviated versions of the downhill experience, and they're still quite an experience. (But don't even think about it if you're not a skillful cyclist.) The **Haleakala Bike Company** (Haiku Marketplace, 810 Haiku Rd.; ☎ 888/922-2453 or 808/575-9575; www.bikemaui.com) will rent you a bike and a crash helmet, then drop you off just outside of the entrance to Haleakala National Park, at 6,500 feet. Then you're free to coast at your own pace back down to the sea. It's pretty much downhill all the way, through 29 switchbacks, past the truck farms and ranches of upcountry, and back to the company's shop, 28 miles from where you start. It takes most people about 2 hours, but you can take as much time as you like. The cost is $70 per person, but if you book online it drops to $60. Deluxe versions include a van ride to the summit to watch the sunrise for $110, or a later tour of the summit without the sunrise for $90. Book either online and save 15%.

If you're hell bent on riding a bike from the summit to the sea, and you know somebody who can give you a ride to the top, you can still do it. Only the commercial tours have been banned. **Haleakala Bike Company** rents its downhill cruisers for $34 a day or $130 a week. In Kahului, near the airport, **The Island Biker** (415 Dairy Rd.; ☎ 808/877-7744; www.islandbikermaui.com) rents road bikes and mountain bikes for $50 for the first day, $20 for each additional day, or $150 per week.

If you just want to bum around on a fat-tired, wide-seated beach cruiser, **South Maui Bicycles** (1993 S. Kihei Rd., Kihei; ☎ 808/874-0068) has them for $22 per day or $99 per week, including lock and helmet. Road bikes go for $30 to $50 per day or $130 to $150 per week, including patch kit, saddle bags, and helmet. In Lahaina, **West Maui Cycles** (1087 Limahana Place, Lahaina; ☎ 808/661-9005; www.westmauicycles.com) offers even better rates on cruisers: $15 per day or $60 per week. Road bikes rent for $50 per day or $200 per week, while mountain bikes go for $40 to $50 per day or $160 to $200 per week. Bicycles built for two rent for $50 to $60 per day or $160 to $200 per week, in both road-bike and mountain-bike styles.

Free Maps

Free detailed hiking maps of the trails in Haleakala National Park are available at any of the park's visitor centers.

Warning: Some hard-core bicyclists pack their bike shoes and pedals and bike all over Maui (a hardy few come specifically to climb Haleakala—the ultimate way to save money on a Haleakala downhill bike ride). But Maui lacks a good system of bike paths and has no lack of drivers oblivious to bicyclists, which makes bicycling an unappealing means of traveling long distances on Maui. Don't try to use bikes as your main transportation mode unless you are a very experienced biker.

TENNIS

Many condos and resorts on Maui have tennis courts for their guests. You'll also find free public courts at a dozen county parks, including five courts at **Lahaina Civic Center** (1840 Honoapiilani Hwy., Lahaina), four courts at **Kalama Park** (1910 S. Kihei Rd., Kihei), and four courts at **Waipulani Tennis Courts** (Waipulani St., Kihei, behind Maui Sunset condominium). First come, first served.

At the **Wailea Tennis Club** kids (131 Wailea Ike Place; ☎ 808/879-1958; www.waileatennis.com), you'll find 11 lovely courts among the rolling golf courses of the ritzy Wailea Resort. The rate is $15 per player per hour (or hour-and-a-half for doubles) for guaranteed court time, with free play afterward if you can find an open court. Resort guests get a discount, and every two paying players can bring along one player 12 or younger for free. The club rents rackets, shoes, and ball hoppers for $8 to $10 each, and a ball machine for $40 per hour, including the court. Adult and advance clinics, as well as stamina drills set to music, are offered 6 days a week for $20 to $35.

In West Maui, the **Kapalua Tennis Garden** (100 Kapalua Dr., Kapalua; ☎ 808/665-9112; www.kapaluamaui.com) boasts 10 gorgeous courts on a terraced hillside next to the Ritz-Carlton hotel. At $16 per person for the day, the court fees are steeper than those of the Wailea Tennis Club, but the rentals are mostly cheaper: Rackets are $6, shoes are $3, ball hoppers are $8, and ball machines are $30 per hour. A fun and affordable option here is to show up for drop-in tennis, a round-robin-like event where you compete with a variety of other players at your skill level. Drop-in tennis costs just $8 and takes place Monday and Wednesday from 4 to 6pm, and on Saturday from 8 to 11am.

MAUI GOLF

Maui has 16 golf courses, most of which are championship courses. Greens fees on Maui range from $25 at the Waiehu Municipal Golf Course to $295 at The Plantation Course at the Kapalua Resort, with rates dropping in the afternoon (see the "Golf Deals" sidebar, below).

The Home Time-Zone Advantage

The best time to visit the summit of Haleakala in order to see the sunrise—whether you're riding a bike back down or not—is shortly after you arrive on the island, while you're still accustomed to an earlier time zone.

County Courts

For the complete list of Maui County parks with tennis courts—where you can play for free—go to www.co.maui.hi.us/youth/maui/athletics/tennis.htm. For more information, call the Parks & Recreation Department (☎ 808/270-7383).

The Courses

Pukalani Country Club (360 Pukalani St., Pukalani; ☎ 808/572-1314; www.pukalanigolf.com) is an 18-hole, par-72, 6,962-yard public course where you can escape from the exorbitant greens fees of the resort courses. Located 1,100 feet up the slopes of Haleakala, you'll need a sweater on chilly mornings here. Rates are $78 for 18 holes before 11am, $73 from 11am to 1:30pm, and $63 after 1:30pm. Check the website for discounts; the club offers various specials on its website. Nine holes cost $45.

You'll find the best deal for Maui golf at one of the local golfers' favorite spots, **Waiehu Municipal Golf Course** (Halewai View Rd.; ☎ 808/270-7400), an 18-hole, par-72, 6,330-yard municipal course, with more ocean-side holes than on all of Maui's other courses combined. What this historic course (the first 9 holes date back to the late 1920s) lacks in modern maintenance equipment, it makes up for in character and affordability. It's an easy course with difficult winds. Rates are $50 on weekdays and $55 on weekends and holidays. Cart rental $19. After 3pm, there's a 9-hole special for $25 on weekdays or $35 on weekends and holidays.

You can play a handful of other courses for under $100, including the 6,649-yard, par-72 **Kahili Golf Course** (2500 Honoapiilani Hwy., Wailuku; ☎ 808/242-4653). It sits among the sandalwood trees on the side of the West Maui Mountains, and features sloping fairways, strong trade winds, and plenty of local and state tournaments. Rates are $125, except after 2pm when they're $85.

For just under $100, try **The Dunes at Maui Lani** (1333 Mauilani Pkwy., Kahului; ☎ 808/873-0422; www.dunesatmauilani.com). The only Maui course built on sand dunes (and ancient, noncoastal ones, at that), this is the only one where sand traps are part of the natural terrain. The Irish linksland-style course requires more thought than brawn. Rates are $99, or $75 after 2pm.

The Elleair Maui Golf Club (1345 Piilani Hwy., Kihei; ☎ 808/874-0777) is South Maui's only public course. It has ocean views from most of the greens, and many holes bring the wind into play. This course has something for players of every handicap. Rates are $125, or $100 after 1pm.

Makena Golf Club (5415 Makena Alanui Rd., Makena; ☎ 808/879-3344; www.makenagolf.com) features two 18-hole courses. The 6,914-yard, par-72 North Course travels up and down the green slopes of Haleakala, around and through ancient Hawaiian rock walls, gullies, gulches, streambeds, and lava flows, as it climbs from sea level to 800 feet. The South Course sticks around sea level, and offers the only oceanfront greens in South Maui. Play either for $175, or $155 after 1pm.

The Kaanapali Golf Resort (Kaanapali Beach Resort; ☎ 808/661-3691; www.kaanapali-golf.com) features two choices: the wide bunkers, long tees, and

Free Road Tour

For hard-core road riders, a free group ride leaves from The Island Biker (p. 311) parking lot every Thursday and Saturday at 7am. Where and how far it goes depends on the wind and the speed of the group, which tends to be pretty fast. This is not a tourist activity. It's an opportunity for serious gearheads to rack up mileage on a 2-hour ride that returns by 9am sharp, so the store's owner, Bob, can open the shop. And it's BYOB—bring your own bike.

convoluted greens of the par-71, 6,700-yard Royal Kaanapali Course, and the par-70, 6,388-yard Kaanapali Kai Course, which is rated a couple of strokes easier despite its big water hazard on the final hole. Royal Kaanapali rates are $225, or $110 after 2pm. Rates at the more affordable Kai course are $185, or $85 after 2pm.

Kapalua Golf Club (Kapalua Resort; ☎ 877/527-2582; www.kapaluamaui.com/golf) has two courses: the Bay Course, a par-72, 6,600-yard course with gently rolling fairways and ample greens, and The Plantation Course, site of the PGA Tour Mercedes Championships every January. Bay Course rates are $215, or $130 at twilight, and Plantation Course rates are $295, or $150 at twilight. After 3:30pm you can play 9 holes on these exclusive links for $75 to $85.

The Wailea Resort (100 Wailea Gold Club Dr.; ☎ 888/328-MAUI; www.waileagolf.com) offers another three courses. The **Wailea Emerald Course,** a 6,825-yard, par-72 course, was ranked by *Golf for Women* magazine among the top 10 "Friendliest in the Nation." The par-72 **Wailea Gold Course** measures 7,700 yards, and its fairways are framed by lava rock, kiawe forest, tall indigenous Hawaiian grasses, and ancient Hawaiian rock walls. **Wailea Blue Course** has generous fairways, and large fast greens that appeal to a broad range of players. Blue Course rates are $175, with a noon twilight rate of $130; Emerald and Gold courses are $200, with no twilight. Discounts are offered during the May-through-October "value season."

Miniature Golf

For golf on a smaller scale, you can play 18 phosphorescent holes at **Glow Putt Mini Golf** (kids) (Lahaina Center, 900 Front St.; ☎ 808/667-2010; Mon–Sat 11am–11pm, Sun noon–10pm). In the heart of old Lahaina town, it's got heavy air-conditioning, prizes for holes-in-one, and golf balls that glow in the dark. It also offers group discounts and birthday packages. Otherwise, it's $8 for the first round and $5 for subsequent rounds. For children 5 and under, it's $6. And everybody gets a glowing bracelet.

Maui Golf & Sports Park (kids) (80 Maalaea Rd.; ☎ 808/242-7818; daily 10am–10pm) features two outdoor 18-hole miniature golf courses, as well as bumper boats, a two-story rock-climbing pillar, and a bungee trampoline. The golf courses both cut through a cave in a pretend volcano. Unlimited golf costs $15 for adults and $12 for children ages 4 to 12; tickets for the other activities run $9 for adults and $6 for children. A package including golf and tickets for any three activities (such as bumper boats, rock climbing, and bungee trampoline) costs $25 for adults and $22 for children.

YOGA

Another way to bask in Maui's fitness culture, and to spend time with flexible, well-toned people who actually live on the island, is to drop in on a yoga class. Maui is crazy for yoga, and it supports about a dozen studios. These include **Maui Yoga Shala** (618 Hana Hwy., Paia; ☎ 808/283-4123; www.maui-yoga.com) in Paia, where you may find yourself practicing ujia breathing alongside professional windsurfers and legendary tow-in surfers. Drop-in classes are a costly $20, and 10-class passes run $170. For better rates, check the schedule for "Community Yoga," where a $10 donation to the Paia Youth & Cultural Center gets you a 90-minute class, twice a week. The owner, Nadia, keeps things sweaty with a blend of Ashtanga and Iyengar yoga. Other instructors lead a variety of yoga and nonyoga classes, including Teen Hip-Hop, Brazilian Samba, and Capoeria, the Afro-Brazilian marshal art.

Despite all the wonderful, funky, independently run yoga studios on the island, my guilty favorite is a franchise in a Lahaina shopping mall called **Bikram Yoga Lahaina** (900 Front St., Ste. F17; ☎ 808/250-1220). Not only do you get a highly scripted, copyright protected, 90-minute, 26-posture, incredibly sweaty workout; but if you're a tourist, the director, Mary Kay, will sell you a $50 unlimited weekly pass. Start the day with yoga every day for a week, and not only will

Golf Deals

For the best bargains on golf, consider:

Last-Minute Tee Times Call **Stand-by Golf** (☎ 888/645-BOOK; www.stand-bygolf.com) to get discounts of $10 to $40 off standard rates. Stand-by Golf works with 8 of Maui's 16 courses. Call between 7am and noon for same-day golf, or between 5:30 and 9:30pm for next-day golf.

Twilight Rates As the trade winds pick up in the afternoon, greens fees fall—sometimes by as much as 50%. You won't necessarily have enough daylight to play 18 holes, but you'll be out there swinging. On golf courses, "twilight" starts in early or midafternoon.

Playing Off Season The resort courses typically raise their rates $10 or more during peak tourist season, which generally runs from the week before Christmas until early May.

Package Deals Stay at one of Maui's exclusive resort hotels or condominiums, and you'll get a substantial discount off their courses.

Play a Short Course If you don't mind playing just 9 holes late in the day, you get a taste of exclusive resort greens for as little as $75.

you leave the island more limber than when you arrived, you'll also get the best yoga deal on Maui ($7 per session). Otherwise, drop-in classes cost $16. In Bikram yoga, the studio is filled with space heaters that simulate baking-hot Bombay-style conditions. So you may need two bottles of water.

ATTENTION, SHOPPERS!

Shopping abounds on Maui. In between the cheap and the absurdly expensive is a vast retail universe, stretching from the "I Got Lei'd on Maui" T-shirts on Front Street in Lahaina to a $7,000 Louis Vuitton handbag at The Shops in Wailea. For the discerning, budget-oriented shopper, rich finds await among the wide variety of Maui-made gifts and souvenirs. It's easy to zero in on the Maui-made stuff. The chamber of commerce has devised a "Made-in-Maui" seal, and it's affixed to the food, clothing, flowers, soaps, lotions, potions, and whatnot of more than 70 local companies. Pahoa berry jam, turbinado sugar packets, macadamia-nut-flavored cigars, macadamia-nut cookies, mumus and other dresses, aloha shirts, Hawaiian-music CDs, hand-carved boxes and bowls, and artwork of all sorts and prices are among the wares.

Kihei and Lahaina are filled with small gift shops and souvenir stands, hawking Made-in-Maui items side by side with faux Hawaiian trinkets made in Malaysia or the Philippines. Kahului has box stores galore and two big shopping malls, while neighboring Wailuku has an old downtown shopping district with an eclectic mix of antiques stores, pawn shops, and other mom-and-pop operations. Paia has a colorful collection of small shops and fun boutiques, while upcountry has galleries in Makawao and all sorts of agricultural operations with gift shops throughout the rest of the area. The resorts have resort-area shops with resort-area prices.

KAHULUI

Kahului's box stores—such as **Wal-Mart** (1011 Pakaula St.; ☎ 808/871-7820), Kmart (424 Dairy Rd.; ☎ 808/871-8553), and **Costco** (540 Haleakala Hwy.; ☎ 808/877-5421)—line the route from the airport to the sunny beaches of West and South Maui. While your vision of the ideal Maui shopping experience might not include the likes of Wal-Mart, the one in Kahului actually has a great souvenir section with pretty good prices. Likewise, **Borders** (Maui Marketplace, 270 Dairy Rd.; ☎ 808/877-6160) has a fantastic Hawaiian-music section and a broad selection of books on Hawaii. Many visitors staying in condos, and saving on food by cooking for themselves, head straight from the airport to Costco or **Safeway** (170 E. Kamehameha Ave.; ☎ 808/877-3377) to stock up on provisions.

Kahului's two major malls sit on the route to neighboring Wailuku. With approximately 50 shops and department stores, **Queen Kaahumanu Center** (275 Kaahumanu Ave.; ☎ 808/877-4325) offers something for everyone, residents and visitors alike. Plus on Friday, a great **farmers market** (9am–5pm) sets up in the parking lot.

At the **Maui Mall** (70 E. Kaahumanu Ave.; ☎ 808/872-4320), you'll find coins, clothing, crystals, nail care, and cellphones, among other wares. You'll also find guri-guri, a delicious cross between ice cream and sherbet, at **Tasaka Guri Guri Shop** (☎ 808/871-4513; Mon–Thurs and Sat 9am–6pm, Fri 9am–8pm, Sun 10am–4pm), Hawaii's most famous purveyor of the cold treat. As lore has it, guri-guri

Buy Practically Anything at Longs

Longs Drug Store is Maui's latter-day general store, where you can pick up sunscreen, film, fishing poles, prescriptions, beach towels, beer, sunglasses, magazines, eggs, onions, insecticides, and so on. Longs also has an especially well-stocked section of Made-in-Maui gifts and souvenirs.

You'll find three Longs in Maui: one at Kihei Center (1215 S. Kihei Rd., Kihei; ☎ 808/879-2259), one at Lahaina Cannery Mall (1221 Honoapiilani Hwy., Lahaina; ☎ 808/667-4384), and one at the Maui Mall (70 E. Kaahumanu Ave., Kahului; ☎ 808/877-0041).

was originally called "goodie-goodie" when it was sold to Japanese workers in the plantation days, but the workers' pronunciation stuck.

Every Saturday, the **Maui Swap Meet** (Maui Community College, 310 W. Kaahumanu Hwy.; ☎ 808/877-3100; 7am–noon; admission 50¢) opens its gate to some of the most fertile bargain-hunting grounds on the island. Among all the T-shirts, CDs, sarongs, homemade cookies, carpet remnants, plate lunches, paperbacks, DVDs, flowers, fruit cakes, license plates, rusty tools, vintage postcards, and Makawao mushrooms, you're sure to find something you weren't expecting. I scored imitation Maui Jim sunglasses for $5.

WAILUKU

Wailuku, once the island's retail capital, has long since been eclipsed by its younger, sprawling neighbor, Kahului. But the shopping in Wailuku merely changed, it didn't die. Wailuku's old downtown has an assortment of locally owned stores selling art, antiques, books, music, leather, trophies, jewelry, aloha shirts, and other stuff that people typically hawk at pawn shops. And they're all concentrated around North Market Street, within walking distance of each other.

Don't miss the gift shop at **Bailey House Museum** (2375-A Main St.; ☎ 808/244-3326; 10am–4pm Mon–Sat; $5 admission, $1 ages 7–12), which is filled with books, wooden bowls, and other high-quality goods. It's one of Maui's best gift shops, and the museum is worth a look, too, featuring the island's best collection of ancient Hawaiian and missionary-era artifacts.

KIHEI

Kihei—a 7-mile strip of shopping plazas and condominiums—doesn't have a downtown. Its closest approximation to a town center is Kalama Park, a 36-acre beach park with a life-size whale sculpture that everyone refers to as "The Big Whale." Across the street from The Big Whale is **Kihei Kalama Village** (1913 S. Kihei Rd.), a collection of bars, restaurants, shops, and souvenir stands that you should poke around in if you're in the market for bric-a-brac. Check out **Cary's of Maui** (☎ 808/891-2117), where the goods range from vanilla-macadamia-nut-flavored cigars to ukuleles. The latter start at $20 for a souvenir-grade uke and climb quickly to $480 for a fine, handmade koa instrument.

Down the road a few blocks at another souvenir bazaar, **Aloha Marketplace** (1794 S. Kihei Rd.), you can get an even cheaper ukulele for $12. You may never get it perfectly tuned, but if you really knew how to play, you wouldn't want one like this anyway. Aloha Marketplace is a smaller assembly of T-shirt and trinket vendors than Kihei Kalama Village, but you'll find all the touristy basics here, such as grass skirts with coconut-shell bras ($8.95 for the adult size, $9.95 extra-large). This is also one of the places where you can pick up a Mail-a-Nut. A twist on the traditional postcard, it's a coconut with a Hawaiian scene painted on it, and space set aside for postage, an address, and a message, which you write with a magic marker. The smallest Mail-a-Nut costs about $10 and the largest costs about $20. Postage adds an extra $4 to $15.

How would you like to return from Maui proudly displaying a vintage pair of grimacing little Hawaiian tikis, which turn out to actually be salt-and-pepper shakers? Or a deck of Kodak hula girl playing cards, circa 1960? Or a lamp made from the inflated body of the deadly puffer fish? Well, I won't promise that you'll find any of that at the **Rainbow Attic** (Kihei Foodland Town Center, 1881 S. Kihei Rd.; ☎ 808/874-0884; 9am–9pm daily), but if the thrifter in you itches to hunt for gems among Kihei's cast-off Polynesian curiosities, you'll definitely want to take a spin through the place. Tucked away in the corner of one of Kihei's many strip malls, The Attic is like a constantly mutating museum devoted to the island's condominium culture, a world saturated in bamboo, rattan, sea shells, plastic houseplants, and surfboard-shaped serving dishes. As well as, naturally, alohawear. Maui's largest "consignment boutique" is the place to go for that $8 aloha shirt or $13 mumu that no one but you ever needs to know was pre-owned—unless you want to brag about it.

LAHAINA

Most retail in Lahaina is concentrated in two locations: the historic district and an old pineapple cannery transformed into a shopping mall called **Lahaina Cannery Mall** (1221 Honoapiilani Hwy.). The town of Lahaina is long on T-shirt shops, art galleries, jewelry stores, and activity discounters peddling timeshares, but short on stores with originality, bargains, or much appeal. Many of the most interesting shops started elsewhere, then opened a store in the area—or, in the case of **Crazy Shirts** (865 Front St., ☎ 808/661-4775; Whalers Village, ☎ 808/661-0117; Lahaina Cannery Mall, ☎ 808/661-4788; and Wharf Cinema Center Shops, ☎ 808/661-4712), opened four stores in the area.

Crazy Shirts started in Honolulu in 1964 when the first baby boomers were hitting college and starting to dabble with T-shirts as a form of self-expression. Early designs tended toward surf-company logos ("Surfboards Hawaii"), drug and alcohol references ("Suck 'Em Up"), and political statements, sometimes mixed with drug or alcohol references ("Draft Beer Not Students"). Shirts today start at $23 and come with a broad assortment of messages and images, many of them related to Hawaii. But if quantity rather than quality drives your T-shirt buying, skip Crazy Shirts and browse the shops and stands along Front Street, where you'll find shirts for less than $12. There's a wide variety, but the higher-quality Crazy Shirts T-shirts will last longer.

The surfer/artist who owns the surf shop **Maui Tropix** (786 Front St., Lahaina; ☎ 808/661-9296; also 215 Piikea Ave., Kihei; ☎ 808/879-6868; and 261 Dairy

Rd., Kahului; ☎ 808/871-8726) is an indefatigable sloganeer who constantly coins catchy new phrases and releases them into the Islands via T-shirt and bumper sticker. Locals love them. "It's All About Me" T-shirts have been spreading lately. "Slow Down, This Ain't the Mainland," is a perennial bumper-sticker favorite.

PAIA

Groovy little Paia on the north shore has Maui's most interesting assortment of unique, locally owned boutiques, shops, and galleries. The shopping scene, combined with the town's fantastic restaurants and the nearby world-renowned windsurfing beach, Hookipa, make Paia a place where you'll want to spend at least a couple of hours.

If you haven't already found one of the other three locations of **Maui Hands** (84 Hana Hwy.; ☎ 808/579-9245; also at 3620 Baldwin Ave., Makawao; ☎ 808/572-5194; and 612 Front St., Lahaina; ☎ 808/667-9898; and in the Hyatt Regency hotel in Kaanapali; ☎ 808/667-7997), take a look around the Paia store. Maui Hands is a consignment shop that sells prints, paintings, carvings, pottery, jewelry, hardwood bowls, and all sorts of other locally crafted, handmade things. Any one of the Maui Hands stores is an excellent place to find genuine Hawaii-made gifts on Maui.

Go to **Hemp House** (16 Baldwin Ave., Paia; ☎ 808/579-8880; www.hemphousemaui.com) and you'll come away with the strong suspicion that anything can be made from hemp. Not only is this shop full of casual hemp wear for men and women (hemp tops, hemp bottoms, hemp boxers, hemp hoodies), and hemp accessories (hemp hats, hemp handbags), it's also got a surprising assortment of hemp bath and body products (hemp soaps, hemp massage oils, hemp moisturizers, hemp shampoos, hemp conditioners), as well as hemp pet products (hemp leashes, hemp collars, hemp cat food, hemp doggie bones), miscellaneous hemp items (hemp candles, hemp incense), and hemp educational materials (a hemp T-shirt filled with hemp facts, such as: "Ben Franklin owned a mill that made

Maui's Nifty Bikini Boutique

The best bikini store on Maui, and possibly in Hawaii, is **Maui Girl & Co.** (12 Baldwin Ave.; ☎ 800/579-9266; www.maui-girl.com), a small beachwear boutique with some 4,000 mix-and-match tops and bottoms in stock, and, when I was there, a half-dozen women going mad over them. Styles range from modest to quite the contrary, with a heavy Brazilian influence. Some of the Brazilian surfers who make the winter big-wave pilgrimage to Maui pack their suitcases filled with the latest swimwear from Rio, which finds its way onto Maui Girl's racks. Maui Girl's owner swipes what she likes and re-creates it under the Maui Girl label. "I see what's really hot, and then make a zillion of them," she says. Prices start at about $38 for a separate and go way up. Call to find out about sales, which sometimes knock prices down by 50%.

Maui Wines & Cheese

You can find bottles of wine from Maui's only winery at liquor stores around the island, but it's more fun to buy it where it's produced. **Tedeschi Vineyards** (Kula Hwy., 5 miles south of Grandma's Coffee House in Keokea; ☎ 877/878-6058 or 808/878-6058; tasting room open 9am–5pm daily; www.mauiwine.com) is on the historic grounds of Ulupalakua Ranch. At the tasting room, in a guesthouse constructed for King Kalakaua, you can sample a table wine, a blush, two pineapple wines, and three sparkling wines. I had low expectations for the pineapple wines, but they weren't nearly as bad as I anticipated. Still, I chose the Ulupalakua Red, and left with a nice bottle of it for $10, as well as a handsome canvas wine tote for $12 (which, together, made a nice gift with a few bars of organic chocolate thrown in). Wines range from $9 for the blush to $18 for a sparkling variety. Try to arrive in time for one of the free tours, held daily at 10:30am, 1:30pm, and 3pm. The grounds are beautiful.

hemp paper" and "Henry Ford made a hemp car that would not smash with a sledgehammer"). Hemp prices run from $3.95 for hemp lip balm, to $45 for a men's hemp hoodie, to $65 for women's hemp beach pants. I like the optimistic slogan about hemp's durability: "It doesn't wear out, it wears in."

UPCOUNTRY

For a cowboy town, Makawao sure has a lot of arts and crafts. Galleries displaying the works of wood turners, painters, potters, and other artists and artisans line the town's two Old West–style streets. For budget shoppers, most of these galleries offer little more than browsing—with a few exceptions. At **Hot Island Glass** (3620 Baldwin Ave.; ☎ 808/572-4527), a big jellyfish sculpture might cost upward of $6,000, but you can also pick up a colorful glass paperweight or a shallow glass bowl for around $15. Before buying, you'll get to watch glassblowers mold and inflate molten glass into vases, bowls, and sea creatures.

Deeper into upcountry the lavender farm **Alii Kula Lavender** ★★ (1100 Waipoli Rd., Kula; ☎ 808/878-3004; www.aliikulalavender.com; daily 9am–4pm) has a gift shop filled with an assortment of goods made from the lavender grown on-site. Lavender is in everything here: bath gel, body butter, body spritzer, coffee (regular and decaf), shortbread cookies, honey, jelly, candles, even lavender-scented note cards and a satin eye pillow filled with lavender. Most lavender items are reasonably priced, between $10 and $25. The farm also offers tours of the lavender grounds, which include a light lavender lunch (for example: lavender herb–seasoned chicken with lavender rolls; $65) or tea (lavender, of course; $40). Call ☎ 808/878-8090 for reservations. The best time to visit is summer, when the fields are in full bloom.

More so than lavender, upcountry is famous for protea, the strange and beautiful flower of the tropical African shrub with the same name. Several farms specialize in protea, which ships well fresh and dries out beautifully. Check out

Proteas of Hawaii (417 Mauna Place, Kula; ☎ 808/878-2533; www.proteasofhawaii.com). Prices start at $1.50 a stem and go up to around $100 for shipping a large basket to the mainland via FedEx. You can order by phone, but it's better to go in person so you can explore the University of Hawaii's protea garden (7:30am–3:30pm; free) across the street.

For Maui-grown coffee, stop at **Grandma's Coffee House** (Kula Hwy., Keokea; ☎ 808/878-2140), a small deli and organic-coffee roaster. When people think of Hawaiian coffee, the Kona district of the Big Island is the first thing that usually springs to mind. But coffee flourishes in other parts of Hawaii, too, including upcountry. Like pure Kona coffee, pure upcountry coffee comes with a premium price: $35 for 10 ounces of Grandma's brand organic. But you can get away with a 10-ounce blend for just $11. If you're lucky, you'll walk in when they've got the ancient roaster fired up and the transcendent aroma of coffee fills the store. Yet another upcountry spot with products unique to Maui is **Surfing Goat Dairy** (3651 Omaopio Rd., Kula; ☎ 808/878-2870; Mon–Sat 10am–5pm, Sun 10am–2pm), whose resident ruminants are responsible for more than 20 gourmet cheeses. Try the aged Maui goat cheese with jalapenos, Thai dragon chilies, Buddha's Hand citron, and Malabar peppercorns in olive oil with garlic ($12 per 8-oz. jar). Or pick up some of the fresh chèvre, which comes plain or with additions such as apple, bananas, curry, tuna, and wasabi, or Maui lavender (in Upcountry Maui lavender goes into everything).

RESORT SHOPPING

You can safely skip the outrageously expensive and dull shops at both Whalers Village in Kaanapali and the Kapalua Shops in Kapalua. But **The Shops at Wailea** (3750 Wailea Alanui Dr.; ☎ 808/891-6770) are worth a look. You won't find many bargains among the 60-plus upscale stores, galleries, and restaurants at this enormous, high-toned outdoor mall, but browsing is pleasant enough and parking is free. Mixed in with the same old high-end, resort-area designer outlets (such as Louis Vuitton and Prada) are a bunch of fun, locally owned places. The **Célébritiés Fine Art Gallery** (☎ 808/875-6565) displays artwork either by or about celebrities, with an emphasis on baby-boomer favorites like Ronnie Wood, John Lennon, Miles Davis, David Bowie, and even Paul Stanley of KISS—all of whom, as it turns out, are visual artists as well as musical ones. Jerry Garcia, who lived for a spell in Lahaina, did a psychedelic-colored painting of a banyan tree. The gallery attendant told me that, while there's no proof, she's certain it's a portrait of the famous banyan at Lahaina Banyan Tree Park. It didn't look like it to me, but I can understand how at a place like Célébritiés, the idea of a celebrity artist doing a portrait of a celebrity tree is irresistible.

Another fun store in the mall is **Enchantress Boutique** (☎ 808/891-6360), which describes itself as a "beautiful, romantic goddess boutique." It sells the kind of loose, flowing, ruffled things that Stevie Nicks might wear. When I offered this observation to the shopkeeper, she told me that, in fact, Stevie Nicks recently came by and bought five loose, flowing, ruffled Azima silk coats.

NIGHTLIFE ON MAUI

From a sandy-floored beach bar with cover bands and dollar mai tais to a symphony hall filled with Tchaikovsky or Gershwin, to a luau stage covered with smiling hula girls and flaming fire-knife dancers, Maui's nightlife ranges across diverse terrain. Most of it is concentrated along the island's west and south shores, where most of the visitors are concentrated. The dinner shows, the sunset cruises, and the majority of bars and clubs are found along the coastal strips running from Wailea to Maalaea, and from Lahaina to Kaanapali. Less extensive but no less intriguing after-dark scenes also occur in Wailuku and Kahului, in Paia on the north shore, and even in Makawao, on the cool, upcountry slopes of Haleakala.

To check out all the possibilities, pick up a Thursday edition of the ***Maui News*** and read its Maui Scene insert, which has the week's entertainment schedule. Or save the 50¢ and grab the free alternative weekly, ***Maui Time,*** which also lists the week's happenings.

SUNSET CRUISES

Many of the same boats that offer snorkeling and whale-watching tours also offer sunset cruises. In the evening, large and small power craft and sailing vessels take 25 to 150 passengers offshore to watch the Maui sun slip beneath the horizon. Most cruises last 2 hours and depart from either Lahaina or Maalaea harbors, with a few sailing catamarans leaving from Kaanapali Beach. The cocktail cruises generally cost around $50, and they're the best deal. Not only do they include open bars, but you can fill up on pupu, too. The dinner cruises add another $30 or so to the ticket—and that money is better spent on dinner served closer to the kitchen. Every activity discounter on the island handles sunset cruises, so it's easy to find deals. For more information, check out www.tombarefoot.com.

Note: With any boat tour in Hawaii—snorkeling trips, whale-watching, and sunset cruises—be prepared to also pay the state's 4% general excise tax, as well as an additional charge to cover the 3.5% harbor fee.

Here's a sunset-cruise sampler that illustrates the variety of what's out there:

Pacific Whale Foundation (Lahaina Harbor, slip 1; ☎ 808/249-8811) carries 40 passengers aboard a 50-foot, double-decked sailing catamaran on cocktail cruises ($45), and 100 people aboard its 65-foot, double-decked motor cat on dinner cruises ($90) in waters off Lahaina.

Slack-Key Guitar & Stories

For an equally entertaining but more authentic Hawaiian cultural experience than a luau—and a less pricey one—check out the **Masters of Hawaiian Slack Key Guitar Concert Series** ★★ (Napili Kai Beach Resort, in Napili; ☎ 888/669-3858 or 808/669-3858; Wed at 7:30pm; $45; www.slackkey.com). Hosted by George Kahumoku, Jr., a slack-key master and storyteller of considerable gifts, this series features a changing roster of guest musicians from the highest ranks of the Hawaiian music industry. Somehow, the 150-seat theater and its resort setting melt away, leaving the impression that you're hanging with Kahumoku and his friends in a garage as they drink beer, talk story, and crack jokes between songs. Recordings of the shows have won two Grammy's.

Hawaii's History Dramatized

The lavish stage show **Ulalena** ★ (Lahaina Myth and Magic Theatre, 878 Front St., Lahaina; ☎ 877/688-4800 or 808/661-9913; www.mauitheatre.com; Tues–Sat 6:30–7:45pm; $60 adults, $40 children 3–15) takes a sweeping spin through 1,500 years of Hawaii's history and culture. It moves from the area's mythological origins, when the demigod Maui fished the islands from the sea with his magic fish hook, to the beginning of the cultural renaissance in the 1970s, when disaffected young Hawaiians began turning to the past like never before. The story is told with traditional hula and modern choreography, with dancers sprinting through the aisles, musicians appearing where you don't expect them, drumming, chanting, acrobatics, and mesmerizing stage effects that include a goddess dancing on the moon and a lava flow that engulfs the entire theater.

The entire presentation unfolds without a word of dialogue, but with refreshments in the lobby, including beer. If you go, and you should, you must study the playbill beforehand to familiarize yourself with the characters. Otherwise you'll have no idea that the lusty swine in one hilarious scene, for instance, is the pig god, Kamapuaa, and the lady with the crazy hair he's trying to seduce is the volcano goddess, Madame Pele. An even better way to ensure you don't get lost along the way is to buy the $10 souvenir program guide, which has color photos of who's who. My only objection to Ulalena is Captain Cook. It's fine to hold up Cook as proxy for Western civilization, enticing the wide-eyed natives with baubles, finery, and musketry, but portraying him as a flighty fop (played by a woman, no less) seems like an unnecessary affront to a great, if controversial, explorer.

***America II* Sailing Charters** ★★★ (Lahaina Harbor, slip 6; ☎ 808/667-2195; www.sailingonmaui.com) offers a rare opportunity to sail aboard one of the most highly pedigreed racing yachts on the planet—and for one of the most affordable sunset-cruise rates ($40). Okay, technically this isn't really a sunset cruise. It's simply a late afternoon sail on a really fast sailboat. How fast? *America II* is the ultra-sleek, 65-foot, $10-million yacht that represented the United States in the 1987 America's Cup Challenge—the Super Bowl of Sailing. Morning and afternoon cruises are offered. If you take the afternoon cruise in the winter, you'll just happen to be out on the water as the sun goes down, making it a de facto sunset cruise. Unlike the actual sunset cruises, you won't have Hawaiian musicians or a wet bar to enjoy. But you're welcome to bring your own beer (in cans), if you like. And in any case, *America II* heels heavily under sail, and you'll be too busy gripping the rail and getting drenched with sea spray to miss the music and mai tais.

The *Pride of Maui* (Maalaea Harbor, main loading dock; ☎ 808/242-0955 or 808/244-2100), a 65-foot motor catamaran, packs 110 people onto its sunset dinner cruises ($60 or $30 kids) and plies the waters of Maalaea Bay or travels along rocky Pali coastline toward Lahaina, depending on weather conditions and the captain's inclination. Live Hawaiian music and an open bar.

The Maui Film Festival

The **Maui Film Festival** (☎ 808/572-3456 for recorded info; www.mauifilmfestival.com) is two things: 1) an ongoing Wednesday-night screening of critically acclaimed films at the Maui Arts & Cultural Center in Kahului, and 2) a weeklong summer festival at the Wailea Resort, with celebrity soirees, haute cuisine, five screens, 50 or 60 films, and a growing buzz. The best screen is the Celestial Cinema, set up under the stars on a driving range, with the imposing outline of Haleakala framing the screen and the ocean at your back. It's like being at a drive-in movie theater, with a really good movie showing, without any cars around, and on Maui.

EXPERIENCING A LUAU

For many visitors, a trip to Hawaii wouldn't be complete without a luau. This power of the luau over the tourist perplexes many residents, who can't understand why anybody would spend $75 (the typical luau price) for a hotel buffet, an inauthentic and not particularly good hula, and a sunset. They point out that sunsets are free, plate-lunch joints sell heaps of Hawaiian food for $10, and not only are the hula dancers at luaus notoriously out of sync, they're not even doing hula half the time, considering all the Tahitian, Samoan, and other Pacific dance forms thrown into the mix.

But don't worry what the luau bashers think. If you want to do a luau—and you're not put off by the ticket price—by all means, do a luau. Just forget about the ones offered by the resort hotels and go to **Old Lahaina Luau** ★ (1251 Front St., Lahaina; across from Cannery Mall; ☎ 808/667-1998; www.oldlahainaluau.com; events typically begin at 5:45pm, but times vary, so call for details; $92 adults, $62 kids 12 and younger). Set on its own 1-acre oceanfront luau grounds done up like a Hawaiian village that's laced with pathways, thatched hales, and native plants, it's staffed with genuinely enthusiastic hosts and hostesses, bartenders, servers, and dancers (it's one of the most coveted service-industry jobs on the island, so everybody's pretty happy to be here). The food is several cuts above what you'd scoop out of the sorry hotel trays at some luaus (at this one, be sure to try the pulehu steak, the mahimahi, and the chicken long rice), and the open bar turns out skillful and generous concoctions. Unlike the Polynesian reviews typical of hotel luaus, which include dance from throughout the Pacific and offer an excuse to include fire-knife dancers (that's a Samoan thing), the dance at Old Hawaiian Luau is strictly hula. (The dancers may not always be in sync, but if I hadn't pointed it out, you probably wouldn't have noticed.) Seating for Old Lahaina Luau fills up well in advance, so make reservations as early as possible. This is not only the best luau on the island, it's the best in the state.

If you can't accept the idea of a luau without a fire-knife dancer, the same company that does Old Lahaina Luau also presents **The Feast at Lele** ★★ (505 Front St., Lahaina; ☎ 808/667-5353 or 866/244-5353; www.feastatlele.com; reservations required), which has grafted fine dining onto the trunk of a conventional luau. You're still greeted at the door with a lei and a mai tai, but instead of family-style seating, you're seated at a private, tablecloth-draped table. As the sun sets, a server brings the first of four main courses to your table and dancers take the stage. They move through four styles of Polynesian dance—Hawaiian, Tahitian, New Zealand, and Samoan—with each dance accompanied by a gourmet treatment of the region's cuisine. This is a smaller, more intimate seaside setting than the mass feeds at most luaus. Unlike Old Lahaina Luau, it's got a fire-knife dancer. At $110 a head ($80 for children 12 and under), this is Maui's premium-priced luau—but it's worth the splurge if a memorable haute-cuisine luau is the Hawaiian experience you have your heart set on.

Through discounters (such as www.tombarefoot.com), you can easily get $10 off luau tickets at the resort hotels, but you won't find Feast at Lele or Old Lahaina Luau discounted. The demand for these luaus is too high. If you're willing to forgo the food (which isn't necessarily a bad idea), you can just watch the show (with fire-knife dancers) at **The Royal Lahaina Luau** (2780 Kekaa Dr., Kaanapali; ☎ 808/661-3611; www.royallahainaluau.org) for $37.

PERFORMING ARTS IN MAUI

If listening to Gershwin or Tchaikovsky is your idea of a good time, check the online schedule for the **Maui Arts & Cultural Center** (1 Cameron Way, Kahului; ☎ 808/242-7469; www.mauiarts.org). Home to the Maui Symphony Orchestra, this $32-million entertainment complex perched on a hill overlooking Kahului Bay is the envy of performing-arts communities on all the other Hawaiian islands. In addition to the symphony, the MACC hosts a rich and diverse variety of shows, which have included big-name rock bands, touring Broadway musicals and dance troupes, local stand-up comedians, and Hawaiian cultural performances. It also presents a weekly film series. While waiting for the show to begin, you can sip a beer outside the theater in the softly lit Candlelight Café.

Also, at the Maui Arts & Cultural Center you might catch a touring Broadway show in the 1,200-seat main theater, a major rock concert in the outdoor amphitheater, or a homegrown stand-up comic in the intimate black-box theater. Something is almost always going on at the MACC, even if it's only a good movie. The center also has a cafe where audiences like to gather before and after the shows. Go online before you get to Maui and find out who will be performing while you're on the island. If you're staying for a while, you can save 20% on prices by getting tickets for six shows at a time.

BARS & CLUBS

In South Maui

When night falls upon the well-manicured, well-mannered Wailea Resort, quiet settles in—with one notable exception: **Mulligan's on the Blue** ★★★ (100

Cover Charges

Cover charges at Maui's various bars and clubs with DJs or live music range from $2 to $3 during the week (if there's a cover at all), and from $5 to $10 on weekends, unless a big-name band is playing, and then the price goes even higher.

The Wildly Talented Mr. Willie K

Immensely popular and ridiculously versatile, Hawaiian singer, songwriter, and musician **Willie K** ★★★ flat out rocks. He plays Hawaiian music, jazz, salsa, country, and whatever else he chooses equally well. Everyone on Maui seems to love Willie K, and he hasn't gone unnoticed by the rest of the world. He's sat in with or opened for the likes of B.B. King, Santana, Prince, Bonnie Raitt, Jimmy Buffet, Willie Nelson, and Crosby, Stills and Nash, not to mention the halftime show he performed on *Monday Night Football*. Monday is Willie K Night at the Charley P. Woofer Saloon (p. 329; show is $15), and it's not to be missed.

Kaukahi St., on the Wailea Blue golf course; ☎ 808/874-1131; www.mulligansontheblue.com). The live music, dancing, and noisy, young crowd that packs into this unlikely Irish pub on a golf course in the middle of the North Pacific gives the place, when you first approach it, a surreal quality, as if it were a nighttime mirage on the fairway. But it's all real and a lot of fun. There's contemporary Irish and Celtic music on the weekends, jazz on Monday, country and Hawaiian on Tuesday, and Island-style solo acoustic on Wednesday and Thursday, with various artists on Fridays. Mulligan's rarely imposes a cover charge, and always pours perfect pints of Guinness.

If you're going out at night in Kihei, you shouldn't—and, because of the location, pretty much can't—miss the cluster of bars across the street from The Big Whale sculpture in Kalama Park. The proper name for the place is **Kihei Kalama Village** (1913 S. Kihei Rd.), and it's a souvenir bazaar by day. At night, I think of it as "Bar Land" because each of its various bars has a different theme, making the whole thing like a theme park for drinkers. Bar Land is the closest thing Kihei has to a town center. Yeah, I know, that's kind of sad for Kihei. But you don't live there. And it's a great place to party.

The cornerstone bar, which sits prominently on the corner of North Kihei Road and Keala Place, **Life's a Beach** ★★ (☎ 808/891-8010) has neon palms on the walls and real sand on the floors. The crowd tends to be young and partial to shots of Jägermeister and chilled Patron. There's loud, live music (rock, reggae, Hawaiian, blues, cover bands) every night but Monday, which is open-mic music night. I strongly recommend the mai tais at Life's a Beach, and so do the readers of the weekly newspaper *Maui Time,* who have declared them Best Mai Tai's on Maui in the paper's reader polls. Go during happy hour (4–7pm) and get a small mai tai for $1, a big one for $2, or a really big one (1 liter) for $6.

If Life's a Beach is too bold and brassy for you, perhaps you'd prefer the intimate, dimly lit little lounge next door. **Ambrosia** (☎ 808/891-1011) isn't much bigger than a two-car garage, but it's got ceilings high enough for an enormous flat-screen TV to continuously show film classics above the bar. And somehow jazz, blues, and other musicians manage to set up their instruments and jam throughout the week. There certainly isn't a dance floor, but if the music's good and the crowd is so moved, people manage to carve out enough space for a little tight-quarter boogying. It's amazing what you can do with not much when you're motivated.

Nearby, the **South Shore Tiki Lounge** (☎ 808/874-6444) has a big outdoor deck and dance floor with nightly entertainment. Live traditional and contemporary Hawaiian music accompanies the 4-to-6pm happy hour (during which beer, well drinks, and house margaritas are $4), and a variety of bands and DJs takes over from 10pm until 1:15am (last call). As you might expect in a Tiki bar, you'll find fruity drinks served in Tiki mugs with umbrellas and pineapple spears, lots of bamboo, grimacing Tikis, and blazing Tiki torches. The black-velvet Elvis, the puffer-fish lampshades, the flat-screen TV with surf videos, and the menu that includes pizza ($4 per slice) are all bonuses.

The biggest bar in Bar Land is **Lu Lu's** (☎ 808/879-9944), an open-air, second-story tropical lanai, with a young, loud crowd, a dance floor, dart boards, pool tables, and other amusements, plus an extensive pub menu (don't be fooled by the bucket of fries, though—the big galvanized pail bursting with fries that you may see going by has a false bottom). Live bands play on Saturdays starting around 7pm, and DJs spin Thursday and Friday from 10pm until the wee hours.

Within walking distance of Bar Land, the Kihei location of **Sansei Seafood Restaurant and Sushi Bar** ★ (Kihei Town Center, 1881 S. Kihei Rd.; ☎ 808/879-0004) is another lively hub of nightlife on Maui's south shore. A thick crowd of residents and visitors crams itself into Sansei for the late-night discounts (50% off sushi and appetizers 10pm–1am Thurs–Sat) and the laser karaoke (I never realized it before I went to Sansei, but karaoke machines change pitch so the music matches the vocal range of the singer. Crazy!). **Sansei's Kapalua location** (The Shops at Kapalua, 115 By Dr.; ☎ 808/669-6286) also has karaoke and late-night specials, but the resort crowd there is a little mellower (see the full review on p. 263).

IN WEST MAUI

Bar Land in Kihei notwithstanding, the best place to bar-hop on Maui is along Front Street in Lahaina, which is lined with restaurants, bars, live-music venues, and dancing. Front Street is always pretty lively, but never more so than on Friday (with the exception of Halloween, when Lahaina becomes "The Mardi Gras of the Pacific"). Lahaina kicks off every weekend with "Friday Night is Art Night" (see p. 298), where the downtown galleries whip up enthusiasm, foot traffic, and hopefully business with live music, free pupu, and appearances by artists.

Among Lahaina hot spots is **Moose McGillycuddy's** (844 Front St.; ☎ 808/667-7758), a popular meat-market-type place with a dance floor and a second-story location overlooking the foot and vehicular traffic on Front Street. It's got a varying schedule of live music and DJs, with no regular cover charge except on

Eating Late in Lahaina

For a late-night bite to eat in Lahaina head to **Lahaina Coolers** (180 Dickenson St.; ☎ 808/661-7082), which serves dinner until midnight. All the restaurant staffers seem to gather here after hours. Prices range from $6 for pupu to $22 for the nightly fish special. Go on Friday night and swing your natty dreads to Hawaii-style reggae from 10pm until 1am.

Tuesday, when it's $5 and drinks are $1 from 9pm to 1am. ***Sneaky trick:*** Get in the door before 9pm, and there's no cover.

Don't be fooled by the mollusks at the **Lahaina Store Grille & Oyster Bar** (744 Front St.; ☎ 808/661-9090). It's just as much of a meat market as Moose McGillycuddy's. You might have to wait 20 minutes to get in the door, but who knows, you might also meet that sweaty special someone on the dance floor who enjoys Irish Car Bombs and Red Headed Sluts just as much as you do.

For good microbrewed beer, in a cool, dimly lit, dark-wood-paneled setting, drive north of Lahaina to the Kahana Gateway Shopping Mall and grab a bar stool at the **Maui Brewing Co.** (4405 Honoapiilani Hwy.; ☎ 808/669-3474; www.mauibrewingco.com). This restaurant (p. 265) and nominal sports bar is also a microbrewery that creates its own beers in small, seven-barrel batches. The beer lineup changes, but try the Double Overhead IPA if it's available. It's smooth, hoppy, and strong, with a name that plays off both its 4-month fermentation process (rather than the normal 2 months) and a system that surfers use to measure wave heights. Happy hour runs 3pm to 5pm.

IN UPCOUNTRY

In the cool, sleepy upcountry town of Makawao, **Casanova's Italian Restaurant & Deli** (1188 Makawao Ave.; ☎ 808/572-0220; www.casanovamaui.com) goes through an unusual evolution each day. It starts out as a casual coffeehouse and deli in the mornings and afternoons. At dinner, it turns into a reasonably priced, family-oriented Italian place. After the tables are cleared and the children packed off to bed, it cranks up the music, draws in the late-night crowd, and turns into

The Sly Mongoose

Lahaina's Front Street has some rowdy, divey bars, like Moose McGillycuddy's, but it doesn't have any true dive bars—places that serve canned beer and potato chips, and where regulars show up with casserole dishes of beef Stroganoff to share because they know they're going to stay a while. There's only one place like that left in Lahaina: **The Sly Mongoose** ★ (1036 Limahana Place; ☎ 808/661-8097). Hidden away on a back street on the *mauka* side of Honoapiilani Highway, the Sly Mongoose elicits either affection or derision, depending on who's talking about it. When a friend and I sought directions from a young mainland transplant working at a Front Street activities kiosk, he warned us to stay away from the place or we'd probably get beaten up. We went anyway and stayed far longer than we intended. When we finally tore ourselves away, we took with us a Sly Mongoose baseball cap, a Sly Mongoose woman's tank top, a half-dozen Sly Mongoose bumper stickers, two good beer buzzes, and the life stories of several Sly Mongoose regulars, including the bartender, all of whom had become our new friends, and none of whom even once suggested we fight. We probably could have had some beef Stroganoff, too, but the regulars ate it all before we got there.

Free Shows at Kaanapali

At **Whalers Village** (2435 Kaanapali Pkwy.), two beachfront restaurant-bars have musicians whom anyone walking by or hanging out on the grass outside can see and hear perfectly well. Don't feel badly about enjoying the music for free—lots of people do it, and nobody minds. At the **Hula Grill** (☎ 808/667-6636), Hawaiian musicians take the stage daily from 3 to 5pm and 7 to 9:30pm. At **Leilani's on the Beach** (☎ 808/661-4495), there's live soft rock and oldies Friday through Sunday from 3 to 5pm. Pick whichever act sounds best, plop down outside, and enjoy the free show. I'd especially recommend going at sunset. For hula, stroll north along the beach walk fronting the hotels until you reach the **Kaanapali Beach Hotel** (2525 Kaanapali Pkwy., Lahaina; ☎ 800/262-8450 or 808/661-0011; www.kbhmaui.com), which brings out dancers every night from 6:30 to 7:30pm to entertain whoever cares to attend, free of charge. The music starts at 6pm and lasts until 9pm. If you continue north to the end of the beach walk, you'll come to Black Rock, aka Puu Kekaa, where the **Sheraton Maui Resort** (2605 Kaanapali Pkwy.; ☎ 808/661-0031) has been holding a free sunset torch lighting and cliff-diving ceremony every evening for the last 3 decades.

one of Maui's hippest, most intimate nightclubs. Makawao's proximity to Paia, the international crossroads for windsurfers, ensures that Casanova's crowd always has a tanned, toned, European flavor to it with no particular allegiance to the current time zone. Casanova's Wild Wahine Wednesdays is Maui's undisputed champion of ladies' nights. Friday and Saturday nights are for live music, including a monthly salsa and samba happening.

ON THE NORTH SHORE

In Paia town, **Charley P. Woofer Saloon** (142 Hana Hwy.; ☎ 808/579-8085) undergoes a similar daily transmutation, starting the day as a breakfast place where cops, windsurfers, and Hana-bound tourists enjoy oversize pancakes and eggs Benedict. It serves lunch and dinner through the rest of the day, then puts on its honky-tonk pants, cracks open the beer, and cranks up the country-western. This being Hawaii, it also cranks up the reggae, the rock, and the contemporary Hawaiian. Everyone will tell you that this is the place you're most likely to see Willie Nelson, who lives around here and who's a close friend of the owner. And even if you miss Willie, you'll see his gold and platinum records displayed on the wall, and an enormous replica of his guitar. The bar is trying to get the Guinness Book of World Records to recognize the monster-size instrument as the world's largest guitar. Maui's other Wille—Willie K (p. 326)—takes the stage every Monday night.

A few steps from Charley's, you'll find the epicenter of north-shore nightlife: **Jacques Northshore Bistro** ★ (120 Hana Hwy., Paia; ☎ 808/579-8844). In case you were wondering where all the windsurfers, kiteboarders, surfers, and other

Paia beach creatures go after dark to eat raw fish, down exotic drinks, and tear up the gentle night on the dance floor, this is the place. Lit by torches and tucked behind bamboo fencing, with outdoor seating under a big-top canopy ceiling, Jacques has a DJ on Friday and Saturday around 9pm, after its kitchen and the sushi bar close.

CENTRAL MAUI

Meanwhile, in Wailuku, the hippest nightspot in town is **Café Marc Aurel** (28 N. Market St.; ☎ 808/244-0852; Mon–Sat 4–9pm or later; www.cafemarcaurel.com). After starting out as an Internet cafe and coffee bar, it has grown up into a wine bar, too, with more than 80 wines by the glass ($5 and up), as well as gourmet cheeses and port. Marc, the young owner, has a laid-back manner and a forgiving attitude toward patrons who order a wine they don't like. "My motto is if you don't like it, that's okay—I'll drink it and bring you something else," he says cheerfully. During the Saturday wine tastings (3–5pm; flights start at $11) Marc will sit at your table with you and talk about what you're drinking. Mondays are open-mic nights, and Thursdays are reserved for live jazz and blues.

ABCs of Maui

American Express Offices are located in South Maui at the **Grand Wailea Resort** (☎ **808/875-4526**), and in West Maui at the **Westin Maui at Kaanapali Beach** (☎ **808/661-7155**).

Dentists Emergency dental care is available at **Kihei Dental Center,** 1847 S. Kihei Rd., Kihei (☎ **808/874-8401**), or in **Lahaina at the Aloha Lahaina Dentists,** 134 Luakini St. (in the Maui Medical Group Building), Lahaina (☎ **808/661-4005**).

Doctors **West Maui Healthcare Center,** Whalers Village, 2435 Kaanapali Pkwy., Suite H-7 (near Leilani's Restaurant), Kaanapali (☎ **808/667-9721;** fax 808/661-1584), is open 365 days a year until 10pm nightly; no appointment is necessary. In Kihei call **Urgent Care Maui,** 1325 S. Kihei Rd., Suite 103 (at Lipoa St., across from Star Market; ☎ **808/879-7781**), which is open daily from 6am to midnight.

Emergencies Call ☎ **911** for police, fire, and ambulance service. District stations are located in Lahaina (☎ 808/661-4441) and in Hana (☎ 808/248-8311).

Hospitals In Central Maui, **Maui Memorial Hospital** is at 221 Mahalani, Wailuku (☎ **808/244-9056**). East Maui's **Hana Medical Center** is on Hana Highway (☎ **808/248-8924**). In upcountry Maui, **Kula Hospital** is at 204 Kula Hwy., Kula (☎ **808/878-1221**).

Post Office To find the nearest post office, call ☎ 800/ASK-USPS. In Lahaina, there are branches at the Lahaina Civic Center, 1760 Honoapiilani Hwy., and at the Lahaina Shopping Center, 132 Papalaua St. In Kahului, there's a branch at 138 S. Puunene Ave.; and in Kihei, there's one at 1254 S. Kihei Rd.

Weather For the current weather, call ☎ 808/871-5054; for Haleakala National Park weather, call ☎ 808/572-9306; for marine weather and surf and wave conditions, call ☎ 808/877-3477.

7 Hawaii: The Big Island

With black sand & red-hot lava, the Big Island is bigger than all the other Hawaiian islands combined—& still growing.

by David Thompson

I HAVE A FRIEND ON THE BIG ISLAND WHO LIVES NEAR THE SPOT WHERE AN old palm grove once grew along a black-sand beach on the edge of a beautiful bay. In 1990, a lava flow burned the trees, buried the black sand, and created a raw new coastline where the mouth of the bay used to be. My friend had a crying rock out there where she liked to sit when things weren't going well. She once took me to see it, and we found that an enormous fissure had opened up along the shore, threatening to dump the crying rock and a huge slice of the new coastline it sat on into the pounding surf.

That's how the Big Island is: sometimes beautiful, sometimes menacing, and always on the verge of change.

The party responsible for the island's ever-morphing face is currently a hyperactive volcano called Kilauea. Since 1983, Kilauea has erupted almost continuously, and it's showing no signs of letting up. The smooth-flowing, generally non-explosive nature of the eruption means you can sometimes inch up as close to the red hot lava as you could get to an open blast furnace. When you wander through the steaming, otherworldly landscape Kilauea has created at Hawaii Volcanoes National Park—the island's top visitor attraction—you feel the yin-yang nature of creation and destruction on a massive, blackened, sulfuric scale.

Erosion has yet to catch up with expansion on the Big Island. At 4,028 square miles and growing, it's bigger than all of the other Hawaiian Islands combined. It's the island with breathing room. That and amazing geographic diversity. Thanks to two of the largest mountains in the Pacific, Mauna Kea and Mauana Loa, which rise from sea level to nearly 14,000 feet, the Big Island has 11 of the world's 13 climate zones. That means you'll find coastal deserts where ancient petroglyphs and Hawaiian archaeological sites slowly age in the sun, steamy rainforests with more waterfalls than you can count, cool upland ranches where cowboys roam, and sometimes even snow-covered alpine peaks. As for beaches, Big Island's tend to be rocky and made of black sand. But there is a stretch of coast graced with golden sandy beaches that rival anything Maui, Oahu, or Kauai have to offer.

DON'T LEAVE THE BIG ISLAND WITHOUT . . .

Visiting a volcano. Kilauea (p. 394) is not only one of the world's most active volcanoes, it's one of the world's tamest—comparatively speaking. On the right days, you can hike out onto the flow field and stand as close to molten lava as you dare.

Eating a volcano. At Sushi Rock (p. 361), on the northern tip of the island, a sushi chef, unrestrained by traditional training, makes a roll called the Mauna Loa Eruption: ahi, smoked salmon, and a seasonal Hawaiian white fish made into a shield volcano with scallion cream and fiery orange tobiko pouring down its sides.

Swimming through an underwater park. Kealakekua Bay (p. 403) is a state park, a marine-life conservation district, and one of the best places to snorkel in Hawaii.

Making it to the ancient Place of Refuge. At the remarkably well-preserved sanctuary of Puuhonua o Honaunau (p. 378), noncombatants could find safety in wartime and *kapu* (taboo) breakers could find a second chance. To visit the site today is to come face to face with ancient Hawaii, grimacing idols and all.

Drinking Kava with Hawaiians & hippies. Join the laid-back and motley crowd of regulars from the wilds of rural Puna (p. 398) to partake in the mildly narcotic but perfectly legal pleasures of the awa root.

A BRIEF HISTORY

At just under a million years old, the Big Island is the youngest of the Hawaiian Islands. Culturally, though, it is where Hawaii began. The first Polynesians to settle the Hawaiian archipelago started here, at South Point, the remote, wind-swept southernmost tip of both the island and the United States. Throughout the Big Island, you'll find more remnants of the ancient world these first people created than anywhere else in Hawaii. Some are carved in stone, thousands of times, in the densest petroglyph fields of the Pacific. There are also ancient fishponds to see, *heiau* (temples), and village sites, as well as Puuhonua O Honaunau, where Hawaiians could find refuge in times of war or redemption if they had broken a *kapu.*

This is the island from which King Kamehameha came, the first Hawaiian king to rule all of Hawaii. Today you can hike to the place he was born, drive to the massive war *heiau* he built, and attend a luau at what were once the grounds of his royal compound, where he died.

BEACHES & VOLCANOES

The Big Island is too young to have much of its 282 miles of coastline adorned with beaches, but the beaches it does have are real gems. In addition to powdery white- or golden-sand beaches, it's got black-sand beaches, hallmarks of a volcanic island still in the fiery throes of development. The Big Island's most famous black-sand beach, Kaimu Beach, disappeared in 1990 beneath a lava flow from Kilauea. A new beach, however, is forming in the area, and you can hike out over the lava at the end of the road (which was also covered) in Puna to see it.

A Note on Terminology & Organization

Hawaii is the proper name for the Big Island, but most people use the latter name to distinguish the island from the state. The ancient Hawaiians divided the Big Island into six districts, which are still recognized today: Kona, Kohala, Hilo, Hamakua, Puna, and Kau. I've divided the sections of this chapter in two: east Hawaii and west Hawaii. West Hawaii includes Kona and Kohala, where most visitors stay. East Hawaii takes in the rest. To balance east and west, I've given South Point, the southernmost tip of the island, to East Hawaii, though it could have logically gone to the other side. The northern part of the island, inaccessible from the east side, falls clearly into west Hawaii. Mauna Kea, which looms large over both sides of the island, looms largest over east Hawaii, so that's where I placed it.

Two active volcanoes—Kilauea and Mauna Loa—keep things interesting on the Big Island. While Mauna Loa hasn't spilled lava since 1984, it hasn't exactly been quiet. Scientists using finely calibrated GPS instruments have been watching the 13,677-foot tall mountain slowly swell and shrink over the decades, inflating and deflating like a lung. It's almost as if the mountain, which makes up more than half of the whole island, were slowly breathing, perhaps catching its breath before its next big show.

Kilauea is a smaller volcano growing out of the side of Mauna Loa. It's the hyperactive youngster that simply can't sit still. Since it began erupting 1983, it's destroyed palm groves, rainforests, beaches, highways, ancient Hawaiian sties, an ill-conceived modern subdivision, and the fishing village of Kalapana. It's also added 600 acres of new land to the island, and it continues to add more. Located mostly within Hawaii Volcanoes National Park, you can, on a good day, hike out to where molten lava oozes, pools, and cascades across the flow field, sometimes pouring from 80-foot cliffs into the sea. On Kilauea's summit, you can watch volcanic gasses rise from 400-foot-deep Halemaumau Crater, where the Hawaiian volcano goddess Pele dwells.

Pele's rival, the goddess of snow, Poliahu, makes her home atop Mauna Kea (another of the island's major mountains). Historically, these two goddesses haven't gotten along. It's been 3,500 years or so since Pele last invaded Poliahu's territory, with a series of explosive late-stage eruptions that left Mauna Kea's summit covered with pimply cinder cones. But a few times each year, Poliahu continues to taunt Pele by dusting the smooth black dome of Mauna Loa with snow. Pele hasn't answered for some time, but since Mauna Kea is classified as dormant, not extinct, I wouldn't count her out.

Pele may quietly seethe when it snows on Mauna Loa, but only astronomers get upset when it snows on Mauna Kea. They can wait years for a few precious hours at one of the 13 telescopes on the summit, the best place for astronomy on the planet, and if it snows on their nights, they're out of luck. Others on the island love the snow. They dash up to the summit with snowboards and inner tubes, and fill the beds of their pickups with powder so they can make snowmen at the beach.

With a four-wheel-drive rental, or on a tour, you can get to the top of Mauna Kea to ponder the universe from a point above so much of the earth's atmosphere, the stars don't twinkle. Or you can drive as far as 9,200 feet, to the visitor center, which is still plenty high. That's where I once went to watch the sunrise. As the sky lightened that morning, my chattering teeth relaxed, and slowly the clouds beneath me began to part and thin. I could see patches of ocean glaring white with sunlight, and then parts of the coastline. It would be warm at the beach for sure, and I thought about maybe heading there next. Either way, it would in all likelihood turn out to be another beautiful day on the Big Island.

LAY OF THE LAND

Here are the highlights of the Big Island's major areas.

WEST HAWAII

Kona

On the sunny west side of the island, Kona is the center of Big Island tourism, with its sunset cruises, marlin fishing, luaus, historic sites, and abundance of places to shop, eat, stay, and lounge around in the sun. Dormant Hualalai volcano, rising to 8,275 feet, dominates the north part of Kona, including the main town, Kailua-Kona (so named to distinguish it from Kailua, Oahu). Kailua-Kona has its charms (which you'll find mostly along or in the ocean) but it suffers from heat, dust, traffic, and tackiness. Nicer, mellower, cooler towns, such as Holualoa and Kealakekua, lie in Kona's upland areas, where Kona coffee comes from.

Kona has some of the best snorkeling spots on the island, including Kealakekua Bay, where Captain Cook was killed, and Honaunau Bay, home to the ancient Place of Refuge. The north part of Kona is covered with miles of desolate black lava fields, which have some startlingly beautiful beaches along them, as well as an alarmingly expensive resort development, the first along the so-called Gold Coast.

Kohala

The string of Gold Coast resorts continues north of Kona into Kohala, where dazzling beaches share the shoreline with exclusive hotels, all along the edge of a vast lava desert. Rooms at these resorts tend to cost more than most dollar-wise travelers would ever pay, but great deals can sometimes be found and are worth looking for. Note, too, that the beaches in this area are accessible; they're public and open to everyone, as are all beaches in Hawaii.

North of the resorts, you can visit the enormous war *heiau* (temple) that Kamehameha built at Kawaihae, where the west side's only deep-draft harbor is. Inland, and set among velvety green hills and pastures at the base of the 4,120-foot Kohala Mountains, is Waimea, an old cowboy town gone upscale. This is the home of the enormous 225,000-acre Parker Ranch (which you can tour by horseback, ATV, or covered wagon).

At the northern tip of the island, on the other side of the Kohala Mountains, there are more ancient Hawaiian sites to see, including Kamehameha's birthplace, as well as former plantation towns like Hawi, and the lush Pololu Valley, with a beach that threatens swimmers but rewards beachcombers.

EAST HAWAII

Hilo-Hamakua Coast

Through the former sugar-cane-growing region on the northeastern side of the island, there's a great drive along the rugged coastline that runs 50 miles into the districts of Hamakua and Hilo. It takes in the overlook at Waipio Valley to the north, where Hawaiians still grow the taro they use to make poi, and runs to the city of Hilo. The route passes through rainforest and by waterfalls, including 440-foot Akaka Falls, with scenic detours along the way.

Hilo

The city of Hilo, predominant feature of the Hilo District, sits along crescent-shaped Hilo Bay, where cruise and cargo ships dock. Although rainy old Hilo is the second-largest population center in Hawaii, it has somehow maintained the feel of old Hawaii. Its frumpish downtown has some unusual shops and great restaurants, the island's best farmers market, and attractions including the Pacific Tsunami Museum (tsunamis have hit the city several times) and the well-kept old Lyman Mission House. Hilo is only about 40 minutes from Hawaii Volcanoes National Park, and a great stopping point for those headed to the park. Just out of town, on the way to the volcano, there's the Panaewa Rainforest Zoo, where visitors may borrow umbrellas and stroll the tropical grounds in any weather.

Hawaii Volcanoes National Park

The 333,000-acre park is the state's top tourist attraction, drawing some 2.5 million visitors per year. It stretches from sea level to the 13,677-foot summit of Mauna Loa, the largest volcano both on earth and in the known solar system, and includes much of Kilauea, the island's other, more active volcano. Just outside the park, Volcano Village has some bed-and-breakfasts and great restaurants, spread out though the misty cool rainforest.

Puna & Kau

Kilauea straddles the enormous rural districts of Puna and Kau. The volcanic hazards have kept real-estate prices comparatively low, drawing back-to-the-landers, hippies, pot growers, New Agers, and a general variety of free spirits for decades. Lower Puna, in particular, is the land of alternative communities and realities. The central hub, Pahoa, has a boardwalk-lined main street and several great, cheap restaurants. A hot pond, a nude beach, a lively farmers market, and a newly forming black-sand beach (replacing one the volcano swallowed) are among the area's visitor attractions. To the south, Kau has the island's most accessible black-sand beach, at Punaluu Beach Park, as well as the southernmost point in the United States, South Point, and Green Sands Beach, which takes some effort to get to but really does have green sand.

GETTING TO & AROUND THE BIG ISLAND

The Big Island has two airports. If you're going to spend time on both sides of the island, consider arriving at one and departing from the other. A steep rental-car drop-off fee of $65 or so will apply, but you'll save hours of driving and be able to make a more logical tour of the island.

The Big Island

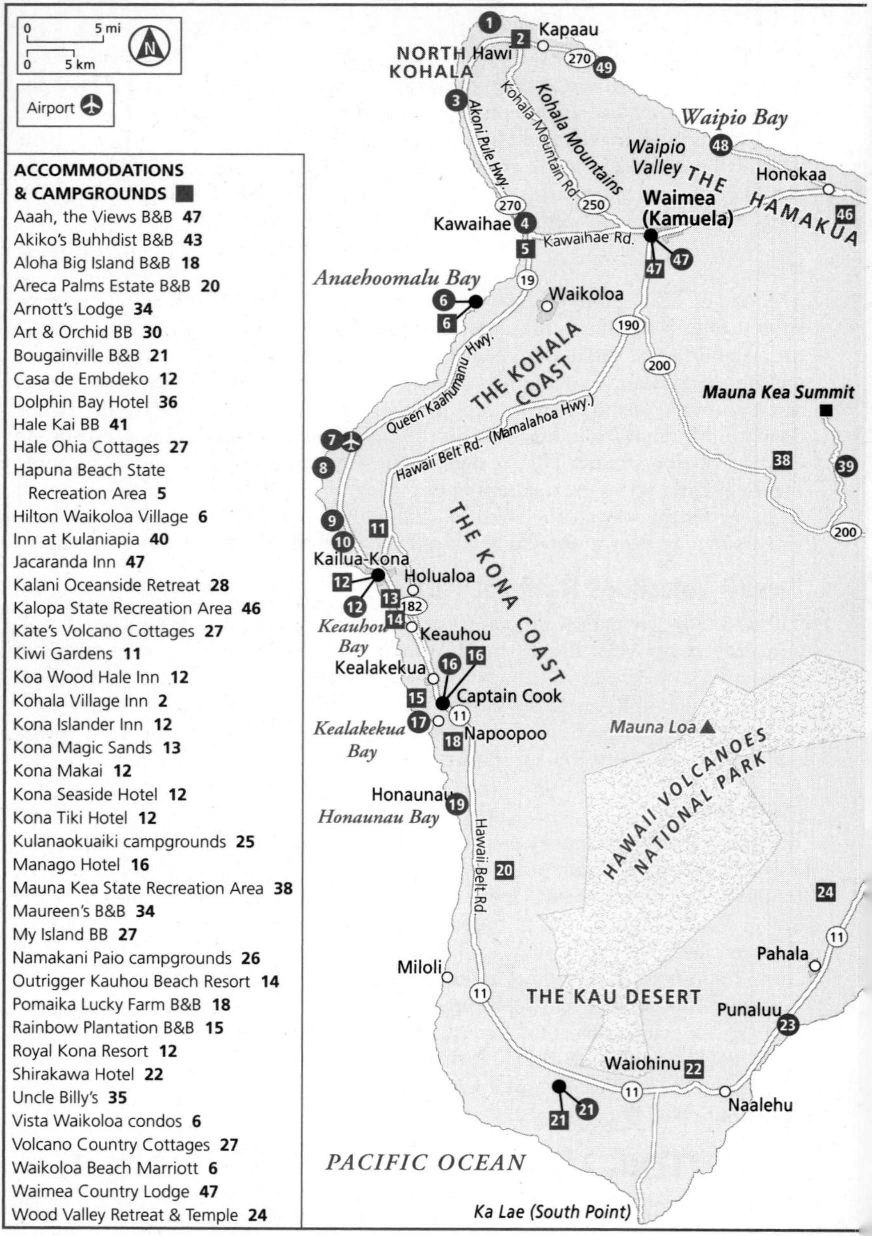

ACCOMMODATIONS & CAMPGROUNDS ■

- Aaah, the Views B&B **47**
- Akiko's Buhhdist B&B **43**
- Aloha Big Island B&B **18**
- Areca Palms Estate B&B **20**
- Arnott's Lodge **34**
- Art & Orchid BB **30**
- Bougainville B&B **21**
- Casa de Embdeko **12**
- Dolphin Bay Hotel **36**
- Hale Kai BB **41**
- Hale Ohia Cottages **27**
- Hapuna Beach State Recreation Area **5**
- Hilton Waikoloa Village **6**
- Inn at Kulaniapia **40**
- Jacaranda Inn **47**
- Kalani Oceanside Retreat **28**
- Kalopa State Recreation Area **46**
- Kate's Volcano Cottages **27**
- Kiwi Gardens **11**
- Koa Wood Hale Inn **12**
- Kohala Village Inn **2**
- Kona Islander Inn **12**
- Kona Magic Sands **13**
- Kona Makai **12**
- Kona Seaside Hotel **12**
- Kona Tiki Hotel **12**
- Kulanaokuaiki campgrounds **25**
- Manago Hotel **16**
- Mauna Kea State Recreation Area **38**
- Maureen's B&B **34**
- My Island BB **27**
- Namakani Paio campgrounds **26**
- Outrigger Kauhou Beach Resort **14**
- Pomaika Lucky Farm B&B **18**
- Rainbow Plantation B&B **15**
- Royal Kona Resort **12**
- Shirakawa Hotel **22**
- Uncle Billy's **35**
- Vista Waikoloa condos **6**
- Volcano Country Cottages **27**
- Waikoloa Beach Marriott **6**
- Waimea Country Lodge **47**
- Wood Valley Retreat & Temple **24**

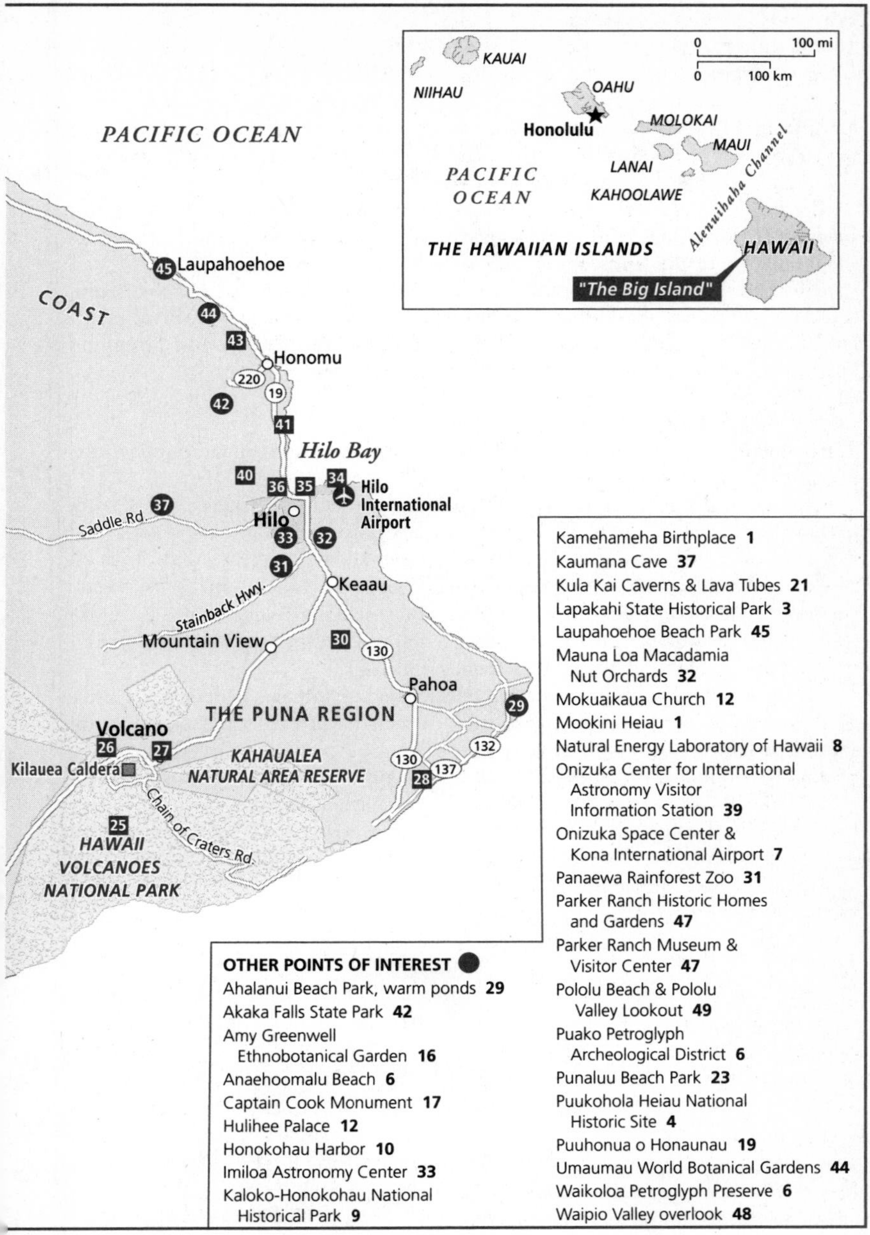

PACIFIC OCEAN
COAST
Laupahoehoe
Honomu
Hilo Bay
Hilo
Hilo International Airport
Saddle Rd.
Stainback Hwy.
Keaau
Mountain View
Pahoa
THE PUNA REGION
Volcano
Kilauea Caldera
KAHAUALEA NATURAL AREA RESERVE
Chain of Craters Rd.
HAWAII VOLCANOES NATIONAL PARK
220
19
130
132
137
45
44
43
42
41
40
36
35
34
37
33
32
31
30
29
26
27
28
25
KAUAI
NIIHAU
OAHU
Honolulu
MOLOKAI
MAUI
LANAI
KAHOOLAWE
PACIFIC OCEAN
Alenuihaha Channel
HAWAII
THE HAWAIIAN ISLANDS
"The Big Island"
0
100 mi
100 km
OTHER POINTS OF INTEREST
Ahalanui Beach Park, warm ponds 29
Akaka Falls State Park 42
Amy Greenwell Ethnobotanical Garden 16
Anaehoomalu Beach 6
Captain Cook Monument 17
Hulihee Palace 12
Honokohau Harbor 10
Imiloa Astronomy Center 33
Kaloko-Honokohau National Historical Park 9
Kamehameha Birthplace 1
Kaumana Cave 37
Kula Kai Caverns & Lava Tubes 21
Lapakahi State Historical Park 3
Laupahoehoe Beach Park 45
Mauna Loa Macadamia Nut Orchards 32
Mokuaikaua Church 12
Mookini Heiau 1
Natural Energy Laboratory of Hawaii 8
Onizuka Center for International Astronomy Visitor Information Station 39
Onizuka Space Center & Kona International Airport 7
Panaewa Rainforest Zoo 31
Parker Ranch Historic Homes and Gardens 47
Parker Ranch Museum & Visitor Center 47
Pololu Beach & Pololu Valley Lookout 49
Puako Petroglyph Archeological District 6
Punaluu Beach Park 23
Puukohola Heiau National Historic Site 4
Puuhonua o Honaunau 19
Umaumau World Botanical Gardens 44
Waikoloa Petroglyph Preserve 6
Waipio Valley overlook 48

GETTING TO & FROM THE AIRPORTS

Kona International Airport at Keahole (☎ 808/329-3423), in West Hawaii, is where most visitors land. It has direct flights from San Francisco, Los Angeles, and Oakland, though most fly in making a stop first in either Maui or Oahu. **Island Air** (☎ 808/484-2222; www.islandair.com) tends to have the least expensive flights from those two islands (on average of $145 round-trip), so check its prices if you have to change planes (and most will).

Located 7 miles north of Kailua-Kona, the runway sits partially on a lava flow from 1801. First-time visitors are sometimes aghast when they land, stunned by the desolation of the landscape. Don't worry; it's not all like this.

Hilo International Airport (☎ 808/934-5801), on the east side of the island, is located within the city limits, 10 minutes from downtown. It gets direct mainland flights from Oakland, and has indirect flights from Maui and Honolulu (again with Island Air offering the best fares; see above).

GETTING AROUND

You really need a rental car on the Big Island. Distances are great and public transportation is practically nonexistent.

In Kona and Hilo, Alamo, Avis, Budget, Dollar, Hertz, National, and Thrifty all have cars available at Kona International Airport. Of these, I've found that **Budget** (www.budgetrentacar.com; about $40 per day for an economy car with all taxes) tends to have the best prices for daily rentals, while **Alamo** (www.alamo.com; about $218 per week) beats the others on weeklong rentals. Since prices do shift often, however, be sure to shop around before renting, as it can mean big savings—between $40 and $100 dollars when I looked.

Note: If you're planning to drive Saddle Road, a somewhat dangerous drive (with a steep climb up and down), only National will come and pick you up should you break down (you drive at your own risk if you book a car through one of the other rental companies). The deal's the same to South Point, however not even National will venture out there should you have a problem—you're on your own. So, if you're considering driving one of these roads or up to the summit of Mauna Kea, turn to **Harpers Car and Truck Rental** (☎ 800/852-9993 or

The Ferry on the Way

At press time, **Hawaii Super Ferry** (www.hawaiisuperferry.com) had just begun offering ferry service—something Hawaii has been sorely lacking—between Honolulu, Maui, and Kauai. Service between Oahu and the Big Island is expected to begin in early 2009. Walk-on passengers fares of $56 Friday through Monday, and $47 Tuesday through Thursday, appear to be a better deal than airfare; however, a fuel surcharge that varies monthly (it was 37% at press time) is likely to wipe out any savings. Still, traveling between islands by boat is a fun way to go (when it's actually operating). You can trim the cost a bit by booking 14 days in advance and getting a $5 discount, and by booking online for an additional $3 off. See p. 231 and p. 430, for more on the ferry (and its quirks).

A Note on Maps

Some of the accommodations and some of the restaurants reviewed in this chapter lie outside of the near-scale maps of Kailua-Kona and Hilo on p. 368 and p. 373, respectively. For additional and more detailed maps, pick up one of the ubiquitous free visitor booklets such as ***Big Island Gold, This Week Big Island,*** and especially ***Big Island Maps, Beaches & Tours.*** You'll find them in the racks stuffed with colorful visitor-activity brochures that you'll run into everywhere, starting at the airports. These handy, pocket-size publications pinpoint many of the places to stay and eat on the island that you won't find listed on the maps here.

808/969-1478; www.harpershawaii.com). It's the only company that will cover you wherever you drive, as well as the only one to allow its four-wheel-drive vehicles to be driven to the summit of Mauna Kea. It's at the airport at Kona, and has a free shuttle to its offices for those who fly into Hilo.

Taxis on the Big Island charge $2.40 per mile with a $3 drop fee. A cab ride from the airport to Kailua-Kona costs about $24. **SpeediShuttle** (☎ 877/242-5777 or 808/242-7777; www.speedishuttle.co), which runs passengers from the Kona airport to points around the island, charges about the same.

Arnott's Lodge and the Hawaii Naniloa Hotel send shuttles to the Hilo airport. No other shuttle or bus service is available. A taxi to the Banyan Drive Hotels of Hilo from the Hilo airport costs about $11; to downtown about $12; and to Volcano Village about $73.

ACCOMMODATIONS, BOTH STANDARD & NOT

by Pauline Frommer & David Thompson

When it comes to accommodations, the Big Island could be called the Budget Island. Nightly rates, except at the properties along the Kohala Coast, tend to be a good 15% to 20% lower than what you'd find for similar properties on Maui, Kauai, or Oahu.

That being said, the Big Island has less of a variety of accommodations within certain areas than the other islands do. Just as the topography of the Big Island shifts from area to area (and is continuing to shift as the mighty Pele adds acreage hour by hour with her lava flow), so the various kinds of accommodations shift dramatically from region to region. In Kailua-Kona, for instance, condominiums outnumber hotels 10 to 1, making condos the lodging of choice. South of Kona and in the town of Waimea, small B&Bs predominate; to the north, along the Kohala coast, it's all fantastically decadent and expensive luxury resorts; and for those looking to stay on the east side of the island, the outlook gets even wackier, with rustic campgrounds and Buddhist retreats competing with more standard options. Since the methods for finding nonhotel properties can be as important as picking the property itself, look for the boxes below that profile some of the top condo- and vacation-rental agencies. Be sure to cross-reference as you read, and compare the many options for lodging on the Big Island before making your final decision on where to stay

Finding Your Place to Stay

The accommodations in the following sections can be found on the map on p. 336.

WEST HAWAII

Kona

A honky-tonk of a town, Kailua-Kona is the Big Island's answer to Lahaina in Maui or Fort Lauderdale in Florida. Its central strip, beachfront Alii Drive, is lined with T-shirt shops, trinket stores, and such "yikes, this must be a really touristy place" red flags as the Bubba Gump Shrimp Company and the Hard Rock Cafe. Like much of the Big Island, there are only a scattering of sandy beaches; all the lodgings in Kona sit on the rocky shore, though a handful (as noted in reviews) are next to small patches of sand.

But if you're looking for reasonably priced, oceanfront accommodations, this area can be a mecca; there are affordable condos by the score, as well as a handful of hotels that provide excellent value for the money. Kona will also appeal to travelers who enjoy having a wide variety of shops, restaurants, and bars within easy reach.

CONDOS

As I said before, condos are the name of the game in Kona. For the most part, they offer an excellent value because they provide a full kitchen (which trims food costs), never charge extra for parking, and often come equipped with boogie boards and other beach items. Decorated by individual owners, it's nearly impossible to guarantee what you'll get in terms of looks, but after recently touring dozens of units in Kona, I found them all pleasant enough on the eyes, usually with a variation on the palm-tree and tropical-fish themes for the bedspreads and curtains; some type of rattan or wicker set of furniture in the living room; and framed nautical prints along the walls. I didn't find a single bed that was too soft or saggy, though I did see some that had minor upkeep problems (a slightly stained rug, a chipped chair). Those owned by folks who spend some portion of the year in them tend to be a tad nicer and better maintained than those with absentee landlords. (***Note:*** When you book, try to inquire about the owner's involvement.) All of the condos in this area can be booked through the major rental agencies in town (see box); or perhaps for a greater savings, through those direct-access websites that pair owners with renters such as **VRBO** (www.vrbo.com), **Rentalo** (www.rentalo.com), and **Home Away** (www.homeawy.com). If price is your priority, this may be the way to go, though if you're unhappy with your condo, you won't have the same ability to switch as you would when dealing with a rental agent who handles dozens of properties.

$–$$ The cheapest decent condos can be found at the **Kona Islander Inn** (75–5776 Kuakini Hwy., south of Hualalai Rd.; see "Top Condo-Rental Companies in Kona" box, p. 341, for information on booking), a complex of six three-story buildings centered around a small oval pool and communal barbecue grill. Motel-like in

Top Condo-Rental Companies in Kona

Three big fish (spinner dolphins, perhaps?) are active in the Kona rental market, and you'll probably find yourself booking with one of them if you decide to go the condo route.

Hawaii Resort Management, Inc. (75-5776 Kuakini Hwy., in the lobby of the Islander Inn; ☎ 800/244-4752 or 808/329-3333; www.konarentals.com; daily 8am–8pm; DISC, MC, V) is the most proudly "budget" of the three, representing properties that run the gamut from top-of-the-line to slightly frayed around the edges. Unlike the other companies, which base prices solely on view, number of bedrooms, and season, this renter factors decor and upkeep into its prices, charging a bit less for places that might have a scuff mark on the wall or an older couch. "People come here to explore the Big Island, so they're looking for a clean, affordable place to stay," owner Jim Metcalf told me. "Price is what sells." All in all, HRM represents upwards of 250 condos all around Kona and a handful of vacation homes.

Knutson Realty (☎ 800/800-6202 or 808/329-6311; www.konahawaiirentals.com; Mon–Fri 8am–4:30pm; MC, V) is highly selective in the properties it represents. "I don't believe you should come 5,000 miles and sleep on a musty pillow," laughed owner Marilyn Knutson when we last spoke. "We have a reputation to uphold and most of our business is repeat customers, so I try and choose places that people will really love." To that end, Knutson only represents condos on the oceanfront side of Alii Drive and is militant about upkeep. Each of the condo owners gives her $200, which she can use for on-the-spot upgrades if needed, things like replacement shower curtains or new clock radios. Knutson and her staff also try to put customer service first. "I'm not hard as nails," says Knutson. "If someone doesn't like their place, I'll do everything in my power to move them and make sure they have an enjoyable vacation."

Sunquest Vacations (77-6435 Kuakini Hwy.; ☎ 800/367-5169 or 808/329-6438; www.sunquest-hawaii.com; Mon–Fri 8am–6pm; DISC, MC, V) represents a large range of properties at most of the resorts and in all price ranges. I've found the service here to be a bit lacking (late returns on phone calls, less than helpful with directions), but because they're the gatekeepers for upwards of 200 properties, you're going to want to contact them when shopping around.

its looks, all the units are studios, and small ones at that, with kitchenettes instead of kitchens, two-seater lanais, and tiny showers wedged into Lilliputian bathrooms. In its favor, the landscaping is quite lush, with abundant plants and trees lining the paths. Some units have ocean views (though distant ones; the condo is across the street from the ocean) and the Islander is within walking distance of all the downtown shops. Rooms rent for between $69 and $105 per night, though the price can

The Fine Print on Condos

Before making a reservation, be sure to:

- Read the cancellation policy. For most condo rentals, full payment is due in advance of the stay and a cancellation can lead to a forfeiture if the rental agency is unable to rebook the unit. That's why it's usually a good idea to buy travel insurance, and you should be sure to get it from an outside source, as you don't want to lose your money if the condo-rental agency goes belly-up.
- Calculate the cleaning fees. These will vary from unit to unit and can add between $60 and $90 to the ultimate cost of your stay, so factor these in before booking.
- Check for any additional fees. Get all costs up front, before booking. You don't want to be surprised by a "reservations fee," or some other additional charge, at the end of your stay.

drop to $49 a night at the slower times of the year (mostly in midautumn, with weeklong bookings only). Hawaii Resort Management (see above) represents the most units here (not surprising, as its offices are on property), though other companies also take a piece of the pie.

$–$$$$ A step up, both in price and ambience, is **Kona Magic Sands** ★★ (77-6452 Alii Dr.; see "Top Condo-Rental Companies in Kona" box, p. 341, for information on booking), whose major selling point is its magnificent sea views. Every unit has a lanai that overlooks the water. Though this place is one of many properties on the strip, its location gives the illusion that you're all alone with the sea and the spinner dolphins and whales you can watch from your balcony. As for the rooms, they're about a third bigger than those at the Islander Inn (above), with full usable kitchens and good-size bathrooms. In front of the complex is a handsome small pool that juts out over the ocean; if you want the real thing, you can simply stroll next door to the small sandy beach adjoining the property. The only place you may not want to "swim" is in your shower, as the water never seems to get beyond lukewarm. Still, for between $110 and $189 per night for an oceanfront condo (sometimes down to just $85), who's complaining? Also on-site is a very fine, white-tablecloth seafood restaurant.

$–$$$$ Two pools, including one nifty rock-hewn saltwater pool overlooking the sea, are the crowning glory of the **Casa de Emdeko** ★ kids (75-6082 Alii Dr.; see "Top Condo-Rental Companies in Kona" box, above, for information on booking). This nicely landscaped older property is about a mile from the hustle and bustle of town. Midsize one- and two-bedroom units are a good value here, spacious enough for families and renting for between $87 and $130 for the smaller units, and $142 and $200 for the two-bedrooms. An on-site convenience store and deli are a plus for those who don't want to hit the traffic-clogged road into town.

$\$$–$\$\$\$$ I like the **Kona Makai** ★★ (kids) (5–6026 Alii Dr.; see "Top Condo-Rental Companies in Kona" box, above, for information on booking) as much for its grounds as for its one- and two-bedroom apartments. Forming a rectangular box, with the ocean at one end, the property has a large, luxuriant grass lawn in the middle, with a medium-size pool at the ocean end and a hot tub to one side. In one of the complexes are two tiny gyms (one for weights, the other cardio), a Ping-Pong table, and well-maintained tennis courts. As for the units (approximately 600 sq. ft.), they're perfectly pleasant, with sea-view lanais. But it's the seaside location and all the outdoor entertainments here that make this property a particularly good deal at $100 to $150 a night (sometimes dipping to $92 for longer stays) for a one-bedroom, and about $15 more per night for a one-bedroom unit with an attached sleeping loft.

HOTELS & B&Bs

$–$$ Kona has a half-dozen reasonably priced hotels, but I think the smallest, cheapest one is the best. You're not going to get Frette linens at the **Kona Tiki Hotel** ★★★ 75–5968 Alii Dr.; ☎ 808/329-1425; www.konatiki.com; cash only; book far in advance) or a decor that's anything but motel-simple. But you will be staying right on the ocean for as little as $69 a night (up to $92 for kitchenette units), and you'll have the pleasure of lodging at what has to be one of the most convivial, service-oriented small hotels in Hawaii. To put it simply, the people who work here are darn nice and go out of their way to please the guests—by giving great advice on local hot spots, keeping the place immaculate, supplying visitors with free beach toys, and providing an abundant (and included) fruit-laden continental breakfast each morning. This lends the Kona Tiki a clubby atmosphere, and most weeks the guests (70% returnees) throw potluck dinners, impromptu ukulele singalongs, and game nights, or simply gather to cook together at the communal BBQ grill. One of the guests blows a ceremonial conch to mark the moment of sunset. The only downside to this place—though those seeking a real escape from the world will think this an upside—is the lack of TVs and telephones. It costs an extra $6 for children ages 2 to 12 to stay in their parents' rooms, extra adults are $10.

$–$$ While not nearly as special, the **Kona Seaside Hotel** (kids) (75–5646 Palani Rd., at Kuakini Hwy.; ☎ 800/560-5558 or 808/329-2455; www.konaseasidehotel.com; AE, DISC, MC, V) is also a value, and Hawaiian-owned, so you know you're doing the right thing by staying here. Its mountain-view rooms (read: overlooking the street) are a steal starting at just $88; quieter ones, with views of the interior gardens, come in at a reasonable $98. The key to booking here is to use the hotel's website, where there are nearly always specials, slashing a good 30% off the published rates even in high season. The rooms themselves are standard-looking and can vary widely in decor from building to building in this complex, so if you don't like what you're offered, ask to see another (there are 225 in total). On the grounds are two small swimming pools, a restaurant, and a bar; each well-maintained room comes equipped with air-conditioning, cable TV, and a fridge. Children under 12 stay free.

Staying Connected

The Big Island is a bit behind the mainland when it comes to offering Wi-Fi capability at hotels and other lodgings. In general, Wi-Fi won't be available, though I've noted the hotels that do have it.

$$ My favorite B&B in Kona—and there aren't that many to choose from—is **Kiwi Gardens** (74-4920 Kiwi St.; ☎ 877/526-8352 or 808/885-6651; www.kiwigardens.com; DISC, D, MC, V), a secluded, gated retreat 3 miles into the mountains above Kona. It's a bit of an odd place—the living room is outfitted to look something like a 1950s ice cream parlor, with an actual soda fountain and round leatherette booth—but the three guest rooms here are tremendously comfortable, especially the massive master suite ($125 per night), which looks out onto its own private section of a porch and beyond to the distant sea. Two smaller but still generously proportioned rooms go for $105 and $115 and share a bathroom. You'll get pretty accurate pictures of the rooms on the website. The daily breakfast, included in the price, is picked from the organic garden at back by the friendly horticulturist host, whose day job is at the nearby golf club, overseeing the landscaping there. Though the fruits may look gnarled, they're exquisitely sweet. ***Note:*** Occasionally, this B&B's owner drops the price to $90 a night for those over the age of 60; ask.

$$–$$$ If you happen to come to Hawaii on an air/hotel package, you're likely to be lodged at the **Royal Kona Resort** (75-5852 Alii Dr.; ☎ 800/22-ALOHA or 808/329-3111; www.hawaiianhotelsandresorts.com; AE, DISC, MC, V), which used to be owned by Pleasant Hawaiian Holidays and still hosts its customers (as well as those of other group travel companies). An older property, its appeal is retro-groovy, in the manner of Austin Powers: hip but somewhat bucktoothed. The on-site restaurant is a tiki bar gone wild, with massive faux Polynesian wooden sculptures. Guest rooms feature such nostalgic touches as chairs with pineapples carved into their backs, Chinese dragons lamps, and Asian-accented bureaus. If you ignore the published rates and go to the website, it's easy to get a garden-view room for between $130 and $145. (The hotel is right over the water, so this may be the place to splurge on an oceanview room at $155 and up.) The resort throws a twice-weekly luau; it also boasts a private saltwater swimming lagoon and small freshwater pool. There's Wi-Fi in the lobby, but not yet in the rooms.

$$$–$$$$ My final choice in Kona looks like a splurge from afar. It's a full-service resort with a spa, two sleek restaurants, tennis courts, four bars (with nightly live entertainment), and a golf course a short drive away. The rooms are handsomely appointed with teak and wicker furniture, plush beds, celadon green walls, and unusual square bathtub/showers. The grounds are fascinating to wander; they contain an ancient fertility spring in one grove of trees, and a series of tide pools much beloved by green turtles (forming an impromptu zoo at the front of the hotel). Hotel guests are also blessed with one of the best snorkeling beaches on the island, just next door to the resort. But the **Outrigger Keauhou Beach Resort** ★★ kids

(78–6740 Alii Dr.; ☎ 800/OUTRIGGER or 808/322-3441; www.outrigger.com; AE, DISC, MC, V) is actually a bargain hunter's paradise. Though it advertises rates starting at $249 a night, it's a snap to find these same garden-view rooms for just $145, mostly through Expedia.com, which gets the best rates at this property (better than what you'll find by calling direct). Those who'd prefer a glimpse of the ocean will spend $20 to $60 more, depending on the rate and season, which is still a good deal for a resort of this quality.

A HOSTEL OPTION

$ The only hostel in Kona is the **Koa Wood Hale Inn** (75–184 Ala Onaona St.; ☎ 808/326-7018; MC, V), a somewhat grubby place in an iffy neighborhood far from the water. When I last visited, the manager was making a lot of noises about improving it, though that hasn't happened yet. Still, if you need something ultra-cheap, at $25 a night for a dorm-room bed, you won't do better in Kona. Some of the mattresses are just fine, while others will tattoo their every spring into your back, so ask to switch beds if you're uncomfortable. The inn also has some private bedrooms ($55–$75/night with shared bath), but they aren't as nice as similarly priced ones closer to the ocean.

The South Kona Coast

For an area as caffeinated as this one—the South Kona Coast is home to the Big Island's major coffee plantations—this is a remarkably laid-back region of small towns, winding mountain roads, and breathtaking sea vistas. Stay here if you'd like to have the shopping and restaurants of Kailua-Kona within easy reach but want to avoid the crowds. It's also the best place to decamp if you plan to spend a significant amount of time at the Place of Refuge (p. 378), the Big Island's second-most important tourist sight. Snorkeling is another huge draw in the Place of Refuge area, and while none of the lodgings below are directly on the beach, they're all an easy 5- to 10-minute drive away.

$ Lodgings in this area consist primarily of B&Bs. The one exception is the **Manago Hotel** (P.O. Box 145, Captain Cook; ☎ 808/323-2642; www.managohotel.com; DISC, MC, V), a ramshackle old joint which was opened in 1917 with rooms in the older part of the hotel that look like they were lifted from a documentary on the Great Depression: peeling paint, sagging beds in cell-like rooms, a chipped lonely dresser huddled against a wall. These double rooms, which attract a number of permanent residents, all share communal bathrooms and go for just $37 per night, making them perhaps the cheapest private rooms on the island. But if that sounds a bit too hard-core, the hotel has a newer section at the back that boasts firm beds (mattresses are moved from here to the cheaper part of the hotel when they wear out), spic-and-span bathrooms, and lanais with lovely ocean views (especially from the top floor) for between $58 and $63 a night. There are no phones or TVs in either area of the hotel.

$–$$$ The truth is, B&Bs aren't necessarily super expensive, and there are delightful ones in this area. **The Aloha Big Island B&B** ★ kids (83–5410 Middle Ke'ei Rd., Captain Cook; ☎ 877/328-8053 or 808/328-8053; www.konabednbreakfast.com; MC, V), for example, is a hidden hillside retreat with a pool (plus a hot tub) larger than many of the condo pools in Kona, where guests have a choice of four pretty rooms with colorful quilts on comfy beds and lots of plush armchairs to sink into, starting at just $70 for a loft room with private bathroom (larger rooms range from $95 to $140, with occasional off-season discounts between Apr and Sept). Another find, the **Belle Vue B&B** ★ (P.O. Box 670, Kealakekua; ☎ 800/772-5044 or 808/328-9898; www.kona-bed-breakfast.com; AE, DISC, MC, V) is aptly named: The view from the front lawn, ideal for birdwatching, is one of the loveliest I've seen on the island. Two pastel rooms are for rent, each with its own fully functional kitchen, good firm beds, and lanais shaded by a beautiful rose trellis (the Swiss owner also dots the rooms with fresh-cut flowers). Rooms go for $115 to $165 per night, but can drop to as little as $95 for stays of a week or longer. Both properties are family-friendly, with pull-out couches to accommodate extra guests (ask about additional fees), barbecue grills and generous Hawaiian continental breakfast spreads in the mornings that feature fruits plucked from trees on the property.

$$ The **Rainbow Plantation B&B** ★ (81-6327B Mamalahoa Hwy., Captain Cook; ☎ 800/494-2829 or 808/323-2393; www.rainbowplantation.com; AE, MC, V) is its own peaceable kingdom tucked away in a very junglelike nook of Captain Cook, down the hill a bit and off the main highway. A menagerie of friendly beasts roam the property—miniature horses, a potbellied pig named Cleopatra, turkeys, chickens, peacocks, and parrots—and the rooms and tiny cottages ($88–$108/night) have a rustic charm, with hand-painted murals on the walls, good beds, TVs, and an eclectic collection of furnishings. My favorite is an actual 34-foot fishing boat that the owners have moored on the hillside; it has a decent-size living room at front, blessed with spectacular sunset views, and a small queen-size berth in back for sleeping ($89/night; there's also a futon couch on which to sleep in the front for those who might be a bit claustrophobic). Rates include a large modified continental breakfast (along with the usual fruits and breads, the owner boils up her chickens' multicolored eggs). Guests have use of a serviceable and covered outdoor kitchen. High-speed Internet access is free.

$–$$ Equally oddball (and I think charming) is the coffee shack at the **Pomaikai "Lucky Farm" B&B** ★ (83-5465 Mamalahoa Hwy., Captain Cook; ☎ 808/328-2112; www.luckyfarm.com; AE, MC, V). Once used for storing coffee, it's an actual shack, but a fairly spacious one, with a corrugated tin roof and walls that are really mosquito screens, so you have an unimpeded view into the rainforest on three sides. Don't worry: When it rains here, the drops come down vertically, so those sleeping inside don't get wet (and the platform queen-size bed is comfortable). A private toilet and washbasin are behind a small wall in the shack; just outside is an outdoor shower (with privacy-protecting walls). It's a unique setting and affordable at $85 a night (up to $95 between mid-Dec and Mar). The B&B also has three other fairly standard but nice rooms for $70 to $80, and all guests get a generous, cooked breakfast in the mornings. Guests can also snack on the macadamia nuts that blanket the grounds of this 4-acre working farm.

$$–$$$ I saved the best for last. The **Areca Palms Estate Bed & Breakfast** ★★★ (P.O. Box 489, Captain Cook; ☎ 800/545-4390 or 808/323-2276; www.konabedandbreakfast.com; no guests under age 10; cash or travelers checks) is where you stay when you're celebrating something—or simply want to turn your vacation into a celebration. This handsome, deep-brown cedar house with cathedral ceilings surrounded by areca palms (hence the name) has four guest rooms ($115–$145 per night) that are individually decorated with lovely quilts and pretty plates on the walls, quality Tempur-Pedic mattresses, and cable TVs with VCRs. Innkeepers Janice and Steven Glass work diligently to make their guests comfortable. In addition to providing a different type of breakfast each morning (including such scrumptious treats as Hawaiian sweet-bread French toast, stuffed with sour cream), they put out tea and cookies in the late afternoon, lend guests everything they'd need for a day at the beach, and fill the house with amusements from board games to books about the island to a video-tape library for guests' use. There's also a hot tub out back. But what really sticks with me are the ambrosial smells of the place: In the afternoon, the wind brings in the scent of coffee roasting from neighboring plantations and, in the morning and evenings, the blossoms from the Belladonna trees on this property perfume the air. A top pick.

EAST HAWAII

The Kohala Coast (aka The Gold Coast)

Massive, self-contained luxury resorts are the draw on the Kohala Coast, and those who stay here pay dearly for the experience, with rooms averaging $350 to $450 a night, with extra fees for food, activities, and anything else a hotel can think to charge you for. Still, if you want to be cocooned in luxury, swim with dolphins, and plunge down water slides, these are the only places on the island that will fully satisfy your cravings.

I've found that there are very few real discounts to be had by calling the resorts directly, visiting in low season, or even contacting the standard discounters. However, if you can book through opaque websites (where you won't know what you're getting until after you pay) such as Priceline.com or Hotwire.com, you can score terrific deals, with nightly rates dropping to as little as $125 to $140 in high season! (If you don't believe me, visit the website BiddingForTravel.com, where users dish about how much they paid and which resorts they got when booking with Priceline). It's actually not that big a risk: Every resort on this coast is superb, and since all beaches in Hawaii are open to the public by law, you can visit the properties you're not staying at.

$$$$ I'll focus on the properties that Priceline and Hotwire users score most often: the **Hilton Waikoloa Village** ★★ kids (425 Waikoloa Beach Dr.; ☎ 800/HILTONS or 808/886-1234; www.hiltonwaikoloavillage.com; AE,DISC, D, MC, V) and the **Waikoloa Beach Marriott** ★ (69–275 Waikoloa Beach Dr., Waikoloa; ☎ 800/922-5533 or 808/886-6789; www.marriotthotels.com; AE,DISC, D, MC, V). The **Hilton** is simply humongous, so big, in fact, that guests ride a monorail and canal boats to get around its 62-acre grounds. The main lobby looks like something the ancient Sumerians might have built—a soaring space with huge slabs of stone, designed to impress. Along with all the standard luxury shops, restaurants, spas, tennis courts, two golf courses (one designed by Robert Trent Jones, Jr.), a small man-made beach, and swimming pools, you'll find a children's pool with a sandy bottom, intricate water slides, waterfalls in which you can swim, and a special little lake where one can swim with dolphins for a steep fee ($185 and 2-month advance reservations required). Standard rooms are midsize, pleasantly decorated with Hilton's copyrighted "Sweet Dreams" pillowtop mattresses (so comfy that they're now available for purchase). Room gadgets include cable TV with Nintendo and VCR and MP3 alarm clocks so you can program your wake-up music in advance.

The **Marriott** is less impressive, though much more intimate, and it does have one of the nicest beaches in the area, along with a top-rated luau (featuring an open bar, which is a big plus). Here you'll find two pools (one is for adults only, and one has a sandy bottom), tennis courts, two restaurants, and a 5,700-square-foot spa. Some room and meal packages are available, but not through Priceline, so they're probably not worth the cost.

$$$–$$$$ Another reasonably priced option for travelers in this area—and as I said before, there aren't many—are condo rentals. I particularly like the **Vista Waikoloa Condos** ★ (69-1010 Keana Place). For booking information, contact **South Kohala Management** (P.O. Box 384900, Waikoloa; ☎ 800/822-4252 or 808/883-8500; www.southkohala.com; DISC, MC, V), a rental company that handles the largest number of units on this property, or cruise to VRBO.com. Right near the Marriott, these condos are pleasantly laid out (all are spacious two- and three-bedroom units with good-size lanais, logical designs, and quality furnishings) and standards are strictly upheld. The nice on-site pool and convenient footpath to the beach are bonuses. Nightly rates average $225, but the price drops to $185 a night for weekly rentals and down to $165 for longer stays. In pricey Waikoloa, these rates are budget (believe it or not).

Waimea, Hawi & the Hamakua Coast

This is cowboy country; expect rodeos, horseback riding, and wide-open pastures that look somewhat like Montana (albeit with sparkling blue seas abutting the pasturelands). It's also a good hopping-off point for the Kohala coast and its beaches, which are just a 15-minute drive away—and you'll pay much less to stay at the reasonably priced B&Bs and motels here. Waimea boasts some of the best restaurants on the island.

$–$$$ Killer views are as common as cowboy boots in scenic Waimea, and the town's top budget bed-and-breakfast—**Aaah, the Views B&B** ★ (kids) (P.O. Box 6593, Waimea; ☎ 808/885-3455; www.aaahtheviews.com. MC, V)—really lives up to its name. It overlooks a burbling stream backed by wide-open country vistas, and the placement of the house makes you feel like this is the only property on this bit of Hawaiian prairie. Three of the four rooms ($105–$175, 10% discount for weeklong stays, $10 off for solo travelers) feature sleeping lofts as well as regular beds, making them ideal for families. The kids will love bunking down in the glassed-in lofts, and they'll find play opportunities galore, as the owners have two grade-schoolers of their own. There's also a lovely deck out back for alfresco breakfasts, which are part of the price and include, along with a multitude of fruits, breads, and spreads, some kind of home-baked chocolate treat ("It's our trademark here," says owner Erika Stuart with a twinkle). Cable TVs with VCRs and Wi-Fi are also part of the package, and for $75 extra, Erika's husband, Derek, will unfold his massage table and unknot your back (he's a licensed massage therapist).

Our Man in Waimea

Sometimes it's who you know, and if you get to know rental broker/travel agent/former politician **James K. Dahlberg** (of Kamuela Travel, P.O. Box 309; ☎ 877/526-8352; www.kamuelatravel.com; DISC, D, MC, V), you're more or less assured of getting a good rate on a vacation rental or a package. Representing some 31 properties around the island (of which he owns about half), Dahlberg's prices are among the fairest on the island, whether you're looking at a cute, fully furnished two-bedroom in Waimea for $115 a night; or a full house on a spectacular black-sand beach in Kau for $175. With ties to the Hawaiian-owned hotels (perhaps from his days as a politico?), he can arrange astonishingly good room and car packages, dropping the price of a stay at the Royal Kona (p. 344), for example, to just $105 a night, including a compact-car rental. James is a good resource, so factor him in when you're pricing vacations.

$$ You'll find more standard accommodations at the **Waimea Country Lodge** (65–120 Lindsay Rd., Kamuela; ☎ 808/885-4100; www.castleresorts.com; AE, DISC, D, MC, V), a spic-and-span motel with a friendly staff and rooms that feature sloping knotty-pine ceilings, good-quality beds, lovely mountain views, and cable TV—all for $115 a night.

Hawi

$–$$ At the northernmost tip of the island is a small plantation town called Hawi. Here, you have just one lodging option, but it's a cute one: **Kohala Village Inn** ★ (55–514 Hawi Rd., Hawi; ☎ 808/889-0404; www.kohalavillageinn.com; DISC, MC, V), a spiffed-up former motel which has all kinds of modern bells and whistles including Wi-Fi, cable TV, truly stylish teak furnishings, and surprisingly fine bedding and beds. It's also white-glove clean. Rooms are available in all sorts of configurations from decent-size singles ($65) to doubles ($75) to regular doubles with pull-out couches ($85–$100), and there's no charge for extra adults or children in the room. In the morning, the inn will send you on your way with a bagel breakfast, included in the cost. The only downside is the lighting: Rooms are off of a center courtyard, and the light from the walkway surrounding that courtyard shone through my thin curtains all night (but I'm hoping they'll soon fix this flaw; it's a lovely little inn otherwise).

Along the Hamakua Coast

$ Farther south on the Hamakua Coast, about 10 miles north of Hilo, in the tiny former sugar town of Wailea, my choice for cheap sleeps is **Akiko's Buddhist Bed and Breakfast** ★ (P.O. Box 272, Hakalau; ☎ 808/963-6422; www.alternative-hawaii.com/akiko; children 13 and older only; cash only). You don't have to meditate or be Buddhist to stay here, though all guests are welcome to join Akiko at 5am for her daily sessions of Zen meditation (there are also evening sessions 3 nights a week, as well as periodic workshops). Akiko wants to attract all

A Worthy Splurge

$$$ Waimea is home to one of the island's most romantic lodgings, the **Jacaranda Inn** ★★★ (65–1444 Kawaihae Rd., Kamuela; ☎ 808/885-8813; www.jacarandainn.com; MC, V). Set on a 12-acre estate, the centerpiece here is the grand 1897 home built for the Parker Ranch's manager. Though it's comparing apples and oranges, to my mind, this inn offers a far more unique—and less expensive—experience than any of the megaresorts along the nearby Kohala coast, and therefore may be a good middle ground for those who want a taste of luxury at a price within the realm of reason.

Today, guests will find a collection of nine cushy rooms and cottages, each imaginatively decorated with furniture and linens from the U.S. mainland and Indonesia. Some rooms look like they've been lifted from New England, with antique four-poster beds, jewel-toned wallpaper, and Oriental rugs. Others, such as the Southwestern room, have quirky touches like chandeliers made of antlers; or, in the Southeast Asian–inspired digs, hand-painted Balinese armoires and elaborately carved statuary. Bathrooms in each are oversize, with Jacuzzi tubs and fine fixtures. Prices range from $149 to $169, with one suite going for $199 and an on-property cottage for $450. For those planning a really special occasion, there's a lovely chapel on the property for wedding ceremonies, as well as a scenic waterfall that's a perfect backdrop for wedding photos.

sorts of guests, and she's created different types of lodgings out of this former tofu factory, garage, and plantation, which she's "reincarnated" to house them all. "As long as they're decent human beings," Akiko says of prospective guests, "they are welcome here."

For a true retreat experience, try the Monastery House, a place for guests to "get in touch with themselves and be grounded," according to Akiko. The digs are austere: shared bathrooms, tatami-matted rooms with no furnishings except for sleeping futons, and a code of silence between 6:30pm and 6am daily. Next door, the Pu'uhonua House is more of a traditional B&B, a five-bedroom plantation house with Western-style beds covered in quilts, wooden dressers, and lace curtains shading the windows. Bathrooms are shared here, too, as is the outdoor shower house (with water heated by solar energy). Stays at both properties are $65 for a single, and $75 for a double (dropping down to $55 and $65 for stays of 3 or more nights). Recently, Akiko built two attractive small studio cottages, which are comfortably furnished and a bit set off from the rest, sharing one kitchen and bathroom between them; the smaller one costs $65 per night and the larger house is $85. Both are entirely solar powered.

In the morning, all guests gather for a healthy breakfast (oatmeal, hard-boiled eggs, fruits from the garden, dozens of teas) and speak to one another in hushed voices, often pitching in on the dishes. Some hang around the property for workshops, others take the 10-minute-stroll to a lovely nearby beach or bike into Hilo, but what they all share is the conviction that this is a very special, extraordinarily serene place. I would have to agree.

Hilo

Hawaii's second-largest metropolis after Honolulu, Hilo serves as a good gateway to the rainforest, and is used by many as a home base when visiting Volcanoes National Park, a half-hour drive south of here. Though the downtown has been drained of much of its vitality by the development of massive shopping centers on the outskirts, it has a number of lovely neighborhoods filled with historic homes.

$$ If hotels are your speed, you can't do better than the **Dolphin Bay Hotel** ★★ (kids) (333 Iliahi St.; ☎ 877/935-1466 or 808/935-1466; www.dolphinbayhotel.com; MC, V). Although it looks like your standard cinder-block motel from the outside, it is in fact a terrifically well-maintained, friendly place with more amenities than you can usually get at these prices (rooms start at $99, with a studio apartment for $10 more, and one- and two-bedroom apartments about $30–$50 more). First off, each room is actually a minisuite with a snappily decorated, good-size bedroom on one side, a bathroom in the middle, and a usable kitchenette on the other; those that are listed as one-bedrooms also have a living room with a fold-out couch. On the property is a small walking trail, and a grove of fruit trees that guests are encouraged to snack from. Finally, the staff is an attentive, knowledgeable bunch who post daily information on volcano activity (the owner is an amateur volcanologist) and can help set up tours. When was the last time you got all that for less than $100? Book far in advance, as this place gets lots of repeat business. "The first time people come here, they stay for 2 days," the desk clerk told me. "Next time, they book for a week."

$$ With its ocean views, recently renovated rooms, and kind-to-the-back mattresses, **Uncle Billy's** ★ (87 Banyan Dr.; ☎ 800/367-5102 or 808/961-5818; www.unclebilly.com; AE, DISC, D, MC, V) is another fine choice, the only "budget hotel" (standard rooms go for $104) on Hilo's main hotel strip, Banyan Drive, but the one offering the best values nonetheless (some of the neighboring ones weren't nearly as tidy when I last came to town). A family affair—Uncle Billy is still active at his hotel in Kona, and this one is run by one of his seven children—this place is low-key and friendly, with a small pool out front, a bar/restaurant on-site, and washer/dryers for guests' use. Booking online can often drop the nightly rate to $89 including breakfast (kitchenette rooms and ocean views cost $15 more).

$–$$ If you'd like to lodge in a true historic beauty, go directly to **Maureen's B&B** ★ (1896 Kalaniana'ole Ave, Hilo; ☎ 800/935-9018 or 808/935-9018; www.maureenbnb.com; AE, DISC, MC, V), a baronial-looking redwood and cedar mansion built at the turn of the last century to house a Japanese businessman and his seven children (the family's teahouse is on-site as well as a lovingly tended Japanese garden with a koi pond out back). Maureen Goto, the lively, friendly owner, has filled the house with attractive antiques, period wallpapers, and squishy couches. It's a delightful place to stay, across the street from a nice beach (where turtles will swim with you; don't touch them though, because that's illegal) and in one of Hilo's many microclimate zones that gets significantly less rain than the rest of the surrounding areas. All rooms share bathrooms and range from $65 (single) to between $90 to $115 (double). Prices include breakfast (usually a quiche or waffles) each morning.

$$–$$$ For rooms with more of a view—spectacular ones, actually—I'd suggest the **Hale Kai B&B** ★★ (111 Honolii Place; ☎ 808/935-6330; www.halekaihawaii.com; MC,V) or the Inn at Kulaniapia Falls (below). Set on a cliff overlooking the ocean, Hale Kai B&B has four sea-view guest rooms with floor to ceiling windows, colorfully decorated with hand-stenciled walls and original photos by the owner. Each room has its own small semi-private seating area out front, great for whale-watching, and prices range from $135 to $155 including a gourmet breakfast (basil frittata, anyone?) and Wi-Fi. If that isn't enough to sell you, there's a small pool in the front and a black-sand beach just down the hill.

$$–$$$$ The **Inn at Kulaniapia Falls** ★★ (P.O. Box 646; ☎ 866/935-6789 or 808/936-6789; AE, MC, V) is another top choice with the most Hawaiian of all accessories: a majestic waterfall, in which you can swim, as well as extensive grounds for hiking (a second, smaller waterfall is sided by a wooden deck for picnics). Although it's a 20-minute drive from the center of Hilo on narrow roads past macadamia-nut farms, the effort is more than justified by the property's superb setting, and the price is ultrareasonable at $109 per room (two with queen-size beds, two with kings) including a generous breakfast buffet and Wi-Fi. There's also a pagoda-like guesthouse with its own kitchen that can sleep up to four and goes for $175 a night ($225 with four guests, or $275 with six). And there's a recently added Chinese-style guest house filled with furnishings the owners hand picked on their travels through China; its five rooms each go for $139.

A HOSTEL OPTION

$ Of the two hostels in Hilo, **Arnott's Lodge** (98 Apapane Rd., off Hwy. 19; ☎ 808/969-7097; www.arnottslodge.com) has more character and offers better value than its competitor. It's a bit out of the way, but offers free pickup and drop-off from/to the airport, rents bikes for just $3 a day, and runs a number of well-priced tours to Mauna Kea and the volcano. In addition to hostel rooms (clean, sleeping six, sturdily built bunks, $25/person), there's also a lawn for campers to pitch a tent ($10/person) and semiprivate rooms with shared bathrooms ($60 double), privates ($70). Character comes in because of all the extras here, including a large outdoor patio for lounging, a small theater filled with couches where guests can watch DVDs for free, and a "guest appreciation party" every Saturday night featuring free beer and pizza (and if that ain't heaven for a backpacker, I don't know what is).

Puna

If you want to get a way from it all—I mean really get away—go to Puna, where the tourist presence is next to nil and folks spend their days hiking through the rainforest and bathing in thermal pools (heated by mighty Pele). An enormous rural district (you could fit the entire island of Oahu into it) between Hilo and Kilauea volcano, Puna may well be one of the least known playgrounds in Hawaii.

$$ Because of this area's off-the-beaten-path nature, I only recommend two places here. There's **Art and Orchids B&B** ★ (16–1504 39th Ave., Keaau; ☎ 877/393-1894 or 808/982-8197; www.artandorchids.com; ☎; MC, V), a cute yearling with three rooms ($90–$115 each). The hosts of this property are making a name for themselves with their "above and beyond" hospitality style. Along with abundant and delicious breakfasts, they've been known to throw in free dinners for folks who arrive hungry and will pack up a box breakfast for those who need to leave early (guests also have use of the kitchen and can cook for themselves). The house is stocked with dozens of books and DVDs for guests' use (each room comes with its own DVD player and high-end cable TV) plus snorkels, beach towels, and other beach toys are lent to guests free of charge. They even offer on-site babysitting and art classes to those who come with children. There's an art studio out back (hence the name) and the owner Markie will teach interested guests how to make paper and do other crafts ($15/hour). All in all, this is a cute, unpretentious B&B decorated with the owner's handmade turtle mosaics. One final selling point: This place has Jacuzzi bathtubs and a hot tub out back.

$–$$$$ The other place I recommend is for those who want to lose themselves in a sprawling, diversity-honoring, wellness-oriented jungle getaway by the sea. **Kalani Oceanside Retreat** ★ (12-6860 Kalapana-Kapoho Beach Rd.; ☎ 800/965-7828 or 808/965-0468; www.kalani.com) has lodging priced for every wallet, ranging from $40 tent sites to $260 treehouses. There are also shared dorm rooms for $70, private rooms in lodges with community kitchens for $110–$145, and secluded cottages nestled into jungle clearings for $170. (Stay for a week and save 10%.) Kalani has deep roots in both gay culture and the world of alternative healing, but it's not exclusive to any particular orientation or persuasion. As long as you're cool with nudity around the chlorine-free swimming pool and generally elevated levels of Woo Woo, you'll feel perfectly at home there. A small army of masseurs, masseuses, foot reflexologists, aromatherapists, reiki specialists, and other bodyworkers is available to unblock your chakras and free your energy flow, and there's even a house psychic you can consult. Yoga classes, Pilates, hula lessons, volleyball, and other group activities happen all the time, and every Sunday morning island residents and Kalani guests gather for a sweaty, DJ-driven, free-form gala called Ecstatic Dance. (There are two rules: no talking and no shoes.) Afterword, many of the dancers spend the afternoon stretched out on the black sand at clothing-optional Kahena Beach (p. 375), just down the road. Three times a day, someone in Kalani's kitchen pops outside to blow a conch shell, sounding the call to meals. The vegetarian-friendly breakfasts, lunches, and dinners are served buffet style, on a community veranda. And they're fantastic.

Volcano-Area Housing

Because the area around Volcanoes National Park isn't connected to the municipal water supply and has to rely on catchment water, it hasn't fallen prey to overdevelopment—there simply isn't enough water here to support massive luxury hotels. What you have instead are a dozen or so charming, smaller places, transforming a visit to Hawaii's top tourist attraction into a remarkably intimate experience. Don't make the mistake of staying at the large hotel within the park itself, as it's overpriced, with an unpleasant staff. You'll do better in the gateway community of Volcano or at the lovely campground within the park (see "A House of One's Own," below, and the "Camping & Cabins" sidebar, p. 356).

$–$$ For a true B&B stay, but with a free-standing cottage and apartment units available as well, the hugely popular **My Island Bed and Breakfast Inn** ★★ (P.O. Box 100, Volcano; ☎ 808/967-7216; www.myislandinnhawaii.com; DISC, MC, V) is an excellent pick. Run for more than 20 years by the gracious Morse family (Gordon Morse is a volcano expert and supplies guests with excellent written itineraries for all sorts of different adventures in the vicinity), there are options here for every type of traveler and group, from cozy double rooms (also sold as singles for slightly less), to family rooms where up to five can bunk down in the same room, to an entire three-bedroom house.

There are too many price permutations to list here (go to the website for full information), but the cheapest single goes for $60 a night and the cheapest double is $75. Apartments range from $80 to $100, and the house cost $150, double occupancy. Prices go up by $20 for each extra person 16 or older, and by $10 for 15 or younger. Whichever you pick, you can be assured you'll get spotlessly clean digs with homey furnishings (Amish-like quilts, rocking chairs, wooden dressers), and such nice touches as fresh flowers in vases and brand-new digital alarm clocks. The cottages also have cable TVs, VCRs, and phones, and the main house has Wi-Fi; all guests can partake of a generous breakfast at the main house. The main house is a historic New England–style missionaries' home, built in 1886, with original paned glass and one of Hawaii's first bathtubs built right into the wall and still very much in use. Be sure to ask for a tour.

$$–$$$$ **Hale Ohia Cottages** ★★★ (P.O. Box 758, Volcano Village; ☎ 800/455-3803 or 808/967-7986; www.haleohia.com; MC, V) offers travelers a chic, boutiquey alternative, with Neiman Marcus–like linens, classy antique furniture, and whimsical architecture. One small, round cottage was created from a 1930s redwood water tank and transformed into a surprisingly elegant space; another has its own enclosed tropical garden at front, with a skylight over the bed; still another room, in the main house, transforms what must have been a family parlor into a lovely bedroom, with the bed nestled up against the bay window. The cheapest room here goes for $110, including breakfast, with larger digs costing between $120 and $210 for a three-bedroom house. With seven lodgings altogether, there are a number of variations to choose from here. The only downside: a higher-than-normal charge of $25 per person for extra guests over 2 years old in the rooms.

A House of One's Own

The listings here just scratch the surface of all the affordable vacation-home rentals in Volcano Village. To book one of the free-standing, private homes—and they can be quite nice, with lovely redwood walls, full kitchens, and spacious bedrooms—take a peek at the **Volcano Directory** (http://volcanogallery.com) and **Hawaii Volcano Vacations** (http://hawaiivolcanovacations.com), two helpful compendium booking sites.

$$–$$$ Another nicely private option, the **Volcano Country Cottages** ★ (P.O. Box 545; ☎ 888/446-3910 or 808/967-7960; www.volcanocottages.com; AE, DISC, MC, V), is a collection of four free-standing houses run like a B&B. A fruit-and-pastries breakfast (included in the room rates) is brought to each house the evening before. Not that you need to rely on your hosts to eat: three of the cottages have kitchens (stocked with condiments, coffees, and teas). All have pleasant furnishings—pretty area rugs, comfy armchairs, and brightly colored quilts on firm beds. The smallest house, a good-size studio, is just $105 a night (it's very rare to get a full house for that price); there are also one- or two-bedroom cottages $132 a night (plus $15 for every extra person over two). The final touch is a hidden hot tub down a path out back, in its own enclosure with candles galore for nighttime tubbing (electric lights would attract moths).

$$–$$$$ **Kate's Volcano Cottages** ★ (P.O. Box 159, Volcano; ☎ 877/967-7790 or 808/967-7990; www.volcanoplaces.com; MC, V) offer a similar experience, with four picturesque free-standing houses, enveloped in the rainforest, but here you have the added advantage of dealing with Kate herself, who is a dynamo, very helpful, and extremely knowledgeable about the area. She also provides the fixings for a light, make-your-own breakfast, and her four cute properties (again nicely furnished with full kitchens and lanais) go for $115, $145, and $240 a night, with a 15% discount for stays of 3 nights or more. The $240 property is the splurge of the bunch, an adult one-bedroom playhouse, very elegant with open beamed ceilings, an indoor Jacuzzi, full entertainment center, and covered lanai. All four properties have Wi-Fi.

Kau

South Point, the southernmost point in the United States, is the big attraction here, though there are also some lovely black-sand beaches and thermal ponds. Remote Kau doesn't get all that much tourism, compared with Kona and Hilo, but it actually makes quite a logical jumping-off point for people who want to visit both the volcano and the Place of Refuge, as it sits smack dab in the middle.

$–$$ Standard lodgings can be found at both the **Bougainvillea B&B** ★ (P.O. Box 6045, Ocean View; ☎ 800/688-1763 or 808/929-7089; www.bougainvilleabedandbreakfast.com; AE, DISC, MC, V) and the **Shirakawa Motel** (P.O. Box 467, Naalehu; ☎ 808/929-7462; www.shirakawamotel.com; cash or travelers check only), farther south along the coast. The **Bougainvillea** is a green oasis amidst a sea of black lava, with a good-size swimming pool and access to a nearby beach. The chatty owners do their best to keep guests amused with a full collection of DVDs and videos, Ping-Pong tables, an incredibly starry sky at night, and a gourmet breakfast each morn. Of the four rooms here, I happen to think those on the first floor are better looking—just a tad brighter—than those up above, but the owner charges the same for all ($79 single; $89 double) and, as a rule, doesn't allow guests to request specific rooms (though you can certainly try). Those on a stricter budget can turn to the **Shirakawa Motel,** which bills itself as "The Southernmost Motel in America," but in fact feels like a motel at the end of the world. It's clean, the beds are okay, and the owners are friendly, but everything is extremely worn—the walls are as thin as palm fronds. Still it's tremendously affordable at $50 a night for a double with private bathroom, and $60 for a kitchenette unit.

Camping & Cabins

Ecological wonders—hot ponds, lava streams, deeply green rainforests—are the reason why so many visit the Big Island. And the best way to get up close and personal with all this splendor is to camp out in its midst. Here are my recommendations for campgrounds and cabins:

Hapuna Beach State Recreation Area (on the South Kohala Coast; ☎ 808/587-0300; http://www.hawaii.gov/dlnr/dsp/hawaii.html): A basic shelter, with mattressless platforms, is available here for $20 a night for up to four. Six can stay here, but there's an extra charge of $5 per person. The reason to do it: direct access to one of the nicest beaches on the island.

Kalopa State Recreation Area (on the Hamakua Coast; ☎ 808/587-0300; http://www.hawaii.gov/dlnr/dsp/hawaii.html): Four rooms worth of bunk beds with mattresses, plus communal bathrooms and kitchens are available here for $55 a night for up to eight campers ($5 more for each additional person). Though there's also outdoor tenting ($5/night for up to five people), you're going to want to be indoors in this misty, rainy, very beautiful forest area.

Mauna Kea State Recreational Area ★★ (along Saddle Rd.; ☎ 808/587-0300; http://www.hawaii.gov/dlnr/dsp/hawaii.html): Cabin camping is available on Friday, Saturday, and Sunday nights only for $35 to $45 a night for up to four people. You'll get nice, newly renovated cabins with mattressed bunks, but because of the remote location, you'll have to bring

$ Peacocks preen, stone lions growl, and Buddhas grin beneficently at my favorite lodging in the area: the **Wood Valley Retreat and Temple** ★★ (P. O. Box 250, Pahala; ☎ 808/928-8539; www.nechung.org; AE, DISC, MC, V). This Tibetan Buddhist monastery was created from a classic pagoda/Japanese temple that's now over 100 years old. It's set in a serene, hidden valley at the base of Mauna Loa. As with Akiko's Buddhist B&B (p. 349), you don't have to be Buddhist to stay, though if you do want to engage in meditation, it's less hard-core here than at Akiko's, with residents and guests gathering to meditate at the civilized hour of 8am. Also highly civilized are the accommodations, each of which is decorated with linens and art from some area of the Asian Buddhist world (there's an India room, a Chinese room, and so on). The rooms are quite pretty, with good-quality Western beds, and nightly stays go for $50 for a single to $75 for a double (with 10% off for stays of 3 days or more). I very much enjoyed my time here, meeting with the elfin leader of the temple, Michael Schwab, a charming, very witty fellow who, if you ask nicely, will show you the opulent room the Dalai Lama uses when he comes to stay.

in your own water. The draw here is the area, which is sublimely beautiful and looks more like the high desert of eastern Oregon than Hawaii. Also noteworthy is the spectacular star show at this 6,500-foot elevation. Camping is available as well, for $5 a night (for up to five people).

Namakani Paio and Kulanaokuaiki ✪ (in Volcanoes National Park; ☎ 808/985-6000; http://www.nps.gov/havo/home.htm): You'll find free campgrounds within this park (though you'll have to buy a $10/week permit to enter the park). Namakani is in a peaceful eucalyptus grove, basically a large meadow with a paved loop along which you can camp. There's not a lot of privacy here, but it's still pleasant, as are the on-site cabins (which each feature one double bed, a bunk bed, a picnic table at front, and a barbecue grill; $50/night). Farther into the park, with a lot more privacy, Kulanakuaiki is 5 miles down Hilina Pali Road at 2,700 feet elevation. It offers just eight campsites (also free with an entrance permit) with a vaultlike toilet; there's no water available at this site. Bring your own.

Wilderness camping within Volcanoes National Park (☎ 808/985-6011; www.nps.gov): You'll have to contact the rangers on the day of your hike to ascertain which areas will be appropriate for pitching a tent (as the terrain significantly shifts here). Permits for wilderness camping are free, but note that there's no water in most parts of the park, so you'll have to bring in your own.

DINING FOR ALL TASTES

IN WEST HAWAII

Tourist meccas breed one-shot restaurants, places that charge too much for mediocre fare because they know there's an endless procession of transient diners to disappoint. West Hawaii suffers from this, though it also has a resistant strain of establishments that actually try to please their customers. Here are some of my favorites.

Kailua-Kona

$–$$ You have to be in-the-know to find the simple but popular local eatery called **Kona Mix Plate** (75–5660 Kopiko St.; ☎ 808/329-8104; 10am–8pm Mon–Sat; cash only), tucked away as it is in a back-street strip mall. It's not far from the tourist strip, but you'd never find it if you didn't know to go looking. Kona Mix Plate specializes in the plate lunch, Hawaii's carb-and-protein rich cheap eats of choice. Styrofoam plates are heaped with two scoops of rice, one scoop of macaroni salad, and a generous portion of the main attraction, such as teriyaki

Finding a Place to Eat

The restaurants in the following sections can be found on the maps starting on p. 368.

chicken, tempura shrimp, spicy pork, kalbi ribs, or breaded scallops, and the like. In the patois of the plate lunch, "mix plate" simply means "combo plate," and ordering multiple entrees is encouraged (two choices $9.75, three choices $13). There are tons of other plate lunch eateries on the island, but Kona Mix Plate is a tad more upscale than most, given that it's indoors, air conditioned, and spotlessly clean. Most meals run between $8.50 and $9.75, but you can get a mini-plate for around $6.60 and still feel as filled up as if you just ate a big, fat sandwich.

$–$$ Island Lava Java ★★★ (75-5799 Alii Dr., at Coconut Grove Marketplace, Kona; ☎ 808/327-2161; 6am–9:30pm daily; AE, DISC, MC, V) is a coffeehouse with mostly outdoor seating, Wi-Fi, and a kitchen turning out surprisingly nice meals on heavy plates with delicate garnishes. For dinner, choose from a variety of huge salads (about $9), burgers with a variety of toppings ($8.95), pork tacos with black beans and chipotle aioli ($11), or fish tacos with the same ($12). The market sets the rate for the grilled fish specials ($15 for ahi when I was last there), which are just as good as what other restaurants in Hawaii might charge $10 more for. In the morning, you can laze about sipping Kona coffee while triathletes cycle and run along Alii Drive, or occasionally swim by in the ocean beyond. Try one of the beautiful breakfast wraps, with eggs and your choice of three vegetables, either a la carte ($8.50) or with fried red potatoes and bacon or Portuguese sausage ($9.75)—but no Spam, which is how you know it's not a truly local place.

$–$$ It's not that I don't appreciate a fish taco, but too many Mexican restaurants in Hawaii serve the Americanized version of Mexican cuisine, with a heavy hand on the cheese grater, and healthful fish or tofu fillings displacing traditional chorizo and carne asada. That's not the case at **Tacos El Unico Mexican Food** (75-5725 Alii Dr. at the Kona Marketplace; ☎ 808/326-4033;8am–10pm daily; cash only), a fairly clean, brightly lit Mexican kitchen where English is the second language, weekends mean menudo, and chorizo, adobada, carnitas, pollo, and even lengua fill the tacos ($2.50 apiece). Although it's in the heart of Kailua-Kona, it's hidden in the back of the Kona Marketplace, invisible from Alii Drive, so you have to look for it. It's got counter service and some outdoor seating, as well as free delivery within 2 miles. Most dinners cost $8.50 or less. Pick up a six-pack of Corona, get carryout here, sit by the ocean, and bear in mind that you're dining at 19°N latitude, on the same parallel as Mexico City.

$–$$ Manago Hotel Restaurant (heart of the town of Captain Cook; ☎ 808/323-2642; 7am–9am, 11am–20m, 5–7pm, closed Mon; reservations suggested; DISC, MC, V) serves simple, home-style meals in the old dining hall of a hotel founded by a Japanese immigrant in 1917. Everything besides the New York strip

($14) and the sautéed shrimp ($12) costs $11 or less, and comes with steamed rice and three side dishes, such as peas and carrots, broccoli, and squash. This hotel is like an unsealed time capsule from Hawaii's plantation era. While enjoying a meal, you can gather clues for fathoming how those earlier times on the islands have influenced the Hawaii of today. Try the liver, or better yet, the big, fat pork chops (both $8). This place is famous for its pork chops. Say "Manago Hotel Restaurant" to anyone from Kona, and there's a good chance they'll reply, "pork chops."

$$–$$$ Teshima Restaurant (79-7251 Mamalahoa Hwy., Honalo; ☎ 808/322-9140; about 15 min. south of Kailua-Kona; 6:30am–1:45pm, 5–9pm daily; cash or travelers check only) has changed little since it opened in 1940. When I visited, 100-year-old Grandma Teshima (I kid you not), who started the place, was still working the floor, wiping off tables, and keeping the rest of the family on its toes. The restaurant, like its proprietress, has a unassuming air, with its straight-backed wooden booths, kitchen tables circa 1950, and proudly displayed artwork by one of the grandsons. For dinner, try the shrimp or vegetable tempura ($15, and $13), or get the beef teriyaki and shrimp tempura ($18). It's on the high end of the menu, but it's worth the splurge.

$$ Located at Honokohau Harbor, where most of Kona's sportsfishing fleet berths, the **Harbor House** (74-425 Kealakehe Pkwy., Kona; ☎ 808/326-4166; 11am–7pm Mon–Sat, 11am–5:30pm Sun; AE, MC, V) is as close to its food suppliers as a seafood restaurant can get. I like the grilled-fish sandwiches ($9.75), tall stacks of buns, lettuce, and fish—mahimahi, ono, or whatever else just came in. The fish and chips ($9.95) and the grilled-fish dinner ($11) are good choices, too. The open-air dining room lets in the warm sea breeze and the rhythmic clanking of halyards on masts, as well as birds looking for french fries. The bar draws a batch of sun-weathered regulars, and serves cold beer in 18-ounce schooners ($2.50 domestic during happy hour, 4–6pm). The Harbor House closes early, most nights at 7pm, and 5:30pm on Sunday, because this is a bona fide fishermen's hangout, and fishermen don't stay up late.

$$ The Big Island Grill (75-5702 Kuakini Hwy., 1 block *makai* of tourist central on Alii Dr., Kona; ☎ 808/326-1153; 6am–10am, 11am–9pm. Mon–Sat; AE, MC, V) has so many happy local diners seated elbow-to-elbow that there seems to be no room left for decor. This popular family spot offers massive sandwiches, burgers, and servings of island favorites such as *loco moco* (bowl of rice topped with a hamburger patty and a fried egg, then smothered in gravy). If you're given a choice of mashed potatoes, baked potato, or french fries, get the mashers—they're unusually rich and fluffy. Come here only if you have a good appetite and some time—the portions are huge and there's often a wait to get in.

$$ One of the hallmarks of Kona's coffee-shack architecture is the use of stilts, which enable construction on otherwise impossibly steep slopes. A restaurant called **The Coffee Shack** (83-5799 Mamalahoa Hwy., between mile markers 108 and 109, Captain Cook; ☎ 808/328-9555; www.coffeeshack.com; 7:30am–3pm daily; AE, D, DISC, MC, V) exemplifies this style, jutting so precipitously over a plunging hillside that it almost seems to float on the vog (volcanic smog, see

Pupu with a Sunset

$$$–$$$$ A good sunset dinner can be one of the highlights of a stay in West Hawaii, and **Huggo's** ★★ (75-5828 Kahakai Rd., Kona; ☎ 808/329-1493; www.huggos.com; 11;30am–2pm Mon–Sat, 5:30–10pm daily; AE, DISC, MC, V) is one of the best restaurants in Kailua-Kona from which to watch the sun's burning bald head slide beneath the wet edge of the Pacific. Pilings sunk into the lava shoreline (county building codes once prevented such a thing) carry Huggo's open dining room out to the very edge of the island, where waves either crash or lap beneath the tables of diners, depending on surf conditions. The servers are warm and attentive, something not to be taken for granted in Kailua-Kona. After the sun goes down and the Tiki torches are lit, the darkened dining areas, laid out across three levels, become even more alluring. The Hawaii Regional Cuisine here includes teriyaki steak ($25, and a long-standing local favorite), seafood linguine with a macadamia-nut pesto and sherry-cream sauce ($30), and ono encrusted with crabmeat mixed with mozzarella and Parmesan cheeses ($33). Instead of a full dinner, you can join the pianist in the lounge, pretend like Huggo's is a tapas bar, and order off the pizza and pupu menu. Do what I recently did with a companion: Order two glasses of the house cabernet sauvignon ($7 apiece), and share the Caesar salad ($11), a little skillet of sizzling shrimp and bay scallops ($16 and delicious), and an order of Asian-style mushrooms ($8.95). You'll get the essence of a Huggo's experience for under $50. Plus, you can chat with the piano player.

p. 436) above Kealakekua Bay, far, far below. The clamor of diners on the tiny lanai and in the enclosed little dining room doesn't interfere with the lofty, breezy calm that prevails way up there, but the arrival of the generously prepared pizza or sandwich you ordered can snap you out of a reverie. Try the corned-beef Rueben on fresh-baked rye bread ($8.95), or the 8-inch pepperoni pizza ($12). Sadly, the place closes in the afternoon, so sunsets go unseen from this perch. Those looking for the same type of comfort food later in the evening head to **Kona Brewing Co. & Brewpub** (p. 416). The fare is standard pub grub but the beer is exceptional.

$$–$$$$ If you enjoy sushi, you'll appreciate the native selection at **Wasabi's** ★★ (kids) (Coconut Grove Marketplace, 75-5803 Alii Dr., Kona; ☎ 808/326-2352; 11am–9pm Sun–Thurs, 11am–10pm Fri–Sat.; AE, MC, V), which features fish plucked from the waters off Hawaii—marlin, ono, ahi, you name it. Tremendously fresh with nightly changing specials, this is a great place for sushi despite the simple decor and rushed service (they try to move you in and out quickly as it's usually packed with customers). There's also a children's menu, for those traveling with picky youngsters.

Kawaihae on the Kohala Coast

Kawaihae, site of the west side's only deep draft harbor, is the closest stop for Gold Coast hotel guests who want to get away from their rarified resorts for a meal. A few great eateries have sprung up among the harbor's fishing fleet, shipping containers, and interisland tugs. I have two favorites:

$$–$$$$ There's something about fried calamari and cold beer on a hot tropical day that puts me into the most pleasant languor, and I know of no better place in Hawaii to get in this condition than **The Seafood Bar** (61-3642 Kawaihae Rd.; ☎ 808/880-9393; www.theseafoodbar.com; 11:30–10:30pm Sun–Thurs, 11:30am–11:30pm Fri–Sat; MC, V). It's a cool, shady spot where the walls have been covered with *lauhala* mats, tiki lights, and Don Ho albums, and the second-story view looks out on the harbor's sunny, industrial landscape. The menu is heavy on pupu and light fare, such as the king crab broiled in sake, shoyu, and ginger and served on a sesame rice cake ($17); sautéed crab cakes ($13); and, of course, golden brown calamari ($9).

$$–$$$$ **Café Pesto** (Kawaihae Shopping Center; ☎ 808/882-1071; www.cafepesto.com; also in Hilo; 11am–9pm Sun–Thurs, 11am–10pm Fri–Sat; AE, DISC, DC, MC, V) features Pacific fusion seafood, pastas, organic salads, and wood-fired pizzas with unusual toppings, such as shiitake mushrooms. Try the Pizza Luau: kalua pork, Hawaiian sweet onions, and fresh pineapple ($8.95 for a 9-in. pie). The least expensive entree, Linguine al Pesto ($15), also happens to be my favorite. It's got grilled smoked-chicken apple sausage with a roasted tomato-basil marinara. This dish, with a wild-green salad ($4.95) and a glass of wine, usually does it for me, though I can't say I haven't been tempted by the Hot Keanakolu Apple Crisp, with a macadamia-nut crumb topping ($5.95).

Rockin' Sushi

$–$$$ On the northernmost tip of the island, in the former sugar town of Hawi, the old plantation-era mom-and-pop mercantiles have given way to galleries, boutiques, and restaurants. The best restaurant is **Sushi Rock** ★★ (downtown Hawi; ☎ 808/889-5900; closed Wed and open until 9pm Fri–Sat., otherwise noon–3pm, and 5:30–8pm; MC, V), which started life as a simple gift shop carrying Asian kitchenware, then had a sushi bar grafted on. You can still buy sake sets, teapots, and fancy chopsticks here, but sushi has become the main attraction. Traditional sushi like unagi nigiri (two savory pieces of freshwater eel, $4) stands alongside original creations like an inside-out roll called the Makai (roasted mahimahi, macadamia nuts, avocado, and scallions rolled in sesame seeds and tobiko, aka flying fish roe; eight pieces for $8). The young and talented chef, unconstrained by formal training in traditional Japanese sushi preparation, has fun with the plate presentations. For a specialty roll he calls the Mauna Loa Eruption, he uses ahi, smoked salmon, and a seasonal Hawaiian white fish to construct a shield volcano, then sends scallion cream and fiery orange tobiko pouring down its sides.

Waimea & Hawi

The upscale old cowboy town of Waimea, in the heart of Parker Ranch country, has so much fine dining that it's called "The Gourmet Ghetto."

$ For something less expensive, go Mexican. Ordinarily, I would avoid a restaurant with a pun in the name, but not in the case of **Tako Taco** ★ (64–1066 Mamalahoa Hwy., Waimea; ☎ 808/887-1717; 11am–8:30pm Mon–Sat, noon–8pm Sun; DISC, MC, V). This taqueria originally served octopus (tako in Japanese) tacos, but they were too hard to chew and taken off the menu. Nonetheless, the name stuck. Try the veggie burrito ($6.25), which comes with black beans, cheese, cabbage, guacamole, and a pico de gallo tomato salsa. Or order the tofu taco ($3.50), which, in addition to the alliteration, has a nice filling marinated in a grilled tomato ranchero sauce.

IN EAST HAWAII

East Hawaii has many excellent and reasonably priced restaurants.

Hilo

$–$$ For less ambience and more food, go to **Ken's House of Pancakes** ★★ kids (1730 Kamehameha Ave.; corner of Hwy. 11 and Hwy. 19; ☎ 808/935-8711; AE, DC, DISC, MC, V), a bustling 24-hour diner near the airport and hotels, with plenty of seating. Ken's serves breakfast at all hours, along with dozens of lunch and dinner entrees. The tiny print on its dense menu resembles the typeface of a phonebook. I like the variations Ken's offers on the traditional loco moco (bowl of rice, hamburger patty, fried egg, and gravy; $5.75), such as the mahimahi loco moco, in which fish takes the place of the burger. For heavy eaters, any moco can be sumo-sized. Sumos come with *six* scoops of rice, two patties, three eggs, and some fanfare—as it's carried to your table, the cook rings a ship's bell and the whole kitchen cries "Sumo!," ensuring that your appetite won't go unnoticed. Wednesday is prime-rib night (8 oz. $15, 12 oz. $16), Tuesday is all-you-can-eat taco night (adults $9.95, kids $6.25), Sunday all-you-can-eat spaghetti ($9.25 adults, $6.25 kids), and Thursday Hawaiian food (the price varies).

$–$$ Hilo's most distinctive building, the Imiloa Astronomy Center of Hawaii (p. 387), features three enormous, inverted, titanium-sheathed cones that go from steely-blue to silvery-white with the changing colors of the sky. One cone rises above the lobby, and another houses the planetarium. The third holds the **Sky Garden** (☎ 808/969-9753; www.imiloahawaii.org; 7am–4pm Tues–Sun; AE, DISC, MC, V), where tourists, school kids, and astronomers mingle in a circular cafeteria with glass walls overlooking a Native Hawaiian garden. Generously portioned breakfasts ($8.50 or less) are served all day, and lunch—in addition to a nice selection of soups, salads, sandwiches, and burgers (all for less than $9)—includes an all-you-can eat buffet (11am–2pm; $11 Tues–Fri, $13 Sat–Sun). A family of Chinese restaurateurs, the Chengs, runs the place, so the buffet always has a good selection of Chinese entrees, along with American and local dishes like roast beef and teriyaki chicken. At press time, the Chengs planned to add dinner, pending the approval of their liquor license.

$–$$$ Hidden away on a back street of downtown Hilo, **Garden Snack Club** ★ (82 Kilauea Ave.; ☎ 808/933-9664; BYOB, with no corkage fee; 11am–9:30pm Tues–Sat; MC, V) is a humble sit-down or carryout place with long waits for your food and big payoffs when it finally comes. The Snack Club has a passionate following of Hilo diners hooked on its healthy, unusual specialties, such the garlic-shrimp sandwich (served with organic greens, cucumber, tomato, and pineapple; $7), or Ocean in the Jungle (salmon, squid, shrimp, and pineapple served over spinach with curry sauce; $18). The owner, Tina, comes from Thailand. But the food is really a cuisine unto itself, one which Tina invented in her woks and skillets, with lots of spinach and sweet potatoes and carrots. Try her Thai pizza—spinach, Thai basil, pineapple, onion, red curry, coconut milk, and cheddar cheese layered between two spinach tortillas, like a giant curried quesadilla. It comes with tofu ($12), shrimp ($15), or fish ($18). It's big enough for two, and good enough for you to try and re-create when you get home. A word to the wise: Tina takes her time when she cooks. If you have any time constraints, call your order in before you arrive. Or bring a bottle of wine and enjoy the wait.

$$ Right next door to the Garden Snack Club is another tiny eatery with a big following, **Naung Mai Thai Kitchen** ★★ (86 Kilauea Ave.; ☎ 808/934-7540; closed Sun; reservations suggested; BYOB, with no corkage fee; 11am–2pm Mon–Fri,5–8:30pm Mon–Thurs, 5–9pm Fri–Sat; MC, V). Naung Mai does delightful things with a traditional Thai menu—cucumber salads, tom yum soups, pad Thai—and doesn't put MSG in any of the food. I'm particularly fond of the beef massaman curry. All the curries come with a vegetarian, chicken, beef, pork, or shrimp option, and all cost less than $10, unless you go with shrimp, in which case the price jumps to $12. Naung Mai's small kitchen opens onto its small dining room, which has three high-backed booths and five little tables, each with finely textured Thai silk tablecloths beneath glass overlays and warm spotlighting. This is a nice place for a quiet, intimate evening, where you can drink whatever beer or wine you carry in the door.

$$ On the edge of tranquil Waiakea Pond, behind the sprawling and seedy Waiakea Villas condominium complex, is the untraditional and obscurely located Japanese restaurant **Miyo's** ★ (400 Hualani St.; ☎ 808/935-2273; 11am–2pm and 5:30–8:30pm daily except Sun; MC, V). To find it, look for a bar called Our Karaoke; Miyo's is in the building right behind it, upstairs. When you enter Miyo's for the first time, you feel as if you've stepped into some back-alley Japanese speakeasy, hidden from the general public but filled with those in-the-know. The fare is Japanesevia the local organic farm—a pile of fresh mixed greens is stacked next to most entrees. What to order? It's all good, but I tend to crave the tempura-and-sesame-chicken ($12)—it hits the spot while leaving you light on your feet—and the salad with broiled mackerel ($9.95) (an even lighter but still satisfying way to go). Lunches are cheaper than dinner, and the daylight offers nice views of the pond and its oddball collection of waterfowl, including some wayward Canadian geese, that seem to have given up on migration after making the major navigational error that landed them here.

$–$$ Puka means "hole" in Hawaiian, and **Puka Puka Kitchen** ★★★ (270 Kamehameha Ave.; ☎ 808/933-2121; 11am–2:30 pm daily except Sun, 5:30–8:30pm Thurs–Sat; MC, V) is a hole-in-the-wall lunch spot along the Bay Front area of downtown Hilo. With its three-table dining room, Puka Puka is the runt of Hilo's downtown restaurant litter, though one with culinary gifts and talents far in excess of its tiny stature. I'm crazy for the pitas with lamb or falafel here, as well as with ahi, beef, or chicken ($7.50–$8.95). I also go nuts over the plates of sautéed ahi ($11) or sautéed lamb ($12), served with delicious sautéed rice, a mountain of greens, and a beautiful plate presentation.

$$–$$$ The sushi chef at **Restaurant Miwa** ★ (1261 Kilauea Ave., Suite 230, corner of Kekuanaoa St.; ☎ 808/961-4454; 11am–2pm, 5–9:30pm Mon–Sat, 5–8:30pm Sun, closed first Sun each month; AE, D, DISC, MC, V) is a quiet, circumspect guy named Shigeo. He's also the owner, and a regular face at both the Suisan Company Ltd.'s fish auction, where he picks up fresh ahi before dawn, and at the Hilo Farmers Market, where he loads up on fresh produce. From his sushi bar, get the combination platter (market price), and let Shigeo decide what's best. The other items on the menu are okay, but the sushi and the haupia cream-cheese pie for dessert ($4.50) really stand out. Haupia is a Hawaiian custardlike treat made with coconut and sugar, and the haupia cream-cheese pie alone is worth the effort it takes to get to Restaurant Miwa (it's in an obscure spot, at the end of a dark hall in the elbow of the L-shaped Hilo Shopping Center). Don't try to share a slice of the haupia cream-cheese pie with someone—you'll just end up fighting for the last bite, or resenting that you gave it up.

$$–$$$$ Hilo's hippest eatery is a small bistro tucked between two cellphone stores at a shopping center dominated by Wal-Mart and OfficeMax. This may seem like an unlikely location for anything even remotely hip, but the **Hilo Bay Cafe** ★ (315 Makaala St.; ☎ 808/935-4939; at the Waiakea Center; 11am–9pm

Grazing at the Farmers Market

Twice a week you can grab a bite or gather the makings of a picnic at **Hilo Farmers Market** (corner of Mamo St. and Kamehameha Ave.; ☎ 808/933-1000; Sat and Wed, crack of dawn until 3pm). Not only will you find the Big Island's entire lineup of locally grown produce, but you can also purchase Japanese bentos (box lunches); Spam *musubi* (a slice of Spam tied to a Spam-shaped block of rice with a belt of dried seaweed—don't knock it 'till you try it); Peruvian tamales (chicken, cheese, or tofu, sold by a grumpy Peruvian woman); Filipino empanadas, and other exotic treats that don't cost more than a few bucks. For beverages, there's fresh carrot juice, spirulina drinks, and sometimes a kid with a machete opening coconuts and sticking straws in them so you can sip the sweet milk inside. For dessert, try a mango, a tangerine, or the exotic Southeast Asian rambutan, which is like an enormous grape inside of a rubbery husk covered with red tentacles. It's good. Honest.

Great Steaks, Weird Vibe

$$$ Henri's on Kapiolani ★★ (139 Kapiolani St.; ☎ 808/961-9272; Mon–Sat 5:30–7:30pm; reservations strongly recommended; cash only) arguably is the best place on the Big Island to get a steak. It is without question the oddest. Unlike other restaurants, which strive to attract customers, this one seems to be hiding: It keeps extremely limited hours, never advertises, and is in such a strange location—hidden atop a nondescript three-story walk-up apartment building in a back neighborhood—that only a handful of Hilo residents know it exists. Despite that Henri and his waitstaff hate it—*hate it*—when people show up without reservations, even when the place is empty. And then there's the menu, written in such an enormous Gothic font that it leaves room for just four entrees. When I ate here, only two of them were available—the T-bone steak ($15) and the porterhouse steak ($17), both served with rice and a small iceberg lettuce salad. (I had the porterhouse, and I'm looking forward to the day I go back and have it again.) Did I mention the 1970s-time-capsule decor and Tiny, Henri's friendly, needle-toothed little dog, who may tug at your pant leg or jump in your lap if not shooed away. Finally, there's Henri, himself. If a drowsy, shirtless, pot-bellied guy wanders into the dining room and plops down at the head of a table full of regulars, that's him. Henri's is not for everyone. But for those who love red meat and can handle eccentricity, it's a great place. Just don't forget to make reservations.

Mon–Sat, 5–9pm Sun; AE, DISC, MC, V) is too damn cool to care. The menu reflects the chef's strong San Francisco, Asian, and regional Hawaiian influences, as well as his Midwestern roots (appetizers include ricotta tater tots with a Hawaiian ohelo-berry-and-jalapeno-pepper marmalade). The kitchen works on two tiers: an upper one, where it prepares entrees like the potato-crusted fresh catch, a top grade of fish seared in a sheath of rough chopped potatoes and served with a beurre blanc sauce ($22); and a more affordable one, where you'll find an enormous chicken or vegan pot pie with a marvelously flaky crust ($10). The warm, sensuous lighting and the minimalist, contemporary decor help everyone and everything look their best. Thanks to the darkly tinted windows, after a few glasses of something from the well-rounded wine list, you'll forget all about the box stores outside.

Pahoa

$$$ Hilo used to have an extraordinary Thai restaurant on Mamo Street called Royal Siam. It's still there, but it lost all appeal when the cook, Ning, left in 2002. Fortunately, for those who were hooked on Royal Siam's curry, she didn't go far: just down to the little town of Pahoa in the Puna District, where she opened her own restaurant, **Ning's Thai Cuisine** ★ (15-2955 Pahoa Rd., in the heart of the little downtown; ☎ 808/965-7611; 3–9pm Mon–Sat, 6–9pm Sun; DC, DISC, MC, V).

Grab a table and have some summer rolls with peanut sauce ($7.95), while you wait for the curry (massaman, red, yellow, or green, $8.95–$13) that causes so many of her Hilo followers to forsake Royal Siam for the half-hour drive to Pahoa. Ning's softly cheerful presence fills her kitchen and small, warmly lit dining room, which opens directly onto the Pahoa's Old West–style boardwalk, and is adorned with elephants, Buddhas, and, for some reason, photos of Jimmy Stewart.

In or Near Volcano Village

$$–$$$ Kiawe Kitchen ★ (next to The Volcano Store, corner of Old Volcano Rd. and Haunani Rd.; ☎ 808/967-7711; 5:30–9pm daily; MC, V) is named for the Hawaiian word for mesquite, which burns in the brick oven where the pizzas bake, with their crispy, cracker-thin crusts ($13–$15, plus toppings). I found the white pizza, with olive oil, garlic, fresh mozzarella, and pecorino Romano cheese, to be absolutely delicious—and I don't particularly like pizza. On my last visit, the couple sitting next to me said the red sauce on their pizza lacked zest, but they were from Louisiana. Sandwiches include roast lamb, tenderized in the same oven, laid on a freshly baked baguette, drizzled with aioli, and served with a big side salad. Beyond these dishes, you'll find huge sandwiches at lunch ($10–$12), huge pastas at dinner ($17–$22), and huge salads at lunch and dinner ($5–$12). The warm lighting in Kiawe Kitchen's small dining room, the tomato-soup-colored walls, and the soft jazz of a Seattle Internet radio station in the background give this place a comforting, happy-to-be-in-Volcano feeling.

$$–$$$ Thai Thai Restaurant (19-4084 Old Volcano Rd.; ☎ 808/967-7969; 4:30–8:30pm; AE, DISC, MC, V) is a well-regarded place that does a bustling dinner business in a less-relaxed setting than Kiawe Kitchen. All entrees run between $10 and $23. Thai Thai Curry with Mahi-Mahi is the signature dish, and a pretty good one, for $20. You can get the exact same thing with chicken, beef, pork, or tofu for $13. My favorite is the eggplant with basil entree, to which I like to add beef ($13).

$$$$ Albert Jeyte was once a Hollywood makeup artist. He won an Emmy for his work on the old Hawaii-based detective show Magnum P.I. Now he's a chef and restaurateur, and he's created one of the finest restaurants, with one of the most unique menus, on the Big Island. At his **Kilauea Lodge ★★★** (Old Volcano Hwy.; ☎ 808/967-7366; www.kilauealodge.com; 5:30–9pm daily; AE, MC, V), you'll find traditional German dishes, such as hasenpfeffer (braised rabbit), along with French classics such as duck l'orange and paupiettes of beef (both $29), and some choices even more exotic to Hawaii, such as venison ($36) and ostrich filet ($33). You might guess as I did, incorrectly, that ostrich tastes something like chicken. It actually tastes more like beef, really tender beef, and if it's on the menu when you're here, I recommend it. Kilauea Lodge occupies an old Boy Scout lodge in the misty rainforest near the entrance to Hawaii Volcanoes National Park. It's filled with warm lighting and luxurious native hardwoods, and when the temperature drops, the Scouts' old "Friendship Fireplace," built with stones from around the world, is stoked. Jeyte also runs a bed-and-breakfast here.

WHY YOU'RE HERE: THE BIG ISLAND'S BEACHES

The Big Island has a large supply of beaches, but they differ dramatically according to the area where they're found.

THE WEST SIDE

The west side has almost all of the island's white- and golden-sand beaches. What follows is a guide to the best of this area's places to swim, snorkel, and lounge by the sea, starting in the south and working up the coast.

South Kona District

Located just north of the ancient Place of Refuge (p. 378), **Two Step** (Keala O Keawe Rd., off Hwy. 11 at mile marker 104, south of Kailua-Kona; just north of Puuhonua O Honaunau National Historic Park) teems with snorkelers, scuba divers, and skin divers drawn to its coral reef, clear waters, sudden near-shore drop-off, and turtle cleaning station. Located in **Honaunau Bay,** Two Step has a tiny, sandy beach, beside a boat ramp, where parents let children loose. Apart from this sheltered beach, the shore is dominated by a broad, smooth, rock ledge, where most beachgoers set up their beach chairs and towels if they're not at one of the few picnic tables under the trees. The ledge drops straight into 15 feet of water, and within a few hundred yards from shore the bottom drops precipitously. Free divers from around the world, who descend to depths of 200 feet and more while holding their breath, train here throughout the year and sometimes hold competitions where world records are set. Two Step takes its name from a giant steplike formation in the lava, which makes it easy to get in and out of the water here. At the turtle cleaning station, green sea turtles lie motionlessly on the seafloor while brightly colored reef fish nibble the algae off their shells. To witness this hygiene-for-greens arrangement, start at the giant lava step and swim about 150 feet offshore toward the tip of Honaunau Bay's southern point; if the cleaning station is in operation, you can swim right over it.

North Kona District

Kahaluu Beach Park (south of Kailua-Kona on Alii Dr., at mile marker 5) is an easily accessible salt-and-pepper beach set along a rocky shore. There are tide pools for kids, protected waters with decent snorkeling, plenty of turtles, plenty of parking, plenty of other beachgoers, and a nearby surf spot that's good for beginners. The rocky bottom here makes Kahaluu better suited to snorkeling and turtle watching than swimming, but you can swim safely if you watch your toes. If you need beach gear or hot dogs, you'll find them here. On the lava flat to the south, several ancient Hawaiian petroglyphs appear at low tide. They include human figures, abstract designs, and phalluses.

The Big Island's ficklest beach, **White Sands Beach Park** (south on Alii Dr., mile marker 4), comes and goes with the big winter swells, which is how it got its popular name, Magic Sands Beach, or sometimes Disappearing Sands Beach. When the sand vanishes, a forbidding rocky cove remains. When the sand reappears, it takes the form of a short, broad beach, which draws hundreds of people to bodysurf, boogie board, sunbathe, and play beach volleyball. This is Kailua-Kona's foremost bodysurfing beach, and a good spot to get a taste of Kona's surf

Kailua-Kona Downtown

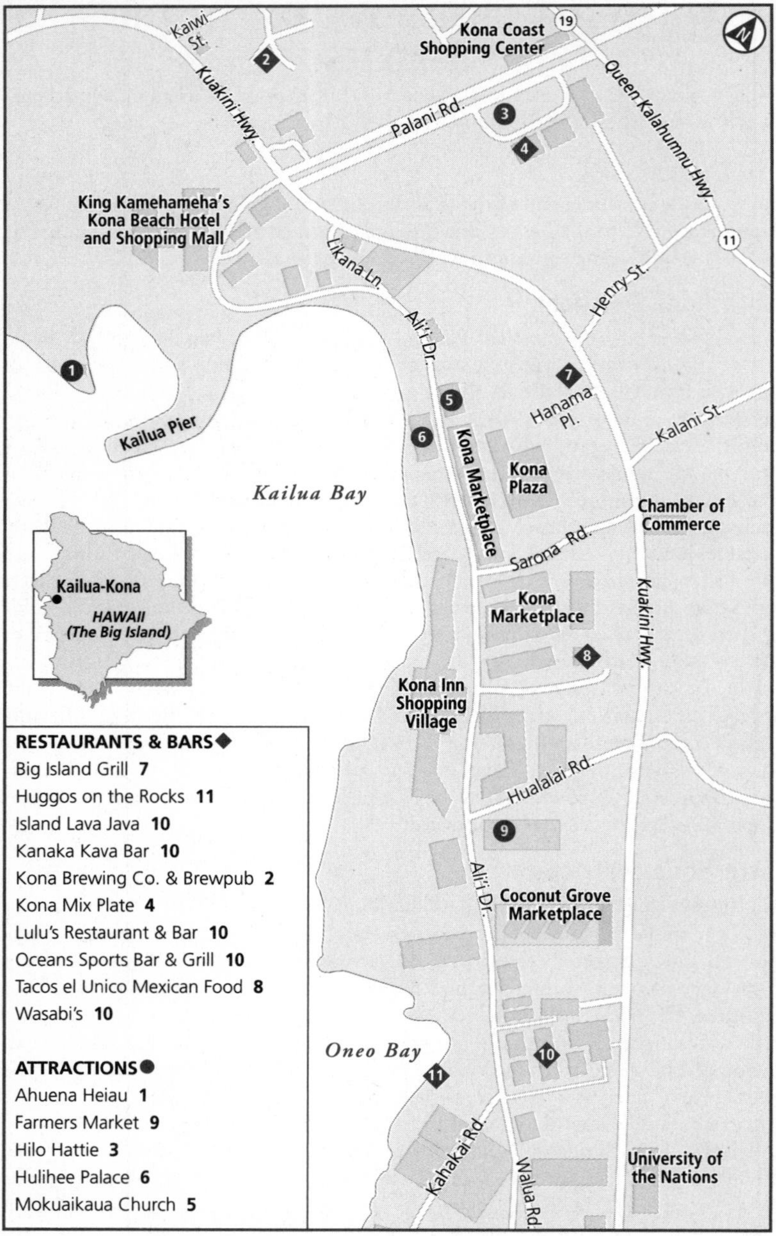

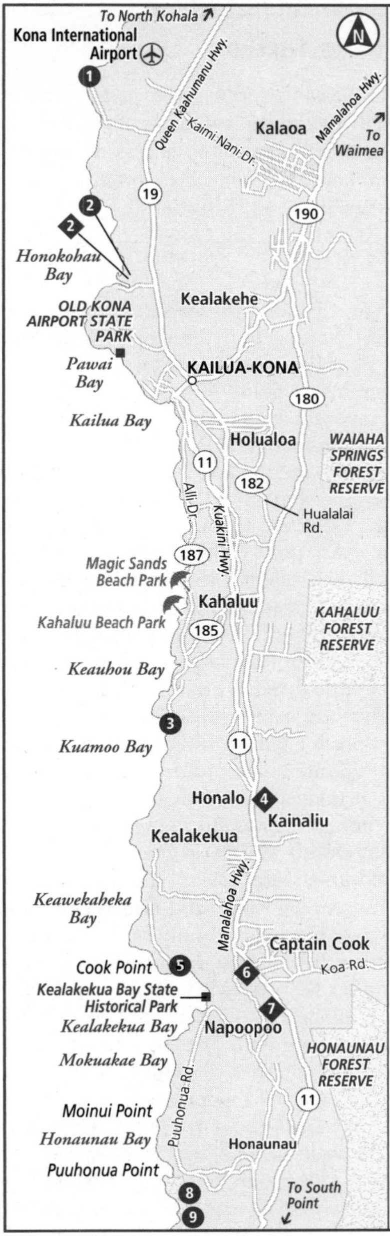

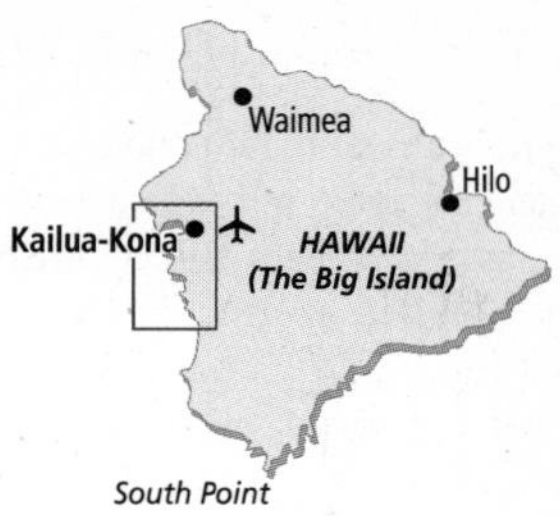

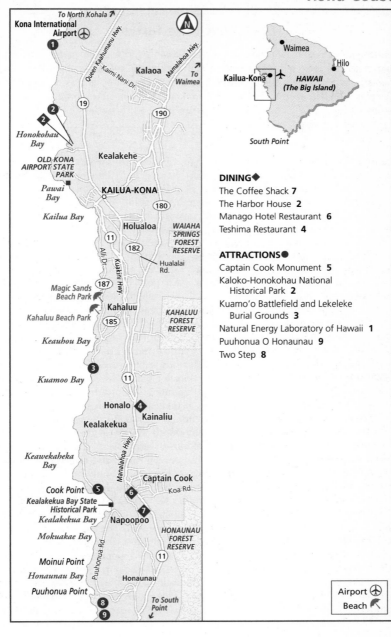

DINING◆

The Coffee Shack **7**
The Harbor House **2**
Manago Hotel Restaurant **6**
Teshima Restaurant **4**

ATTRACTIONS●

Captain Cook Monument **5**
Kaloko-Honokohau National Historical Park **2**
Kuamo'o Battlefield and Lekeleke Burial Grounds **3**
Natural Energy Laboratory of Hawaii **1**
Puuhonua O Honaunau **9**
Two Step **8**

Airport
Beach

Don't Touch the Turtles

Warning: State and federal laws protect Hawaii's turtles from harassment with big fines, so look but don't touch. And give them space. Occasionally, good Samaritans try to help turtles onshore back into the water, mistaking egg-laden females who are staking out nesting grounds in their slow, turtlelike way for stranded turtles. It's always hands-off when it comes to turtles.

culture, if you can time your appearance to coincide with the sand and the waves. The waves break suddenly and violently, waiting until they've almost reached shore before shoaling up and exploding all at once in the shallows.

Water safety tip: Study the ocean here before going in (not a bad idea at any beach). Long lulls between wave sets can give you a false impression of calm seas, a mistake you discover only after you've been lured out and the terrifying mountains of water start rolling in. Even small waves here can give you a good thrashing.

If you have a four-wheel-drive vehicle (and don't mind violating the rental-car agreement that prohibits you from taking it off-road), or you're up for a 2-mile hike across a lava desert to a tropical oasis of a beach, go to **Mahaiula Beach** ★★★ (off Hwy. 19 at sign for KEKAHAKAI STATE PARK, near mile marker 90). It's a gentle 600-foot crescent of golden sand, with overhanging trees casting shade along one edge and turquoise waters lapping along the other. The difficulty of getting here keeps the crowds away, and the beach is long enough for everyone who does show up to have space to themselves. The hike takes a little determination and a lot of bottled water, and the slow drive is along one of the most hellish roads on the island. At the end, there's a parking lot with some port-a-potties, but no drinking water—so bring your own supply. The beach is about a 10-minute walk north from the parking lot. Wild billy goats frequent the area, staring blankly at the beachgoers.

If Mahaiula Beach isn't quite remote enough for you, hike northward along the coast for about 20 minutes to **Makalawena Beach** ★★★ (at the end of Mahaiula Beach, take the trail that runs past the old rusty water tower). The beach has two big white-sand coves, with a minicove in between them, and fingers of lava jutting out here and there. If you find anyone here, they'll only be a few intrepid beachgoers like yourselves, unless there's a swell, and then the surfers turn up, too. It takes fortitude to get to this beach, and it's well rewarded.

Farther north you'll find more beautiful beaches that require neither four-wheel-drive nor grueling treks across the lava to get to. The first one you'll hit is **Kua Bay** ★ (Hwy. 19 at mile marker 88, across from West Hawaii Veteran Cemetery, open 9am–7pm), which has a short sandy beach that's popular with bodysurfers. Underwater pinnacles attract fish and snorkelers off the north point. The beach is backed by sandy ledges set among the lava rock like box seats in a theater. There are Hawaiian village ruins behind the beach, along with brand-new restrooms and showers, a newly paved parking lot, and a newly paved road connecting it all to the highway. The blacktop has brought more people to Kua Bay than when it was at the end of a rough dirt road, but it's still beautiful.

North Kohala

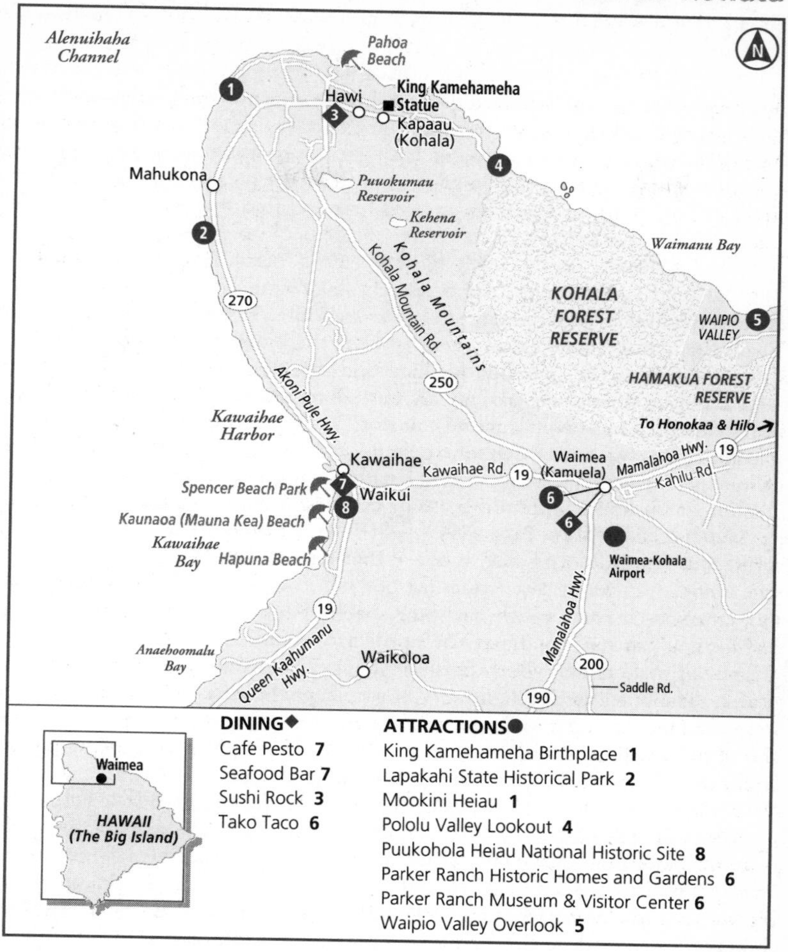

South Kohala

When Hawaiian royalty sailed along the South Kohala coast, they stopped at **Anaehoomalu Bay,** aka A-Bay ★ kids (at Waikokloa Beach Resort, off Hwy. 19 at mile marker 76; open from dawn until dusk), where a large fishpond was stocked with mullet, just for them. The fishpond is still there, as is the long sandy beach where the canoes landed. The beach is backed by a palm grove, and shared by the general public with guests of the Marriott and other hotels at the Waikoloa Beach Resort. **Ocean Sports** (☎ 808/886-6666), a beach concession service, rents windsurfers, sailboats, kayaks, snorkeling gear, and hydro-bikes, and it offers sunset cruises and whale-watching tours. The waters here are well protected and especially good for children. You'll pass the Waikoloa Petroglyph Preserve (p. 377), a highly recommended (and free!) stop. Anaehoomalu Bay takes it name from its ancient use: *anae* meaning mullet, and *hoomalu* meaning protected.

Next, you'll come to **Puako Beach Drive** (off Hwy. 19 near mile marker 70), where a collection of condos and beach houses sit on a scenic cove, and where blue beach-access signs mark the public access ways to the water. The beachfront is a mixture of jagged lava and sand, with great deep-water snorkeling and diving for those comfortable getting in and out of the water on the rocks. You can often walk down one of the beach access ways here and find that you're the only ones on the beach. For kids, there are plenty of tide pools to explore.

Waialea Beach, aka 69 Beach (Hwy. 19 to Puako Beach Dr., then right on Old Puako Rd.) is really like three beaches: a small sandy cove to the north, a rocky area in the middle, and a sandy stretch to the south. There are plenty of trees for shade, including some gnarled ones that lie in the water at high tide. The water is usually pretty gentle and good for kids, and there are newly installed restrooms and a shower. Before the parking lot was paved and a sign put up, finding this beach involved locating telephone pole no. 71, which, before the county did some renumbering, was once telephone pole no. 69, the beach's namesake. Four telephone poles to the north, you'll find a path leading to **67 Beach,** a smaller, more remote beach where nudism prevails by convention, if not county sanction.

Hapuna Beach State Park ★★★ (Hwy. 19 near mile marker 69, just south of Hapuna Beach Prince Hotel) is one of the best-loved and worst-kept beaches on the island. A finger of lava divides the beach in two. The longer south part fronts a county beach park, which has some shabby but popular nonetheless A-frame cabins you can rent (p. 356). The north part of the beach fronts the luxurious Hapuna Prince Hotel, which puts out lounge chairs on the public beach for its guests. The hotel keeps its property in top shape, but the county, unfortunately, doesn't. The beach park is known for having one of the most beautiful beaches, but some of the most disgusting restrooms, on the Big Island—though last time I checked, they weren't nearly as bad as the time before that.

Mauna Kea Beach, aka Kaunaoa Beach ★ (at Mauna Kea Beach Hotel, Hwy. 19 near mile marker 68) is a long, perfect crescent of sand, with gentle swimming waters, snorkeling areas, and plenty of turtles. Unlike nearby Hapuna Beach, where a resort hotel keeps off to itself at one end, this beach is dominated by a resort hotel, the Mauna Kea Beach Hotel. You might get the feeling here that the hotel thinks it owns the beach, but keep in mind that there are no privately owned beaches in Hawaii—all are open to the public. Still, there's no state or county parking lot here, and the hotel has set aside just 42 public parking spots, which fill up fast. The trick here is to show up early, especially on weekends.

A protective reef and a breakwater built for the harbor at Kawaihae shelter the waters at **Spencer Beach Park** (Hwy. 270, between mile markers 2 and 3), making them ideal for young swimmers. This sunny park, popular with local families, has restrooms, barbecue grills, a basketball court, lots of sand, and some snorkeling possibilities at the rocky south end. A short walk down the trail gets you to **Puukohola Heiau,** looming on the hillside nearby (p. 381). The kids will like its beach, and you can explain the historic site's immense importance to them.

North Kohala

Highway 270 in North Kohala hooks around the northern tip of the island from the west side to the east side, ending at Pololu Valley, where you'll find **Pololu**

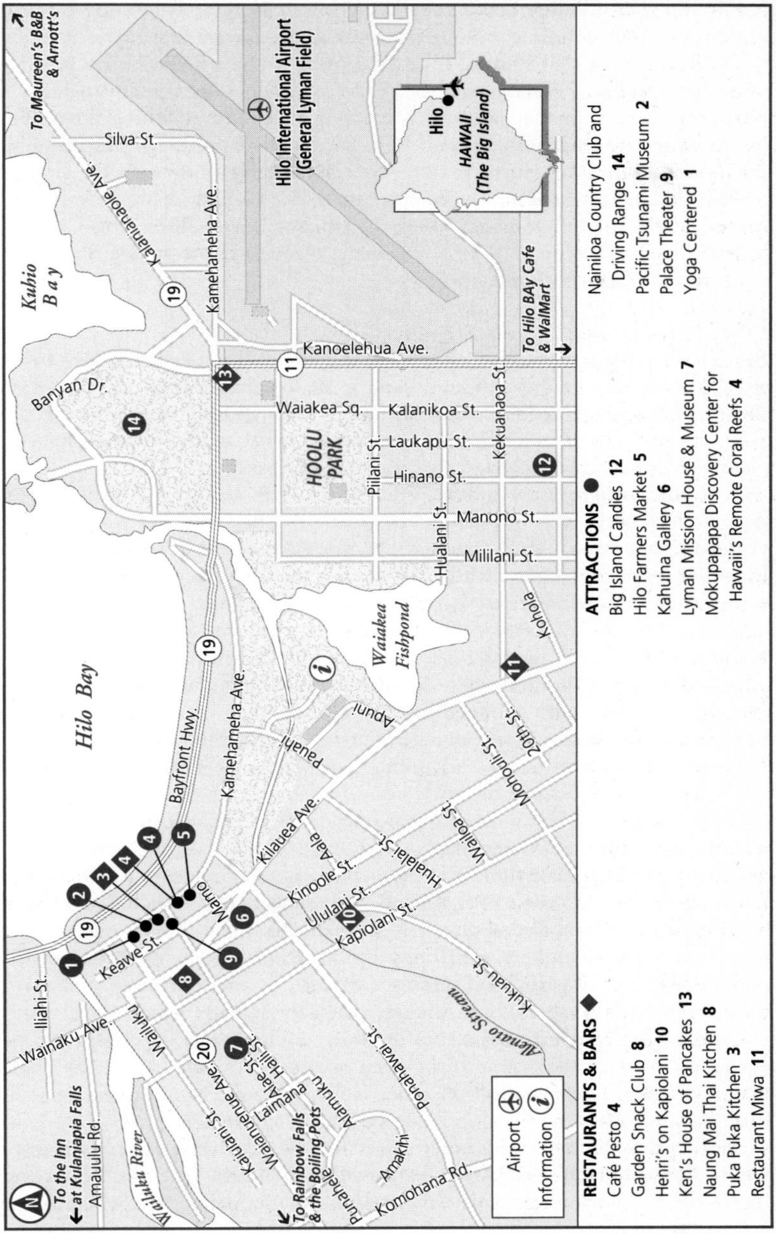

RESTAURANTS & BARS ◆
Café Pesto 4
Garden Snack Club 8
Henri's on Kapiolani 10
Ken's House of Pancakes 13
Naung Mai Thai Kitchen 8
Puka Puka Kitchen 3
Restaurant Miwa 11
ATTRACTIONS ●
Big Island Candies 12
Hilo Farmers Market 5
Kahuina Gallery 6
Lyman Mission House & Museum 7
Mokupapapa Discovery Center for Hawaii's Remote Coral Reefs 4
Nainiloa Country Club and Driving Range 14
Pacific Tsunami Museum 2
Palace Theater 9
Yoga Centered 1
Airport
Information
Hilo Bay
Kuhio Bay
Waiakea Fishpond
HOOLU PARK
Hilo International Airport (General Lyman Field)
HAWAII (The Big Island)
Hilo
To Maureen's B&B & Arnott's
To Hilo BAy Cafe & WalMart
To the Inn at Kulaniapia Falls
To Rainbow Falls & the Boiling Pots
Wailuku River
Alenaio Stream
Silva St.
Kalanianaole Ave.
Kamehameha Ave.
Kanoelehua Ave.
Banyan Dr.
Waiakea Sq.
Kalanikoa St.
Laukapu St.
Hinano St.
Manono St.
Mililani St.
Piilani St.
Hualani St.
Kekuanaoa St.
Kohola
Apuni
Pauahi
Bayfront Hwy.
Kilauea Ave.
Aala
Kinoole St.
Hualalai St.
Ululani St.
Kapiolani St.
Mamo
Keawe St.
Iliahi St.
Wainaku Ave.
Wailuku
Waianuenue Ave.
Kaiulani St.
Laimana
Alae St.
Haili St.
Alamuku
Punahele
Amakihi
Komohana Rd.
Ponahawai St.
Kukuau St.
Waioa St.
Mohouli St.
20th St.
Amauulu Rd.

Beach and **Pololu Valley Lookout** (end of Hwy. 270). The swimming is terrible, but the beachcombing is the best on the island. A steep trail takes you down into the valley (about a 20–30 min. hike) to a long, rough windward beach, littered with driftwood and other flotsam. On rare occasions, the flotsam includes old blue-green glass balls that Japanese fishermen once used as fishing floats. These increasingly rare floats broke loose from their nets decades ago and have been doing laps around the North Pacific ever since, riding along with the clockwise current that runs west along the equator, up to Alaska past Japan, down the west coast of the Americas, and back along the equator again. (***Note:*** This is really an east-side beach, but since it's only accessible through the west side, I've stuck it with the other west-side beaches.)

THE EAST SIDE

Beaches are rare on the rugged east side of the island. What beaches there are tend toward black sand, if they have any sand at all, and many have chilly freshwater springs just offshore, making the water colder than you might expect in Hawaii. Still, the beaches of east Hawaii, fronting a stretch of ocean unbroken until Central America, are lovely and well worth seeking out.

The cold, rocky waters of **Honolii Cove** (Hwy. 19, turn at Alae Point subdivision, 1 mile north of Hilo) make for dreadful swimming, but the year-round northeast trade-wind swell makes it the most consistent surf spot on the Big Island. In Hawaiian legend, this is where the mischievous demigod Maui died, after turning into an eel, chasing a girl up a tree, and getting smashed to pieces by a kahuna with a club. Nowadays, the only shape-shifting going on involves the black sand, which occasionally changes from a river-mouth sand spit into a offshore sand bar, then back again. **Onekahakaha Beach Park** (kids) (Kalanianaole Ave., about a mile past entrance to Hilo Harbor) has a broad, sheltered, sandy-bottomed swimming area behind a hefty break wall of boulders, which subdue an otherwise tumultuous ocean and calm the water enough to teach an infant to swim. There are also some nice tide pools to explore, which kids love, plenty of parking, and an old Hawaiian graveyard nearby with ceramic photos of some of the occupants on their headstones.

The proper name for the next beach you'll come to is **James Kealoha Beach Park,** but everybody calls it **Four Mile** ★ (Kalanianaole Ave., 2 miles past the Hilo Harbor entrance). You can sit on the cool green grass here, or on a warm, smooth lava rock, but the only sand you'll find is on the bottom of the lagoon, which is sheltered by a small island and some rocky reef. Freshwater springs make swimming a brisk affair, especially at low tide when the warmer seawater is in retreat. The easiest way to get in and out of the water is via a short flight of metal steps at the end of the park closest to the open ocean. This beach is precisely 4 miles from Hilo's downtown post office, which is the zero point for measuring distances from the city.

Farther down the road is a beach that could be called Five Mile but is instead known as **Richardson's** ★★ (Kalaniaole Ave., a mile past Four Mile). It's a popular spot, with ancient Hawaiian fishponds, a tiny pocket of sand where you can get in and out of the water easily, lots of rocky shore, good snorkeling, and boogie boarding over a shallow, razor-sharp reef.

Puna District

Along the Puna District's vast, wild coastline, there's a beach park with a pond in it where seawater mixes with fresh, volcanically heated spring water. The temperature in the pond at **Ahalanui Beach Park** (2 miles S. on Hwy. 137 from intersection of Pahoa-Kapoho Rd.) varies from disappointingly warm to startlingly hot. It's hottest during low tide, when the cooler seawater subsides. There's a lifeguard, restrooms, and showers, plus occasional closures when bacteria contaminates the heavily used pond. The ebb and flow of the tides generally keeps the pond pretty clean, though. The park closes at night, which is a shame because it would be a wonderful place to sneak into under a full moon and exchange *watsu* (Japanese water massage) with someone you're sweet on. Or so one imagines.

Farther south from the hot pond is **Isaac Hale Beach Park,** aka Pohoiki (junction of Hwy. 137 Pohoiki Rd.). This spot, with its variety of surf breaks, is the center of the Puna surf scene. While it's a good place for a quick stop to check the waves and maybe inspect a port-a-potty, it's a lousy place to swim and a dangerous place for novice surfers. The unpaved parking lot, one of Puna's social centers, isn't the most inviting spot for visitors to hang out, but it's all you'll find here. Still, if there's a good south swell running, it's fun to watch the surfers for a while.

Farther south, you'll come to **Kahena Beach** (Hwy. 137 near mile marker 19). You'll know it because there's a cliff-side lookout here with a few parking spots, and all sorts of overflow parking on either side of the road. This is Puna's nude beach, and another social center, as well as one of the few beaches you'll ever find born during the baby boom in 1955. A massive lava flow poured into the ocean nearby, forming the jagged black point to the east. As the flow hit the sea, steam explosions threw up tons of glassy, sand-size ash, which accumulated here and created this black-sand beach. In 1975, when an immense earthquake altered the

A Beach Is Born

The 1990 lava flow that destroyed the fishing village at Kalapana also wiped out the famous black-sand beach at Kaimu. That much-loved and -photographed beach, along with the coastline it occupied, now lies beneath about 70 feet of lava. However, you can visit the new black-sand beach forming at **Kaimu** ★★ (where Hwy. 137 dead ends at the lava flow, just past the intersection with Ahia Rd.), not far from where the old one was. Highway 137 ends at a place known as Uncle Robert's (p. 398), where there's an outdoor exhibit illustrating the destruction of Kalapana and the beach, as well as an awa bar. Uncle Robert's place was on the edge of Kalapana and was just missed by the flow.

From the parking area, follow the trail across the lava field, about 15 minutes (although this isn't a good hike for you if you have bad ankles). Hundreds of young coconut trees have been planted along the way, but they grow slowly on the arid landscape. The beach itself is hot and shadeless, with a steep drop-off into a rough ocean wracked with dangerous currents. Although swimming here isn't safe, it's fascinating to sit for a while on the baking hot sand at one of the rawest, newest beaches on the planet.

Puna and Kau coastline, Kahena Beach dropped by about 3 feet. The sand remained, however, and the nudists never stopped coming. Nowadays, leathery hippies older than the beach itself share the sand and shade beneath the ironwoods with nouveau tribalists, nubile students from the University of Hawaii at Hilo, an ever-present contingent of gay sunbathers, and a regular parade of passing gawkers (weekends are the worst).

The swimming here can be treacherous, with a sharp drop-off promoting rip currents and powerful breakers rolling ankle-smashing rocks up and down the steep beach. Some days are so rough that waves wash over the entire beach, forcing it to close down. On calm days, the deep blue ocean just offshore is hard to resist, and the occasional pod of spinner dolphins passes by. On Sunday, a drum circle materializes and carries the beat into the night.

Kau District

Twenty-seven miles south from the entrance to Hawaii Volcanoes National Park, along the vast, undeveloped coastline of the Kau District, you'll find **Punaluu Beach Park** (Hwy. 11 to Punaluu Rd. near mile marker 56). It has a gorgeous black-sand beach you can drive up to, generally rough water made cold by underwater springs, and a rich history. Punaluu means "spring dived for," and was so named because the ancient Hawaiians used to plug gourds with their fingers, dive with them to the underwater springs, and fill them up with fresh water from the seafloor. There's plenty here to see, including a large *heiau* (temple) on the northeast point, the ruins of a sugar mill, the ruins of a failed Polynesian-style tourist trap, and a little monument to the first Hawaiian Christian, Henry Opukahaia. After seeing his parents killed in a war raid, and later suspecting that the kahuna had him in mind as a prospective human sacrifice, a young Opukahaia swam out to a passing fur trader anchored here in 1809 and signed on as a cabin boy. He embraced Christianity, attended school in New England, started translating the Bible into Hawaiian, and died of typhoid fever, inspiring the first wave of young missionaries who set off for Hawaii a few years later. (Opukahaia himself was buried in Connecticut for 185 years before he finally got back to Hawaii.) Green sea turtles gather at Punaluu, and the occasional hawksbill turtle, the rarest turtle in the Pacific, nests here in the spring and summer. When the hawksbills show up, so do volunteers with the Hawksbill Turtle Monitoring Program, who sit with the nests and protect them from predators and misplaced human footsteps.

Black isn't the only unusual color that Big Island beaches come in. They also come in green. Like the eroding iron-rich cinder cone nourishing a red-sand beach on Maui, an eroding cinder cone rich in olivine, a glassy, olive-green mineral, gives the black sand at this Big Island beach its unusual tint. Located near South Point, the southernmost tip of both the United States and the island, **Green Sands Beach** (take South Point Rd. to the fork and bear left; go until road ends at the boat ramp; by foot, follow the rutted trail 2½ miles to the cliffs, then pick your way down the trail to the beach) takes some effort to get to. Most car-rental companies won't cover you if your car breaks down out here or if it's broken into, and break-ins aren't uncommon. The area's remote and windblown, with treacherous waters much of the time, especially if you get very far from shore, where swift currents whip whatever they find near shore far out to sea. During big south swells, waves sometimes inundate the beach, closing it entirely. It has no facilities

A Cutworm's Comeuppance

The unusual flat-topped hills located a few miles inland from **Punaluu Beach Park** were once ridges, which erosion has long since cut into segments. Hawaiian legend attaches its own significance to the hills: Punaluu, a beautiful young woman who once lived here, married a handsome stranger, who was secretly a shape shifter. At night he would turn into a cutworm and inch off to feast on sweet-potato leaves. After changing back into human form, he'd sleep all day, doing nothing to provide for his wife. When he caught Punaluu spying on him, he destroyed all the sweet-potato patches in the area. The aggrieved populace then appealed to the god Kane, who killed the shiftless shape shifter and chopped him into pieces, reminiscent of the flat-topped hills visible from Punaluu Beach Park today.

or shade, and it takes a good 40 minutes to hike to. But in spite of these drawbacks, it gets a fair share of visitors, drawn by the wildness and the novelty of lounging on green sand.

THE TOP SIGHTS & ATTRACTIONS

I'll deal first with the historical and cultural sites, then with the natural wonders.

WEST HAWAII

History comes first. The Big Island has more ancient Hawaiian sites, and more easily accessible ancient Hawaiian sites, than any of the other islands. Among these are petroglyph fields, where Hawaiians carved enduring images and designs in smooth pahoehoe lava.

Historical Sights

Where you find one petroglyph, you usually find many more, not unlike graffiti. The most extensive accumulation of these carvings in the Pacific is at the **Puako Petroglyph Archeological District** ★ kids (at the Mauna Lani Resort, Hwy. 11 between mile markers 73 and 74; follow signs to parking area; walk about ½ mile along marked trail). About 3,000 carvings have been found here, including paddlers, marchers, dancers, dogs, chickens, turtles, and Polynesian crab-claw sails. The earliest carvings date to around A.D. 1200, and the latest—such as images of the horses and cattle Europeans introduced to the islands—date to the early 1800s. A lot of circles within circles were also carved here. They are believed to have been used to stash the umbilical cords of newborns, which tied the infant to the land and helped ensure it health and longevity. ***Beware:*** The trail leads through a thorny kiawe (aka mesquite) forest, so protect your feet.

You'll find another vast assembly of petroglyphs, surrounded by a golf course, in the **Waikoloa Petroglyph Preserve** ★ kids (Waikoloa Beach Resort, off Hwy. 19 near mile marker 76; petroglyph area is well marked, just before Kings' Shops). Among the canoes, animals, and other traditional themes, there's a carving here of a *paniolo,* a Hawaiian cowboy, on horseback. You can wander the cinder pathways through the field on your own, but you'll learn more if you take the free **tour**

Finding Places to See & Go

The sights and attractions in the following sections can be found on the maps starting on p. 336.

(☎ 808/886-8811) that's offered daily. It meets at 10:30am at the nearby Kings' Shops, in front of the food pavilion, and lasts about an hour. The tour walks along a section of the King's Trail, which once circled the island (petroglyphs are typically found along trails). After the tour, go to nearby **Anaehoomalu Bay** (p. 371) to see the ancient Hawaiian fishpond and to take a swim in the ocean.

At many ancient Hawaiian sites, it takes some imagination to see how the piles of stones lying about would have been used by the people who originally piled them. That's not the case at **Puuhonua o Honaunau** ★★★ (Keala O Keawe Rd., off Hwy. 11 at mile marker 104, south of Kailua-Kona; ☎ 808/328-2288; visitor center open daily 8am–4pm, grounds open 7am–8pm; admission $5 per car with up to 4 occupants, $3 per additional person; admission good for one week; all National Park Service passes accepted; www.nps.gov/puho), where original structures have been reconstructed or so well preserved that you'll have no trouble at all seeing how things were. In ancient times, this was a place of refuge, a *puuhonua,* where noncombatants could go in times of war, where warriors on the losing side of a battle could find safety, and where *kapu* breakers in mortal danger might find a second chance. The kahuna at a place of refuge could absolve *kapu* breakers of their sins, freeing them to return to society without fear of retribution. Otherwise, they might face death. ***Cash saving tip:*** Visit early or late in the day and get in free. Admission is charged only while the visitor center is open. ***Bonus tip:*** Puuhonua o Honaunau is a great place to watch the sunset.

Each island had puuhonua, and the Big Island had at least six. This one has survived, and offers a visceral sense of what some of the human landscape of ancient Hawaii looked like. A 1,000-foot-long mortarless rock wall, 10 feet high and 17 feet deep, is in perfect shape, with lava rock arranged into long, clean, tapered lines. The wall seals off a broad point of land upon which waves crash and a *heiau* (temple) and royal mausoleum stand, complete with prayer tower and grimacing idols. Near the base for another *heiau,* there's a flat stone used as a game board for *konone,* the Hawaiian version of checkers. Small black-lava and white-coral playing pieces fill niches carved into the top of the board, and it's not hard to imagine refugees gathered around it, whiling away the time.

Outside of the wall is a royal village compound with fishponds, thatched structures, and a sandy canoe landing cut naturally in the rock (keep an eye out for turtles). It takes about half an hour to do the self-guided tour with a brochure you can pick up at the visitor center where you enter. But it can get pretty hot and sunny here, so bring water and a hat. Afterward, walk over to Two Step (p. 367), a nearby snorkeling and scuba-diving spot where you can jump in the water to cool off.

Unlike well-preserved **Puuhonua o Honaunau** (see above), many of the ancient sites spread across the 1,160 acres of lava desert and shoreline of **Kaloko-Honokohau National Historical Park** ★ (Hwy. 19 between mile markers 96 and

97; ☎ 808/329-6881; visitor center open 8:30am–4pm, Kaloko Rd. gate open 8am–5pm; free admission; www.nps.gov/kaho) take either an archaeologist's eye to appreciate, or at least the free map and interpretive brochure handed out at the visitor center. Also, unlike Puuhonua o Honaunau, which gets a half million visitors a year, scarcely anyone seems to come here, even though it's just 3 miles north of Kailua town. A network of age-old trails runs through the park, but the shimmering air rising off the sun-baked lava discourages all but the most ardent (and well-hydrated) hikers, or those who come early or late in the day. It seems as if no one could have ever lived there, but hundreds of Hawaiians once did. They were concentrated along the shore, where they tended fishponds, grew crops in raised beds (using coconut husks soaked in fresh water for irrigation), and traded what they harvested from the sea for what people living in the green upslope areas grew.

If you visit, you'll find all sorts of ancient structures, including two huge fishponds, a large fish trap (fish swam in at high tide and got stuck when the tide dropped), and a *heiau,* plus house sites, planters, and stone cairns that mark the boundary between the *ahupua'a* of Kaloko and Honokohau, the two ancient land divisions that met here. From the visitor center it's about a half-mile walk through the lava field to the fish trap and the sea. A full loop through the park takes about 2 hours. Bear in mind that this is a rugged lava desert, where sturdy shoes, good sun protection, and plenty of water are in order. You can also get into Kaloko-Honokohau by parking on the north side of Honokohau Harbor, which is the way to go if you want to beat the heat by hiking in the late afternoon, since the two official parking areas are gated by 5pm. Just be sure to stop at the visitor center in advance to pick up a map and brochure.

Another good place to get an idea of the human scale of ancient Hawaii is **Lapakahi State Historical Park** (Hwy. 270, near mile marker 14; ☎ 808/882-6207; 8am–4pm daily; free admission), on the north end of the island. Here you'll see the partially reconstructed remains of a fishing village founded some 600 years ago. It sits on a desolate, windblown stretch of coastline, and feels like a Stone Age ghost town. A 45-minute self-guided tour (you can cheat and shorten it) takes you past 23 points of interest, including house and burial sites, a canoe shed, and a fishing shrine. The self-guided tour brochure has a mystical tone that suits the place perfectly. Take, for example, this quote: "You will feel the presence—you will look for things that are but cannot be seen."

Petroglyph Protocol

For years, people have taken rubbings and castings of Hawaii's more accessible petroglyphs, which seems harmless enough, but actually damages the carvings. These days, it's a look-but-don't-touch policy with petroglyphs, except for a special area in the Puako Petroglyph Archeological District where you can take rubbings from replicas, if you like. A better way to record what's there is with a camera. The long shadows of the late afternoon make the carvings stand out best, and offer the best viewing and photo opportunities.

The Captain Cook Monument

Captain James Cook, on an expedition in search of the fabled Northwest Passage, became the first known European to reach Hawaiian waters. He spent 2½ weeks at Kealakekua Bay in 1779, provisioning his two ships for a journey to the Arctic. Things went well enough with the Hawaiians at first, who initially suspected he must be a god. They quickly figured out he wasn't. Cook left on good terms, but when he was forced back to the bay to make repairs to a broken mast, everything descended into chaos. The British, in trying to recover a stolen cutter, killed an *alii,* inciting a skirmish in which Cook was stoned, stabbed, clubbed, held under water, and beaten in the head with a rock.

The Captain Cook Monument, a 27-foot obelisk, stands near the spot where he died. A small plaque in shallow water marks the actual spot where he's believed to have fallen. The hard-to-reach point where the monument is located is part of Kealakekua Bay State Historic Park, which is also a marine conservation district and one of the best snorkeling spots in Hawaii. Ruins of the village of Kaawaloa lie in the thick kiawe forest behind the shore.

On the very northernmost tip of the island stands **Mookini Heiau** (Hwy. 270 to Upolu Rd., at mile marker 20; at the airfield, turn left onto the unpaved road and go about 1 miles), staring across choppy Alenuihaha Channel at the dark shores of northeastern Maui. This *heiau* (temple), nearly the size of a football field and 30-feet tall in places, was dedicated to Ku, the god of war. Surprisingly, the descendants of the high priests who built the *heiau* around A.D. 480 and oversaw it through the centuries still oversee it today (p. 397).

About 1,000 yards away is the **King Kamehameha Birthplace** (½ mile farther along the dirt road). The Hawaiians weren't going by the Gregorian calendar then, but the year of Kamehameha's birth has been pinpointed through chants that refer to a mysterious star appearing in the sky at the time of the future king's birth, an omen now presumed to have been Haley's comet, which appeared in 1758. As the story goes, a prophecy foretold that Kamehameha would one day rule the Big Island, even though he was not in the royal line of succession. As a precautionary measure, a high chief from the east side sent warriors to kill the infant, but Kamehameha's mother vanished with him after his birth and raised him in hiding. You can walk to the birth site from the *heiau* and see smooth birthing stones lying within a double-walled enclosure. You can't drive to these sites without a four-wheel-drive vehicle, but the 3-mile round-trip hike along the road is easy and pleasant enough.

In the nearby town of Kapaau stands a bronze **statue of King Kamehameha** (front lawn of the Kapaau Courthouse) with a spear in one hand, and sometimes a fresh flower lei in the outstretched palm of his other. Identical statues can be found in Honolulu and Hilo. This is the original, commissioned in 1878 and lost when the ship carrying it from Paris, where it was cast, sank off the Falkland Islands. A replacement was commissioned, and arrived in Honolulu safely. A few weeks later, a ship showed up in Honolulu harbor carrying the original. The captain had found it in a Port Stanley junkyard, where it wound up after someone salvaged the wreck.

As the story goes, prophecy held that Kamehameha would conquer all of the Hawaiian Islands only after he built a temple to his family war god. The enormous structure he constructed at Kawaihae is now **Puukohola Heiau National Historic Site** ★★ (Hwy. 270, near Kawaihae Harbor; ☎ 808/882-7218; www.nps.gov/puhe; visitor center open 7:30am–4pm daily; free admission). This impressive place is right next to Spencer Beach Park, a convenient spot to take a dip after hiking around the parched 77-acre site. Puukohola was constructed between 1790 and 1791. For its dedication, Kamehameha invited his cousin and rival from east Hawaii, Keoua. When Keoua's canoes landed at Puukohola, he was attacked and killed, his corpse prepared as the *heiau*'s first sacrifice. It's possible that Keoua knew what he was in for. As his troops passed Kilauea volcano on their return home from an earlier battle with Kamehameha, an explosive eruption buried many of them in scalding ash. A high-level admonishment like this from the gods—in this case the fearsome volcano goddess Pele—could have demoralized Keoua so thoroughly that he simply resigned himself to his fate at Puukohola. In any case, his death ended opposition to Kamehameha on the Big Island, and fulfillment of the prophecy got off to a quick start.

Two other *heiau* occupy this site, though you'll only see one, **Mailekini Heiau,** an older temple that Kamehameha converted into a fort with cannons he acquired from Western traders. The other is **Hale O Kapuni,** built in the sea just offshore and dedicated to sharks, who breed in these waters (don't worry, they don't bother swimmers in the protected waters at the nearby beach park). This *heiau* once stood above the waves, but has since fallen beneath them.

Across Highway 270 from Puukohola Heiau, you'll find the **homestead of John Young** (ask for directions at the visitor center), one of Kamehameha's two British advisors. Young and his associate, Isaac Davis, started out as ordinary seamen and ended up as chiefs in the Hawaiian Kingdom. They taught the Hawaiians how to use cannons and muskets, which gave Kamehameha a colossal advantage in battle, and they provided the king invaluable insight into the minds of the European traders, who were showing up increasingly in Hawaiian waters. Young's house very well might have been the first structure ever built with mortar in Hawaii. The foundation and remnants of the walls remain, along with those of a half-dozen other buildings. One was a traditional Hawaiian *hale* (house), where Young's royal-blooded Hawaiian wife resided. She apparently didn't think mortared stone was necessarily an improvement on what Hawaiians already had.

Kamehameha spent his final years presiding over his kingdom and fishing at **Kamakahonu** (now the grounds of the King Kamehameha's Kona Beach Hotel, 75-5660 Palani Rd.; Kailua-Kona), his royal compound on Kailua Bay, where he died in 1819. After his death, his son and heir to the throne, Liholiho, sat down to dinner here with Queen Kaahumanu and other women, breaking a fundamental *kapu* (taboo) that prohibited the sexes from eating together, and symbolically shattering the *kapu* system, the age-old religious order. Nothing remains of the royal compound except the **Ahuena Heiau,** which is a reconstruction. It looks authentic enough, but it's a fraction of the original's size.

A Walking Tour

The **Kona Historical Society** (call ☎ 808/938-8825; tours Tues and Thurs at 9:30am, or by appointment for groups of 4 or more; $15; reservations required) conducts a 75 minute walking tour of historic sites around downtown Kailua-Kona. The walk starts at King Kamehameha's old royal compound, Kamakahonu, where the King Kamehameha's Kona Beach Hotel stands today. It then heads toward Mokuaikaua Church, and finishes across the street at Hulihee Palace. The guides brim with ideas and information, and the price includes booklet with maps and historic photos.

Liholiho's abandonment of the *kapu* system set off an insurrection against him, led by his cousin Kekuaokalani. In the battle that followed, Kekuaokalani and many of his warriors were killed and the uprising was quashed. At the end of Alii Drive, past the Kona Country Club, you'll find **Kuamo'o Battlefield and Lekeleke Burial Grounds** (7 miles south of Kailua town), a lava plain between a steep hillside and rugged sea cliffs, where 300 or so Hawaiians died in the battle. At first, all you'll see is a chaotic jumble of heaving, crumbling *a'a'* lava. Then, your eyes start to notice the stone cairns filled with the dead that cover the battlefield, their clean rock lines bringing order to the tortured landscape. Nowadays, this is a popular spot for picnics and sunsets.

Eighteen-nineteen was an important year in Hawaiian history. Kamehameha died, the *kapu* system was abandoned, and while everybody was still reeling from those developments, the brigantine *Thaddeus* anchored off Kailua-Kona with a strange group of passengers on board—Congregationalist Christian missionaries. They weren't immediately welcomed ashore, but after some negotiations they won permission to stay on a trial basis. The first church they put up was a thatched hut, which they replaced in 1837 with a more permanent building, constructed with the stones of an abandoned *heiau* and called **Mokuaikaua Church** (75-5713 Alii Dr.; ☎ 808/329-0655). Today its steeple rises above the souvenir shops and restaurants of Kailua-Kona's deepest tourist zone. It's open from dawn until dusk, and you should take a look around. Check out how the posts and beams are joined with notches and pegs. The missionaries didn't have nails, which is a good thing since nails would have rusted away by now. Don't be put off if there's a service in progress (Sun at 8 and 10:30am); you can still poke around unnoticed in the vestibule, where there are some historic displays, including an enormous model of the *Thaddeus*.

Directly across the street from Mokuaikaua Church sits **Hulihee Palace** ★★★ (75-5718 Alii Dr.; ☎ 808/329-1877; www.huliheepalace.org; $6 adults, $1 children 18 and younger; 9am–4pm daily), built the year after the church was completed by High Chief Kuakini, governor of the island, and used by subsequent generations of *alii* as a seaside retreat. After the fall of the Hawaiian monarchy, the palace fell into disrepair. It was saved from demolition in 1920 by the Daughters of Hawaii, a women's society founded by seven missionary daughters, who restored it and have maintained it since. The society also hosts free afternoon concerts and hula performances here. Visit the website for details and schedules.

The palace is filled with some of its original furnishings, as well as artifacts such as a 22-foot spear that belonged to Kamehameha himself, and an enormous hat box made for Princess Ruth from the trunk of a coconut tree. When you stand at the front gate and face Hulihee Palace, with its neat, quiet grounds, and the glimmering sea beyond, it's easy to forget for a moment the world of mass tourism swirling behind you along Alii Drive. Kailua-Kona is once again a sleepy village built on a lava shoreline, and Hawaii an island kingdom, whose vacationing royals considered this spot especially beautiful, even though they all came from beautiful places. ***Note:*** Slow-going repair work following a 2006 earthquake that badly rattled the building has closed public access to some rooms, but the palace is still open daily.

Farmers in ancient Hawaii created the Kona Field System, a network of terraced agricultural lands spread across 30 square miles of rich volcanic slopes. You can see remnants of these gardens and groves at the **Amy Greenwell Ethnobotanical Garden** (Hwy. 11 at mile marker 11, Captain Cook; ☎ 808/323-3318; weekdays 8:30am–5pm; $4). All 250 of the plant species on these tranquil 15-acre grounds are either native or endemic to the islands, or were introduced by the first Polynesian settlers. The Hawaiians had uses for just about all of them, such as the tall fan-shaped loulu palm, which was used for thatch, spears, and its edible seeds. You can walk the gardens on your own, but you'll learn more on one of the guided tours, offered Wednesday and Friday at 1pm for $5. There's a free tour the second Saturday of every month at 10am

Cultural Sights

One of the most extensive private art collections in Hawaii belongs to one of the most exclusive private schools in the world, Hawaii Preparatory Academy in Waimea. At the **Isaacs Art Center Museum and Gallery** (65-1268 Kawaihae Rd., Waimea; ☎ 808/885-5884; Tues–Sat 10am–5pm), you can view some of the multimillion-dollar collection. On display are pieces by renowned Hawaii artists such

Coffee Country

The upper regions of Kona have sunny mornings, cloudy afternoons, mild nights, and rich volcanic soil—all of which coffee plants adore. Kona coffee grows at elevations between 500 and 3,000 feet in the mile-wide, 30-mile-long Kona Coffee Belt. For 1 week in the fall, the **Kona Coffee Cultural Festival** (www.konacoffeefest.com) celebrates the island-grown bean with a tasting and coffee cherry (as the ripe red beans are called) picking competitions, a Miss Kona Coffee pageant, floral displays, lei-making contests, luncheons, running races, talent shows, craft workshops, art exhibits, and more.

Note: Ask at any concierge's desk for the free brochure that provides a self-guided driving tour of the coffee belt.

Parker Ranch: Historic Homes & Fun on the Range

Beef came to Hawaii when the explorer Captain George Vancouver gave cattle to King Kamehameha as a gift. Kamehameha turned them loose to reproduce, issuing a *kapu* protecting them from harm. They bred like crazy, and before long Hawaii had a wild-cattle problem, with the beasts destroying forests, trampling crops, and threatening people. To bring the beasts under control, Kamehameha hired John Palmer Parker, a young American sailor who had jumped ship. Parker Ranch arose from the animals and the land near Waimea that Kamehameha granted to Parker for his efforts. It grew to become one of the largest ranches in the United States.

In Waimea, the **Parker Ranch Museum & Visitor Center** (67-1185 Mamalahoa Hwy., behind the Parker Ranch Shopping Center; ☎ 808/885-7655; www.parkerranch.com; admission $8 adults, $6 children 4–12), offers a good overview of the history of the ranch and the evolution of the *paniolo* (Hawaiian cowboy). Nearby, the **Parker Ranch Historic Homes and Gardens** (Hwy. 190, outside Waimea; ☎ 808/885-5433; admission $9 adults, $8 children 4–12; closed Sun) preserves the home John Parker built for himself and the high-ranking Hawaiian he married, as well as the opulent mansion where subsequent generations dwelled. Parker's house, known as Mana Hale, is a New England saltbox with a shiplike interior finished in rich koa wood. It was moved, board by board, from its original location and reassembled here, next door to **Puopelo,** the family estate. The last person to live in Puopelo was Richard Smart, Parker's great-great grandson, a Broadway and cabaret performer, and the end of the family bloodline. When he died in 1992, the ranch was taken over by a trust, which manages it for the benefit of several Waimea community groups. Highlights of the two homes include Smart's collection of antiques, Peking glassware, and French Impressionist paintings, including works by Degas. Twenty-minute lectures on the Parker family are given at the top of the hour throughout the day. Be sure to pop into the powder room, which Smart turned into something of a shrine to his theater days.

A 45-minute **wagon ride** (☎ 808/885-7655; $15 adults, $12 children 4–12; Tues–Sat 10am–2pm tours depart from the visitor center on the hour) will give you a peek at the more traditional side of ranching; it's also possible to **tour the ranch by horseback or ATV** (☎ 808/885-7655; $79 by hoof, $95 on wheels). Both types of tours last 2 hours and happen at 8:15am and 12:15pm daily. Both also offer a 1½-hour sunset tour at 4:15pm.

Money-saving tip: If you buy tickets for the museum, the historic homes, and the wagon ride all at once, you'll save $3.

as Jean Charlot, Madge Tennent, and Herb Kane, as well as works by others such as 16th-century printmaker Albrecht Dürer. The gallery itself occupies the town's old public school building, which was built in 1915 and slated for demolition in 2002. The community rallied to save the schoolhouse from a passive-aggressive state Department of Education that was determined to raze the place. In the end, it came down to a sympathetic demolition contractor, who exercised a right-of-salvage clause in his contract to salvage the entire building, moving it in sections a few blocks through town to the private school site. State officials were chagrined when they discovered the building hadn't ended up in the landfill, but there was nothing they could do about it. The building was saved and put to good use.

Space, Technology & Marine Matters

Unless you're a space buff, don't go out of your way to see the **Onizuka Space Center** (at Kona International Airport, between Aloha and Hawaiian airlines; ☎ 808/329-3441; daily 8:30am–4:30pm; $3 adults, $1 children 12 and under). But if you have a long wait at the airport, the space center is a pleasant—and conveniently located—place to kill time, especially if you're traveling with kids. It's filled with space and science games and toys (though much of the hands-on stuff was out-of-order when I visited). Exhibits include the Apollo 13 space suit worn by astronaut Fred Haise, and a gravity well that demonstrates orbital motion. The center is dedicated to Ellison Onizuka, a Big Island boy who grew up to be an astronaut and perished when the Space Shuttle Challenger exploded in 1986. (Don't confuse the Onizuka Space Center with the Onizuka Center for International Astronomy on Mauna Kea, p. 389. They're named after the same Onizuka, but they're unrelated.)

Manta Rays: Flying Mouths of the Sea

Because manta rays are impossible to keep in captivity and difficult to study in the wild, marine scientists know little about them. One thing is clear though: Manta rays love zooplankton, those microscopic, often larval, critters of the sea. If you shine a bright light into the ocean, zooplankton will flock to it like bugs to a headlight, and the mantas in Kailua-Kona usually follow. The **Sheraton Keauhou Bay Resort & Spa** (78–128 Ehukai St.; ☎ 808/930-4900), built on a rocky promontory south of Kailua-Kona, shines a light into the water just off its Crystal Blue Lounge, drawing mantas to feed and people to watch them. The mantas, which resemble flying mouths, don't show up every night, but they do at least half the time, usually after 8pm. (***Tip:*** Low tide is the best time to see them.) On Wednesday and Friday at 7:30 pm, there's a free manta ray briefing at the Crystal Blue Lounge, where manta experts discuss mantas and their behavior, or what's known of it anyway.

EAST HAWAII

Again we'll focus primarily on history and culture, but this time we'll discuss the attractions found in the eastern part of the Big Island.

Historical Sights

Three weeks after they married in 1832, two idealistic young New Englanders, David and Sarah Lyman, set sail for Hawaii to work as Christian missionaries. At the home they built near Hilo Bay, they taught young Hawaiians to read, write, and do arithmetic. They entertained Hawaiian royalty and hosted visiting Westerners, including VIPs like Mark Twain and Robert Louis Stevenson. The **Lyman Mission House** (276 Haili St., Hilo; ☎ 808/935-5021; www.lymanmuseum.org; Mon–Sat 9:30am–4:30pm; admission $10 adults, $3 children 6–17) has survived to become the oldest wood-framed building in Hawaii. It's open for half-hour guided tours Monday through Saturday at 11am, 1pm, and 3pm.

Right next door stands the **Lyman Museum**, which has cultural, geologic, and astronomy exhibits. Admission to the mission house gets you into the museum as well. The house is filled with furniture, clothing, and artifacts from the Lymans' days, and it retains the spirit of its original occupants, who lived here until their work on Earth was done. He died in 1884, and she in 1885.

Natural Science Wonders

The mostly uninhabited islets and atolls of the northwestern Hawaiian Islands, which extend 1,000 miles beyond Kauai, make up two-thirds of the Hawaiian archipelago. They also contain 70% of all the coral reefs in U.S. waters, which, like sensitive coral reefs everywhere, have suffered from environmental degradation. The National Oceanic and Atmospheric Administration's coral reef museum, **Mokupapapa Discovery Center for Hawaii's Remote Coral Reefs** ★ kids (308 Kamehameha Ave., downtown Hilo; ☎ 808/933-8195; http://hawaiireef.noaa.gov/center/welcome.html; 9am–4pm Tues–Sat; free), is dedicated to these far-flung Hawaiian ecosystems. One of the center's goals is to inspire kids to care about coral reefs and the life they support, and advocate for them when they're grown. But the place is hardly just for kids. One push-button exhibit demonstrates the lifecycle of Hawaiian islands, showing how they go from enormous, fiery places like the Big Island—too young to have much coral—to tiny remnants like Kure Atoll, at the westernmost end of the island chain, where the original island has long since vanished and the fringing coral reef is all that remains. Of all the exhibits, my favorite is the mock-up of the *Pisces V* submersible, a deep sea research vessel with working robot arms that you can use to grab things off the ocean floor.

If there's only one thing you take away from a visit to the **Pacific Tsunami Museum** (130 Kamehameha Ave., downtown Hilo; ☎ 808/935-0926; www.tsunami.org; Mon–Sat 9am–4pm; $7 admission, or $2 ages 6–17), hopefully it will be this: If the ocean suddenly and freakishly recedes, as it sometimes does when a tsunami approaches, don't wander out onto the exposed seafloor to investigate. Run for your life. Densely populated and located along a bay that amplifies tsunamis, Hilo was hit hard by two big 20th-century tsunamis, one in 1946 and one in 1960, as well as some smaller ones. This unusual little museum serves as a memorial to the people killed, while doing what it can to educate the living about tsunamis so fewer people will be killed in the next ones. Despite the grave mission, the museum's filled with good, clean, scientific fun. At one exhibit, you get

World's Biggest Hula Happening

The missionaries did their best to stop hula, but they only succeeded in driving it underground. By the time Hawaii's last king, David Kalakaua, took the throne, the missionaries were gone but the hula remained. King Kalakaua liked the hula. He had dancers perform at his coronation in 1883, the first public hula in ages. His love of the dance, along with his general flair for fun, earned him his nickname, the Merrie Monarch.

Nowadays, for 1 week each spring, hula troops from all over Hawaii, the mainland, and Japan, converge in normally sleepy Hilo for a gargantuan hula gathering named in Kalakaua's honor, **The Merrie Monarch Festival** (☎ 808/935-9168; http://merriemonarchfestival.org; $25 reserved seating, $15 general admission). The festival kicks off on Easter Sunday and continues through Wednesday with a series of free events. On Thursday, things get serious, with paid seating and smiling but fiercely competitive female dancers vying for the title of Miss Aloha Hula. Male and female *halau,* as hula troops are known, compete in the traditional dance category, and on Friday they compete in the modern Hawaiian dance, with the awards ceremony afterward.

Tickets for the 3 days of competition go on sale after Christmas and are available by mail only. If you want to go, send a cashier's check or money order, postmarked on or after December 26, to: The Merrie Monarch Festival, c/o Hawaii Naniloa Hotel, 93 Banyan Dr., Hilo, HI 96720. Only two tickets per person are allowed. Merrie Monarch is a time of tremendous Hawaiian pride and a great week to be in Hilo. But it's a terrible time to try to find a hotel room or a rental car. If you can't get a ticket, or you like your hula in smaller doses, you can watch the festival on television. It's broadcast live throughout the islands.

to play the director of the Pacific Tsunami Warning Center, who has to decide whether or not to evacuate Hawaii's coastlines as a potentially devastating tsunami approaches. If you make the right call, you save lots of lives; if you blow it, either people die or you cost the state $50 million for a false alarm. Unlike the real director, you get to pick the location and magnitude of the earthquake that generates the waves—and you can shrug it off if you make a bad call.

In a classic culture clash, Native Hawaiians are perennially at odds with astronomers over Mauna Kea, the highest mountain in the Pacific. For astronomers, the mountain is one of the best places on the Earth to peer into space. For many Hawaiians, the cluster of observatories on the summit desecrate a sacred place. The conflict has resulted in a boon for visitors to Hilo, the **Imiloa Astronomy Center of Hawaii** ★ (600 Imiloa Place, Hilo; ☎ 808/969-9700; www.imiloahawaii.org; admission $15, $7.50 ages 4–12). The idea behind the $28-million center was to demonstrate that Hawaiians and astronomers share a lot in common. Ancient Polynesians were seafaring explorers who kept their eyes on the stars as they sailed into the unknown. Modern astronomers are explorers with eyes fixed on the stars as they push deeper into the unknown. Politically, the center has been more of a lighting rod for controversy than a bridge across the cultural divide. But for visitors, it's a great place to kill an hour and a half or so while learning a little about both Hawaii and the cosmos (don't expect to hear about the culture clash through—that's all behind the scenes). Housed in three giant titanium-covered cones built on the hillside above town, the center has loads of astronomical and Hawaiian cultural exhibits, as well a planetarium where dizzying movies about space and Hawaii play on the enormous dome shaped ceiling. Go online or call to check the film showing in the planetarium so you can time your visit right, and keep in mind there's a great place to eat there (p. 362).

The World of Water & a Zoo

The Wailuku River flows through Hilo and gives it an unusual feature for a city: an 80-foot waterfall. **Rainbow Falls** (west, meaning uphill, on Wainuenue Ave., watch for sign) plunges into a large round pool with an enormous cavern behind its impact zone. According to legend, this cavern is where Hina, mother of the mischievous demigod Maui, lived. Swimming is off-limits at Rainbow Falls, but it's technically off limits at **Boiling Pots** (half a mile up Wainuenue from Rainbow Falls), too, but a lot of people swim there anyway if the river isn't running too high. A series of plunge pools make up Boiling Pots. When the river runs high, water cascades from one to the next. In times of drought, water drains through fissures from one to another, whirlpooling and roiling as it goes, and looking something like boiling pots. You can swim here when the river's running low, but not otherwise.

A few miles south of Hilo, on the road to Hawaii Volcanoes National Park, you'll pass a turnoff for the **Panaewa Rainforest Zoo** ★★★ (kids) (Makami St., off Hwy. 11; ☎ 808/959-9233; www.hilozoo.com; daily 9am–4pm; free admission), a lush 12 acres of plants and animals, with free loaner umbrellas at the entrance so you can stroll about in any weather. More than 80 animals live here, including monkeys, butterflies, giant anteaters, sloth, lemurs, toucans, water buffalo, a pygmy hippopotamus, and a rare white Bengal tiger. The zoo grounds are actually a botanical garden, planted with palms, orchids, bamboos, tropical rhododendrons, and strange things like the enormous Indonesian corpse flower, which attracts its insect pollinators with a smell like rotting flesh. As if this wasn't already a great place for kids, there's also a petting zoo on Saturday from 1:30 to 2:30pm. Tiger feeding time: 3:30pm daily.

Natural Wonders

MAUNA KEA: THE TALLEST PEAK

Towering 13,796 feet above the Pacific, the **summit of Mauna Kea** ★★★ (from Hwy. 200, Saddle Rd., turn onto John A. Burns Way and start climbing; drive time to the summit from Kailua-Kona is about 2½ hr., and from Hilo about 1½ hr.) is the highest mountain peak in the Pacific Ocean. The dry, stable, clean air at that altitude makes it one of the best places on Earth to peer into the cosmos, and various nations have built the 13 astronomical observatories here. The ancient Hawaiians considered the summit to be the realm of the gods. The presence of the telescopes and proposals to develop new ones cause perennial friction between

An Inside Look at the Big Island: Lava Tubes

The Big Island is laced with lava tubes, underground conduits, through which molten lava once traveled—and still does, around Kilauea. Here are three good, deactivated ones you can travel through:

Kaumana Cave (Kaumana Drive, 5 miles from downtown Hilo; free) is an enormous, rugged tube that daring explorers with flashlights can walk or crawl 3,000 feet into. It's usually dripping wet inside, with stalactites, lava drips, and roots growing through the ceiling that form habitats for spiders and insects. This is where I discovered why spelunkers wear helmets and not baseball caps. I almost knocked myself unconscious here walking into the ceiling, which snuck down to head level, unbeknownst to my eyes concealed behind the bill of my cap.

Thurston Lava Tube (at Volcanoes National Park; $10 per car entrance fee; p. 393) is the tamest and easiest lava tube to explore, with its graded path and lighting. It's big enough for a subway train, and open at either end. An additional unlit section continues for several hundred more feet, which you can visit with a flashlight.

Kula Kai Caverns and Lava Tubes (near South Point; ☎ 808/929-7539 or 808/929-9375; www.kulakaicaverns.com; by appointment only) is a 1,000-year-old underground labyrinth on private land, with guided tours that take you as far as 2 miles into the earth. The easy ½-hour tour costs $15 for adults and $10 for children (age 6–12, 5 and under free), and a 2- to 3-hour journey costs $95 for adults and $65 for kids age 8 to 12.

Hawaiian activists and astronomers. On clear days you can see some of the telescopes from sea level, where you get no sense whatsoever that the tiny, shining domes on the mountain are actually hundreds of feet tall, or that they're such a source of contention.

The summit is open to the public, but a four-wheel-drive vehicle is needed to safely get to the summit and back, and the only car rental company on the island that will let you take its 4X4s up there is **Harper Car & Truck Rentals of Hawaii** (locations in Hilo and Kona; ☎ 800/852-9993 or 808/969-1478; www.harpershawaii.com). Without a 4X4, you can drive as far as 9,200 feet, still well above the clouds, and visit the **Onizuka Center for International Astronomy Visitor Information Station** ★★★ (☎ 808/961-2180; www.ifa.hawaii.edu/info/vis; 9am–10pm daily). Whether or not you're going all the way up, you should stop here to get acclimated to the thin, high-altitude air. Shoot straight to the top without acclimatizing along the way, and you're begging for the nasty hangover-like symptoms of altitude sickness. But you wouldn't want to miss the visitor center, anyway. During the day, a solar telescope is trained on the sun, and you can see solar flares and sometimes sunspots through it. More public telescopes are put out at night, and a couple of eager and knowledgeable interpretive guides are usually around day and night to chat. On the first Saturday of the month, in a free lecture series called **The Universe Tonight,** astronomers give presentations on their latest discoveries. The talks begin at 6pm. **Free summit tours** are conducted on Saturday and Sunday, leaving from the visitor information station at 1pm, and visiting two telescopes on the summit. The catch is that you have to get yourself to the top, and again, that requires a 4X4. The tour has other restrictions as well (see the "Altitude Problems" box, below). ***Tip:*** Take a short walk through the enclosed area behind the visitor center. You'll find silversword growing there, a rare plant found nowhere in the world but Mauna Kea, Mauna Loa, and Haleakala. They're fenced here to protect them from feral goats and sheep that have nibbled them nearly to extinction.

If you make it to the top on your own, head for the visitors gallery at the **W.M. Keck Observatory** (☎ 808/885-7887; www.keckobservatory.com; 10am–4:30pm Mon–Fri), which has twin telescopes peering into the deepest space like close-set eyeballs (you'll know it when you see it). At the visitors gallery, you can look into one of the telescope's domes to see what's going on inside, and watch a video. If you arranged it beforehand, you can also tour the **Subaru Telescope** (www.naoj.org), Japan's national astronomical observatory and Mauna Kea's newest telescope. You can see this $400-million marvel of Japanese construction, engineering, and miniaturization on free guided tours, 15 days a month at 10:30am, 11:30am, and 1:30pm. Reservations are required, they can only be made online, and they have to be made at least a week in advance. And again, transportation to the summit is up to you.

THE HILO-HAMAKUA COAST

The lush, green drive along the 50-mile Hilo-Hamakua Coast, on the island's northeast side, is sort of like Maui's long, winding drive to Hana (p. 290), except the road is straighter, faster, and not jammed with caravans of rental cars. This was once the most productive sugar region in Hawaii, a rolling patchwork of rainforest and green tasseled cane fields that stretched for 50 miles from Hilo in the south to Waipio Valley in the north. The rainy Hilo-Hamakua Coast runs between the cinder red upper slopes of Mauna Kea and jungle-fringed sea cliffs. Dozens of deep gorges cut through the landscape, concealing spectacular waterfalls. As the last sugar mills shut down in the 1990s, small farmers began moving in, planting things like sweet potato, macadamia nuts, bananas, coffee, vanilla, gourmet mushrooms, and oolong tea, much of which turns up at the **Hilo Farmers Market** (p. 412). The most prominent crop you'll see is the eucalyptus tree—there are 14,000 acres of them—which will likely be cut for pulp someday.

Dress for the Cold on Mauna Kea

While it's 80°F (27°C) at the beach, it might be 50°F (10°C) at Mauna Kea's summit—and even colder after dark. Temperatures can drop below freezing up there, and occasionally it snows. Bring warm clothing no matter what time of year you visit. And brace yourself for the wind. For the summit's weather and road report, call ☎ 808/935-6268.

Altitude Problems

The summit of Mauna Kea, jutting above 40% of the earth's atmosphere, is not safe for everyone to visit. The office that manages the telescope complex strongly discourages people with heart and breathing problems, pregnant women, and children under 16 from going beyond the visitor center at 9,200 feet. Also, scuba divers risk the bends if they fail to wait 24 hours after diving before climbing to the summit. Everyone else headed to the top should linger at the visitor center for 20 minutes to an hour to get acclimated to the thin air before continuing. After all, nothing ruins a good trip to the top of the world quite the like the nausea and headache that come with altitude sickness.

If you can't get to the summit on your own, you can take a commercial tour, which will carry you to the top in time for the sunset, then linger for star gazing. The best deal on tours is offered by **Arnott's Lodge and Hiking Adventures** ★ (☎ 808/969-7097; www.arnottslodge.com; tours Mon, Wed, and Fri, departing Hilo between 2 and 3pm, depending on time of sunset), which hauls passengers up in four-wheel-drive vans out of Hilo. Guests of Arnott's Lodge pay $75 including tax, and nonguests pay $120. Bring warm clothing and food; at about 8 hours, it's a long tour and it gets cold. Other companies offer summit tours as well, and some feed you dinner, but they all charge more than $180.

The population along the coast is concentrated in small towns and old plantation camps. The largest, with about 2,500 residents, is Honokaa in the north, sitting 1,114 feet above sea level with an elevated view across rough Alenuihaha Channel to Maui, on clear days anyway. Honokaa withered when its sugar mill closed, but it has sprung back with restaurants, shops, galleries, bed-and-breakfasts, and a restored movie house.

If you have time to explore: Look for turnoffs along the way for Old Mamalahoa Highway, the original coastal route; segments of it still remain, and you'll find streams, waterfalls, parks, and old towns along it that you won't see from Highway 19.

The paved road along the Hilo-Hamakua Coast ends about 15 minutes north of Honokaa, at the **Waipio Valley Overlook,** poised almost 2,000 feet above the mile-wide mouth of **Waipio Valley.** The view may look familiar. It's one of Hawaii's iconic postcard vistas. This rainforest valley has a wild gray-sand beach, good for strolling, but not so safe for swimming. While the valley's a mile wide, it's got a network of canyons nearly 6 miles deep, and it's large enough to support a scraggly population of semi-wild horses. From within the valley, you can see Hiilawe Falls and Hakalaoa Falls, aka the Twin Falls of Hiilawe, cascading for 1,000 feet down sheer cliffs at the back of the valley.

In ancient times, Waipio Valley was a major population center and home to many Hawaiian rulers. It's known as the Valley of Kings. Today just a handful of people live there, mostly Hawaiians, who tend ancient taro fields they've restored. They can seem a little grumpy, which you can understand with all the tourists tromping through what would otherwise be an idyllic land. If you go without a tour, be sure to respect the KEEP OUT signs. And beware of dogs, whether signs are posted or not.

Heading south along the Hilo-Hamakua Coast toward the city of Hilo, you'll come to **Laupahoehoe Beach Park** (off Hwy. 19, near mile marker 27) near the little town of Laupahoehoe, which sits high above the park on the cliff. The beach park is a peaceful windblown spot on a broad fan of lava protruding from the mouth of a valley. It's a beautiful place to breathe sea air and contemplate ironwood trees after driving for a while. The cliff-lined Hamakua Coast's only boat ramp is here, but the seas are often too rough to launch boats, and swimming is out of the question. You'll encounter a sad little monument to the 24 people killed in the 1946 April Fools' Day tsunami that slammed into the valley. Most of the victims were children, who perished when their schoolhouse was knocked off its foundation and washed away.

Another good stop is **Umauma World Botanical Gardens** (kids) (Hwy. 19 near mile marker 16; ☎ 808/963-5427; www.worldbotanicalgardens.com; Mon–Sat 9am–5:30pm; $13 adults, $3 children ages 5–12, $6 children ages 13–17). The 300 acres of former sugar-cane land here has been transformed into Hawaii's largest botanical gardens. It's wheelchair accessible, and it's a great place for kids.

There's a big hedge maze, but it's kept trimmed to about 5 feet so parents can locate hopelessly lost children. Check out the Hawaiian wellness garden, the ethnobotanical garden, the arboretum, and especially the phylogenetic garden, where species are grouped in roughly the order in which they appeared on earth. A quarter-mile walk leads to an overlook facing the 300-foot triple-tiered **Umauma Falls.**

Return of the Kings?

Waipio Valley is rich in history and legend, and possibly involved in a museum heist. In 1994, a pair of coconut-fiber baskets containing the bones of two Hawaiian kings disappeared from the Bishop Museum on Oahu. They've never been recovered. It's widely believed that the two kings have been reinterred somewhere in Waipio Valley, from which many Hawaiians say they were stolen to begin with.

You need a four-wheel-drive vehicle to get down the horrendously steep road into the valley, and to get around once you're there, but all of the car-rental companies on the island (except Harpers) put the valley off-limits for their four-wheel-drive vehicles. A better way to go anyway is with **Waipio Valley Shuttle & Tours** (☎ 808/775-7121; Mon–Sat 9am–4pm; $50 adults, $25 children 3-11), which leaves from the overlook on 90-minute tours. A more unusual way to see the valley is by horse-drawn wagon, the way **Waipio Valley Wagon Tour** (☎ 808/775-9518; Mon–Sat 10:30am, 12:30pm, 2:30pm, and 3:30pm; $55 adults, $25 children 4–12) does it. Tours are 90 minutes, 30 of which are spent in a 4X4 van getting down to the valley stables and back. Two companies offer 2½-hour horseback-riding tours through the valley, both charging $85: **Waipio on Horseback** (☎ 877/775-7291 or 808/775-7291; Mon–Fri, 9:30am and 1:30pm) and **Waipio Naalapa Trail Rides** (☎ 808/775-0419; Mon–Sat 9am and 12:30pm).

A Scenic Detour

The Hilo-Hamakua Coast's thick tropical greenery gets even thicker just south of Honomu, or 8 miles north of Hilo, on this **4-mile scenic drive** (between mile markers 7 and 11). The drive follows a segment of Old Mamalahoa Highway—a slow, winding route that people took along the coast before modern Highway 19 was built. This worthwhile detour runs through dark green tunnels of enveloping jungle and over single-lane bridges crossing streams and cascades that you can stop to explore.

The best waterfall to seek out along the Hilo-Hamakua Coast is at **Akaka Falls State Park** ★★★ (turn left at Honomu and drive 3½ miles inland on Akaka Falls Rd.; free). An easy half-mile paved loop leads to and from the 440-foot falls, through rainforest. Do it counterclockwise and you'll come to 100-foot **Kahuna Falls** first, a nice warm-up waterfall. Depending how much rain there's been, the falls may roar with awesome force or cascade gracefully. Either way, you've got a good chance of catching a rainbow. The little town of **Honomu** that you pass through to get to the falls has a few shops and food vendors.

HAWAII VOLCANOES NATIONAL PARK

When the firey cradle of creation calls, what can you do but grab your camera and go investigate? Known as the world's only drive-up volcano, **Kilauea volcano** is remarkably visitor-friendly, as far as volcanoes go. You can actually drive all the way around the 11-mile rim of the main crater, or lace up your hiking boots and trudge right through it, past scalding steam vents and tortured lavascapes. Sometimes you can even hike to the current lava flow and inch up as close to the oozing, pooling, and cascading molten rock as the scorching heat will allow. Located mostly within **Hawaii Volcanoes National Park** ★★★ ($10 per vehicle park entrance fee; ☎ 808/985-6000; www.nps.gov/havo; open 24 hr.), Kilauea is the island's top visitor attraction.

It's the smooth-flowing, fluid nature of Hawaiian magma (as lava's called before it surfaces) that makes Kilauea so accessible. Hawaiian magma releases gasses easily, rather than trapping them like the sticky magma found in other, more violent volcanoes. Gas-trapping magma leads to explosive eruptions, such as the big 1981 blow-up of Mount St. Helens, while Hawaiian magma tends to promote the kind of long, easy-going eruptions that allow this national park to have two of the world's most active volcanoes—Mauna Loa and Kilauea—and 2.5 million visitors a year.

From Hilo the volcanoes park is a 45-minute drive southwest on Highway 11. From Kailua-Kona, it's a 2½-hour drive southeast on Highway 11, or a 3-hour drive north, through Waimea and down the Hilo-Hamakua Coast, via Highways 19 and 11. Bring something to wear in case it rains—it's often wet at the 4,000-foot summit of the volcano, and, believe it or not, cold.

At press time, Mauna Loa hadn't erupted since 1984, and then the enormous lava flow that spilled down its northeast flank, coming within 4 miles of Hilo, did so outside of the park's boundaries. Kilauea, a much smaller volcano embedded in

Eruption Activity Updates

To find out whether or not flowing lava is accessible on a given day, call or go online for an **eruption activity update** (☎ 808/985-6000 ext. 1; http://volcano.wr.usgs.gov/hvostatus.php). As you near the park, listen to 530 AM on your car radio for the latest park info.

Mauna Loa's side and sitting largely within the park, began erupting in 1983. Lava has been pouring out of it almost continuously since. Conditions change all the time. Often, it's possible to walk right to spots where lava has broken out, inching up as close to it as you dare. Other times, the lava's in areas inaccessible to the public.

Give yourself at least a day at the 333,000-acre volcanoes park; with its more than 150 miles of hiking trails and backcountry campgrounds, you could spend weeks exploring. If you have only a few hours to devote to the park, do a counterclockwise loop along 11-mile **Crater Rim Drive.** If you have more time, do Crater Rim Drive and the 40-mile round-trip **Chain of Craters Road,** which dead-ends where the current flow has buried the asphalt and is sending a stream of lava into the sea (often releasing huge plumes of steam).

A Kilauea Driving Tour

Start: The Entrance Station (Hwy. 11 near the 28-mile marker).

Finish: The Entrance Station (Hwy. 11 near the 28-mile marker).

Best Time: If you're just doing Crater Rim Drive, early morning is best for beating the crowds. If you're headed for the lava flow at the end of Chain of Craters Road, hike out onto the flow field just before sunset. Lava viewing is far more dramatic after dark.

Note: Bring water and snacks with you on this tour. Hawaii Volcanoes National Park (open 24 hours) is vast, and the Volcano House Hotel and Kilauea Military Camp, both near the park entrance, are the only places in the park where you'll find provisions. After that, you're on your own.

❶ The Entrance Station

Upon arrival, pay the $10 per-car fee, which is good for unlimited reentry here or entry to **Puuhonua o Honaunau** (p. 378) for 7 days. The park ranger will give you a quick eruption update if you ask, and a fact-laden, fold-out brochure with detailed maps of the park, whether you ask or not.

Head straight to:

❷ Kilauea Visitor Center

Stop here, just inside the park entrance along Crater Rim Drive, to get your bearings and get up to speed on solfatara fields, pit craters, calderas, cinder cones, spatter cones, fumaroles, and the other volcanic features you'll soon encounter. There's a bulletin board with notices on special events, lectures, and ranger-led hikes. You can also get camping permits and find out about hiking in the park. At the gift shop (open 7:45am–5pm), you can pick up an activity book for kids and they can work through it as you drive around the park.

Across the street from the visitor center is:

3 Volcano House Hotel

The Volcano House has accommodations, a restaurant, a bar, and your first opportunity to see Kilauea Crater, an immense charred pit 3 miles long and 2 miles wide, where the volcano's activity was centered through most of the 19th and 20th centuries.

Next door to the visitor center is:

4 Volcano Art Center ★★

This a good place to find original gifts and souvenirs. See p. 413.

Continue counterclockwise around:

5 Crater Rim Drive ★★★

Kilauea's eruptive center used to be concentrated in Kilauea Caldera, one of the park's main features. Crater Rim Drive begins at the park entrance and runs around and across part of the 450-foot-deep caldera. The drive cuts through rainforest and across the crater floor and its lava desert, passing all sorts of volcanic wonders along the way.

At the end of a cul-de-sac, just after Volcano Art Center, you'll find:

6 The Sulfur Banks

Sulfuric gas fills the air with the stink of rotting eggs here, at the most accessible solfatara field in the park.

A short hop farther along Crater Rim Drive brings you to:

7 The Steam Vents

Rainwater seeps into Kilauea's nether reaches, vaporizes, and returns to the atmosphere through fissures and holes here on the crater rim.

Keep driving and you'll come to:

8 Jaggar Museum

Perched on the edge of the caldera, the Jaggar Museum (8:30am–5pm) shares a building with the Hawaiian Volcano Observatory, where scientists monitor the vital signs of Mauna Loa and Kilauea with instruments such as seismographs, tiltmeters, and their naked eyes. The observatory isn't open to the public, but there's a window in the museum through which you can view seismographs as they record the constant swarms of earthquakes, usually too far beneath the earth's surface to feel, on great rolling drums of paper.

Drive farther and you'll reach:

9 Halemaumau Overlook

Halemaumau is a crater within the crater. Early in the 20th century, it was known worldwide as the Hawaiian Fire Pit, a roiling, sputtering lake of lava, whose levels rose and fell over the years, sometimes overflowing its banks entirely. In 1924, it suddenly drained. Its walls crumbled and collapsed, then rainwater entered cracks and set off a series of enormous steam explosions that lasted a week and a half. In the end, the crater doubled in width to 3,000 feet. The bottom is now crusted over, and it's 400 feet deep. Halemaumau is known as home of Pele, the volcano goddess. At the lookout, you may see ti-leaf-wrapped offerings left by Hawaiians. Leave them alone, and leave the offering of offerings to the Hawaiians. There's a particular protocol involved in honoring Pele, and it's not the kind of thing you want to do wrong.

Continue onward (past the turnoff for Chain of Craters Rd.), and you'll come to:

⑩ Thurston Lava Tube

A paved trail leads through an ohia forest and a fern grove, passing through a well-lit lava tube wide enough for a subway car to pass through (p. 389).

A short distance farther brings you to:

⑪ Kilauea Iki Overlook

This crater was once a boiling pool of lava, from which 1,900-foot fountains of lava arose in a 1959 eruption. Now there's a nice 2-hour hike here (p. 397).

If you're headed for the lava flow, take:

⑫ Chain of Craters Road ★★★

To get to where the latest volcanic activity is occurring, take Chain of Craters Road, which descends 3,700 feet from rainforest to coastal desert, stopping where the latest lava flow crossed the road. The road is about 20 miles long, but it can get shorter because lava-viewing conditions change all the time. Some days a half-hour hike from the end of Chain of Craters Road gets you there. Some days, it's a 3-hour round-trip hike. Some days, the outbreaks aren't accessible at all.

The hike crosses jagged, crumbling, sweltering terrain, some of which may have formed just a few days earlier and not fully cooled. Not everyone can or should be out there. Falling there is like falling on glass, and people come away with ugly wounds all the time. It's already hot in this desert wasteland, and then you get close to the molten lava and it's like standing in a sauna. Instead of a sauna's healthy steam, though, sulfuric acid and sulfur dioxide hang heavily in the air, making your eyes water and your lungs burn.

Two tips: If you're headed for the flow, bring sensible shoes and lots of water. If you're going to be out there after dark—when every magma-filled crack and fissure strikingly reveals itself in incandescent orange—bring a flashlight. Hiking out before sunset and back after dark is a good strategy and a popular thing to do.

Another Way to See Kilauea

Several companies offer helicopters tours over the Hawaii Volcanoes National Park, providing bird's-eye views of Kilauea and points in the park you can't readily get to afoot, like Puu Oo vent. In general, the smaller the helicopter, the lower the price. Most leave out of Hilo.

Tropical Helicopters (Hilo International Airport; ☎ 808/961-6810) has the best deal: $142 per person for a 35-minute tour of the volcano, tax included. For a 45-minute tour that takes in the volcano and a waterfall, the cost is $165.

Volcanic Air Pollution

Volcanic gasses in the park can make breathing difficult, especially near Halemaumau and on the lower end of Chain of Craters Road. People with respiratory conditions or heart problems, as well as pregnant women and infants, should be especially cautious.

Hikes & Walks in Hawaii Volcanoes National Park

More than 150 miles of trails run through the park, offering long hikes that can last for days or short hikes that you can accomplish in a few hours or less. Among the best day hikes are:

Halemaumau Trail (off Crater Rim Dr.), which runs 6½ miles back and forth across the floor of Kilauea Crater between the Volcano House and the Halemaumau parking lot. Cairns mark the way through the bizarre volcanic landscape.

Kilauea Iki (off Crater Rim Dr.), a 4-mile loop that runs across the crater floor, up the side, and back through rainforest along the crater rim. Kilauea Iki, or "Little Kilauea," was the center of a 1959 eruption that shot a fountain of lava 1,900 feet into the air.

Devastation Trail (off Crater Rim Dr.), a mile-long trail through skeletal remains of a rainforest scorched when ash and pumice rained down upon it during the 1959 eruption of Kilauea Iki. The trail winds among skeleton-like trees bleached as white as bone.

Puu Loa Petroglyph Field (Chain of Craters Rd., near the 15-mile marker), a 1-mile hike to an extensive petroglyph field. A boardwalk runs around the field.

THE OTHER BIG ISLAND

The Big Island offers a broad band of non-traditional Hawaii experiences for those who seek them. From drinking awa with Hawaiians and hippies deep in the jungle, to doling out Gatorade to sweaty triathletes dashing through touristy Kailua-Kona, there are all sorts detours from the well-beaten visitor path that will enrich your appreciation of island life.

VOLUNTOURISM

OK, I know that weed pulling may not sound like the ideal Hawaiian vacation to you. But when you show up at **Mookini Heiau** for **"Weed Pulling/Oral History Day,"** (☎ 808/373-8000; call in advance), you get a lot more than dirt under your fingernails. On the third Saturday of each month (excluding Nov–Jan), people from around the island gather at this enormous ancient Hawaiian temple in North Kohala to do groundskeeping at one of the most important Native Hawaiian religious sites there is. The *heiau,* which was dedicated to Ku, the god of war, is nearly the size of a football field, so there are plenty of grounds to keep. And plenty of locals showing aloha for the land to hang with. Leimomi Mookini Lum, the *heiau*'s gaurdian, oversees the event. Work begins at 9am and goes until around 11:30am, when Lum calls everyone together to talk about the history and tradition of the place. And there's no one better on that subject than her, since she

Kava Mellows the Mind, Numbs the Gums

Drinking Kava is an old Polynesian tradition that's making a big comeback in Hawaii. A mildly narcotic but entirely legal drink made from the root of the kava plant, it calms the mind without dulling it and numbs the palate without diminishing its ability to detect the bitterness of the drink. The ancient Hawaiians drank kava (they called it awa) for medicinal as well as recreational purposes. Today, the places where it's drunk regularly are very local and very social, and trying it is a wonderful and quick way to get to know a certain subset of locals.

The easiest place to find it in Kona is at the **Kanaka Kava Bar** (75–5803 Alii Dr., at Coconut Grove Marketplace; ☎ 808/327-1660; 10:30am–10:30pm daily), a small, open-air bar near the outdoor volleyball court. The owner, Zack, grows his own kava along the Hamakua Coast, and he serves it in individual coconut shells for $4, or in large calabashes (five shells worth) for $12, both with fresh pineapple on the side. Like the regulars at a neighborhood tavern who keep their personal beer mugs behind the bar, Kanaka Kava regulars keep shells imprinted with their names on a shelf behind the counter. Guzzling the first shell as quickly as you can is the customary way to get started. You can nurse the next ones after that, though kava's bitterness discourages sipping and encourages quaffing.

When the sun goes down in rural Puna, devotees of the bitter root converge in the front yard of Uncle Robert Keliihoomalu, Sr. to partake. At Keliihoomalu's very informal, open-air awa bar, known as **Uncle's Awa**

is the direct descendant in the line of *kahuna* (priests), who have overseen this *heiau* for 1,500 years. Don't expect to hear everything, though. Much of the knowledge that's passed down through the ages is sacred and secret and not part of the deal. The work lasts only a couple hours, but the experience will stick with you a long time.

Mookini Heiau isn't the only place to get your hands dirty volunteering. Once or twice a month, Big Island conservationists, heeding the call of **The Nature Conservancy,** turn out for a day of reforestation, invasive-species eradication, or maybe trail clearing. If you join them—and they'll be happy to see you—you might plant koa and ohia seedlings in the Nature Conservancy's Kona Hema Preserve, 8,061 acres up the slope of Mauna Loa in South Kona. The preserve is an astonishingly beautiful part of the island that you would never get to see unless you were volunteering. You might even catch a glimpse of an endangered Hawaiian hawk, an endangered Hawaiian hoary bat, or other rare species that call the place home. Contact volunteer coordinator Dore Centeio (☎ 808/885-1786; dcenteio@tnc.org).

Maybe you're not one of the superfit elite who can wake up in the morning and swim 2½ miles in the ocean, bike 112 miles through a lava desert, and then run a marathon, like the hundreds of triathletes who come to Kona each October

Club ★ (dead end of Hwy. 137, where lava closed the road; 5pm–whenever; closed Sun), regulars sip the dishwater-like drink and converse in soothing tones well into the wee hours. You pay $5 for one coconut shell cup or $10 to drink until closing, which on a good night might not be until 4am. Best nights to go are Friday and Saturday, when Hawaiian musicians tend to turn up and Hawaiian food is sometimes served.

Uncle Robert lives in Kalapana, or what's left of Kalapana after a 1990 lava flow buried much of the place. During the day, tourists on their way to the nearby black-sand beach of Kaimu—also destroyed, but making a tremendous comeback—tromp through Uncle Robert's yard to see a small interpretive exhibit on the lava flow that edges up to Robert's property. As lava poured over a rock wall into Uncle Robert's yard, his wife stood in its path, crying and praying for the family's home. Robert urged her to leave, but she stood her ground, and it apparently worked. The flow suddenly changed direction and headed for the sea, sparing the house.

Uncle Robert's extended-family gatherings frequently overlap the Awa Club operation, offering discerning visitors a glimpse into contemporary Hawaiian culture that's as warm with aloha as it gets. But the scene is not geared toward tourists, and it's definitely not for everyone. Photography is forbidden. They key to fitting in is to adopt a quiet, unpresuming approach, and to act as if you're visiting someone's home—which, in fact, you are. Otherwise, you might stir up a silent who-let-this-one-out-of-the-cage vibe that no amount of awa will dispel.

for the **Ironman Triathlon World Championship** (75-5722 Kuakini Hwy.; ☎ 808/329-0063; www.ironmanlive.com). But as a race volunteer, you can tap directly into the endorphin-soused, behind-the-scenes fun of it all—and maybe even end up at an after party. A staggering 7,000 volunteers are needed for everything from sticking IVs into the arms of those the course crushes (if you're a medical professional) to passing out T-shirts to the finishers (no particular skill required). You have to be 16 or older, and you can sign up online or just walk into the race office in the lobby of King Kamehameha's Kona Beach Hotel (75-5660 Palani Rd.) during race week and say, "Hi, what can I do?"

EYE-OPENING CLASSES & PRESENTATIONS

With 13 of the world's most powerful telescopes clustered in the thin air atop Mauna Kea, the Big Island has a thriving community of resident and transient space scientists. Once or twice a month, a world-renowned astronomer, astrophysicist, or the like participates in the **AstroTalk lecture series** (various lecture halls at the University of Hawaii at Hilo; ☎ 808/932-2328; www.astroday.net), a joint effort of the University of Hawaii at Hilo's Department of Physics and Astronomy and the UH Institute of Astronomy. The lectures are fascinating, free, and tailored for a lay audience. Past topics have included "Dark Energy and the

Runaway Universe," "New Moons of Giant Planets," and "Fragment X: Untold Tales of Comet Shoemaker-Levy 9."

At Hawaii Volcanoes National Park, an evening lecture series called **After Dark in the Park** (Kilauea Visitor Center Auditorium, Hawaii Volcanoes National Park; ☎ 808/985-6011; www.nps.gov/havo/afterdark/adip.htm; $1 donation, plus $10 per vehicle weekly park entrance fee) sometimes leaves the auditorium behind for, perhaps, a nighttime stroll along the steaming sulfur banks, or a full-moon hike through a giant pit crater (park officials generally discourage night hiking, due to the risk of disappearing forever into a crack in the earth, but you'll be pretty safe if you're with After Dark in the Park). Other times the series hunkers down indoors, but in either case it concentrates on the culture, history, geology, and biology of Hawaii. It usually happens on the second or third Tuesday of the month, beginning at 7pm, but check the website for the schedule.

Artists have long washed up on the shores of the Big Island, and many of them have taken root on the east side, which is more conducive to an artistic lifestyle (it's cheaper) than the west side. The collectively run **Kahuina Gallery** kids (128 Kilauea St., corner of Kilauea and Mamo sts.; ☎ 808/935-4420; www.kahuina.org; any time between 10am and 4pm) is a haven for them. Located in a funky old plantation-era building smack in the heart of downtown Hilo, Kahuina is as much community center as anything, and always a good bet for meeting painters, sculptors, musicians, and other right-brainers. Throughout the week there are events dealing with religion, politics, peace and justice, and, naturally, the arts. Call for the latest. On Saturdays, you can drop in any time during the day for an art class with Ken Charon, one of the eight members of this colorful artist cooperative. Whether you've been painting for years or you're still struggling with stick figures, you'll fit right in. It costs $10 per session, and you bring whatever art supplies you'd like to use. A pencil and notebook will do fine. Artistic kids especially seem to love this.

What happens when creative scientists and entrepreneurs have unlimited sunshine and an endless flow of super chilly seawater to work with? They become aquaculturalists and farm cold-water seafoods like abalone, flounder, and Maine lobster. They produce electricity, nutritional supplements, pharmaceuticals, black pearls, and sea horses. And they desalinate seawater, bottle it, and sell it to the Japanese at astronomical prices. At least that's what they do at the **Natural Energy Laboratory of Hawaii Authority** (off Hwy. 11 just south of Kona International Airport; ☎ 808/329-7341; www.nelha.org). Located on sun-drenched Keahole Point, the sunniest coastal area in the United States, NELHA is an 870-acre, state-funded technology park where tenants have access to a constant supply of 43°F (6°C) seawater pumped from depths of 2,000 and 3,000 feet. For an inside look at what goes on there, drop by the visitor center, a futuristic-looking building with the enormous solar panels that jut skyward like insect wings, for one of the **public presentations** (10am–11:30am, Tues–Thurs; $8 per person, $5 students and seniors, free for 8 and younger). After a briefing on the history of NELHA and an overview of the various businesses and research projects underway, you'll drive through the park to an outdoor exhibit area. Among the wonders there are delicate strawberries, tomatoes, and periwinkle growing under the merciless Keahole Point sun, their roots cooled and watered by condensation on the plastic hoses that circulate cold seawater through their raised beds. It's all pretty ingenious and utterly cool.

ACTIVE HAWAII

If you want to do more on the Big Island than sunbathe on a beach or meander through the sights, this list of active vacations is for you.

WEST SIDE ACTIVITIES

The Big Island's west side has the sunniest days, the best beaches, the calmest seas, the clearest waters, the greatest number of visitors, and, consequently, most of the outfits offering outdoor activities. Discounts abound. Look for coupons in the ubiquitous free **visitors' publications,** such as *Big Island Gold* and *This Week Big Island.* Also look online, particularly at **Tom Barefoot's Cashback Tours** ★ (☎ 888/222-3601; www.tombarefoot.com). The discounts here are generally modest, usually around 5%, but they can go as high as 20%. Check the website first, then call the toll-free number with questions.

Expedia!Fun (☎ 800/770-0326; www.expedia.com) is another dependable online discounter—though not quite as user-friendly as Tom Barefoot's site. It takes a few clicks to navigate to the Big Island, then you enter the dates you'll be in Hawaii, and Expedia gives you a list of activities available at the time. Around Kailua town, Expedia!Fun also has **activities desks** (in the lobbies of the King Kamehameha's Kona Beach Hotel, 75–5660 Palani Rd.; the Keauhou Beach Resort, 78–6740 Alii Dr.; and the Royal Sea Cliffs, 75–6040 Alii Dr.) where you can get the same discounts offered online, but in person.

Snorkeling

The generally calm, clear waters of the Kona and Kohala coasts are well known for their abundance of marine life and incredible visibility. Exploring these waters with a mask and snorkel can be a highlight of a trip to Hawaii, as well as some of the simplest, cheapest fun you can have.

You can rent a mask, snorkel, and fins (and a variety of other beach gear) at **Kona Boys** (79-7536 Hwy. 11, Kealakekua; ☎ 808/328-1234). Snorkel gear here goes for $7 per day or $25 per week. In Kailua-Kona, you can rent snorkel gear at **Jack's Diving Locker** (75-5813 Alii Dr., at Coconut Grove Marketplace; ☎ 808/329-7585) for $7.50 per day, with the price dropping to $6 per day if you hold on to it for at least 5 days. **Snorkel Bob's** (75-5831 Kahakai Rd.; ☎ 808/329-0770) has the cheapest rates around, but the cheapest-quality gear, too, at $2.50 per day or $9 per week. Bob's will, however, try to persuade you to upgrade to better-quality gear, for as much as $8 per day and $32 per week. ***Tip:*** The quality of the snorkel gear isn't nearly as important as how well the mask seals against your face. To test the seal, place the mask on your face and inhale through your nose. If a vacuum forms that holds the mask in place, you've got a good fit. A bad fit will leak. If you plan to use your snorkel gear for a week or longer, it makes sense to buy it; go to **Wal-Mart** (75-1015 Henry St.; ☎ 808/334-0466).

Among the better West Hawaii snorkeling spots, check out these five favorites:

Kahaluu (kids) (p. 367) is a popular beach where the near-shore reef's fragile coral has been pretty thoroughly trampled to death. But fish still thrive. The best snorkeling is in the deeper waters to the immediate north, where the coral is alive and too deep to step on.

Hononaunau Bay, aka Two Step (p. 367), has clear blue waters, a sudden drop-off, and a turtle cleaning station, where sea turtles let tiny fish nibble their shells clean. This is one of the most popular scuba and snorkeling spots on the island. Finding free parking can be a headache on weekends, but there's a private pay lot that charges $2.

Puako Beach Drive (p. 372) has lots of spots to chose from (look for the blue beach access signs), and chances are usually good you can get one all to yourself. It's tricky getting in and out of the water over the rocks at most of the sites, but excellent snorkeling awaits, especially near the Church of Ascension. There's an easier entry point at Puako Village End, at the end of the road.

Kua Bay (p. 370) has underwater pinnacles that draw a lot of fish, off the north point.

At **Hapuna Beach** (p. 372), if you walk to the northern end, in front of the Hapuna Beach Prince Hotel, and snorkel around the point, you'll discover a private little cove with lots of fish.

Kayaking Kealakekua

The state is considering a restriction on individual kayak rentals on the bay, which is a protected conservation zone. But kayak tours, where guides can steer kayakers around resting dolphins rather than right through them, would still be allowed. (For updates, call the State of Hawaii, Department of Land and Natural Resources at ☎ 808/587-0440. If you can't get a straight answer there, any Kona-area kayaking- or snorkel-tour company can fill you in.)

In the meantime, kayak rentals are widely available along Highway 11 between Kailua-Kona and Kealakekua Bay. **Kona Boys** (79-7536 Hwy. 11, Kealakekua; ☎ 808/328-1234), for instance, rents individual kayaks for $47 per day, and doubles for $67, and gives good briefings on low-impact dolphin interactions. The launching area at Napoopoo Wharf is a mile away from the snorkeling area at Cook's monument.

Snorkeler Etiquette: Hands Off Coral, Turtles & Dolphins

- The living part of a coral reef is a thin membrane of fragile, tiny organisms that die en masse when stepped on or even touched gently by hand. Snorkel lightly.
- Snorkelers in Hawaii often encounter green sea turtles going about their day. Touching or chasing them is not only rude as far as the turtles are concerned, but it can be construed as harassment under state and federal law, both of which carry heavy fines on offenders.
- Misguided snorkelers chase dolphins, which is illegal. Enlightened snorkelers enjoy dolphins from afar, hoping the pod will come their way. Lucky snorkelers mind their own business, and suddenly dolphins appear.

A Historic Bay with Spectacular Snorkeling

Kealakekua Bay ★★★ (10 miles south of Kailua Kona, near the town of Captain Cook at the bottom of Napoopoo Rd.) has some of the best snorkeling on the Big Island. On the north end, at Kaawaloa Cove, colorful coral gardens filled with fish and other sea creatures sit at the top of a drop-off plunging to 100 feet and creating a dramatic snorkel spot. The waters are generally protected and crystal clear. This is where Captain Cook was killed in a skirmish with Hawaiians in 1779. A 29-foot-tall monument to Cook erected by the Commonwealth of Australia in 1878 stands near the spot where he fell, and right before the very best snorkeling area. Most visitors get to this remote end of the bay on commercial snorkeling tours, which range in price from $75 to $120, although you can also hike there for free (p. 405).

Pod problems: Kealakekua Bay has dolphins, but don't get your hopes up for an up-close interspecies encounter. The dolphins use the bay's protected waters to rest between hunts. Unfortunately for them, some of the bay's hundreds of daily human visitors are drawn to the dolphins' bedrooms to see if any of them want to play. As you can imagine, you, as a resting dolphin, might find it hard to get the rest you need with such interruptions. The human impact seems to be taking a toll. An increase in the number of snorkelers visiting Kealakekua Bay has coincided with a decrease in the number of dolphins. At press time, the state was mulling over restrictions on access to the bay to protect the dolphins and other marine life. In the meantime, it's best to appreciate dolphins from afar. If you see them, resist the urge to swim into their midst. They might come to you, but if not, it's not meant to be.

Several outfits offer kayak tours, including **Adventures in Paradise** (81-6367 Hwy. 11; ☎ 808/323-3005 or 888/371-6035; www.bigislandkayak.com; daily morning and afternoon tours), run by a husband-and-wife team who lead great 4-hour tours without disturbing sleeping dolphins, snacks and snorkeling included, for $130 per person.

Kealakekua Tour Boats

Four tour-boat operators have permits to do business in Kealakekua Bay, one using catamarans and the others using inflatable rafts. All offer morning and afternoon tours. Snorkeling is best in the morning, before the winds come up. Tours are cheaper in the afternoon, when most of the companies lower their rates. Here are the island's four companies:

Fair Wind Cruises ★★★ (Keahou Bay; ☎ 808/322-2788; www.fair-wind.com) carries 100 passengers aboard its 65-foot catamaran. Morning costs are $119 for adults, $75 for children 4–12, and $29 for children 3 and younger. Afternoon tours cost $75 for adults, $45 for 4–12 year olds, and free for kids 3 and younger. Fair Wind Cruises has the largest, most comfortable boat. It also carries the largest crowd of other snorkelers with it, which is the trade-off.

Two Ways to Explore the Deep Without Leaving Your Seat

One of the most interesting and unusual tours on the Big Island is the submarine exploration of a 25-acre reef in Kailua Bay. The 65-foot ***Atlantis VII* submarine** ★★ (Kailua Pier; ☎ 800/548-6262 or 808/329-6626; adults $89, children 11 and younger $45) dives to over 100 feet and quietly hums about the reef, past scores of fish who seem indifferent toward the capsule full of alien species in their midst. A tender takes you out to the sub, which dives at various spots on different days, ranging from a half-mile offshore to more than a mile. The whole tour takes an hour, with about 35 minutes spent underwater. When business is slow and the sub only half full, it might dive along a ledge just offshore; this is the most spectacular dive site, but the captain will go there only if all of the passengers fit onto one side of the vessel, so everyone gets a front-row view of the vertical wall outside their porthole.

For a more budget-oriented look at Kona's underwater world, take a ride on the **glass-bottom boat *Marian*** (departs from Kailua Pier; ☎ 808/324-1749; adults $30, children ages 6–13 $15; www.konaglassbottomboat). The tours, which last just under an hour, leave at 10:30, 11:30am, and 12:30pm Monday through Saturday. The *Marian* has the graceful lines of an old admiral's tender, with her wide, low-slung beam, her rounded bow and stern, and her elliptical portholes. She's actually a modern boat, though, that the captain built in his backyard. Forty-four passengers can sit comfortably in her shady cabin, peering out at the reef 15 to 20 feet below.

Sea Quest (Keahou Bay; ☎ 808/329-7238; www.seaquesthawaii.com) carries 6 to 12 people aboard its inflatable rafts, charging $89 for adults and $72 for children 12 and under for the 4-hour morning trips, and $69 for adults and $59 for children for the 3-hour afternoon outings. The morning trips include a second snorkeling stop farther down the coast, at Honaunau Bay. The rafts explore sea caves, lava tubes, and a blow hole along the coast on the way there. Look for $10-off coupons in the free visitor magazines all around the Big Island, or book online and get a healthy $15 off per person.

Captain Zodiac (Honokohau Harbor; ☎ 808/329-3199; www.captainzodiac.com) carries up to 16 people on its rafts. The 4-hour tours cost $90 for adults, $75 for kids 12 and younger. You can knock $10 off the adult price with the Captain Zodiac coupons available in the free visitors' magazines you'll find all over the island, but the company's pirate-themed website has an even better discount: $15 off adults, and $5 off for kids. The truth is, you don't even need to go online to get the Web discount. Just mention it when you're booking a trip, and it's yours.

Dolphin Discoveries (Kealakekua Bay; ☎ 808/322-8000; www.dolphin discoveries.com) stops first at Kealakekua Bay; then, when Fair Wind Cruises shows up with its crowd, it sets off down the coast for a second snorkel at Honaunau Bay. It charges $93 for adults, and $73 for children. The afternoon tours, which stay in Kealakekua Bay, cost $73 for everyone. Web specials cut $10 off the morning rates and $5 off afternoon rates.

Kealakekua by Foot

It's possible to hike down to the Captain Cook Monument, but it's not an easy walk. From Highway 11, turn onto Napoopoo Road; the trail begins about 750 feet from the intersection, at the second telephone pole. It's about an hour-long hike down, with a constant 1,300-foot descent along an unmaintained trail. Go early, while it's cool, bring food and water, and make a day of it. Then hike back up after it's cooled off. The trail can be a challenge when the weather's cool, and utterly miserable when it's hot.

Deep-Sea Fishing

With generally calm seas and a seafloor that plunges to open ocean depths just a few miles from shore, Kailua-Kona has perfect conditions for deep-sea fishing. The majority of west Hawaii's sportsfishing fleet ties up at Honokohau Harbor, 5 miles north of Kailua-Kona. Hundreds of charter boats here offer fishing trips, lasting from 4 to 8 hours and varying widely in price. Some are outlandishly well-appointed yachts with air-conditioning, satellite TV, and attentive crews. Others are tiny work-a-day vessels with no shade, oily bilge water sloshing about, and curmudgeonly captains who wouldn't pay a crew even if they could find one. Most boats fall in between. A good way to make sure you don't end up on a dog is to book through **The Charter Desk** (Honokohau Harbor; ☎ 888/566-2487 or 808/329-5735). It handles about 60 boats, all over 30 feet, and all vetted to weed out vessels of dubious character. Four-hour private charters range in price from $400 to $550, 6-hour charters run from $500 to $650, and 8-hour charters run from $700 to $1,200. The boats carry up to six guests and generally have four rods out. If you're serious about fishing, a private charter is the way to go. Otherwise, consider a shared charter, where you don't get the whole boat to yourself, but you generally pay less. The 38-foot ***Sea Wife II*** (☎ 808/329-1806), for instance, carries up to eight anglers on 4-hour morning or afternoon tours for $95 per fisherman, with ride-alongs boarding for $50. You have to share the rods and the chairs with the other guests, but whatever beer you bring is all yours.

Who Gets the Fish?

In Hawaii, it's customary for the charter fishing boat to keep the fish. This may seem unfair to the fisherman who paid to catch the thing, but it's an almost universal practice. Sometimes, a boat will divvy up the catch and send you back to the hotel with, maybe, 20 pounds of ahi—which raises another question: What do you do in a hotel with so much fish?

Surf Lessons

The Big Island doesn't have the abundance of surf spots or the nice sandy surfing beaches that Oahu has. But it does have surf and a large population of surfers who follow it closely. If you want to take lessons, a handful of schools offer them. **Hawaii Lifeguard Surf Instructors** (75-159 Lunapule St., Kailua-Kona; ☎ 808/324-0442; www.surflessonshawaii.com) has, as the name suggests, instructors who are current or retired county lifeguards. A group lesson costs $70 for a 1-hour session or $115 for a 2-hour session (2 hr. is the way to go). Private lessons, for $95 to $165, are offered too. But with Hawaii Lifeguard's 3-to-1 student-teacher ratio, you're not missing anything by taking a group lesson. Students surf at Kahaluu Beach, the best beginners' spot in Kailua-Kona.

Ocean Eco Tours (74-425 Kealakehe Pkwy.; ☎ 808/324-7873; www.oceanecotours.com) offers 2- to 3-hour lessons (depending on how long students' paddling arms last) at 8:30am and 11:30am for $95, with a student-to-teacher ratio of no more than 4 to 1. ***Pauline Frommer's Hawaii special:*** Show this book at Ocean Eco Tours and you'll get 10% off of surf lessons, or any of the company's other activities, including scuba and whale-watching tours.

Jet-Skiing

If you want to buzz around Kailua Bay on a jet ski, there's only one jet-ski operator in town: **Aloha Jet Ski** (☎ 808/329-2754; Kailua Pier; 9am-4pm). Call for reservations or just show up at the pier and find the white truck with ALOHA JET SKI written all over it (if a cruise ship is in port, definitely call for reservations). It costs $95 per hour including tax, or $65 per half-hour. Up to two adult riders can board the jet ski, or one adult and two kids, for $15 per extra rider. Go before 10am and you'll save $10.

Parasailing

To get up above the ocean, you can parasail with **UFO Parasail** (☎ 808/325-5836; Kailua Pier; www.ufoparasail.net; reservations required). Parasailing requires no skill on the part of the parasailor whatsoever. You just sit there, hanging from a parachute-like canopy at the end of a line hooked to a speed boat, which reels you out and back in as it tows you through the air. It costs $65 for a 7-minute ride to 400 feet and $75 for a 10-minute ride to 800 feet. The whole outing takes about an hour, and tours leave every hour on the hour from 8am until sometime in the afternoon, which changes depending upon demand. Save $5 by going on the 8am boat.

Tennis Anyone?

The best public courts in Kona are located at **Old Airport Park,** just north of town. Covered public courts in rainy Hilo are at the Edith Kanakaole Tennis Stadium on Kalanikoa Street. Both of these courts are free (as are all municipal courts in Hawaii). For a detailed list of all Hawaii County courts, contact Hawaii County Department of Parks and Recreation (25 Apuni St., Hilo, HI, 96720; ☎ 808/961-8720; www.hawaii-county.com/parks/parks.htm).

A Driving Range

If you approach Kailua-Kona at night along Mamalahoa Highway from the north, the brightest lights you'll see come from a driving range called the **Swing Zone** (74–5562 Makala Blvd., corner of Kuikini Hwy.; ☎ 808/329-6909; 8am–8pm daily). You can get a 60-ball bucket for $7, which you can lug through the free putting green and chipping area before hitting the driving range itself. For another $7, you can putt your way through an 18-hole putting course shaped like the Big Island, and for $14 you get unlimited access to the 6-hole, par 6 golf course. Golf clubs aren't the only things you can swing at the Swing Zone. In the batting cages, $2 will buy you 15 baseballs.

Horseback Riding

See p. 384 and 392.

Golf

Most of the Big Island's famed links lie on fields of black lava that would be devoid of any green had they not been transformed into some of the best golf courses in the world. The majority of the west-side courses belong to the Gold Coast resorts, along the Kohala Coast, where greens fees can exceed $200. But the price falls to more reasonable heights when the winds pick up and the "twilight" rates kick in, often after noon or 1pm. The other way to get onto these deluxe links without paying full rate is through **Stand-by Golf** ★★★ (☎ 888/645-BOOK). Call between 7am and noon for same-day golf, and between 5:30 and 9pm, except Saturday, for next-day golf. Discounts range from 10% to 40%.

IN KOHALA

Of the oceanfront Gold Coast resorts, the **Hapuna Golf Course** (Hapuna Beach Prince Hotel; ☎ 808/880-3000; www.hapunabeachprince.com) has the lowest greens fees, at $165, with seasonal twilight rates. *Golf* magazine named this par-72, 6,029-yard course, which runs from the ocean to 700 feet, as Hawaii's most environmentally sensitive course.

Mauna Lani Frances I'I Brown Championship Courses (Mauna Lani Resort; ☎ 808/885-6655; www.maunalani.com) started out as a single course that was later split in two, with 9 holes added to each half. The popular, par-72, 5,940-yard South Course fronts the sea. The par-72, 6,086-yard North Course makes good use of lava rocks and sharp-thorned kiawe trees. Greens fees for both are $210, with a $145 twilight rate.

The Waikoloa Beach Resort Courses (Waikoloa Resort; ☎ 877/924-5656 or 808/886-7888; www.waikoloabeachresort.com) have challenging holes, $195 greens fees, and variable twilight rates. The par-70, 6,566-yard Waikoloa Beach Course has plenty of white-sand bunkers and water features. The par-72, 7074-yard Waikoloa King's Course has broad, undulating fields snaking through the raw lava landscape.

Get Your Yoga On

Every Saturday morning in a lovely park beside the sea, Big Island yoga people gather to do **yoga at the beach** (Pahoehoe Beach Park, on Alii Dr. near mile marker 4; 8–9:30am; $10). It's organized through **Shambhava School of Yoga** (77–447 Seaview Circle, Kailua-Kona; ☎ 808/331-1147; www.shoshoni.org), which is part of an ashram for followers of the guru Rishi Mahamandalashwar Sri Shambhavananda. Yoga classes are held throughout the week on a beautiful covered deck with an upper-slope ocean view (class times vary, so check the website or call for the latest schedules). On Thursdays at 7pm, enthusiasts of Kirtan, the esoteric but increasingly popular practice of ecstatic Sanskrit chant, meet here for an hour to rhythmically repeat the various names of God, over and over, starting out slowly and working up into an emotional crescendo.

The **Waikoloa Village Gold Club's** (Waikoloa Resort; ☎ 808/883-9621; www.waikoloa.org) par-72, 6,791-yard course is the central feature of the oddly located lava desert community of Waikoloa (it was built as affordable housing for workers at the nearby resorts). It has reasonable $80 greens fees, and holes challenging enough for serious golfers but not off-putting for beginners. The twilight rate drops to just $40.

IN KONA

In Kona, the par-72, 7034-yard **Big Island Country Club** (71–1420 Mamalahoa Hwy., Kailua-Kona; ☎ 808/325-5044) has a dramatic layout 2,500 feet up the slope of Hualalai volcano, and a pro shop in a yurt. Greens fees run $169, with a $109 twilight rate.

The **Kona Country Club** (7000 Alii Dr., Kailua-Kona; ☎ 808/322-2595) has a par-72, 6,281-yard ocean course with wild parrots running about, and $165 greens fees (with discounted rates of $107 at twilight, and $60 for 9 holes after 3pm). Greens fees at the par-72, 5,976 mountain course run $150, with a $97 twilight rate.

The **Makalei Hawaii Country Club** (72-3890 Hawaii Belt Rd.; ☎ 808/325-6625) has peacocks, pheasants, and turkeys on a par-72, 6,161-yard course that climbs to nearly 3,000 feet on the slope of Hualalai. Greens fees run $89, with a $65 twilight rate.

IN WAIMEA

Outside of town on the cool, wet side of Waimea is the **Waimea Country Club** (47-5220 Mamalahoa Hwy; ☎ 808/885-8053), a par-72, 6,661-yard country course, in the middle of cattle country and looking as much like Scotland as anywhere in Hawaii possibly could. Greens fees run $95, with a $75 twilight rate.

EAST SIDE ACTIVITIES

The rainy weather and choppy waters on the Windward Side of the island limit the appeal of ocean activities to visitors. You'll find some horseback riding and hiking tours, but vacation activities on this side of the island are mostly self-directed. There is, of course, golf.

Golf is cheaper and more naturally green on the wetter east side of the island, where local golfers outnumber visitors.

Golf

ALONG THE HAMAKUA COAST

At the **Hamakua County Club** (ocean side of Hwy. 19, Honokaa; ☎ 808/775-7244), you don't need a tee time. Just show up, drop $15 into the box, and play. It's got an unusual layout with 9 holes crisscrossing each other on a steep hillside fit for walkers only.

IN HILO

The **Hilo Municipal Golf Course** (340 Haihai St.; ☎ 808/959-7711) is a popular, often soggy, par-71, 6006-yard course with greens fees of $29 on weekdays and $34 on weekends. Carts cost $16. The biggest challenge here is simply getting a tee time. Weekdays are your best bet.

Near downtown Hilo, the **Naniloa Country Club and Driving Range** (120 Banyan Dr.; ☎ 808/934-0044) is a 9-hole course that you can play twice. If you count both laps, it's a par-70, 5,615-yard course. Greens fees are $25 for 9 holes or $45 for 18 holes if you walk, and $45 to $54 with a cart. At the driving range, you get a bucket with 30 balls for $1.25.

IN VOLCANO VILLAGE

The par-72, 6547-yard **Volcano Golf & Country Club** (Piimauna Dr., off Hwy. 11 between mile markers 30 and 31, just past entrance to Hawaii Volcanoes National Park; ☎ 808/967-7331) is set among a misty pine and ohia forest at 4,200 feet, where the ball travels farther than you might expect due to the altitude, and where you're a just a mile from Kilauea Crater. Greens fees run $65, with a $52 twilight rate after noon.

ATTENTION, SHOPPERS!

Souvenir shops are everywhere, but the better, more authentic purchases require pinpoint accuracy.

WEST HAWAII

If you're looking for a dashboard hula dancer, a shot glass printed with your name in Hawaiian, or matching aloha wear for the whole family, the tourist-thick heart of Kailua-Kona along Alii Drive has plenty of shops for you. But you'll find better deals a few blocks away. I hate to say it, but Kona's **Wal-Mart** (75-1015 Henry St.; ☎ 808/334-0466) has a big selection of Hawaii souvenirs at reasonable prices, as well as aloha shirts, muumuu, and macadamia nuts. A better place to head is **Hilo Hattie—The Store of Hawaii** (75-5597A Palani Rd., at Kopiko Plaza, behind Burger King, Kailua-Kona; ☎ 808/329-7200), which has prices comparable to Wal-Mart's but a more extensive selection of stuff. In fact, Hilo Hattie (which also has a store in Hilo, and stores on all the other major islands) has possibly the largest pile of Hawaii kitsch in the world.

Weavings Like No Other

Some of Kona's best shopping experiences happen in outlying communities such as Holualoa, Captain Cook, and Honaunau. The old coffee-country town of Holualoa, 1,400 feet above Kailua town, has a solid collection of art galleries and unusual shops, such as **Kimura Lauhala Shop** (intersection of Hwy. 182 and Hwy. 180; ☎ 808/324-0053). Here, the age-old craft of weaving long, durable fronds of the hala tree into usable things, *lauhala* in Hawaiian, hangs on by a few thin fibers. The creation of *lauhala* was widely practiced in Hawaii before the introduction of Western fabrics undercut the need. Kimura Lauhala Shop started out in 1914 as a general store run by Japanese immigrants, the Kimuras, who bartered with Hawaiian *lauhala* weavers for mats, hats, and baskets, which went straight onto the store shelves. The *lauhala* trade grew so brisk that the Kimuras eventually turned their general store over entirely to *lauhala*. The family's fourth generation now runs the place, selling enough *lauhala* to keep the craft alive among a small group of weavers. Custom *lauhala* hats, modeled after any other hat in the world, can be ordered here ($90–$160). When I stopped by, there was a *lauhala* replica of the 10-gallon monster worn by Hoss, the lumbering cowhand in the 1960s TV Western *Bonanza*. You can also find floor mats, pillows, Kleenex box covers, door stoppers, napkin boxes, trivets, beer can holders, and a Kimura Lauhala Shop T-shirt—a rare concession to cotton.

Nearby you'll find the most dignified souvenir shop in Kailua-Kona, the **Hulihee Palace Gift Shop** (75-5718 Alii Dr.; ☎ 808/329-6558; at Hulihee Palace). This tiny shop, unobtrusively tucked away on the grounds where Hawaiian royalty once dwelled, faces the sea and seems further removed than it actually is from the tumult along Alii Drive. Volunteers with The Daughters of Hawaii, whose 2,000 members all have family connections to Hawaii dating to at least 1880, run the palace and the gift shop. Among the finds are note cards with historic photographs of old Hawaii ($1.50), koa doorstops ($8.95), rare Niihau shell earrings (starting at $24), handmade Hawaiian dolls (starting at $14), and a small but thoughtful selection of books, including hard-to-find works such as David Malo's "Hawaiian Antiquities." Raised in the royal court and taught to read by missionaries at age 42, Malo put into writing much of what is known about the ways of ancient Hawaii today.

The **Kona Farmers' Market** (75-7544 Alii Dr., the corner of Hualalai Rd.; Thurs–Sun, 8am–5pm; www.konafarmersmarket.com) is a great place to pick up flowers, coffee, produce, and souvenirs on the cheap. You can get mangoes, papayas, avocados, macadamia nuts, macramé bracelets, monkeypod wood bowls, and grass skirts with coconut shell bras, at reasonable prices and in a colorful, clamoring marketplace right in the center of downtown Kailua-Kona. Farther south along Alii Drive, but too far to walk from town, you'll find another farmers market, **Alii Gardens Market Place** (75-6129 Alii Dr.; ☎ 808/334-1381). In a more peaceful, and permanent, location, this market sells somewhat more upscale souvenirs at somewhat more upscale prices.

For a gift unique to the Big Island, or just a guilty pleasure to eat while driving, stop at **Kona Chips** (Hwy. 11; heart of the town of Captain Cook, next to Manago Hotel; ☎ 808/323-3785; www.konachips.net) and pick up a bag, pail, or box of Big Island potato chips. They're made on-site, with the skin left on and a lot of the frying oil spun off by centrifugal force. You can pick up a 4.25-ounce bag of chips for $3.25, a 5-quart pail of them for $13, or a 4-gallon gift box for $26. You can get sweet potato chips, too.

For good deals on macadamia nuts, keep traveling south on Highway 11 past Kona Chips to the town of Holualoa and the **Kona Coast Macadamia Nut & Candy Factory** (turn right on Middle Keei Rd. and you can't miss it; ☎ 808/328-8141). At the little gift shop of this working mac-nut orchard and processing plant, you can buy 1-pound bags of roasted nuts for $8.25. The Nutty Hawaiian Bark, a 3-ounce shingle of dark chocolate or milk chocolate infused with mac nuts, for $4.60, is a popular concoction. There's a miniature working model of a macadamia-nut husking machine that demonstrates how the husking is done. It works just like the big husker in the factory here, only one nut at a time.

Hundreds of independent growers harvest the celebrated Kona coffee bean within the coffee-friendly micro-climate known as The Kona Coffee Belt. The little guys sell their crops to a handful of big guys, who process the freshly picked cherry, as it's called, into brewable coffee. **Greenwell Farms** (Hwy. 11 between mile markers 111 and 112, Kealakekua; ☎ 808/323-2275; closed Sun) is one of the larger big guys. It dries and roasts 20% of the world's Kona coffee supply. For all its clout as an industry titan, it's a remarkably laid-back operation, which you can see for yourself on the free 20- to 30-minute tours held throughout the day. The place is so laid back tours have no scheduled times. They just happen when people show up to take them (though you do have to show up from 8:30am–4pm Mon–Fri, or 8:30am–3pm Sat). Tour or no tour, Greenwell Farms is a good place to stop to pick up some top quality Kona coffee. Prices—which fluctuate like crude oil—are as good here as anywhere.

About 75 Big Island artisans, artists, and farmers sell their handiwork on consignment at the **Kealia Ranch Store** (86-4181 Mamalahoa Hwy., aka Hwy. 11, at mile marker 101; ☎ 808/328-8744). Located in the country in an old Hawaii-style ranch home, the store has a rich selection of locally produced gifts, souvenirs, and foods, including grass-fed beef raised on the Kealia Ranch. You can pick up an 8-ounce jar of honey for $10. It comes in a bunch of different flavors, including macadamia nut and eucalyptus. And $24 will buy a CD holder or small photo album with covers made from retired Hawaii license plates. A $3,000 handmade Hawaiian quilt may be out of reach, but you can take home a packet of Hawaiian quilt napkins for just $3. And if you're staying in a place with cooking facilities, and have a taste for duck eggs, you can pick up a dozen of them for $6.

EAST HAWAII

Hilo

On the east side of the island, most of the best shopping is concentrated in Hilo, with some worthwhile points of retail interest in outlying areas. For souvenirs, check out **Hilo Hattie—The Store of Hawaii** (Prince Kuhio Plaza shopping mall, corner of E. Makaala and Hwy. 11; ☎ 808/961-3077), a windowless and well-stocked emporium of kitchy Hawaiiana. It's out in Hilo's box-store and mall district. You'll find more enjoyable shopping ambience in Hilo's old, low-rise downtown, which has an abundance of mom-and-pop shops catering to visitors and residents alike. Most are located along Kamehameha Avenue, which follows the broad arc of Hilo Bay.

If you're in Hilo on a Wednesday or a Saturday, walk around the **Hilo Farmers Market** ★★★ (corner of Kamehameha Ave. and Mamo St., downtown Hilo; ☎ 808/933-1000; crack of dawn until 3pm). When the last sugar mill on the Big Island closed in the 1990s and the plantation era officially ended, a new era of diversified agriculture began. Small farmers, many from the Philippines, now grow all sorts of fruits and vegetables on former cane land. A lot of this produce ends up spread out on the tables here, including familiar items like lettuce, papayas, and eggplant, as well as exotic edibles like rambutan—an oversized grape inside a rubbery husk covered with red tentacles (they're good). In addition to produce, you'll find palm reading, chair massage, cheap T-shirts, and all the fruits of the Big Island's diversified arts-and-crafts industry.

For super cheap items woven from natural fibers, check the well-stocked aisles of **Dolly's Handicrafts** (50 Mamo St.; ☎ 808/933-9356; right next to Hilo Farmers Market). At this simple corner shop, fluorescently lit and loaded with bargain kitsch, you'll find handbags large and small, hats, *lauhala* boxes of various sizes, woven place mats, and coconuts carved into monkeys.

The Hawaiian Force (140 Kilauea Ave.; ☎ 808/934-7171), offers a line of clothing and stickers popular among Native Hawaiians and sold nowhere else. All of it's designed by Craig Neff, the Hawaiian owner, who you'll typically find behind the counter. Many of the T-shirts ($17) and stickers ($1–$5) bear themes reflecting the deep resentments of many Hawaiians, but not everything is political. There's a "Got Poi?" shirt, Hawaii's spin on the American dairy industry's much mimicked "Got Milk?" campaign. A "Hilo" shirt takes up the three meanings of the word, each shedding light on the town. (As Neff will explain, one meaning is "to twist or braid," which relates to the legend involving demigod Maui, who twisted ti leaf into a line to tie his canoe here; another meaning is the name of an ancient Tahitian navigator, who is said to have found his way to Hilo's shores; and the third is the name for the first day after the new moon, when the moon is a narrow sliver not unlike the crescent of Hilo Bay).

Makuu Farmers Market

The **Makuu Farmers Market** ★ (Hwy. 130, after mile marker 7; Sun) is part crafts fair, part swap meet, part roadside produce extravaganza, and pure Puna. I'm talking crystals, carrot juice, cutlery, used books, free kittens, quack medicine, hot tamales, Hawaiian food, folk singers, pogs, kava for a dollar a cup, and good deals on souvenir Hawaii T-shirts ($7 apiece or four for $20). You'll also be able to pick up fresh, cheap organic produce. The market is off the highway in the middle of nowhere, but it's an excellent place to observe a cross-section of Puna's motley community of free-spirited souls.

Creative Minds in the Fiery Cradle of Creation

The earth's fiery creation process—and the 1.5 million visitors a year who visit Kilauea to see it—provide inspiration and a market for the Big Island's artistic community. About 300 artists display their works at the **Volcano Art Center** ★★ (in Hawaii Volcanoes National Park; ☎ 808/967-8222; www.volanoartcenter.org $10 per vehicle park entrance fee), which occupies the old Volcano House, a 19th-century lodge moved from the crater rim when the new Volcano House was built. Look for works by Dietrich Varez, the amiable but reclusive printmaker whose work draws largely from Hawaiian mythology, and whose studio, at the rainforest homestead he rarely leaves, looks out on Puu Oo, Kilauea's very active 600-foot cinder cone, which smolders just 8 miles away. Unlike most printmakers, who raise the value of their work by producing it in limited editions, Varez prints with the same hand-carved blocks indefinitely or until they wear out. That keeps his prices down. His smallest hand-printed, signed works sell for just $5. The largest go for $20. "Printmaking is pop art," Varez says. "And pop art should be affordable for everyone."

The Hawaiians followed the moon closely, giving it 30 different names, one for each night of the month. At **Basically Books** ★★★ (160 Kamehameha Ave.; ☎ 808/961-0144), all the moon's names are included on the ancient Hawaiian lunar calendar ($11), which correlates each night of the month with the fishing and farming activity best undertaken or avoided then (pole fishing's good on a new moon, for example, but you wouldn't want to plant taro or sweet potatoes then). Basically Books is loaded with cool stuff like this poster, among its rich stock of maps, nautical charts, postcards, CDs, toys, games, knickknacks (thin koa bookmarks shaped like surfboards for $9.95), and, of course, books.

Nearby, **The Most Irresistible Shop** ★ (256 Kamehameha Ave.; ☎ 808/935-9644) has a delightful collection of mostly Hawaiian and Asian odds-and-ends and curios with pleasantly reasonable prices, all squeezed into a surprisingly small space. Hats, handbags, postcards, pocket charms, cookbooks, women's clothing, dishware, body care potions, and jewelry (including cute sterling silver post earrings with a petroglyph turtle design for $12) are among the wares.

A short drive from downtown **Big Island Candies** (585 Hinano St.; ☎ 808/935-8890; www.bigislandcandies.com), is a bonanza of goodies, with free samples of all the different sweets they make (the chocolate-dipped shortbread is great). Along with buying, you can also watch it being made.

Six miles south of Hilo, fill up on free macadamia-nut treats at **Mauna Loa Macadamia Nut Corp.** (6 miles south of Hilo, on Macadamia Rd., off Hwy. 11; ☎ 808/966-8618) and view the inner workings of the macadamia-nut processing plant. My favorite activity here, though, is driving the long road through the 2,500-acre macadamia-nut orchard surrounding the factory.

Pahoa

Twenty miles south of Hilo, the curious little town of Pahoa serves as the commercial hub for scores of Big Island bohemians pursuing alternative lifestyles in the rainforests, jungles, and perpetual summer of the vast Puna District. The town's boardwalk-lined main street has plenty of eating places and a handful of places to shop, including **Puna Style** (15-2903 Pahoa Village Rd.; ☎ 808/965-7592), which knows what Puna people like. Puna people like loose, flowing, cotton clothing. They like handmade handbags and backpacks, incense, wind chimes, flutes, and candles. They like things made in India, Bali, and Thailand, and they like things made with hemp. Puna Style also knows that it's a rare Punatic, as Puna people like to call themselves, who has $40 to spend on a pair of pants, so things here are priced accordingly.

The Volcano Area

Sending flowers from Hawaii to someone on the mainland is a time-honored way of saying, "Wish you were here," as well as "Hawaii's awesome—you're really missing out!" **Volcano Store** (19-4005 Haunani Rd., Volcano Village; ☎ 808/967-7210; next to the post office) has sensible prices on cut flowers, such as anthurium, though shipping ratchets up the bill. For about $60, you can send a bouquet of two orchids and a dozen anthurium to the mainland. If the occasion calls for something more enduring than a bouquet, stop outside of Volcano Village at **Akatsuka Orchid Garden** (Volcano Hwy. between mile markers 22 and 23; ☎ 808/967-8234; daily 8:30am–5pm) and get a potted orchid. For about $45, you can have a modest one shipped to the mainland, root ball and all.

The **Volcano Winery** (35 Pii Mana Rd., off Hwy. 11 near mile marker 30; ☎ 808/967-7479) offers free tasting of its six wines: two made the traditional way with grapes, one made with Big Island macadamia nut honey and no grapes, and three made with grapes and guava or jaboticaba (a South American fruit). Bottles range in price from $16 to $17. The gift shop is loaded with Big Island–made goods, such as handmade ceramic tiles intended as drink coasters and jewelry made from olivine, the green volcanic mineral responsible for the unusual tint of the Big Island's Green Sands Beach (p. 376).

NIGHTLIFE ON THE BIG ISLAND

Believe it or not, there's quite a bit to do after (or just before) the sun sets.

WEST HAWAII

Sunset Cruises

A nice way to end a day and begin an evening is out on the ocean, sailing or motoring offshore as the sun sinks beneath the horizon. A dozen or more commercial boats offer sunset cruises, some with dinner and some without.

Body Glove Cruises (☎ 808/329-4807) offers the always popular booze cruise with dancing. For $73 including tax, you can sail aboard one of two double-decker

---

Finding a Place to Unwind

The nightclubs and bars in the following sections can be found on the maps starting on p. 368.

Bar Hours

Bars in Hawaii can serve alcohol until 2am. Many Kona-area nightspots will stay open that late when they're busy and close by 1am when they're slow.

trimarans, the ***Kanoa*** and the ***Kanoa II,*** which have high profiles like sea-going SUVs. They've got live music (usually rock), two dance floors (one on each deck), and open bars. The hard-working *Kanoa I* and *II* do snorkel trips to Pawai Bay during the day, and booze cruises at night that carry 85 passengers.

For Kona's largest and most shameless sunset cruise, check out **Captain Beans' Cruises** (☎ 808/329-2955; www.robertshawaii.com). Captain Beans' 150-foot steel-hulled *Tamure* isn't the most elegant vessel on the waters—it looks like an over-lit drilling platform masquerading as a Polynesian voyaging canoe, with it's rust-colored twin hulls and ridiculously undersized crab claw sails—but it costs just $69 for adults and $39 for kids 4 to 11 years old (with discount coupons widely available in the visitors' magazine), and it includes a so-so dinner (teriyaki beef and chicken, garlic bread, and salad). It carries 200 guests at a time, who board at Kailua Pier at 4:45pm and slowly motor offshore for 2 hours. There's a Polynesian dance review, and (I'm pretty sure) watered-down drinks (the first one's included with dinner). It's pure mass-tourism fun.

Luaus

With their shell-lei greetings, their fire dancers, and all the other conventions of the genre, Big Island luaus are lively and corny affairs. There are plenty here, but in my mind any one is as good, or as bad, as another. What's intriguing about the **Island Breeze Luau** (75-5660 Palani Rd., on grounds of the King Kamehameha Kona Beach Hotel; ☎ 808/326-4969; www.islandbreezeluau.com) is the historic setting. The luau grounds were once part of Kamakahonu (p. 381), the royal compound where King Kamehameha spent his last days, and where the most pivotal meal in Hawaiian history was eaten, the one in which Queen Kaahumanu persuaded Kamehameha's heir to the throne, Liholiho, to dine with women, breaking a fundamental *kapu* prohibiting men and women from dining together and shattering the age-old religious order.

These days, every Tuesday, Wednesday, Thursday, and Sunday, from 5 to 8pm or so, some 350 male and female luau-goers gather here for kalua pig, mai tais, and a Polynesian dance show. Most have no idea of the dining tradition they're carrying on—or that, at one time, enjoying an all-you-can-eat buffet with the opposite sex might have cost them far more dearly than the current rates ($70 for adults, $35 for children ages 5 to 12; $45 if you want to watch the show but not eat; coupons for luaus abound in the free tourist booklets around town, so there's no need to pay full price). The pig that's served roasts in the ground all day. If you go by in the morning, you can watch the cooks prepare it and, at 9:30am, drop it into the *imu,* the underground oven filled with rocks, banana leaves, and banana stalks.

Nightclubs & Bars

Huggo's on the Rocks (75-5828 Kahakai Rd.; ☎ 808/329-1493; right off Alii Dr.) has a thatched roof over its open-air bar, a sand floor, and a torch-lit waterfront location, all of which give it its postcard-perfect tropical allure. A hula dancer appears each evening from 6:30 to 8:30pm, and everybody gets to dance from 8:30pm onward, with a band playing contemporary Hawaiian and oldies. It's a swell nightspot in every respect except for the steep drink prices ($7 for a little 12-oz. beer in a plastic cup). Thank goodness for the periodic drink specials.

Drinks are cheaper nearby, at **Lulu's Restaurant & Bar** (75-5819 Alii Dr.; ☎ 808/331-2633; at the Coconut Grove Market); its dance floor attracts a young and sometimes rowdy crowd Thursdays through Saturdays (when the DJs are spinning). Cash prizes are up for grabs on Wednesday, game night, with a changing lineup of events that range from free-throw shooting to booty shaking. On karaoke Tuesday, crooners belt their hearts out for $1 a song. On karaoke Sunday the house actually *pays* customers to sing, $1 a song.

Toward the back of Coconut Grove Marketplace, behind the outdoor volleyball court, **Oceans Sports Bar & Grill** (75-5819 Alii Dr.; ☎ 808/327-9494) is a dark and roomy place with two brightly lit pool tables and more TV screens devoted to surfing than basketball, football, or hockey—as it should be in Hawaii. Bands play or DJs spin Wednesday through Thursday and crowds throng the dance floor. Happy hour runs from 3 to 6pm daily, with beers in the $2 to $3 price range, well drinks for $2.50, $2 off other mixed drinks, and pupu for $2 off. It's got some outdoor seating in the restaurant area, where kids are allowed, making it a family-oriented kind of bar.

When well-known bands come to town, chances are they'll appear at a somewhat hard-to-find venue in Kona's old industrial area, the **Kona Brewing Co. & Brewpub** (75-5629 Kuakini Hwy., go north on Kuakini Hwy. to intersection with Kaiwi St., turn right on Kaiwi, turn right on Pawai St., and go to end of Pawai; ☎ 808/334-2739; www.konabrewingco.com). Check the website for a map and to see who's scheduled to play. Regardless of the entertainment schedule, this place is worth finding if you're into microbrewed beer. The bartenders pour nine regular brews, including the light and delicate Big Wave Golden Ale, the mildly hoppy Longboard Lager, and the full-bodied Castaway IPA (my favorite). Pints cost $5, except for the "beer of the week," which goes for $3.75. During happy hour, Monday through Friday from 3 to 5pm, all pints are $3.75. On Sunday there's live local music—Hawaiian, classical guitar, blues, or something along those lines. If the indoor seating gets too loud, the outdoor seating—set amid tiki torches and

Beach Volleyball after Dark

For a pickup game of volleyball, or for a nice place to sit on the grass and watch others play volleyball, check out the sand court at Coconut Grove Marketplace, right next to the **Hard Rock Cafe** (75-5815 Alii Dr.; ☎ 808/329-8866). People play all day, but the games really heat up after dark, when the weather cools down.

Pupu to You

It wasn't so long ago in Hawaii when cocktail lounges throughout the islands commonly served free pupu with your second or third round of drinks. Times have changed and free pupu have gotten harder and harder to find. But the tradition is alive and well in slow-to-change Hilo at a handful of laid-back places. My all-time favorite is **Kim's Karaoke Lounge** (☎ 808/935-7552), a blue-collar, after-work, sports-bar-type place where tourists almost never enter. If you go, be prepared for some looks. A friend and I once encamped at Kim's, and after the third round of drinks, seven exquisite little pupu platters appeared at our booth: bacon-wrapped asparagus, caramelized weenies, pork 'n tofu, chicken katsu, chicken with peanut sauce, tempura sweet potatoes and onions, and an enormous pile of ahi sashimi on a bed of freshly grated cabbage with mustard sauce. The variety of pupu at a place like Kim's might vary, and the spread can range from humble to lavish, but it invariably includes ahi sashimi.

There is protocol involved in partaking of the free pupu. First, never refer to them as "free pupu." Second, don't mention pupu at all until at least your second round of drinks. Third, once it's established that you're there to stay a while and spend some money on drinks, casually say something like, "You guys got pupu?" Fourth, just leave it at that—don't ask any more questions. You have no control, at this point, over what shows up at your table anyway. Fifth, tip generously (because, you know, freedom has a price).

tropical foliage—will be mellower. If you're a real beer nut, you can come back during the day for the **free brewery tour,** daily at 10:30am and 3pm.

EAST HAWAII

East Hawaii nightlife is not quite an oxymoron, but it's close; it's definitely not what this side of the island is known for. The free pupu bars (above) are where much of the local population heads after dark. You should also consider the following:

The **University of Hawaii at Hilo Performing Arts Center** (200 E. Kaiwili St.; ☎ 808/974-7310; http://artscenter.uhh.hawaii.edu, click "coming events") offers a regular series of concerts, dramas, musicals, Hawaiian cultural performances, and other events throughout the spring and fall. Student productions of standards like *Oklahoma* share the schedule with visiting performers from the mainland and beyond.

Like a lot of downtown Hilo, the **Palace Theater** (38 Haili St.; ☎ 808/934-7777; www.hilopalace.com) is a restoration work in progress, and in this case, one with the paint peeling and the Grecian urns missing from its neoclassical facade. I get the feeling that it might never be completed, but it doesn't really matter; in the meantime, there's a full schedule of films and live performances throughout the year. The lineup ranges from community productions to international acts. Built in 1925, the Palace was once the biggest thing in entertainment in east Hawaii. While much of its glory has faded, its purpose endures.

ABCs of the Big Island

American Express There's an office on the Kohala Coast at the Hilton Waikoloa Village (☎ 808/886-7958) and The Fairmont Orchid in Mauna Lani Resort (☎ 808/885-2000). To report lost or stolen traveler's checks, call ☎ 800/221-7282.

Dentists In an emergency, contact Dr. Craig C. Kimura at **Kamuela Office Center** (☎ **808/885-5947**); in Kona, call **Dr. Frank Sayre,** Frame 10 Center, behind Lanihau Shopping Center on Palani Road (☎ **808/329-8067**); in Hilo, call **Hawaii Smile Center,** Hilo Lagoon Center, 101 Aupuni St. (☎ **808/961-9181**).

Doctors In Hilo, the **Hilo Medical Center** is at 1190 Waianuenue Ave. (☎ **808/974-4700**); on the Kona side, call **Hualalai Urgent Care,** 75–1028 Henry St., across the street from Safeway (☎ **808/327-HELP**).

Emergencies For ambulance, fire, and rescue services, dial ☎ **911** or call ☎ 808/961-6022. To contact the **Hawaii Police Department,** call ☎ **808/326-4646 in Kona,** ☎ **808/961-2213 in Hilo.** The **Poison Control Center** hot line is ☎ **800/362-3585.**

Hospitals Hospitals offering 24-hour urgent-care facilities include the **Hilo Medical Center,** 1190 Waianuenue Ave., Hilo (☎ **808/974-4700**); **North Hawaii Community Hospital,** Waimea, 67 1125 Mamalahoa Hwy. (☎ **808/885-4444**); and **Kona Community Hospital,** on the Kona Coast in Kealakekua (☎ **808/322-9311**).

Post Office All calls to the U.S. Post Office can be directed to ☎ 800/275-8777. There are local branches in Hilo at 1299 Kekuanaoa Ave., in Kailua-Kona at 74–5577 Palani Rd., and in Waimea on Lindsey Road.

Weather For conditions in and around Hilo, call ☎ 808/935-8555; for the rest of the Big Island, call ☎ 808/961-5582. For marine forecasts, call ☎ 808/935-9883.

8 The Essentials of Planning

by David Thompson

A PERENNIALLY POPULAR T-SHIRT IN HAWAII HAS A SIMPLE TWO-WORD message that captures the spirit of the islands perfectly: "Hang Loose." Tapping into that spirit comes naturally to people. Just go, kick back, and relax.

Nonetheless, tending to some nuts and bolts before you arrive in the islands will enhance your experience and save you money. This chapter sums up the basics that you'll need to plan your trip.

WHEN TO VISIT

There really isn't a bad time to visit the islands. Hawaii does, however, have a 6-month wet season and a 6-month dry season, known within the islands as "winter" and "summer." Winter begins in October and runs through April, while summer begins in May and runs through September. There's no discernable spring or fall. While it rains in the mountains year-round, you're more likely to get rained out at the beach during the winter wet season. It doesn't happen much, but it happens.

Hawaii's coolest months are February and March, and its warmest months are August and September. But generally speaking, the year-round temperature doesn't vary much. At the beach, the average daytime high in summer is 85°F (29°C), while the average daytime high in winter is 78°F (26°C); nighttime lows are usually about 10°F (–12°C) cooler. But how warm it is on any given day really depends on where you are on which island.

The biggest surf occurs in the winter, on the north shores. In summer, south shores get the waves. Hurricane season in the North Pacific runs from June into November. Most hurricanes pass at sea, causing stormy weather but no serious problems. Occasionally one makes land. The last, Hurricane Iniki, hit Kauai in 1992, killing eight people and causing $2 billion in damage.

HIGH SEASON & LOW TOURIST SEASONS

If you have any control over what time of year to go to Hawaii, plan to visit the islands in the spring or fall. Those are the low seasons for tourism, when crowds are at their thinnest and prices at their lowest. Both accommodations and airfares tend to cost less from mid-April to mid-June, and from mid-September to mid-December. Family travelers in June, July, and August account for the summer high season, while holiday travelers and snowbirds drive the high season that lasts from mid-December to mid-April, as well as the mini–high season that lasts for a week around Thanksgiving.

WHALE SEASON

The biggest drawback of hitting Hawaii during the low seasons is that you tend to miss the whales. Each winter an estimated 5,000 humpback whales migrate from cold Arctic waters to mate, calve, socialize, and generally make a big splash in Hawaiian waters. They appear off all of the Hawaiian Islands, but they're particularly fond of the protected shallow waters off Maui's south shores. Whale season officially runs from mid-December until mid-May (so it overlaps a little with the spring low season, but with dwindling numbers of whales). February is the peak month. All sorts of boats around the islands, especially out of Maui's Lahaina and Maalaea harbors, offer whale-watching tours. You can easily spot whales from shore (for free), especially when seas are calm. On rough choppy days, look for their telltale "blows," clouds of mist that appear on the surface as they purge their blow holes. You'll notice when whale-watching that humpbacks have some very deliberate and defined moves. These include:

- **Head rises,** aka **sky hops.** Whale holds enormous head out of the water, vertically, probably for a look around.
- **Breaches.** Whale launches itself out of the water and lands on its back, making an enormous splash.
- **Tail slaps.** Whale smacks flukes on surface of water, usually repeatedly. Possibly a warning.
- **Peduncle slaps.** Like the tail slap, but involving the whole rear section of the whale.
- **Blows.** Clouds of mist released when whale purges its blow hole upon surfacing. Adult humpbacks breathe every 10 to 15 minutes, although they can hold their breath as long as 45 minutes. Calves breath more often.

Warning: Humpback whales are protected under the Endangered Species Act, and harassing, injuring, killing, or approaching within 300 feet of them is prohibited.

The Climate at a Glance

The main Hawaiian Islands sit high in the Tropics, just beneath the Tropic of Cancer. Hawaii's weather is characterized by mild temperatures, moderate humidity, northeasterly trade winds, and the occasional severe storm. Snow, hail, tornadoes, hurricanes, thunderstorms, lightning, flooding, and droughts all occur, but not with the frequency or severity that they do on the mainland. Hawaii's mountains are responsible for a highly variable climate that, within the space of a few miles, can include rainforest, deserts, and alpine tundra. The Big Island, with the two tallest mountains, Mauna Loa and Mauna Kea, has terrain so varied it includes 11 of the world's 13 climatic zones. Hawaiian mountains interrupt the flow of moist ocean air blowing across the North Pacific, wresting precipitation from it that keep the windward and mountain areas green. The leeward sides of the islands tend to be drier, because the majority of moisture has been stripped from the wind by the time it crosses the mountains.

Visitor Information

The Hawaii Visitors and Convention Bureau (☎ 800/464-2924; www.gohawaii.com), along with its neighbor island branches, is the state's official source for visitor information—but not a very good one, at least over the phone (the website is more useful). If you dial the information line, the operators will tell you about the weather, they'll read from the members list of the Hawaii Visitors and Convention Bureau, and they'll refer you to the Web. It's like pulling teeth to get much more from them. Less constrained, more informal, and more helpful are the people who work at the information booths at the airports. They're mainly there to answer the same question over and over again—um, where are the rental cars?—but they'll take a stab at anything, and they answer questions over the phone. Here are the numbers:

- Hilo International Airport (☎ 808/934-5838)
- Honolulu International Airport (☎ 808/836-6413)
- Kahului Airport (☎ 808/872-3893)
- Kona International Airport (☎ 808/329-3423)
- Lihue Airport (☎ 808/246-1448)
- Molokai Airport (☎ 808/567-6361)

Hawaii's Visit-Worthy Annual Events

Hawaii has events and festivals throughout the year, and I've listed some of the most popular annual ones here. The Hawaii Visitors and Convention Bureau's website (www.gohawaii.com) provides up-to-date calendars (one of the more useful services of the HVCB).

January

Mercedes Championships. Winners of the PGA Tour events meet at Kapalua's Plantation Course on Maui. For more information, call ☎ 866/669-2440.

Ka Molokai Makahiki. At the Kaunakakai Town Baseball Park on Molokai, the ancient harvest festival of makahiki, a time of peace and tribute to the *alii,* is reenacted with hula, games, sports, crafts, and food. Held in late January. Call ☎ 808/553-3876 for details.

Morey World Bodyboarding Championship. The world's most skilled and gutsy body boarders shoot Oahu's Banzai Pipeline on their bellies and knees. Date depends on surf conditions.

February

Hula Bowl. A competition held in the War Memorial Stadium on Oahu, in January or February, between the nation's top college football players. Go to www.hulabowlhawaii.com for more information.

NFL Pro Bowl. A week after the Super Bowl, the best players from the NFC face off against the all-stars of the AFC in Oahu's Aloha Stadium. Visit www.nfl.com/probowl for details.

Sony Open. The Waialae County Club hosts the first full-field event in the PGA Tour, with proceeds going to Hawaii charities. See www.sonyopeninhawaii.com.

Slack-key Guitar Around the Islands

Fans of slack-key, the uniquely Hawaiian approach to playing the guitar, know Gabby Pahinui as one of the giants of the form. Two years after his death in 1980, his friends staged a music festival at the beach park near his home in Waimanalo, Oahu. The event was a smash—2,000 people turned out—and it's been back every year since. Over time, the ★★★ **Hawaiian Slack-Key Guitar Festival** (☎ 808/226-2697; www.slackkeyfestival.com) has grown to include one-day events on Maui, Kauai, the Big Island, and sometimes Molokai. It has occasionally shipped out overseas, as well, with visits to Germany, Japan, Great Britain, Canada, France, and the continental U.S.

The schedule and venues change from year to year, but the Hawaii events typically fall between June and November. Before your visit to the islands, check the website for the schedule, and if your visit coincides with a date, count yourselves lucky. The festivals are a real slice of Hawaiian life, always picnic-on-the-grass casual, filled with living legends of Hawaiian music, and absolutely free.

Great Aloha Run. This annual 8.15-mile footrace starts at Aloha Tower in downtown Honolulu and ends at Aloha Stadium; it's a big, inclusive event—with elite runners, parents with strollers, people in wheelchairs, and people who walk but don't run. Proceeds go to local charities. To get more information, call ☎ 808/528-7388 or go to www.greataloharun.com.

Panaewa Stampede Rodeo (next to the Panaewa Rainforest Zoo, south of Hilo). This Big Island event features amateurs and pros, young and old, and all the traditional rodeo events, plus Cowboy Poker, in which players sit at a table in a bull ring with an aggravated bull. The last one at the table wins.

March

Run to the Sun. Sinewy ultra-distance runners hoof it 36.2 miles from sea level to the summit of Maui's Haleakala at 10,023 feet. To lace up or find out more about watching the race, call ☎ 808/573-7584.

Turtle Bay Championship. A 36-hole, 2-day golf tournament in which four-person amateur teams are paired with pros on the PGA Championship Tour. Call ☎ 808/479-3548.

The Hawaiian Music Awards. This 4-day music festival brings out Hawaii's top musicians; the public votes for the winners online. Call ☎ 808/951-6699 or go to www.hawaiianmusicawards.com.

Kona Brewers Festival. For 40 bucks a ticket, you'll get a glass, some beers, and all you can eat at this event that brings Hawaii's microbrewers and those who support them together on the Big Island for food, music, dance, and, most importantly, beer. For more information, call ☎ 808/331-3033 or visit www.konabrewersfestival.com.

Kona Chocolate Festival. Expect live music, wine, champagne, local chefs, caterers, ice cream makers, and gourmet chocolatiers at this Big Island festival. Go to www.konachocolatefestival.com for details.

April

East Maui Taro Festival. This 2-day celebration of the staple of ancient Hawaii includes cultural demonstrations, food booths, arts and crafts, and a big taro-pancake breakfast. Held at the ballpark in rural Hana on Maui. Call ☎ 808/264-1553 for more information.

Hawaii Invitational Music Festival. Junior high, high school, and college drill teams, choirs, orchestras, and jazz bands come together for a week of free shows and friendly competition in Waikiki.

The Merry Monarch Festival. The world's largest hula competition, held at Edith Kanakaole Tennis Stadium in Hilo lasts 1 week, starting on Easter Sunday, and it's the worst possible time to try to find accommodations or automobile rentals in Hilo on the Big Island. Call ☎ 808/935-9168 for details.

May

International Festival of Canoes. Master carvers from around the Pacific turn logs into canoes before your eyes—although slowly, very slowly. At Banyan Tree Park on Maui. To learn more, call ☎ 888/310-1117 or 808/667-9175 or go to www.mauicanoefest.com.

Honolulu Triathlon. Triathletes from around the world spend the day swimming, running, and cycling in this event, usually held in April or May. Call ☎ 866/454-6561 or go to www.honolulutriathlon.com to learn more.

Astroday. This event on the Big Island brings astronomers down from the telescope complex atop Mauna Kea to mingle with the general public at Prince Kuhio Mall in Hilo; includes all sorts of neat science stuff, as well as Hawaiian cultural presentations. For further information, call ☎ 808/932-2328 or 808/969-9101, or visit www.astroday.net.

June

Kamehameha Day, June 11. Hawaii is the only state with a holiday honoring a king, and it does so on this day with a variety of events including a parade that fills the streets of Honolulu with floats, glamorous Pau riders, and marching bands, with an awards presentation at the end of the line. Festivities on the Big Island are equally compelling in North Kohala, where the boy who would be king was born. The fun begins at 8am, when 22-foot leis are draped around the statue of the king in the little town of Kapaau.

July

Makawao Parade & Rodeo. A traditional event in upcountry Maui, where the cowboys still roam. For more info, call ☎ 808/244-3530.

Kapalua Wine & Food Festival. Cooking demonstrations, wine-tasting seminars, and winemaker dinners are some of the highlights of this event, an extended banquet of fine dining and bold, compelling New World wines. For details, call ☎ 808/KAPALUA or go to www.kapalua.com.

Annual Molokai to Oahu Paddleboard Race. Paddlers from all over the world race 32 miles across the channel to Oahu, usually on the last Sunday of July. For details, call Mike Takahashi at ☎ 808/638-8208.

Queen Liliuokalani Keiki Hula Competition. More than 500 youngsters from two dozen hula *halau* dance in honor of Hawaii's deposed queen at the Neal Blaisdell Center in Honolulu. Call ☎ 808/521-6905 for more information.

Ukulele Festival Hawaii. If you had any doubts that the ukulele was alive and well, they'll be gone by the time a ukulele orchestra, made up of 800 musicians, mostly children, leaves the stage at the Kapiolani Park Bandstand in Waikiki. For details, call ☎ 808/732-3739 or go to www.ukulele-roysakuma.com.

Prince Lot Hula Festival. Ancient and modern hula is presented at a beautiful location (the Moanalua Gardens in Honolulu), and held in honor of a Hawaiian monarch who ignored Western critics in his efforts to promote Hawaiian culture. Third Saturday of July.

Turtle Independence Day. On July 4, scores of endangered green sea turtles, raised in the ancient Hawaiian fishponds on the grounds of the Mauna Lani Resort in the Kohala District, are released into the wild. To learn more, call ☎ 808/885-6677 or visit www.maunalani.com.

Great Waikoloa Food, Wine & Music Festival. On the weekend closest to July 4, top Hawaii chefs and some from the mainland come together to present food, paired with wines from around the world. The event is accompanied by jazz and fireworks. For more information, call ☎ 808/886-1234 or go to www.hiltonwaikoloavillage.com.

Parker Ranch Rodeo. Hawaii's *paniolo* (cowboys) exhibit their considerable skills in Waimea, the heart of cowboy country. Find out more by calling ☎ 808/885-7311 or visiting www.rodeohawaii.com.

Crater Rim Run & Marathon. This event in Hawaii Volcanoes National Park traverses the volcanic landscape in 5-, 10-, and 26.2-mile races, or walks for the less competitive. Call ☎ 808/967-8222.

August

Admission Day. A state holiday commemorating the day in 1959 when the Territory of Hawaii became the state of Hawaii. Celebrated statewide; third Friday in August.

Hawaii State Farm Fair. Hawaii's unique version of the state fair, held at Aloha Stadium in Honolulu, with farm animals, a Ferris wheel, and Spam musubi (a slice of fried Spam fastened to a Spam-shaped block of rice with a belt of seaweed—a local favorite). Dates vary by year, for more information, call ☎ 808/531-3531.

Puu Kohola Heiau National Historic Site Anniversary Celebration. Hawaiian workshops, performances, and pride at the massive war temple King Kamehameha built near Kawaihae Harbor. Mid-month, phone ☎ 808/882-7218.

Annual Hawaiian International Billfish Tournament. Competitors from around the globe compete in the waters of Kailua-Kona at a sport where a strike is a good thing. To get more information, call ☎ 808/329-7311 or visit www.konabillfish.com.

September

Aloha Festivals. A widely disbursed series of parades and other events throughout the islands. For details, call ☎ 800/852-7960 or go to www.alohafestivals.com.

Great Molokai Mule Drag & Hoolaulea. Molokai's favorite beasts of burden are raced through the center of town in Kaunakakai, if you can call dragging a mule down the street by the reigns a race. To learn more, call ☎ 800/800-6367 or check out www.molokai-hawaii.com.

Taste of Lahaina. A festival built around Maui's most illustrious chefs, with plenty of entertainment, beer and wine, and 10,000 attendees. Get more info by calling ☎ 888/310-1117.

October

Halloween in Lahaina. Front Street is closed to cars and turned over to 20,000 creatures of the night, when Lahaina thinks it's New Orleans at Mardi Gras. On October 31 each year.

Aloha Classic Wave Championships. Windsurfers launch from cresting waves and catch big air at the most illustrious windsurfing beach in the world, Hookipa Beach park, in the Pro World Tour's final event. See www.alohaclassicwindsurfing.com.

Maui County Fair. Hawaii takes the mainland county fair and makes it its own. To learn more, call ☎ 808/244-3530.

Molokai Hoe Outrigger World Championship Race. A 40-mile Hawaiian canoe race across the rough channel between Molokai and Oahu and ending in Waikiki. Check out http://holoholo.org/hoe.

Emalani Festival. A forest festival at Kokee State Park in honor of the Hawaiian monarch Queen Emma, who made a famous trek to the festival site with a large retinue in 1871. For details, call ☎ 808/245-3971.

Ironman Triathlon World Championship. Some 1,500 tawny, driven triathletes swim 2.4 miles, bike 112 miles, then run 26.2 miles, in a grueling all-day race under the Kona sun. If you get to the seawall on Alii Drive before 5:30am, you might succeed in staking out a spot to watch the 7am water start. To learn more, call ☎ 808/329-0063 or visit www.ironmanlive.com.

Hamakua Music Festival. The lush Hamakua Coast is the setting for live blues, jazz, rock, Hawaiian, and classical music performances. Go to www.hamakuamusicfestival.org.

November

Hawaii International Film Festival (various locations throughout state). A celebration of cinema from Asia, the Pacific Islands, and the United States, during the first 2 weeks of November. For details, call ☎ 808/528-FILM or visit www.hiff.org.

Vans Triple Crown of Surfing. The three big events in pro-surfing—the Op Pro Hawaii, the O'Neill World Cup, and The Rip Curl Pro Pipeline Masters—run from November into December, with holding periods for each, when participants pray for surf and usually get it. Check out www.triplecrownofsurfing.com.

MasterCard PGA Grand Slam (last weekend of Nov). Top golfers and $1 million in prizes meet in Kauai at the Poipu Bay Resort Golf Course. For details, call ☎ 888/744-0888 or visit www.pga.com.

Annual Kona Coffee Cultural Festival (all over Kailua-Kona). Harvest time in Kona is marked with coffee tasting, picking contests, the Miss Kona Coffee pageant, and other tributes to the bean. Go to www.konacoffeefest.com.

Big Island Festival (early Nov). Four days and nights of food, golf and other sports, spa specials, Hawaiian music, and farm exhibits on the Big Island's Gold Coast. For details, phone ☎ 877/817-0460 or 808/964-5067 or visit www.bigislandfestival.com.

December

First Light. So many Hollywood heavyweights spend the holidays on Maui that film studios with dreams of Oscars and Golden Globes have taken to premiering their late-in-the-year award hopefuls there, at the Maui Arts and Cultural Center in Kahului. To get more information, call ☎ 808/579-9996 or visit www.mauifilmfestival.com.

Old-Fashioned Holiday Celebration. Crafts, carolers, Christmas cookies, and Santa Claus are what you'll find on the second Saturday in December, under Hawaii's most famous tree at the Banyan Tree Park in Lahaina. For details, call ☎ 808/310-1117.

Quiksilver in Memory of Eddie Aikau. A big-wave surf contest held at Waimea Bay and named in honor of a revered Hawaiian waterman lost at sea while trying to save others. The holding period for this 1-day event starts in December and runs into February. Waimea must be breaking at least 20 feet for the contest to go on—the bay calls the day, as they say. Go to www.quicksilver.com/eddie for specifics.

Honolulu Marathon. This is one of the world's largest marathons, with more than 30,000 runners. To sign up or to get the low down on spectating, call ☎ 808/734-7200 or go to www.honolulumarathon.com.

Festival of Trees. Downtown Honolulu becomes an unlikely wonderland of Christmas trees in an annual benefit for Queens Medical Center. Lighting of the tree occurs on the first or second week of December. To learn more, call ☎ 808/547-4307.

Aloha Bowl. Pac-10 meets the Big 12 on Christmas Day in a nationally televised college classic at the Aloha Stadium in Honolulu. For details, call ☎ 808/545-7171.

Rainbow Classic. The NCAA's best basketball teams play at the University of Hawaii's Special Events Arena in Honolulu during the week after Christmas. To get more information, call ☎ 808/965-6501.

Whales on the Web

For background on humpbacks and the Hawaiian Islands Humpback Whale National Marine Sanctuary, visit www.hawaiihumpbackwhale.noaa.gov.

ENTRY REQUIREMENTS

Be sure to check with the U.S. embassy or consulate for the very latest in entry requirements, as these continue to shift. Full information can be found at the **U.S. State Department's website** (travel.state.gov).

VISAS

As of this writing, citizens of western and central Europe, Australia, New Zealand, and Singapore need only a valid passport and a round-trip air ticket or cruise ticket to enter the United States. Canadian citizens can also enter without a visa; they simply need to show proof of residence.

Citizens of all other countries will need to obtain a tourist visa from the U.S. consulate; depending on your country of origin, there may or may not be a charge attached (and you may or may not have to apply in person). To get the visa, along with a passport valid for at least 6 months from the end of your scheduled U.S. visit, you'll need to complete an application and submit a 1½-inch-square photo. It's usually possible to obtain a visa within 24 hours, except during holiday periods or the summer rush.

For information about U.S. visas, go to http://travel.state.gov and click on "Visas."

PASSPORTS

To enter the United States, international visitors must have a valid passport that expires at least 6 months later than the scheduled end of their visit.

For Residents of Australia. You can pick up an application from your local post office or any branch of Passports Australia, but you must schedule an interview at the passport office to present your application materials. Call the Australian Passport Information Service (☎ 131-232), or visit the government website at www.passports.gov.au.

For Residents of Canada. Passport applications are available at travel agencies throughout Canada or from the central Passport Office (Department of Foreign Affairs and International Trade, Ottawa, ON K1A 0G3; ☎ 800/567-6868; www.ppt.gc.ca). ***Note:*** Canadian children who travel must have their own passports. However, if you hold a valid Canadian passport issued before December 11, 2001, that bears the name of your child, the passport remains valid for you and your child until it expires.

For Residents of Ireland. You can apply for a 10-year passport at the Passport Office (Setanta Centre, Molesworth Street, Dublin 2; ☎ 01/671-1633; www.irlgov.ie/iveagh). Those under age 18 and over 65 must apply for a €12 3-year passport. You can also apply at 1A South Mall, Cork (☎ 021/272-525), or at most main post offices.

For Residents of New Zealand. You can pick up a passport application at any New Zealand Passports Office or download it from their website. Contact the Passports Office (☎ 0800/225-050 or 04/474-8100; www.passports.govt.nz).

For Residents of the United Kingdom. To pick up an application for a standard 10-year passport (5-year passport for children under 16), visit your nearest passport office, major post office, or travel agency or contact the United Kingdom Passport Service (☎ 0870/521-0410; www.ukpa.gov.uk).

MEDICAL REQUIREMENTS

No inoculations or vaccinations are required to enter the United States, unless you're arriving from an area that is suffering from an epidemic (cholera or yellow fever, in particular). A valid, signed prescription is required for those travelers in need of syringe-administered medications or medical treatment that involves narcotics. It is extremely important to obtain the correct documentation in these cases as your medications could be confiscated; and if you are found to be carrying an illegal substance, you could be subject to significant penalties. Those who are HIV-positive may also require a special waiver in order to enter the country (as you will be asked on your visa application whether you're a carrier of any communicable diseases). The best thing to do is contact **AIDSinfo** (☎ 800/448-0440 or 301/519-6616 or www.aidsinfo.nih.gov) for up-to-date information.

CUSTOMS REGULATIONS

Strict regulations govern what can and can't be brought into the United States—and what you can take back home with you.

WHAT YOU CAN BRING INTO HAWAII

Every visitor more than 21 years of age may bring in, free of duty, the following: (1) 1 liter of wine or hard liquor; (2) 200 cigarettes, 100 cigars (but not from Cuba), or 3 pounds of smoking tobacco; and (3) $100 worth of gifts. These exemptions are offered to travelers who spend at least 72 hours in the United States and who have not claimed them within the preceding 6 months. It is altogether forbidden to bring into the country foodstuffs (particularly fruit, cooked meats, and canned goods) and plants (vegetables, seeds, tropical plants, and the like). Foreign tourists may carry in or out up to $10,000 in U.S. or foreign currency with no formalities; larger sums must be declared to U.S. Customs on entering or leaving, which includes filing form CM 4790. For details regarding U.S. Customs and Border Protection, consult your nearest U.S. embassy or consulate, or **U.S. Customs** (☎ 202/927-1770; www.customs.ustreas.gov).

WHAT YOU CAN TAKE HOME FROM HAWAII

For a clear summary of Canadian rules, write for the booklet *I Declare,* issued by the **Canada Border Services Agency** (☎ 800/461-9999 in Canada, or 204/983-3500; www.cbsa-asfc.gc.ca).

For information, U.K. citizens can contact **HM Customs & Excise** (☎ 0845/010-9000 or, from outside the U.K., 020/8929-0152; www.hmce.gov.uk).

A helpful brochure for Australians that's available from Australian consulates or Customs offices is *Know Before You Go.* For more information, call the **Australian Customs Service** (☎ 1300/363-263; www.customs.gov.au).

Most questions regarding New Zealand rules are answered in a free pamphlet available at New Zealand consulates and Customs offices called *New Zealand Customs Guide for Travellers, Notice no. 4.* For more information, contact **New Zealand Customs** (The Customhouse, 17–21 Whitmore St., Box 2218, Wellington; ☎ 04/473-6099 or 0800/428-786; www.customs.govt.nz).

FINDING A GOOD AIRFARE TO HAWAII

Because Hawaii is such a wildly popular destination, discounted airfares are elusive. And if you're thinking you might cash in on your frequent-flier miles, think again—the airlines are notorious for leaving Hawaii off the list of destinations where frequent fliers can reap their rewards. There are, however, some strategies you can employ to help shave a few bucks off of your plane tickets:

- **Fly local.** Hawaiian Airlines frequently runs special sales, and often beats the majors with its fares. The number of gateways it serves are limited, but in certain instances it will be less expensive to fly to one of its Western gateways—Las Vegas, Los Angeles, Oakland, Orange County, Phoenix, Sacramento, San Jose, Seattle, Reno, San Diego—and then transfer to a Hawaiian Airlines flight.
- **Fly when the business travelers are on the ground.** Those who fly midweek and midday and who stay over a Saturday night generally pay far less than those who fly at more popular times.
- **Book at sale time.** Consider booking on a Wednesday as well—that's the day when most airfare sales traditionally come out. Be sure to watch such sites such as Frommers.com and SmarterTravel.com, which highlight fare sales.
- **Try booking through a consolidator.** Those traveling to Hawaii from a country other than the United States may wish to use a consolidator, or

go!—New Airline Offers Low Rates in Hawaii

In June 2006, Mesa Air Group's new carrier called **go!** began operating interisland flights between Honolulu and Lihue, Kahului, Hilo, and Kailua-Kona. It regularly offered interisland fares as low as $39, touching off a nasty airfare war that had only just started to quiet down in early 2008, when one of its main competitors, Aloha Airlines, went under. With fewer seats on the market, prices are expected to rise, but go! continues to call itself the "new discount airline in town," and you still stand a chance of saving some bucks by checking its rates before booking with another airline. Call ☎ 888/IFLYGO2 or go to www.iflygo.com.

Trouble in Paradise

As this guide went to press, Hawaii was reeling from a series of blows to its tourist industry. In 2007, Maui county (encompassing Maui, Lanai, and Molokai) began to crack down on unlicensed B&Bs, closing most of them and forcing others to scramble for permits (p. 246). Then, in early 2008, Molokai Ranch, which owns a large amount of property on Molokai and was a major employer on the island, shut down. Along with the closure of the 22-room Molokai Lodge and the 40 tentalows at Kaupoa Beach Village—the only "luxury" options on the island—the shutdown also shuttered Molokai's sole movie theater and its only 18-hole golf course.

And as if that weren't enough, both Aloha Airlines and ATA ceased operations in March of 2008. Aloha was one of the primary providers of interisland flights, along with go!, Island Air, and Hawaiian Airlines. Price wars between the four had driven the price of tickets down to a historic low of $19 per flight, in some instances. With Aloha out of the picture, Hawaii has about 30,000 fewer interisland seats available each week. Hawaiian Airlines, Island Air, and go! were adding some flights as we went to press, but for the near future, at least, interisland seats will be harder to buy and prices higher (in just one week, the average interisland flight jumped from $49 to $70). Many experts are suggesting that travelers pick a single island for the duration of their trip, simply to keep costs low and hassles at a minimum. For those still planning interisland hops, it's more important to buy tickets well in advance of travel. Flights between the mainland of the United States and Hawaii are also pricier. As we go to press, the average airfare from the West Coast of the U.S. to Oahu has nearly doubled, going from $400 to $700. Hopefully, as other carriers step in to fill the hole left by Aloha and ATA, prices will stabilize, but for now, it's more important than ever to be smart about searching for the lowest airfares (see p. 251 for more on that).

Adding more uncertainty to the mix, the much-vaunted (or much-derided, depending on who you talk to) Hawaii Superferry (p. 430) has been in and out of dry dock. In theory, the Superferry provides a fairly cheap, albeit slow, alternative to the airlines when you need to get between certain islands. But with frequent cancellations due to weather—and sometimes long periods spent out of service for repairs—we can't recommend basing any critical plans around it at this time.

What does this mean for someone traveling to Hawaii in the near future? Plan carefully. If you book with a B&B, make sure it's licensed when you place your reservation (all properties in this book, unless otherwise noted, were). If you plan to stay on Molokai, and there are any activities or establishments you have your heart set on visiting, call ahead to make sure they'll be open during your visit. Every effort was made to ensure the Molokai information provided in this guide was accurate, but the island was still in a state of flux at presstime, and the effects of Molokai Ranch's closing will likely be felt for quite some time.

Hawaii Superferry: The Newest Interisland Travel Alternative

Island hopping aboard the new **Hawaii Superferry** (☎ 877/443-3779; www.hawaiisuperferry.com) isn't the fastest way to get around Hawaii, and it may not be the cheapest. But taking a leisurely little sea voyage between islands will give you a fresh perspective on how isolated and precious these specks of land in the middle of North Pacific are.

At first glance, ferry fares appear to be competitive with airline tickets. But there's a catch—the fuel surcharge. At press time the surcharge added a walloping 37% to the regular $56 (including tax) base fare between Oahu and Maui or Kauai, destroying all hope of saving money while traveling by sea. The surcharge can fluctuate monthly, but unless it comes way down, air travel is likely to remain the more economical way to go.

Still, there are ways to shave a few bucks off the cost of a ferry ride. First of all, travel on Tuesday, Wednesday, or Thursday—the off-peak days of the week. Off-peak fares from Oahu to Maui or Kauai cost $47 for adults (including tax, but not the fuel surcharge). Furthermore, you can save $5 by booking at least 14 days in advance, and you can save another $3 by booking online.

At this writing, planes may also be a more sure-fire way of getting from island to island. In early 2008, the ferry wound up in drydock for several months for repairs. And in the first few months of operation, turbulent seas forced it to cancel its crossings a number of times (so even though the 349-foot superferry carries cars, rental car agencies are forbidding their clients from bringing them aboard currently, as they don't want to

"bucket shop," to snag a ticket. These companies buy tickets in bulk and pass savings along to their customers. If you reside in Europe, the best way to find one that services your area is to go to the website www.cheapflights.co.uk, which serves as a clearinghouse for all sorts of buckets shops, both large and small. Many will also advertise in the Sunday papers. Be careful though: Some charge outrageous change fees, so read the fine print before you purchase your ticket. Bucket shops will not be useful for those flying within the United States as they are not generally able to undercut standard pricing on domestic travel.

- **Search, search & search some more.** Try such Web search engines as Sidestep.com, Kayak.com, or Momondo.com, which search airline sites directly, adding no service charges and often finding fares that the larger travel-agent sites miss.
- **Consider an air-hotel package.** Often by booking your airfare and hotel together, you'll pay less than you would if you had booked these elements separately. See below.

deal with cars abandoned on other islands when ferry cancellations occur). Water conditions should be less of a problem in the summer months.

Another source of delays had been the anti-superferry movement in Hawaii, which had raised questions about the impact of the ferry on neighbor island traffic and about the risk the ferry's speed poses for whales. A legal challenge on Maui and protestors in the water on Kauai delayed the start of ferry service to late 2007 (everyone on Oahu seems to love the ferry). The state legislature, which passed a law allowing the superferry to operate while an environmental assessment is conducted, removed the legal obstacle blocking the superferry. The U.S. Coast Guard, after some brainstorming on how to deal with nimble anti-superferry activists on surfboards, cleared the human obstacles in the superferry's path.

Overall, the superferry is a comfortable ride. It's got leather seats and sofas, flat screen TVs, video games, a play area for kids, and three dining areas serving soups, sandwiches, and island pupu. The superferry's catamaran design makes it relatively stable at sea, but sea sickness, especially when winter's northern swells come rolling in, can be an issue. If you're prone to hanging over the rail, fly or take your motion sickness preventative of choice (Dramamine is a standard pharmaceutical solution, but some people swear by raw potatoes).

Superferry service between Oahu and the Big Island is scheduled to begin in 2009. There are no plans for stops at Molokai or Lanai. Expect to spend 3 to 4 hours aboard the ferry traveling between Oahu and Maui or Kauai, and 4 to 5 hours between Oahu and the Big Island.

- **Travel during off season.** Airfares rise and fall with demand. During Hawaii's off seasons—from mid-April to mid-June, and mid-September to mid-December (Thanksgiving excepted)—demand slackens.

BOOKING PACKAGES TO HAWAII

Because its shorelines are covered with thousands of hotel rooms needing to be filled, the Hawaiian Islands are one of the world's hot spots for travel packages, in which airfares, accommodations, vehicle rentals, and often extras like golf or luaus, are sold in discounted bundles. With a good travel package, you might save upwards of $100 per day on your vacation. The rooms in the cheapest packages aren't likely to be at the cushier hotels, but big savings can compensate for lackluster lodgings. Even the pricey resort hotels, though, offer packages, so remember that packages aren't only for budget travelers.

You can customize some travel packages, picking your dates of travel, certain hotels, rental-car makes and models, and whatnot. But the more flexible you are with travel times and accommodations, the more likely you are to land a deal. For more specifics, read the following list and take a look at p. 106.

Here are some hints to keep in mind when considering air/hotel packages:

- When an ad for a travel package says "from $500 on up," it means "from $500 on up, but not including the taxes and fees that jack the price up further." Be sure to take that into account when shopping around.
- The best-priced packages depart from the West Coast. If you live east of California, factor in the added cost of getting to the West Coast.
- Packages are always based on double-occupancy rooms. Single travelers usually have to pay a supplement, which will often wipe out any savings. Again, crunch the numbers carefully, especially if you're flying solo.
- Package rates can vary greatly from one day to the next, so if you find a good deal, grab it. It might be gone tomorrow.
- If you're getting travel insurance, don't get it with the travel package. Get it from an outside source (p. 434). That way, if the company you're dealing with goes under, it won't take your travel insurance with it.

THE HOW-TOS OF HOME EXCHANGES

Whether you're a homeowner or a renter, you can reap big savings on accommodations by doing a home exchange with someone who lives in Hawaii. Among the handful of home-exchange networks, **Intervac USA** (☎ 800/756-HOME; www.intervacus.com) is the oldest. Founded in 1953, it claims 10,000 members in 52 countries. A 1-year online membership starts at $65 and allows you to find potential home-swap partners, with whom you then work directly. You can go online and search for available properties, without the contact information, for free.

Another company, **HomeLink International** (☎ 800/638-3841; www.homelink.org), claims to have the largest home-exchange registry, with 13,000 members. Like Intervac, you can browse HomeLink's listings online, minus the contact information. Web-only membership costs $110 per year, while "full" membership, with two directories, costs $170. But before committing to either Intervac or HomeLink, click on "housing swap" at **www.craigslist.com**—a free, online, global classified ads of sorts, with discussion groups. You may luck out. When doing a home swap, don't be shy about asking a potential home-swap partner for references—many home-swappers have done it before, and a third party can help you triangulate the suitability of a particular home. ***Heads Up Sin City:*** People in Hawaii are crazy for Vegas. Your chances of finding someone in Hawaii who wants to stay where you live increase exponentially if you reside in Las Vegas.

PACKING

The dress code in Hawaii is highly casual. Shorts, T-shirts, and flip-flops (or "slippers" as they're called in the islands) are acceptable in most settings. For dressier occasions, khakis and aloha shirts, and dresses or muumuus, with just about any kind of shoe, usually suffice. Aloha wear or a sports coat will do in the finest dining establishments. Most golf courses require players to wear collared shirts.

Long-sleeved shirts, sunglasses, and wide-brimmed hats are sensible for sun protection (along with regular applications of sunscreen). It can get cool in the evening; pack a light jacket, windbreaker, or sweater. Bring something in case of rain, and bring a water-resistant windbreaker if you might head out on a boat—it can get wet and windy out on the sea, especially in the late afternoon.

If you're headed into the mountains, particularly up Haleakala on Maui or Mauna Kea on the Big Island, bring warm layers. A rule of thumb in Hawaii is that temperatures drop 3 degrees for every 1,000 feet of elevation. If it's 86°F (30°C) on the beach in Kona, it might be 47°F (8°C) atop 13,796-foot Mauna Kea. Layers are definitely the way to go, as temperatures will get cooler and cooler as you go up the mountain, and warmer and warmer as you come down.

For spotting whales, dolphins, or big-wave surfers, pack binoculars. For horseback riding, pack long pants. For hiking—especially hiking on lava—bring appropriate footwear.

MONEY MATTERS

ATM machines and debit cards—which work in Hawaii just like they do everywhere else—have supplanted the need for traveler's checks. ATMs are all over the islands, with surcharges of $2 and up.

All car-rental companies and many hotels and condos require credit cards. By the same token, some smaller restaurants and accommodations don't accept them, so call ahead if Visa's all you've got. Out-of-state checks aren't generally accepted.

Foreign currency can be exchanged at Honolulu International Airport, at some of the larger hotels, and at banks. Banking hours are generally from 8:30am to 4:30pm Monday through Friday, with some open until 6pm on Friday, and from 9am until noon on Saturday.

TIPS & TAXES

Hawaii doesn't technically have a sales tax, but it does have a 4.16% general excise tax, which is, for all intents and purposes, a sales tax. It's attached to all retail sales, including food, as well as commissions, rental income, and services. In addition, accommodations incur a 7.25% room tax, and rental cars come with a $3-per-day state surcharge, and a 35¢-per-day vehicle-registration and weight tax, as well as the general excise tax, and in most cases an Airport Concession Recovery Fee (11.11% at Honolulu International Airport, and 8.1% in Hilo, Kona, Kahului, and Molokai). It adds up fast.

If You Get There & Your Luggage Doesn't . . .

You and your lost luggage stand a better chance of a speedy reunification if it's labeled with not only your home address, but also the name, address, and phone number of the place you'll be staying in Hawaii.

Airlines are required to deliver late-arriving luggage to you. It's standard for them to tell you your missing bags are on the next flight, encouraging you to wait around (when they may or may not be right). If waiting doesn't suit you, don't. The airline will deliver your bags when (and if) they arrive. But before leaving the airport, make sure to get a lost-luggage claim form, the phone number to call to check on your luggage, and an estimated time of delivery.

What Things Cost

Groceries, gasoline, housing, and most things in general tend to cost more in Hawaii than they do on the mainland. Shipping is blamed for some costs, scarcity of land for others. Some things just seem to cost more because everything else does. In national cost-of-living surveys, Honolulu is never far from the top of the list, and imported goods on the neighboring islands are typically a bit more expensive because of the cost of shipping them from Honolulu, where they enter the state. Here's a random sampling of consumer goods on the Big Island to give you an idea of what to expect:

Cup of coffee at Ken's House of Pancakes, Hilo	$1.95
4-ounce tube of Colgate toothpaste	$4.29
Tampax, box of 40	$7.79
4 fluid-ounce bottle of Bausch & Lomb ReNu brand lens solution	$4.99
Huggies disposable diapers, box of 34	$14.69
Bottle of Coors at Kim's Karaoke, Hilo	$3
Pint of Longboard Lager at Kona Brewing Co. & Brewpub, Kona	$5
Typical plate lunch in Hawaii	$6–$9
Banana Boat Sport Quik Bloc sunscreen, SPF 50	$9.99
Movie ticket	$8–$8.75
Honolulu Advertiser on Oahu	75¢
Honolulu Advertiser on neighbor islands	$1

In addition to factoring taxes into your budget, you need to factor in tips. Standard tips are: 15% to 20% at restaurants and bars; $1 per bag for luggage handlers; $1 to $2 per night for room maids; 15% for cabdrivers; and 10% for really good surf lessons.

TRAVEL INSURANCE

Should you buy travel insurance before coming to Hawaii? Maybe, but not necessarily. Your existing insurance policies and credit cards may already cover such items as lost luggage, canceled tickets, and medical expenses. And because hotels usually allow you to cancel reservations with at least 24 hours notice, insurance isn't necessary to protect you against financial loss should you abort your trip at the last minute. However, if you're not already covered and have bought airline tickets well in advance, are renting a vacation home, or taking a cruise, you might consider trip-cancellation insurance, which protects you if you have to scrub a trip or if your travel agency goes belly up. You might also consider lost-luggage insurance. Checked baggage is covered up to $2,800 per ticketed passenger on domestic flights. On international flights, including U.S. legs of international flights, coverage is limited to about $635 per checked bag. If you're lugging valuables worth more than the standard coverage and your other insurance policies don't have a lost-luggage clause, you'd be wise to protect yourself. Also, if you're a not a U.S. citizen, you might consider medical insurance to cover unforeseen doctor visits, since healthcare is very expensive in the States. In general, you can expect to pay between 5% and 8% of the total cost of your vacation on travel insurance. The website www.insuremytrip.com allows you to compare travel-insurance policies of the major companies, such as:

- Access America (☎ 866/807-3982; www.accessamerica.com)
- Travel Guard International (☎ 800/807-3982; www.travelguard.com)
- CSA Travel Protection (☎ 800/873-9844; www.csatravelprotection.com)

HEALTH & SAFETY

Many people consider Hawaii to be paradise, but even in paradise, good vacations can go bad. The Four Horsemen of the Hawaiian Vacation Apocalypse are Sunburn, Crime, Auto Accidents, and Drowning.

SUN PROTECTION

The Hawaiian sun can be brutal, and every year hapless visitors end up in the emergency room with second-degree burns. First-degree burns can be treated with cool baths, moisturizers, and over-the-counter hydrocortisone cream. Aspirin may help as well. Beachgoers—and especially fair-skinned beachgoers—should wear wide-brimmed hats and use sunblock creams or lotions of at least SPF 15. Apply sunblock in the morning, and periodically reapply it through the day—especially between the hours of 10am and 3pm, when the sun's rays are most intense. Ultraviolet rays penetrate clouds, so don't go without sunblock just because it's cloudy. Out on the water, UV rays reflected off the sea can fry your undersides, so be sure to put sunblock under your nose, not just on top of it. Babies should be kept out of the sun. If that's impossible, protect babies with sunblock and light-colored, lightweight clothing, and always keep their little heads covered.

CRIME AVOIDANCE

Hawaii ranks low in violent crime but high in property crime when compared with the other states. Much of Hawaii's property crime is driven by its problem with crystal methamphetamine—or "ice." Hawaii has one of the worst ice problems in

How to Escape a Rip Current

If you get caught in a current, don't try to fight it by swimming against it. You'll just get worn out. Instead, swim perpendicular to the current's direction of flow. Eventually you'll find the edge. For example, if you find yourself getting carried away from the beach, do not try and swim toward the beach. Instead, swim parallel to the beach until you escape the current. Then head back in. Here's another way to put it: Swim across currents, not against them.

Volcanic Smog, aka Vog

Kilauea volcano is Hawaii's leading polluter and would be a major violator of federal clean-air standards if the EPA had any authority over it. The volcano dumps an estimated 1,000 metric tons of sulfur doxide into the atmosphere on an average day—worse than any U.S. industrial polluter. Sulfur dioxide reacts chemically with sunlight, oxygen, dust, and water to form an acidic haze known as vog, for "volcanic smog." Vog can irritate the eyes, nose, throat, and lungs.

People with breathing problems, particularly the elderly and children with asthma, are among those most acutely affected by vog. Vog can hang in the air over all of the islands. It's especially noticeable on the west side of the Big Island, where the prevailing northeast trade winds wrap around the southern tip of the island and carry it up the Kona Coast. When the trade winds abate, Hilo, on the east side, gets the vog. The Hawaii State Department of Health operates the **Vog Index Hotline** (☎ 808/885-7143; Mon–Fri), which rates air quality on a scale of 0 to 10. The higher the number, the worse the vog.

the United States. Tourists and their rental cars are favorite targets. It's easy to let your guard down while on vacation, but you shouldn't. Hang loose, but keep an eye on your belongings, especially at the beach, where stuff gets nipped all the time. Never leave anything of value in an unattended rental car, and don't fool yourself into thinking that stuff locked in the trunk is safe. Every thief on the rental-car circuit knows about the latch in the driving compartment that unlocks the trunks of many cars, and, lacking one of those, that the trunk can be easily popped with a crowbar. To gauge the frequency of car break-ins at a particular parking area, look around the ground for broken window glass. Consider buying a small, waterproof plastic container which can be hung around your neck while swimming and which can hold car keys and cash. You'll find these containers from such travel stores as Magellans.com and at many shops in the islands.

HIGHWAY SAFETY

Hawaii is very much an automobile society, with way too many people driving far too fast. You may see bumper stickers that say, "Slow Down: This Ain't the Mainland," but the truth is that Hawaii drivers are as bad as drivers anywhere. The result is about 130 traffic fatalities per year. Honolulu, with its L.A.-style freeways, and the Big Island with its long, two-lane country roads, always take the grim lead in numbers. In addition, there are some 12,000 traffic-related injuries. Drive carefully.

WATER SAFETY

Err on the side of caution in and around Hawaiian waters. Each year, about 60 people drown in Hawaii, and nearly half of them are visitors. Kauai has the largest numbers of drownings of any of the islands.

Coral Reef Etiquette

Not only are people at risk for harm in Hawaii's marine environment, they can inadvertently inflict harm upon it. Be careful and mindful of your surroundings.

Snorkel lightly. Corals reefs are made from colonies of tiny coral polyps that dwell on the outer surface of the hard coral structures they create, one thin layer at a time, over centuries. Coral polyps are extremely sensitive. Merely laying your hands on a head of coral can transfer enough residue from your skin to screw up the delicate mucous membranes that protect the colonies from disease and parasites. Standing on coral simply crushes the coral polyps en masse. If you need to stand while snorkeling or swimming in Hawaii, find a sandy spot. If you're not a strong swimmer, consider snorkeling with a flotation device under your chest to help keep your swim fins from becoming weapons of mass coral polyp destruction. The main idea is to float horizontally on the surface; don't touch the coral.

Leave the turtles alone. You shouldn't touch them. Turtles are protected by law from harassment, and in any case, it's just not nice.

Let resting dolphins rest. When dolphins come near shore, they do so to rest after long and hard deep-water hunting trips. The impact of well-meaning visitors looking for one-on-ones with the dolphins has had a huge impact on dolphin populations in places such as Kealakekua Bay on the Big Island, where the numbers have fallen as visitor numbers have increased. The impact of humans swimming among pods of resting wild dolphins has become a big political issue in Hawaii, and the state is struggling to balance the interests of the visitor industry, which promotes the romantically appealing idea of dolphin swims, with the interests of conservationists, who are trying to promote the idea that dolphins need a good, uninterrupted day's sleep to function effectively in the wild. The dolphin-encounter issue, as a matter of public policy, has yet to be resolved. In the meantime, the sensible thing to do if you spot dolphins in the water is to play hard to get. Hold your ground, think positive thoughts, and hope for the best. Maybe you'll be blessed with a visit from the pod. If not, at least you caused no harm.

At the beach: Ocean conditions can be deceptive. What might look like a safe swimming area can actually be wracked by dangerous undertows or rip currents. Sneaker waves can wash you off of cliffs. If there's a lifeguard around, say hi and ask about swimming conditions before getting in the water. Hawaii lifeguards are remarkable watermen, and good people to talk to, anyway.

Along streams: When hiking along mountain streams, beware of flash flooding. After periods of sustained rain or during sudden heavy downpours, streams can swell suddenly, trapping you on the wrong side or, worse, washing you away. Check the weather forecast before striking out into the mountains.

A note on drinking water: The Hawaii State Department of Health recommends that you drink 16 ounces of water per hour to avoid dehydration when out in the sun. Don't drink from mountain streams or you might get the tropical bacterial disease leptospirosis. Hawaii averages about 44 cases of the disease a year, with one suspected death in 2002. Symptoms include high fever, severe headache, chills, muscle aches, vomiting, jaundice, abdominal pain, and diarrhea—any one of which could single-handedly ruin a vacation. Tap water is safe.

SPECIALIZED TRAVEL RESOURCES

FAMILIES

Hawaii is a very family friendly destination, and children are welcome wherever they go, whether it be the beach or a fancy restaurant. It's no secret either that there's much for the little ones to do, from exploring the critters in tide pools, to snorkeling, to learning how to surf. If you want some time to yourself, most large hotels and resorts in Hawaii have supervised children's programs, where travelers can deposit their tyke, then go off and do other things. If you're not staying at one of those places, try **People Attentive to Children (PATCH)** (www.patchhawaii.org), which can refer trained babysitters in the islands. Call them on Oahu at ☎ 808/839-1988; on Maui at ☎ 808/242-9232; on Kauai at ☎ 808/246-0622; and on the Big Island at ☎ 808/325-3864 (Kona) or 808/961-3169 (Hilo). To rent baby paraphernalia such as cribs, strollers, and playpens, check with **Baby's Away** (www.babysaway.com) on Oahu at ☎ 800/496-6386 or 808/685-4299; on Maui at ☎ 800/942-9030 or 808/875-9030; and on the Big Island at ☎ 800/996-9030 or 808/987-9236.

TRAVELERS WITH DISABILITIES

In general, Oahu and Maui are good on accessibility. Kauai and the Big Island have a way to go, and Molokai and Lanai have a long way to go. Accessible rental vans are available on Oahu, Kauai, Maui, and the Big Island through **Access Aloha Travel** (☎ 800/480-1143 or 808/545-1143; www.accessalohatravel.com). This company specializes in booking vacations for people with disabilities, helping with accommodations, cruise-ship trips, tours, and whatnot. Hand-controlled cars can be rented from **Avis** (☎ 800/331-1212) and **Hertz** (☎ 800/654-3131), but availability is limited, so book as far in advance as you can. Hawaii has long had a 4-month quarantine on all dogs entering the state, including Seeing Eye dogs, but the rules have been modified to allow animals that have documented rabies shots and meet other state requirements to enter without delay. The specifics are available at www.hawaii.gov/hdoa/ai/aqs/info, or by calling the **Animal Quarantine Facility** (☎ 808/483-7171). For general information on traveling with a Seeing Eye dog, contact the **American Foundation for the Blind** (☎ 800/232-5463; www.afb.org).

On Oahu, the therapeutic recreation unit of the **Honolulu Department of Parks and Recreation** (☎ 808/768-3027) has Landeez All-Terrain Wheelchairs available, free of charge, at the following beaches: Ala Moana Regional Park, Hanauma Bay Nature Preserve, Sans Souci Beach Park, Kualoa Regional Park, Kailua Beach Park, Fort DeRussy Beach Park, and Pokai Bay Beach Park. The **Golden Access Passport** (☎ 888/GO-PARKS; www.nationalparks.org), which gives U.S. residents with permanent disabilities 50% discounts on all federal user fees, will save you money at Hawaii Volcanoes National Park and Puuhonua o Honaunau National Historical Park on the Big Island, Haleakala National Park on Maui, and the USS *Arizona* Memorial at Pearl Harbor on Oahu.

SENIORS

Many accommodations and restaurants in Hawaii give discounts to card-carrying members of AARP. Just be sure to ask for the discount before they ring up the charges. And make sure that the discount you're getting is the deepest one (sometimes other sources of discounts may be better).

The **Elderhostel Program** (11 Avenue de Lafayette, Boston, MA 020110-1746; ☎ 877/426-8056; www.elderhostel.org) has a delightful variety of opportunities for seniors to get to know Hawaii in ways not open to other visitors. The range of educational, cultural, and volunteer programs has in the past included: scrubbing, sanding, painting, and greasing the battleship *Missouri*—The Mighty MO—in Pearl Harbor; studying astronomy and volcanology at the University of Hawaii at Hilo; and exploring historic homes and gardens on Kauai.

The **National Parks Lifetime Senior Pass** (☎ 888/GO-PARKS; www.nps.gov) allows seniors (ages 62 and up) and three of their companions, free entrance to National Parks across the U.S. (including Hawaii). To get one, you pay a one-time $10 fee, at a National Park. In addition to free entrance, seniors get a 50% discounts on all federal user fees. So this could mean big savings at such Hawaiian hotspots as Hawaii Volcanoes National Park and Puuhonua o Honaunau National Historical Park on the Big Island, Haleakala National Park on Maui, and the USS *Arizona* Memorial at Pearl Harbor on Oahu.

GAY & LESBIAN TRAVELERS

Waikiki is where Hawaii's main gay and lesbian scene is, with such queer landmarks as **Hula's Bar & Lei Stand** (134 Kapahulu Ave.; ☎ 808/923-0669) and the stretch of shoreline known as Queen's Surf Beach (which had that name long before it went gay). The Puna District of the Big Island has been growing as a gay destination, with gay-friendly getaways such as **Kalani Eco-Resort** (☎ 808/965-7828; www.kalani.com). *The Odyssey* (www.odysseyhawaii.com) is a free gay publication available at gay-friendly spots throughout the islands. For general information, check www.gayhawaii.com, which has a directory of beaches, businesses, and community resources, broken down by island.

BRIDES & GROOMS

Hawaii is a fine place to tie the nuptial knot, and the state has done an uncharacteristically good job at minimizing the red tape for weddings. The main requirement, apart from a fiancé, is a marriage license. To get one, you must fill out a marriage-license application, and you and your betrothed, together, must hand it to a licensed marriage agent, along with $60 (so no surprising your beloved with an on-the-spot wedding). To locate a licensed marriage agent call:

- Oahu: ☎ 808/586-4544
- Big Island: ☎ 808/974-6008
- Kauai: ☎ 808/241-3498
- Maui: ☎ 808/984-8210
- Molokai: ☎ 808/553-3663
- Lanai: ☎ 808/565-6411

You can get the application for a marriage license from a licensed marriage agent, or you can download one at www.hawaii.gov/health.

There are no blood-test requirements, state residency requirements, or U.S. citizenship requirements to marry in Hawaii. There are gender requirements, since Hawaii hasn't legalized gay marriage (although it came close). You do have to be at least 18, unless you're 16 or 17 and have convinced your parents, legal guardians, or a family-court judge to sign consent forms, or if you're 15 and have convinced your parents or legal guardians *and* a family-court judge to sign consent forms. Regardless of your age, you need birth certificates, valid IDs or driver's licenses, and the full names, including maiden names, of your parents. The marriage license is good for 30 days throughout Hawaii.

If you'd like to use a wedding planner (many of whom are also licensed marriage agents), you can find a list of them at www.gohawaii.com, the website of the state's official source of tourism information, the Hawaii Visitors and Convention Bureau. Wedding-planner charges start around $250 and go way up. If your need for a wedding planner is too urgent to shop around, try: on Oahu, **Aloha Wedding Planners** (☎ 800/288-8309 or 808/943-2711; www.alohawedding planners.com); on Maui, **A Paradise Dream Wedding** (☎ 888/286-5979 or 808/875-9503; www.mauiwedding.net); on Kauai, **Coconut Coast Weddings and Photography** (☎ 800/585-5595 or 808/826-5557; www.kauaiwedding.com); and on the Big Island, **Paradise Weddings Hawaii** (☎ 800/428-5844 or 808/883-9067; www.paradiseweddingshawaii.com).

If you'd like to bypass the wedding planner and make your own arrangements before you arrive, the www.gohawaii.com website lists facilities and venues, caterers, florists, formal wear, photographers and videographers, and limousines, as well as ministers. You'll find only the members of the Hawaii Visitors and Convention Bureau listed there, but that includes just about everybody in Hawaii's wedding industry, so it's a pretty complete. For an even more in-depth list—or say, if you absolutely must have tom yum soup at the reception—go to www.superpages.com, where you can pull up everything from florists in Hilo to Thai caterers in Honolulu.

PETS

At one time, all dogs and cats entering the islands, including Seeing Eye dogs, had to go through an onerous 4-month quarantine, an eternity in dog years. Nowadays, dogs and cats can get around hard time in quarantine by having documented rabies shots and meeting other state requirements, all of which are spelled out at www.hawaii.gov/hdoa/ai/aqs/info, or by contacting the **Animal Quarantine Facility** (☎ 808/483-7171).

STAYING WIRED (OR WIRELESS) WHILE AWAY

Many hotels in Hawaii have Internet access and some have Wi-Fi. Honolulu is the Wi-Fi capital of the islands, but you won't find it as widely available as it is in comparably sized mainland cities. Wi-Fi hotspots are still scarce on the neighboring islands, although the Starbucks and the Borders throughout the state serve as Wi-Fi sites for T-Mobile (www.t-mobile.com), which offers 7 days of broadband Internet access for $20. If you're not lugging a laptop, your best bet for online access is among the multitude of Internet cafes found everywhere on all islands.

RECOMMENDED READING

If you're a bibliophile, like me, you probably abhor the idea of going someplace you've never been without reading up on it first. Any one of the readings from the abbreviated but carefully selected bibliography we offer here will illuminate Hawaii for travelers. You can find these books at bookstores and some gift shops in the islands, and you stand a good chance of finding them off-island through www.amazon.com or www.powells.com.

- ***'Olelo No'eau: Hawaiian Proverbs & Poetical Sayings,*** by Mary Kawena Pukui (who's full name is Mary Abigail Kawena ula-oka-lani-a-Hi'iaka-i-ka-poli-o-Pele-ka-wahine-'ai-honua Na-lei-lehua-a-Pele Wiggin Pukui). This extensive collection of Hawaiian proverbs offers unmatched insight into the wisdom, concerns, and lyrical cast of mind of the ancient Hawaiians. Illustrated by Dietrich Varez.
- ***Hawaiian Antiquities,*** by David Malo. Born on the Big Island in 1795 and raised among chiefs, priests, artisans, and scholars in the court of King Kamehameha, Malo wrote one of the few primary sources on the ancient beliefs and practices of Hawaiians.
- ***Hawaii's Story by Hawaii's Queen,*** by Queen Liliuokalani. Queen Liliuokalani, the last Hawaiian monarch, who was deposed by a band of mostly white subjects, explains what happened in a Victorian style that can put off some 21st-century readers but will tear your heart out if you stick with it.
- ***To Steal a Kingdom,*** by Michael Dougherty. Presents carefully researched profiles of major players in post-Cookian Hawaiian history—monarchs, missionaries, businessmen, and even literary characters such as Herman Melville—and fits them into the currents of change that ultimately led to the overthrow of Queen Liliuokalani.
- ***Shoal of Time: A History of the Hawaii Islands,*** by Gavan Daws. Fills in the details between the arrival of Captain Cook in 1777 and the arrival of statehood in 1959.
- ***A World Between Waves,*** edited by Frank Stewart. Writings on Hawaii's rich natural history by Peter Matthiessen, Diane Ackerman, James D. Houston, Maxine Hong Kingston, John McPhee, W. S. Merwin, Gavan Daws, Victoria Nelson, Kenneth Brower, Pamela Frierson, John L Culliney, Kenneth S. Norris, and Thomas Farber.

Online Resources

www.hawaii.gov State website; includes details on getting married, online camping permits, hiking, vacation planning, and a greeting from the governor.

www.gohawaii.com The state's official tourism site, where the Hawaii Visitors and Convention Bureau has a fairly thorough listing of events, activities, tours, lodging, and wedding and honeymoon resources.

www.visitmaui.com Maui County Visitors Bureau, including Lanai and Molokai.

www.visit-oahu.com Oahu Visitors Bureau.

www.kauaidiscovery.com Kauai Visitors Bureau.

www.kauai-hawaii.com Kauai County's website, with lots of resources for visitors.

www.molokai-hawaii.com Lists happenings, accommodations, activities, and so forth on Molokai.

www.alternative-hawaii.com Fairly comprehensive listing of activities, events, and so forth with very brief descriptions and an attempted emphasis on eco-tourism.

www.prh.noaa.gov/hnl/pages/SRF.php Provides the National Weather Service surf forecast.

www.nws.noaa.gov National Weather Service weather forecasts.

www.hawaiihumpbackwhale.noaa.gov Offers information on humpback whales and the Hawaiian Islands Humpback Whale National Marine Sanctuary.

http://hawaiianlanguage.com Basic online language lessons, pronunciation and common mispronunciations, the meaning of aloha, and so on.

www.hawaii-nation.org Lots of background on the movement to return Hawaii to an independent nation.

www.honoluluadvertiser.com Daily news from the state's largest newspaper.

- ***da word,*** by Lee Tonouchi (aka "Da Pidgin Guerilla"). A collection of short stories, written entirely in pidgin English (aka Hawaiian Creole English, or the Hawaiian Ebonics) by pidgin's leading academic proponent.
- ***Roadside Geology of Hawaii,*** by Richard W. Hazlett and Donald W. Hyndman. Illuminates the landscape in astounding and easily accessible ways.

www.star-bulletin.com Daily news from the state's second-largest daily newspaper.

www.honoluluweekly.com Oahu's alternative weekly newspaper, with up-to-date guide to arts, entertainment, and happenings.

http://ilind.net Retired Honolulu investigative reporter Ian Lind offers insightful commentary on local media and politics, and lots of photos of his cats.

www.mauinews.com Maui's daily newspaper.

www.mauitime.com Maui's alternative weekly newspaper, with the latest on Valley Isle arts, entertainment, and happenings.

www.westhawaiitoday.com West Hawaii's daily newspaper.

www.hawaiitribune-herald.com East Hawaii's daily newspaper.

www.hawaiiislandjournal.com The Big Island's alternative newspaper, with calendar of island events and happenings.

www.kauaiworld.com Kauai's daily newspaper, the *Garden Island.*

www.nps.gov/havo Hawaii Volcanoes National Park.

http://hvo.wr.usgs.gov U.S. Geological Survey Hawaiian Volcano Observatory site, with eruption updates, current hazards, history, and links to other volcano observatories.

http://hvo.wr.usgs.gov/cam Live panorama of Pu'u O'o vent, from webcam mounted on the rim of Kilauea volcano's very active crater.

www.cfht.hawaii.edu/webcams Webcam on summit of Mauna Kea, mounted on dome of the Canada-France-Hawaii Telescope, pointed at Gemini Observatory.

http://cfht.hawaii.edu/webcam/cfhtdome Webcam on summit of Mauna Kea, mounted on Gemini Observatory, pointed at Canada-France-Hawaii Telescope.

- ***The Colony,*** by John Tayman. A fascinating and heartrending history of Molokai's famed leper colony.
- ***Kilauea: The Newest Land on Earth,*** by Christina Heliker. A geologist with the Hawaiian Volcano Observatory covers the history of the volcano, richly illustrated with the work of photographer Dorian Weisel.

The ABCs of Hawaii

AAA Hawaii's only American Automobile Association (AAA) office is at 1130 N. Nimitz, Suite A-170, in Honolulu (☎ 808/593-2221). Some car-rental agencies now provide auto-club-type services, so you should inquire about their availability when you rent your car.

American Express For 24-hour traveler's-check refunds and purchase information, call ☎ 800/221-7282.

Area Code All the Hawaiian Islands are in the 808 area code. Note that if you're calling one island from another, you'll have to dial 1-808 first.

Business Hours Most offices are open Monday through Friday from 8am to 5pm. Bank hours are Monday through Thursday from 8:30am to 3pm and Friday from 8:30am to 6pm; some banks are open on Saturday as well. Shopping centers are open Monday through Friday from 10am to 9pm, Saturday 10am to 5:30pm, and Sunday from noon to 5 or 6pm.

Electricity The United States uses 110–120 volts AC (60 cycles), compared to 220–240 volts AC (50 cycles), the standard in Europe, Australia, and New Zealand. Adapters to use with appliances from these nations are difficult to find in Hawaii. Bring adapters with you if you're traveling from outside the U.S. with small appliances.

Emergencies Dial ☎ **911** for police, fire, or ambulance.

Liquor Laws The legal drinking age in Hawaii is 21. Bars are allowed to stay open daily until 2am; places with cabaret licenses are able to keep the booze flowing until 4am. Grocery and convenience stores are allowed to sell beer, wine, and liquor 7 days a week.

Smoking Hawaii has one of the toughest smoking bans in the U.S. State law prohibits smoking in almost all public places, including restaurants, bars, and nightclubs. It also prohibits smoking within 20 feet of the entrance to any business or office. The law allows hotels to designate up to 20% of their rooms for smokers, but increasingly hotels are simply doing away with smoking rooms altogether. Most bed-and-breakfasts prohibit smoking indoors.

Taxes Hawaii's sales tax is 4%. The hotel-occupancy tax is 7.25%, and hoteliers are allowed by the state to tack on an additional 0.1666% excise tax. Thus, expect taxes of about 11.42% to be added to your hotel bill.

Time Zone Hawaii is 2 hours behind Pacific Standard Time and 5 hours behind Eastern Standard Time. In other words, when it's noon in Hawaii, it's 2pm in California and 5pm in New York during standard time on the mainland. There's no daylight saving time here, so when daylight saving time is in effect on the mainland, Hawaii is 3 hours behind the West Coast and 6 hours behind the East Coast; in summer, when it's noon in Hawaii, it's 3pm in California and 6pm in New York.

Hawaii is east of the International Date Line, putting it on the same day as the U.S. mainland and Canada, and a day behind Australia, New Zealand, and Asia.

9 Hawaiian Terms & Phrases

THE HAWAIIAN ALPHABET

The Hawaiian alphabet, created by missionaries in the early 19th century as they tried to capture a nonwritten language in print, consists of just 12 letters: a, e, i, o, u, h, k, l, m, n, p and w.

The following is a very general guide to Hawaiian pronunciation:

a — ah, as in far: *hale*
e — ay, as in way: *nene*
i — ee, as in see: *pali*
o — oh, as in no: *taro*
u — as in moon: *kapu*

COMMON HAWAIIAN TERMS

As you explore the islands, you'll probably encounter some common Hawaiian words and sayings. Here's a brief list of the local lingo, organized alphabetically:

ahi Hawaiian tuna fishes, especially the yellowfin tuna

ahupua'a land division usually extending from uplands to the sea

aina land, earth

akamai smart, clever

Alii chief, chieftess, king, queen, noble; royal, kingly; to rule or act as chief

aloha love, mercy, compassion, pity; greeting; loved one; to love; to greet, hail; greetings; good-bye

anuenue rainbow

aole no, not; to have none

apu coconut shell cup

aua stingy

ewa crooked, out of shape, imperfect; place name for area west of Honolulu, used as a directional term

hahalua manta ray

haiku flower

hailepo sting ray

hala the pandanus or screw pine

halau long house, as for canoes or hula instruction

hale house, building; to have a house

hale pili house thatched with pili grass.

hale pule church, chapel

haleu toilet paper; to wipe, as with toilet paper

hana hou to do again, repeat; encore

hanai foster child, adopted child

haole white person; formerly any foreigner; introduced, of foreign origin

Do You Have to Speak Hawaiian in Hawaii?

by Jeanette Foster

Almost everyone here speaks English. But many folks in Hawaii now speak Hawaiian as well. All visitors will hear the words *aloha* and *mahalo* (thank you). If you've just arrived, you're a *malihini*. Someone who's been here a long time is a *kamaaina*. When you finish a job or your meal, you are *pau* (finished). On Friday it's *pau hana,* work finished. You eat *pupu* (Hawaii's version of hors d'oeuvres) when you go *pau hana*.

If you venture beyond the tourist areas, you might hear another local tongue: pidgin English, a conglomeration of slang and words from the Hawaiian language. "Broke da mouth" (tastes really good) is the favorite pidgin phrase and one you might hear; "'Eh fo'real, brah" means "It's true, brother." You could be invited to hear an elder "talk story" (relating myths and memories). But because pidgin is really the province of the locals, your visit to Hawaii is likely to pass without your hearing much pidgin at all.

hapa portion, fragment, part; person of mixed blood

hapa haole part white person; of part-white blood; part white and part Hawaiian, as an individual or phenomenon

hau kea snow

haupia pudding made from coconut cream, formerly thickened with arrowroot, now usually with cornstarch

heiau pre-Christian place of worship

hele to go, come, walk; to move, as in a game; going, moving

hele mai come

hele wale to go naked; to go without fixed purpose

hepa idiot

hihimanu various sting rays and eagle rays; lavish, magnificent, elegant

hoa hele traveling companion, fellow traveler

holo hele to run here and there

holoholo to go for a walk, ride, or sail; to go out on pleasure

honu general name for the turtle

ho'o-haole to act like a white person, to ape the white people, or assume airs of superiority

hooilo winter, rainy season

hui club, association, firm, partnership, union; to form a society or organization; to meet

hukilau seine; to fish with a seine

hula Hawaiian form of dance

iwi bone; shell, as of coconut, candlenut, gourd, egg, shellfish

iwi po'o skull

kahu honored attendant, guardian, keeper, administrator, pastor of a church; one who has a dog, cat, or any pet

kahuna priest, minister, sorcerer, expert in any profession

kai sea, seawater

kamaaina native born

kanaka human being, man, human, mankind, person, individual, subject, as of a chief; Hawaiian

kane male, husband, male sweetheart, man

kapakahi one-sided, crooked, lopsided; biased

kapu taboo, prohibition; sacred, holy, consecrated

Kau summer

keiki child, offspring

koa brave, fearless; soldier; an endemic forest tree, the largest and most valued of the native trees

koko blood; rainbow-hued

kumu bottom, base, foundation; teacher

lau leaf

laulau wrapping, wrapped package; individual servings of pork or beef, salted fish, and taro tops, wrapped in ti leaves of banana leaves, and baked in a ground oven, steamed, or broiled

lei garland, wreath; necklace of flowers, leaves, shells, ivory, feathers, or paper; any ornament worn around the neck

limu general name for all kinds of plants living underwater

loa distance, length, height; distant, long, far, permanent

lolo feeble minded

lomilomi kneaded, worked until softened; in cuisine, raw fish is softened through the use of an acidic marinade, like ceviche

lua hole, pit, grave, den, cave, mine, crater; toilet

luakini large heiau where ruling chiefs prayed and human sacrifices were offered

luau young taro tops, especially baked with coconut cream and chicken or octopus; Hawaiian feast

mahalo thanks, gratitude, to thank

mahimahi broad-headed game fish called dolphin

maile a native twining shrub, with tiny fragrant leaves, a favorite for decorations and lei

makahiki ancient festival beginning about the middle of October and lasting about 4 months, with sports and religious festivities and kapu on war

Makahiki Hou New Year (Hau'oli Makahiki Hou: Happy New Year)

makai toward the sea, in the direction of the sea (see mauka)

make to die, defeated, death

malama to take care of, care for, preserve, fidelity, loyalty

malihini stranger, newcomer, guest, one unfamiliar with a place or custom

mana supernatural or divine power

manini small, stripped sturgeon fish; stingy

maoli native, indigenous, genuine, true, real

mauka inland

Menehune legendary race of small people, who worked at night building fishponds, roads, temples; if the work was not finished in one night, it remained unfinished

nalu wave, surf, full of waves

noni Indian mulberry, a small tree or shrub formerly useful to Hawaiians as a source of dyes, food, and medicine

nui big, large, great, important

ohana family

oheo a small, native shrub, in the cranberry family, bearing small, red or yellow edible berries

ono delicious, tasty, savory

opala trash, rubbish

opu belly, stomach, abdomen

pali cliff, steep hill

pau finished, over, completed, all done

Pele lava flow, volcano eruption; the volcano goddess

piko navel, umbilical cord, genitals; summit of a hill or mountain, crown of the head, ear tip, end of a rope

pipi beef, cattle

poi the Hawaiian staff of life, made from cooked taro corms

pono goodness, morality, moral qualities, correct or proper procedure; right, just, fair

puka hole

pule prayer, church service, to pray

pupu relish, snack, hors d'oeuvre

umi umi whiskers, beard

wahine woman, lady, wife, female, feminine

wai water or liquid of any kind, other than sea water

wiki, wikiwiki to hurry, hasten; quick

Source: New Pocket Hawaiian Dictionary, Mary Kawena Pukui and Samuel H. Elbert (University of Hawaii Press).

A HAWAIIAN SEAFOOD PRIMER

ahi yellowfin or big-eye tuna, important for its use in sashimi and poke at sushi bars and in Hawaii Regional Cuisine

aku skipjack tuna, heavily used by local families in home cooking and poke

ehu red snapper, delicate and sumptuous, yet lesser known than opakapaka

hapuupuu grouper, a sea bass whose use is expanding

hebi spearfish, mildly flavored, and frequently featured as the "catch of the day" in upscale restaurants

kajiki Pacific blue marlin, also called *au,* with a firm flesh and high fat content that make it a plausible substitute for tuna

kumu goatfish, a luxury item on Chinese and upscale menus, served *en papillote* or steamed whole, Oriental style, with scallions, ginger, and garlic

mahimahi dolphin fish (the game fish, not the mammal) or dorado, a classic sweet, white-fleshed fish requiring vigilance among purists because it's often disguised as fresh when it's actually "fresh-frozen"—a big difference

monchong bigscale or sickle pomfret, an exotic, tasty fish, scarce but gaining a higher profile on Hawaiian Island menus

nairagi striped marlin, also called *au,* good as sashimi and in poke, and often substituted for ahi in raw-fish products

onaga ruby snapper, a luxury fish, versatile, moist, and flaky

ono wahoo, firmer and drier than the snappers, often served grilled and in sandwiches

opah moonfish, rich and fatty, and versatile—cooked, raw, smoked, and broiled

opakapaka pink snapper, light, flaky, and luxurious, suited for sashimi, poaching, sautéing, and baking; the best-known upscale fish

papio jack trevally, light, firm, and flavorful, and favored in Island cookery

shutome broadbill swordfish, of beeflike texture and rich flavor

tombo albacore tuna, with a high fat content, suitable for grilling

uhu parrotfish, most often encountered steamed, Chinese style

uku gray snapper of clear, pale-pink flesh, delicately flavored and moist

ulua large jack trevally, firm-fleshed and versatile

10 The Natural Wonder That Is Hawaii

by Jeanette Foster

WHEN THE FIRST POLYNESIANS ARRIVED IN HAWAII BETWEEN A.D. 500 AND 800, scientists say they found some 67 varieties of endemic Hawaiian birds, a third of which are now believed to be extinct. They did not find any reptiles, amphibians, mosquitoes, lice, fleas, or even a cockroach.

There were only two endemic mammals: the hoary bat and the monk seal. The **hoary bat** must have accidentally blown to Hawaii at some point, from either North or South America. It can still be seen during its early evening forays, especially around the Kilauea Crater on the Big Island.

The **Hawaiian monk seal,** a relative of warm-water seals found in the Caribbean and the Mediterranean, was nearly slaughtered into extinction for its skin and oil during the 19th century. These seals have recently experienced a minor population explosion and can be seen at various beaches throughout the state. They're protected under federal law. If you're fortunate enough to see a monk seal, just look; don't disturb one of Hawaii's living treasures.

The first Polynesians brought a few animals from home: dogs, pigs, and chickens (all were for eating), as well as rats (stowaways). All four species are still found in the Hawaiian wild today.

BIRDS

More species of native birds have become extinct in Hawaii in the last 200 years than anywhere else on the planet. Of 67 native species, 23 are extinct and 30 are endangered. Even the Hawaiian crow, the **alala,** is threatened.

The **aeo,** or Hawaiian stilt—a 16-inch-long bird with a black head, black coat, white underside, and long pink legs—can be found in protected wetlands like the Kanaha Wildlife Sanctuary and Kealia Pond on Maui, and the Hanalei National Wildlife Refuge on Kauai, which is also home to the Hawaiian duck. Another great birding venue is Kokee State Park on Kauai. Native birds spotted here include some of the 22 species of the native honey creepers. Frequently seen are the **apapane** (a red bird with black wings and a curved black bill), **iiwi** (also red with black wings but with orange legs and a salmon-colored bill), **amakihi** (a plain olive-green bird with a long, straight bill), and **anianiau** (a tiny yellow bird with a thin, curved bill). Also in the forest is the **elepaio,** a small gray flycatcher with an orange breast and an erect tail. The most common native bird at Kokee is the **moa,** or red jungle fowl, a chicken brought to Hawaii by the Polynesians.

To get a good glimpse of the seabirds that frequent Hawaii, drive to Kilauea Point on Kauai's North Shore. Here you can easily spot **red-** and **white-footed**

Leapin' Lizards!

Geckos are harmless, soft-skinned, insect-eating lizards that come equipped with suction pads on their feet, enabling them to climb walls and windows to reach tasty insects such as mosquitoes and cockroaches. You'll see them on windows outside a lighted room at night or hear their cheerful chirp.

boobies, wedge-tailed shearwaters, frigate birds, red-tailed tropic birds, and the **Laysan albatross.**

Hawaii's state bird is the **nene.** It's being brought back from the brink of extinction through strenuous protection laws and captive breeding. A relative of the Canada goose, the nene stands about 2 feet high and has a black head and yellow cheeks. The approximately 500 nenes in existence can be seen in only three places: on Maui at Haleakala National Park, and on the Big Island at Mauna Kea State Recreation Area bird sanctuary and on the slopes of Mauna Kea.

The Hawaiian short-eared owl, the **pueo,** which grows to between 12 and 17 inches, can be seen at dawn and dusk on Kauai, Maui, and the Big Island. According to legend, spotting a pueo is a good omen.

SEA LIFE

Approximately 680 species of fish are known to inhabit the waters around the Hawaiian Islands. Of those, approximately 450 species stay close to the reef and inshore areas.

CORAL Coral reefs take thousands of years to develop. They attract and support fish and crustaceans, which use them for food and habitat. The corals most frequently seen in Hawaii are hard, rocklike formations named for their familiar shapes: antler, cauliflower, finger, plate, and razor coral. Some coral appears soft, such as tube coral; it can be found in the ceilings of caves. Black coral, which resembles winter-bare trees or shrubs, is found at depths of more than 100 feet.

REEF FISH During the millions of years it took for the islands to sprout up from the sea, ocean currents—mainly from Southeast Asia—carried thousands of marine animals and plants to Hawaii's reef; of those, approximately 100 species adapted and thrived. Today, Hawaii's waters host 450 types of reef fish, 27% of which are found nowhere else. Here are the ones you're most likely to spot:

Angelfish can be distinguished by the spine, located low on the gill plate. These fish are very shy; several species live in colonies close to coral.

Blennies are small, elongated fish, ranging from 2 to 10 inches long. Blennies are so small they can live in tide pools; you might have a hard time spotting one.

Butterfly fish, among the most colorful of the reef fish, are usually seen in pairs (scientists believe they mate for life). There are 22 species of which three (bluestripe, lemon or milletseed, and multiband or pebbled butterfly fish) are endemic. Most butterfly fish have a dark band through the eye and a spot near the tail resembling an eye, meant to confuse predators (moray eels love to eat them).

Moray and **conger eels** are the most common eels seen in Hawaii. Morays are usually docile except when provoked or when there's food around. Unfortunately, some morays have been fed by divers and now associate divers with food; thus, they can become aggressive. While morays may look menacing, conger eels look downright happy, with big lips and pectoral fins (situated so that they look like big ears) that give them the appearance of a perpetually smiling face.

Parrotfish, one of the largest and most colorful of the reef fish, can grow up to 40 inches long. They're easy to spot—their front teeth are fused together, protruding like buck teeth that allow them to feed by scraping algae from rocks and coral. The rocks and coral pass through the parrotfish's system, resulting in fine sand. In fact, most of the white sand found in Hawaii is parrotfish waste; one large parrotfish can produce a ton of sand a year.

Scorpion fish are what scientists call "ambush predators": They hide under camouflaged exteriors and ambush their prey. Several kinds sport a venomous dorsal spine so be careful when putting you feet or hands in the water. These fish don't have a gas bladder, so when they stop swimming, they sink—that's why you usually find them "resting" on ledges and on the ocean bottom.

Surgeonfish, sometimes called *tang,* get their name from the scalpel-like spines located on each side of the body near the base of the tail. Several surgeonfish, such as the brightly colored yellow tang, are boldly colored; others are adorned in more conservative shades of gray, brown, or black. The only endemic surgeonfish—and the most abundant in Hawaiian waters—is the convict tang, a pale white fish with vertical black stripes (like a convict's uniform).

Wrasses are a very diverse family of fish, ranging in length from 2 to 15 inches. Wrasses can change gender from female to male. Some have brilliant coloration that changes as they age.

GAME FISH Hawaii is known around the globe as *the* place for big-game fish—marlin, swordfish, and tuna. Six kinds of **billfish** are found in the offshore waters around the islands: Pacific blue marlin, black marlin, sailfish, broadbill swordfish, striped marlin, and shortbill spearfish. Tuna ranges in size from 1 lb. or less mackeral tuna to the 250-pound yellowfin ahi tuna (you'll also find big-eye, albacore, kawakawa and skipjack).

Other types of fish, also excellent for eating, include **mahimahi; rainbow runner;** and **wahoo** (ono). Shoreline fishermen are always on the lookout for **trevally, bonefish, ladyfish, threadfin, leatherfish,** and **goatfish.** Bottom fishermen pursue a range of **snapper** as well as **sea bass** (the state record is a whopping 563 lb.) and **amberjack** (which weigh up to 100 lb.).

WHALES Humpback whales come to Hawaii to mate and calve every year, beginning in November and staying until spring—April or so—when they return to Alaska. They grow to up to 45 feet long, so when one breaches (jumps out of the water), you can see it for miles. Other whales—such as pilot, sperm, false killer, melon-headed, pygmy killer, and beaked—can be seen year-round.

SHARKS About 40 different species of sharks inhabit the waters surrounding Hawaii, ranging from the totally harmless whale shark (at 60 ft., the world's largest fish), which has no teeth and is so docile that it frequently lets divers ride on its back, to the not-so-docile, extremely uncommon great white shark. The most common sharks seen in Hawaii are white-tip or gray reef sharks (about 5 ft. long) and black-tip reef sharks (about 6 ft. long).

THE FLORA OF THE ISLANDS

Hawaii is filled with sweet-smelling flowers, lush vegetation, and exotic plant life.

AFRICAN TULIP TREES Even from afar, you can see the flaming red flowers on these large trees, which can grow to be more than 50 feet tall. The buds hold water, and Hawaiian children use the flowers as water pistols.

ANGEL'S TRUMPETS These small trees can grow up to 20 feet tall, with an abundance of large (up to 10-in. diameter) pendants—white or pink flowers that resemble, well, trumpets. ***Warning:*** All parts of the plant are poisonous and contain a strong narcotic.

ANTHURIUMS There are more than 550 species, but the most popular are the heart-shaped red, orange, pink, white, and purple flowers with tail-like spathes.

BANYAN TREES Among the world's largest trees, banyans have branches that grow out and away from the trunk, forming descending roots that grow down to the ground to feed and form additional trunks, making the tree very stable during tropical storms.

BIRDS-OF-PARADISE These natives of Africa have become something of a trademark of Hawaii. They're easily recognizable by the orange and blue flowers nestled in gray-green bracts, looking somewhat like birds in flight.

BOUGAINVILLEA Originally from Brazil, these vines feature tissue-thin bracts, ranging in color from majestic purple to fiery orange, that hide tiny white flowers.

BREADFRUIT TREES A large tree—more than 60 feet tall—with broad, sculpted, dark-green leaves, the famous breadfruit produces a round, head-size green fruit that's a staple in the diets of all Polynesians. When roasted or baked, the whitish-yellow meat tastes somewhat like a sweet potato.

BROMELIADS Of the 1,400 species of bromeliads, the pineapple plant is the best known. Generally spiky, bromeliads ranging in size from a few inches to several feet in diameter and are popular for their strange and wonderful flowers.

COFFEE Hawaii is the only state that produces coffee commercially. Coffee is an evergreen shrub with shiny, waxy, dark-green pointed leaves. The flower is a small, fragrant white blossom that develops into ½-inch berries that turn bright red when ripe.

GINGER White and yellow ginger flowers are perhaps the most fragrant in Hawaii. Usually found in clumps growing 4 to 7 feet tall in areas blessed by rain, these sweet-smelling, 3-inch-wide flowers are composed of three dainty petal-like stamens and three long, thin petals. Ginger was introduced to Hawaii in the 19th century from the Indonesia-Malaysia area. Other members of the ginger family frequently seen in Hawaii include red, shell, and torch ginger.

HELICONIA Some 80 species of the colorful heliconia family came to Hawaii from the Caribbean and Central and South America. The bright yellow, red, green, and orange bracts overlap and appear to unfold like origami birds.

HIBISCUS The 4- to 6-inch hibiscus flowers bloom year-round and come in a range of colors, from lily white to lipstick red. The flowers resemble crepe paper, with stamens and pistils protruding spirelike from the center. Hibiscus hedges can grow up to 15 feet tall. The yellow hibiscus is Hawaii's official state flower.

JACARANDA From March to early May, these huge lacy-leaved trees metamorphose into large clusters of spectacular lavender-blue sprays.

MACADAMIA A transplant from Australia, macadamia nuts have become a commercial crop in recent decades in Hawaii, especially on the Big Island and Maui. The large trees—up to 60 feet tall—bear a hard-shelled nut encased in a leathery husk, which splits open and dries when the nut is ripe.

MONKEYPOD TREES One of Hawaii's most majestic trees, growing more than 80 feet tall and 100 feet across, its wood is a favorite of local artisans.

NIGHT-BLOOMING CEREUS Look along rock walls for this spectacular night-blooming flower. Originally from Central America, this vinelike member of the cactus family has green scalloped edges and produces foot-long white flowers that open as darkness falls and wither as the sun rises.

ORCHIDS To many minds, nothing says Hawaii more than orchids. The most widely grown variety—and the major source of flowers for leis and garnish for tropical libations—is the vanda orchid. The vandas used in Hawaii's commercial flower industry are generally lavender or white, but they grow in a rainbow of colors, shapes, and sizes.

PANDANUS (HALA) Called *hala* by Hawaiians, pandanus is native to Polynesia. Thanks to its thick trunk, stiltlike supporting roots, and crown of long, swordlike leaves, it's easy to recognize. Hawaiians weave the *lau* (leaves) of the hala into hats, baskets, mats, bags, and the like.

PLUMERIA Also known as frangipani, this sweet-smelling, five-petal flower is the most popular choice of lei makers. The Singapore plumeria has five creamy-white petals, with a touch of yellow in the center. Another popular variety, ruba—with flowers from soft pink to flaming red—is also used in leis.

PROTEA Originally from South Africa, this unusual oversize shrub comes in more than 40 different varieties. The flowers of one species resemble pincushions; those of another look like a bouquet of feathers. Once dried, proteas last for years.

TARO Around pools, near streams, and in neatly planted fields, you'll see these green heart-shaped leaves, whose dense roots are a Polynesian staple. The ancient Hawaiians pounded the roots into poi. Originally from Sri Lanka, taro not only is a food crop, but is also grown for ornamental reasons.

Index

See also Accommodations and Restaurant indexes, below.

GENERAL INDEX

ACCOMMODATIONS

RESTAURANTS